Historical and Conceptual Issues in Psychology

Second edition

Marc Brysbaert and
Kathy Rastle

PEARSON

Harlow, England • London • New York • Boston • San Francisco • Toronto • Sydney
Auckland • Singapore • Hong Kong • Tokyo • Seoul • Taipei • New Delhi
Cape Town • São Paulo • Mexico City • Madrid • Amsterdam • Munich • Paris • Milan

Pearson Education Limited
Edinburgh Gate
Harlow
Essex CM20 2JE
England

and Associated Companies throughout the world

Visit us on the World Wide Web at:
www.pearson.com/uk

First published 2009 (print)
Second edition published 2013 (print and electronic)

© Pearson Education Limited 2009, 2013

ISBN 978-0-273-74367-5 (print)
    978-0-273-74368-2 (ebook)
    978-0-273-78684-5 (etext)

British Library Cataloguing-in-Publication Data
A catalogue record for this book is available from the British Library

Library of Congress Cataloging-in-Publication Data
A catalog record for this book is available from the Library of Congress

10 9 8 7 6 5 4 3 2 1
16 15 14 13 12

Typeset in 10/12 Monotype Sabon by 75
Printed by Ashford Colour Press Ltd, Gosport

Brief contents

Contents

Companion Website

For open-access **student resources** specifically written to complement this textbook and support your learning, please visit **www.pearsoned.co.uk/brysbaert**

Lecturer Resources

For password-protected online resources tailored to support the use of this textbook in teaching, please visit **www.pearsoned.co.uk/brysbaert**

Edited preface to the first edition

From time to time it is good to pause and wonder how we got where we are now. For instance, why did you open this book? How did you become interested in psychology? But also: for how long has one been able to study psychology? Why has this book been published? Why do all good degrees of psychology today include a course on historical and conceptual issues? What is the position of psychology in society? Is psychology really a science? What is a science?

These are some of the questions addressed in this book (although you will not be surprised to hear that many of them cannot be fully answered on the basis of present knowledge). They refer to the foundations of psychology, which consist of historical and conceptual issues.

Historical issues refer to the past of the discipline and can be approached in many different ways (see Chapter 10). One distinction is whether history is studied to find out what people at different points in time thought and knew, or whether history is studied to gain insight into how the present situation came about as the result of certain developments and choices in the past. The latter is the approach taken in this book, because it is of particular relevance to everyone wanting to become a psychologist.

Conceptual issues are more difficult to define. Basically, they refer to the big questions underlying a discipline. For psychology, these are questions like: 'What is the human mind?', 'Is it possible to know the mind of someone else?', 'Is it possible to know my own mind?', 'Is such information reliable and useful?' Importantly, these issues cannot readily be addressed in the way scientists love to do: by collecting data and testing new predictions made on the basis of the available knowledge (see Chapter 9). Conceptual issues relate to the convictions and opinions that underlie a particular discipline and that determine the meanings of the terms used (e.g. the meanings of 'consciousness', 'process' and 'personality'). Conceptual issues are shared by the researchers and practitioners of a discipline and are imposed on all newcomers. However, they usually remain tacit. They exert their influence by reliance on common understanding rather than explicit teaching (if this sounds a bit woolly at the moment, come back to this section after you have read the part on paradigms in Chapter 9). Indeed, even for us authors, writing this book has been eye-opening at times. Quite often we found ourselves saying 'Oh, that's where it comes from! That's what it means!'

Needless to say, historical and conceptual issues are closely intertwined. Historical developments depended on the conceptual issues at the time and, in turn, had an impact on the concepts and the convictions shared by the next generations. For instance, many psychologists today talk about 'cognitive processes' and 'cognitive representations'. However, they would find it hard to define what exactly they mean by these terms. They just know that every psychologist is taught them and that the words refer to information-processing in the brain. Where these terms came from, why at a certain point in time they were introduced, and why they subsequently conquered the complete discipline are questions that are left out of consideration in most teachings (e.g. you don't find them in introductory books on psychology). One reason for this is that you need a certain amount of historical, philosophical, and technical background before you can address them.

The main danger of a book on historical and conceptual issues is that it tries to cover too much. Just imagine: everything that ever happened and that was ever thought of is a possible topic that could be included! Every chapter of this book could easily have been expanded into a 500-page book. Indeed, the most common complaint about courses of historical and conceptual issues is that lecturers try to cram too much into a short period of time. To tackle this problem head-on, we decided not to try to write a 'complete book' (which is impossible anyway), but to start from the question of what is feasible for a series of 12 two-hour lectures. Which are the main issues that must be covered? What is informative and interesting for psychology students (rather than what is known to historians and philosophers of science)? Therefore, do not expect to find everything in this book. Our purpose is simply to provide you with a basis. If this book entices you to want to know more, then we have achieved our goal. To help you with this, each chapter includes a list of the relevant books we found interesting. There is also a lot of information freely available on the internet, links to which you can find on our website at **www.pearsoned. co.uk/brysbaert**.

Although the writing of this book has been exceedingly fluent, we are aware that the current text is much better than the initial draft we had in mind. This is to a considerable degree due to the feedback we got from a group of dedicated and conscientious reviewers, who would not let anything substandard go unnoticed. Although it was impossible to respond to each and every individual comment, whenever there was convergence on a weakness we took it into account to improve the coverage. All in all, nearly half of the current text was rewritten, rearranged, or added as a result of the comments we got.

We also would like to say a big thank you to our commissioning editor, Janey Webb, who not only was one of the best reviewers, but also cheerfully guided us through the many dreadful details that have to be attended to in the conversion from an idea into a reader-friendly, printed book.

Finally, we thank our families for giving us the freedom and the time to write a book like this, even though the only compensation they got out of it was that on many nights they were free to choose what they wanted to watch on television.

Preface to the second edition

Since the completion of the previous edition, we have done a lot of reading. Apparently there is some truth in the saying that history can become addictive once you have covered the basics (so, beware!).

The extra reading has allowed us to update and streamline the discussion of several chapters. It also showed us that the historical part of the book tended to be a bit short (which was one of the few criticisms we received of the previous edition). As a result, we have added a chapter and now cover the emergence of the natural sciences and psychology in more detail. This also gives lecturers more choice of topics (because they can more easily drop a chapter now).

For the rest, we noticed two more patterns. The first is that many ideas and findings tend to be considerably older than we had thought. There is a tendency to attribute views and insights to specific time periods, whereas it is often possible to find precursors centuries earlier. Throughout the book we give examples of this bias.

The second, related pattern is that we often have simplistic views about the knowledge at a certain time. When reading the original publications, the degree of sophistication and perspective is invariably much higher than assumed nowadays. In a few cases this had led to the formation of outright myths, not all of which we were able to avoid in our previous edition. Therefore, we have introduced a new feature, myth-busting, in which we review the origin of widespread convictions that turn out to be wrong.

Reviewers liked the new feature so much they urged us to find more. We resisted this temptation, wary that it might increase the risk of us inventing myths so that we could bust them! Myths are damaging, because they distort our understanding of events. So, the fewer of them there are, the better. However, if you come across a genuine myth we have missed, please let us know. We will be more than happy to include it in the next edition and acknowledge your input. After all, this is the only way to avoid real mistakes in the understanding of our past.

Guided tour

This chapter will cover gives a brief outline of the main points of each chapter, to help you understand what you'll learn.

Each chapter opens with a range of **questions to consider** in relation to the historical and conceptual issues raised. These give an idea of topics covered and encourage students to critically reflect on them.

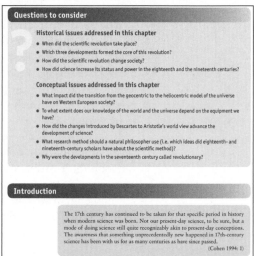

Questions to consider

Historical issues addressed in this chapter
● When did the scientific revolution take place?
● Which three developments formed the core of this revolution?
● How did the scientific revolution change society?
● How did science increase its status and power in the eighteenth and the nineteenth centuries?

Conceptual issues addressed in this chapter
● What impact did the transition from the geocentric to the heliocentric model of the universe have on Western European society?
● To what extent does our knowledge of the world and the universe depend on the equipment we have?
● How did the changes introduced by Descartes to Aristotle's world view advance the development of science?
● What research method should a natural philosopher use (i.e. which ideas did eighteenth- and nineteenth-century scholars have about the scientific method)?
● Why were the developments in the seventeenth century called revolutionary?

Introduction

> The 17th century has continued to be taken for that specific period in history when modern science was born. Not our present-day science, to be sure, but a mode of doing science still quite recognizably akin to present-day conceptions. The awareness that something unprecedentedly new happened in 17th-century science has been with us for as many centuries as have since passed.
>
> (Cohen 1994: 1)

The **introduction** to every chapter opens with a quote or example to provide background and stimulate interest in the topic.

Just how anti-science were the Romantics?

Romanticism took place in the late eighteenth and early nineteenth centuries. According to the *Encyclopaedia Britannica* it emphasised the individual, the subjective, the irrational, the imaginative, the personal, the spontaneous, the emotional, the visionary, the natural and the transcendental. It started in Germany when a group of young academics and artists distanced themselves from the emphasis on reason and mechanical order that characterised Enlightenment. According to Berlin (1999), Romanticism originated out of envy of the French intellectual triumph at a moment when the German-speaking estates and kingdoms experienced a low. Whereas the Enlightenment claimed that all questions were knowable and answerable in a coherent way by reason and science, the Romantics held that there were no eternal truths, eternal institutions or eternal values, suitable for everyone and everywhere. Values

The new **myth busting** boxes highlight and explore common misconceptions in psychology.

? What do you think?

Arguably the most vivid illustration of idealism is provided by the first film of *The Matrix* trilogy (1999). In this film the main character discovers that the world he has been living in is fake. In reality, he – like all other people he is interacting with – is floating in a liquid-filled pod, serving as an energy source for machines, and his brain is being fed with a virtual reality by means of wires. The whole outside world, which felt very real to him, turned out to be nothing but an imagination. What do you think: is it possible that the world we are living in does not really exist? Are you as real on the internet as in daily life?

What do you think? boxes offer students the chance to pause and reflect on what they've read, and to consider their own opinions.

KEY FIGURE Charles Darwin

- British biologist (1809–1882).
- Famous for his contributions to biology:
  - description of new species
  - importance of cross-fertilisation
  - development of the evolutionary theory.
- Impact for the advancement of science:
  - focused on the similarities among animals and humans
  - pointed to the importance of heredity
  - developed a theory of how life adapts to changing situations.

Source: FPG/Getty Images.

Key figure boxes sum up the main facts about important people in the field of psychology, and their contribution to our understanding of the subject.

Interim summary

- In France, psychology was seen as part of the humanities as a result of Comte's writings. This was questioned by Ribot, who pointed to the developments in the UK and the German lands.
- Another towering figure in France was Charcot, a neurologist best known in psychology for his research on hysteria. Trusted entirely on his clinical expertise, which turned out to be wrong in the case of hypnosis.
- Binet and Simon's development of the first valid test of intelligence is France's best-known contribution to early psychology.

Interim summaries provide a recap and revision tool to help students get to grips with the main points.

Recommended literature

Most handbooks of neuropsychology contain a chapter on the history of the discipline. In addition, an increasing number of the original publications are becoming available on the internet. Interesting books on the history of neurophysiology are Finger, S. (1994) *Origins of neuroscience: A history of explorations into brain function* (Oxford: Oxford University Press), Gross, C.G. (1998) *Brain, vision, memory: Tales in the history of neuroscience* (Cambridge, MA: The MIT Press) and Clarke, E. & Jacyna, L.S. (1987) *Nineteenth-century origins of neuroscientific concepts* (Berteley, CA: University of California Press). A classic textbook of cognitive neuropsychology is Ellis, A.W. & Young, A.W. (1988) *Human cognitive neuropsychology* (Hove, UK: Psychology Press). Good books about cognitive neuroscience are Gazzaniga, M.S. (2008) *Cognitive neuroscience: The biology of the mind* (New York: W.W. Norton & Co.) and Ward, J. (2010) *The student's guide to cognitive neuroscience* (2nd edition) (Hove, UK: Psychology Press).

Recommended literature offers useful and manageable suggestions for further study of the topics covered in each chapter.

Acknowledgements

We are grateful to the following for permission to reproduce copyright material:

Cartoons

Cartoon on page 233 from Boston Diagnostic Aphasia Examination–Third Edition (BDAE-3), by Goodglass, H. in collaboration with Kaplan, E. and Barresi, B., 2001, Austin, TX: PRO-ED. Copyright 2001 by PRO-ED, Inc. Reprinted with permission.

Figures

Figure 1.1 from *The universal history of numbers: From prehistory to the invention of the computer,* Ifrah, G. Copyright © 1998 The Harvill Press. Reproduced with permission of John Wiley & Sons, Inc. and Éditions Robert Laffont; Figure 1.1 from The *Universal History of Numbers: The Computer and the Information Revolution* by *George Ifrah.* Published by The Harvill Press. Reprinted by permission of The Random House Group Limited. Figure 1.2 from *The mathematical brain,* Macmillan (Butterworth, B. 1999) Fig. 2.3, p. 91; Figure 1.5 from Aristotelian cosmology, 1524, Royal Astronomical Society/Science Photo Library (V700/432); Figure 2.1 from http://vikdhillon.staff.shef.ac.uk/teaching/phy105/celsphere/phy105_ptolemy.html, ©Vik Dhillon, 30th September 2009; Figure 3.2 from Quantitative visual psychophysics during the period of European enlightenment. The studies of astronomer and mathematician Tobias Mayer (1723–1762) on visual acuity and colour perception, *Documenta Ophthalmologica,* 71, pp. 93–111 (Grüsser, O.J. 1989), With kind permission from Springer Science+Business Media; Figure 5.3 from *Animal intelligence: Experimental studies* (Thorndike, E.L. 1911) Figure 2, p.39, Copyright 1911 by Transaction Publishers. Reprinted by permission of the publisher; Figure 6.1 from *The Edwin Smith Sugical Papyrus,* Vol. 2 (Breasted, J.H. 1930) Plates XVII and XVIIA Courtesy of the Oriental Institute of the University of Chicago; Figure 6.4 from The withdrawal arc by Descartes, Stock Montage Inc. Reproduced with permission; Figure 6.5 reprinted from *The outline of science: A plain story simply told,* G.P. Putnam's Sons (Thomson, J.A. 1922); Figures 6.7, 6.8 adapted from Language and the brain, *Scientific American,* 226, 4, p. 78 (Geschwind, N. 1972) © The Estate of Bunji Tagawa; Figure 6.9 from *Nineteenth century origins of neuroscientific concepts,* Berkeley, California: University of California Press (Clarke, E. and Jacyna, L.S. 1987); Figures 6.10, 6.16 from *Psychologie,* Academia Press (Brysbaert, M. 2006); Figure 6.11 reproduced from Disturbance of vision by cerebral lesions, *British Journal of Opthalmology,* Holmes, G.M., 2, p. 355 Copyright 1918 with permission from BMJ Publishing Group Ltd; Figures 6.12, 6.13 adapted from Morton, J. and Patterson, K., 'A new attempt at an interpretation, or, an attempt at a new interpretation' in, *Deep Dyslexia* (Coltheart, M., et al. (eds.) 1980) Copyright 1980, Routledge and Kegan Paul. Reproduced by permission of Taylor & Francis Books UK; Figure 6.14 reprinted from *EEG & Clinical Neurophysiology,* Supp. 28, Berger, H., Hans Berger on the electroencephalogram of man: The fourteen original reports on the human electroencephalogram, Copyright 1969; Figure 6.18 from Gross, Charles G., *Brain, vision, memory: Tales in the history of neuroscience,* Figure on page 54, © 1998 Massachusetts Institute of Technology, by permission of The MIT Press; Figure 6.19 from Social cognitive neuroscience: A review of the core processes, *Annual Review of Psychology,* 58, pp. 259–89 (Lieberman, M.D. 2007); Figure 6.20 adapted from Capgras delusion: a window on face recogntion, *Trends in Cognitive Science,* 5(4), Figure 4 (Ellis, H.D. & Lewis, M.B. 2001) Copyright 2001, with permission from Elsevier; Figure 7.1 from Affective discrimination of stimuli that cannot be recognized, *Science,* 207, pp. 557–8 (Kunst-Wilson, W.R., and Zajonc, R.B. 1980). Reprinted with permission from AAAS; Figure 7.2 reprinted from *Cognitive Psychology,* 15(4), Marcel, A.J., Conscious and unconscious cognitive perception: experiments on visual masking and word recognition, pp. 197–237, Copyright 1983, with permission from Elsevier; Figure 7.3 reprinted from *Trends in Cognitive Sciences,* 9(6), Haggard, P., Conscious intention and motor cognition, pp. 290–5, Copyright 2005, with permission from Elsevier; Figure 7.5 adapted by permission from Macmillan Publishers Ltd: Brain mechanisms linking language and action, *Nature Reviews Neuroscience,* 6(7), July, pp. 576–82 (Pulvermuller, F. 2005), Figure 1 Schematic illustration of the cortical systems for language and action, Copyright 2005; Figure 7.6 from On making the right choice: The deliberation-without-attention effect, *Science,* 311, pp. 1005–7

(Dijksterhuis, A., Bos, M.W., Nordgren, L.F., & Van Baaren, R.B. 2006). Reprinted with permission from AAAS; Figure 8.4 from Pseudohistory and pseudoscience, *Science & Education*, 13, 179–95 (Allchin, D. 2004), With kind permission of Springer Science+Business Media; Figures 9.1, 9.2 from Edith Brysbaert; Figure 9.7 With kind permission from Springer Science+Business Media: *Perception and Psychophysics*, Ambiguity of form: Old and new, Vol. 4, 1968, p. 191, Fisher, G.H., Figure 3.6; Figures 9.8 and 9.9 with permission of Isa Brysbaert; Figure 10.1 from Mapping the backbone of science, *Scientometrics*, 64, pp. 351–374, Figure 4 on p. 365 Map of science generated using the IC-Jaccard similarity measure (Boyack. K.W., Klavans, R. and Borner, K. 2005), with kind permission from Springer Science+Business Media; Figure 10.2 republished with permission of National Science Teachers Association from Scientists - Geeks and Nerds? Dispelling teachers stereotypes of scientists., *Science and Children*, 38, pp. 16–19 (McDuffie, T.E. 2001), permission conveyed through Copyright Clearance Center Inc.; Figure 11.1 Reproduced from *British Medical Journal*, 'Mortality in relation to smoking: 50 years' observations on male British doctors', Doll, R., Peto, R., Boreham, J. and Sutherland, I., Vol. 328, pp. 1519–28, © 2004 with permission from BMJ Publishing Group Ltd. Figure 12.1 adapted from A rose by any other name would it smell as sweet?, *Journal of Neurophysiology*, 99, pp. 386–93 (Djordevic, J. et al. 2008).

Tables

Table 6.1 from Gross, Charles G., *Brain, vision, memory: Tales in the history of neuroscience*, Table from page 21, © 1998 Massachusetts Institute of Technology, by permission of The MIT Press; Table 8.2 based on Figure 2.11b "Multiple comparisons of mean performance on the science scale" from OECD (2007), PISA 2006: Science Competencies for Tomorrow's World: Volume 1: Analysis, PISA, OECD Publishing. http://dx.doi. org/10.1787/9789264040014-en; Table 8.3 reprinted from Organizational Dynamics, Vol. 13, Weisbord, M.R., Participative work design: A personal odessey, pp. 4–20, Copyright 1985, with permission from Elsevier, itself adapted from *The evolution of socio-technical systems – A conceptual framework and an action research program*, Toronto, Canada: Ontario Ministry of Labour (Trist, E. 1981) Ontario Quality of Working Life Centre, Occasional Paper 2, © Queen's Printer for Ontario, 1981. Adapted and reproduced with permission.; Table 11.3 from Artificial intelligence and other approaches to speech understanding: reflections on methodology, Ward, N., *Journal of Experimental and Theoretical Artificial Intelligence*, 1998 Taylor & Francis Ltd, reprinted by permission of the publisher (Taylor & Francis Ltd, http://

www.tandf.co.uk/journals); Table 11.7 adapted from Starks, H. and Trinidad, S.B., Choose you method: a comparison of phenomenology, discourse analysis and grounded theory, *Qualitative Health Research*, 17, pp. 1372–80, copyright © 2007 by SAGE PUBLICATIONS. Reprinted by permission of SAGE Publications; Table 12.2 adapted from Geert Hofstede, Gert Jan Hofstede, Michael Minkov, *Cultures and organizations: Software of the mind*, Third Revised Edition, McGrawHill 2010, ISBN 0-07-166418-1. © Geert Hofstede B.V. quoted with permission.

Text

Extract on pages 49–50 from book review of *Galileo Antichrist: A Biography* by Michael White, *The Guardian*, 04/08/2007 (Callow, S.), Copyright Guardian News & Media Ltd 2007; Extract on pages 131–2 from The psychological Laboratory at Leipsic, *Mind*, 13, pp. 37–51 (Cattell, J.M. 1888), Mind by MIND ASSOCIATION Reproduced with permission of OXFORD UNIVERSITY PRESS; Extract on pages 129–30 from Wundt's laboratory at Leipzig in 1891, *History of Psychology*, 2, 194–203 (Nicolas, S. & Ferrand, L. 1999), Copyright © 1999 by the American Psychological Association. Reproduced with permission. The official citation that should be used in referencing this material is Wundt's laboratory at Leipzig in 1891, History of Psychology, 2, 194–203 (Nicolas, S. & Ferrand, L. 1999). The use of this information does not imply endorsement by the publisher; Interview questions on pages 455–6 Copyright © 2007 by the American Psychological Association. Reproduced with permission. The official citation that should be used in referencing this material is Interview questions, p. 15 from Schraw, G., Wadkins, T. & Olafson, L. (2007). Doing the things we do: A grounded theory of academic procrastination. *Journal of Educational Psychology*, 99(1), 12–25. No further reproduction or distribution is permitted without written permission from the American Psychological Association. Extract on pages 348–9 excerpt from *The Times*, November 20th 2007. Copyright © NI Syndication Limited.

Picture Credits

The publisher would like to thank the following for their kind permission to reproduce their photographs:

(Key: b-bottom; c-centre; l-left; r-right; t-top)

Alamy Images: Daniel Templeton 223tr; The Art Archive 22br © **David M. Buss, all rights reserved.:** 492; **Corbis:** Bettmann 193, Roger Ressmeyer 315; **Cornell University Library/Rare & Manuscript Collections:** 141; **Getty Images:** Bill Pierce / Time&Life Pictures 395b, FPG 113, Hulton Archive 395t, Popperfoto 335, Raymond Koch /

Photonica 252b; **Harry Whittaker:** 248b; **Institute and Museum of the History of Science, Florence, Italy. :** 55t; **Mary Evans Picture Library:** Interfoto / Sammlung Rauch 225br; © 2007 by the Massachusetts Institute of Technology: 225b; **Neuropsychologia:** 253c; **Science & Society Picture Library:** 115; **Science Photo Library Ltd:** A J Photo / Hop Americain 251, 138, BSIP / Jacopin 232, CCi Archives 56br, Detlev Van Ravenswaay 51, Dr Jurgen Scriba 251b, Geoff Kidd 83, Humanities and Social Services Library / New York Public Library 188, National Library of Medicine 155, RIA Novosti 189, Royal Astronomical Society 54, UC Regents / Lick Oberservatory 375, University of Durham /

Simon Fraser 254, US National Library of Medicine 134, 151; **TBGS Observatory/Chris Proctor:** 49; **Wellcome Library, London:** 225, 225t, Heidi Cartwright 223tl; **Yale Pictorial Records & Collections:** Robert Mearns Yerkes Papers 187

Cover images: *Front:* **Antony Gormley**

All other images © Pearson Education

In some instances we have been unable to trace the owners of copyright material, and we would appreciate any information that would enable us to do so.

1 The wider picture
Where did it all start?

Questions to consider

?

Historical issues addressed in this chapter

- When did the first writing systems appear?
- When did the first number systems appear, and what did they look like?
- Did the Ancient Greek civilisation end after it was conquered by the Romans?
- How did information from the Greek and Roman cultures survive the Dark Ages?
- How long did the Middle Ages last?
- Why did countries such as the UK, parts of Germany and the Netherlands at a certain point become more productive than the other European countries?

Conceptual issues addressed in this chapter

- In what ways does the availability of written records change human thought?
- In what ways do current writing systems differ from the first ones? Is this an improvement?
- Can education change the way in which we read texts?
- How does arithmetic depend on the code that is used to represent numbers?
- Why were Christian schools after the fall of the Roman Empire unable to prevent a sharp decline in scientific knowledge?
- Is it possible to write a complete history of science?
- To what extent does our current scientific knowledge depend on the contribution of a small number of geniuses who achieved the major scientific breakthroughs?

Introduction

If you, reader, had been born, say, two or more centuries ago, the chances are that you would have been poor, indeed extremely poor. You would have spent your whole life working the land, with no hope or prospect of change. Except for the odd tenacious survivor, your numerous children would have predeceased you. You would have taken it for granted that you would probably not live beyond the age of about forty-five. Your home would have been a country hovel, heated in winter with whatever firewood you had managed to gather. The only source of other comforts would have been the few coppers you had hoarded. Apart from everyday conversation, infant wailing and the clucking of chickens, you would have been surrounded by silence, broken every so often by a clap of thunder, communal singing, the occasional drums and trumpets of passing armies, or perhaps the tolling of a solitary bell. You would have believed firmly and unquestioningly in the literal existence of spirits or gods, or a single God, as the guiding or all-determining force in life and especially after death.

(Cohen 2010)

Human life has changed profoundly in the last few centuries, due to the growing impact of science on our lives. If you look around, it is easy to see how society is filled with scientific products and scientifically-based solutions to social problems. Because of the ubiquity of science, we often forget how recent this state of affairs really is.

This book describes the growth of psychology as an independent branch of learning and tries to comprehend the essence of the discipline. Because it deals with fundamental and long-standing questions, we begin rather a long time ago. We begin by discussing the invention of writing and numerical systems, as these were critical developments that allowed the accumulation of knowledge and understanding. We then present a short account of the ancient civilisations – the Greeks, the Romans, the Byzantine and Arab empires – and consider the role each played in the evolution of knowledge. In particular, we focus on the key figures whose ideas and philosophies have had a strong impact on Western civilisation. We end with a brief description of the Renaissance. We focus on those events that shaped the emergence of the scientific approach as we now know it. Our review starts thousands of years ago and ends on the eve of the scientific revolution in the seventeenth century.

1.1 The invention of writing

The introduction of written records represents one of the most important moments in the development of science. Therefore, it is important to know when and where writing systems were invented and what is so important about them.

The preliterate culture

preliterate civilisation
civilisation before writing was invented

One way that we can start to answer why the invention of writing was so significant in the development of science is by exploring the nature of preliterate civilisations. Though these civilisations have not left us with written testimonies, it is possible to discern several important features of them by studying existing cultures that do not use writing, as advanced by Lindberg (1992). His research revealed three important characteristics of knowledge in these kinds of cultures.

First, Lindberg observed that although cultures without literacy know how to make tools, start fires, obtain shelter, hunt, fish, and gather fruit and vegetables, their skills are not based on an understanding of how things work, but rather on practical rules of thumb of what to do when. Their knowledge is confined to 'know-how' without theoretical understanding of the underlying principles.

A second characteristic of a culture without written records is the fluidity of knowledge. Knowledge of the actual history of the tribe is limited to two generations and the function of the oral tradition mainly is the transmission of practical skills.

A third feature of these cultures is the existence of a collection of myths and stories about the beginning of the universe, life and natural phenomena, in which human traits are projected onto objects and events (e.g. in the form of gods). The belief that objects and nature are inhabited by spirits with human-like characteristics, which cause events to happen, is called animism. The term was introduced by Sir Edward Burnett Tylor (1832–1917), one of the first anthropologists, to draw a distinction between the thinking of 'primitive people' as opposed to the then growing 'scientific thinking' in the Western world. In Tylor's view, primitives (as they were

animism
explanation of the workings of the world and the universe by means of spirits with human-like characteristics

called) looked at the world like children and endowed all things, even inanimate ones, with a nature analogous to their own (Bird-David 1999).

Lindberg (1992) looked down upon the animistic thinking of preliterate civilisations less than Tylor did. For him, the myths and stories reinforced the values and attitudes of the community and fulfilled the human need for explanatory principles capable of bringing order, unity and meaning to events. In general, the myths are also related to the treatment of illnesses: the person with the greatest knowledge of the myths is the person to whom people turn when they have an ailment. At the same time, Lindberg noticed that myths often contradict each other and contain inconsistencies, without any evidence that this hinders the preliterate people. Each story stands on its own. It is only when information is written down that patterns start to emerge and incompatibilities become visible. Therefore, Lindberg argued, scientific thinking cannot occur without written records.

The first writing systems

Written language appeared separately in at least four cultures: in China (around 6,000 BCE)[1], Egypt (around 3,200 BCE), Sumer (also around 3,200 BCE) and America (Olmec and Mayan, 300 BCE). These four written languages were preceded by proto-writing, the use of symbols to represent entities without linguistic information linking them.

Characteristics of writing systems

pictogram

an information-conveying sign that consists of a picture resembling the person, animal or object it represents

phonogram

a sign that represents a sound or a syllable of spoken language; forms the basis of writing systems

logograph

a sign representing a spoken word, which no longer has a physical resemblance to the word's meaning

From an early stage, writing systems were a combination of pictograms (pictures that resemble the persons, animals and objects they represent) and phonograms (signs to represent sounds of the spoken language). The Egyptian hieroglyphs, for instance, could only be deciphered when scientists realised that most hieroglyphs represented spoken syllables. The phonograms were gradually replaced by simpler signs symbolising meaningful sounds in the language (phonemes) or syllables. The use of phonograms to represent phonemes led to the alphabetic writing systems, starting with the Phoenician alphabet that formed the basis of the Arabic, Hebrew and Greek alphabets. The writing system that has remained closest to the pictograms is Chinese, where the correspondence between the physical signs and the word meanings they represented rapidly decreased, so that the writing system became logographic rather than pictographic (words are represented by written signs – characters – that no longer resemble the meanings they stand for). However, in this language as well, most written words consist of two characters that have a relationship to the word's meaning and that often include cues to the pronunciation.

Written documents form an external memory

Writing and the accumulation of knowledge

The importance of writing lies in the external memory written records provide about the knowledge available at a certain point in time. This is important because it allows an accumulation of knowledge. New thinkers do not have to rediscover what was previously thought; they can simply read what their predecessors wrote. This does not mean that insights are never overlooked (certainly not when a lot is published and not always readily available), but it usually implies that the insights can be retrieved if one is motivated to look for them (the history of science is full of rediscoveries of seminal teachers who were only known to a small circle of ex-students).

A particularly revealing excerpt illustrating the importance of written documents is provided by a remark made by Socrates. Socrates (*c.* 470–399 BCE) was an important philosopher in Ancient Greece, who was not at all interested in keeping written records of his thoughts. In a dialogue with a young student (Phaedrus) Socrates recounted how the god Thoth of Egypt offered the king of Egypt all types of inventions, including dice, checkers, numbers, geometry, astronomy and writing. The god and the king discussed the merits and drawbacks of the various gifts and were in general agreement until they reached the gift of writing. Whereas the god stressed the advantage of being able to remember information, the king objected: 'If men learn this, it will implant forgetfulness in their souls; they will cease to exercise memory because they will rely on that which is written, calling things to remembrance no longer from within themselves, but by means of external marks.' From the remainder of the dialogue it is clear that Socrates wholeheartedly agreed with the king of Egypt and thought that the availability of books made students lazy and discouraged them from properly studying.

What do you think?

Very much the same criticism is made nowadays about the use of the internet by students. Because all information is easily available, there is no need for them to learn it any more. What do you think? Is the internet changing our thinking in the same way as the invention of writing did?

The irony of the dialogue is that we would never have heard of this, or indeed of any of Socrates' other memorable dialogues, if they had not been documented by his student, Plato. An oral tradition would most certainly have changed the wording of the story and in all likelihood it would not have survived up to today. In addition, the dialogue would not have been included in the present book, if it had not been present in Manguel's (1996) *A history of reading* (on page 58), which we read in the preparation of this chapter.

Written records not only made more information available; they also subtly changed the way in which knowledge was preserved. Before the advent of writing, important legends were memorised as verses, because the rhythm and the rhyme of the poem helped the narrator to remember the correct phrases, so that the contents did not change too dramatically from one storyteller to the next. Written texts allowed cultures to relax the formal constraints and concentrate on the content.

The reader

Who can read?

Written records only have an impact if there is somebody to read them. For most of human history the number of people who could read was relatively small (it still is nowadays in some communities). For many centuries a large proportion of the population was excluded from acquiring reading skills. In addition, the early scripts lacked an important characteristic that makes alphabetic languages easier to read: spaces between the words. Even the ancient Greek and Latin texts were written in so-called *scriptio continua* (continuous script). Only in the eighth century did writers start to put spaces between the words. Saenger (1997) argues that this quality of texts made silent reading possible. Before, nearly all readers read aloud or at least had to mumble while reading (a practice that was still widespread in the nineteenth century). In 383 Aurelius Augustine (known as Saint Augustine in the Catholic Church) expressed his surprise when he met the bishop of Milan and saw that he could read silently. 'When he read,' said Augustine, 'his eyes scanned the page and his heart sought out the meaning, but his voice was silent and his tongue was still' (as cited in Manguel 1996: 42).

The influence of orthography

Reading is still a demanding skill, as is illustrated by the many efforts beginning readers have to invest to acquire it. Reading acquisition is easiest in languages with a transparent relationship between spelling and sound, such as Spanish, Italian, Serbo-Croatian, German and Korean, where most children 'crack the code' in less than a year (although they need many more years of practice before the processes become automatic). In languages with a more opaque correspondence, such as English and Hebrew, children need up to four years in order to reach the same level of performance and are more likely to be confronted with reading difficulties (Hanley *et al.* 2004; Ziegler *et al.* 2010).

Reading without critical thinking

Readers in the past differed in one more aspect from present-day scientific readers. For a long time students were taught to read and understand texts exactly as they were. They were in no way encouraged (and were often discouraged) to question the writings or to compare them with other writings. Books were the world's wisdom that had to be transmitted in its original form from generation to generation. As Manguel (1996: 74) noted:

scholastic method
study method in which students unquestioningly memorise and recite texts that are thought to convey unchanging truths

> Essentially the **scholastic method** consisted in little more than training the students to consider a text according to certain pre-established, officially approved criteria which were painstakingly and painfully drilled into them. As far as the teaching of reading was concerned, the success of the method depended more on the students' perseverance than on their intelligence.

The scholastic method was prevalent in schools up to the twentieth century. Even in 1932, Gupta complained that Indian education was still adversely affected by the remnants of the ancient Indian system of requiring pupils first to learn a book by heart and only then to receive an explanation of it.

?

What do you think?

Currently psychology textbooks emphasise 'critical thinking'. From our discussion of the scholastic method, you can understand why this is the case. However, could such an emphasis be exaggerated? Is it possible to think critically without first knowing the facts? What do you think of the arguments in the following quote?

In the past 15–20 years, the most important buzz words . . . . , from kindergardens to graduate schools, have been 'critical thinking'. When it comes up, it is either from a stance of attack ('You are not teaching students enough critical thinking skills!'), or a stance of pride ('We emphasize critical thinking in all our classes!'). The need to teach these skills is felt strongly, and the attitude accompanying it is definitely one of a teacher–student relationship. It is assumed that the teachers can do it, but that most students cannot, and that the best means to get students to do it is through explicit instruction of some type. This burden is not felt equally by professors in all disciplines; often such rhetoric is strongest in the social sciences. As a result, teaching 'critical thinking' is a declared goal of most Introductory Psychology professors. Alas, the goal of teaching critical thinking is inherently flawed; the teacher–student attitude does not create an environment that supports critical thinking; instead, it creates an environment in which the task is to reflect the teacher's critique of the issues, which itself cannot be criticized . . . Rather than trying to set up artificial situations in which students are told to challenge particular views, class should be a context in which students begin to master the knowledge that makes up the field of psychology, which will aid them in challenging things on their own in later classes.

(Charles 2008: Problem 2)

Interim summary

- Features of the preliterate civilisation:
  - knowledge confined to 'know-how' without theoretical knowledge of the underlying principles
  - fluidity of knowledge
  - collection of myths and stories about the beginning of the universe (animism).
- Written language appeared separately in at least four cultures; in each case it was preceded by proto-writing.
- Writing consists of a combination of pictograms and phonograms.
- Written records form an external memory, which allows an accumulation of knowledge.
- For a long time the number of readers was limited. In addition, they were not encouraged to think critically about what they were reading (scholastic method).

1.2 The discovery of numbers

Another development that has been crucial for the growth of knowledge is the discovery of numbers. When we do a simple arithmetic operation, we rarely realise how much insight and knowledge are hidden behind the procedures we use. Interestingly enough, the history of numbers and numerical operations remained largely unexplored until the French maths teacher Georges Ifrah decided to take the issue in hand, a quest that took him over 10 years to finish (see Ifrah 1998).

The limits of visual perception and the special status of the number five

The ease of understanding the numbers one to three

The possession of goods required the ability to count them. The earliest archaeological evidence of counting dates back to 35,000–20,000 BCE and has been found in Africa (Powell & Frankenstein 1997). The evidence consists of lines or other markings carved in bones and stones, as for example found on the Ishango bone (Huylebrouck 2006). It is reasonable to assume that quite early in their evolution humans could make distinctions up to three, which were represented by one, two and three markings. Newborn babies and all kinds of animals can distinguish between one, two and three entities, a phenomenon that is known as *subitising*. Also, a number of isolated tribes have been described as having a number naming system that essentially consisted of three terms: one, two and many.

Larger numbers and the need for grouping the tallies

A problem with tallies to represent numbers is that they rapidly exceed the limits of perception. Whereas nobody has difficulties understanding the symbols I, II and III, the use of an analogue code (i.e. a code that represents numbers by a physical magnitude) rapidly starts to fall apart for larger quantities. Number representations like IIIIII and IIIIIIII are not very useful, even though they are still limited to quantities as small as six and eight. A first solution to this problem was a grouping of the tallies, as we still do when we write ⦀⦀ I or ⦀⦀ III. This method was used independently in several cultures. The most popular grouping had a base five (as in the example above). There are two reasons why this base appeared in many places. First, the number five is the first entity that really exceeds the perceptual limits (it is possible to grasp a grouping of four perceptually without counting the tallies, as in IIII). The number five also coincides with the number of fingers on a hand. Gradually, the base number five started to get a different symbol. For instance, the Etruscan civilisation used the following symbols for the numbers one to five in the sixth to the fourth centuries BCE: I, II, III, IIII, Λ (notice the similarity to the Roman numerals; the Etruscans lived in ancient Italy before they were conquered by the Romans).

Giving numbers names and symbols

The names one to ten

An analysis of the origin of the number names gives some indication of the struggle humans had before they could come up with a handy numerical system. For instance, it is probably no coincidence that the number nine is related to the word 'new' in the Indo-European family of languages. At some point in time, this probably was a newly discovered number. The fact that all Indo-European languages share the same roots for the numbers one to ten further suggests that their names already existed before the original language began to split into its many branches around 2,000 BCE. On the basis of the similarities of the number names in over 20 languages as divergent as Sanskrit, Russian and Spanish, Ifrah (1998: 32) postulates the following original number-set:

1. oino, oiko, oiwo
2. dwo, dwu, dwoi

3. tri

4. kwetwores, kwetesres, kwetwor

5. penkwe, kwenkwe

6. seks, sweks

7. septm

8. okto, oktu

9. newn

10. dekm

Notice how little these names have changed in the 4,000 or so years since.

The problem of naming the teens

Another feature of many of the Indo-European number names is the irregularity of the number names of the teens (i.e. the numbers 11–19). It is clear that some of these numbers were given their names before the base 10 of the number system was fully grasped. Due to the groupings of the tallies, at some point it was realised that large numbers were best represented as multiples of smaller numbers, so-called base numbers. The most frequently chosen base number was 10 (double five, not coincidentally the numbers of fingers on our two hands). However, the Sumerian number system had a base 60, the consequences of which we still experience in our time units (1 hr = 60 min = 60 × 60 s) and the French number names betray the fact that at some time a base 20 was used (97 = quatre-vingt dix-sept [four-twenty ten-seven]).

The names of the teens in the Indo-European languages illustrate the struggle humans had to integrate the base 10 system in their number names. So, instead of calling the number 11 'ten-one' (analogous to twenty-one), the English name turned out to be 'eleven'. This name is still related to the counting of the fingers (it comes from 'one left' [when the fingers of both hands have been counted]; the same is true for twelve, 'two left'), but the structure of the name betrays that it came into being before it was realised that the best way to represent numbers above ten was to treat them as combinations of tens and units. The irregular naming of the teens is not present in the Chinese number system, which according to some researchers may be one of the reasons why Chinese children have less of a problem understanding the base 10 system of numbers.

Representing numbers by symbols

Once the different numbers had their names, it was a small step to represent them by different symbols. From 600 BCE the Greeks developed a written system for the numbers 1–24 based on the 24 letters of their alphabet, going from alpha (1) to omega (24). This system is still in use in Hebrew for expressing the date by the Hebrew calendar, for chapters and verses of the Torah, and sometimes for the page numbers of books.

The fact that numbers in Ancient Greece could be represented by letters does not mean that such a notation was used for calculations. This would have created insurmountable difficulties as it would suggest a base system of 24. Instead, the Greeks used a notation that was in line with a base 10 structure, which they adapted from previous cultures. This notation is shown in Figure 1.1. Notice the similarity to Roman numerals.

1 **ı**	100 **H**	10,000 **M**
2 **ıı**	200 **HH**	20,000 **MM**
3 **ııı**	300 **HHH**	30,000 **MMM**
4 **ıııı**	400 **HHHH**	40,000 **MMMM**
5 **Γ**	500 **ᴘ**	50,000 **ᴘ**
6 **Γı**	600 **ᴘH**	60,000 **ᴘ M**
7 **Γıı**	700 **ᴘHH**	70,000 **ᴘ MM**
8 **Γııı**	800 **ᴘHHH**	80,000 **ᴘ MMM**
9 **Γıııı**	900 **ᴘHHHH**	90,000 **ᴘ MMMM**
10 **Δ**	1,000 **X**	
20 **ΔΔ**	2,000 **XX**	
30 **ΔΔΔ**	3,000 **XXX**	
40 **ΔΔΔΔ**	4,000 **XXXX**	
50 **ᴘ**	5,000 **ᴘ**	
60 **ᴘΔ**	6,000 **ᴘ X**	
70 **ᴘΔΔ**	7,000 **ᴘXX**	
80 **ᴘΔΔΔ**	8,000 **ᴘXXX**	
90 **ᴘΔΔΔΔ**	9,000 **ᴘXXXX**	

Figure 1.1 Number notation used by the Ancient Greeks (from 500 BCE onwards).

Apart from the vertical line for 1, all symbols are the first letter of the number names (Γ is the archaic form of pi, standing for Πεντε [Pente, five]; Δ stands for Δεκα [Deka, ten]; H for Ηεκατον [Hekaton, hundred], X for Χιλιοι [Khilioi, thousand]; M for Μυριοι [Murioi, ten thousand].
Source: Ifrah (1998: 182).

The discovery of place coding

Although the Greek and the Roman number notation was a major achievement, it was not the most parsimonious or transparent system, because the length of the symbol series was not systematically related to the base 10 structure of the numbers (e.g. 38 was represented by seven symbols, XXXVIII, whereas the number 50 was represented by a single symbol, L).

A much better system was developed in India. There people started to work with nine different symbols to represent the numbers one to nine. In addition, they used the place of the symbols in the digit string to represent powers of 10. The first digit represented the units, the second digit the tens, the third digit the hundreds, and so on. So, 'thirty-two' no longer consisted of two vertical lines to represent the two units and three symbols of ten to represent the 30, but became a symbol of 2 in the units position and a symbol of 3 in the tens position. Such a place coding system only works properly if there is a symbol for the absence of a quantity at a certain slot. Otherwise, it is impossible to know whether the digit string 22 refers to the number 22 or to 202, 220, 2020, 2200, or to any other combination of two 2s and voids. In the beginning this problem was solved by inserting spaces between the symbols. Eventually, a symbol for 0 was invented. There is evidence that this system – with the symbol for 0 – was fully in use by 500 CE (see Ifrah (1998) for a review; see also Seife (2000) for a discussion of the history of the number 0). The system was adopted and extended by the Arabs and subsequently taken up in Western Europe. The transition via the Arabs changed the order of the digits (i.e. the rightmost stood for the units, the second rightmost for the tens, etc.) and resulted in our current practice of calling them Arabic numerals (Figure 1.2).

place coding system

system in which the meaning of a sign not only depends on its form but also on its position in a string; is used for instance in Arabic numerals

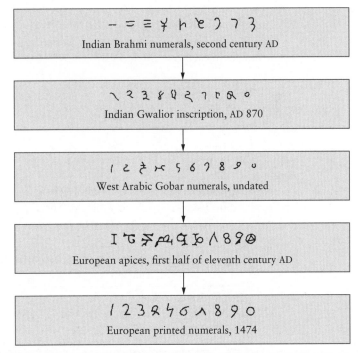

Figure 1.2 The history of Hindu-Arabic numbers.

This figure shows how digits were written in various periods of time. Notice that the number 0 was not initially part of numbering systems.

Source: Butterworth (1999: 91).

Was calculation difficult for the Greeks and the Romans?

In many books (including the first edition of this book!) you can read that the Greek and the Roman number notation hindered the development of mathematics in these cultures, because their number notation made calculations difficult. The argument is that IX + CXI (C = hundred, X = ten, I = one) is much more difficult to solve than 9 + 111, and that IX × CXI is more difficult to solve than 9 × 111.

Schlimm and Neth (2008) took issue with this view. As they wrote:

> Our initial motivation to compare the Arabic and Roman number systems was rooted in surprise and disbelief. Given the myth that Roman numerals are unsuited for arithmetic computations it is puzzling how Romans could conduct commerce, administer armies, or rule an empire.

Schlimm and Neth started their argument by claiming that we have incorrect ideas about the Roman number system. For instance, the Romans did not use the symbols IV and IX to refer to four and nine. These notations were used in the Middle Ages. Rather, the Romans used IIII and VIIII.

Next, Schlimm and Neth showed that it is possible to come up with rather simple algorithms to do addition and multiplication with Roman numerals. For example, to solve the problem VIIII + CXI, all you have to do is make separate rows for each type of symbol in the Roman system and count the number of instances in each row. So, for VIIII + CXI we get:

Row C (100):   C
Row L (50):   –
Row X (10):   X
Row V (5):   V
Row I (1):   I I I I I

Next, whenever there are five symbols in the rows C, X or I, these have to be replaced by a symbol in the row above. The same is true for two symbols in the rows V and L. So, the rows have to be rewritten as:

	Initial situation	Replace IIIII by V	Replace VV by X	End result
Row C (100):	C	C	C	CXX
Row L (50):	–	–	–	
Row X (10):	X	X	X X	
Row V (5):	V	V V	–	
Row I (1):	I I I I I	–	–	

Schlimm and Neth (2008) argued that this calculation is no more difficult (and sometimes even easier) than the addition of Arabic numerals.

To multiply two Roman numerals, one needs a multiplication table, which includes the outcome for all pairs of symbols. So, for the symbols up to C one would use the following table (in which D = 500, M = 1000, v = 5000, x = 10000):

×	I	V	X	L	C
I	I	V	X	L	C
V	V	XXV	L	CCL	D
X	X	L	C	D	M
L	L	CCL	D	MMD	$\bar{v}$
C	C	D	M	v	|x|

To multiply VIIII by CXI, one must read out the multiplication of each symbol of the first numeral with each symbol of the second numeral. So,

V × C = D	I × C = C	I × C = C	I × C = C	I × C = C
V × X = L	I × X = X	I × X = X	I × X = X	I × X = X
V × I = V	I × I = I	I × I = I	I × I = I	I × I = I

All the symbols are added by means of the line system we saw above. Thus,

Row D (500):   D
Row C (100):   C C C C
Row L (50):   L
Row X (10):   X X X X
Row V (5):   V
Row I (1):   I I I I

This gives a total of DCCCCLXXXXVIIII or 999. According to Schlimm and Neth, once one is familiar with the operations, they are no more difficult to perform than those for the multiplication of Arabic numerals.

Interim summary

- Knowledge depends on counting and measuring. The first written forms of counting consisted of lines (tallies) in bones and stones.
- Because it is difficult to discern more than four lines in a glance, the tallies were grouped. The grouping usually occurred in fives (i.e. base 5 system).
- Gradually a separate symbol was used for five and multiples of five.
- Later number systems were based on multiples of 10 (i.e. base 10 system).
- Number names indicate that the invention of numbers was a slow process; it took quite some time before a useful system was discovered.
- The Greek and Roman number systems were suboptimal because their notation did not assign a meaning to the place of the digits. Such a place coding system was developed in India. This required the invention of a symbol for 0.

1.3 The Fertile Crescent

The presence of written records marks the distinction between prehistory and history. As indicated above, the invention of writing happened independently in China, Egypt, Sumer and America. Because only the developments in Egypt and Sumer are important within the history of psychology, we will limit our discussion to these civilisations and the ones that followed them.

The Sumerian and Egyptian cultures were part of the so-called Fertile Crescent. This is a region south-east of the Mediterranean Sea (Figure 1.3), which included Ancient Mesopotamia (Sumerian culture: 3,500–2,300 BCE; Babylonian culture: 2,000–500 BCE) and Ancient Egypt (3,200–340 BCE). One of the many innovations coming from this region was the use of the wheel in the fifth millennium BCE.

Fertile Crescent

region in the Middle East with a high level of civilisation around 3,000 BCE; included the Ancient Mesopotamian and the Ancient Egyptian civilisations

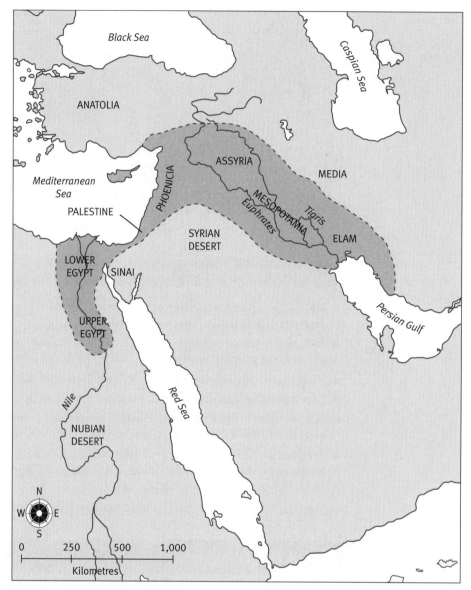

Figure 1.3 The Fertile Crescent.

Mesopotamia and Egypt also started keeping written records and developed a number system. Whether the inventions in both regions occurred independently, or whether the cultures influenced each other, is still a matter of debate.

Ancient Egypt

Two other main contributions from the Egyptians were geometrical knowledge (e.g. calculating the area of a triangle and a circle or determining the volume of a pyramid) and the devising of a calendar consisting of 12 months of 30 days and an extra 5 days at the end of the year.

Ancient Mesopotamia

Mathematical knowledge was more sophisticated in Mesopotamia. In Babylonia, for instance, the number system was superior and they also mastered the basics of algebraic equations. One of the areas in which they applied their mathematical knowledge was astronomy, which they used for their calendar and to determine the times for planting and harvesting (in addition to astrology used to predict the king's fate). They kept maps of the heavens, which allowed them to gain insight into the motions of the 'wandering stars' – the Sun, the Moon, Mercury, Venus, Mars, Jupiter and Saturn. Some of their maps were used millennia later to search for recurring patterns in, for instance, eclipses and comets.

Conditions for growth in knowledge

Contemplating the conditions that made the growth of science possible in the cultures of the Fertile Crescent, Lindberg (1992) identified the following qualities: political stability, urbanisation, patronage and the availability of a writing system that was easy enough to be learned by enough people so that a critical mass could be reached. He claimed that the same factors explained why other cultures experienced similar spurts of knowledge.

What do you think?

Lindberg described several factors that were of importance for the growth of science. Can you order them? For instance, how important is political stability? As we will see in the next chapter, the scientific revolution started in the seventeenth century. Was this a less turbulent century in Europe than the sixteenth or the eighteenth century?

Interim summary

- Civilisations in the Fertile Crescent:
  - Ancient Mesopotamia: mathematics (algebra, astronomy, calendar)
  - Ancient Egypt: geometrical knowledge, calendar, hieroglyphs.

1.4 The Greeks

Without doubt, in the beginning the Ancient Greeks borrowed heavily from Egypt and Mesopotamia. However, they soon added their own knowledge. A famous example in this respect was the physician Hippocrates (460–370 BCE). Although his work likely was embedded within existing traditions, he wrote and edited a collection of treatises on medical conditions and treatments, the *Corpus Hippocraticum,* which had such an impact on medical practice that Hippocrates is generally considered to be the father of (modern) medicine.

The start of philosophy

philosophy
critical reflection on the universe and human functioning; started in Ancient Greece

Ancient Greece was probably the first culture that started to ask serious questions about the nature of the world they lived in. This was the beginning of philosophy around 600 BCE. One of the questions pondered was whether the foundations of life were constant or ever-changing. Heraclitus (535–475 BCE), for instance, argued that everything was constantly changing and that even if you did the same thing twice, it was different because the conditions were no longer exactly the same. Others argued that at the end of the explanatory road of the perceivable changing phenomena, there had to be something fixed and unchangeable. The most famous of them was Plato who, together with Aristotle, has had an enormous influence on Western thought.

Plato

Plato (427–348 BCE) was the first thinker to call philosophy a distinct approach with its own subject and method. He is regarded as the one who coined the word 'philosophy', defined as 'love of wisdom'. A remarkable aspect of his texts is that they consist of dialogues of persons discussing philosophical matters. One of the participants was usually Socrates, Plato's mentor. Because of the dialogue format, it is never entirely clear whether Plato shared the position articulated by his characters, or used the dialogue to raise the argument for the reader. Because of the format there are also notable inconsistencies between the ideas/arguments put forward in different books. As a result, many generations of philosophers have debated about what can be seen as the essence of Plato's philosophy. Below, we review some of the topics about which there is consensus.

The realm of the ideal forms

The first important element of Plato's philosophy was the distinction he made between the realm of eternal, never-changing ideal forms and the realm of the ever-changing material reality in which the forms or ideas are imperfectly realised and which we perceive. According to Plato, we perceive nothing but the shadows of the objects. Plato further considered the soul and the body as two distinct and radically different kinds of entity, and he saw the soul as the entity defining the person. The soul was immortal, made of the leftovers of the cosmos-soul. It travelled between the stars and the human body it temporarily inhabited. Because human souls were part of the cosmos-soul, they had knowledge of the perfect realm. Therefore, humans could get access to the true ideas (e.g. about goodness, beauty, equality, change) by focusing on the innate knowledge brought by the immortal soul. For Plato, the true path to knowledge was the inward path of reasoning rather than the outward path of perception. The excerpt below summarises Plato's view (from *The Republic*):

> The starry heaven which we behold is the finest and most perfect of visible things, but it must necessarily be deemed to be greatly inferior, just because they are visible, to the true motions of absolute swiftness and absolute slowness, which are relative to each other. The true realities of velocities are found in pure number and in every perfect figure. Now, these are to be apprehended by reason and intelligence, but not by sight.

For Plato, the most prestigious knowledge was mathematical and geometrical knowledge, because in these disciplines new information is derived from a set of principles by means of reasoning.

The three parts of the soul

In some of his writings, Plato (or rather one of the characters in the dialogue) defended the idea that the soul was divided into three parts. The first part comprised reason, as discussed above. It allowed humans to get access to the realm of the ideal forms. It guided them to a virtuous life in search of abstract, non-worldly perfection, which was the ideal fulfilment of human nature. According to Plato, reason was situated in the brain. The second part of the soul dealt with sensation and emotions such as anger, fear, pride and courage. It was mortal and situated in the heart. To avoid it polluting the divine soul, a neck separated the two. Finally, the lower part of the soul dealt with appetite and the lower passions, such as lust, greed and desire. It was localised in the liver (Figure 1.4).

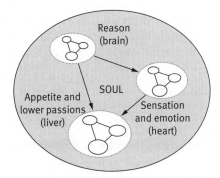

Figure 1.4 In some of his writings, Plato distinguished three parts in the soul.

The first part comprised reason, allowing humans to get access to the realm of the ideal forms. The second part dealt with sensation and emotions such as anger, fear and pride. The last part dealt with appetite and lower passions such as lust, greed and desire. The parts were situated in different organs of the human body, respectively the brain, the heart and the liver.

KEY FIGURE Plato

- Greek philosopher (427–348 BCE).
- Founder of the Academy in Athens.
- Recorded the dialogues of Socrates.
- Made a distinction between the realm of eternal, never-changing ideal forms and the realm of the ever-changing material reality in which these forms or ideas are imperfectly realised (an analogy used here is that we are in a cave and only see the shadows of the real forms).
- Method of knowledge: rationalism (truth is based on thinking, not on information from the senses; humans have innate knowledge that can be recovered through deductive reasoning).
- Made a distinction between three parts of the soul: reason (brain), sensation plus emotion (heart), and appetite plus lower passions (liver).
- Plato's views appealed to the Christian churches and, therefore, his books were among the most widely available in the late Roman Empires and the Middle Ages.
- Also strongly influenced René Descartes (see Chapter 2).

Aristotle

A second towering figure in Ancient Greece was Aristotle (384–322 BCE). He was a student of Plato, but deviated in important ways from his mentor (e.g. he did not postulate an independent realm of ideal forms). He was also an inspiring teacher, who usually started by reviewing the available evidence and then supplementing it with new insights. The scope and variety of the topics he covered was breathtaking, as can be deduced from the titles of his works: *On Justice, On the Poets, On Wealth, On the Soul, On Pleasure, On the Sciences, On Species and Genus, Deductions, Definitions, Lectures on Political Theory, The Art of Rhetoric, On the Pythagoreans, On Animals, Dissections, On Plants, On Motion, On Astronomy, Homeric Problems, On Magnets, Proverbs, On the River Nile,* and so on. Sadly, nearly all the books he published have been lost, and what we know of his philosophy mostly stems from lecture notes, which were hidden in a cave. Needless to say, these lecture notes are often rather difficult to understand without the oral explanations that would have accompanied them. Also, some of them may have been written or edited by students, rather than by Aristotle himself. As Barnes (2000: 5) notes:

> . . . it will hardly be a surprise to find that the style of Aristotle's works is often rugged. Plato's dialogues are finished literary artefacts, the subtleties of their thought matched by the tricks of their language. Aristotle's writings for the most part are terse. His arguments are concise. There are abrupt transitions, inelegant repetitions, obscure allusions. . . .

This again has given rise to century-long debates about what exactly Aristotle wrote and meant.

Three types of knowledge

Aristotle divided knowledge into three kinds: productive, practical and theoretical. *Productive knowledge* was concerned with making things, such as farming, engineering, art or rhetoric. *Practical knowledge* referred to how men ought to act in various circumstances, both in private and public life (e.g. ethical and political knowledge). Finally, the goal of *theoretical knowledge* was neither production nor action, but truth. It was further subdivided into three classes: mathematics, natural science (including biology, psychology, meteorology, chemistry, physics) and theology (including astronomy, the substances divine in the heavens and – arguably – logic [2]).

Theoretical knowledge starts with axioms

According to Aristotle, theoretical knowledge consisted of a series of axioms from which the remaining knowledge was derived by means of logic (notice the influence of Plato and geometry). The axioms were self-evident truths about nature, which were acquired through observation and intuition, and of which the final cause could be discerned. Final causes referred to the purpose of things within the universe. Aristotle's universe consisted of the Earth in the centre, surrounded by the Moon, Mercury, Venus, the Sun, Mars, Jupiter, Saturn and the Fixed Stars (Figure 1.5).

Two regions were distinguished in the universe: one from the Earth up to the Moon (the sub-lunar region) and one from the Moon to the end of the universe (the super-lunar region). The super-lunar region was filled with aether, a divine and incorruptible element. This region contained immaculate stars moving in perfect harmony. The sub-lunar region was less orderly. Everything there was a mixture of four

As Barnes (2000) noted, Aristotle was an indefatigable collector of facts – whether zoological, astronomical, meteorological, historical and sociological. The next quote also illustrates the importance Aristotle attached to observation (*Posterior analytics,* Book II, Part 13):

> To resume our account of the right method of investigation: We must start by observing a set of similar – i.e. specifically identical – individuals, and consider what element they have in common. We must then apply the same process to another set of individuals which belong to one species and are generically but not specifically identical with the former set. When we have established what the common element is in all members of this second species, and likewise in members of further species, we should again consider whether the results established possess any identity, and persevere until we reach a single formula, since this will be the definition of the thing. But if we reach not one formula but two or more, evidently the definiendum cannot be one thing but must be more than one.

On the other hand, Aristotle was equally clear that observation alone was not enough for true knowledge. Theoretical knowledge for Aristotle first consisted of knowledge derived from axioms by means of logic. Observation helped to formulate the axioms, but was not enough, as can be seen in the following quote (Aristotle, *Posterior analytics,* Book I, Part 3):

> Our own doctrine is that not all knowledge is demonstrative: on the contrary, knowledge of the immediate premises is independent of demonstration. (The necessity of this is obvious: for since we must know the prior premises from which the demonstration is drawn, and since the regress must end in immediate truths, those truths must be indemonstrable.) Such, then, is our doctrine, and in addition we maintain that besides scientific knowledge there is its originative source which enables us to recognize the definitions. [3]

The axioms were more fundamental than observations. They defined the essence of things, what it was to be that thing within the universe. Or as Aristotle wrote (*Posterior analytics,* Book I, Part 2):

> . . . the premises of demonstrated knowledge must be true, primary, immediate, better known than and prior to the conclusion, which is further related to them as effect to cause. . . . The premises must be the causes of the conclusion, better known than it, and prior to it. . . . Now 'prior' and 'better known' are ambiguous terms, . . . In saying that the premises of demonstrated knowledge must be primary, I mean that they must be 'appropriate' basic truths, for I identify primary premise with basic truth. A 'basic truth' in a demonstration is an immediate proposition. An immediate proposition is one which has no other proposition prior to it.

Perception was the source of knowledge, but was not knowledge itself. As Aristotle remarked, all animals have perception, but they do not have theoretical knowledge. The subservient role of observation to knowledge became clear when there was a mismatch between an observation and an existing theory. This is how Barnes (2000: 90–1) summarised Aristotle's view of deviating observations:

> Did he leave any room for chance in nature? He certainly believed . . . that in nature many things happen not invariably but only for the most part. If something happens one way for the most part, then it must happen another way for the least part. Aristotle identified 'the accidental' with such exceptions to what happens for the most part. . . . Aristotle adds that such accidental happenings are beyond the purview of science. . . . there are accidental phenomena in nature, and they are not subject to scientific knowledge.

As we will see in later chapters, the relationship between observation and theory has remained a contentious issue in the philosophy of science up to the present day. However, currently deviating observations are no longer considered as 'exceptions' that can happen, but rather as an indication that the prevailing theory may be false (see Chapter 9).

On the soul

In the treatise *On the soul*, Aristotle further introduced the existence of an animating force in the universe. This force was called *psyche* (*anima* in Latin translations) and it was what discriminated living from non-living things. It consisted of three kinds. The lowest, the *vegetative soul*, was present in all living things, including plants. It enabled organisms to nourish themselves and to reproduce. Animals and humans further had *animal souls* (or sensitive souls), which provided them with locomotion, sensation, memory and imagination. Finally, humans also had *rational souls*, enabling them to reason consciously and to lead virtuous lives.

What do you think?

In a previous section we saw that the preliterate culture was characterised by animistic thinking. Do you consider Aristotle's inclusion of a soul in the universe an example of animism as well? If you don't know, type 'Aristotle' and 'animism' in your internet search engine. What do you get?

KEY FIGURE Aristotle

Source: The Art Archive/ Alamy.

- Greek philosopher (384–322 BCE).
- Student of Plato.
- Founder of the Lyceum in Athens.
- Contributed to many subjects, such as:
  - biology (careful descriptions of animals and plants)
  - view of the universe (model of the universe consisting of the earth surrounded by different spheres; the existence of five basic elements: aether, air, earth, fire, water)
  - logic (was the first to define propositions, syllogisms, and the rules that result in necessarily true conclusions)
  - psychology (his book *On the soul* would be central in teachings on psychology well into the eighteenth century).
- Knowledge less based on reason than with Plato; also room for observation.
- Would become the most popular author in the Renaissance; initially led to some tensions with the Roman Catholic Church.

The foundation of schools

Something else the Greek society introduced was a class of literate individuals who hired themselves out for teaching and who transferred the culture. As a result, reading and writing were quite widespread in Ancient Greece. In addition, it resulted in the creation of four prestigious schools, which continued to educate pupils for centuries. The first was the *Academy,* founded by Plato in 388 BCE. The second was the *Lyceum,* established by Aristotle in 335 BCE. Previously, Aristotle had been a member of Plato's school for 20 years, but some years after Plato's death he established his own school, presumably because his opinions started to deviate too much from the Platonian view.

Plato's and Aristotle's schools were later joined by the *Stoa* (312 BCE) and the *Garden of Epicurus* (307 BCE), which are both still famous for the lifestyle they promoted (the Stoic approach based on self-control, fortitude and detachment from distracting emotions vs. the Epicurean approach based on a virtuous and temperate life with the enjoyment of simple pleasures obtained by knowledge and friendship).

The shift to Alexandria

The Greek culture underwent a big expansion under Alexander the Great (356–323 BCE). As a result of his military successes, the Greek culture was propagated over a much wider area, expanding from Egypt to India, and including the whole Fertile Crescent. This created a completely new dynamic of interactions, which became known as the Hellenistic culture, and which continued after Alexander the Great's death when the empire fell apart into different states governed by his generals and when the Romans occupied the Hellenistic world (see Figure 1.6).

Much of the new dynamic took place in Alexandria, a city created by Alexander the Great in Egypt that was famous for its massive library. Here thinking was more influenced by mathematics and became much more specialised than the grand, universal philosophies of Plato and Aristotle (Cohen 2010). The names of the scholars working in this tradition are the ones we usually find in history books of mathematics and sciences. These are a few names:

- **Euclid** (around 300 BCE): best known for his work on geometry, which resulted in the organisation of all available evidence within a coherent framework, known as Euclidian geometry.
- **Herophilos** (335–280 BCE) and **Erasistratos** (304–250 BCE): physicians who extended Aristotle's work on the human anatomy (based on dissections of human bodies). They founded the medical school in Alexandria.
- **Archimedes** (287–212 BCE): contributed greatly to geometry and also made major contributions to physics, often resulting in new or improved machines.
- **Ptolemy** (*c.* 90–*c.* 168 CE): best known for his book *Almagest,* which was the most comprehensive treatise on astronomy, along the lines of the Aristotelian universe (Figure 1.5) but more detailed in the description of the movements of the (wandering) stars.

Interim summary

- Ancient Greece was the birthplace of philosophy (Heraclitus, Socrates, Plato, Aristotle). It also saw major advances in medicine (Hippocrates).
- Two great philosophers were Plato and Aristotle.

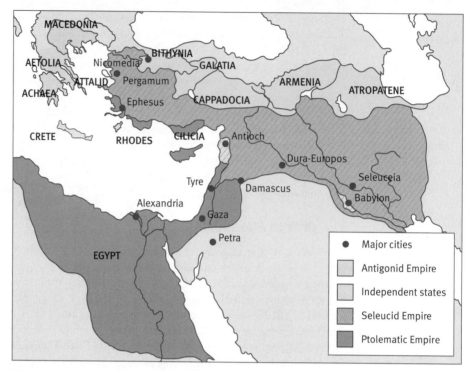

Figure 1.6 The Hellenistic world, cities and empires in 240 BCE.

Interim summary (continued)

- Plato and Aristotle also founded schools (respectively the Academy and the Lyceum), which together with two other schools would educate students for centuries. The two other schools were the Stoa (which had an emphasis on self-control) and the Garden of Epicurus (which emphasised the enjoyment of simple pleasures).

- Under Alexander the Great, there was significant expansion and interaction with other cultures, leading to what is called the Hellenistic culture and a shift to Alexandria, where knowledge became more mathematical and specialised (Euclid, Archimedes, Ptolemy).

1.5 Developments from the Roman Empire to the end of the Middle Ages

The Romans

Assimilation of Greek culture

By 200 BCE the Roman Empire had already expanded well outside the Italian peninsula and had started to annex the Greek provinces (Figure 1.7). Because the Romans had much admiration for and interest in the Greek culture, this did not lead to its

Figure 1.7 The Roman Empire at its largest (around 100 CE).

collapse. Rather, the Greek methods and learning were transferred to Rome, where there was already quite a strong Greek presence and where many educated people mastered Ancient Greek and visited the Greek schools as part of their education. According to the Roman writer Horace, Rome might have captured Greece militarily and politically, but the artistic and intellectual conquest belonged to the Greeks (as cited in Lindberg 1992: 134).

A typical example of the interactions between the Roman and the Greek cultures is the physician Galen of Pergamon (129–*c.* 200 CE). Born and educated in Pergamon (part of present-day Turkey), he travelled to Corinth, Crete, Cyprus and finally Alexandria, where he joined the medical school. After another brief stay in Pergamon, where he was responsible for the treatment of gladiators, in 162 CE he went to Rome, where he became one of the best-known practicing physicians. As we will see in Chapter 7, his writings had an enormous impact on medical thinking until well into the second millennium of the Common Era, which is why Galen is usually mentioned as a founder of modern medicine, together with Hippocrates.

Emphasis on practical knowledge

One major difference between the Romans and the Greeks was that the Romans were much more interested in practical questions than the philosophical debates that preoccupied the Greeks. Therefore, the transfer of Greek knowledge did not so much involve the subtleties of philosophy or the advanced levels of Greek mathematics, astronomy and anatomy, but subjects of practical value and intrinsic appeal. For the same reason, the Roman legacy is much more dominated by technological inventions and improvements (e.g. their road-building and invention of road maps) than by their profound philosophical writings.

The wittiest account of the differences between the ancient Romans and Greeks has undoubtedly been written by Cubberley (1920: 74–5). Enjoy for yourself:

> The contrast between the Greeks and the Romans is marked in almost every particular. The Greeks were an imaginative, subjective, artistic, and idealistic people, with little administrative ability and few practical tendencies. The Romans, on the other hand, were an unimaginative, concrete, practical, and constructive nation. Greece made its great contribution to world civilization in literature and philosophy and art; Rome in law and order and government. . . .
>
> As a result the Romans developed no great scholarly or literary atmosphere, as the Greeks had done at Athens. They built up no great speculative philosophies, and framed no great theories of government. Even their literature was, in part, an imitation of the Greek, though possessing many elements of native strength and beauty. They were a people who knew how to accomplish results rather than to speculate about means and ends. Usefulness and effectiveness were with them the criteria of the worth of any idea or project. They subdued and annexed an empire, they gave law and order to a primitive world, they civilized and Romanized barbarian tribes, they built roads connecting all parts of their Empire that were the best the world had ever known, their aqueducts and bridges were wonders of engineering skill, their public buildings and monuments still excite admiration and envy, in many of the skilled trades they developed tools and processes of large future usefulness, and their agriculture was the best the world had known up to that time. They were strong where the Greeks were weak, and weak where the Greeks were strong. . . .
>
> The Greeks were an imaginative, impulsive, and a joyous people; the Romans sedate, severe, and superior to the Greeks in persistence and moral force. The Greeks were ever young; the Romans were always grown and serious men.

? What do you think?

Something we usually do not realise when we read about the Greek and the Roman civilisations is how small these populations were. The Roman Empire counted some 4 million citizens out of a total of 50–60 million people in the Roman Empire. Athens counted some 100,000 citizens out of a total of 250–300,000 inhabitants. Given that only citizens were likely to receive education and take part in intellectual life, this puts their achievements in a new perspective. To what extent could the current rate of scientific progress be a sheer consequence of the number of people involved in research? What other factors might impact on scientific progress?

The Byzantine Empire

Towards the end of the second century CE, the political stability and patronage in the Roman Empire began to fade away. Civil wars gave rise to a division between an East and a West Empire around 300. Rome remained the capital of the West Empire, but the heart of the civilisation shifted to the east, the Hellenistic world, where the Byzantine Empire was founded (Figure 1.8). Its capital was Constantinople (now Istanbul in Turkey). During much of its history it was also known as the Empire of the Greeks because of the dominance of the Greek language and culture. It lasted

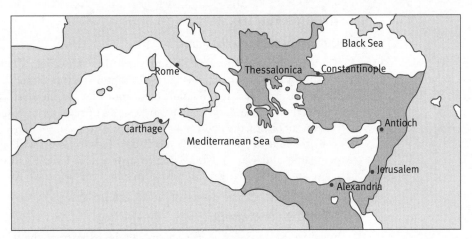

Figure 1.8 The Byzantine Empire around 500 CE.

till 1453 when Constantinople fell to the Ottoman Turks (although there had been a few upheavals in the thirteenth century when Constantinople was attacked and the Crusaders established the Latin Empire between 1204 and 1261).

Preservation of the Ancient Greek legacy

Intriguingly, despite nearly 1,000 years of relative prosperity and political stability, Byzantine science never reached the same level as that of the Ancient Greeks. The main contribution of Byzantium to the history of science seems to have been the preservation of the legacy of the Ancient Greeks.

Role of religion

The main factor that is quoted for the decline of scientific advancement (also in Western Europe) is the emergence and eventual dominance of the Christian religion (see e.g. Lindberg 1992). Although it has often been claimed that the halting of science was the result of active opposition by the Christian religion, this does not seem to be true (although there are examples of unpleasant standoffs, as we will see further on). For centuries, religious orders and schools were the main conservators and proponents of the intellectual achievements. A more likely explanation is that they simply were not interested in natural science and considered it to be inferior knowledge (on a par with manual skills). Their attention was much more directed towards religion-related and cultural topics. Not only did the Christian religion have to defend its position against rival contenders, there were also internal divisions, which eventually led to the schism between Roman Catholicism and Eastern Orthodoxy in the eleventh century. As a consequence of the change of focus, the brightest pupils were directed away from scientific issues and science was often associated with paganism.

? What do you think?

How has science been presented in your primary and secondary education? Was it seen as less or more interesting and creative than literature, art and rational thinking?

The Arab Empire

Expansion of the Arab Empire

The Arabian peninsula had been untouched by Alexander's military campaigns. As a result, it was not much affected by Byzantine culture either. In one of the cities of the peninsula, Mecca, Mohammed was born late in the sixth century. He preached a new religion, Islam, on the basis of a series of revelations, which were preserved in the Koran, one of the first books written in Arabic.

By the time of Mohammed's death in 632 his followers had taken over the Arabian peninsula and were pushing northwards. By 661 they had occupied the Fertile Crescent and Persia. By 750 they controlled the north of Africa and nearly all of Spain, where Cordoba and Toledo became important intellectual centres (Figure 1.9).

Scientific achievements

Interest in science increased when in 749 the dynasty of the Abbasid family came to power and a period began of stronger political stability and patronage. Around this time the translation of Greek works into Arabic started. Agents were sent to Byzantium in search of manuscripts and a research institute was founded in Baghdad: the *House of Wisdom* (ninth century). At the same time, Islamic scholars advanced Greek knowledge in medicine, astronomy, mathematics and optics. For instance, Ibn al-Haytham's book *Optics,* written in the eleventh century, far surpassed its predecessors. As we have seen in a previous section, they also adopted the Indian number system and turned it into a much more efficient mathematical system than what the Greeks and the Romans had achieved. In particular, al-Khwarizmi's book *Algebra* (around 820) was a milestone.

The remains of the Western Roman Empire

Science arguably received its biggest blow in the Western part of the Roman Empire, including Rome itself. Already before the Roman Empire fell to the German tribes there was a sharp decline in scientific endeavour because of the political upheaval and economic downfall.

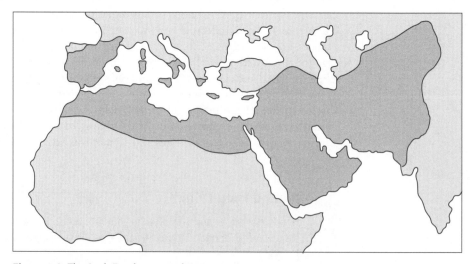

Figure 1.9 The Arab Empire around 750 CE.

Decreased access to Greek knowledge

One factor that contributed to this decline was the diminishing knowledge of the Greek language. As argued by Myers-Scotton (2006), the motivation to learn a second language decreases as a function of economic dominance. In particular, members of non-dominant groups are eager to learn a language in addition to their mother tongue, in order to improve their life circumstances and (in the case of scientists) to enlarge their audience. As a consequence, Myers-Scotton argues, the 'universal language' (lingua franca) of science has always closely followed the shifts in economic dominance (and is likely to continue to do so in the future). Because the Romans dominated the other nations, it became increasingly unnecessary to study languages other than Latin, whereas more and more individuals became inclined to learn Latin as a second language, rather than Greek. As a result, a language barrier emerged between the Romans and Greek science. This was partly alleviated by an increased availability of Latin translations, but translations did not conserve the full richness of the Greek legacy. Only the works that were thought to be of interest to the Romans made it into Latin and were preserved. For instance, when Christianity became the dominant religion in the third century, there was much more interest in Plato's writings than in those of the other philosophers, because Plato's views of a higher, ideal world of which we only see the shadows, coincided with the Church's view. As a consequence, Plato's works were among the most widely available.

The contribution of the Catholic Church

After the fall of Rome in 476 and the takeover by Germanic tribes, the Catholic Church became the patron of learning through the creation and support of schools. As in the Byzantine Empire, however, science was not at the forefront of the education (to put it mildly), which was centred on theological, ecclesiastical and literary knowledge. In addition, Catholic education was not the sort to foster critical thinking in students. As a result, scientific knowledge not only stalled but fell back from the level it had reached at the height of the Roman Empire. For this reason, scholars in the fourteenth and the fifteenth centuries tended to refer to the Middle Ages in Western Europe as the 'Dark Ages'.

Dark Ages
name given in the Renaissance to the Middle Ages, to refer to the lack of independent and scientific thinking in that age

Interim summary

- Ancient Romans:
  - assimilated the Greek methods and knowledge
  - were more interested in technological advances than in philosophy.
- Byzantine Empire:
  - eastern part of the Roman Empire; capital Constantinople; lasted till 1453
  - preservation of the legacy of the Ancient Greeks.
- Arab Empire:
  - founded on Islam; contained the Fertile Crescent
  - translation and extension of the Greek works
  - particularly strong on medicine, astronomy, mathematics (algebra) and optics
  - occupied most of Spain.

Interim summary (continued)

- Western Roman Empire:
  - largest decline in scientific knowledge
  - Catholic Church main preserver; not very science-oriented
  - in the Renaissance referred to as the 'Dark Ages'.

Just how dark were the Middle Ages?

A phenomenon often observed in history is that the proponents of a new movement despise the time period before them. Sometimes this results in lasting negative views of that period. This is what happened to the Middle Ages. After they were called the Dark Ages by the Italian humanists (who wanted a return to the great ancient civilisations), there has been a tendency to exaggerate just how dark they were, which gave rise to a number of myths. Below we discuss some. If you want to read more, have a look at Numbers (2009) and Hannam (2009).

Myth 1: Nothing was invented in the Middle Ages

The Middle Ages saw major advancements in farming, which led to a considerable growth in the European population. Particularly important were the development of the plough, the horse collar (so that horses and oxen could pull heavier weights), the three-field rotation (so that better crops were grown on the fields) and windmills. Further, the weaponry of the armies was constantly updated, so that countries had varying success in their wars. Eventually this led to the development of weapons that could destroy the strongest defence walls, which was one of the factors leading to the demise of the feudal system with castle lords and serfs. Towards the end of the Middle Ages, spectacles and the mechanical clock were added to the list of new instruments.

Myth 2: Medieval people thought that the earth was flat

Aristotle had already given proof of the sphericity of the earth and this was repeated by nearly all early-medieval writers. Medieval scholars also knew that moonlight was reflected from the Sun.

Myth 3: The medieval church prohibited dissection and thereby stifled medical progress

Medieval church did not prohibit dissection at all. As a matter of fact, the religious authorities did it themselves (e.g. they embalmed bodies and they dissected the bodies of saints to distribute the relics). Opposition usually came from family and local governments. The strongest evidence for Church interference came from Pope Boniface VIII, who in 1299 forbade under pain of excommunication a funerary practice that was becoming increasingly frequent. However, this practice consisted of cutting up the corpse and boiling the flesh off the bones, in order to make it easier to transport for distant burial (a procedure that had gained currency among the Crusaders).

> **Myth 4: The rise of Christianity was responsible for the demise of ancient science**
>
> The demise of ancient science in the West was due to the fall of the Roman Empire. For centuries the Church was the only institution interested in education and preservation of the old texts. From the twelfth century on, the Church also actively promoted the foundation of universities for the education of the higher clergy. In these universities natural philosophy was studied and many theologians considered it an essential part of their training. Because nature had been created by God, man could learn about its creator by studying nature. It is true that Christianity saw natural philosophy not as a legitimate end in itself, but as a means to other ends. Natural philosophy had to accept a subordinate position as the handmaiden of theology and religion, the temporal serving the eternal, but clergy were not prohibited from studying natural philosophy, and many did so.

1.6 Turning the tide in the West

The foundation of schools and universities

The revival of learning in the West has a long history. Lindberg (1992) identifies a whole series of small steps. First, there were efforts by Charles the Great around 800 to improve the education in his Carolingian Empire, in particular in the capital, Aachen. Second, as a result of better agricultural techniques there was a population explosion between 1000 and 1200. This resulted in renewed urbanisation and the foundation of larger cathedral schools with broader educational aims. These schools in turn increased the appetite for knowledge in the intellectually able, which created a market for independent teachers, called masters. To improve their living conditions, the teachers organised themselves in guilds, which they called 'universities'. Bit by bit the guilds acquired wealth and started to lobby for tax exemptions and patronage. The first charters leading to independent university status were awarded in Bologna (1150), Paris (1200) and Oxford (1220).

Students who finished the master's programme at the universities had the right to teach everywhere (*ius ubique docendi*), which led to increased mobility of the masters and a harmonisation of the curricula. At the same time, scholars became aware of the much richer cultures on the outskirts of Western Europe and the translation of Arabic and Greek texts into Latin reached a high point. The former mainly happened in Spain, the latter in Italy.

Inclusion of Greek and Arabic texts in the curricula

Many of the Greek and Arabic books were integrated within the curriculum without problems, as they were clearly superior to what was available and often filled a void. This was, for instance, the case for Euclid's *Elements,* Ptolemy's *Almagest,* al-Khwarizmi's *Algebra,* Ibn al-Haytham's *Optics,* the Greek and Arabic works on medicine and the *Canon of medicine* written by the Arab scholar Avicenna. There were more difficulties with Aristotle's works. For many scientifically-minded scholars, his views and methodology were more inspiring than those of Plato and the Christian theology that had been built on it. This led to some skirmishes at the University of Paris (but not at other universities), where the teaching of Aristotle was forbidden first by the Catholic bishop in 1210 and later by the papal legate. However, in practice this did not prevent the works from being widely available, and by 1255 the University of Paris followed the other universities and put Aristotle at the centre of its teaching in philosophy.

One of the problems with Aristotle was that he claimed that the universe, including the Earth, was eternal, without beginning or end, whereas the Bible clearly indicated the beginning (Genesis) and the end of life (the Last Judgement). This aspect of Aristotle's view called into question the dependence of life on God, the creator, and His power to intervene in worldly matters. Another problem was that Aristotle saw the soul as the actualisation of the potentialities of the body, which could be interpreted as meaning that the soul was unable to exist without a body and, therefore, ended together with the body. Needless to say, such a view was incompatible with the Christian doctrine of an independent and immortal soul.

Most universities sailed around these contentious issues by not including them in the parts of Aristotle they were teaching. However, the issues were more than isolated differences of view. They arose because Aristotle had come to his conclusions on the basis of observation and reasoning (logic) rather than biblical revelation and church tradition. As these were the elements in Aristotle's philosophy that attracted the scholars, other disagreements were soon to follow. By 1277 the Catholic bishop of Paris, Etienne Tempier, already had a list of 219 propositions related to Aristotelian philosophy that he would not allow to be taught at the University of Paris.

A cultural movement based on imitation of the Greek and Roman civilisations

Renaissance
cultural movement from the fourteenth to the seventeenth century based on a rediscovery and imitation of the classical Greek and Roman civilisations

The availability of the ancient texts not only influenced scientists but also society as a whole. Slowly but surely the Middle Ages gave way to the Renaissance, a cultural movement based on an imitation of the classical Greek and Roman civilisations. This started in Italy in the fourteenth century and lasted until well into the seventeenth century. Its presence was most visible in architecture and painting (where perspective was discovered) and it produced artists such as Jan van Eyck (*c.* 1395–1441), Leonardo da Vinci (1452–1519), Michelangelo (1475–1564), and Raphael (1483–1520).

This period also saw the return of scientists in Western Europe of a stature high enough to be remembered today. One of them was Nicolaus Copernicus (1473–1543), who started to question Aristotle's and Ptolemy's conviction that the Earth was the centre of the universe and who we will meet again in Chapter 2. Other noteworthy names were Andreas Vesalius (1514–1564), who restarted and dramatically extended the Greek studies on human anatomy (including dissection), and Gerardus Mercator (1512–1594) who developed a technique to make more accurate maps of the world.

The Protestant Reformation

Protestant Reformation
movement against the Roman Catholic Church, which was important for the development of science, because it emphasised the need for education, critical thinking, hard work and worldly success

The Renaissance also saw the birth of Martin Luther who revolted against the perceived greed and corruption of the Papacy. Eventually, this led to the Protestant Reformation, starting in 1516, which resulted in large parts of Europe no longer being under the control of the Roman Catholic Church (most of present-day Germany,

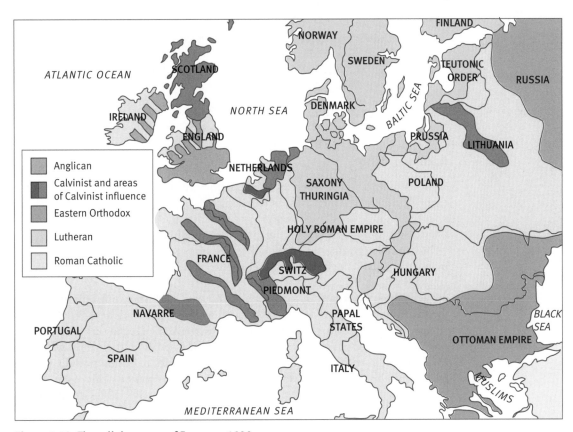

Figure 1.10 *The religious map of Europe c. 1600.*

the Netherlands, Scandinavia and Switzerland, see Figure 1.10). In the middle of the upheaval, Henry VIII of England founded the Church of England and joined the Reformed movement, although the Church of England always kept its independence from the other Protestant movements. The Reformed Churches stressed much more than the Roman Catholic Church the need for education and critical thinking (in order to be able to read and understand the Bible) and the importance of hard work and worldly success.

According to the German sociologist Max Weber (1864–1920), the Protestant ethic was one of the reasons why the Protestant countries started to outperform the Catholic countries economically. As he wrote (Weber 1904/1905: 3–6):

> A glance at the occupational statistics of any country of mixed religious composition brings to light with remarkable frequency a situation which has several times provoked discussion in the Catholic press and literature, and in Catholic congresses in Germany, namely, the fact that business leaders and owners of capital, as well as the higher grades of skilled labour, and even more the higher technically and commercially trained personnel of modern enterprises, are overwhelmingly Protestant. . . .
>
> Thus, to mention only a few facts: there is a great difference discoverable in Baden, in Bavaria, in Hungary, in the type of higher education which Catholic parents, as opposed to Protestant, give their children. That the percentage of Catholics among the students and graduates of higher educational institutions in general lags behind

their proportion of the total population, may, to be sure, be largely explicable in terms of inherited differences of wealth. But among the Catholic graduates themselves the percentage of those graduating from the institutions preparing, in particular, for technical studies and industrial and commercial occupations, but in general from those preparing for middle-class business life, lags still farther behind the percentage of Protestants. On the other hand, Catholics prefer the sort of training which the humanistic Gymnasium affords.

Book printing

Interwoven with all these developments (both at the origin of them and heavily relied on by them) was the introduction of book printing in Europe. First (by 1300), letters were carved in a woodblock and printed on cloth (a technique originally invented in China), which allowed mass production of a small number of pages. Later (around 1450) movable printing was invented by Johannes Gutenberg, a technique in which individual metal letters were placed in a matrix and could be recycled for other texts. This allowed cheap production of all types of texts, leading to a rapid and massive availability of information to everyone who was interested, not only in Latin but increasingly in the native languages as well. Millions of books were printed and distributed in a short period of time. An often overlooked factor in this process was the production of paper, something the Europeans learned from the Arabs, who in turn had probably been inspired by the initial Chinese invention. Printing would never have been so easy or prevalent if printers had been forced to print on cloth or parchment.

The importance of (book) printing for the developments discussed in this book can hardly be overestimated. Here are just four ways in which printing changed the lives of people interested in knowledge.

First, knowledge came much more within reach. Before the introduction of printed books, scholars only had access to the few books in the library of the institute to which they were attached. If they wanted to consult a book that was not in the library (and there were many of them), they had to travel for weeks, sometimes months, on hazardous roads. This meant that access to knowledge was very limited indeed.

Second, because books were so rare, there was a constant danger of loss or destruction. Scholars had almost a full-time job preserving and copying the existing knowledge, so that it could be transferred to the next generation. This also frequently meant the eternal loss of books from authors who for one reason or another temporarily became less popular.

Third, manually copied books contained many transcription errors, particularly when they involved scientific materials. Humans are extremely error-prone, certainly when they have to copy text they do not understand. As a result, either the scholars had to copy the books themselves or they had to fleece the exemplar made by a scrivener to correct the errors that had been made. This was especially a problem for mathematical treatises where small changes in equations can lead to major interpretation problems. Book printing avoided this problem because the first print was proofread by the author (or someone else knowledgeable). Indeed, in the first decades of printing, very often new, corrected, editions were needed because of errors discovered in the manuscript that had been used for the original print.

Finally, for the first time scholars could work on the same copy of a book. This made it much easier to correspond and collaborate with each other. For instance, in 1578 the French publisher Henri Etienne produced the first printed edition of Plato's works. This made it possible to refer precisely to a passage in the dialogues, because everyone had the same pagination. As a matter of fact, the pagination of the first edition is still used by scholars of Plato to refer to passages in the dialogues (Annas 2003).

What do you think?

The introduction of the internet is sometimes claimed to be of equal importance to the introduction of book printing, because it makes information even more accessible to everyone who is interested. Do you think this will have an impact on our thinking? In what ways? Do you have other ideas now than when the same question was asked before we discussed the impact of book printing?

Colonisation of the world

Finally, the European powers had started their exploration and colonisation of the world, beginning with the occupation of shores in Africa and Asia, and the discovery of America in 1492. This would rapidly turn into a race between the different nations to conquer as much as possible of the newly discovered territories, increasing the demand for technical and scientific inventions that could be of use.

The new explorations also brought the European countries in contact with other cultures and inventions. In addition, it led to one of the very first firm indications that Aristotle was not infallible (given the prestige Aristotle enjoyed, this was a major blow to the world view of many scholars). According to Aristotle, the Earth was divided into five different climate zones. The two extreme zones, the northern and the southern pole, were too cold and icy for life. The middle zone around the equator was uninhabitable as well, because it was boiling hot there. Only in the two zones between the poles and the equator was the climate temperate enough to sustain life.

Aristotle was proven wrong when the Portuguese started to occupy parts of Africa, and in 1473 crossed the equator by sea in their search for a trade route to Asia (the route across land was controlled by the Arabs). Given that this fallacy could not easily be explained away by an interpretation error on the part of the reader, it raised the question of whether Aristotle had been wrong on other aspects as well.

Interim summary

- Post-medieval developments in Western Europe:
  - the establishment of (cathedral) schools and universities
  - increased mobility of the scholars
  - discovery of the Ancient Greek and Arabic texts
  - growing impact of Aristotle's works.
- A cultural movement:
  - increased interest in and imitation of the Ancient Greek and Roman cultures (Renaissance)
  - increasing status of science and scientists.

Interim summary (continued)

- The Protestant Reformation:
  - rebellion against the dominance of the Catholic Church
  - more importance given to education, critical thinking, hard work and worldly success.
- Book printing:
  - rapid and massive availability of reliable information.
- Colonisation of the world:
  - need for technological and scientific innovations
  - discovery of new worlds.

1.7 *Focus on*: The limits of history writing

In the preceding sections we have depicted the broad lines of the history of science up to the seventeenth century, as it can be found in current history books. However, we do not want to conclude this chapter without giving consideration to the limits of history writing that have become clear in the past decades and which have questioned history writing as the unearthing of the truth. First, we discuss some biases that are – often implicitly – present in nearly all historical accounts. Then we discuss the implications for this particular chapter and the historical chapters that are still to follow.

What do you think?

Which type of history writing do you prefer? One focusing on individuals and their struggles to get their ideas accepted, or one focusing on the ideas themselves and the impact they had? List the pros and cons of each approach and keep them close to hand as we progress through the book.

Biases in history writing

Looking at historical writings, it is not difficult to discern a number of biases in them. Here we discuss just a few of the most important.

Too much centred on persons

A typical characteristic of historical writings is that they tend to focus on individuals. As a result, the history of science is presented as a succession of discoveries and insights made by geniuses that far exceeded the intellectual level around them. For instance, in Chapter 2 we will discuss the ground-breaking contributions of Galilei and Newton. After reading them you might wonder what would have happened to science if they had never lived. The answer, however, in all likelihood is that it would not have mattered much. As Gratzer (2002) reflects in the introduction of his book *Eurekas and euphorias: The Oxford book of scientific anecdotes*:

> Science differs from other realms of human endeavour in that its substance does not derive from the activity of those who practise it; the nature of the atom or the structure

of DNA would have been discovered if Bohr and Rutherford, and Watson and Crick had not lived. It would merely have taken longer. Science is above all a collective activity. *L'art c'est moi, la science c'est nous,* was how Claude Bernard, the father of modern physiology, put it. In this sense individuals are of minor importance.

Centring histories of writing on individual scientists makes the reading more interesting, as magisterially demonstrated by Bill Bryson (2003) in his science history directed at a wide audience, but is essentially wrong. It has been shown over and over again that discoveries have been prepared over a long time (and often have happened independently at several places) and that the time was simply right for them to come to the foreground. Of course, there was the genius of the individual who brought everything together and made the decisive move, but in all likelihood other individuals would have come to the same conclusion around the same time or shortly after (as again ironically illustrated in Bryson's book, when he amusingly tells how virtually no discovery is entirely due to the person history remembers for it). In this respect, historians sometimes talk about the importance of the zeitgeist, a German word that refers to the spirit of the age, the intellectual climate of the period.

zeitgeist

word used in the history of science to indicate that the time was right for a certain discovery; the discovery did not originate from a single genius, but from a much wider development leading to the discovery

The Matthew effect

One of the reasons why histories of science are centred on individuals is that more credit is given to eminent scientists than they actually deserve. Contributions from less well-known colleagues and contemporaries are ascribed to the most famous person of the era, a tendency known as the Matthew effect (the effect got its name from a line of the Matthew Gospel in the Bible: 'For unto every one that hath shall be given, and he shall have abundance: but from him that hath not shall be taken away even that which he hath'). As a result of the Matthew effect, individuals become the condensation of the intellectual climate that was shared by a larger group.

Matthew effect

the tendency to give more credit to well-known scientists than they deserve; increases the perceived impact of these scientists

Hindsight bias

Another reason why individual scholars get more prominence in history books than they usually deserve is that we have a tendency to assume that they knew more than they actually did. On the basis of what we now know, we assume that the same knowledge was shared by the person who first described the phenomenon. We also have a tendency to believe that the evidence presented by that individual was much more convincing than it actually was. After all, classical discoveries must be clear-cut discoveries, not a slow and messy unearthing of evidence that took decennia to sort out.

Ethnocentrism

Another feature of history writing is that authors have a tendency to attach excessive weight to the contribution of their own group and the group of their readers. So, Anglo-Saxon reviews of the history of science are too much centred on the contribution of the Ancient Greek, Latin, British and American scholars. The Matthew effect and the hindsight bias are applied to increase the dominance of one's own research group over that of other groups. In addition, writings about their contributions are much more easily available. This results in a tendency to give too much credit to the input of economically dominant groups. For instance, at several places in this book we were struck by how much easier it is to find information about the American situation than about the developments in other countries, which to some extent biased our coverage of topics.

? What do you think?

One of the first instances in which a science book was purposely chauvinistic was written by Mary Somerville in 1834 and titled *On the connexion of the physical sciences*. The early 1800s were a time in which British science was perceived as lagging behind that in Continental Europe. Whereas other scientists wrote pamphlets pointing to the gravity of the situation and how much more advanced science was in Continental Europe, Somerville wrote a book focusing nearly exclusively on British science, in order to stir enthusiasm in the British audience. What do you think? Are you also more interested in scientific findings from your own country? Would you object having to study a textbook that describes the history of psychology as it happened in Lithuania, Switzerland, Turkey or South Korea?

History reviews are summaries of summaries

The biases described in the preceding paragraphs are particularly strong because very few general history books (including the present chapter!) are based on a full analysis of the original sources. Rather, they build on other books that summarise part of the history to be described and try to maximise the clarity and the persuasiveness of the message. As a result, an error in one book can be exaggerated and pervade the knowledge of a complete community. This is particularly the case if the information is 'too good not to be true' (see Chapter 7).

History writing: rewriting or streamlining the past?

History writing and reshaping the past

The big question, of course, is whether the above biases result in such a distorted account of the past that history writing becomes a reinterpretation of what happened. Such a position has been defended by Thomas Kuhn, one of the main philosophers of science, who we will encounter again in Chapters 6 and 10, when we talk about what makes science. In Kuhn's view, science does not progress via a linear accumulation of new knowledge, and science as we know it now is only one of the possible interpretations of reality. As a result, the present review of the history of science is the view of twenty-first-century scientific psychologists writing for an Anglo-Saxon audience. It gives the illusion of an objective and straightforward account of the progress in science in the past 10,000 years, but may have no overlap at all with the history of science as it will be written in 400 years by an Indian physicist. This is because both histories are just that: interpretations of what may have happened directed by the current set of convictions that are shared within a particular research community.

History writing and simplifying the past

The alternative position is that all the biases mentioned above indeed happen, but are motivated by the need to make the knowledge digestible given the constraints under which it has to be transmitted. According to this position, the present chapter is a simplification of what has happened because it has to be summarised in a chapter of 20,000 words. Although it may contain elements that do not stand up to further scrutiny, these inaccuracies are not meant to reinterpret the past and do not detract from the basic message. They are the result of a streamlining of the rich and often conflicting raw materials that are just too much for us to grasp. For instance, it could rightly be objected that Plato's and Aristotle's writings are much more contradictory and contain many more ambiguous passages than has been suggested here. Indeed, large numbers of scholars have debated for over 2,000 years about what exactly Plato and Aristotle may have meant in some of their passages, and to what extent their methods of knowledge resemble and differ from the scientific method as we know it now. However, we do not think that any of these nuances would add much to our basic messages: that Plato and Aristotle have had a large impact on the way scientific thinking emerged and that scholars at a certain point in time struggled to overcome their limitations.

A nice illustration of the limits and the strengths of history writing has been documented by Endersby (2007) in his book *A guinea pig's history of biology: The plants and animals who taught us the facts of life* (although we hasten to say that similar accounts can be found elsewhere). When he discusses Mendel's contribution to genetics in the second half of the nineteenth century, he first mentions a story that can be found in many (popular) books:

> [Gregor] Mendel was obscure in his lifetime, but today most people are aware that he was a simple, uneducated Austrian monk who, while playing around with pea plants in his garden, discovered the basic laws of modern genetics. Yet this breakthrough was ignored, partly because he was cut off from the scientific world of his day, but also because the one famous scientist he contacted, the botanist Carl von Nägeli, sent Mendel off on a wild goose chase to investigate the genetics of hawkweeds. Nägeli may even have done this deliberately: jealous of his younger rival's brilliance, he set poor, innocent Mendel to work on a famously intractable group of plants, confident that the monk would never be able to sort them out. Frustrated by his failure, Mendel died in heartbroken obscurity. One final ironic twist to the story is added by the fact that Mendel . . . sent a copy of his paper on peas to Charles Darwin, who never read it.
>
> (Endersby 2007: 103–4)

This is the type of heartbreaking story that makes history books worthwhile reading! Unfortunately, Endersby goes on to show that nearly every detail is wrong. Here are just a few facts:

- Mendel was not Austrian.
- Mendel had studied both biology and mathematical physics at the University of Vienna, where he had been taught by some of the best-known scientists of the day.
- Mendel did not discover anything by accident; he performed carefully planned and well-designed experiments, for which he could rely on several helpers.
- The scientific society he belonged to had many distinguished members and its journal was widely read; as a consequence, Mendel's work was mentioned in the *Encyclopaedia Britannica*.
- Mendel never sent a copy to Darwin (or at least there is no evidence that he ever did so).
- One of the reasons why Mendel did not pursue his work was that he became the abbot of the abbey.

- Mendel was interested in hawkweeds, because he believed that the big variety in this species would give him more insight.

- The main reason why Mendel did not have the impact he may have wanted, is that he did not understand what was going on. He carefully noted and published the results of his experiments, but was at a loss to explain the underlying mechanisms. The explanation of alleles on chromosomes coming from the father and the mother and leading to dominant or recessive inheritance, with which we are now familiar and which we attribute to Mendel, only became clear many decades later (involving a whole series of scientists never mentioned except in specialised books). Only then did researchers realise the full importance of Mendel's findings and he was crowned as the father of genetics (the reasons why hawkweeds behave so differently from other plants took nearly a century to be understood).

The story of Mendel nicely illustrates the biases we have mentioned (try to find them!). At the same time, it illustrates that although nearly all the details are wrong, the summary still conveys the basic message that at some point in time (zeitgeist) science was advanced enough to begin to question the mechanisms of inheritance and to look for answers. It is sensationalising and dramatising the history of Mendel to a point that is no longer acceptable in scientific terms (although see Chapter 8), but is still not reinterpreting the past.

Similarly, we are confident that our summary in its broad brushstrokes will stand up to time, despite its unavoidable selectiveness and biases (although we hope to have done better than the Mendel example!). However, nothing prevents you from reading much more about the history of science and filling in the many omissions that give the present chapter a much smoother appearance than is warranted by history.

Interim summary

- History writing always involves simplification and streamlining.
- Therefore, biases easily slip in:
  - centred on persons rather than on zeitgeist
  - too much credit is given to a small number of people (Matthew effect)
  - facts are interpreted on the basis of what happened afterwards (hindsight bias)
  - too much attention is given to the contribution of the author's own group (ethnocentrism)
  - history writers often rely on summaries and interpretations made by other writers.

Recommended literature

History is one of the topics well covered in encyclopaedias. For instance, a lot of additional information can be found on **www.wikipedia.org,** of which we have made use as well. If you prefer books, here are some recommendations:

Writing

As you probably observed, we relied on Manguel (1996), included in the reference list. If you want to read more

about psychological research on reading and writing, see Harley, T.A. (2007) *The psychology of language: From data to theory* (3rd edition) (Hove: Psychology Press).

Numbers

The best book for the history of numerical systems is Ifrah (1998), included in the reference list. Easy to read introductions to the psychology of number processing can be found in Dehaene, S. (2000) *The number sense: How the mind creates mathematics* (Oxford: Oxford University Press), and Butterworth, B. (1999) *The mathematical brain* (Basingstoke: Macmillan).

History of science

The book we found most useful, in addition to the ones mentioned in Chapter 2, was Lindberg (1992; see the reference list). For specific topics, the *Very short introductions* from Oxford University Press often are a good point of departure. In this chapter we used the very short introductions to Plato (Annas 2003) and Aristotle (Barnes 2000). Another very interesting book is Cubberley's (1920) *The history of education,* which you can find on the internet. This book is also interesting because it gives examples of a writing style that was common up to the first half of the twentieth century but is no longer acceptable nowadays (with blissfully ignorant passages of chauvinistic Anglo-Saxon thinking).

References

Annas, J. (2003) *Plato: A very short introduction.* Oxford: Oxford University Press.

Barnes, J. (2000) *Aristotle: A very short introduction.* Oxford: Oxford University Press.

Bird-David, N. (1999) '"Animism" revisited: Personhood, environment, and relational epistemology', *Current Anthropology,* **40**: S67–S91.

Bryson, B. (2003) *A short history of nearly everything.* London: Doubleday.

Butterworth, B. (1999) *The mathematical brain.* London: Macmillan.

Charles, E.P. (2008) 'Eight things wrong with introductory psychology courses in America: A warning to my European colleagues', *Journal für Psychologie,* 16(1). At www.journal-fuer-psychologie.de

Cohen, H.F. (2010) *How modern science came into the world: Four civilizations, one 17th-century breakthrough.* Amsterdam: Amsterdam University Press.

Cubberley, E.P. (1920) *The history of education.* London: Constable & Co.

Endersby, J. (2007) *A guinea pig's history of biology: The plants and animals who taught us the facts of life.* London: William Heinemann.

Gratzer, W. (2002) *Eurekas and euphorias: The Oxford book of scientific anecdotes.* Oxford: Oxford University Press.

Hanley, J.R., Masterson, J., Spencer, L.H. & Evans, D. (2004) 'How long do the advantages of learning to read a transparent orthography last? An investigation of the reading skills and reading impairment of Welsh children at 10 years of age', *Quarterly Journal of Experimental Psychology,* 57A: 1393–410.

Hannam, J. (2009) *God's philosophers: How the medieval world lay the foundations of modern science.* London: Icon Books.

Huylebrouck, D. (2006) 'Mathematics in (central) Africa before colonization', *Anthropologica et Praehistorica,* **117**: 135–62.

Ifrah, G. (1998) *The universal history of numbers: From prehistory to the invention of the computer.* London: The Harvill Press. (Translation of the French original (1994): *Histoire Universelle des chiffres.* Paris: Editions Robert Laffont.)

Lindberg, D.C. (1992) *The beginnings of Western science: The European scientific tradition in philosophical, religious, and institutional context, 600 BC to AD 1450.* Chicago: The University of Chicago Press.

Manguel, A. (1996) *A history of reading.* London: HarperCollins.

Minto, W. (1893) *Logic: Inductive and deductive.* London: John Murray.

Myers-Scotton, C. (2006) *Multiple voices: An introduction to bilingualism.* Malden, MA: Blackwell Publishing.

Numbers, R.L. (2009) *Galileo goes to jail and other myths about science and religion.* Boston, MA: Harvard University Press.

Powell, A.G. & Frankenstein, M. (1997) *Ethnomathematics: Challenging Eurocentrism in mathematics education.* New York: SUNY Press.

Saenger, P. (1997) *Space between words: The origins of silent reading.* Stanford, CA: Stanford University Press.

Schlimm, D. & Neth, H. (2008) 'Modeling ancient and modern arithmetic practices: Addition and multiplication with Arabic and Roman numerals'. In V. Sloutsky, B. Love and K. McRae (eds) *Proceedings of the 30th Annual Meeting of the Cognitive Science Society.* Austin, TX: Cognitive Science Society, pp. 2007–12.

Seife, C. (2000) *Zero: The biography of a dangerous idea.* London: Souvenir Press.

Weber, M. (1904/1905) 'Die protestantische Ethik und der Geist des Kapitalismus' (translated in 1905 as 'The protestant ethic and the spirit of capitalism'). *Archiv für Sozialwissenschaft und Sozialpolitik,* **20**: 1–54; **21**: 1–110.

Ziegler, J.C., Bertrand, D., Toth, D., Csepe, V. *et al.* (2010) 'Orthographic depth and its impact on universal predictors of reading: A cross-language investigation', *Psychological Science,* **21**: 551–9.

2 The scientific revolution of the seventeenth century and its aftermath

This chapter will cover . . .

Questions to consider

?

Historical issues addressed in this chapter

- When did the scientific revolution take place?
- Which three developments formed the core of this revolution?
- How did the scientific revolution change society?
- How did science increase its status and power in the eighteenth and the nineteenth centuries?

Conceptual issues addressed in this chapter

- What impact did the transition from the geocentric to the heliocentric model of the universe have on Western European society?
- To what extent does our knowledge of the world and the universe depend on the equipment we have?
- How did the changes introduced by Descartes to Aristotle's world view advance the development of science?
- What research method should a natural philosopher use (i.e. which ideas did eighteenth- and nineteenth-century scholars have about the scientific method)?
- Why were the developments in the seventeenth century called revolutionary?

Introduction

> The 17th century has continued to be taken for that specific period in history when modern science was born. Not our present-day science, to be sure, but a mode of doing science still quite recognizably akin to present-day conceptions. The awareness that something unprecedentedly new happened in 17th-century science has been with us for as many centuries as have since passed.
>
> (Cohen 1994: 1)

In this chapter we continue our quest for the origins of psychology. The word psychology did not appear in the literature before 1500 and was not used in the title of an influential book until the 1730s. What happened between the Renaissance and the eighteenth century that made authors use this particular word?

It is now generally accepted in history writings that intellectual developments in the seventeenth century changed the course of human thinking and initiated scientific research as we currently know it. A name often given to this period is the **scientific revolution**. Although a thousand-page book could be written (and has been written) about the many facets of the scientific revolution and the various people involved, we will limit ourselves to the core developments, which altered human thought and two centuries later made psychology, as the scientific study of human mind, possible.

scientific revolution
name given to a series of discoveries in the seventeenth century, involving Galilei, Descartes and Newton, that enhanced the status of science in society

We discuss three critical insights that came to the foreground during the scientific revolution:

1. The realisation that the Earth did not form the centre of the universe.
2. The realisation that many things on Earth (including the human body) could be understood as (complicated) machines.
3. The actual demonstration that many movements on Earth and in the universe could be described using a handful of relatively simple mathematical equations, which became known as the laws of physics.

After a brief description of the main developments we will see what consequences the scientific revolution had on Western thought and Western society. We will also ask ourselves whether the seventeenth-century developments really were unprecedented enough to deserve the name 'revolution'.

What do you think?

The three events at the centre of the scientific revolution are usually associated with the names of (1) Copernicus and Galilei, (2) Descartes, and (3) Newton, even though they were broad events, involving hundreds and possibly thousands of thinkers. Have a look at the biases in history writing described in Chapter 1 and try to understand why such condensation took place.

2.1   From a geocentric to a heliocentric model of the universe

In the sixteenth century there was increasing interest in astronomy because the Julian calendar, used since the days of Julius Caesar, was getting out of phase with reality. Because a year comprises 365.2425 days, the Julian calendar (based on three years of 365 days and one leap year of 366 days) underestimated the length of a year by 11 minutes, meaning that one day was 'missed' every 134 years. As a consequence, by the sixteenth century the calendar was already 11 days short of target. Eventually, this was corrected when in 1582 the Julian calendar was replaced by the Gregorian calendar in the Roman Catholic world and Thursday 4 October was followed by Friday 15 October.[1] In order to get the new calendar right, a lot of fine-grained astronomic observations and calculations were needed. One of the people who was involved in this effort was the Polish astronomer Nicolaus Copernicus (1473–1543).

The geocentric model of the universe in the sixteenth century

The Earth as the centre of the universe

The model of the universe used in the sixteenth century was the model described by Aristotle (who built on others) and elaborated by Ptolemy. As we saw in Chapter 1 (Figure 1.5), Aristotle's universe was a limited universe with the Earth in the middle.

It was surrounded by the fixed stars which circled in perfect harmony. Between the Earth and the fixed stars were the seven wandering stars (the Moon, Mercury, Venus, the Sun, Mars, Jupiter, and Saturn). This model of the universe is called a geocentric model because the Earth was seen as the centre.

geocentric universe

model of the universe in which the Earth is at the centre; was dominant until the seventeenth century

The following quote from Ptolemy's *Almagest* nicely summarises the then available knowledge and the reasons brought forward for a stationary Earth in the centre of the universe:

> The earth is a sphere, situated in the center of the heavens; if it were not, one side of the heavens would appear nearer to us than the other, and the stars would be larger there. The earth is but a point in comparison to the heavens, because the stars appear of the same magnitude and at the same distance *inter se*, no matter where the observer goes on the earth. It has no motion of translation . . . . If there were a motion, it would be proportionate to the great mass of the earth and would leave behind animals and objects thrown into the air. This also disproves the suggestion made by some, that the earth, while immovable in space, turns round on its own axis.
>
> (translation: Cubberley 1920: 385)

The addition of epicycles

A key problem within the Aristotelian universe was the movements of some of the wandering stars. If one looks on successive nights at Mercury, Venus, Mars, Jupiter or Saturn (always at the same time), in general they have moved a bit to the east relative to the previous night. However, the displacements are not fixed, as would be expected if these stars were circling around the Earth. Instead, the displacement frequently seems to slow down, to stop, to turn into a displacement in the opposite direction, then again to stop and resume the usual eastward movement. (These are movements you can easily observe for yourself if you have enough spare nights.)

To explain the strange movements, Ptolemy used the notion of 'epicycles', first introduced by Appolonius of Perga (*c.* 262 BCE–*c.* 190 BCE). Epicycles are small cycles made by the wandering stars in addition to their main orbit around the Earth (Figure 2.1). The use of epicycles allowed Ptolemy to develop a model with a better fit to reality, but it did not take away all the oddities. To correct for these, Ptolemy introduced higher order epicycles (i.e. epicycles on epicycles).

The Catholic Church and the Islamic faith adopted Ptolemy's model of the universe without modification. However, because of the calendar issue a renewed interest in the precise movements in the universe grew. This resulted in improved translations of Ptolemy's main work, *Almagest*, and an eagerness to read the Arab commentaries on this book.

Copernicus's alternative heliocentric model

The Sun as the centre of the universe

Aristotle's model was not the only one that had been proposed in ancient cultures. Several authors had suggested the possibility of the Earth orbiting the Sun rather than the reverse, but their views had never been taken seriously. Copernicus became interested in this model and saw it as a valid alternative (Figure 2.2). In Copernicus's heliocentric model, there was first the Sun, then Mercury, Venus, the Earth (orbited by the Moon), followed by Mars, Jupiter, Saturn and the sphere of immobile stars. Other features of the model were that one turn of the Earth around

heliocentric model

model of the universe in which the Sun is at the centre

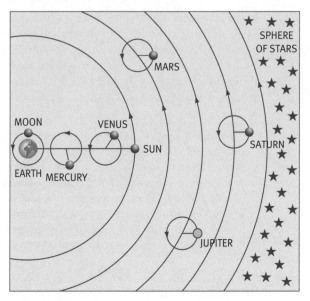

Figure 2.1 Ptolemy's model of the universe with simplified epicycles.
Source: Vik Dhillon. Reproduced with permission.

the Sun took one year (instead of the daily orbit of the Sun around the Earth) and that the Earth spun around its axis in one day, causing the alternation of day and night and the movements of the fixed stars. Later, Copernicus also had to add epicycles to his model, in order to predict the movements of Mercury, Venus, Mars, Jupiter and Saturn more precisely.

Why Copernicus waited to publish his model

Copernicus wrote a short commentary on his heliocentric model in 1514 and made it available to a few friends, who had approached him with respect to the calendar problems. Although the model was widely discussed, Copernicus was not yet interested in publishing it. Only shortly before his death (in 1543) was he persuaded to have the book printed. The popular story is that Copernicus was afraid of the response he would get from the Roman Catholic Church (which was his employer). Another reason may have been that Copernicus did not feel the evidence for his model was strong enough to justify publication. Chalmers (1999) reports the following objections Copernicus could have expected from his colleagues, who had studied Ptolemy:

- What is the practical utility of the model relative to Ptolemy's? (In the end, both were nearly of the same complexity, because of the need for epicycles.)
- If the Earth moves and spins around its axis, why is it that if you throw a stone from a high tower, it ends exactly at the bottom of the tower (and not a few metres away from the tower, as you would expect if the Earth moved so rapidly)?
- If the Earth spins around its axis, why is it that people and objects are not flung from the surface (as would happen if they stood on a spinning wheel)?

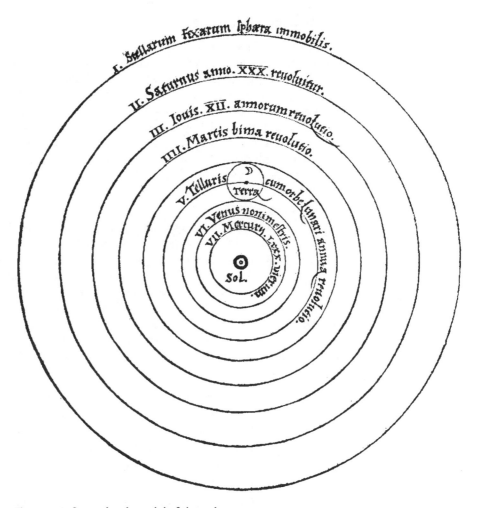

Figure 2.2 Copernicus's model of the universe.

This picture does not include the epicycles Copernicus had to add in order to fit the movements of the wandering stars.

- Would this model not predict that the stars should appear to increase and decrease in magnitude as a function of where the Earth is (nearby or far away)?
- Why does the Moon keep following the Earth? Why is it not orbiting the Sun as well?

What do you think?

Do you know the answers to some of the objections against Copernicus's heliocentric model? For instance, why does a stone thrown from a tower land at the bottom of the tower instead of some distance from it? If you are in a fast-moving train and you drop a pen, does the pen fall straight down or is there a displacement due to the movement of the train? Why?

Galilei uses a telescope

Because of the many problems with Copernicus's model, it failed to have much impact, and it was Ptolemy's model that was used to calculate the Gregorian calendar. If Copernicus's model was taught, it was mentioned as an example of a faulty model. The first person to take Copernicus's model seriously was the German astronomer Johannes Kepler (1571–1630), who around 1600 realised that he could get rid of the epicycles in the model by using elliptical orbits instead of circular ones, and who developed the three laws of planetary motion that would considerably simplify astronomy. Kepler's insights, however, were overlooked for decades by, among others, Galilei and Descartes.

Galilei's observations

Copernicus's heliocentric model received strong impetus when the Italian natural philosopher Galileo Galilei (1564–1642) in 1609 heard of Dutch inventors who had made a 'telescope' by using a combination of a convex and a concave lens. Apparently this telescope made it possible for distant objects to look nearer and larger.

Galilei[2] was not only one of the finest scholars of his time; he was also a handy craftsman. In less than a week he built his own telescope. Although he immediately saw the military use of the instrument (and seized the opportunity to get a permanent position at the University of Padua with a big salary increase), he quickly turned his eyes to the sky. Even though the telescope only magnified ninefold, he saw some amazing things:

1. There were many more stars than were visible to the naked eye.
2. The surface of the Moon was not smooth, as claimed by Aristotle, but comprised mountains and craters (Galilei could discern the mountains because some surfaces in the dark half were lit when he looked at a half-moon).
3. Jupiter had four orbiting moons, so that the Earth's moon was no longer the only heavenly body failing to turn around the centre of the universe.
4. The sizes of Mars and Venus appeared to increase and decrease in cycles, suggesting that their distances to the Earth changed over time. In addition, Venus had phases just like the Moon (Figure 2.3).

Response of the Roman Catholic Church

On the basis of this evidence Galilei started to argue in letters that Copernicus's heliocentric model was much more likely than Ptolemy's geocentric model. In 1615 one of these letters made a Dominican friar file a written complaint with the Inquisition in Rome. This resulted in an investigation of a year, after which Galilei received a private warning to stop defending Copernicus's model. Around the same time, Copernicus's book was put on the Index of Prohibited Books until it would be revised.

Galilei followed the warning until in 1632, at the age of 68, he published a book in dialogue form, in which one of the characters defended the heliocentric model. Galilei ventured that such a format would be acceptable, also because the pope at that time was someone who had expressed his admiration for Galilei's work before. Unfortunately for Galilei, the Vatican decided to take action for questioning their doctrine. Galilei was summoned to Rome and put under house arrest for the final years of his life.

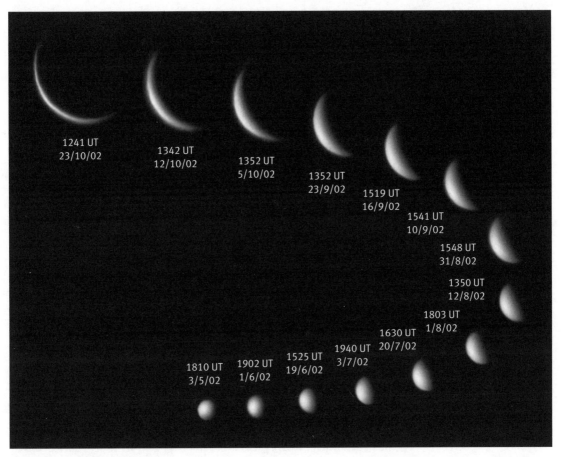

Figure 2.3 Changes in the magnitude and phases of Venus showing that Venus orbits the Sun with a diameter smaller than that of the Earth.

Source: TBGS observatory/Chris Proctor.

The popular account of this episode is that of a religion fanatically (and desperately) defending its position against the growing influence of science, as illustrated by the following excerpt:

In June 1633, Galileo Galilei, unquestionably the greatest scientist of his age, was formally humiliated by the Roman Catholic church for promulgating the heretical doctrine that the Earth revolved around the Sun. He was not burned at the stake, nor was he imprisoned, but he was officially muzzled and confined under house arrest for the rest of his life. This action threw the intellectual community in Catholic lands into a state of fear and circumspection, just as it had been intended to. Elsewhere, however, the church's grand symbolic gesture was greeted with a mixture of ridicule and outrage, galvanising the movement towards the secularisation of science that would reach its final destination in the 19th century . . .

A treasurable typographical error in [Michael White's] book refers to a 'Professor of Scared Scripture', and that of course is what the authorities were. They understood that to challenge any orthodoxy threatened, like pulling a stray thread of wool in a cardigan, to unravel the whole false fabric of theology. It is impossible not to read the transcript of the trial without wanting to shout out in rage: Italy produced no physical scientist of the slightest importance for two centuries after Galileo.

(S. Callow, *The Guardian*, 4 August 2007; book review of *Galileo antichrist: A biography* by Michael White. Copyright Guardian News & Media 2007.)

As is often the case, a closer look at the historical evidence seems to point to a slightly more moderate picture. These circumstances were why Galilei received a particularly strong rebuttal from the Vatican:

- The Roman Catholic Church had been confronted by the Reformation and did not want to be seen as weak. In addition, the pope was involved in wars to defend and extend his territories. (Italy in those days did not exist, but was divided into several city-states.)
- Galilei ridiculed the Catholic Church in his book by putting the views of the Church in the mouth of an individual called Simplicius (simple-minded).
- Not everyone in the Roman Catholic Church agreed with the developments. Before, during and after his trial, Galilei was helped by cardinals who did not approve of what happened.
- Disagreements between scientists and the establishment have not been limited to the Roman Catholic Church, as we will see later.

? What do you think?

The criticism of the role of the Roman Catholic Church in the development of science has been most scathing in Anglo-Saxon literature. To what extent could this be because the English-speaking countries dissociated themselves from the influence of the Roman Catholic Church?

What do you think of the following statement (Hannam 2009: 3)?

The waters were muddled further by the desire of [the seventeenth-century] Protestant writers not to give an ounce of credit to the Catholics. It suited them to maintain that nothing of value had been taught at universities before the Reformation. Galileo, who thanks to his trial before the Inquisition was counted as an honorary Protestant, was about the only Catholic natural philosopher to be accorded a place in English-language histories of science.

Independent of the Church's reaction, the main outcome of Galilei's research was that the evidence he presented (and which could easily be verified by others once they had a telescope) was so convincing that the heliocentric view rapidly came to dominate astronomy (although it was not until 1822 that Pope Pius VII would allow the printing of works based on the heliocentric theory in Rome). As such, the episode was an important triumph for natural philosophy.

Interim summary

- The need for an improved calendar renewed interest in the motions of the Earth, the Moon and the Sun relative to one another.
- The model of the universe that was used was the geocentric model of Aristotle and Ptolemy. This model has the Earth at the centre of the universe.
- Copernicus became interested in an alternative heliocentric model with the Sun at the centre. He did not publish this model until the year of his death, partly because he thought the evidence was not convincing enough and partly because he did not want to upset the Roman Catholic Church.
- Nearly a century later Galileo Galilei used a telescope to look at the night sky and observed several phenomena that were easier to explain on the basis of a heliocentric model than on the basis of a geocentric model. In doing so, he upset the Roman Catholic Church.
- Because the evidence was so convincing and could be verified by others, the heliocentric model rapidly came to dominate astronomy despite the Roman Catholic Church's resistance.

KEY FIGURE Galileo Galilei

Source: Detlev van Ravenswaay/Science Photo Library Ltd.

- Italian scholar (1564–1642).
- Famous for his contributions to:
  - astronomy: heliocentric model, discovery of Jupiter's largest moons
  - physics: experiments on and mathematical descriptions of motions of bodies (e.g. falling objects and the trajectories traversed by cannonballs)
  - technology: improved several pieces of equipment (e.g. the telescope).
- Controversy with the Roman Catholic Church:
  - first tried to convince the Church authorities of the heliocentric model in 1616. Was not successful
  - published a book on heliocentrism in 1632 after the election of his friend Cardinal Barberini as Pope Urban VIII. However, he offended the Pope and was confronted with a Church that saw a need to defend its stance
  - ordered to stand trial on suspicion of heresy in 1633. Had to recant his ideas, was put under house arrest, and saw his book banned.
- Importance for the advancement of science:
  - promoted the Copernican view of the organisation of the universe
  - the fact that the heliocentric model prevailed despite the resistance of the Church authorities is generally considered to be the turning point in the advancement of science.
- Two main works:
  - *Dialogue concerning the two chief world systems* (1632), book in which he put forward a heliocentric view of the universe
  - *Discourses and mathematical demonstrations relating to two new sciences* (1638), particularly known for its law of falling bodies (also see Chapter 10).

2.2 Mechanisation of the world view

Descartes' philosophy of man

One of the first people to be affected by the Roman Catholic Church's harsh treatment of Galilei was René Descartes (1596–1650), a French scholar and philosopher who lived in the Netherlands. He was about to publish a book of his world view, *Le monde,* which also included a heliocentric model of the universe. Although he was physically quite safe in the Netherlands, which were dominated by the Protestants, he decided to shelve the study. (It was only published more than 10 years after his death.) However, the result of Descartes' decision was not that he stopped thinking about natural philosophy, as arguably the Roman Catholic Church had hoped, but that he started to look at how he could build a new philosophy, which would reconcile the Church with natural philosophy. In the end, this turned out to be equally devastating for the status of the religious world view.

Dualism

Descartes identified the soul as being divine and independent of everything else. His first move, therefore, was to clearly separate the human soul from the rest of the universe, as had been done before by Plato and the Catholic Church. Because the human soul was divine, human thoughts and feelings could not be studied by the natural sciences and fell under the remit of philosophy and religion. In line with Plato, Descartes was convinced that the soul had innate knowledge, which could be recovered on the basis of reasoning (see rationalism below). The assumption of a sharp distinction between the immaterial mind and the material body is known as dualism. We will return to the relationship between mind and body in Chapter 7.

dualism
view of the mind–body relation according to which the mind is immaterial and completely independent of the body; central within religions and also in Descartes' philosophy

Mechanistic view of the universe, including the human body

Descartes' second move was to view the universe and all the matter in it (including the human body) as one big, sophisticated machine that could be studied by humans. Descartes believed that God had created a self-perpetuating machine, so that He did not have to continuously look after His creation. Humans were endowed with reason so that they could grasp the workings of the machinery. In this respect, Descartes was strongly influenced by the views of Dutch Protestant philosophers, in particular Isaac Beeckman (1588–1637).

To understand why the mechanistic view was important for the development of science, we must have a look at the Aristotelian model it replaced. Although Aristotle's writings were much more appealing to scholars than those of Plato and the Catholic Church, they did not coincide with modern science. As we saw in Chapter 1, Aristotle's views centred on the purposes of things within the universe (the final causes) and on the fact that living things were driven by souls. As a result, everything and everybody had a purpose. Aristotelian explanations of nature depended on the perceived goals and aims of things (e.g. the final cause of rain was to let the plants grow) and Aristotle's thinking with respect to living organisms was plainly animistic (i.e. their workings were explained by means of spirits with humanlike characteristics). Descartes rejected all goals, emotions and intelligence in nature and claimed that everything in the universe was a perfectly designed mechanism, made to function

mechanistic view
world view according to which everything in the material universe can be understood as a complicated machine; discards the notion that things have goals and intentions as assumed by the animistic view; identified with Descartes

KEY FIGURE René Descartes

- French scholar living in the Netherlands (1596–1650).
- Famous for his contributions to:
  - mathematics: Cartesian geometry, exponential notations
  - philosophy: rationalism, dualism, the undeniable existence of thought ('I think, therefore I am' [*cogito, ergo sum*]).
- Impact for the advancement of science:
  - mechanistic world view
  - body can be studied scientifically
  - idea of innate knowledge and the importance of deductive reasoning (rationalism).

Source: Royal Astronomical Society/Science Photo Library Ltd.

independently, so that God did not have to attend to it any more. Natural philosophers could study these mechanisms.

The only exception Descartes made to the mechanistic world was the human soul, as superbly summarised by Fancher (1996: 22):

> As Descartes summarized to a friend, 'The soul of beasts is nothing but their blood.' But Descartes would not go so far regarding human beings in spite of the fact that their bodies resembled the bodies of animals in many ways, and obviously operated like machines as well. The point of difference lay in the human capacities for *consciousness* and *volition*. It seemed obvious to him that his own actions often occurred because he *wanted them to,* or because he freely chose them following rational deliberation. This supremely important, subjective side of human experience did not seem to lend itself to mechanistic analysis. Accordingly, Descartes attributed it to the presence of a soul or mind, which he thought interacted with the bodily machine in human beings. In sum, he got rid of the Aristotelian vegetative and animal souls, but retained the rational soul.

Implications for the advancement of science

Although Descartes meant to make a sharp division between religion and science, thereby protecting one from the other, his views primarily benefited science. Not only did the mechanistic view of the world invite further scrutiny of its workings (as was intended); very soon questions were asked about how the soul could steer the mechanism of the human body if it was separated from it. Descartes conjectured that the soul could influence the body via the pineal gland (a small gland in the middle of the brain), but rapidly this view was found to be unconvincing. As a consequence, the 'soul' got dragged into the mechanical part of the universe and became the subject of natural investigations as well, as we will see in the next chapters.

Interim summary

- The response of the Roman Catholic Church to Galilei encouraged René Descartes to build a new philosophy of man.
- In this philosophy a clear distinction was made between the soul, which was divine and could not be studied with scientific methods, and the rest of the universe (including the

Interim summary (continued)

body), which was a complex machine that could be studied scientifically. This became known as (Cartesian) dualism.

● The mechanistic view of the world came to replace Aristotle's view, which still contained animistic elements.

2.3 The formulation of the first laws of physics

Why is the Earth orbiting the Sun?

One of the big mysteries of the heliocentric universe was why the planets orbited the Sun and why some planets were orbited by one or more moons. Remember that in the Aristotelian universe there were only two 'natural' movements: one downwards to the centre of the Earth (applicable to earth and water) and one upwards to the edge of the sub-lunar region (fire and air). All other movements needed an external cause. According to some medieval views this meant that the Sun and the stars were constantly being pushed by angels. However, what was pushing the Earth around the Sun?

Movements are the result of forces

It would take the genius of the British scholar Isaac Newton (1643–1727) to bring all the available evidence together and formulate an account that in hindsight was so elegant and simple that it is hard to believe no-one else had come to the insight before. (It is thought by some that Descartes came close when he aborted his studies of physics and turned to his philosophical treatise about the nature of the universe and the place of man in it.) Newton's starting point consisted of studies by Galilei (yes, him) on the trajectory of cannonballs. Galilei noticed that the path of a cannonball was a parabola, the curvature of which depended on the force with which the ball had been propelled: The stronger the force, the further the ball went (Figure 2.4). This relationship could be described mathematically.

Newton's clever insight was that if you placed the cannon on a mountain and shot the ball with enough force, then it would not fall fast enough to touch the Earth but would circle around it (Figure 2.5). In addition, if you took away the friction of the air, the motion would continue ad infinitum. Could this be the reason why the Moon orbited the Earth?

But why were the cannonball and the Moon attracted to the Earth? Why is the trajectory of the cannonball not a straight path out of the mouth of the cannon? These questions brought Newton to another important insight: objects were attracting each other. The Earth attracted the cannonball and the cannonball attracted the Earth. Because of the big difference in mass, however, the pulling force (called the gravitational force) of the Earth on the cannonball was immensely larger than the other way around.

The *Principia mathematica*

All that was left for Newton to do was to calculate the exact magnitudes of the different forces. The end result was a book, *Philosophiae naturalis principia mathematica*,

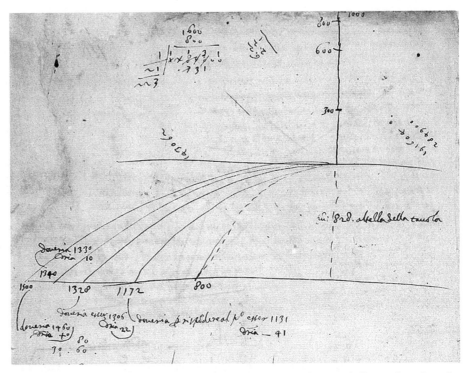

Figure 2.4 Drawing by Galilei of the parabolic trajectories of cannonballs as a function of the propelling force.

Source: Institute and Museum of the History of Science, Florence, Italy.

Figure 2.5 Newton's insight that a cannonball will orbit the Earth if it is fired with the right force.

published in 1687, in which all known movements in the Copernican universe were adequately described on the basis of three laws and the postulation of a gravitational force. Each of the components was described in mathematical terms, allowing precise calculations of the orbits, which fully agreed with the laws of planetary motion Kepler had discovered 80 years before.

Principia mathematica

book in which Newton presented his laws of physics (1687); considered to be the primary reason for the increased status of science

The magnitude of the impact of the *Principia mathematica* (as it is usually abbreviated) can hardly be exaggerated. For decades scholars had argued that the universe could be thought of as a perfect machine, the workings of which could be studied and understood by natural philosophy. Suddenly they had their wildest dreams fulfilled: here was a book that described all motions (both on Earth and in the universe) on the basis of a handful of equations that could be understood by everyone with a bit of mathematical sophistication! The mechanisms of the universe were laid bare to the human eye. It was only a matter of time before similar equations would be discovered for the other parts of the machine.

The boost science got from Newton's *tour de force* persists till today. Scientists after Newton felt much less need to keep abreast of philosophical issues than before. In contrast, philosophers without scientific knowledge saw their status sharply decreased. (Although for the sake of completeness it must be added that Newton's theory has since been upgraded by Einstein's relativity theory, and that physicists still do not know how celestial bodies can attract each other over large distances without any apparent matter between them.)

Interim summary

- Newton explained why planets orbit the Sun and moons orbit planets.
- In doing so, he not only defined the relevant forces, but described them in such detail that they could be calculated precisely.
- The resulting mathematical equations were the first laws of physics, published in the *Principia mathematica,* convincing scholars that science could uncover the mechanisms underlying the universe.

KEY FIGURE Isaac Newton

- British physicist and mathematician (1643–1727).
- Famous for his contributions to:
  - mathematics: development of calculus
  - optics: showed that white light is the sum of all the colours of the rainbow
  - physics: described gravitation and three laws of motion that would form the basis of mechanics and the scientific understanding of the universe for the next two centuries.
- Impact for the advancement of science:
  - showed that science could uncover the mechanisms underlying reality
  - seemed to suggest that all scientific knowledge could be summarised in mathematical laws.

Source: CCI Archives/Science Photo Library Ltd.

2.4 What set off the scientific revolution in seventeenth-century Europe?

Ever since the term *scientific revolution* was coined (see below), historians have tried to find the reasons why the revolution took place in seventeenth-century Europe. Why did it not happen in Ancient Greece? Or in Rome? In China? In the Arab Empire?

Factors that contributed to the scientific revolution

Many of the factors that are thought to have contributed to the scientific revolution of the seventeenth century are the same as those mentioned for the emergence of the Renaissance three centuries earlier (Chapter 1). The list below is based mainly on Cohen (1994), occasionally supplemented with interesting thoughts we found elsewhere.

Demographic changes

Europe's population nearly halved in the fourteenth century as a result of the Great Famine (starting in 1315), the Hundred Years War (1337–1453), and the Black Death (1348–1350). At the end of the fifteenth century a new growth began. Around the same time, the feudal system came to an end, partly as a result of the Crusades, which depleted the aristocracy. The cities grew and installed more democratic regimes.

Particularly important was the emergence of a large group of merchants that formed a link between the hand workers and the intellectual elite. In previous civilisations there had been a big gap between mechanics (done by slaves) and scholarship (done by the elite). Artisans made numerous mechanical discoveries, but they lacked the analytical skill to systematise their discoveries and raise them from rules of thumb of practical knowledge to the plane of scientific laws. Scholars had the intellectual capacities but their knowledge lacked practical application and did not profit from the existing know-how. Technical information had been available, but the merchant mentality was needed to overcome the gulf between scholar and artisan. According to Cohen (2010), this may have been a reason why the scientific revolution did not take place in China. There, the bureaucrats succeeded in preventing the merchants from becoming a social group with an autonomous power base in society.

Absence of stifling pressure from religion or authority

Another factor contributing to the emergence of science was the absence of a repressive religion or authority. Church authority was first hollowed out by the Western Schism from 1378 to 1417, when the cardinals could not decide on whom to elect for office and two popes held office simultaneously (one in Rome and one in Avignon). It was dealt another blow in 1517 when Martin Luther (1483–1546) started the Protestant Reformation. As a result, the actions of the Roman Catholic Church against Galilei were limited in their impact. Galilei's books remained freely available in countries not controlled by the Roman Catholic Church and the Vatican's response was exploited by the Protestants as part of their own legitimacy efforts.

According to Holland (2008), the crisis in the Catholic Church began in the eleventh century. Before this century people had been waiting for the Day of Judgment, the moment when normal life would end, the dead would be resurrected and every person judged according to the quality of their relationship with God. Both the years 1000 and 1033 (one thousand years after Christ's death) seemed plausible times for the Last Judgment. They both passed, however, and people found themselves confronted with the need for a new project. In Holland's words (2008: xxviii):

> For a long while, the notion that the world would be brought to an end, that Christ would come again, that a new Jerusalem would descend from the heavens, had been a kind of answer. With the disappointment of that expectation, the Christian people of Western Europe found themselves with no choice but to arrive at solutions bred of their own restlessness and ingenuity: to set to the heroic task of building a heavenly Jerusalem on earth themselves.

Christian religion left another opening for scientific advance. Because it made a strict distinction between the worldly and the heavenly, it resulted in two different authorities, who tended to keep each other in check. For religious matters, there was the Church with the pope as its leader; for worldly affairs, kings ruled. There was not a single force taking complete control of people. Quite often, Church and court disagreed with each other. They also had different regulations and laws. To some extent, it may be argued that these two instances personalised (and possibly reinforced) the dualistic view of mankind, with the mind belonging to the church and the body to the king. Science could take advantage of the ambiguities in this state of affairs.

New inventions

In Chapter 1 we mentioned the impact of the invention of paper and printing. This made information abundantly available and relieved scholars from the burden of preserving the information from the previous generation. As Cohen (1994: 363) wrote: 'During the scribal age, a never-ending effort to prevent and halt as best one could the ongoing corruption, decay, and destruction of texts was the primary concern of scholars.' Information also became available in the vernacular, as important texts were translated into different languages. Galilei, for instance, was one of the first authors to publish his books in Italian.

The invention of the mechanical clock (in the fourteenth century) also had an impact, because it provided philosophers with a working example of a mechanical world (cf. Descartes' views). It further resulted in the establishment of a professional group of clock- and watchmakers, who could make the high-precision equipment needed for the scientific experiments that were to come.

The introduction of the compass, the telescope and the microscope were other factors convincing the ruling powers of the importance of new inventions, because of their impact on war and trade. States could be made more efficient and gather extra wealth by learning more about nature. As we have seen in the case of Galilei, these inventions also had implications for the development of science. Suddenly, scholars could see more than they had been able to perceive before.

The existence of universities and patronage

Another variable that may have helped the emergence of scientific thought was the existence of universities. They provided a place for natural philosophers in society and conveyed the message that the pursuit of knowledge about nature was a worthwhile activity in its own right. This in turn increased the chances of patronage by wealthy families or even the involvement of those families in the expansion of science. The experiments had the additional attraction that they often baffled the audience, which more easily lent itself to the popularisation of knowledge than the writings of religious and humanistic thinkers. All over Europe, kings and aristocrats took an interest in the new experimental science and provided the instruments and laboratories by means of which experiments could be carried out.

This is not to say that universities were invariably at the forefront of new discoveries. As a matter of fact, they have been criticised for being too conservative, clinging to the old philosophical texts and the scholastic teaching method, as can be seen in the following excerpt from Cubberley (1920: 394):

> During the seventeenth century, and largely during the eighteenth as well, the extreme conservatism of the universities, their continued control by their theological faculties, and their continued devotion to theological controversy and the teachings of state orthodoxy rather than the advancement of knowledge, served to make of them such inhospitable places for the new scientific method that practically all the leading workers with it were found outside the universities.

In particular, the universities largely continued to use the Socratic disputations that were popular in Ancient Greece (Chapter 1) to settle issues, as described by Shapin (1996: 121):

> The disputatiousness of traditional natural philosophy was frequently blamed on the dominant role of university scholars and traditional scholar ways of establishing and justifying knowledge. A typical form of philosophical exchange in the universities was the ritual disputation, in which opposing scholars deployed sophisticated logical and rhetorical tools to defend their theses and defeat those of their opponents, the results to be judged by a philosophical master. So when moderns insisted they would mind not words but things, they were referring quite specifically to the verbose and wrangling style of natural philosophy in the Schools.

Yet, of the four central people we mentioned above, two found a position at a university (Galilei and Newton). One was largely financed by the Roman Catholic Church (Copernicus) and one had independent means (Descartes).

Massive enrichment from the Greek and Arab civilisations

In the sixteenth century, many more texts became available than those of Plato and Aristotle. For instance, the translation of Archimedes' books on mathematics gave mechanics an impetus and prepared the ground for the mathematisation of the world. Other information that became available were the thoughts of Democritus (c. 460 BCE–c. 380 BCE), Epicurus (341 BCE–270 BCE) and Lucretius (c. 99 BCE–c. 55 BCE), according to whom the world consisted of atoms moving in empty space. This presented an alternative to the Aristotelian view of the universe and strongly influenced the thinking of Descartes. One of the factors contributing to the increased access to Greek writings was the fall of Constantinople in 1453 and the subsequent flight of Greek scholars to Italy.

Interestingly, of all the factors Cohen mentioned in 1994, the availability of information from the Greek and the Arab civilisations seems to have retained the most importance in the book on the same topic he published in 2010. According to Cohen (2010), major breakthroughs happen (or can happen) when two main civilisations interact. This creates a fluidity and dynamism in which new ideas can grow. It happened to some extent when the Greek and the Roman civilisations met, when the Greek and Arab cultures met, when the Arab and Chinese cultures met; and it happened when the Western, Greek and Arab cultures met.

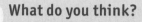

What do you think?

Currently we are experiencing a massive exchange between the Western world and the Asian cultures. Is this creating a dynamism that can lead to new breakthroughs? Are these more likely to happen in the West or in Asia?

Natural philosophy became detached from the big philosophical questions

For centuries education in Europe had been dominated by teachings on big philosophical and religious issues. Knowledge of nature was thought to make sense only in the framework of a comprehensive view of the universe and man's place in it, as provided by the Church, Plato and Aristotle. Gradually, natural philosophers became detached from these views and felt allowed to study a phenomenon without prior knowledge of the totality of things. To a large extent, this evolution resembled the shift from Athens to Alexandria in the Greek culture (Cohen 2010).

Factors that helped the fledgling science grow

Maybe equally important as the question of why modern scientific thoughts emerged is the question of how they could survive and gain in power. After all, the world had known impressive civilisations for thousands of years without the contribution of science. If things had evolved slightly differently, we could have continued to live in the world of Ancient Persia, Egypt, China, Greece, Rome or the Arabic world. So, what happened?

The absence of disaster

One element that most certainly contributed to the survival of scientific thought is the absence of major disasters in the fifteenth to nineteenth centuries. For instance, one might wonder what would have happened if the Mongol troops had continued their invasion of Western Europe in 1241, rather than returned to Mongolia when their king, the Great Khan, died. Would the devastation of Western Europe have prevented the scientific revolution? There is good evidence, for instance, that war was one of the factors preventing Arab science from reaching its full potential.

Another disaster that did not happen was an epidemic of the same scale as in the fourteenth century. According to Hannam (2009) medieval thought at the end of the thirteenth century came very close to the thinking of the early seventeenth century (see below), but it was cut short because so many people died of the plague. Similarly, a major natural disaster at the end of the seventeenth century could have prevented the thoughts of Galilei, Descartes and Newton from having a lasting impact.

A benevolent religion

As indicated above, science also profited from the Protestant Reformation. Ironically, this may have been partly because of what happened to Galilei. The Protestant Churches not only encouraged followers to study the Bible, but some also encouraged them to study science to set themselves apart from the Roman Catholic Church. There are many writings in which the positive interactions between natural philosophy and Protestant religion were praised. Teaching science was an element that distinguished the new Protestant schools from the established Catholic schools.

It is important to realise that the Protestant Reformation did not in the first place encourage the innovative thinking we currently associate with science. Rather, it stressed arduous work and an orientation to worldly success, which still turned out to be good breeding grounds for scientific progress. This is how Weber (1904/1905: 4–11) summarised the Protestant view:

> . . . it is necessary to note, what has often been forgotten, that the Reformation meant not the elimination of the Church's control over everyday life, but rather the substitution of a new form of control for the previous one. . . . The rule of Calvinism [. . .], as it was enforced in the sixteenth century in Geneva and in Scotland, at the turn of the sixteenth and the seventeenth centuries in large parts of the Netherlands, in the seventeenth in New England, and for a time in England itself, would be for us the most absolutely unbearable form of ecclesiastical control of the individual which could possibly exist. . . .
>
> . . . the spirit of hard work, of progress, or whatever else it may be called, the awakening of which one is inclined to ascribe to Protestantism, must not be understood, as there is a tendency to do, as joy of living nor in any other sense as connected with the Enlightenment. The old Protestantism of Luther, Calvin, Knox, Voet, had precious little to do with what to-day is called progress. To whole aspects of modern life which the most extreme religionist would not wish to suppress to-day, it was directly hostile.

The establishment of learned societies

Natural philosophers also established structures to advance and solidify their status. This partly happened through the creation of ever more universities, but also through the foundation of learned societies, such as the *Accademia dei Lincei* (Italy, 1603), the *Académie Française* (1635) and the *Royal Society of London* (1660). These societies offered a place for natural philosophers to meet regularly and share ideas. They also published proceedings that allowed researchers to disseminate their ideas.

Maybe as a result of their culture of gentlemen's clubs, most research groups in Britain founded a society as soon as they had enough members. So, in addition to the Royal Society of London, the Royal Society of Edinburgh (1783), the Linnean Society of London (1788, devoted to the description of biological species), the Geological Society of London (1807), the Royal Astronomical Society (1820), the Royal Statistical Society (1834), the British Archaeological Association (1843), the Ethnological Society of London (1843) and many, many more were formed.

? What do you think?

According to Taleb (2007), lists of factors that made historical events possible are meaningless. Most high-impact episodes are random events that happen purely by chance (Taleb calls them 'black swans'). When we try to establish variables that 'caused' previous developments, we are simply looking at independent events that happened around the same time, and we are deluding ourselves by thinking that they help us to understand the past and to predict the future. The fact that twenty years ago virtually no-one could foresee the present state of affairs (as becomes painfully clear when you read old science-fiction literature) should teach us that we have no knowledge of what may – randomly – happen in the next 20 years. What do you think? Are the factors listed in this section merely hindsight interpretations of society changes that happened to coincide with the scientific revolution, or are they factors that genuinely increased the probability of the scientific revolution taking place and surviving?

Interim summary

- The following factors are thought to have precipitated the scientific revolution in seventeenth-century Europe:
  - the growth of the population, urbanisation, and the emergence of a considerable class of merchants
  - a crisis of religion
  - new inventions that made information more easily available, that led to new questions, and that included the promise of scientific discoveries leading to wealth and power
  - the existence of universities and patronage
  - massive enrichment from the Greek and Arab civilisations
  - the idea that small issues could be solved without the need of an overall view that explained everything in the universe.
- The scientific revolution could also have died prematurely if:
  - a major disaster or war had happened
  - religion had been able to suppress the new thinking
  - natural philosophers had not been able to organise themselves and create structures that solidified their progress.

2.5 The new method of the natural philosopher

The scientific revolution could not take place unless something fundamental changed in the way scholars approached knowledge-gathering. Unfortunately, as we will see in this section and in Chapter 9, it is not easy to describe what exactly demarcated the new 'scientific' method used by the natural philosophers.

What do you think?

The question of what exactly science is will be a theme throughout this book. It may be a good idea at this moment to write down your opinions. What do scientists do? What methods do they use? In what ways does scientific knowledge differ from other types of knowledge? Keep your answers at hand and compare them with the text below and the following chapters (in particular Chapter 9).

Although it is tempting to use the word 'scientist' in our discussion below, historically this would not be correct, as the word was only coined in 1833 by the British philosopher of science William Whewell (1794–1866). Before, learned men interested in sciences called themselves natural philosophers or (later) men of science. The word science itself is much older. It is derived from the Latin word 'scientia' and was – together with natural philosophy – used in the Middle Ages and the Renaissance to refer to Aristotle's theoretical knowledge.

Francis Bacon and the importance of the interaction between perception and reason

Traditionally, science was associated with knowledge that depended on reasoning. This was true for all sciences from antiquity: mathematics, geometry, optics, astronomy. Philosophers like Plato and Aristotle were quite clear that scientific knowledge could not be built on observation, because the perceptible world was too volatile, unlike the permanent principles science sought to discover. Also, perception could be deceptive: people sometimes perceived things not present (e.g., in their dreams). As we saw above, mistrust in perceptual information formed the cornerstone of Descartes' thinking as well. For him, the divine soul had innate knowledge which could be made explicit by thinking. Descartes did not deny the existence of sensory experiences, but he minimised their significance:

> I cannot doubt that there is in me a certain passive faculty of perceiving, that is, of receiving and recognizing the ideas of sensible objects; but it would be valueless to me and I could in no way use it if there were not also in me or in something else, another active faculty capable of forming and producing these ideas.
>
> (as translated in Gardner 1987: 52)

The *New organon*

The person usually associated with the change in scientific method is the English lawyer and polymath Francis Bacon (1561–1626), although chances are high that in reality he was the exponent of a much wider movement. (For instance, in 1600 the astronomer William Gilbert published a book on magnetic and electrical phenomena, called *De magnete,* based on a series of experiments very similar to the type of studies promoted by Bacon.)

In 1620 Bacon published a book, *Novum organum* (*New organon*), in which he described the new view of science, as opposed to Aristotle's approach (which was taught at universities on the basis of Aristotle's six books on logic, together referred to as the *Organum* [the Latin word for instrument, tool]; hence Bacon's title *Novum organum*). Because of its importance in the growth of science, it is worthwhile to describe Bacon's book in some detail.

Bacon started by claiming that neither perception nor reasoning alone provides progress. Interaction between both is required. The limits of reasoning can be seen in Aristotle's axioms or first principles, which according to Bacon were the weakest part of Aristotle's theoretical knowledge:

> The syllogism consists of propositions, propositions consist of words, words are symbols of notions. Therefore if the notions themselves (which is the root of the matter) are confused and overhastily abstracted from the facts, there can be no firmness in the superstructure. Our only hope therefore lies in a true induction.
>
> (Book I, Aphorism XIV)

According to Bacon, perception is limited as well. A first weakness is that it tends to be biased by people's convictions:

> The human understanding is of its own nature prone to suppose the existence of more order and regularity in the world than it finds. . . .
>
> The human understanding when it has once adopted an opinion (either as being the received opinion or as being agreeable to itself) draws all things else to support and agree with it. And though there be a greater number and weight of instances

to be found on the other side, yet these it either neglects and despises, or else by some distinction sets aside and rejects, in order that by this great and pernicious predetermination the authority of its former conclusions may remain inviolate. . . .

(Book I, Aphorisms XLV–XLVI)

To correct for the confirmation bias, Bacon advised that particular attention be paid to deviating observations:

> . . . it is the peculiar and perpetual error of the human intellect to be more moved and excited by affirmatives than by negatives; whereas it ought properly to hold itself indifferently disposed toward both alike. Indeed, in the establishment of any true axiom, the negative instance is the more forcible of the two.
>
> (Book I, Aphorism XLVI)

A further problem with perception is the limitation of the senses: people do not observe everything correctly:

> But by far the greatest hindrance and aberration of the human understanding proceeds from the dullness, incompetency, and deceptions of the senses . . . the sense by itself is a thing infirm and erring.
>
> (Book I, Aphorism L)

Finally, even when observations are veridical they do not result in useful knowledge unless they are accompanied by reasoning and understanding. In this respect, Bacon referred to the works of alchemists whose experiments were based on observations but whose enterprise was haphazard because it lacked a coherent theoretical framework:

> To those therefore who are daily busied with these experiments and have infected their imagination with them, such a philosophy seems probable and all but certain; to all men else incredible and vain. Of this there is a notable instance in the alchemists and their dogmas . . .
>
> (Book I, Aphorism LXIV)

To overcome the deficiencies of observations, Bacon recommended putting them on a firmer basis by a tougher coupling between observation and reason:

> Those who have handled sciences have been either men of experiment or men of dogmas. The men of experiment are like the ant, they only collect and use; the reasoners resemble spiders, who make cobwebs out of their own substance. But the bee takes a middle course: it gathers its material from the flowers of the garden and of the field, but transforms and digests it by a power of its own. Not unlike this is the true business of [natural] philosophy; for it neither relies solely or chiefly on the powers of the mind, nor does it take the matter which it gathers from natural history and mechanical experiments and lay it up in the memory whole, as it finds it, but lays it up in the understanding altered and digested.
>
> (Book I, Aphorism XXVII, XCV)

Bacon also urged his readers to make observations much more systematic than was done at his time, so that there would be a firmer empirical basis for thinking to build upon:

> Now for grounds of experience – since to experience we must come – we have as yet had either none or very weak ones; no search has been made to collect a store of

particular observations sufficient either in number, or in kind, or in certainty, to inform the understanding, or in any way adequate. On the contrary, men of learning, but easy withal and idle, have taken for the construction or for the confirmation of their philosophy certain rumours and vague fames or airs of experience, and allowed to these the weight of lawful evidence. And just as if some kingdom or state were to direct its counsels and affairs not by letters and reports from ambassadors and trustworthy messengers, but by the gossip of the streets; such exactly is the system of management introduced into philosophy with relation to experience. Nothing duly investigated, nothing verified, nothing counted, weighed, or measured, is to be found in natural history . . .

(Book I, Aphorism XCVIII)

Bacon further took inspiration from technological research (which he called the 'mechanical arts') and argued that natural philosophers, just like craftsmen, should experiment to see which changes worked and which not, without bothering about the implications for the totality of the universe. However, natural philosophers should go beyond the experiments mechanics set up to solve practical problems (which Bacon called *experimenta fructifera*, fruit-bearing experiments). They should additionally use clarifying experiments to determine the true causes of phenomena, experiments which Bacon called *experimenta lucifera* (light-bringing experiments):

> . . . the mechanic, not troubling himself with the investigation of truth, confines his attention to those things which bear upon his particular work, and will not either raise his mind or stretch out his hand for anything else. But then only will there be good ground of hope for the further advance of knowledge when there shall be received and gathered together into natural history a variety of experiments which are of no use in themselves but simply serve to discover causes and axioms, which I call *Experimenta lucifera*, experiments of *light*, to distinguish them from those which I call *fructifera*, experiments of *fruit*.
>
> Now experiments of this kind have one admirable property and condition: they never miss or fail. For since they are applied, not for the purpose of producing any particular effect, but only of discovering the natural cause of some effect, they answer the end equally well whichever way they turn out; for they settle the question.

(Book I, Aphorism XCIX)

Ultimately, observations and clarifying experiments must result in deeper understanding. In Bacon's words, natural philosophers must go from *particulars* (or *works*) to *axioms*, which in turn will lead to new particulars:

> But after this store of particulars has been set out duly and in order before our eyes, we are not to pass at once to the investigation and discovery of new particulars or works; or at any rate if we do so we must not stop there. For although I do not deny that when all the experiments of all the arts shall have been collected and digested, and brought within one man's knowledge and judgment, the mere transferring of the experiments of one art to others may lead, by means of that experience which I term literate, to the discovery of many new things of service to the life and state of man, . . . from the new light of axioms, which having been educed from those particulars by a certain method and rule, shall in their turn point out the way again to new particulars . . . For our road does not lie on a level, but ascends and descends; first ascending to axioms, then descending to works.

(Book I, Aphorism CIII)

The existence of axioms also allows natural philosophers to purposely search for new phenomena, rather than having to rely on chance findings:

> And this consideration occurs at once – that if many useful discoveries have been made by accident or upon occasion, when men were not seeking for them but were busy about other things, no one can doubt but that when they apply themselves to seek and make this their business, . . . they will discover far more. For although it may happen once or twice that a man shall stumble on a thing by accident which, when taking great pains to search for it, he could not find, yet upon the whole it unquestionably falls out the other way.
>
> (Book I, Aphorism CVIII)

Sometimes an observation or a clarifying experiment may even decide between two alternative explanations. Bacon called such instances *crucial instances*:

> Sometimes in the search for a nature the intellect is poised in equilibrium and cannot decide to which of two or (occasionally) more natures it should attribute or assessing the cause of the nature under investigation . . . in these circumstances crucial instances reveal that the fellowship of one of the natures with the nature under investigation is constant and indissoluble, while that of the other is fitful and occasional. This ends the search as the former nature is taken as the cause and the other dismissed and rejected.
>
> (Book II, Aphorism XXXVI)

The link between particulars and axioms, however, must be much closer than in Aristotle's thinking. To achieve this, Bacon recommended working with a hierarchy of axioms, starting with lesser axioms (staying close to the observations), going over middle axioms (which are true and solid axioms on which the affairs and fortunes of men depend), to the highest axioms (which are general and abstract).

> In establishing axioms, another form of induction must be devised than has hitherto been employed, and it must be used for proving and discovering not first principles (as they are called) only, but also the lesser axioms, and the middle, and indeed all.
>
> (Book I, Aphorism CV)

More than anything else, the adoption of Bacon's research method was the reason why science became so successful from the seventeenth century on. One of the first research areas to profit from the application of the method was chemistry. Whereas before it was a widely erratic business, known as alchemy (to which Newton devoted more time than to physics!), the introduction of scientific rigour in a few decades turned it into a respectable science, with the rapid discovery of chemical elements and the laws that governed their behaviour. A central figure in this transition was the British scholar Robert Boyle (1627–1691), who in 1662 published one of the first laws of gas and who is seen by many (especially chemists) as another central figure in the scientific revolution. Boyle, for example, stressed that scientific experiments should be performed publicly and reported in such detail that everyone could replicate them.

To honour Bacon's role in the scientific revolution, historians sometimes call the new sciences based on close interactions between observation and reasoning 'Baconian sciences'.

Inductive vs. deductive reasoning

To better understand the novelty of Bacon's writings, it is helpful to be aware of the distinction between deductive and inductive reasoning drawn in logic.

deductive reasoning

form of reasoning in which one starts from a number of indisputable premises, from which new, true conclusions can be drawn if the rules of logic are followed

Deductive reasoning is a way of reasoning in which one starts from a number of indisputable premises from which new conclusions are drawn. The conclusions are guaranteed to be true if the premises are right and the correct logical rules have been followed. As we saw in Chapter 1, this was clearly the reasoning of Plato. It got further impetus when Aristotle defined the syllogisms and the rules to follow. It was also embraced by the Catholic Church and Descartes.

Because deductive reasoning requires indisputable premises to start from, it usually defends some form of innate knowledge, knowledge people seem to have intuitively. One source of such knowledge is the wisdom brought by the Soul, which explains the appeal deductive reasoning has for religious authorities.

The new scientific method proposed by Bacon, however, was much closer to inductive reasoning, a form of reasoning in which likely conclusions are drawn on the basis of a series of converging observations.

inductive reasoning

form of reasoning in which one starts from observations and tries to reach general conclusions on the basis of convergences in the observations; is needed in science to turn observed phenomena into scientific laws, but does not guarantee that the conclusions are true

Bacon stressed inductive reasoning because of his unhappiness with the indisputable premises in the systems of Plato and Aristotle. For him, the innate knowledge postulated by Plato and Aristotle was questionable and should be replaced by knowledge based on observation and induction. Descartes also found the first premises of Plato and Aristotle unsatisfying, but he tried to find new and improved ones. This brought him to his first premise 'I think, therefore I am' [*cogito, ergo sum*], because everything is doubtable (including perception) except for the fact of doubting itself. From this first axiom, Descartes came to the distinction between Soul (the doubting entity) and body and, henceforth, to the existence of God, who stood for the innate ideas of perfection, unity and infinity.

Experimental histories to extract the truth from Nature

It is important to realise that Bacon did not simply argue that deductive reasoning should be replaced by inductive reasoning. He was too well aware of the limitations of perception and inductive reasoning. Rather, as we have seen, he proposed a much closer coupling between perception and axiom, in which observations were used to formulate *and* evaluate axioms, and in which axioms were used to guide perception.

More than two centuries later, Whewell (1837) also observed that Aristotle's problem was not that he refused to use observation and inductive logic (as a matter of fact, Aristotle was the one who introduced the term!), but that he failed to integrate his observations and theoretical knowledge. Both were isolated, belonging to two different realms. The precedence of deductive logic was so incontestable that it could not be tainted by mere observations, which were subject to perceptual error and the risk of faulty reasoning.

experimental history

method introduced by Bacon in which the natural philosopher extracts the truth from Nature by active manipulation and examining the consequences of the intervention

In another publication of 1620, *Preparative toward natural and experimental history*, Francis Bacon made a cleaner distinction between his method of knowledge-gathering and mere observation. He called the process of careful observation and the formulation of lower and middle axioms through inductive reasoning a *natural history*. He contrasted this with an **experimental history** in which the natural philosopher examined the truth of the axioms and attempted to get to higher axioms by means of clarifying experiments. Natural philosophers had to take an active role in order to find the most likely interpretation of a phenomenon. In experimental histories, the situation was not passively observed, but elements of it were actively manipulated to see which effects this had on the phenomenon. Science had to extract the secrets from Nature, not passively observe them.

The importance of experimental histories was given further impetus in 1665 when the British scholar Robert Hooke (1635–1703) translated Bacon's crucial instance into *experimentum crucis* (critical experiment) and defined it as the experiment that was able to determine decisively whether a particular hypothesis or theory was better than its alternatives. Newton in 1672 claimed to have performed such an *experimentum crucis,* when he first dispersed a beam of white light into the colours of the rainbow using a prism and then converged the various colours back into a white beam with another prism. This, according to Newton, definitely proved that white light was the sum of all rainbow colours.

Are scientific theories always observation-based?

Although Bacon's writings had a great impact on the development of natural philosophy, to some extent they underestimated the importance of reasoning beyond observation in scientific research. Galilei and Newton again provide beautiful examples.

If people before Galilei felt happy about the geocentric model of the universe, this was not in the first place because it agreed with the Scripture, but because it agreed with their own senses. After all, no-one had the impression of moving with an incredible speed through space and making a full turn of the earth every 24 hours! So, when Copernicus started to consider the heliocentric model as an alternative, it was not because the heliocentric model of the universe agreed better with his perception, but because for some time it seemed to simplify matters for calculating the movements of the wandering stars. Similarly, Galilei had great difficulty convincing his audience that a moving earth was not necessarily in contradiction with their perception. Among other things, he had to evoke the analogy of travelling in the cabin of a ship. There, too, one can have the impression of being immobile while in reality one is moving over the waters.

Newton's *Principia mathematica* was another case in point. In this study, Newton happily postulated invisible forces that governed the movements of planets in the universe. The reasons Newton felt comfortable with these forces had more to do with his religious convictions (God could initiate whichever force he wanted) than with the scientific method advanced by Bacon.

In general, Newton was a notoriously sloppy experimenter. Virtually none of his breakthroughs were based on careful observation. Rather, Newton seemed first to postulate a mathematical theory and then to verify its truth by checking whether the predictions of the theory more or less matched the measurements. Newton's lack of empirical work was a major argument used by the German poet and polymath Johann Wolfgang von Goethe (1749–1832) when in 1792 he questioned Newton's theory of colour and put forward an alternative theory. According to Goethe, Newton had failed with respect to the scientific method, because he did not work cooperatively with other observers and because he did not conduct and replicate a large number of experiments to make sure they formed a converging pattern. As Goethe wrote (translation from Richards 2002: 437–438):

> My intention is to collect all experience in this area, to perform all experiments myself, and to do so throughout all their varieties, and thereby make it easy to repeat them and thus allow other researchers the chance to observe them. In this way, I hope to establish from a higher standpoint the propositions that express these observations and to determine whether such propositions can be brought under a yet higher principle.

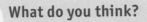

? What do you think?

Goethe's theory of colour vision failed to have much impact. Why would this be the case, given that Goethe followed Bacon's advice much more closely than Newton? After all, don't we all learn nowadays that scientific advance consists of convergent findings from many different studies involving different methods, different variables that are manipulated, and different variables measured?

In a revealing and amusing book from 1863, the German chemist Justus von Liebig (1803–1873) showed that even Bacon did not often use the Baconian method in his scientific writings. Most of the time Bacon started from his thoughts and searched in the literature for converging evidence (often without acknowledging the source), completely in line with the confirmation bias he had warned against. Liebig also noted that Bacon exhibited an almost pathological fear of mathematics in his writings.

We will return to the tension between theory and observation in Chapter 9, when we discuss current ideas about what makes a science. However, it is important to keep in mind that the first natural philosophers knew the limitations of perceptual information as the basis of knowledge. And indeed some of the very first scientific breakthroughs were testimony to these limits. After all, didn't the perception of a fixed world give humans the false impression of a geocentric universe? And were the failures to see differences in the brightness of Venus and to detect the moons around Jupiter not the reasons why Copernicus's heliocentric theory had been disregarded for almost a century? And who could have thought on the basis of the visual sense that white light was the sum of all colours of the rainbow? Human perception was both fallible and limited. The limitations of human vision were again brought to the foreground when the Dutch merchant and natural philosopher Antoni van Leeuwenhoek (1632–1723) in the 1670s published his findings with the microscope: Surfaces that to the naked eye looked uniform contained many more organisms than ever dreamed of.

Knowledge is to be discovered and not to be retrieved from antiquity

Besides the realisation that scientific thinking should be based on experimentation, another important element in the scientific revolution was the growing awareness that a lot of knowledge was still to be discovered. For centuries, scholars in Europe had lived with the conviction that mankind started with much more information than was left at the time. This was partly due to the extraordinary Greek civilisation (a lot of which was lost by the beginning of the Renaissance) and partly due to the Jewish-Catholic religion, which believed that God had created Man with access to all wisdom, but that this knowledge had been lost when Adam and Eve were chased out of the Garden of Eden. Because of this conviction, for a long time natural philosophy consisted of trying to reconstruct the vanished knowledge from ancient times on the basis of the fragments that had survived.

Gradually natural philosophers started to realise that the ancient civilisations did not know everything and that some of their knowledge was plainly wrong. Several of the new inventions had never been described or alluded to in the past, and the geography of the world, which became available through the new expeditions and explorations, looked very different from the writings of the Ancient Greeks. So, a lot of novel knowledge still had to be unearthed, just like it was possible to come across a previously unknown continent on an expedition around the earth. As Richards (1981) noted:

> Up to the scientific revolution, people held a static view of knowledge: God had infused certain men (such as Adam or Moses) with scientific knowledge, which was passed on to successive generations. This view accorded with the Renaissance presumption that ancient thought embodied the highest standards of knowledge. Even Newton contended that his Principia was a recovery of wisdom known to the ancients. After the scientific revolution, scientist changed to a growth model: Scientific knowledge is only at its beginnings.

Some of the knowledge growth model can be found in Bacon's *New organon*, although he still stayed very close to the traditional assumption that humans in ancient times knew much more than people in contemporary times. So, when he criticised Plato and Aristotle, Bacon did not point in the first place to the new knowledge generated, but to the fact that there seemed to have been older information more reliable than Plato's and Aristotle's. In his own words:

> The sciences which we possess come for the most part from the Greeks. For what has been added by Roman, Arabic, or later writers is not much nor of much importance; and whatever it is, it is built on the foundation of Greek discoveries. . . . But the elder of the Greek philosophers, Empedocles, Anaxagoras, Leucippus, Democritus, Parmenides, Heraclitus, Xenophanes, Philolaus, . . . betook themselves to the inquisition of truth. And therefore they were in my judgment more successful; only that their works were in the course of time obscured by those slighter persons [Plato and Aristotle] who had more which suits and pleases the capacity and tastes of the vulgar; time, like a river, bringing down to us things which are light and puffed up, but letting weighty matters sink.
>
> (Book I, Aphorism LXXI)

Because of the revision of the past, for a natural philosopher the truth of statements could no longer be based on the authority of history and tradition. This meant the end of the type of arguments used by the Italian astronomer Francesco Sizi in 1611 to question Galilei's claim that Jupiter had moons, and so there might be more than seven wandering stars:

> There are seven windows in the head, two nostrils, two ears, two eyes and a mouth; so in the heavens there are two favorable stars, two unpropitious, two luminaries, and Mercury alone undecided and indifferent. From which and many other similar phenomena of nature such as the seven metals, etc., which it were tedious to enumerate, we gather that the number of planets is necessarily seven. . . . Besides, the Jews and other ancient nations, as well as modern Europeans, have adopted the division of the week into seven days, and have named them from the seven planets: now if we increase the number of planets, this whole system falls to the ground. . . . Moreover, the satellites are invisible to the naked eye and therefore can have no influence on the earth and therefore would be useless and therefore do not exist.
>
> (translation from Stanovich 2010: 9)

? What do you think?

Was it a coincidence that the awareness of a lot of knowledge still to be discovered arose when scholars became freed from copying the old manuscripts in order to preserve the information for the next generations?

Interim summary

The method of the natural philosopher:

- in particular, the writings of Francis Bacon were important in making the new method of the natural philosopher (the predecessor of the scientist) explicit.
- Bacon's advice comprised the following elements:
  - observation and inductive reasoning are much more important in science than acknowledged by Aristotle
  - systematic observation is important to have a good understanding of the phenomena and to come to correct axioms; it is also important to spot evidence against the prevailing axioms and convictions
  - because of the limitations of observations, they must be supplemented by experimental histories to extract the truth from Nature (rather than passively observe Nature); observation and understanding must constantly interact.
- Bacon's view was able to explain quite well the developments that resulted in the scientific revolution, but the emphasis on observation and experimental histories did not explain the ways in which Galilei and Newton sometimes came to their conclusions.
- Another major change was that natural philosophers started to realise that not all knowledge had been known in ancient times and that much still remained to be discovered.

2.6 Changes in society as a result of the scientific revolution

The impact of science on daily life

Science and prosperity

Although the practical implications of natural philosophy remained very limited in the first 200 years after Bacon's writings (against the initial promises), by the nineteenth century the new thinking started to alter everyday life, because the technological changes (in particular, the invention of steam engine) began to affect the socioeconomic conditions of people, a process which became known as the **industrial revolution**.

industrial revolution

name to refer to the socioeconomic and cultural changes in the nineteenth century caused by the invention of machines; involved, among other things, the replacement of the labour of peasants and craftsmen by mass production in factories and the resulting massive relocation from the countryside to the towns

Kagan (2009) listed five positive outcomes of the impact of science on society:

1. Mechanical devices lightened the burden of manual labour and increased the production of goods.

2. People started to live longer on average.

3. Most people had better health.

4. People became more literate.

5. They also knew more about the world.

Scientific advances undeniably increased the affluence of the countries involved. People gained access to more goods and needed less time to invest in the fulfilment of their basic needs, so that more time became available for education. At the same time the improvements in nutrition, hygiene and medical care made humans healthier and live longer. Due to new communication methods (the first newspapers appeared in the seventeenth century), people were more aware of what happened in the world.

The positive effects were to some extent offset by the negative impacts of science. Certainly in the beginning the working conditions of the labourers were rarely enviable (although they must be compared to the pre-industrial situation). The technological changes also came with a serious pollution problem and there was growing concern that the rapid production would lead to the exhaustion of natural resources.

As science gained in standing, a scientific career also became a means of upward social mobility. The cleverest and most dynamic elements of the lower classes could improve their status through a scientific career. At the same time, a new type of skill was promoted, because scientific research required strong intellectual capacities. This put the emphasis on the individual rather than the family of origin. As Young (1994: 20) argued, society is a battleground between two great principles: selection by family and selection by merit. Science clearly favoured the latter: individual capacities were more important than the class one came from. Selection by personal merit also meant prominence of short-term gains, rather than attention to long-term preservation, which is more of an issue for landlords and their families.

What do you think?

Do you agree with Young that people have been able to progress in science irrespective of background/class, and that science has been a way of upward social mobility?

Science and specialisation

Scientific advances led to a further differentiation of occupations people could hold. Increasingly they also had to train for these jobs, because these involved specialised knowledge and skills. This made society more complex and also, progressively, led to what Schütz (1964) called the use of *recipe knowledge*. Individuals knew how to operate new tools and to integrate new inventions into their life, but they had only the faintest knowledge of their workings. When something broke, people could no longer mend it themselves, but had to consult an 'expert'. Knowledge became distributed.

What do you think?

Do you make use of recipe knowledge as well? Or do you have an idea of the precise workings of the tools around you? If you think the latter, could you be subject to what Keil (2003) has called 'the illusion of knowledge depth', the tendency people have to overestimate their explanatory understanding? Do you know how a computer functions? And could you be more specific than saying that you enter input and commands which are processed?

Proposals to ground society in the natural sciences

The Age of Enlightenment

The more successful science grew, the more intellectuals in the Western world began to see it as a way not only to gather knowledge, but also to organise society. Autonomous and scientific thinking were considered better sources of legitimacy than the authority of existing institutions, customs and morals. This led to the so-called Age of Enlightenment in the eighteenth century, and played a role in the outbreak of the American War of Independence (1775–1783) and the French Revolution (1789–1799); both were intended to replace the ruling powers by a more reasonable government inspired by the scientific method.

One of the elements that attracted intellectuals to the natural sciences was the belief that knowledge provided by these disciplines was objective, based on a method in which practitioners set aside their personal passions and interests to come to the best possible solution, free from political and moral values. Scientists were perceived as reasonable people who settled their disagreements with empirical data and experiments instead of persuasion and brute force. Human intellect had the power to understand the world and to provide value-free solutions to social problems if it followed the method of the natural sciences.

Age of Enlightenment

name given to the Western philosophy and cultural life of the eighteenth century, in which autonomous thinking and observation became advocated as the primary sources of knowledge, rather than reliance on authority

Positivism

The movement that promoted the social value of science the most became known as positivism. Adherents of this philosophical movement maintained that science was the only source of true knowledge and that the only possible objects of knowledge consisted of observable facts and scientific laws. Driven by the success of the industrial revolution, it maintained that science and technology formed the new grand project of human life.

The term positivism was introduced by the French philosopher Henri de Saint-Simon, but is associated with his disciple Auguste Comte (1798–1857), who is seen as the founder (or at least one of the founders) of sociology. In a series of publications Comte advanced the hypothesis that civilisations pass through three progressive stages. In the first stage, which he called the theocratic stage, gods and spirits dominate the culture. Within this stage there was a transition from animism (present in primitive societies), to polytheism (the belief of the ancient civilisations) to monotheism (as present in the Jewish-Catholic religion and in Islam). The second stage was called the metaphysical stage, because at this stage philosophical explanations predominated. Metaphysics is a branch of philosophy that aims to explain the fundamental nature of the world and the (human) being. Finally, the third stage was the positivistic stage, in which explanations were provided by the natural sciences. A society reached maturity when scientific explanations became the motor of progress. As was customary for this era, Comte did not call his hypothesis the theory of three stages but the *Law of three stages,* to convey the message that his insight was on the same par as Newton's laws of physics.

positivism

view that authentic knowledge can only be obtained by means of the scientific method; saw religion and philosophy as inferior forms of explanation

? What do you think?

Do you agree with Comte's assessment that scientific explanations are more educated than religious or philosophical explanations? Is this true for all types of questions?

Ironically (and maybe a sign of how fundamental the transition was) Comte did not recommend a science-based society in his third stage as we would conceive it now. Rather, science for Comte had to become a religion, in order to keep the cohesive function religion traditionally had. So, Comte set up a new Religion of Humanity, with its own calendar and rituals. This made it very difficult for his British followers, such as John Stuart Mill (1806–1873), to promote positivism in the Anglo-Saxon world. The 'real' scientists ridiculed Comte, although some followers did establish British churches of positivist worship (Wright 2008). None of the positivistic churches survived long.

New claims about the status of scientific knowledge

Together with the assertion that the sciences provided the only valid knowledge, positivists also upped the virtues of the scientific method in their communication to the wider public. In particular, they downplayed the problems of fallible perception and wrong theorising, because these did not agree with the message that scientific information was always true knowledge. So, the messages sent to the wider public were the following:

1. Because science is based on observation and experimentation, and not on opinion and authority, it is always right.
2. Scientific theories are summaries of observations and, therefore, are always correct as well.
3. Because scientific knowledge is always true, it should be the motor of all progress (i.e. it must decide all choices to be made).

The following excerpt from a school textbook on natural philosophy shows how these messages were also conveyed by the self-confident rhetoric of the scientists themselves, who looked proudly at the many achievements realised in the previous few hundreds of years:

> Why is it that the most acute mathematicians and metaphysicians the world has ever produced for two thousand years made so little advance in knowledge, and why have the last two centuries produced such a wonderful revolution in human affairs ? It is from the lesson first taught by Lord Bacon, that, so liable to fallacy are the operations of the intellect, experiment must always be the great engine of human discovery, and, therefore, of human advancement.
>
> (Draper 1847: v–vi)

Indeed, as science gained in power, it was the scientists who started to spread the message that their knowledge was superior to that of non-scientists. They no longer required the approval of positivists (who after all were 'only' philosophers and journalists writing about science):

> What has made positivism so appealing to scientists with an interest in the past of science is that this doctrine fits in beautifully with working scientists' virtually inborn prejudices regarding the achievement of their predecessors. Almost inevitably, successful scientists tend to regard the truths they have discovered as necessary truths. In retrospect, the achievements of earlier generations seem self-evident, and it requires a real effort of the mind to place ourselves in the position of those to whom 'truth' had not yet become manifest.
>
> (Cohen 1994: 39)

The counter forces

Not everyone was happy with the rise in status and power of science. As is often the case, the gain of one group was the loss of another. Therefore, some segments of society had little cause to support the scientific case.

The Roman Catholic Church

As we saw above, the first institute to challenge science's ascent was the Roman Catholic Church. Even though Galilei was not tortured and quite likely not even threatened with torture, the message was sent out that this *could* have happened. In combination with the real torture taking place in the hands of the Inquisition, this was a powerful signal that a commanding segment of the Roman Catholic Church had little sympathy for the natural sciences. The Church was the most powerful organisation in Europe and it was ready to defend its position.

The main message conveyed by the Roman Catholic Church, however, was not one of science being heretic. Rather, clergy presented scientific knowledge as second-rank, detracting individuals from real wisdom, and potentially dangerous if not restrained by religious morals. Scientists, like other lay people, lacked the knowledge and the authority to tamper with God's creation. An important channel for the message was the dominant position the Roman Catholic Church enjoyed in the education systems of many countries. This is how Catholic schools publicised their teaching:

> The great object studied in St. Patrick's Schools, is to train up the children in the genuine principles of their own holy religion; and to give them not merely worldly science; but, as they have a God to serve, and souls to be saved, to teach them their duty as Catholic Christians; and to instruct them in that heavenly science, which Jesus Christ himself came down upon our earth to teach; and without which all worldly science is vain.
>
> (*Catholicon* 1815: 127)

To counter the appeal of the Protestant Reformation and strengthen the Roman Catholic standing in education, a new religious order was founded in 1540: the Society of Jesus, better known as the Jesuits. The order combined a strong intellectual zeal with a highly effective organisation, resulting in the establishment of hundreds of secondary schools, universities and training seminaries, in which Latin, Greek, poetry, philosophy, modern languages, arts and sciences were taught.

In several countries of Europe the strong position of the Church in education was part of the struggle between the proponents of enlightenment and the traditionalists. One of the consequences of the French Revolution, for instance, was the establishment of religion-neutral state schools and universities.

The Protestant Churches

Because the new Protestant Churches still had to establish their power base, many tended to see science as an ally rather than an adversary (although this was far from a general approach; it is not difficult to find a strong anti-science text for every pro-science stance written). At the same time, there was little doubt that scientific knowledge dealt with worldly matters and, hence, was the handmaiden of the heavenly wisdom from the Scripture and the Church Fathers. For the Protestants as well scientific knowledge was dangerous knowledge if not guided by religion, as can be seen in the excerpts below:

> Religion without science will leave the race degraded, but science without religion would conduct it onwards to a remediless curse. As long as men shall believe in God

there will be some hope of their attaining a true appreciation of their own nature; when they shall come to believe only in themselves, elevation will no longer be possible; expectation will be a despair, and memory a remorse.

(Tait 1854: 495)

. . . science without religion – reason and truth without the moral vigour and judgment to wield them, thus creating a fertile source of evil in the fermentation of the intellectual elements without the restraining force of religious and moral discipline – impelling the people to employ their knowledge in crude misdirected combinations, in a restless and morbid activity to equal those above them, whom they believe they equal in point of intellect; – letting loose, in short, a fearful power when unregulated by moral cultivations and religious discipline.

(*The Imperial Magazine* 1834, Vol. IV: 284)

. . . the best processes to educate a child physically are the best to educate him intellectually, and that the best to educate him physically and intellectually are the best to educate him religiously and morally. There is no antagonism; but all attempts to separate science and religion are ruinous. They were made to go hand in hand, the mistress and the handmaiden. Science, without religion, would be cold-hearted infidelity; religion, without science, would be narrow-hearted bigotry. Every lesson in arithmetic, and grammar, and geography should not only make our children wiser, but better. Every lesson should point upward to man's higher and holier destiny. All our instruction ought to be in moral truth. When we go before our pupils, armed with these truths, our teaching will have some effect. Nothing but the religion of Jesus Christ is to reform the world.

(*American normal schools: Their theory, their workings, and their results, as embodied in the Proceedings of the First Annual Convention of the American Normal School Association,* 1859: 97)

Many Protestant Churches enjoyed good relationships with science. Ministers took part in scientific discussions, providing scientists with moral and religious counsel. Some were natural philosophers themselves, just like most scientists were deeply religious men. After all, didn't Bacon, Descartes, Newton and many others propose a 'sacred science', a science inspired by religion and for the greater benefit of faith?

The relationship between Protestant religion and science deteriorated in the 1870s, when scientists began to react against what they felt to be the patronising attitude of church authorities (Garoutte 2003). One cause of disagreement grew out of the estimates of the Earth's age. The general belief of the Church was that Creation had taken place in six days some four or at most ten thousand years before the birth of Christ. This did not agree with the geological fossil findings that became available, and was further questioned in 1859 when Darwin published his book on evolutionary theory (see Chapter 3).

In a short period of time several books and journals, such as the *Popular Science Monthly* and *Scientific American,* were published which not only exalted the many breakthroughs of science, but also raised suspicion about extent to which scientific progress had been hindered by religion. Two particularly influential writers were John William Draper (1811–1882) and Andrew Dickson White (1832–1918). The latter was co-founder of Cornell University, which was established as 'an asylum for Science', in contrast to the other private American universities that were religious institutions focused on the liberal arts and religious training. In response to the criticism and innuendo White received from religious leaders, he wrote two books: *The warfare of science* (1876) and *A history of warfare of science with theology in Christendom* (1896), in which he argued that Christian religion had a long history of opposing scientific progress in the interest of dogmatic theology. John William Draper is particularly known for his book *History of the conflict between religion and science* (1874), in which he above all criticised the role of the Roman Catholic Church in the suppression of science. It is becoming clear that many of our current views of an unavoidable hostility between religion and science trace back to these publications (Ferngren 2002; Garoutte 2003; Hannam 2009; Numbers 2009).

? What do you think?

According to sociologists, groups and organisations in societies try to defend and increase their power at the expense of others. This is done through conflict and oppression when the group is strong enough, through alliance formation with other groups when that is perceived as instrumental to achieve their own goals, and through exclusion of individuals who do not belong to the group (they are typically denounced as 'unqualified'). Can you apply these insights to the struggles between science and religion?

The humanities

humanities

academic disciplines that continued the traditional study of the ancient classics, increasingly supplemented with teachings of contemporary literature and art

Also outside religion there was a large segment of the population that preferred to keep away from the scientific realm. They were people interested in literature, culture, art, law, history and 'real' philosophy (as opposed to natural philosophy). These disciplines became known as the humanities, studies of the human condition on the basis of reading, thought and emotion. They were the continuation of the medieval and Renaissance teachings, based on the study of the ancient classics, increasingly supplemented with teachings of contemporary literature and art, to reach a universal human culture:

> The term *umanista* was used, in fifteenth-century Italian jargon, to describe a teacher or student of classical literature and the arts associated with it, including that of rhetoric. The English equivalent 'humanist' makes its appearance in the late sixteenth century with a very similar meaning. Only in the nineteenth century, however, and probably for the first time in Germany in 1809, is the attribute transformed into a substantive: humanism, standing for devotion to the literatures of ancient Greece and Rome, and the humane values that may be derived from them.
>
> (Mann 1996: 1–2)

An important text within the humanistic movement was the book *Reflections on the revolution in France,* which the Irish-British politician Edmund Burke (1729–1797) wrote in 1790. After having supported the American War of Independence because it restored the rights of the people against a tyrannical king, he initially felt sympathetic to the French Revolution as well, until he saw the scale of the upheaval and the extent to which the ruling classes suffered from the fight against traditional institutes and values. Burke argued that societies had grown spontaneously and that the prevalent customs and beliefs were the time-honoured outcome of this organic process and formed a bond between the living, the dead, and those who are yet to be born. A drastic breach with traditions tore apart the existing social tissue, made people unsettled, and was a jump into the unknown, even when based on scientific knowledge. It was an illusion to think that human social life could be built on reason alone.

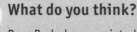

What do you think?

Does Burke have a point when he claims that society contains an implicit wisdom as a result of its century-long growth and evolution, and that we risk destroying this if we try to change the existing customs too often and too drastically on the basis of the newest insights?

Does your opinion change if you are told that Burke is generally considered the philosophical founder of modern conservatism? If so, why? If not, why not?

Romanticism

Romantic movement

movement in the late 1700s to early 1800s that reacted against the mechanistic world view and the emphasis on reason preached by Enlightenment; it saw the universe as a changing organism and stressed everything that deviated from rationalism: the individual, the irrational, the imaginative, the emotional, the natural and the transcendental

Leahey (2004: 188–9) also included the **Romantic movement** as a main force against science. In his words:

> Although we usually think of romanticism as a movement in the arts, it was much more; it carried on the protests of the Counter-Enlightenment against the Cartesian–Newtonian world view. . . . The romantics regarded Cartesian claims for the supremacy of reason as overweening, and combated them with paeans to strong feeling and non-rational intuition. . . . the romantics fervently believed there was more in the universe than atoms and the void, and, by unleashing passion and intuition, one might reach a world beyond the material. . . .
>
> In contrast to the rather bloodless and mechanical picture of the mind advanced by many philosophers, . . . the romantics depicted the mind as free and spontaneously active.

Although it is true that the Romantics in many aspects were closer to the humanists than to the natural philosophers, historical research in the last decade has made clear that the attitudes of the Romantics to science were much more ambivalent than thought by Leahey. Indeed, some of the strongest claims about the anti-science standing of the Romantic movement have turned out to be myths rather than facts, as shown in the myth-busting box below.

Just how anti-science were the Romantics?

Romanticism took place in the late eighteenth and early nineteenth centuries. According to the *Encyclopaedia Britannica* it emphasised the individual, the subjective, the irrational, the imaginative, the personal, the spontaneous, the emotional, the visionary, the natural and the transcendental. It started in Germany when a group of young academics and artists distanced themselves from the emphasis on reason and mechanical order that characterised Enlightenment. According to Berlin (1999), Romanticism originated out of envy of the French intellectual triumph at a moment when the German-speaking estates and kingdoms experienced a low. Whereas the Enlightenment claimed that all questions were knowable and answerable in a coherent way by reason and science, the Romantics held that there were no eternal truths, eternal institutions or eternal values, suitable for everyone and everywhere. Values and customs were context-dependent and often inherently in conflict with each other. The universe was constantly changing like a living organism and, therefore, could not be understood as a machine that operated according to fixed, eternal principles. The Romantic movement spread from Germany to the rest of the (Western) world.

The following are some of the examples given to illustrate how diametrically opposed romanticism was to science.

1. The Swiss Romanticist Jean-Jacques Rousseau (1712–1778) praised the 'noble savage', the pure human who lived close to Nature and had not yet become corrupted by civilisation. He honoured primitive people as natural, whereas he saw 'civilised' people as turned away from nature by education, social custom and opinion.

2. The British Romantic poet John Keats (1795–1821) declared that Newton had destroyed all the poetry of the rainbow by reducing it to a prism.[3]

3. The British Romantic novelist Mary Shelley (1797–1851) published a book in 1818, *Frankenstein,* in which she warned against the dangers of mad and evil scientists who followed their obsessions and created monsters.

However, historical research has revealed that none of the above examples is reliable. For a start, there are no writings of Rousseau in which he claimed that primitive tribes had a better life than Westerners (Ellingson 2001). The most likely origin of the noble savage story is a speech the Scottish physician and orientalist John Crawfurd gave in 1859 before the Ethnological Society of London, in which he ridiculed 'Rousseau's' views of primitive people, as part of an attempt to convince the Society that indigenous people were a different species from white people (and, hence, could be exploited without moral scruples).

Keat's 'declaration' was made during a rowdy and alcohol-fuelled dinner to celebrate the first stage of an enormous work by the British painter Benjamin Haydon (Holmes 2008). In a chat about the powers of Reason vs. Imagination, the poet Charles Lamb mocked Newton, describing him as 'a fellow who believed nothing unless it was as clear as the three sides of a triangle'. Keats joined in with his phrase about Newton and the rainbow, which was noted down by Haydon and which would be used later as a piece of evidence for the strong anti-science stance of the Romantic movement.

Mary Shelley's book *Frankenstein* was quite different from the image most people have of it (Holmes 2008), as can easily be verified by everyone who makes the effort to read it. Although the book indeed dealt with the creation of a new person by a man of science, both the scientist, Victor Frankenstein, and his creature were represented as emotion-rich human beings. For instance, a large part of the book described the solitude the creature experienced as a result of his ugliness and which eventually drove him to murder. The book was no great success, until it was adapted for the stage in the 1820s. These adaptations gradually shifted to the caricature image of scientists as depicted by some church authorities and humanists. Victor Frankenstein became a mad and evil scientist, working in a demoniac laboratory with a comic German assistant, and his creature became a dumb monster, without the intellectual and emotional competences he had in the book. Because Mary Shelley needed the money, she did not object to these changes, which made the stage play (and later the film adaptations) a great success.

So, the supposedly strong antithesis between Romanticism and science seems to be based on thin grounds. As a matter of fact, there is good evidence for close contacts between the main proponents of the Romantic movement and natural philosophers. Romanticists were interested in the new scientific findings and often fascinated by them. Similarly, some natural philosophers felt quite at ease with the romantic view of the universe as a living and changing organism rather than a stable machine. At the end of the eighteenth century, for instance, the views of the cosmos started to change. Whereas before the heavens had been seen as static, it became clear that major changes were taking place. Sometimes new stars lit up and disappeared after some time. Also, in 1789 the German-British astronomer Frederick William Herschel (1738–1822) published a treatise in which he described the dynamic nature of the nebulae he observed through his telescope. All these observations were more in line with the Romantic idea of an organic universe than with Descartes' mechanical picture. The romantic idea of the universe would also strike a chord with Darwin's views about evolution and would be one of the reasons why his theory found rapid approval in Germany (Richards 2002).

All in all, it looks like the interactions between the Romantics and the men of science in the eighteenth and nineteenth century were much richer and more ambivalent than fits into the description of a simple dichotomy between cultural movements for or against science.

The two cultures

There is evidence that the divide between science on the one hand and religion/humanities on the other hand increased in the first half of the twentieth century. For instance, in 1959 the British physicist, novelist and administrator Charles P. Snow (1905–1980) gave a talk at the Senate House in Cambridge that would touch a nerve in British society, given the many comments it elicited. (To get an idea of this, type the words *two cultures Snow* in your internet search engine.)

In his talk, Snow bemoaned the gulf that had grown between the scientists and the humanists (or literary intellectuals as he called them). According to Snow, by the middle of the twentieth century the groups had grown apart to such an extent that they barely communicated with each other. He called them 'The Two Cultures' and this is how he described the rift between them:

> It is about three years since I made a sketch in print of a problem which had been on my mind for some time. . . . By training I was a scientist: by training I was a writer. . . . It was a piece of luck, if you like, that arose through coming from a poor home. . . .
>
> There have been plenty of days when I have spent the working hours with scientists and then gone off at night with some literary colleagues. . . . It was through living among these groups and much more, I think, through moving regularly from one to the other and back again that I got preoccupied with the problem of what . . . I christened to myself as the 'two cultures'. For constantly I felt I was moving among two groups – comparable in intelligence, identical in race, not grossly different in social origin, earning about the same incomes, who had almost ceased to communicate at all, who in intellectual, moral and psychological climate had so little in common . . .

> I believe the intellectual life of the whole of Western society is increasingly being split into two polar groups. . . . Literary intellectuals at one pole – at the other scientists . . . Between the two a gulf of mutual incomprehension – sometimes (particularly among the young) hostility and dislike, but most of all lack of understanding. They have a curious distorted image of each other. Their attitudes are so different that, even on the level of emotion, they can't find much common ground.
>
> (Snow 1959/1998)

Snow saw the divide as a loss for society, because in his view both cultures had a lot to learn from each other. He appealed for more communication and cross-fertilisation, for instance, by including both sides in the school curriculum.

? What do you think?

Does the gulf between the two cultures as identified by Snow in 1959 still exist? Or is this gap now bridged? Are sciences and humanities treated equally in current society? And where do psychology and the other behavioural sciences stand?

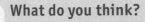

Interim summary

- Science has induced many changes in society, such as:
  - people became more prosperous and knowledgeable
  - a scientific career became a new means of upward social mobility
  - life and knowledge became more differentiated and specialised.
- The reactions to the scientific revolution can roughly be divided into positive and negative ones:

  Positive reactions
  - reason and science should be the basis of social order (the Age of Enlightenment)
  - science is the motor of progress and true knowledge (positivism)
  - scientific knowledge is always true knowledge and should guide the decisions made.

  Negative reactions
  - Roman Catholic Church: scientific knowledge is second-rank and dangerous if not guided by religious morals
  - Protestant Churches: many saw no inherent contradiction between science and religion, but science still had to be guided by religion (led to attacks by positivists around 1870)
  - humanities: the traditional world order and education have proven their use; it is dangerous to overhaul it all with rationality and science
  - romanticists: the mechanistic world view relied on by scientists is wrong; the universe is a living, changing organism.
- The two cultures.
- Snow regretted the gulf that existed between scientists and humanists (whom he called literary intellectuals) in the 1950s.

2.7 *Focus on*: How revolutionary was the scientific revolution?

In the previous sections we described how scientific thinking emerged in Western society and how it profoundly changed human life (in the next chapters we will see how it resulted in the formation of psychology as a new branch of learning based on scientific principles). Interestingly, the scientific advances escaped the attention of nearly all historians up to the first half of the twentieth century. The only histories of science that were written came from scientists and looked more like catalogues of achievements rather than thoughtful reviews of what had made scientific developments possible and what implications they had on peoples' lives.

In hindsight, one can discern three factors that hindered historians' awareness of the impact of science on society:

1. Historians were part of the humanist culture and did not feel much affinity with science.

2. To historians the accumulation of scientific knowledge seemed like a slow, steady process, spanning over three or even four millennia, without interesting twists and turns.

3. Many historians questioned whether there was such a thing as scientific 'progress'. Does history deal with 'progress'? And, if so, to what end? Are the developments in science steps forward or just steps without direction?

Indeed, the first historians of science had a hard time convincing both historians and scientists that studying the history of science was a worthwhile enterprise. They seemed to fall into the void between the two cultures described by Snow. This is how one of them, the Belgian-American chemist and historian George Sarton (1884–1956), described the situation (Sarton 1937: 38–40):

> . . . how is it possible that historians have paid so little attention to [scientific activity] and that old-fashioned 'humanists' have even affected to ignore it altogether and to consider it irrelevant to their purpose?
>
> The explanation is simple enough. That activity is to a large extent inconspicuous and even secret. It is impossible not to see the soldiers marching to war, not to hear the blowing of the trumpets and the noise of the battle; it is impossible not to see the king sitting on his golden throne, the regal and holy processions, bishops blessing the multitude, and many other grand spectacles, which seem to symbolize the whole of life and the best of it. But how many of us will manage to see . . . the scientist meditating in his garret? . . . how many people will ever understand what the scientist meant and did? It is not only his activity which is secret, even the products of it. Sometimes he may appear for a moment in the limelight, but on the whole these occasions are rare and if he be a good man as well as a good scientist he will not wish to multiply them. . . . When scientists are publicly praised, it is more often than not for secondary and inferior achievements.
>
> Two great events happened in the year 1686, the publication of Newton's *Principia* and the constitution of the League of Augsburg.[4] Everybody discussed the latter, but only a relatively small group of men were at once (or ever) aware of the former. The political importance of the League can hardly be exaggerated, but after all, the world wherein we are living to-day, would not have been essentially different if the League had not been brought into being. As to the *Principia*, this was really the foundation stone

of modern thought. Our conception of the world was utterly changed by it; that is, the world itself was changed.

Things started to improve for the science historians in the second half of the twentieth century, partly as a result of the efforts of people like Sarton (he was co-founder of the History of Science Society) and partly as a result of the huge expansion of academic activity and productivity. Another factor that gave the subject a boost was the introduction of the notion *scientific revolution* to refer to the events of the seventeenth century. This concept was launched by the French-Russian philosopher Alexandre Koyré (1892–1964) in 1939.

The idea of a revolution was much more attractive than the previous image of slow, protracted progress. It suggested conflict (one of the historians' specialities), fast developments, and a limited time period. As a result, the seventeenth century became one of the most studied centuries in human history.

Gradually, however, awareness grew that the concept of 'revolution' was far from neutral and tended to bias people's perception, because it suggested a radical breach with the time before. This was not entirely in line with the outcome of more refined archive research. To illustrate, have a look at the following excerpts and try to decide on the most likely author on the basis of what we have seen in this chapter.

1. Therefore, the earth cannot be in the centre . . . and just as the earth is not at the centre of the universe, so the sphere of the fixed stars is not its outer border.

2. If Aristotle had been a god then we must think that he never made a mistake. As he is a man, he has certainly made mistakes just like the rest of us.

3. When someone many times sees the eating of scammony accompanied by the discharge of red bile and he does not see that scammony attracts and draws out red bile, then from the frequent perception of these two visible things [he/she] begins to form a notion of the third, invisible element, that is that scammony is the cause that draws out red bile.

Scammony
Source: Geoff Kidd/Science Photo Library.

4. If you let fall from the same height two weights, one of which is many times heavier than the other, you will see that the relative times required for their drop does not depend on their relative weights . . .

5. In the celestial motions, there is no opposing resistance. Therefore, when God, at the creation, moved each sphere of the heavens with just the velocity he wished, He then ceased to move them Himself and since then those motions have lasted forever due to impetus impressed on the spheres.

Actually, our request to find the most likely seventeenth-century author was a bit of a red herring, because none of these texts were written by these scholars. So, the author of (1) is not Copernicus or Galilei, but Nicholas of Cusa, a cardinal who lived from 1400 to 1464. Similarly, the author of (2) was not Descartes but Albert the Great, who lived in the thirteenth century (*c*. 1200–1280). The author of (3) is not Francis Bacon doing a clarifying experiment, but Grosseteste, an English statesman and bishop who lived from *c.* 1175 till 1253, giving advice on how to obtain knowledge. The author of (4) is not Galilei on the tower of Pisa, but John Philoponus who lived in the sixth century (*c.* 490–570). Finally, Newton did not write (5), although he could have done so, but John Buridan who lived in the fourteenth century (*c.* 1300–*c.*1360).

Hannam (2009) used the examples above to illustrate that the knowledge which took centre stage in the seventeenth century was not all brand-new and completely out of the blue (see also Gauch 2003: 40–72). There had been similar thoughts before, but these had never been put into a coherent framework or reached the critical power to force a breakthrough in human thinking as happened in the seventeenth century. They were, however, recycled by the proponents of the scientific revolution to build their case. As such, they illustrate that although the notion of scientific revolution is exciting and attention-grabbing (which is why we used it in the title of this chapter), it tends to obscure the continuity in thinking that seems to have been present in human history. This, of course, again raises the question to what extent the emergence of scientific thinking was an unavoidable consequence of human intellect, or whether some extraordinary coincidence took place in the seventeenth century without which our world would have looked very different.

Interim summary

- Part of the reason why the notion of *scientific revolution* has gained currency is that it made the history of science more attractive.

- Although many aspects of seventeenth-century thought were innovative and ground-breaking, there has been more continuity in human thought than suggested by the word 'revolution'.

Recommended literature

As in Chapter 1, a lot of extra information on the historical events can readily be found in online encyclopaedias (e.g. **www.wikipedia.org**). The full texts of many of the (old) books described here also are available on the internet (e.g. through **books.google.com**). Below are listed the other texts we used to write the present chapter.

The scientific revolution

The impact of Copernicus and Galilei on the development of science is well described in Chalmers, A.F. (1999), to be found in the reference list. Other interesting books are: Cohen (1994, 2010) and Shapin (1996). Also know that Bacon's *New organon* is freely available on the internet and is well worth reading!

Very readable introductions about the lives, works and times of Galilei, Descartes and Newton are respectively: Sobel, D. (1999) *Galileo's daughter* (London: Fourth Estate); Grayling, A.C. (2005) *Descartes: The life of René Descartes and its place in his times* (London: Pocket Books); and Gleick, J. (2003) *Isaac Newton* (London: Harper Perennial).

Reactions to the rise of science

The books referred to in the chapter are all worth reading. For the reaction of the churches, both Ferngren (2002) and Numbers (2009) are good. For the relationship between science and romanticism, a good start is Holmes (2008), although it does not go beyond the British situation. For the German context, see Richards (2002).

References

Berlin, I. (1999) *The roots of Romanticism* (ed. H. Hardy). London: Pimlico.

Catholicon, or the Christian Philosopher (1815) *Roman Catholic Magazine,* 4 (at books.google.co.uk/books?ei=8zRjT_ipHOWa0QWH0uWKCA&id=yC4EAAAAQAAJ).

Chalmers, A.F. (1999) *What is this thing called science?* (3rd edn). Maidenhead: Open University Press.

Cohen, H.F. (1994) *The scientific revolution: A historiographical inquiry.* Chicago: University of Chicago Press.

Cohen, H.F. (2010) *How modern science came into the world: Four civilizations, one 17th-century breakthrough.* Amsterdam: Amsterdam University Press.

Cubberley, E.P. (1920) *The history of education.* Cambridge, MA: Riverside Press.

Dawkins, R. (1998) *Unweaving the rainbow: Science, delusion, and the appetite for wonder.* Boston: Houghton Mifflin.

Draper, J.W. (1847) *A textbook on natural philosophy for the use of schools and colleges.* New York: Harper & Brothers.

Ellingson, T. (2001) *The myth of the Noble Savage.* Berkeley: University of California Press.

Fancher, R.E. (1996) *Pioneers of psychology (3rd edn).* New York: Norton.

Ferngren, G.B. (2002) *Science & religion: A historical introduction.* Baltimore, MD: The Johns Hopkins University Press.

Gardner, H. (1987) *The mind's new science: A history of the cognitive revolution.* New York: Basic Books.

Garroutte, E.M. (2003) 'The positivist attack on Baconian science and religious knowledge in the 1870s'. In C. Smith (ed.), *The secular revolution: Power, interests, and conflict in the secularization of American public life* (pp. 197–215). Berkeley: University of California Press.

Gauch, H.G. (2003) *Scientific method in practice.* Cambridge: Cambridge University Press.

Hannam, J. (2009) *God's philosophers: How the medieval world laid the foundations of modern science.* London: Icon Books.

Holland, T. (2008) *Millennium.* London: Little, Brown.

Holmes, R. (2008) *The age of wonder: How the Romantic generation discovered the beauty and terror of science.* London: Harper Press.

Kagan, J. (2009) *The three cultures: Natural sciences, social sciences, and the humanities in the 21st century.* Cambridge, MA: Cambridge University Press.

Keil, F.C. (2003) 'Folkscience: Coarse interpretations of a complex reality', *Trends in Cognitive Sciences,* 7: 368–73.

Leahey, T.H. (2004) *A history of psychology.* Upper Saddle River, NJ: Pearson/Prentice Hall.

Mann, N. (1996) 'The origins of humanism'. In J. Kraye (ed.) *The Cambridge companion to Renaissance humanism* (pp. 1–19). Cambridge: Cambridge University Press.

Numbers, R.L. (2009) *Galileo goes to jail and other myths about science and religion.* Cambridge, MA: Harvard University Press.

Proceedings of the First Annual Convention of the American Normal School Association (1859). At http://books.google.co.uk/books?id=-PxBAAAAIAAJ&printsec=frontcover#v=onepage&q&f=false.

Richards, R.J. (1981) 'Natural selection and other models in the historiography of science'. In M.B. Brewer & B.E. Collins (eds) *Scientific inquiry and the social sciences* (pp. 37–76). San Francisco: Jossey-Bass Publishers.

Richards, R.J. (2002) *The Romantic conception of life: Science and philosophy in the age of Goethe.* Chicago: University of Chicago Press.

Sarton, G. (1937) *The history of science and the new humanism.* Cambridge, MA: Harvard University Press.

Schütz, A. (1964) 'The well-informed citizen'. In *Collected papers. Vol. II. Studies in social theory* (ed. A. Broderson). The Hague: Martinus Nijhoff.

Shapin, S. (1996) *The scientific revolution.* Chicago: University of Chicago Press.

Snow, C.P. (1959/1998) *The two cultures.* Cambridge: Cambridge University Press.

Stanovich, K.E. (2010) *How to think straight about psychology.* (9th edn). Harlow, UK: Pearson.

Tait, W. (1854) *Tait's Edinburgh magazine.* Edinburgh: Sutherland & Knox (at www.archive.org/details/taitsedinburghm04taitgoog).

Taleb, N.N. (2007) *The black swan: The impact of the highly improbable.* New York: Random House.

Weber, M. (1904/1905) 'Die protestantische Ethik und der Geist des Kapitalismus' (translated in 1905 as 'The Protestant ethic and the spirit of capitalism'). *Archiv für Sozialwissenschaft und Sozialpolitik,* 20: 1–54; 21: 1–110.

Whewell, W. (1837) *History of inductive sciences.* London: Parker & Strand.

Wright, T.R. (2008) *The religion of humanity: The impact of Comtean positivism on Victorian Britain.* Cambridge: Cambridge University Press.

Young, M. (1994) *The rise of the meritocracy.* London: Transaction Publishers.

3 Eighteenth- and nineteenth-century precursors to a scientific psychology

This chapter will cover . . .

Questions to consider

Historical issues addressed in this chapter

- Which factors made people more aware of their own individuality?
- What were the main developments in philosophical thinking in the eighteenth and nineteenth centuries?
- When did philosophers start to use the word 'psychology'?
- How strong was Aristotle's influence on the first views about psychology?
- Why was Kant an important figure in the early years of psychology?
- When did Darwin propose his evolutionary theory, and which aspects of the context help to explain the formulation of his theory?

Conceptual issues addressed in this chapter

- To what extent was the rise of scientific thinking a cause or an effect of the increasing individualisation of Western society?
- Why did psychology become the fourth part of metaphysics?
- Why did the first authors make a distinction between rational and empirical psychology?
- Why were authors like Kant and Comte convinced that the study of the human mind could not be a science? What alternatives did they propose?
- What are the differences between rationalism, empiricism and idealism? Why did empiricism lead to idealism?
- What contribution did problems in the other sciences have to the emergence of psychology as the scientific study of the human mind?
- Was Comte's positivism a good thing for psychology?
- How did Darwin's evolutionary theory influence psychology?
- In what respects did mathematical thinking and discoveries in the eighteenth to nineteenth centuries affect psychology?

Introduction

Psychology . . . is the fourth part of metaphysics, and consists in the knowledge of the soul in general, and of the soul of man in particular; concerning which, the most profound, the most subtle and abstract researches have been made, that the human reason is capable of producing; and concerning the substance of which, in spite of all these efforts, it is yet extremely difficult to assert any thing that is rational, and still less any thing that is positive and well supported.

(*Encyclopaedia Britannica* 1773, Vol. III: 175)

? What do you think?

In the present and the coming chapters we will discuss how psychology came about and what people at various times thought of it. It may be good for you at this moment to take stock of your own notions and beliefs. What is psychology to you? How would you define it to your friends? Are your views influenced by the way in which psychology has been defined in your first lectures? Or where does your definition come from? Do you think people have always defined psychology as you do now? Why so, or why not?

The first documented record of the term *psychology* is by the Croatian poet Marko Marulié (1450–1524) around 1500. The original document has been lost, but it is referred to in a list of Marulié's treatises made at the time. One of these treatises was entitled *Psichiologia de ratione animae humanae* (Krstić 1964). The next printed record of the word was in a book published in 1590 by the German scholar Rudolf Göcke (1547–1628): ψυχολογια[1] *hoc est de hominis perfectione, anima, ortu,* four years later followed by the book *Psychologia anthropologica* by the German philosopher Otto Casmann (1562–1607). The first book in English with psychology in the title was published by a British chaplain, John Broughton, in 1703: *Psychologia: or, an account of the nature of the rational soul.* Like the previous books, it failed to have much impact. It was summarised as 'a Discourse upon nothing' by a reader (letter from Anthony Collins to John Locke on 30 June 1703).

We report these uses of the word *psychology* to illustrate that the word is considerably older than the date usually quoted as the birth of psychology (1879; see Chapter 4). As a matter of fact, by the 1750s psychology had become quite a common word in book titles and course names. We start this chapter by looking at the changes in Western society that made people more aware of their individuality. Next, we look at the changes in philosophy that made philosophers study the human mind, and we review the first experimental histories concerning mental functioning. We end by discussing how evolutionary theory and statistics contributed to the emergence of psychology as a distinct topic of scientific investigation.

3.1 Individualisation in Western society

individualisation

trend in a society towards looser social relations and a greater focus by individuals on themselves than on the groups they belong to

A characteristic of current Western society is that people derive their self-image and self-esteem from their own qualities and accomplishments rather than from the position of their family in society. They are more likely to agree with statements like, 'If a social group hinders my development, it is better to leave the group' and 'I want to be judged on the basis of my own achievements' than with statements like, 'Children must stay with their parents until they are married' and 'I respect the decisions taken by my family'. Historians believe that this process of individualisation started sometime around the end of the Middle Ages and is still growing. The following factors have been mentioned as contributors.

Increased complexity of society

Richards (2002: 150) conjectured that individualisation has been a consequence of increasing diversity in occupations and complexity of social relations. As long as people stayed in the region and class they were born into, they were content to describe themselves in terms of age, gender, appearance and occupation. At most, Hippocrates' four personality temperaments (phlegmatic, choleric, melancholic and sanguine) were needed for further description of someone's character. However, increased urbanisation and industrialisation put people into more complex and competitive social networks, in which everyone struggled to maintain a sense of dignity and meaning. As the number of occupations and trades grew, people felt a greater need to position themselves relative to others.

Increased control by the state

Another hypothesis about the origin of growing individualisation was put forward by Foucault (1976). According to Foucault, individualisation was a consequence of increased control by the state, the fact that society gathered and stored more and more information about its individuals, which was reported back to the citizens. This information gathering gave people the feeling of standing out of the crowd.

Individuality promoted by Christianity

Kagan (2009) ventured that another reason for increased individualism in Western society was the Christian religion. This religion puts an emphasis on the solitary individual, because each person's private state of faith and relation to God is the essence of piety. The Christian view can be contrasted to Confucianism, the Chinese guide of conduct, according to which each person's collection of social roles and associated obligations to others forms the core of the self.

Pickren and Rutherford (2010) reasoned along the same lines and noted that the Protestant religion made people focus even more on their interior life by the use of devotional aids such as conduct books and diaries documenting the individual's behaviour. These aids enhanced the importance of self-control and also increased the need for education (to make sure people could read and write).

Mirrors, books and letters

Attention to individuals was further increased by some new inventions. For instance, the sixteenth century saw the introduction of mirrors of decent quality, with Venice as an important production centre. Needless to say, the presence of a mirror in the house made people more aware of themselves and the impression they made on others.

Printing further enhanced the interest and fascination for others. The period 1700–1900 saw the birth of the novel, in which characters were depicted with increasing depth, ruminating about their existence and their relations to others. Before, adventures were the centre of the stories and the protagonists were not much more than stylised figures responding in uniform and predictable ways. Only the classic Greek tragedies deviated to some extent from this pattern. Novels from the eighteenth and nineteenth centuries that have stood the test of time are Daniel Defoe's *Robinson Crusoe* (1719), Johann Wolfgang von Goethe's *Die Leiden des jungen Werther* (1774), Jane Austen's *Pride and Prejudice* (1813), Honoré de Balzac's *Comédie humaine* (1842), Emily Brontë's *Wuthering Heights* (1847) and Gustave Flaubert's *Madame Bovary* (1856). Already by the seventeenth century Shakespeare's (1564–1616) plays had a considerable degree of personal depth.

Finally, as literacy increased and postal services improved, letter writing became more common and was no longer limited to formal messages. So-called 'familiar letters' became a way to explore, express and share intimate experiences.

What do you think?

Is individualisation a process that is still going on? Has society changed in the past 30–50 years? Do you feel you attach more importance to individual development and worth than your parents and grandparents did? If you think society is still changing on this front, what factors are driving the current change? Do you think individualisation is a positive development? Are there drawbacks?

Interim summary

Since the end of the Middle Ages there has been increasing individualisation in society. Factors hypothesised to play a role include:

- Increased complexity of society
- Increased control by the state
- Individuality promoted by Christianity
- The increased availability of mirrors, books and letters

3.2 Philosophical studies of the mind

Descartes was the first Western philosopher after the Ancient Greeks to value new and independent thinking (the other philosophers had too much respect for Plato, Aristotle and the teachings of the Church). However, he was by no means the last. The seventeenth century saw a great revival of philosophical thinking. This thinking focused on the nature of knowledge (**epistemology**) and on the human mind (psychology), rather than on the universe, as had been the case for Plato and Aristotle.

epistemology

branch of philosophy concerned with the nature of knowledge

Empiricism instead of rationalism

The traditional rationalist view

As we saw in Chapters 1 and 2, the traditional view of understanding in philosophy was based on **rationalism**: Knowledge came from inside. Plato argued that by focusing on their own thoughts and reason, humans could get in touch with the realm of the never-changing Forms. Although Aristotle did not believe in the existence of ideal Forms, he too considered reason and deduction as the pillars of theoretical knowledge, a conviction embraced by the Catholic Church and nearly all philosophers up to and including Descartes. True knowledge was derived from reason, in order to come to an absolute description of the world, uncontaminated by the observer's fallible experience.

rationalism

view according to which knowledge is obtained by means of reasoning; usually through deductive reasoning on the basis of innate knowledge

Empiricism

As natural philosophers developed the scientific method, observation and inductive reasoning gained importance (see Chapter 2). The 'men of science' pointed to the ambivalent attitude of Aristotle towards observation as a source of knowledge, just like the Arab philosophers Ibn Sina (*c.* 980–1037) and Ibn Tufail (*c.* 1105–1185) had done before them. After all, Aristotle was the first to publish treatises entirely based on careful observation, and in *De anima* he wrote the following passage (Book III, Part 4):

> . . . mind is in a sense potentially whatever is thinkable, though actually it is nothing until it has thought [. . .] What it thinks must be in it just as characters may be said to be on a writing tablet on which as yet nothing actually stands written: this is exactly what happens with mind. [2]

More important than Aristotle's 'blessing' was the success of the Baconian sciences. Particularly in Great Britain, there grew strong opposition to the rationalist approach of knowledge acquisition. This influenced in particular the philosopher and politician John Locke (1632–1740). In 1689 he published a treatise, *An essay concerning human understanding,* which is generally considered as the start of empiricism. Empiricism is the conviction that there is no innate knowledge to start from and that all knowledge arises from sensory experience and induction. The human mind at birth is a blank slate (a *tabula rasa*) on which experiences leave their marks and make associations with the marks already present.

empiricism
view according to which knowledge is obtained by means of perceptual experiences; usually involves the idea of associations between ideas to combine the individual perceptions; also emphasis on inductive reasoning

The following quote from Sir William Lawrence (1783–1867), a British professor of anatomy and surgery, cogently illustrates the empiricist point of view:

> Examine the mind, the grand prerogative of man. Where is the mind of the foetus? Where that of a child just born? Do we not see it actually built up before our eyes by the actions of the five external senses, and of the gradually developed internal faculties? Do we not trace it advancing by a slow progress from infancy and childhood, to the perfect expansion of its faculties in the adult?

(Lawrence 1817: 6)

It is no coincidence that Locke's treatise concerning human understanding appeared two years after the publication of Newton's *Principia mathematica,* which hugely impressed Locke (he was a Fellow of the Royal Society, where he met the British natural philosophers and heard their talks).

Interim summary

Rationalism

- Existence of innate knowledge (nativism)
- Reason is the source of knowledge
- Main research method: deductive reasoning
- Main applications: logic, mathematics
- Main proponents: Plato, Descartes, Leibniz

Empiricism

- No innate knowledge (blank slate)
- Perception is the source of knowledge
- Main research methods: observation, experimentation, inductive reasoning
- Main applications: natural sciences
- Main proponents: natural philosophers, Locke, Berkeley, Hume

Epistemology in troubled waters: idealism

Although John Locke is generally considered to be the father of empiricism, his writings were actually rather cautious. Just like Francis Bacon, he was aware of the limits of perception and inductive logic and, despite the image of a blank slate, he did not really promote the idea of a human mind without any innate potential. For example, he took it for granted that humans could distinguish black from white. He also thought that language was an innate human ability, just like the tendencies to seek happiness and avoid pain. As Leahey (2004: 143) summarised: 'For Locke, the mind was not merely an empty room to be furnished by experience; rather, it was a complex, information-processing device prepared to convert the materials of experience into organized human knowledge.'

Berkeley and Hume

It didn't take long before other philosophers took up Locke's idea of the mind as a blank slate and showed that it could lead to far-reaching, counterintuitive conclusions. In 1709 the 24-year-old Irish student George Berkeley (1685–1753) published a booklet in which he argued that if the contents of the soul entirely consist of impressions acquired through observation, then we have no guarantee, except for God[3], that the contents of the soul are a faithful rendition of the world. Even worse, we have no guarantee that there exists something like an outside world. The contents of our mind could be fully self-generated. For instance, our eyes do not perceive depth (the retinas are flat and respond in the same way to light coming from objects far away as to light coming from nearby objects). Any impression of depth we have is constructed by our brain and although we assume this to be a faithful reconstruction of the outside world, there is no such guarantee. In other words, the method of observation promoted by the men of science did not necessarily lead to a true understanding of the world. It could equally well result in one grand illusion. Berkeley's position became known as idealism and is usually contrasted to realism.

Berkeley's position was expanded by the Scottish philosopher David Hume (1711–1776), who pointed out that idealism questioned the scientific endeavour of unearthing causes and effects. Because causes are never observed directly, we derive them from experiencing the co-occurrence of phenomena. We think that the sun is the cause of light, because the experiences of sun and light coincide, but all the mind has access to is the percept of something called sun and something called light, and the experience that both mostly (always?) co-occur. Thus, the mind simply infers causality from co-occurrence (contiguity) in time and place. When we experience the co-occurrence of events, we tend to see one event as the source of the other. This gives us an illusion of deeper knowledge beyond senses and memory, but actually there is no guarantee that something in the world corresponds to our postulated causal relationship. We assume that our impression of causality is due to the existence of a cause–effect relationship in the outside world, which we have discovered (realism), but from an empiricist perspective there is no guarantee for such an assumption. The link could arise entirely from the mind alone (idealism).

Hume pointed to a second principle humans use to group sensations, namely association by similarity. Because two sensations resemble each other, we assume they come from the same entity in the world. Again, there is no guarantee that this is true if one does not believe in God (Hume was criticised for his atheism, and this is seen as the main reason why he never obtained an academic position at a British university).

idealism

view within philosophy that human knowledge is a construction of the mind and does not necessarily correspond to an outside world; the truth of knowledge depends on the coherence with the rest of the knowledge in the social group

realism

view within philosophy that human knowledge tries to reveal real properties of the outside world; the truth of knowledge is determined by the correspondence of the knowledge with the real world

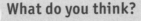

What do you think?

Arguably the most vivid illustration of idealism is provided by the first film of *The Matrix* trilogy (1999). In this film the main character discovers that the world he has been living in is fake. In reality, he – like all other people he is interacting with – is floating in a liquid-filled pod, serving as an energy source for machines, and his brain is being fed with a virtual reality by means of wires. The whole outside world, which felt very real to him, turned out to be nothing but an imagination. What do you think: is it possible that the world we are living in does not really exist? Are you as real on the internet as in daily life?

Kant

Hume's analysis of cause and effect provoked a reaction from the German physicist and philosopher Immanuel Kant (1724–1804) who felt that it awakened him from his 'dogmatic slumbers'. In 1781 he published the first of a series of books, *Kritik der reinen vernunft* (Critique of pure reason) that would become central in epistemology. Kant agreed with Berkeley and Hume that we cannot have direct knowledge of the outside reality (the thing-in-itself) through perception, but he sought to prove that (a) perception is much richer than postulated by Hume and Berkeley, and (b) such perception can only exist in a world of things that is not in contradiction with it.

In the discussion below, it is important to keep in mind that we have considerably simplified Kant's thinking (based on Scruton 2001). Kant is known as one of those philosophers who require a lifetime's devotion to grasp what he may have meant. The temptation is strong to skip Kant's writings in a book like this. However, given the tremendous influence he had on nineteenth-century thinking, this would be a glaring omission. Also, the relevance of the discussion between idealism and realism is very high when it comes to psychology: to what extent is a person's psychological understanding of the world a valid representation of an outside reality or a construction built by the person?

Kant started from the observation that humans are conscious of their perceptions. That is, humans not only perceive, they also think about their perceptions. By combining input from their senses with understanding, they come to concepts and judgments that generalise across the perceived instances and go beyond basic experiences. In doing so, the mind adds knowledge (to sensations) that is not derived from the observation itself and, hence, can be considered innate. The most important types of knowledge added by the mind to incoming stimuli are those of time, space and cause–effect. Because there is continuity in the understanding and the perceptions, the mind can conclude that there must be continuity in time both for the observer and the observed. As a result, perceptions are automatically situated and ordered in time. Second, because sensations are experienced as caused by something from 'outside', there is a sense of space that need not be learned and leads to the postulation of perceptions referring to substances situated in space. Finally, Kant argued, the mind puts forward the assumption that 'every event has a cause'. As a result, the mind sees cause–effect sequences wherever possible.

In summary, according to Kant, human experiences on which knowledge is built are much richer than Hume and Berkeley claimed, because they already contain within themselves the features of time, space, substance and causality.

Next, Kant argued that human perception, as described above, could not arise in an environment completely at odds with the sensations. Even if sensations are subjective, they can only exist if the perceiver inhabits a world that is in line with the input from the senses. Successive sensations must form continuity and unity to be understood, otherwise they are experienced as incoherent and meaningless snapshots. Just like things-in-themselves cannot be known directly, humans do not have direct access to their experiences. All they can observe is the objects of their experiences and these objects require stimulation that remains constant in time (i.e. that continues to exist when unobserved).

Finally, Kant argued, humans are not merely centres of knowledge; they are also agents, operating in the environment on the basis of their knowledge. Not all of these actions are successful, suggesting that an outside reality constrains human activities. Even Hume, in a dialogue published after his death, had one of the characters joke:

> Whether your scepticism be as absolute and sincere as you pretend, we shall learn bye and bye, when the company breaks up: We shall then see, whether you go out at the door or the window; and whether you really doubt, if your body has gravity, or can be injured by its fall; according to popular opinion, derived from our fallacious senses and more fallacious experience.
>
> (Hume 1779, *Dialogues concerning natural religion*).

? What do you think?

To understand Kant's arguments, try to apply them to the *Matrix* film. How is coherence in time and space achieved? Did this require some real entity interacting with the human mind? How were the human tendencies to seek causes and to interact with the environment circumvented? Again, would this be possible without some 'outside reality'?

Scottish common sense

In Scotland, too, there was a feeling that Berkeley and Hume's idealism had gone one step too far and was alienating philosophical epistemology from science's ongoing victory march. In particular, Thomas Reid (1710–1796) argued it was time for a return to what he called 'common sense':

> Philosophy . . . has no other root but the principles of Common Sense; it grows out of them, and draws its nourishment from them. Severed from this root, its honours wither, its sap is dried up, it dies and rots. . . . It is a bold philosophy that rejects, without ceremony, principles which irresistibly govern the belief and the conduct of all mankind in the common concerns of life . . .
>
> (Reid 1764; as cited in Gauch 2003: 64)

Reid thought that the decoupling of mind and reality, initiated by Descartes and Locke, had spun out of control. He urged philosophy to return to the good old Aristotelian view of perception as a simple record of the world as it is. According to him, perception was a direct interaction between the perceiver and the real object, and did not result in a separate stage of perceptual representations, which may or may not be a truthful copy of the outside world.

However, Berkeley's idealism was not so easy to put down. Philosophers kept struggling with it and, as we will see in later chapters, it knew a spectacular revival in postmodernist thinking in the second half of the twentieth century. Certainly when it comes to psychology, the discussions between realists and idealists are still very much alive, as we will see in Chapters 10 and 11.

Rational and empirical psychology

As philosophers became ever more interested in the human mind, the theme 'psychology' was added as the fourth part of metaphysics (see the opening quote of this chapter). Metaphysics involves the study of the nature of the universe (addressing the question 'what is really there?'; Jolley 2005) and usually entails reference to that which is not directly observable (Valentine 2000). It got its name from a treatise by Aristotle, who distinguished three parts in metaphysics:

1. *Ontology*: the study of the universe and its entities
2. *Natural theology*: the study of God(s)
3. *Universal science*: the study of the axioms and demonstrations on which theoretical knowledge is based.

In the early 1700s the study of the human soul was added as the fourth component to Aristotle's list and called psychology. To some extent this was not surprising, given the extraordinary popularity of Aristotle's book *De Anima* throughout the centuries. Psychology rapidly became the main subject of eighteenth- to nineteenth-century philosophical enquiry. Kant characterised it as an inventory of all that is given to humans by pure reason. Other authors saw more scope for an empirical input.

Wolff

A momentum in the rise of psychology as an independent theme of study was the publication of two books by the Polish-German mathematician and philosopher Christian Wolff (1679–1754): *Psychologia empirica* (1732) and *Psychologia rationalis* (1734). Wolff was one of the leading figures of the German Enlightenment and wrote these two books after he had been ousted from the University of Halle in Prussia[4] because of his insufficient religious zeal. At that time he was appointed at the University of Marburg in the nearby Duchy of Saxony (remember that present-day Germany consisted of many different states in the eighteenth century). Our discussion of Wolff's books is based on Richards (1980).

Wolff took ideas from Aristotle, Bacon and Newton to define the subject of psychology. First, he defined *rational psychology* very much as Aristotle had done for theoretical knowledge. It started from axioms (self-evident truths), which had to be derived from more fundamental disciplines, such as physics and metaphysics. On the basis of deductive reasoning, these axioms would lead to the 'demonstration' (in an Aristotelian sense) of new knowledge. This rational approach guaranteed true conclusions about the human soul and allowed the philosopher to penetrate more deeply into the matter than by simple observation. In Wolff's own words (as translated by Richards 1980: 236):

> In rational psychology reason must be given for whatever occurs in the soul or can occur in it. For rational psychology is that part of philosophy concerning itself with the soul. Therefore reason must be given for whatever actually occurs in the soul or can occur in it.

Wolff agreed with Bacon that pure reason without observation entailed a risk of error. Long chains of reasoning without reality checks invited mistakes. Therefore, psychology needed a close interaction between reason and observation, or *empirical psychology*. In Wolff's own words:

> Empirical psychology is similar to experimental physics; for we use experiments – either directly or by deducing something from them – to examine the tenets of dogmatic physics. . . . In this instance the psychologist imitates the astronomer, who derives theory from observations and corroborates theory through observations, and who, by the aid of theory, is led to observations which he otherwise might not make. And thus the demonstrations of rational psychology suggest what ought to be considered in empirical psychology. And wherever empirical psychology is established and rational psychology cultivated, we are enriched by many principles which otherwise would have to be secured with great difficulty. Thus the best thing is for one constantly to join the study of rational psychology with that of empirical psychology . . .
>
> (Wolff in 1732, as translated by Richards 1980: 232–3)

introspection

research method in psychology consisting of a person looking inward and reporting what he/she is experiencing; usually done under controlled circumstances

Empirical psychology according to Wolff was built on introspection, the mind's conscious observations of its own activity. In his view, the human mind could perceive its own operations and use this information to build a science of psychology, as can be seen in the following excerpt (translated by Richards 1980: 231):

> In empirical psychology the characteristics of the human soul are established through experience; but we experience that of which we are aware (cognoscimus) by attending to our perceptions. Hence we come to know the subjects dealt with in empirical psychology by attending to those occurrences in our souls of which we are conscious.

Finally, Wolff suggested that psychology should aim for mathematical demonstrations, similar to Newton's laws of physics. Only then would there be full understanding. He called this approach 'psychometria'.

Wolff's books and definitions were picked up by Diderot and d'Alembert in their famous dictionary of French Enlightenment, *Encyclopédie, ou dictionnaire raisonné des sciences, des arts et des métiers,* published between 1751 and 1772. Wolff's ideas also found their way to the *Encyclopaedia Britannica,* first published between 1768 and 1771 in Edinburgh (cf. the opening quote of this chapter). The impact of the books can further be gauged from the fact that in 1755 the Swiss author Charles Bonnet published a book entitled *Essai de psychologie,* in which he already felt the need to issue an apology for contributing to a field in which 'so many books have been written' (as cited in Hatfield 1998). Clearly, the new, fourth branch of metaphysics was thriving and started to position itself on the side of the blooming natural sciences.

Kant again

Given the importance of psychology in metaphysics by the second half of the eighteenth century, Immanuel Kant was bound to contemplate the issue as well, as part of his struggle to integrate rationalism and empiricism. In doing so, he came to a conclusion that was pretty devastating for the scientific ambitions of psychology, as can be read in his 1786 book with the (translated) title *Metaphysical foundations of natural science.*

For a start, Kant made the by then usual distinction between empirical and rational knowledge. The empirical approach led to a collection of facts, which could be ordered and classified. This led to what Kant called a *historical doctrine of nature,* which was below the level of natural science. In Kant's view, natural science required rational analysis, a system of undisputable axioms and demonstrations. Furthermore (and this was Newton's influence), a *proper* natural science required the axioms and demonstrations to be written as mathematical laws. Because of the latter requirement, Kant classified chemistry as a field that had not yet reached the threshold of a (proper) natural science. Its grounds were still empirical, merely laws of experience, and not yet laws demonstrated by necessity and formulated in mathematical terms. Kant formulated his arguments as follows:

> A rational doctrine of nature thus deserves the name of a natural science, only in case the fundamental natural laws therein are cognized a priori, and are not mere laws of experience. . . . All *proper* natural science therefore requires a *pure* part, on which the apodictic certainty that reason seeks therein can be based. . . . I assert, however, that in any special doctrine of nature there can be only as much *proper* science as there is *mathematics* therein. For, according to the preceding, proper science, and above all proper natural science, requires a pure part lying at the basis of the empirical part, and resting on a priori cognition of natural things.
>
> (Kant 1786, as translated by Friedman 2004; italics in the original).

Needless to say, if chemistry did not qualify as a proper natural science, there was little hope for psychology. And indeed, this was Kant's verdict:

> Yet the empirical doctrine of the soul must remain even further from the rank of a properly so-called natural science than chemistry. In the first place, because mathematics is not applicable to the phenomena of inner sense and their laws, the only option one would have would be to take the *law of continuity* in the flux of inner changes into account – which, however, would be an extension of cognition standing to that which mathematics provides for the doctrine of body approximately as the doctrine of the properties of the straight line stands to the whole of geometry. For the pure inner intuition in which the appearances of the soul are supposed to be constructed is *time,* which has only one dimension. [In the second place,] however, the empirical doctrine of the soul can also never approach chemistry even as a systematic art of analysis or experimental doctrine, for in it the manifold of inner observation can be separated only by mere division in thought, and cannot then be held separate and recombined at will (but still less does another thinking subject suffer himself to be experimented upon to suit our purpose), and even observation by itself already changes and displaces the state of the observed object. Therefore, the empirical doctrine of the soul can never become anything more than an historical doctrine of nature, and, as such, a natural doctrine of inner sense which is as systematic as possible, that is, a natural description of the soul, but never a science of the soul, nor even, indeed, an experimental psychological doctrine.
>
> (Kant 1786, as translated by Friedman 2004)

Kant's objections can be summarised as follows:

1. The outcome of introspection cannot be formulated in mathematical terms because there are no aspects of substance or space in inner observations, only time.
2. Inner observations cannot be separated and recombined at will, as is possible with outside objects.
3. The act of introspection by itself changes and displaces the state of the observed mind.
4. As a result, psychology can never become a natural science (let alone a proper natural science). It can at most be a historical doctrine of nature, a collection of systematically ordered empirical facts.

As a result of Kant's standing within philosophy, his evaluation of psychology was a serious setback for the fledgling branch of learning or at least for its scientific claims. The movement initiated by Wolff was nipped in the bud. Psychology was not part of the emerging natural sciences. At most, it could aim for a systematic classification of empirically observed facts, similar to what historians could do with the facts they observed.

What do you think?

Does Kant have a point when he says that psychology always will be a collection of empirically established facts without a deeper understanding? Or have we proven him wrong over the past 200 years? Is psychology really a science? And does Kant's definition of a science sound OK to you? Return to these questions after you've read Chapters 9 and 10. Do you think any differently now?

Sturm (2006; see also Hatfield 1998) argued that Kant's true standing has been misunderstood. According to Sturm, Kant left open the possibility of psychology as a science, as long as there was a clear connection with stimuli in the environment (see the law of continuity in the excerpt above). After all, Kant knew and approved of some of the first studies of human perceptual capacities. His evaluation of psychology was aimed at contemporary empirical psychologists, such as Alexander Baumgarten and Johann Nicolas Tetens, who defended a strong and uncritical version of introspectionism, according to which psychology could be a science entirely based on this method. Kant thought this was a false trail.

Whatever the correct interpretation of Kant's views, the fact that he explicitly denied psychology the status of science has been used repeatedly against those who wanted to promote psychology's scientific standing (Chapter 10).

Comte

Another high-profile person who denied the scientific status of psychology was Auguste Comte, the proponent of positivism and the founder of sociology (Chapter 2). Psychology was excluded from his hierarchy of sciences because of the problems with the introspective method. This is how Comte formulated it:

> I limit myself to pointing out the principal consideration which proves clearly that this pretended direct contemplation of the mind by itself is a pure illusion. . . . It is in fact evident that, by an invincible necessity, the human mind can observe directly all phenomena except its own proper states. For by whom shall the observation of these be made? It is conceivable that a man might observe himself with respect to the passions that animate him, for the anatomical organs of passion are distinct from those whose function is observation. Though we have all made such observations on ourselves, they can never have much scientific value, and the best mode of knowing the passions will always be that of observing them from without; . . . The thinker cannot divide himself into two, of whom one reasons whilst the other observes him reason. The organ observed and the organ observing being, in this case, identical, how could observation take place? This pretended psychological method is then radically null and void. On the one hand, they advise you to isolate yourself, as far as possible, from every external sensation, especially every intellectual work – for if you were to busy yourself even with the simplest calculation, what would become of internal observation? – on the other hand, after having with the utmost care attained this state of intellectual slumber, you must begin to contemplate the operations going on in your mind, when nothing there takes place! Our descendants will doubtless see such pretensions some day ridiculed upon the stage. The results of so strange a procedure harmonize entirely with its principle. For all the two thousand years during which metaphysicians have thus cultivated psychology, they are not agreed about one intelligible and established proposition. 'Internal observation' gives almost as many divergent results as there are individuals who think they practice it.
>
> (Comte 1830; as translated by James 1890, Vol. I: 188)

The only ways in which the human mind could be studied scientifically, according to Comte, was on the basis of biology and on the basis of observation of the products produced by the mind. As for the former, Comte was particularly impressed by phrenology (the view that mental functions were localised in the brain and that the capacity of a function corresponded to the size of the brain part devoted to it; see Chapter 5). As for the latter, the products of the human mind formed one of the subjects of Comte's new science: sociology.

All in all, Comte came to a hierarchy of six sciences, with the lower levels depending on the laws discovered in the higher and, therefore, likely to take longer before they reached the same level of perfection:

1. mathematics
2. astronomy
3. physics
4. chemistry
5. biology
6. sociology.

In Comte's hierarchy there was no need for a 'science' of psychology, which was better left in philosophy's realm of metaphysics.

Interim summary

Philosophical studies of the mind
Epistemology

- Rise of empiricism (Locke), which questioned the traditional rationalist view.
- In its extreme form empiricism leads to idealism (human knowledge is a construction of the mind, which need not correspond to an outside world), as argued by Berkeley and Hume.
- Kant sought to reconcile rationalism and empiricism by arguing that the mind imposes structure on the incoming sensory experiences and that it requires a coherent and constant input to make sense of the input.
- Idealism was also put aside by Scottish common sense.

Rational and empirical psychology

- Psychology was added as the fourth part of metaphysics.
- Important impetus: two books by Wolff, who made a distinction between rational psychology (based on axioms and deductions) and empirical psychology (based on introspection).
- Kant argued that psychology could not be a proper natural science, because the act of introspection changed the state of the mind, inner observations could not be separated and recombined at will, and could not be formulated in mathematical laws.
- Comte also argued that introspection as a scientific method was flawed and claimed that the human mind could only be studied scientifically by focusing on physiology (done by biologists) and on the products of the human mind (done by sociologists).

3.3   Textbooks of psychology

Because of psychology's increasing impact within philosophy, a growing number of psychology courses were taught at university, not only to philosophy students, but also to students of religious and educational studies. This created a market for textbooks on psychology, which shaped people's views (Hatfield 1998; Smith 2005; Teo 2007). We describe a few of the more interesting ones.

Kant

Kant is not only known for his attempts to synthesise empiricism with rationalism and his claim that psychology did not qualify as a proper natural science, in 1798 he also published a textbook on human functioning, *Anthropologie in pragmatischer Hinsicht,* based on the lecture notes of a course he was teaching. In line with his assessment of psychology, Kant did not treat the topic as a science, but as a collection of narratives. Nor did he call the subject psychology (the study of mind) but anthropology (the study of man). This was the table of contents (as translated in Louden 2006):

Anthropology from a Pragmatic Point of View

Part I: Anthropological Didactic. On the way of cognizing the interior as well as the exterior of the human being

Book I	On the cognitive faculty
Book II	The feeling of pleasure and displeasure
Book III	On the faculty of desire

Part II: Anthropological Characteristic. On the way of cognizing the interior of the human being from the exterior

In this book Kant addressed topics such as self-consciousness, self-observation, unconscious ideas and mental processes, the distinction between sensation and thinking, the role of pleasure and pain in human life, how to define and control emotions and passions, and what the differences were between the characters of the French, British, Spanish, Italians, Germans, Greeks and Armenians.

physiognomy
belief that the personality of an individual can be deduced from their appearance, in particular from the shape of the head and the face

As can be seen in the table of contents, Kant also devoted a part to deriving people's characters from their appearance and behaviour. The former is known as **physiognomy,** the belief that the personality of individuals can be deduced from their appearance. It can be traced back to Ancient Greece and in Kant's time was made popular again by the Swiss pastor Johann Kaspar Lavater (1741–1801) in a series of richly illustrated books. Kant did not fully share Lavater's conviction that the interior of humans could be derived entirely from their looks. Rather, he thought the judgement of a person's interior had to be based on their behaviour in addition to their appearance. These are some of the observations Kant made (as translated in Louden 2006: 198, italics in the original):

When we pursue our observations of human beings as they actually are, it becomes apparent that an exactly measured *conformity to the rule* generally indicates a very ordinary human being who is without spirit. The *mean* seems to be the basic measurement and the basis of beauty; but it is far from being beauty itself, because for this something characteristic is required. . . . one may find fault with a face here, there a forehead, nose, chin, or color of hair, and so on, and yet admit that it is still more pleasing for the individuality of the person than if it were in perfect conformity to the rule, since this generally also carries lack of character with it.

But one should never reproach a face with *ugliness* if in its features it does not betray the expression of a mind corrupted by vice or by a natural but unfortunate propensity to vice; for example, a certain feature of sneering as soon as one begins to speak, or of looking another person in the face with impudence that is untempered by gentleness. . . .

Herbart

Another widely used textbook of psychology was published in 1816 (2nd revised edition 1838) by Johann Friedrich Herbart (1776–1841) when he was Professor at the University of Königsberg (the Chair previously occupied by Kant). The book was entitled *Lehrbuch zur psychologie* and was written in particular for use in educational studies (Herbart is one of the founders of educational sciences). Herbart was convinced that knowledge of psychology was of principal importance to teachers. The table of contents of his textbook was as follows (as translated by Smith 1901):

> **A textbook in psychology**
>
> **Part First**: Fundamental Principles
>
> **Part Second**: Empirical Psychology
>
> > First division: Psychological phenomena, according to the hypothesis of mental faculties
> > Second division: Mental conditions
>
> **Part Third**: Rational psychology
>
> > Section first: Theorems from metaphysics and natural philosophy
> > Section second: Explanations of phenomena

It is interesting to see how closely the structure of Herbart's book follows Wolff's division of empirical and rational psychology. A further peculiarity of the book is that Herbart formulated his theorems as 'mathematical laws', to increase the scientific credentials of his claims, in defiance of Kant's contention that psychology could never be a science with Newtonian rules.

Upham

Not only German-speaking Europe produced textbooks on psychology. There was also a lively scene in the United States, where students had to take courses on moral and mental philosophy. Moral philosophy dealt with ethics and conduct; mental philosophy studied the elements and processes of the mind and how they influenced action. The contents were heavily influenced by Scottish common sense realism (see above), but increasingly took a distinctive American look with locally produced books.

A particularly popular textbook was *Elements of intellectual philosophy*, written in 1827 by the American philosopher Thomas Upham (1799–1872). Over 50 editions of this book were published, and it was retitled *Elements of mental philosophy* in 1832. The table of contents was as follows:

> **Elements of Intellectual Philosophy**
>
> Chapter 1: Utility of intellectual philosophy
> Chapter 2: Primary truths
> Chapter 3: Perception
> Chapter 4: No innate knowledge
> Chapter 5: Origins of simple ideas

Chapter 6: Simple and mixed modes
Chapter 7: Ideas of substance
Chapter 8: Ideas of relations
Chapter 9: Of apparitions
Chapter 10: Origin of signs of thought
Chapter 11: Use of words
Chapter 12: Characteristicks of languages
Chapter 13: Principles of mental associations
Chapter 14: Causal connections of thought
Chapter 15: Of attention
Chapter 16: Of conceptions
Chapter 17: Of abstract ideas
Chapter 18: Of dreaming
Chapter 19: Demonstrative reasoning
Chapter 20: Moral reasoning
Chapter 21: Dialecticks of rules of debate
Chapter 22: Of memory
Chapter 23: Emotions of beauty
Chapter 24: Emotions of sublimity
Chapter 25: Of imagination
Chapter 26: Of wit and humour
Chapter 27: Of instincts
Chapter 28: The will, conscience, &c.
Chapter 29: The passions
Chapter 30: Mental alienation
Chapter 31: Origin of Prejudices
Chapter 32: Evidence of testimony
Chapter 33: Education

Of further interest is the way in which Upham's book starts, which we cannot resist reprinting here. Pay particular attention to the following assertions: (i) that intellectual philosophy is a science, (ii) that it differs from the previous, worthless education in Roman Catholic schools, and (iii) that studying it is not a waste of time. As we will see in later chapters, these have been recurrent themes in psychological textbooks.

Chapter first: Utility of intellectual philosophy

§ 1. *Of the prejudice existing against this science.*

A prejudice prevails against the science of Intellectual Philosophy. It is generally entered upon in our academies and colleges with reluctance, and relinquished without regret. This aversion is not limited to the idle, but includes those, who know the value of time and the importance of mental improvement.

The objections against the Philosophy of the Mind, which have in a great measure given rise to this prejudice, may be principally summed up in two particulars.

§ 2. *Of the metaphysicks of the schools.*

Of these, one is the frivolous character of the metaphysical writings of the Schools.

The origin of those institutions, to which the name of Schools is given, was this. By order of a general Council of the Roman Catholick Church, held at Rome in the year 1179, certain persons were appointed to give instructions either in the cathedrals and monasteries, or in some suitable buildings erected near them. The places of instruction were called by the Latin name Scholae; the teachers were termed Scholastici. . . .

By the Schools, then, are to be understood the European literary and theological institutions, as they were constituted and regulated from about the middle of the twelfth century to the period of the Protestant reformation. By the Scholastick Philosophy, using the terms in a general sense, we mean those topicks, which were most examined and insisted on during that period. . . .

The following are some of the inquiries, which were warmly agitated during the period now under examination.

Whether the Deity can exist in imaginary space no less than in the space, which is real? Whether the Deity loves a possible unexisting angel better, than an insect in actual existence? . . .

Whether angels can visually discern objects in the dark? Or whether they can pass from one point of space to another without passing through the intermediate points?

Such inquiries, it will readily be admitted, were worse than fruitless.

§. 3. *Supposed practical inutility of this science.*

A second ground of the prejudice, existing against this science, is the prevalence of a false opinion of its practical inutility. In studying Intellectual Philosophy, we are supposed in the erroneous opinion, which has been mentioned, to learn in a scientifick form only what we have previously learnt from nature; we acquire nothing new, and the time, therefore, which is occupied in this pursuit, is misspent.

All persons, however ignorant, know what it is, to think, to imagine, to feel, to perceive, to exercise belief. All persons know the fact in Intellectual Philosophy, that memory depends on attention; and when asked, why they have forgotten things, which occurred yesterday in their presence, think it a sufficient answer to say, that they did not attend to them. Every body is practically acquainted with the principles of association, even the groom; who, with all his ignorance of philosophical books, has the sagacity to feed his horses to the sound of the drum and bugle, as a training preparatory to their being employed in military service.

From some facts of this kind, which may safely be admitted to exist, the opinion has arisen of the practical inutility of studying Intellectual Philosophy as a science.

Bain

The United Kingdom also saw an impressive series of psychology-related textbooks published. Arguably the most influential were two books published by the Scottish philosopher and educationalist Alexander Bain (1818–1903): *The senses and the intellect* (1855) and *Emotions and the will* (1859). These books formed the template of nearly all subsequent English psychology textbooks. An important new element Bain introduced was the inclusion of physiology in his books. He was equally interested in the biological basis of mental functioning as in the philosophical writings on the topic. As such, Bain reflected the growing impact of biological and medical research in the nineteenth century (see below and Chapter 6).

These were the tables of contents:

The Senses and the Intellect

Introduction

    Chapter 1: Definition of the mind
    Chapter 2: Of the nervous system

Book I: Movement, sense, and instinct

    Chapter 1: Of spontaneous activity and the feelings of movement
    Chapter 2: Of sensation

Chapter 3: Of the appetites

Chapter 4: Of the instincts

Book II: Intellect

Chapter 1: Law of contiguity

Chapter 2: Law of similarity

Chapter 3: Compound association

Chapter 4: Of constructive association

The Emotions and the Will

The Emotions (15 chapters on emotions of wonder, terror, tenderness, power, intellect, sympathy, aesthetics, ethics, . . .)

The Will (11 chapters on motivation including: the primitive elements of volition, growth of voluntary power, control of feelings and thoughts, conflict of motives, desire, moral habits, prudence, liberty, . . .)

Belief

Consciousness

The first book is particularly interesting because it illustrates the appearance of biology in psychology textbooks (note the second chapter on the nervous system, which has since become a classic in psychology textbooks). It also shows how strongly British ideas of psychology were influenced by empiricism: human knowledge was derived from perceptual experiences and ideas were associated on the basis of contiguity and similarity.

What do you think?

Most of the books discussed above are freely available on the internet. Have a look at them! And compare them to your current introductory textbook of psychology. Which themes have vanished and which have remained to the present times? And are there new themes in your present textbook that were not included in the old ones?

Interim summary

The increased importance of psychology has resulted in the production of textbooks since the late 1700s, which illustrate the themes considered important and which also influenced people's views of psychology. Four books have been discussed:

- Kant: anthropology as a collection of observed facts about humans
- Herbart: attempt to make psychology scientific by introducing mathematical laws
- Upham: claim that intellectual (mental) philosophy is a science worthwhile to be studied
- Bain: introduction of the nervous system and other physiological information in a textbook of psychology

3.4 Scientific studies of 'psychological' functions

While philosophers in metaphysics were debating the status and contents of psychology, some natural philosophers started to run Baconian experimental histories that nowadays would be classified as psychology experiments. In the second half of the nineteenth century, the findings of these experiments would encourage scholars to establish 'laboratories of experimental psychology', specifically devoted to this type of research, as we will see in Chapter 4. One line of study concerned human perceptual capacities; another examined the speed of information-processing in the nervous system.

Human perception

Given the importance of observation in natural science, it was normal for men of science to be interested in the possibilities and limits of (human) perception. Quite a lot was already known about the topic before the scientific revolution, for instance how one could correct acuity difficulties with lenses (a topic extensively described by Roger Bacon in the thirteenth century), and how objects became less visible at large distances. The latter subject had been discussed in tracts on optics since Ancient Egypt and Greece (Wade 2007) and attracted attention from scholars throughout the centuries. For instance, the Spanish scholar (and member of the Inquisition) Benito Daza de Valdes (1591–1634) measured the distance at which a row of mustard seeds could still be counted and small print be read. Astronomers also wondered what resolution was required to see double stars with the naked eye and with telescopes of varying magnifications, an issue that for instance interested René Descartes, who ventured that the retina consisted of nerve fibres and that objects smaller than a fibre could not be disentangled.

In the following we select a few studies that were either exemplary or highly influential in the history of psychology. However, it is important for you to realise that, as with all topics discussed in this book, there were many more scholars and studies involved than the ones we have described and that we have a bias to include Western European thinkers, in particular English-speaking (cf. Chapter 1).

Hooke

Visual acuity interested the seventeenth-century British gentlemen who were so instrumental in carrying on the scientific revolution. In particular, Robert Hooke (1635–1703) was interested in determining the minimal visual angle that could be discriminated. This was important for the use of telescopes and later also determined the degree of detail that could be seen through the newly built microscopes, of which Hooke made extensive use. On the basis of his studies, Hooke concluded that humans could discriminate lines that covered a visual angle of 1 minute of arc, which was later estimated to amount to a retinal width of 0.0035 mm. This is how Hooke announced his conclusion (Hooke 1674; in Wade 2007: 1237):

> Now that any one may presently satisfy himself of the truth of what I assert, concerning the limited power of the naked eye, as to the distinguishing of Angles; Let him take a sheet of white Paper, and thereon draw two parallel Lines, as OO, and PP, in the 28th. [Figure 3.1; reproduced here], at four or five inches distance, then draw as many other small lines between them at right angles to them, and parallel one with another, as he

Figure 3.1 Figure used by Hooke (1674) to show the limits of human visual acuity.

thinks convenient, as aa, bb, cc, dd, ee, ff, gg, hh, ii, &c. and let them be drawn distant from each other an inch, then let him alternately blacken or shadow the spaces between them, as between aa and bb, between cc and dd, between ee and ff, between gg and hh, between ii and kk, between ll and mm, &c. leaving the other alternately white, and then let him expose this Paper against a Wall open to the light, and if it may be so that the Sun may shine on it, and removing himself backwards for the space of 287 1/3 feet, let him try whether he can distinguish it, and number the dark and light spaces. And if his eyes be so good that he can, then let him still go further backwards from the same, till he finds his eyes unable any longer to distinguish those Divisions, then let him make a stand, and measure the distance from his eye to the aforesaid Paper, and try by calculation under what Angle each of those black and white spaces appears to his eye, so by that means it will be manifest how small an Angle his eye is capable of distinguishing, and beyond which it cannot reach.

Mayer

Hooke's research was replicated and much extended nearly a century later by the German astronomer Tobias Mayer (1723–1762), who published his findings in 1755. Mayer used more types of stimuli than Hooke had used (black dots, gratings, checkerboards) and found that for black dots, the limit of vision was nearly half that of Hooke's estimate while the limit for gratings was comparable to Hook's estimate. In addition, Mayer manipulated illumination (by putting a candle at various distances). When doing so, he observed that the relationship between the distance of the candle and the limit of vision was not linear but curvilinear (see Figure 3.2). Using elementary arithmetic, Mayer argued that the limit of vision could be predicted with the following equation:

$$\text{Limit of vision} = k * \sqrt[3]{\text{distance of the candle}}$$

in which k depended on the type of stimulus used (grating, checkerboard, etc.).

We could not find out whether Kant knew of Mayer's study, leaving open the tantalising question whether his appreciation of psychology was made despite Mayer's study, or whether Mayer's study could have changed Kant's assessment if he had known of it. For Mayer's results showed that at least some aspects of psychology could be described by mathematical functions very similar to Newton's laws, which Kant and other philosophers of science thought so fundamental for a 'proper' natural science.

Weber and Fechner

Another person interested in human perception was the German physician and professor at the University of Leipzig, Ernst Heinrich Weber (1795–1878). Unlike most of his colleagues, he was not in the first place interested in vision but in audition and, above all, the tactile senses. He published two treatises in the 1830–1840s that would turn out to be highly influential for the history of psychology, one in Latin and one in German, both translated into English by Ross and Murray (1996).

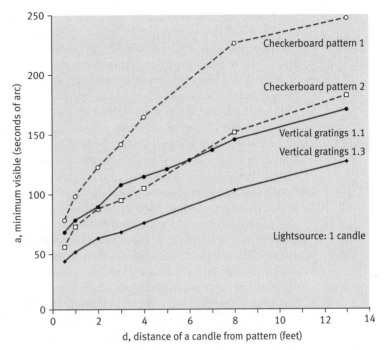

Figure 3.2 Relationship between the limit of vision and the distance of the candle, described by Mayer (1755).

This is exactly the type of Newtonian mathematical relationship psychologists had been searching for and which was impossible according to Kant.

Source: Grüsser (1989).

Weber ran two types of studies. First, he used a compass with blunted points and briefly touched people's skin with them. When the points were far apart, people could clearly feel two different parts being touched (they were blindfolded). When the points were put closer together, from a certain point on, people no longer had the feeling of two different parts being touched but of an elliptic instrument contacting them (i.e. they still could distinguish the axis of the elongation). When the points were brought even closer together, the impression of elongation diminished and, from a certain distance on, was experienced as a single round object touching the person. Weber called the minimal distance required between the two points to be perceived the *two-point threshold*. He further discovered that the two-point threshold was not constant for different body parts: it was much smaller on the tips of the fingers and the tip of the tongue (the two most sensitive areas) than on the arm, the leg or the trunk.[5]

In a second series of experiments Weber examined how good people were at discerning weights between the left and the right arm. He examined this by putting unequal weights in the left and the right hand, asking people which weight was the heavier, and examining the minimal difference that could be perceived. In a series of studies, Weber first discovered that people were much better at discriminating between weights when they were allowed to lift them than when the weights were put in their hands and they had to remain motionless. This, according to Weber, showed the importance of muscles and joints for weight discrimination. Weber further observed that, for most people, weights in the left arm seemed to be heavier than weights in the right arm. So, they felt a distinction faster when the heavier weight was placed in the left hand and the lighter weight in the right hand, than vice versa. Finally, Weber discovered that the difference between the weights had to be larger for heavy weights than for light weights. If persons could discriminate between 32 and 26 oz (1 oz = 28.35 grams) they could also discriminate between 32 and 26 drachms (1 drachm = 1.77 grams). In other words, it was not the absolute difference between the weights that was important, but the ratio between them: 6 oz is slightly less than 1/5th of 32 oz, just as 6 drachms is slightly less than 1/5th of 32 drachms.

Weber's last finding became particularly important, when it inspired his colleague at the University of Leipzig, Gustav Fechner (1801–1887), to develop a mathematical law connecting sensation magnitude to stimulus intensity. Fechner was a physicist with a strong interest in philosophy, religion and aesthetics. He was intrigued by Kant's claim that the human mind did not show the same kind of regularities as nature. As a young man, Fechner had been a very promising academic member of staff in physiology and physics, but at the age of 38 he had a breakdown (partly due to health problems). In the next 12 years he published only a few religious works, but around 1850 started to contemplate the relationship between the outer and the inner world. At some point he realised that there could be a simple equation linking sensation strength to stimulus intensity, which would be in line with Weber's findings of just noticeable differences. This relationship was the logarithmic function.

To understand Fechner's insight, let us assume that Weber's ratio of just noticeable differences for weight is 1/5. Then participants can make a distinction between 30 grams and 30 + 30/5 = 36 grams, between 36 grams and 36 + 36/5 = 43.5 grams, between 43.5 and 43.5/5 = 52.2 grams, and so on. In other words, for the person 30, 36, 43.5 and 52.2 grams correspond to consecutive sensations. Now, for a mathematician it is very easy to show that such a sequence of observations implies that the magnitude of the sensation corresponds to the logarithm of the stimulus magnitude.[6]

In other words, Fechner suddenly realised that there could be a Newtonian mathematical function connecting the magnitude of the sensation to the magnitude of the stimulus. He started a series of experiments to determine whether Weber's ratio applied to a larger continuum of weights and to other senses as well. While running these studies he also devised new and better ways to measure the minimal differences that could be noticed. In 1860 Fechner published a book *Elemente der psychophysik* (Elements of psychophysics), in which he described his measurements and conclusions. This was the birth of **psychophysics**, a branch of research that dealt with the relationship between physical stimuli and their subjective correlates. Although Fechner shortly after the publication of his book became interested in other topics (in particular aesthetic judgment), the new psychophysical methods to establish just noticeable differences and Fechner's logarithmic function (which he called Weber's law) had such an impact on scholars studying human perception that Fechner, in his old age, felt obliged to write several more treatises on the topic.

psychophysics

part of psychological research dealing with the relationship between physical stimuli and the corresponding sensation

The speed of signal transmission in the nervous system and mental chronometry

The personal equation

Two main tasks of astronomers are: precise measurement of the movements of stars and determination of the exact time on earth. Before the development of modern equipment with automatic registration, both tasks required a close coupling of clock reading and star-gazing. Typically, the field of a telescope was divided by cross-wires and astronomers had to determine the time when a target star crossed a given wire.

This was done by looking at a clock shortly before the star began to cross the wire and counting seconds with the beats of the clock. Then the astronomer had to divert his gaze to the telescope and register at which beat the star crossed the wire and how much distance it travelled until the next beat. These two observations were noted and, on the basis of them, the time of the transition was calculated up to a tenth of a second.

Things went reasonably well until 1796 when Nevil Maskelyne, the British Astronomer Royal at Greenwich Observatory, noticed that the times registered by his assistant, David Kinnebrook, were about half a second later than his. By January 1796 the difference had become about eight-tenths of a second and Maskelyne saw himself forced to dismiss Kinnebrook, who returned to his previous job as schoolmaster (Rowe 1983). Maskelyne attributed the event to an unfortunate flaw in his assistant and paid no further attention to it. However, the event was included in a history of Greenwich Observatory written by von Lindenau for the *Zeitschrift für astronomie* in 1816. There it caught the attention of a young astronomer at Königsberg, Friedrich Bessel, who examined whether similar differences existed between himself and other astronomers. They did, and as a result astronomers and other time watchers were persuaded to have their 'personal equation' established, the time they needed to record star transits, so that the error could be corrected. Soon, however, it became apparent that the personal equation was not fixed for a person but showed considerable variability between measurements. Consequently, more energy was directed to the development of better registration methods than to further refinement in the measurement of the personal equation. However, the fact that people differed from each other in the time needed to register precise events (and showed variability in this) became well established among astronomers and other men of science (Weber mentioned it in one of his books on tactile senses). As a result, scholars became interested in the time needed to transfer information in the nervous system and to perform simple mental operations.

What do you think?

Can you see how these research questions arising from the existing sciences slowly but surely eroded Kante's and Comte's claims that nothing of the human mind could be studied scientifically? Can you think of objections Kant and Comte might have formulated?

von Helmholz

Around the time Fechner was elaborating the psychophysical law in Leipzig, his colleague Hermann von Helmholtz (1821–1894) at the University of Königsberg started a series of studies to measure the speed of nerve impulses. For a long time, it had been assumed that information transfer in the brain and the nerves was so fast that it was practically immeasurable, either because the transfer consisted of animal spirits racing through hollow tubes or (a more recent hypothesis) of electricity propagating through the nerves at a rate close to the speed of light (see Chapter 6).

In the 1850s von Helmholtz tested the speed of nerve conduction in a frog by using the motor nerve that runs the length of the leg. By stimulating the nerve at a certain place and measuring the passage of the signal at several distances, he could estimate the conduction speed of the nerve. With this technique von Helmholtz was able to show that the speed was actually rather slow: only 30 metres per second (i.e. slightly more than 100 km/h). This meant that information transmission in the nervous system became measurable and had practical consequences (e.g. a signal in humans from the toe required more time to reach the brain than a stimulus from the shoulder, which von Helmholtz verified by stimulating the skin at different places and noticing the time the participant needed to indicate he felt the stimulus).

Donders

Stimulated by von Helmholtz's findings, the Dutch ophthalmologist Franciscus Cornelis Donders (1818–1889) wondered whether he could use a similar technique to measure the speed with which humans could perform elementary mental tasks. This is how he formulated it (Donders 1868; as translated in Donders 1969: 417):

> Would thought also not have the infinite speed usually associated with it, and would it not be possible to determine the time required for shaping a concept or expressing one's will? For years this question has intrigued me. . . .
>
> The idea occurred to me to interpose into the process of the physiological time some new components of mental action. If I investigated how much this would lengthen the physiological time, this would, I judged, reveal the time required for the interposed term.

Donders first used a very simple task. A single stimulus was presented (e.g. the auditory stimulus 'ki'), and the participant had to repeat it as fast as possible. Donders measured the time between the presentation of the stimulus and the start of the response up to a millisecond (i.e. one-thousandth of a second) accuracy. He found that the mean response time for this simple type of reaction was 197 milliseconds. Then he made the task slightly more difficult. He presented five possible stimuli ('ka, ke, ki, ko and ku') and the participant had to repeat the stimulus as soon as he heard 'ki'. In this condition, there was uncertainty about the stimulus that would be presented but not about the response that had to be made. The mean response time now was 243 milliseconds. By comparing the response times in the two conditions, Donders concluded that the time needed to perceive the identity of the stimulus, was 243 − 197 = 46 milliseconds. Finally, Donders presented a condition in which the participants got the same five stimuli and had to repeat each of them. Now there was uncertainty both with respect to the stimulus that would be presented and the response that had to be given. The response time was now 285 milliseconds, making Donders conclude that the time needed to choose the correct response out of five alternatives was 285 − 243 = 42 milliseconds.[7]

mental chronometry

using reaction times to measure the time needed for various mental tasks; on the basis of a comparison of different tasks, models of the mental processes involved in the tasks are postulated

Donders' technique has been the basis of the **mental chronometry**, the use of reaction times to measure the time needed to perform mental tasks or task components. The technique has been fundamental to psychological research up to this day. Just like Fechner's, it could be implemented without further ado in any laboratory to measure human functioning with the scientific method, which is exactly what happened, as we will see in the next chapter. Fechner and Donders themselves were not interested in this type of research, because they had other priorities.

? What do you think?

If you have had an introductory course of (cognitive) psychology, look up a recent reaction time experiment that was discussed. Can you rephrase the research question and the findings in Donders' terminology? Or do present-day psychologists use a different terminology?

Interim summary

Scientific studies of 'psychological' functions

Characteristics and limitations of human perception and information processing interested the natural philosophers, who began to run Baconian experimental studies. They discussed two lines of research:

- Studies on human perception: the level of detail humans can discern (Hooke), the influence of illumination on this capacity (Mayer), the detection of just noticeable differences between stimuli (Weber, Fechner) and the formulation of a psychophysical theory based on them (Fechner).

- The time needed to perform tasks and the speed of signal transmission in the nervous system: astronomers varied in their estimates of the timing of events (personal equation) and showed variability in them; von Helmholtz could measure the transmission speed of nerves in frogs (and humans), Donders could measure the time needed for simple mental operations (mental chronometry).

3.5 Evolutionary theory

Another nineteenth-century development that would have a profound effect on the growth of psychology as an independent branch of learning was the formulation of the evolutionary theory by Charles Darwin (1809–1882).

Darwin's theory

Many scientists consider Darwin's insights to be the second largest discovery in science (or even the largest). Whereas Newton (and since him, the physicists) discovered the way the universe functions, Darwin (and with him the biologists) unravelled the way life in the universe came about, constantly changes, and adapts itself to changing circumstances.

The right zeitgeist

In hindsight, Darwin's theory about the evolution of species was bound to be discovered around the mid-nineteenth century, most likely in the United Kingdom. Ever since the Swedish physician Carolus Linnaeus had started his work on the classification of plants and animals in the eighteenth century and published his *Systema naturae* (1st edition in 1735, 11 pages; 13th edition in 1770, 3,000 pages), botanists from many countries had contributed to the enterprise, none more enthusiastically than the British (who, as we have seen, established the Linnean Society of London in 1788). The taxonomy of biological species not only confronted the scholars with thorny issues about how to define distinctions and similarities; it also made them wonder how the diversity had originated. Linnaeus himself, for instance, came to the conclusion that he had no other option than to classify humans in the same grouping as primates.

Around the same time, the first writings about fossils started to appear. In 1787 a huge thigh bone was found in New Jersey that did not seem to match any existing animal. It turned out to be from a dinosaur, although it took quite some time (and many more finds) before this was realised. In the United Kingdom, geologists began to look for fossils of small animals and plants to estimate the age of rocks. These findings raised more questions about how all these layers of fossils (some of them unlike existing animals) had come about and disappeared.

In the 1840s the British Prime Minister, Sir Robert Peel, replaced the tax on glass (and other visible signs of wealth) by an income tax. One of the consequences of this abolishment was a vast proliferation of greenhouses in which exquisite, exotic and continuously evolving plants were cultivated. Charles Darwin had several of these greenhouses. As a young man he had spent five years collecting and document-ing specimens of unknown plants and animals, during a voyage on a ship called the *Beagle* to new territories. Darwin had been invited along because the captain, weary of the loneliness of a long expedition, had required a gentleman companion. After the expedition with the *Beagle*, Darwin never again left Britain and he became a recluse in his home, from where he conducted a rich correspondence with friends, family members and scientific colleagues. While pondering his recollections from the voyage and cultivating his exotic plants, Darwin inevitably started to wonder about the origin of the variety he observed.

Cross-fertilisation and natural selection

natural selection
process in Darwin's evolutionary theory by which the environment results in the continuation and multiplication of organisms with certain genetic features and hinders the reproduction of organisms with other genetic features; the first type of features are called favourable (within the prevailing environment), the second type unfavourable

A first observation that struck Darwin was that, although many plants were capable of self-fertilisation, they seemed to avoid it. Furthermore, if it happened, the offspring were on average less healthy. Cross-fertilisation produced variation in the offspring that was more vital and sometimes even resulted in the creation of a new type of flower. (This finding was also of non-academic interest to Darwin, because he had married one of his cousins, as quite often happened in the upper-class families of those times. Later he would become a supporter of measures to dissuade this type of marriage.)

Darwin was at a loss to understand how the new offspring could start to domi-nate and eventually replace the old variety. The breakthrough came when he read a book by the economist Thomas Malthus, who defended the position that if humans did not obey 'moral constraint' their growth would outstrip food production, which would inevitably result in either famine or war. Darwin now realised that the struggle for existence in a world of limited resources was the reason why some variants had an advantage and started to outgrow the variants without that advantage. Later this insight became encapsulated in the phrase natural selection or (more popular, but less correct) survival of the fittest (a term introduced by Herbert Spencer; see Chapter 5).

survival of the fittest
term introduced by Herbert Spencer to describe the outcome of natural selection: only organisms that fit within the environment and can produce viable offspring survive

The origin of species

Darwin was reluctant to publish his insights and only did so at the age of 50, when he was warned that one of his correspondents, Alfred Russel Wallace, was about to publish a very similar thesis. The first edition of the book *On the origin of species by means of natural selection, or the preservation of favoured races in the struggle for life* (usually abbreviated to *The origin of species* or *the Origin*) appeared in 1859.

The origin of species
book by Charles Darwin (1859) in which he presented the evolutionary theory

The dilution problem

Although the book was an instant success and led to lively debates (which Darwin refused to attend), its initial impact was less impressive than we nowadays think. One element that Darwin failed to explain and that would haunt him until his death (and evolutionary theory for nearly half a century longer) was how a single new plant or animal could come to dominate the rest. This criticism was best formulated by the Scottish engineer Fleeming Jenkin. According to Jenkin, when an organism with a new feature is placed amid a group of other organisms, this new feature will not expand but will dilute in the pool of existing features until in the end virtually nothing remains. He gave the example of a white man shipwrecked on an island inhabited by black people. If this man becomes part of the community and has children, his whiteness will never become dominant, even if the trait is better suited to the environment. After a few generations the whiteness of the forefather will have all but vanished because it is overruled by the more prevalent blackness.

Darwin never found a proper answer to Jenkin's dilution argument. In the fifth edition of *the Origin* (1869), he agreed that a single new random variant could not alter the nature of a species and that evolution was only possible when a change in the environment favoured a whole group of individuals at the same time, for instance when a drought favoured birds with strong beaks. Because of the blending problem, the impact of the evolutionary theory on other biological scientists was almost nil around 1900. Only a few decades later, when biologists started to unravel the nature of inheritance and understood that genes are not blended in the process of conception, did the real impact of the evolutionary theory become clear, as we will see in later chapters.

KEY FIGURE Charles Darwin

- British biologist (1809–1882).
- Famous for his contributions to biology:
  - description of new species
  - importance of cross-fertilisation
  - development of the evolutionary theory.
- Impact for the advancement of science:
  - focused on the similarities among animals and humans
  - pointed to the importance of heredity
  - developed a theory of how life adapts to changing situations.

Source: FPG/Getty Images.

 What do you think?

Do some people still doubt Darwin's evolutionary theory? What are their arguments?

Common misunderstandings of evolutionary theory

There is no direction in the genetic changes

Although the evolutionary theory is quite straightforward, it is often misunderstood. One of the misinterpretations is that the genes induce a change in a plant or animal so that it becomes more adapted to the environment. This is wrong, because the genetic material has no knowledge of the environment and so cannot change in a desirable direction. All that happens is that the material now and then has a random alteration. Most of these changes result in offspring that do not differ in an observable way from the parents. Sometimes, a change results in a descendant that is barely viable or that does not result in further offspring. Such a mutation is not passed on to further generations. Occasionally, however, an alteration results in a characteristic that is particularly well adapted to the prevailing environment and that increases the chances of the organism to survive and have descendants. This new variant gradually increases in number at the expense of the variants without the characteristic.

Organisms do not become better or stronger

A second misunderstanding about evolution is that each genetic mutation that survives results in a better, stronger and more complex organism. (How else could humans have evolved from primates? Or how else can we explain that each new generation of humans becomes smarter?) Jones (1999) gave a particularly forceful example of how adaptations need not be for the better. First, he described how predators such as wolves and mammoths dramatically declined (often to extinction) as soon as humans invaded their territory. At the same time, a few species sharply increased in number. These were the species humans kept as pets or for food, such as dogs and pigs. In general, Jones argued, these species are dumber and meeker than the ancestors from which they were bred, because the humans did not want dogs with their own initiative or pigs that were smart. They wanted helpless animals that were lost without the human presence and that constantly showed their affection and dependence. The same would happen if the Earth were suddenly invaded by a new species that kept humans as pets. Those humans who opposed the occupation (because they were too proud, intelligent or aggressive) would be killed and would no longer be able to pass on their genes. In contrast, mentally feeble humans that depended on their masters for survival would be bred, rapidly increase in number, and spread over all planets occupied by the aliens.

An example of Darwin's influence: Galton

One of the first people examining the implications of Darwin's theory for human functioning was the British polymath Francis Galton (1822–1911). He particularly searched to find evidence for the argument that features were inherited. First, he tried unsuccessfully to demonstrate this in rabbits (by transfusing blood from black or white rabbits into silver-grey rabbits and looking at their offspring), then he had some mixed results with sweet peas, but his ultimate goal was to show the heredity of human traits, in particular intelligence. In 1869 he published *Hereditary genius*, in which he claimed that mental qualities were inherited. He did so by pointing to the many family ties that existed between the intellectuals of England (for instance, Galton had a grandfather in common with Darwin; Fancher 2009).

Galton's contemporaries were not impressed, however, because most of them accepted that mental capacities were divine. These capacities set humans apart from animals and were influenced by the health and the habits of the parents. Alcoholism, for instance, was considered a degenerative disease whose effects were inherited, but this was thought to be caused by the fact that drunken parents weakened their minds and bodies and then passed these weaknesses on to their children.

? What do you think?

Is heredity the only possible reason why there were many family ties between the intellectuals of nineteenth-century England?

Because of the resistance Galton encountered, he set out to measure human intelligence. His most ambitious attempt took place in 1884 during the International Health Exhibition in London, attended by over 4 million people. Here he installed an anthropometric laboratory, where various aspects of men were measured: their principal physical dimensions, their hearing power, the accuracy of their eyesight, and various measures of physical speed and strength. Galton was convinced that individual differences in mental ability were due to inherited differences in the quality of the senses and he set out to prove this. During the six months of the exhibition, 17

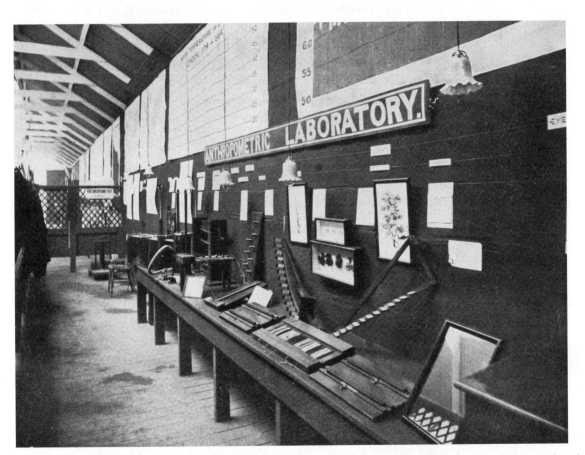

In 1884 Sir Francis Galton opened an anthropometric laboratory at the South Kensington Museum, in which he gathered sensory and physical data from over 4,000 individuals. Before, he had collected measures of over 9,000 visitors at the International Health Exhibition in London. Unfortunately, none of the measures correlated highly with the intelligence of the people, as Galton had hoped.

Source: Photograph plate taken from *The life, letters and labours of Francis Galton* (Vol. 2, 1924) by Karl Pearson. Science and Society Picture Library. Reproduced with permission.

different measures were made of over 9,000 visitors. Afterwards Galton obtained a room in the Science Galleries of the South Kensington Museum, in which the laboratory continued for another six years, gathering data on over 4,000 more individuals. Unfortunately for Galton, his measures again turned out to be far from convincing. As a matter of fact, he never published them. His claims remained based on impressions and anecdotes (Deary 1994). We will return to the development and the use of intelligence tests in later chapters.

Interim summary

Evolutionary theory

- Proposed by Darwin.
- Several developments made the theory likely in the nineteenth century: interest in diversity and correspondence between species, discovery of fossils, cultivation of new flower types.
- Darwin discovered that random variations at birth, together with limited availability of resources, could explain evolution on the basis of natural selection.
- Theory published in *The origin of species* (1859).
- Darwin could not explain how new randomly generated organisms could come to dominate the existing organisms (absence of knowledge of genetics).

Common misunderstandings of evolutionary theory

- The mistaken belief that there is a direction in the genetic changes that cause the initial variation.
- The mistaken belief that evolution results in better or stronger organisms.

An example of Darwin's influence: Galton

- Galton tried to find evidence for the heredity of animal and human features.
- Was not very successful, but inspired subsequent generations to address the issue of intelligence testing.

3.6 The contribution of statistics

Psychological research requires the analysis of many observations to detect the underlying patterns

The development of statistics was another innovation of capital importance for the emergence of psychological research. A crucial difference between physics and psychology is that processes in the former usually yield very much the same outcome each time they are repeated. As a result, research in physics mostly consists of a small number of very precise measurements. In contrast, psychological outcomes often differ between individuals and they also differ when an individual does the same task twice. The latter can easily be shown. When participants are asked to press a response key as quickly as possible when they hear a stimulus (cf. Donders' first task), their responses are not always exactly 197 ms. In some trials their reaction time can be as fast as 150 ms, in others it can be as slow as 300 ms, even when the participants are highly motivated to respond as fast as possible on each trial. This is because psychological measures are embedded in a lot of noise, which can be random (e.g. in some trials the participant was blinking at the moment the stimulus was presented), or due to the influence of some other systematic variable (e.g. the position of the hand relative to the response key).

Because of the intrinsic variability in psychological (and biological) measures, it is not possible to get rid of the noise simply by trying to improve the accuracy of the measurement, as in physics. Discrepancies will always remain between successive observations. This means that the same measurement techniques cannot be used in psychology as in physics (the exception being some aspects of psychophysical research, where methods similar to those in physics can be applied). In physics, good research requires extremely accurate measurements of a few observations; in psychology good research usually consists of a sufficiently large number of observations, so that the inherent noise in the data can be partialled out. This, however, was not known to the first men of science, who tried in vain to apply the methods of physics to research on living organisms.

Quetelet's contribution

The importance of statistical analyses for behavioural data was discovered by Adolphe Quetelet (1796–1874), a Belgian astronomer and professor of mathematics, who analysed crime statistics from several countries. A problem with criminal activities is that it is nearly impossible to predict when and where they will happen (because they are the result of many chance factors). However, what struck Quetelet was that, despite this inherent noise in the individual data points, the sums of the crimes looked very similar year upon year. As he wrote:

> Thus, as I have occasion to repeat already several times, one moves from one year to another with the sad perspective of seeing the same crimes reproduced in the same order, and attracting the same punishments in the same proportions . . . the greater the number of individuals, the more the single individual becomes obliterated and allows general facts to predominate, facts which depend on causes, facts according to which society exists and preserves itself.

> (Quetelet 1835; as translated by Jahoda 2007: 82)

Whereas Quetelet was not able to predict a single crime, he was able to predict how many crimes there would be in the next year and which variables affected this number (e.g. differences between men and women, between countries, between seasons and so on). A similar observation was made by the American mathematician, Elizur Wright (1804–1885), who specialised in life insurance. He wrote: 'While nothing is more uncertain than the duration of a single life, nothing is more certain than the average duration of a thousand lives' (Gerteis 1991). The calculation of totals based on reasonably large samples was but the first step whereby statistics made it possible to analyse behavioural data in meaningful ways. Soon, this step was augmented by other, more sophisticated, statistical measures and techniques.

Statistics help to design a proper study

Statistics not only allowed researchers to analyse their data, they also provided them with information on how to design biological and behavioural studies, so that valid conclusions could be drawn. Before the advent of statistics, researchers only had knowledge of the methods used in physics and chemistry. These were ill-suited for the type of problems tackled by researchers of living organisms, which showed considerable variability, the functioning of which was influenced by several variables at the same time. This became painfully clear when the great British statistician Ronald Fisher (1890–1962) was called upon by the agricultural research institute at Rothamsted to sort out the data mess they had got themselves into (as recounted by Salsburg 2001).

The purpose of the Rothamsted station was to find ways to improve crop cultivation. This was done by trying out different types of fertilisers on different fields. Each year a number of changes were introduced and the harvests were carefully registered. The plan was to compare the outcome with the produce of the years before and with the produce from other fields, sometimes hundreds of yards away. Unfortunately, the outcome became increasingly complex and chaotic, because the weather changed from year to year, the soil differed between the fields, weeding practices were not the same each year, the produce of a field was influenced by what had been planted the year before, and so on. In the end, that it became impossible to decide which fertilisers had worked and which hadn't. Hence, the call for help to Fisher.

In the end, Fisher was able to sort things out to some degree (in the process inventing or massively improving statistical techniques such as time series analysis and multiple regression analysis), but soon he started to explain to the users why the analysis had become so complicated and what could be done to simplify it. All that was needed was that the researchers at Rothamsted split up their fields into many small patches, some of which got the experimental fertiliser and others not. Then, simply by comparing the average harvest of both types of patches, the scientists would know whether the fertiliser had any effect, because all the other confounding variables (weather, soil, weeding practice, compatibility with the crops grown in the previous years, etc.) would be averaged out. Insights like these started a complete new field of research methodology, which allowed scholars to study living organisms and their behaviours.

Interim summary

The contribution of statistics

- Research on living organisms required other data analyses than research in physics and chemistry, because the data were noisy and simultaneously influenced by many different factors.

- Quetelet discovered that, whereas individual data points were impossible to predict, such prediction was possible when the analyses were based on the means of hundreds of observations.

- Fisher further showed how researchers could adapt their methodology so that the influence of confounding variables could easily be factored out in statistical analyses.

3.7   *Focus on*: The status of medicine in the eighteenth and nineteenth centuries

Given that psychology (the study of the mind) is closely related to medicine (the study of the body), it is interesting to know what the status of medicine was when psychology emerged as an independent discipline. We will devote a separate chapter to the input from brain research (Chapter 6). Here we focus on the medical practice, the ways in which patients were treated by their doctors. Our discussion is based on Porter (2006).

Advanced understanding of the body

Without doubt, physicians in the eighteenth and nineteenth centuries knew more about the bodies of their patients than before. In Chapter 1 we discussed the contribution of Vesalius's anatomical studies in the Renaissance. Another major breakthrough was the discovery of how the blood system worked. Since the writings of Galen, physicians had been taught that the main blood flow occurred in the veins, originating in the liver and flowing to the organs where it was consumed. This was called the *natural system*. The arteries formed a second system, the *vital system,* starting in the heart which generated blood for the lungs and from there for the other organs. This system was important to get air (pneuma) and vital spirits into the body and to dispel sooty vapours from the body. Although Galen had argued otherwise, the arteries were not thought to contain much blood, because they tended to be rather empty in anatomical dissections (given that the heart no longer pumped blood through them).

From 1500 on, Galen's views started to be questioned, but they would not be superseded until the British physician William Harvey (1578–1657), on the basis of experiments with animals, claimed that the blood system did not consist of two unidirectional flows, but of two circuits in which the blood continuously circled, with the heart as the pump that kept the circulation going. One of the circuits made blood flow ceaselessly round the body from the veins into the arteries and from the arteries into the veins; the other circuit involved blood flowing from the heart to the lungs and back. This was published in a Latin treatise in 1628 with the translated title *Motion of the heart and blood*. After a period of quite strong resistance and much debate, Harvey's insights became accepted and were taught, along with other new findings, as part of medical degrees at universities.

Medical education

Medicine became taught as a degree around 1200, first in Northern Italy and France, and then in the rest of Europe. First, it was taught at independent institutions of higher learning, but soon the institutions joined the growing universities in order to profit from the privileges these were able to obtain. Medical degrees were among the most demanding (they took seven years), but not the best preparation for medical practice. They started with a full course of arts (taking four years), in which the seven liberal arts were taught: grammar, logic and rhetoric (together referred to as the Trivium), and arithmetic, astronomy, music and geometry (the Quadrivium). The liberal arts were considered the basic education of every free person, and only after successful completion of them did medical teaching start. It mainly consisted of the theoretical study of textbooks, with minimal training in practical skills. Still, the university-educated medical men managed to impose themselves on administrations (increasingly populated by university-educated colleagues) and became the governing body of medicine. They called themselves 'doctors' and often also had private practices for wealthy clients.

Most of the medical care was provided, however, by persons without (higher) school education, who learned the trade as apprentices of existing practitioners. They were apothecaries, general practitioners, surgeons and midwives, who acquired the tricks of the trade from their predecessors. The relationship between doctors and medical practitioners is nicely illustrated by the following quote from Willis (1847) describing the life of William Harvey:

> ... in the early autumn of the same year [1633] we are pleased to find Harvey again at his post in St. Bartholomew's Hospital, engaged in his own province and propounding divers rules and regulations for the better government of the house and its officers, which of themselves give us an excellent insight into the state of the hospital, as well as of the relative positions of the several departments of the healing art two centuries ago. The doctor's treatment of the poor chirurgeons in these rules is sufficiently despotic it must be admitted; but the chirurgeons in their acquiescence showed that they merited no better handling. The only point on which they proved restive, indeed, was the revealment of their Secrets to the physician; a great outrage in days when every man had his secrets, and felt fully justified in keeping them to himself. But surgery in the year 1633 had not shown any good title to an independent existence. The surgeon of those days was but the hand or instrument of the physician; the dignitary mostly applied to his famulus when he required a wen removed, or a limb lopped, or a broken head plastered; though Harvey it seems did not feel himself degraded by taking up the knife or practising midwifery. Nevertheless, in these latter days Royal Colleges of Physicians have been seen arrogating superiority over Royal Colleges of Surgeons, and Royal Colleges both of Physicians and Surgeons combining to keep the practitioner of obstetrics under.
>
> (Willis 1847: xxvi–xxvii)

Medical care up to the twentieth century

According to Shorter (2006), the help medical practitioners were able to provide was very minimal up to the twentieth century, and mainly consisted of a placebo effect (the reassurance patients and their family felt because they were treated by a doctor). Most of the patients to whom practitioners were called (in those days doctors went to their patients) suffered from fever as a result of infection (tuberculosis, syphilis, diphtheria, plague, meningitis, malaria, childbirth fever etc.), for which there was no cure. Because doctors were compelled to do 'something', they usually fell back to the ancient conviction that something wrong had to be discharged from the body and, therefore, resorted to blood-letting, vomiting and purgation. Pills with heavy metals such as mercury and lead also became popular in the eighteenth century, before it was found out that they were poisonous rather than healing. As noticed by Boston's William Douglass in 1755:

> In general, the physical practice [giving medications] in our colonies is so perniciously bad, that excepting in surgery and some very acute cases, it is better to let nature under a proper regimen take her course . . . than to trust the honesty and sagacity of the practitioner. . . . Frequently there is more danger from the physician than from the distemper.
>
> (as quoted in Shorter 2006: 109).

According to Shorter, the only really helpful medicament practitioners had in the eighteenth and nineteenth centuries was the pain-reliever opium, despite its side-effects and the danger of addiction.

Because of the limited medical help physicians could provide to their patients besides diagnosis and prognosis, around 1880 a new movement grew. It was called the 'patient-as-a-person' movement, which held that patients were not helped by medicines, although these had to be given, but by the doctor's psychological support.

A sympathetic doctor who saw his patients as 'persons' and approached them in an understanding way was therapeutic in and of itself. The physician had to be the good old GP (general practitioner) who was willing to sit and listen to his patients and advise them about how to cope with their problems. This movement was based on the observations that the effectiveness of doctors was rarely related to their medical treatment and that a substantial proportion of the patients in primary care failed to show physical ailments but complained of sleeplessness, nervousness, agitation or depression. Proponents of the patient-as-a-person movement were Hermann Nothnagel, professor of medicine in Vienna, and William Osler of the medical school at Johns Hopkins University in Maryland, the United States.

Interim summary

Medical care in the eighteenth and nineteenth centuries

- Most medical care was done by practitioners who learned the trade as apprentices. In addition, there were university-educated doctors whose training often only included theoretical knowledge.

- Effective medicines against the prevailing diseases were lacking and practitioners often resorted to bloodletting, laxatives and purgatives. Towards the end of the nineteenth century, a movement emerged which saw the practitioner as a GP listening to his patients and giving advice about how to cope with the illness (the patient-as-a-person movement).

Recommended literature

Philosophical and physiological developments that led to the emergence of psychology

The book we found most informative in understanding how psychology came about was Leahey, T.H. (2004) *A history of psychology* (Upper Saddle River, NJ: Pearson/ Prentice Hall). Another book that contains many interesting insights and anecdotes is Jahoda, G. (2007) *A history of social psychology* (Cambridge: Cambridge University Press). Also very worthwhile reading, because it takes an approach complementary to ours (from the point of view of the scholars involved), is Fancher, R.E. (1996) *Pioneers of psychology* 3rd edn (New York: Norton & Company).

Darwin and evolutionary theory

The original *Origin of species* is in print and remains a worthwhile read. Jones, S. (1999) *Almost like a whale: The origin of species updated* (London: Doubleday) is an equally readable introduction to the evolutionary theory. Particularly worthwhile reading is Endersby, J. (2007) *A guinea pig's history of biology* (London: William Heinemann), which describes the various plants and animals that have played a central role in working out the mechanisms of the evolutionary theory.

History of medicine

As indicated in the text, we found the book by Porter (2006), mentioned in the References below, very informative.

References

Collins, A. (1703) Letter to John Locke. As cited in Woolhouse, R. S. (2007) *Locke: A biography*, p. 441. Cambridge: Cambridge University Press.

Comte, A. (1830) *Cours de philosophie positive*. Paris: Bachelier.

Deary, I.J. (1994) 'Sensory discrimination and intelligence: Postmortem or resurrection?' *The American Journal of Psychology*, **107**: 95–115.

Donders, F. C. (1969[1868]) 'On the speed of mental processes', *Acta Psychologica*, **30**: 413–21.

Encyclopedia Britannica (1773) London: Dilly.

Fancher, R.E. (2009) 'Scientific cousins: The relationship between Charles Darwin and Francis Galton', *American Psychologist*, **64**: 84–92.

Foucault, M. (1976) *Surveiller et punir: Naissance de la prison*. Paris: Editions Gallimard (English translation: Foucault, M. (1979) *Discipline and punish: The birth of the prison*. New York: Vintage).

Friedman, M. (2004) *Kant: Metaphysical foundations of natural science (Cambridge Texts in the History of Philosophy)*. Cambridge: Cambridge University Press.

Gauch, H.G. (2003) *Scientific method in practice*. Cambridge: Cambridge University Press.

Gerteis, L.S. (1991) 'Book review of *Abolitionist, actuary, atheist: Elizur Wright and the reform impulse*, by Lawrence B. Goodheart', *The Journal of American History*, **77**: 1360–1.

Griffith, C.R. (1921) 'Some neglected aspects of a history of psychology', *Psychological Monographs*, **30**: 17–29 (available on http:// psychclassics.yorku.ca).

Grüsser, O.J. (1989) 'Quantitative visual psychophysics during the period of European enlightenment. The studies of astronomer and mathematician Tobias Mayer (1723–1762) on visual acuity and colour perception', *Documenta Ophthalmologica*, **71**: 93–111.

Hatfield, G. (1998) 'Kant and empirical psychology in the 18th century', *Psychological Science*, **9**: 423–8.

Hume, D. (1779) *Dialogues concerning natural religion* (2nd edn). London.

Jahoda, G. (2007) *A history of social psychology*. Cambridge: Cambridge University Press.

James, W. (1890) *The principles of psychology* (2 vols). New York: Henry Holt (at psychclassics.yorku.ca).

Jolley, N. (2005) *Leibniz*. London: Routledge.

Jones, S. (1999) *Almost like a whale: The origin of species updated*. London: Doubleday.

Kagan, J. (2009) *The three cultures: Natural Sciences, Social Sciences, and the Humanities in the 21st century*. Cambridge, MA: Cambridge University Press.

Kant (1994) *Metaphysical foundations of natural science* (trans. M. Freeman). Cambridge: Cambridge University Press.

Krstić, K. (1964) 'Marko Marulic: The author of the term "psychology"' *Acta Instituti Psychologici Universitatis Zagrabiensis*, **36**: 7–13 (at psychclassics.yorku.ca).

Lawrence, W. (1817) *Lectures on physiology, zoology, and the natural history of man*. London: James Smith.

Leahey, T.H. (2004) *A history of psychology*. Upper Saddle River, NJ: Pearson, Prentice Hall.

Louden, R.B. (ed.) (2006) *Immanuel Kant: Anthropology from a pragmatic point of view*. Cambridge: Cambridge University Press.

Pickren, W.E. & Rutherford, A. (2010) *A history of modern psychology in context*. Hoboker, NJ: John Wiley & Sons.

Pomerantz, J.R. and Kubovy, M. (1986) 'Theoretical approaches in organization', in Boff, J.P. Kaufman, L. and Thomas, J.P. (eds) *Handbook of perception and human performance*. New York, NY: Wiley.

Porter, R. (ed.) (2006) *The Cambridge history of medicine*. Cambridge: Cambridge University Press.

Richards, G. (1996) *Putting psychology in its place: An introduction from a critical historical perspective*. London: Routledge.

Richards, G. (2002) *Putting psychology in its place: A critical historical overview* (2nd edn). London: Routledge.

Richards, R.J. (1980) 'Christian Wolff's prolegomena to empirical and rational psychology: Translation and commentary', *Proceedings of the American Philosophical Society*, **124**: 227–39.

Ross, E.H. & Murray, D.J. (1996) *E.H. Weber on the tactile senses* (2nd edn). Hove, UK: Taylor & Francis.

Rowe, F.B. (1983) 'Whatever became of poor Kinnebrook?' *American Psychologist*, **38**: 851–2.

Salsburg, D. (2001) *The lady tasting tea: How statistics revolutionized science in the twentieth century*. New York: Freeman.

Scruton, R. (2001) *Kant: A very short introduction*. Oxford: Oxford University Press.

Shorter, E. (2006) 'Primary care'. In R. Porter (ed.), *The Cambridge history of medicine* (pp. 103–35). Cambridge: Cambridge University Press.

Smith, M.K. (1901) (translator) *A text-book in psychology: An attempt to found the science of psychology on experience, metaphysics, and mathematics by Johann Friedrich Herbart*. New York: Appleton and Company.

Smith, R. (2005) 'The history of psychological categories', *Studies in History and Philosophy of Biological and Biomedical Sciences*, **36**: 55–94.

Sturm, T. (2006) 'Is there a problem with mathematical psychology in the eighteenth century? A fresh look at Kant's old argument', *Journal of the History of the Behavioral Sciences*, **42**: 353–77.

Teo, T. (2007) 'Local institutionalization, discontinuity, and German textbooks of psychology, 1816–1854', *Journal of the History of the Behavioral Sciences*, **43**: 135–57.

Valentine, E.R. (2000) 'Metaphysics'. In A.E. Kazdin (ed.), *Encyclopedia of psychology*, vol. 5 (pp. 204–9). Oxford: Oxford University Press.

Wade, N.J. (2007) 'Image, eye, and retina (invited review)', *Journal of the Optical Society of America*, **24**: 1229–49.

Willis, R. (1847) *The works of William Harvey, M.D. translated from the Latin with a life of the author*. London: Sydenham Society.

4 Establishing psychology as an independent academic discipline

This chapter will cover . . .

Questions to consider

Historical issues addressed in this chapter

- When did psychology start?
- When and how did the first psychological laboratory come about?
- Which research methods did Wundt use?
- Who were the founders of psychology in the United States?
- When did psychologists start to measure intelligence?
- How did the treatment of mental health problems evolve up to the twentieth century?
- What was Freud's contribution to the development of psychology?
- Why did it take so long for psychology to thrive in the United Kingdom?

Conceptual issues addressed in this chapter

- Can a complex discipline, such as psychology, have a single birthday?
- To what extent do the degrees offered at universities reflect the political and social concerns in a country?
- Does Wundt's fame as the founder of psychology also mean that he has a lasting scientific legacy?
- To what extent has the history of early psychology been misrepresented in textbooks?

Introduction

> Psychology stands in a peculiar relation to the sciences of life and to the physical sciences, for it is one of the youngest of Philosophy's children and, on that account, has fallen heir, as do the successive members of any growing family, to a number of family treasures, some good, some bad, and some indifferent. Among other things, it has inherited from the physical sciences a well-rounded methodology and a refined laboratory technique; and from the sciences of life, a 'genetic' way of regarding mind in its relation to life. Moreover, in the near future, some one will write a history of the development of scientific concepts and it will then be discovered that psychology has fallen heir, also, to scientific ways of regarding the world at large, ways that became established a hundred years or so before mind was brought into the laboratory.
>
> (Griffith 1921: 17)

In the previous chapters we saw how changes in society and progress in knowledge primed the Western world for the scientific study of the human mind. In the present chapter we discuss the first attempts to establish psychology as an independent academic discipline. We start with the establishment of the first psychology laboratory in Germany. Then we discuss how psychology in only a few years came to flourish in the United Status. We also discuss the start of psychology in France, the Austro-Hungarian Empire, and the United Kingdom. As in Chapter 1, we end with a section on how history writing not only describes the past but also to some extent shapes it.

4.1 The foundation of the first laboratory of experimental psychology in Germany

As we saw in Chapter 3, by 1850 there was a thriving literature of psychological sub-jects in Germany. Philosophers studied psychology as the fourth theme of metaphys-ics, and psychology courses were part of the education of teachers and clerics. This created a market for textbooks. At the same time, men of science began to run studies that were informative for the functioning of the human mind. What was lacking for an independent academic discipline, however, was a group of scholars who called themselves psychologists and established research centres specifically devoted to the non-philosophical study of the mind. This would happen after Wilhelm Wundt was appointed as professor at the University of Leipzig, as we will see shortly. First, we need some background information explaining why Wundt was able to start a labora-tory of experimental psychology in the first place.

? What do you think?

The establishment of a new academic discipline usually happens gradually, particularly at traditional universities. If you are studying at a university with a history going back to the nineteenth century, it may be interesting to try to find out (1) when the first course of psychology was taught at your university, (2) when the first laboratory of (experimental) psychology was set up, (3) when the first chair (professorship) in psychology was created, and (4) when the first psychology degree was awarded. Usually, these markers of the establishment of a discipline do not coincide. Sometimes there are several decades in between!

The university reform in Germany

As in other countries, universities in the German states for a long time were domi-nated by the humanities and religion (first the Roman Catholic Church, then one of the Protestant Churches). This was a feature proponents of the Enlightenment fought against. A clear example of this struggle took place at the University of Halle. The university was created in 1694 by Friedrich III of Brandenburg, later the first King of Prussia, and was based on two pillars: the ideas of Enlightenment and Pietism. Pietism was a Protestant movement, promoting a revival of practical and devout Christianity, based on spiritual rebirth and advocating charitable and missionary work. Towards the end of the seventeenth century, Pietism and Enlightenment were brothers-in-arms in the struggle against Catholic orthodoxy and doctrine, emphasising good education in German (instead of Latin). The Enlightenment ideas mainly came from a group of academics who had been expelled from the University of Leipzig, because of their critical attitude and modern ways of thinking. The unity of both groups at the University of Halle lasted only a few years, which was to be expected given that Enlightenment sought to demystify religion, whereas Pietism emphasised inward spirituality and the centrality of Scripture. In 1723 the disagreements resulted in the ousting of the philosopher-scientist Christian Wolff (see Chapter 3), one of the Enlightenment proponents, by his colleagues from the theological faculty, who feared that Wolff's views would lead to atheism and who convinced King Friedrich that Wolff's teachings could lead to massive desertion of soldiers without any right of punishment. Eventually Wolff, who had a stellar reputation, was called back to Halle in 1740, after Friedrich died. At that time Aristotelian philosophy based on scholastic teachings was replaced by teaching of the new sciences without interference from the theological faculty.

A further reform took place after the defeat of the Holy Roman Empire in 1805–1806. The Holy Roman Empire was a federation to which the many kingdoms, principalities, duchies and free cities of present-day Germany belonged, together with (at its height) Austria, Hungary, Belgium, the Netherlands, Luxembourg, the Czech Republic and Slovenia. It was a confederation of states, which were more or less sovereign, with occasional battles over land disputes. It broke down in two parts, when Napoleon first defeated a coalition around the Austrians in the south (this part would continue as the Austrian Empire and later as the Austro-Hungarian Empire) and then a coalition around the Prussians in the north (which would later unify into the forerunner of the present-day Federal Republic of Germany).

The defeat by the French particularly upset the Prussians, who decided it was high time to modernise their country. The school system was reorganised and a new university model was installed. Whereas before the universities had been places of education, mainly aimed at the training of physicians, lawyers and clergy, scientific research now became part and parcel of an academic career with its own financing. In Berlin, the capital of Prussia, a new type of university was inaugurated based on two goals: *Wissenschaft* (scholarship and scientific research) and *Bildung* (the making of good citizens). The power of the university was put in the hands of a limited number of professors (chairs) who were given academic freedom and resources to pursue their interests and who had a number of assistants and lecturers under their command.

This type of university rapidly expanded over the entire German federation. The emphasis on scientific research and the freedom given to the professors made the German universities dynamic and open to new areas for scientific investigation. By the end of the nineteenth century, Germany was one of the front-runners in the industrial revolution, attracting students from all over the world. Porter (2006) estimated that over 15,000 American students went to study biology and medicine in Germany between 1850 and World War I.

Wundt and the first laboratory of experimental psychology

Wundt's career

Wilhelm Wundt (1832–1920) was born to an intellectual family (his father was a minister, and on both sides of the family were professors and physicians). He was an unmotivated and rather poor student in secondary school, but pulled himself together when he studied medicine and he began to excel. After his PhD (or at least the equivalent of it), he obtained an assistantship with Hermann von Helmholtz, the man who had started to measure the speed of signal transmission in nerves (Chapter 3). Here Wundt began to identify himself as a scientific psychologist. In 1862 he gave his first course in 'Psychology as a natural science' and in 1874 he published a book on physiological psychology, called *Grundzüge der physiologischen psychologie* (Principles of physiological psychology). In the book, psychology was defined as the study of the way in which persons look upon themselves, on the basis of internal physiological changes that inform them about the phenomena perceived by the external senses. Or as Wundt formulated it, the aim of 'physiological psychology' was:

> first, to investigate those life processes that, standing midway between external and internal experience, require the simultaneous application of both methods of observation, the external and the internal; . . . [This new science] begins with physiological processes and seeks to demonstrate how these influence the domain of internal observation. . . . The name physiological psychology . . . points to psychology as the real subject of our science. If one wishes to place emphasis on methodological characteristics, our science might be called experimental psychology in distinction from the usual science of mind based purely on introspection.
>
> (Wundt 1873: 157, as translated by Leahey 2004: 234)

? What do you think?

For most people a textbook is the first contact with a particular topic. Do you have memories of how a textbook affected your perception of a particular subject? Did you come to dislike a subject because of the way it was presented? And, conversely, did you unexpectedly become interested in a topic because of the textbook used?

Wundt called his psychology 'physiological psychology' not only because he thought physiology should form the basis of psychology, but also because he was convinced that psychology should use the experimental methods that had been pioneered by the physiologists, in particular the measurement of just-noticeable differences as described by Fechner (1860) and the registration of response times, as described by Donders (1868; see Chapter 3).

In 1875 Wundt was appointed Professor of Philosophy in Leipzig (after a short stay in Zurich), the university where Fechner had published his *Elemente der psychophysik* (Elements of psychophysics). Now at last he was able to put into practice what he had preached in his book. He could start a laboratory entirely dedicated to the study of the new physiological psychology, rather than simply publishing books about the viability of such investigations, as textbook writers had done before him. The first laboratory of experimental psychology was officially opened in 1879 and named Institut für Experimentelle Psychologie (Institute for Experimental Psychology). This date became generally accepted as the birth of psychology.

According to Boring (1950), Wundt was able to start a laboratory of experimental psychology, not only because of the incentives German professors had to pursue their own interests, but also because science in nineteenth century Germany had moved away from the mathematical deductive style of investigation prevalent in astronomy and physics. More than in other countries, Germany had embraced the inductive, Baconian research style, which was easily extended to the study of the mind. As Boring (1950: 19–21) wrote:

> The French and the English respected most the mathematical deductive style in science, the manner of Galileo and Newton. At that time biological science did not lend itself so readily to great generalizations, like the law of gravitation, generalizations from which facts could be deduced mathematically for empirical validation. Consequently it was left to the Germans, who have always had a great faith that sufficient pains and care will yield progress, to take up biology and promote it. . . .
>
> So we find in the Germany of the nineteenth century the beginning of a phenomenology, the careful collection of observational fact, that was sound, keen-sighted as to detail, conscientious and thorough. . . .
>
> By [early 19th century] Germany was ready to take over from the French the business of cataloguing facts and to do the job more thoroughly. . . . nineteenth-century experimental physiology was getting itself established. It was more inductive than deductive, more given to the fact-collecting which Francis Bacon recommended for science, . . .
>
> In brief, then, part of the story of how psychology came to join the family of sciences is that the Germans, with their faith in collecting data, welcomed biology to its seat in the circle of sciences, while the French and English hesitated because biology did not fit in with the scientific pattern set by physics and celestial mechanics.

Did psychology start in 1879?

In nearly all introductory psychology textbooks the birth of psychology is firmly placed in 1879, the opening of Wundt's laboratory of experimental psychology. As we have seen in Chapter 3, however, psychology is much older. One could easily claim that the 'true' birth of psychology is 1732, the year in which Christian Wolff published his book *Psychologia empirica* and argued that empirical psychology was similar to experimental physics. On the other hand, if one wanted to point to the first experimental work in psychology, Fechner's publication of the *Elemente der psychophysik* in 1860 would be a more righteous candidate, given the number of experiments in this book and the fact that Wundt built on them.

The reason why 1879 became known as the birth year of psychology was that many American students went to study in Wundt's laboratory. Upon their return to America, they established their own laboratories. This, together with their eagerness to propose psychology as a new discipline, radically different from the epistemological debates in mental philosophy, was the reason why they agreed upon the opening of Wundt's lab as the 'real' start of psychology. Because few scholars in the United States had access to the old, pre-1879 literature and because American textbooks rapidly became used in nearly all countries, everything before Wundt became lost or swept under the carpet as part of psychology's philosophical prehistory.

Only in the past decades, after meticulous analyses by historians and with the massive availability of old books on the internet, is the situation changing.

1879 was a birth year in some respects, because in that year Wundt established a laboratory of psychology, where students could convene and 'become' experimental psychologists. However, it was not *the* start of psychology. At most, it was the start of the type of psychology that the most productive American psychology textbook writers at the end of the nineteenth century wanted to promote.

Research in Wundt's laboratory

One of the reasons why Wundt's laboratory had a strong impact on the creation of psychology is that Wundt used it to actively promote psychological research. He not only created a journal (which he surprisingly called *Philosophische studien* [philosophical studies][1]), but he also set up a six-month introductory course, to which he invited students and colleagues from all over the world. We know quite a lot about the workings of the laboratory, because a few participants published a short account of what happened. The most interesting of these was written by a Belgian professor, Jules-Jean Van Biervliet, who had managed to get his own psychology laboratory at Ghent University and as part of his preparation went for training to Wundt's laboratory. In 1892 he wrote an account of his experiences in French. Because the report itself is so lively, we quote extensively from it.

> Thanks to the generosity of the Saxon government, Mr. Wundt was able to fit out premises, buy essential measuring apparatus, and give the first practical training in psychology. The Leipzig institute, founded about 10 years ago, includes at the moment a relatively large number of workers. During the last summer semester, 24 young persons, among them 8 foreigners, did original research under the close supervision of Mr. Wundt. Several former students of the master have founded laboratories similar to the one at Leipzig at universities such as Göttingen, Freiburg, and Bonn. A very modest laboratory is directed by Professor Ebbinghaus at Berlin. The Americans, always numerous at Wundt's institute (there were five of them last summer), founded about 20 institutes of psychology in their own country. However, Leipzig remains the center in which the most numerous and important works are done . . .
>
> The distinguished professor, as well as his assistants, Messrs. Külpe and Kirschmann, introduced us with the greatest kindness to the smallest details of their scientific installations . . .
>
> The young people who intend to tackle issues of experimental psychology come to the institute with very different backgrounds of theoretical preparation and practical training. In addition to medical students and candidates for a PhD in science, there are philosophy students, lawyers, and even teachers of primary education.
>
> The goal of the introductory course is to introduce this heterogeneous group to the specific aspects of experimental work, to familiarize the newcomer with the main equipment used in the laboratory, and to discuss and criticize the various methods used until now in the collection of data. This course, limited in time – it contains only 15 sessions – is repeated every 6 months. Thus, every semester new students attend the seminar in psychology.
>
> Dr. Külpe is in charge of this preliminary course. The course, intended for a necessarily restricted audience, is conducted in an informal manner. The professor has in front of him the apparatus, of which he explains the use and the function. A blackboard nearby allows the professor to draw curves, to do arithmetic. The audience is often questioned on the way it would run an experiment, to avoid misinterpretations. The

professor discusses the answer, shows the weak points, then himself gives the right answer. The audience is allowed to interrupt the professor, to raise objections, to ask for clarifications. The end of the course is often devoted to running a series of experiments with the equipment previously described, applying the methods just discussed.

When the introductory course is nearing its end, Mr. Külpe proposes to his audience two or three subjects of original research. The students have 8 days to develop a design, to determine the technical arrangement, to choose the methods that, according to them, will give the best solution to the problem.

The last two sessions are devoted to a detailed examination of the different proposals given during the course. This sort of examination allows the professor to estimate the benefit the students have gained from the introductory course . . .

To provide for the numerous needs of the laboratory, Mr. Wundt has an annual sum of money of only 1,500 Deutschmarks at his disposal; it is really insufficient to equip a laboratory consisting each year of more than 20 people. So it would be wrong to expect luxurious installations at Leipzig. Some Americans told us that laboratories of psychology in the United States are far better equipped . . .

Invariably every day, Mr. Wundt spends his afternoon in the laboratory. From time to time he visits the groups of workers; always unassuming and affable, he listens to the remarks, examines the installations, criticizes a detail, suggests an improvement . . .

Indeed, workers are organized in groups. . . . For each project, we name a chief experimenter, some assistants if necessary, and one or several subjects. The experimenter, head of the group, is generally an experienced person; having worked in the laboratory for several semesters, he is familiar with psychophysiological techniques. The apparatuses are familiar to him, the electricity has no more secrets for him. If the reader remembers how workers are recruited, he will understand the necessity of this organization. Besides the physicists and the physiologists, always relatively rare, we find a large number of students in philosophy and law. These students are able to supervise researchers only after a long initiation, after devoting two or three semesters, either as a subject or as an assistant experimenter, to become familiar with the specialized equipment used at the institute.

The head of a group is an important person; the success of the project depends largely upon him, . . . The subject or the subjects also have an important role in this success; the fundamental quality required from them is absolute sincerity. A subject must above all be conscientious; he must react naturally without bias, especially without preconceived ideas. . . . The subject is not always the same. To test a law, it is very often necessary to use a series of subjects. So the assistants, the fellow students of the workers, even the foreigners often serve as subjects of the ongoing experiments . . .

The necessary complement of experimental installations is a good library . . . Among the books in the collection, next to purely philosophical works of Leibnitz, Kant, Herbart, Schopenhauer, we find the works of Fechner, Stumpf, Ribot, Preyer, Taine, Bain, Spencer, Delboeuf, Bucola. The treatises of physiology by Hermann and Wundt, the medical physic of the same author, the works of Helmholtz, Pflüger's archives of physiology, and so forth . . .

(Van Biervliet 1892; as translated by Nicolas and Ferrand 1999: 196–201).

The methods used by Wundt

Van Biervliet's account is in line with what is currently known about Wundt's methodology (as we will see below, Wundt's work has been misrepresented for a long time in history books and introductory books). Wundt used three groups of methods for three different types of problems.

Experimental methods

First, Wundt and his students used experimental methods. These methods included:

1. psychophysical methods to study the connection between physical stimuli and their conscious states,
2. the measurement of the duration of simple mental processes,
3. the accuracy of reproduction in memory tasks.

Wundt was very familiar with Fechner's work on psychophysics (Chapter 3). So, quite a lot of energy was devoted to the psychophysical measurement of just-noticeable differences, i.e. the minimum perceivable difference between two stimuli. The following account by James McKeen Cattell (1888), one of Wundt's best-known American students, gives a flavour of what was investigated and found:

> Ever since Helmholtz published, in 1862, his classical researches on sound, much attention has been given to the perception of musical notes, investigations having been undertaken by Mach, Preyer, Hensen, Stumpf and others. Careful experiments, not yet published, have also been carried on for several years past in the Leipsic laboratory. Luft with tuning-forks and Lorenz with an apparatus on the principle of the harmonium have been investigating the least noticeable difference in pitch in the same manner as the loudness of sound has been studied. We have seen that the ear does not readily distinguish differences in loudness; in pitch, on the contrary, small changes can be noticed with marvellous accuracy, and this whether the observer be 'musical' or not. In the range most easily covered by the human voice (from about c' to c''', 256 to 1024 vibrations per second) successive notes can be distinguished when the difference between the physical stimuli is 1/4 to 1/5 of a vibration per sec. Where the pianoforte machine gives 24 notes the ear can distinguish over 3000.
>
> 'The psychological laboratory at Leipsic', *Mind*, **13**, pp. 37–51 (Cattell, J.M. 1888), Mind by Mind Association. Reproduced with permission of Oxford University Press.

Reaction times were measured to get insight into the mental processes that were required to perform a task. Here again a description by James McKeen Cattell:

> The term psychometry can . . . be confined to . . . the subject which we are about to take up, the measurement of the duration of mental processes. Psychometry has received abundant attention from astronomers, physicists, physiologists and psychologists; nearly half the researches undertaken in the Leipsic laboratory are concerned with this subject. We are naturally glad to find it possible to apply methods of measurement directly to consciousness; there is no doubt but that mental processes take up time, and that this time can be determined. The measurements thus obtained are not psychophysical as those which we have been recently considering, but purely psychological. It may be true that we are in some sort measuring the 'outside' of the mind, but the facts obtained, when we learn how long it takes to perceive, to will, to remember, etc., are in themselves of the same interest to the psychologist, as the distances of the stars to the astronomer or atomic weights to the chemist. But, besides the general interest of psychometrical facts as a part of a complete description of the mind, these times are of further and great use to the psychologist, as they help him in analysing complex mental phenomena, and in studying the nature of attention, volition, etc. It should also be noticed that psychometrical experiment has brought, perhaps, the strongest testimony we have to the complete parallelism of physical and mental phenomena; there is scarcely any doubt but that our determinations measure at once the rate of change in the brain and of change in consciousness. . . .

It will not be necessary to describe at length the psychometrical researches undertaken at Leipsic, as the most recent of these have been printed in [the journal] MIND. Most of the earlier work on this subject was then reviewed; attention should, however, be called to researches by Kraepelin and by Berger. Kraepelin studied the effects of certain drugs on the duration of a reaction and of simple mental processes. These times seem to be at first lengthened and then shortened by ether and chloroform, and at first shortened and then lengthened by alcohol, a difference of action which, perhaps, has less to do with different effects of the drugs on the nervous system than with the method of taking them, ether and chloroform being inhaled and alcohol drunk. Berger, in experimenting with light, sound and electric shock, found the reaction-time to become shorter as the stimulus was taken stronger. According to these experiments, the reaction-time for the several colours is the same.

'The psychological laboratory at Leipsic', *Mind*, **13**, pp. 37–51 (Cattell, J.M. 1888), Mind by Mind Association. Reproduced with permission of Oxford University Press.

These excerpts also show that Wundt's lab did not form an island, but was part of a network of laboratories that did very similar research and communicated intensively with each other. Finally, the fragments (and the larger texts they come from) show how the early psychological researchers tried to apply the methods of physics to their topics. The texts describe extensively the efforts made to reduce the variability in the measurements, both by more accurate measurements and by making use of a small number (sometimes only 1!) of trained participants. What was not yet known at that time was that variability is an inherent characteristic of biological processes and that demand characteristics have a strong influence on psychological findings, even when people try to be conscientious and react naturally without bias and without preconceived ideas. Demand characteristics refer to the fact that participants change their behaviour (often without awareness) when they have information about the experiment's purpose (Rosenthal 1963, 1966).

Introspection

The experimental methods were particularly important in Wundt's early years when he defined physiological psychology and established the laboratory of experimental psychology. However, Wundt also strongly believed in a second method: introspection. As we have seen in Chapter 3, this method was already proposed by Wolff (1732) and consisted of a process by which a person looked inside and reported what he/she was sensing, thinking or feeling. It is based on the belief that people have conscious access to (parts of) their own mental processes and can report them. Well before Wundt's time, the method had already been criticised by Kant and Comte. Wundt thought he could get away with the criticisms by introducing more control into the experimental situation. He made a distinction between *Innere Wahrnehmung* (internal perception) and *Experimentelle selbstbeobachtung* (experimental self-observation). The former referred to armchair introspection as practised by philosophers; the latter pointed to self-observation in highly controlled circumstances, where a stimulus was presented repeatedly and the participants reported their experiences to the stimulus. Wundt claimed that experimental self-observation was a valid scientific method to get information about the contents of consciousness, whereas internal perception was not.

Wundt's affection for introspection became painfully clear when his assistant, Oswald Külpe, in 1893 published his own textbook of experimental psychology, *Grundriss der psychologie* (Outlines of psychology). In this book Külpe defended the thesis that psychology should be a natural science, exclusively based on the experimental method. Psychology should be limited to those psychological processes that are amenable to experimental methods (nearly three-quarters of the book was devoted to sensation). Three years after the publication of Külpe's book, Wundt (by that time already well over 60) published his own book with the same title, in which he aimed to refute Külpe. He emphasised that there was a big difference between the natural sciences and psychology. Whereas the former were concerned with objects, independently of the perception of the subject, the latter dealt with perception itself and the way it was influenced by the person. Very often this could only be studied with introspection, by looking at the contents of the mind from inside. For Wundt this was the way to study the nature of human consciousness, even though he was well aware of the criticisms that had been raised against the method.

What do you think?

The limits of introspection are usually well explained in introductory textbooks. Do you think this method is still used today? If so, why? If not, what has changed since Wundt's time?

The historical method

historical method

one of the three research methods introduced by Wundt; consists of studying the human mind by investigating the products of human cultures; according to Wundt particularly well suited to investigate the 'higher' functions of the mind

Finally, Wundt's third method consisted of a study of the products of the human mind. In particular, towards the end of his life he became a firm believer in the historical method, the study of mental differences as revealed by differences between cultures (both in time and in space). This method was particularly well suited to studying 'higher' psychological functions, such as the social aspects of human thought and behaviour, for which the experimental methods could not be used. Wundt believed that the development of an individual recapitulated the evolution of mankind. So, a person's development could be studied by examining the historical development of the human race. Wundt called this type of psychology *Völkerpsychologie* (psychology of the peoples, or folk psychology), to which he devoted the last two decades of his life (and 10 book volumes). Because of this work, Wundt is also sometimes considered as the founder of anthropology, the study of cultures and societies. In all likelihood, he was influenced in this respect by Comte's writings (Chapter 3).

Wundt's legacy

Despite the fact that Wundt had a career of 65 years, was head of the best laboratory in the world, and was a prolific writer (he published more than 50,000 pages, in a time when texts were still written by hand), his scientific legacy is not very much more than that of being 'the father of experimental psychology'. The main reason for this is that Wundt did not produce a useful theory like Newton or Darwin, or make an empirical discovery that had a wide-ranging, lasting impact (such as Lavoisier's discovery that oxygen was needed for the burning of a substance). Furthermore, although Wundt was considered to be a good teacher, his writings were far from clear and easy to read. Below you find two examples. The first is from one of his 'easiest' books (*Grundriss der psychologie*, 1896), the other is from the *Völkerpsychologie*.

If we apply these considerations to psychology, it is obvious at once, from the very nature of its subject-matter, that exact observation is here possible only in the form of experimental observation; and that psychology can never be a pure science of observation. The contents of this science are exclusively processes, not permanent objects. In order to investigate with exactness the rise and progress of these processes, their composition out of various components, and the interrelations of these components, we must be able first of all to bring about their beginning at will, and purposely to vary the conditions of the same. This is possible here, as in all cases, only through experiment, not through pure introspection. Besides this general reason there is another, peculiar to psychology, that does not apply at all to natural phenomena. In the latter case we purposely abstract from the perceiving subject, and under circumstances, especially when favored by the regularity of the phenomena, as in astronomy, mere observation may succeed in determining with adequate certainty the objective components of the processes.

(Wundt 1896; as translated by Judd 1897: 20–1)

In so far as Völkerpsychologie can find any psychological laws of independent content, these will always be applications of principles valid for individual psychology. But one can also assume that the conditions of mutual mental interaction will bring out new and special manifestations of the general psychic forces that could not be predicted from the mere knowledge of the properties of individual consciousness; these again will augment our insight into the functioning of individual mental life.

(Wundt 1908; as translated by Jahoda 2007: 127)

Finally, there were several contradictions in Wundt's writings over the period of over 60 years in which he wrote, (e.g. in the higher importance he attached to experimental methods in his early writings than in his late writings). The American psychologist William James saw an inverse ratio between Wundt's productivity and his wisdom, and let the following (for him uncharacteristically derisory) quote slip:

He aims at being a Napoleon of the intellectual world. Unfortunately he will never have a Waterloo, for he is Napoleon without genius and with no central idea . . . Whilst they make mincemeat of some of his views by their criticisms, he is meanwhile writing a book on an entirely different subject. Cut him up like a worm, and each fragment crawls; there is no noeud vital in his mental medulla oblongata, so that you can't kill him all at once.

(as cited in Boring 1950: 346)

KEY FIGURE Wilhelm Wundt

- Germany, 1832–1920.
- Studied with von Helmholtz (measurement of reaction times).
- Published a book on physiological psychology in 1874.
- Once he became professor, he founded the first laboratory of experimental psychology at the University of Leipzig in 1879.
- Offered a course in psychological research which would attract many beginning psychologists from all over the world.
- At first mainly promoted experimental methods (reaction time measurement, psychophysics, memory performance). Later stressed the importance of

Source: US National Library of Medicine/Science Photo Library Ltd.

introspection for the study of higher mental processes. Towards the end of his life invested heavily in the historical method.

● His writings were not easy to read, sometimes contradicted each other, and did not contain lasting insights. As a result, his scientific legacy is limited.

Interim summary

● German universities were reformed in the nineteenth century to make them more dynamic and advance the new sciences.

● Wundt was a German physician who became interested in applying the physiological methods to psychological phenomena.

● When he obtained a professorial chair at the University of Leipzig, he established a new laboratory in 1879. This event became seen as the birth of psychology.

● Wundt not only used the experimental methods from physiology, but also thought that introspection was a valid research method and that information about the psychology of individuals could be obtained by looking at cultures (historical method). The impact of the latter two methods increased as he grew older.

● Many psychologists got their initial training in Wundt's laboratory.

4.2 Starting psychology in America: James and Titchener

James's *Principles of psychology*

Introductory psychology courses in the American curricula

In 1875, William James (1842–1910) started to teach a course of psychology at Harvard University. Many colleges and universities in the United States included such a course as part of the philosophy curriculum. The fact that James taught this course was not only testament to the breadth of his interests but to the fact that psychology was not yet considered as an independent academic discipline and could be taught by whoever was interested. James had started to study chemistry and finally settled on medicine. He already taught a course on physiology. At other universities, the introductory psychology course was given by lecturers who primarily taught courses in philosophy, literature or education. For example, at one university it was taught by a member of staff of the Department of English and History, and at another it was delivered by a lecturer with the title 'Professor of anatomy, physiology and geology' (Fuchs 2000).

The impact of the *Principles*

James turned out to be a great success in the classroom. Gradually he planned to write his own textbook and in 1878 signed up to a publisher. What followed was a 12-year struggle to finish his two-volume book, *The principles of psychology* (1890), which may be one of the reasons for the scornful comment about Wundt mentioned above (Wundt published about one volume a year). However, James's book turned out to be what Wundt's writings never were: an accessible and clear account of what was known and conjectured about psychology at the end of the nineteenth century. Within a few years the *Principles* (or rather the shorter, one-volume version that was published in 1892 and known as 'the Jimmy') would become the textbook of choice at many colleges and universities in the English-speaking world. Because of his textbook James has been one of most influential people in the early history of psychology, even though a few years after the book's publication he decided that psychology was not interesting enough and turned towards philosophical issues. As such, James fits more into the tradition of the textbook writers mentioned in Chapter 3 than into the tradition of the psychology researchers. However, because James wrote extensively about ongoing research in the psychological laboratories and because he was instrumental in the development of psychology as a discipline, he is generally considered one of the first psychologists.

James and research methods

For James, introspection was the best available method, despite its limitations:

> Introspective observation is what we have to rely on first and foremost and always. The word introspection need hardly be defined – it means, of course, the looking into our own minds and reporting what we there discover . . . The inaccuracy of introspective observation has been made a subject of debate . . . Some authors take high ground here and claim for it a sort of infallibility . . . Others have gone to the opposite extreme, and maintained that we can have no introspective cognition of our own minds at all. A deliverance of Auguste Comte to this effect has been so often quoted as to be almost classical . . . Our general conclusion [is] that introspection is difficult and fallible; and that the difficulty is simply that of all observation of whatever kind. Something is before us; we do our best to tell what it is, but in spite of our good will we may go astray, and give a description more applicable to some other sort of thing. The only safeguard is in the final consensus of our farther knowledge about the thing in question, later views correcting earlier ones, until at last the harmony of a consistent system is reached. Such a system, gradually worked out, is the best guarantee the psychologist can give for the soundness of any particular psychologic observation which he may report. Such a system we ourselves must strive, as far as may be, to attain.
>
> (James 1890, vol. 1: 185–6, 191–2)

James was not fond of the experimental methods, as the following quote shows (which incidentally is also an example of the humour and the light touch that made the book so digestible):

> But psychology is passing into a less simple phase. Within a few years what one may call a microscopic psychology has arisen in Germany, carried on by experimental methods, asking of course every moment for introspective data, but eliminating their uncertainty by operating on a large scale and taking statistical means. This method taxes patience to the utmost, and could hardly have arisen in a country whose natives could be bored. Such Germans as Weber, Fechner, Vierordt, and Wundt obviously cannot; and their success has brought into the field an array of younger experimental psychologists.
>
> (James 1890, vol. 1: 192)

In the rest of the *Principles* James elaborates on subjects such as:

- the stream of thought
- consciousness of the self

- attention
- discrimination and comparison
- association
- perception of time
- memory
- sensation
- imagination
- perceptions of 'things' and space
- perception of reality
- instinct
- emotions
- the will and
- hypnotism.

The impact of evolutionary theory

James was very familiar with Darwin's evolutionary theory, which had a large following in the United States, and saw the Darwinian ideas as an interesting framework. For James, the human mind had emerged as an adaptation, to increase the chances of survival, as can be seen in the following excerpt:

> We talk, it is true, when we are darwinizing, as if the mere body that owns the brain had interests; we speak about the utilities of its various organs and how they help or hinder the body's survival . . . We forget that in the absence of some such super-added commenting intelligence (whether it be that of the animal itself, or only ours or Mr. Darwin's), the reactions cannot be properly talked of as 'useful' or 'hurtful' at all . . . the moment you bring a consciousness into the midst, survival ceases to be a mere hypothesis . . . Real ends appear for the first time now upon the world's stage . . . Every actually existing consciousness seems to itself at any rate to be a fighter for ends, of which many, but for its presence, would not be ends at all. Its powers of cognition are mainly subservient to these ends, discerning which facts further them and which do not.
>
> (James 1890, vol. 1: 140–1)

For James the precise contents of the mind were less important than what consciousness did, what functions it served for man and animal (in particular with respect to survival). This view struck a chord with many psychologists in the United States, who became known as the **functionalists**, because they were primarily interested in the practical functions of the mind, not what the mind comprised or what structure it had.

functionalism

name given to an approach in early American psychology research, that examined the practical functions of the human mind inspired by the evolutionary theory

James's stress on the adaptive role of the human mind also opened the way to comparative psychology, the comparison of the abilities in various animal species. For instance, the undergraduate Edward Lee Thorndike (1874–1949) became interested in psychology after reading the *Principles* and decided to go to Harvard to study with James. He was interested in children and pedagogy but because of difficulties getting child subjects, he turned to learning in chicks and cats. This research would be the start of his very influential work on instrumental learning, as we will see in Chapter 5.

KEY FIGURE William James

- United States, 1842–1910.
- Wrote a textbook of psychology (*The principles of psychology*, 1890) as part of his teachings. This book included much research done in the previous 10 years and conjectures that inspired further researchers.
- Was also very influential in the foundation and expansion of psychology as a science in the United States.
- Defended introspection as the best available research method.
- Was strongly influenced by evolutionary theory. Sought to outline the functions of the human mind for survival. As such, he was one of the fathers of functionalism.
- Saw continuity between animal behaviour and human behaviour and, therefore, was receptive to comparative psychology (e.g. helped Thorndike).

Source: Science Photo Library Ltd.

Titchener's structuralism

Titchener

Another student of Wundt was the Englishman Edward Bradford Titchener (1867–1927). After studying at Oxford (during which he translated the third edition of Wundt's *Grundzüge der physiologischen psychologie* into English) he went to study with the master himself and obtained a doctorate in 1892. Upon his return to England, he found this country unreceptive to psychologists, crowded as it was with biologists and philosophers. After a short stint as a biology lecturer, Titchener left for the USA to teach at Cornell. We will come back to the situation in the UK later.

Structuralism

structuralism

name given by Titchener to his approach to psychology, consisting of trying to discover the structure of the human mind by means of introspection

Titchener turned Cornell into the centre of **structuralism**. This was an approach that, via introspection, tried to discover the structure of the human mind. Inspired by the British philosophical tradition of empiricism and associationism, Titchener tried to discern which sensation elements formed the basics of knowledge and how they were associated with one another.

Structuralism did not inspire many psychologists (even though Titchener was a successful textbook writer). There were three main reasons for this. The first was that introspection did not intuitively give rise to the experience of elementary sensations. This was first made explicit by the Würzburg school, a group of psychologists at the University of Würzburg, where Külpe for some time was Professor (although the theorising was mainly done by others). While studying the associationist theory, they noticed that the participants (as usual, including themselves) often made associations to stimuli without any intervening conscious process at all. Participants did not seem able to describe these processes; all they could say was that they had had them. This was even true when the processes dealt with decision-making. The researchers found that the participants often came to a conclusion without having a clue of the processes that underlay it. These unconscious processes became known as imageless thoughts, thoughts without a conscious trace. The French psychologist Binet (see below) independently came to the same conclusion as the **Würzburg school**: clear images such as those found in daydreaming were incompatible with the rapid processes of thought; thought was an unconscious act that needed words and images to become conscious (as cited in Mandler 2007: 79). Titchener objected to this criticism that imageless thoughts might be true for naïve individuals, but that participants could be trained to become perceptive of their sensations. As we will see in Chapter 5, this training element further weakened the status of introspection as a valid scientific research method.

The second reason why structuralism never became a big movement in psychology was because it did not address the issues most American psychologists saw as important. Influenced by James and Darwin, they were much more interested in pragmatic issues such as, how could psychology advance the conditions of individuals and of American society? The question of what consciousness was made of might very well be interesting to philosophers, but did not help anybody move forward. Therefore, many more psychologists found themselves interested in functionalism than in structuralism, certainly when Titchener came to the conclusion that there were no fewer than 30,500 basic visual elements.

Finally, Titchener's structuralism even failed to convince the researchers, who remained interested in the contents of consciousness. Very rapidly the objection was made that you cannot discover the nature of the human mind by trying to break it down into its 'atoms'. It would be like trying to understand the perception of a musical chord by breaking it down into its individual tones, or trying to understand a text by focusing on the letters it was made of. Human perception was more than the sum of the individual sensations the stimulus elicited. This countermovement became known as **Gestalt psychology**. According to the Gestalt psychologists the brain had self-organising principles and people experienced the world in terms of gestalts (from the German word *Gestalt*, which translates as 'pattern', 'whole' or 'organisation'). One of the illustrations the Gestalt psychologists used to make their point was the existence of visual illusions, as shown in Figure 4.1. In these illusions we see something different than what is physically presented. We see bendy vertical lines whereas in reality the lines are straight, or we see figures of different sizes that in reality are the same size.

The main proponents of Gestalt psychology were Max Wertheimer (1880–1943), Kurt Koffka (1886–1941) and Wolfgang Köhler (1887–1967). The first two had studied at Würzburg. Gestalt psychology also attracted attention in Scandinavia, with the best known researchers being the Danish psychologist Edgar Rubin (1886–1951), who provided compelling examples of the fact that perception entails a distinction between figure and background (Figure 4.2), and the Swede Gunnar Johansson (1911–1998), who discovered that motion is a strong organising principle in perception. When all you can see of people is a few lights attached to their joints, you still immediately recognise what is going on when they start to perform familiar actions (e.g. walking), despite the fact that the stimulus is extremely poor.

Würzburg school

group of psychologists at the University of Würzburg who used introspection as a research method, but came to different conclusions from those of Wundt and Titchener; in particular they claimed that many thought processes were not available to introspection (imageless thoughts)

Gestalt psychology

group of psychologists who argued that the human mind could not be understood by breaking down the experiences into their constituent elements; perception is more than the sensation of stimuli, it involves organisation

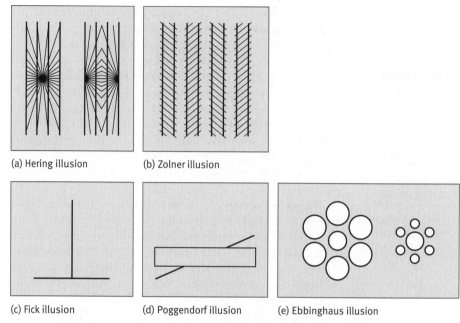

(a) Hering illusion   (b) Zolner illusion

(c) Fick illusion   (d) Poggendorf illusion   (e) Ebbinghaus illusion

Figure 4.1 Illusions used by the Gestalt psychologists as evidence against structuralism.

The Gestalt psychologists argued that humans cannot be understood as simply the sum of the constituent elements. They defended this thesis by pointing to the fact that what we perceive often deviates from the elements that are presented in the stimulus. The vertical lines in the Hering and Zolner illusions are straight (test them with a ruler). The vertical line of the Fick illusion has the same length as the horizontal line. The two oblique line segments in the Poggendorf illusion are in line with each other, and the two inner circles of the Ebbinghaus illusion have the same diameter.

Figure 4.2 Figures made by Edgar Rubin showing that perception involves the separation of figure and background.

Both figures are reversible: either the white part or the blue part can be the figure. In particular the right figure shows that the figure–background assignment can affect the interpretation (a vase vs. two facing faces) despite the fact that the stimulus and the associated sensations remain the same. This illustrates the point the Gestalt psychologists wanted to make, that the interpretation of a stimulus (the perception) is more than a simple sum of the sensations elicited by the stimulus.

Source: (right) Pomerantz, J.R. & Kubovy, M. (1986).

KEY FIGURE Edward Titchener

- Englishman in the USA, 1867–1927.
- Studied with Wundt.
- Promoted structuralism, an approach that tried to discover the structure of the human mind with the use of introspection.
- Was not very influential because of criticism from three sides:
  - Würzburg school and Binet: humans are not aware of many thought processes and cannot report them, let alone dissect them
  - functionalists: not enough practical advantages in knowing the precise structure of the mind
  - Gestalt psychology: humans are more than the sum of their individual sensations (e.g. in perception, interpretation is added to the stimulus).
- Defended introspection as the main research method; thought participants had to be trained to do this properly.
- Was strongly influenced by empiricism and associationism.

Source: Cornell University Library/Rare and Manuscript Collections.

Interim summary

- James was an American physician who became interested in psychology through his teachings. Arguably wrote the most influential textbook of early psychology.
- James was influenced by Darwin's evolutionary theory. This resulted in interest in the survival functions of the human mind and in comparative research of animals and humans.
- Titchener promoted structuralism on the basis of introspection in the USA.
- Had a limited impact because of criticisms of the method (introspection), the limited usefulness of the knowledge (functionalism), and the objection that humans are more than the sum of the individual sensations (Gestalt psychology).

? What do you think?

Can you think of a situation in which the introspection advocated by Titchener is useful? Could it be used to break down a complex reasoning problem into its constituent parts?

4.3 Psychology in France: Ribot, Charcot, Binet

Ribot and Comte's legacy

Psychology was a popular topic in French philosophy as well. However, after Comte's repeated assaults on the scientific status of psychology in the first half of the nineteenth century, there was little doubt in French minds that psychology belonged to the humanities and not to the natural sciences. As we saw in Chapter 2, Comte argued that civilisations went through three stages:

1. the theocratic stage, with animistic/religious explanations of natural phenomena,
2. the metaphysical stage, with theories of nature based on philosophical systems like those of Aristotle and Descartes, and
3. the positivistic stage, with theories based on empirical observation and verification.

According to Comte, the metaphysical stage was an unavoidable transition from the theocratic mode of thought, characteristic of primitive cultures, to the positivistic end state of mature cultures. Psychology was a remnant of the metaphysical stage and its elucidation attempts on the basis of introspection would in time be replaced by proper, scientific explanations provided by biology and sociology (Chapter 3).

What do you think?

Do you agree with Comte's assessment that psychology boils down to biological and social factors? Is the human mind more than the workings of the brain and interactions with other people?

The person to question Comte's view was the French philosopher Théodule Ribot (1839–1916), professor at the Sorbonne in Paris. His strategy consisted of showing his colleagues how out of touch they were with developments in other countries, in particular the UK and the German lands. In 1870 he published *La psychologie anglaise contemporaine* (English contemporary psychology) and in 1879 *La psychologie allemande contemporaine* (German contemporary psychology), in which he praised the recent advances in these cultures. For instance, the book on German contemporary psychology included large parts on Fechner and Wundt.

The book on English contemporary psychology was written mainly with the intent to defuse Comte's assessment of psychology (Guillin 2004). In this book, Ribot tried to convince his readers that one could be a 'good' positivist without accepting all Comte's claims. In the UK several scholars promoted scientific research and called themselves positivists, but disagreed with Comte on several aspects. In particular, the views of John Stuart Mill (1806–1873) and Herbert Spencer (1820–1903) were discussed, who both argued that psychology could be a science and introspection a respectable scientific method. Their arguments were as follows:

1. The mind can attend to more than one impression at the same time. So, why would the mind be unable to attend to its own conscious mental states?

2. Introspection can be based on memories, which allows humans to be aware of their thoughts post hoc even for tasks involving such great effort that simultaneous monitoring is not possible.

3. If one rejects introspection, how can one then study mental functions? How can one find the physiological basis of a mental function, if the latter supposedly does not exist? For instance, phrenology, praised by Comte as the best way to study the biological basis of thought, required the existence of mental faculties, so that the different parts of the brain could be related to them. How were these faculties to be found if one was not allowed to rely on introspection?

4. Introspection is not incompatible with the 'objective method'. On the contrary, to be a truly scientific method (different from what philosophers did), introspection must be combined with empirical observation and verification. There is no sharp divide between psychological and physiological facts, which makes it impossible to study them in interaction, just as there is no absolute distinction between humans and simpler life forms.

In particular, the last argument was used by Ribot to defend the possibility of a new psychology, different from previous metaphysical thinking and also different from Comte's exclusive attention to physiology and the socio-cultural products of the human mind. According to Ribot, this new psychology would study 'psychological phenomena subjectively, using consciousness, memory, and reasoning; and objectively, by relying on the facts, signs, opinions and actions that express them' (Ribot 1870; as translated in Guillin 2004: 178).

In line with most theorists of his time, Ribot never put his programme in to practice. In many respects he was the William James of France. These are the similarities Guillin (2004: 166) noticed among the impacts of James and Ribot in their countries:

- They were the first to wrest control of psychology from the abstract philosophers by adapting study of mental functioning to the methods of physiology.
- They were the first to take up the scientific study of consciousness within the context of the new evolutionary biology.
- They were the first to teach the scientific psychology.
- They were the first to open a laboratory for student instruction and to encourage others to start a research laboratory.
- They were the first to grant a PhD in the new discipline.
- They were the first to write a textbook of psychology from the positivist point of view.
- But they never were experimentalists themselves.

Charcot and the need for methodological rigour

Another major input to the development of psychology in France came from medical research, both related to brain functioning and the treatment of mental illnesses. We will discuss the input from brain research in Chapter 6. Here we focus on psychopathology, the importance of which for the fledging French psychology can be judged from the following quote:

> With relatively few exceptions, the psychologists of my country have left the investigations of psychophysics to the Germans, and the study of comparative

psychology to the English. They have devoted themselves almost entirely to the study of pathological psychology, that is to say psychology affected by disease.
(Binet 1890/1915; as translated in Leahey 2004: 219)

A towering figure in nineteenth-century French psychiatry was Jean-Martin Charcot (1825–1893). He was one of the first neurologists (physicians dealing with disorders of the nervous system; see below) and for most of his professional life was director of the Hôpital de la Salpêtrière in Paris, one of the largest centres in Europe for the treatment of nervous disorders. According to Pickren and Rutherford (2010), Charcot was initially interested in the Salpêtrière because its many chronic patients (who stayed in the hospital until they died) enabled him to do post-mortem brain analyses, so that he could relate clinical symptoms to anatomical brain dysfunctions. As part of his work, Charcot became increasingly interested in hypnosis to understand hysteria.

Hypnosis

Interest in hypnosis started with the German-Austrian physician Franz Anton Mesmer (1734–1815). Mesmer became convinced that movements of the sun, the moon, planets and stars influenced the human body by means of 'animal magnetism', just like the moon and the sun affected the tides of the seas. Before long, Mesmer sought to influence the 'animal magnetism' as a cure for all kinds of illnesses (remember from Chapter 3 that physicians had virtually no effective treatments in these days). First, he let patients touch magnetised iron bars; then he magnetised the objects himself, and finally he came to directly magnetise the patients through touch or stare. He first practiced in Vienna, but was ousted after having claimed that he could cure a blind girl. In 1778 he went to Paris, where his sessions were initially successful among the aristocracy, but were soon questioned by the French Academy of Medicine. In 1784 a commission concluded that animal magnetism did not exist and that any effect ascribed to it was due to the imagination of the patient.

Mesmer was forced to leave Paris and went to Switzerland. However, the interest in 'mesmerism' did not die in Paris, and gradually it was discovered that it was not animal magnetism that was important, but the trance-like, somnambulist state into which patients could be induced. Among others, this state interested surgeons who were searching for anaesthetics to make their surgeries less painful. One of these surgeons, the Scot James Braid, coined the term hypnosis. The interest of surgeons in mesmerism quickly waned once anaesthetic drugs became available, but hypnosis kept on being used by other practitioners to treat patients.

Charcot became interested in hypnosis because he thought it was related to hysteria. The latter referred to a condition of emotional distress often accompanied by physical symptoms for which no organic origin could be found. The condition was observed most often in women (and for a long time was thought to be caused by the uterus). Charcot assumed it was a progressive hereditary degeneration. As part of his examinations, he noticed that hysterical symptoms very much resembled the behaviour that could be elicited from individuals under hypnosis. These individuals too could be made to believe that part of their body was paralysed, that they felt no pain, and afterwards they could not remember what they had done under hypnosis. Charcot ventured that responsiveness to hypnosis was a hereditary degeneration with the same neurological origin as hysteria and, hence, would be particularly strong in hysterical patients. This indeed turned out to be the case, as Charcot sensationally demonstrated in his public lectures, attended by students and distinguished guests from all over the (developed) world.

Charcot also saw similarities between hysteria, epilepsy and hypnosis. In their pure forms (which, admittedly, were rare), the attacks in all three ailments showed a standard sequence of stages. For epilepsy there were three stages: an aura (feeling of the attack's onset), a tonic phase (in which the muscles of the body go rigid and the patient loses consciousness), and a clonic phase (with convulsions). A hysteric attack consisted of four phases. It would start with an epileptoid stage, in which the patient felt the onset of the attack. The second phase was the large movement stage, in which the patient showed big, uncontrolled movements. This was followed by the hallucinatory stage, during which the patient experienced self-generated sensations. The attack would end with a delirious phase of withdrawal characterised by disorganised behaviour and decreased attention. A hysteric fit could be elicited by touching a hysterogenic zone on the body of the patient. For hypnosis Charcot discerned three stages: lethargy (a sleep state), cataplexy (a sudden loss of muscle function), and somnambulism (performing actions in a sleep-like state without recollection afterwards).

Far-reaching claims lead to critical examination

Charcot's ideas about hypnosis were challenged by Ambroise Liébeault (1823–1904) and Hippolyte Bernheim (1840–1919), physicians from the north-eastern French town of Nancy. They both practiced hypnotic techniques and treatments and were convinced that responsiveness to hypnosis was not a disorder, but was present to some degree in nearly everyone. Furthermore, they rarely saw Charcot's three hypnotic stages, and considered hypnosis as a sleep-like state produced by suggestion. The Nancy criticisms gained impetus as Charcot's demonstrations and claims about hypnosis became more extravagant. At some point, Charcot reported that his assistants could reverse the symptoms of hysterics by bringing them under hypnosis, putting them in front of a magnet, and flipping the polarity of the magnet. Reports like these intrigued not only the French intellectuals. They also raised the interest of scholars in nearby countries. One of them was Joseph Delboeuf (1831–1896), a Belgian professor of mathematics and philosophy, who had started his career running psychophysical experiments to test Fechner's psychophysical law (Delboeuf 1873), but over the years had become interested in hypnosis. He was familiar with all (French-speaking) players involved in the dispute and in 1885 decided to go to the Salpêtrière to see the evidence at first hand (Nicolas 2004; Wolf 1964).

However, Delboeuf returned less convinced than he had hoped. What he had witnessed was a patient eager to please Charcot's assistants, who in addition made no effort to disguise their expectations (e.g. the magnet was turned in full vision of the patient and the assistants freely communicated about their expectations during testing, assuming that the patient could not hear them under hypnosis). As Delboeuf summarised four years later:

> All the way to Paris I was reflecting on the experiments to be made, and on the precautions that should be taken to prevent error. On the day of my arrival I saw M. Ribot who presented me to M. Binet who, the following morning, presented me to M. Charcot. The Salpêtrière was open to me.
> There I was a witness to the famous three states – lethargy, catalepsy, and somnambulism; there I saw the half states and the stupefying 'mixed states' . . . even those expressing two contradictory feelings . . . love on the right, hate on the left; there I was shown in action the neuromuscular hyperesthesias; there, finally, I was present at the experiments on transfer. But when I saw how they did these last experiments; when I

> saw that they neglected elementary precautions, for example, not to talk in front of the subjects, but [actually] announcing aloud what was going to happen; that, instead of working with an electromagnet activated without the knowledge of either the subject or of the experimenter, the latter was satisfied to draw from his pocket a heavy horseshoe; when I saw that there was not even a machine-électrique in the laboratory, I was assailed with doubts which, insensibly, undermined my faith in all the rest.
>
> (Delboeuf 1889; as translated by Wolf 1964: 763)

The lack of experimental control upset the experimentalist in Delboeuf, who decided to replicate the studies. What Delboeuf discovered was that hypnotised hysterics could indeed switch their symptoms from one moment to the next, but *only* when the experimenter gave away his expectations. When the polarity of the magnet could be changed secretly, no change in symptoms followed. So Delboeuf, in a series of publications between 1885 and 1889, was one of the first to stress the impact of demand characteristics on the outcome of psychological studies. The story has a further interesting twist, because one of Charcot's young assistants was Alfred Binet, generally considered France's first great psychologist. Wolf (1964) illustrates how Binet first vehemently reacted to Delboeuf's criticism but gradually came to stress the importance of methodological rigour in psychological research. Indeed, in a 1910 review article on hysteria, he would come to the conclusion that:

> Charcot never mistrusted suggestion; he never perceived the disastrous influence that involuntary suggestions can produce in an experiment of hypnotism or during an observation on a hysteric. Far from taking the least precaution, he spoke constantly aloud before the sick ones, announcing what was going to happen, and veritably giving them a lesson on it! It is not astonishing that his opponents had so often reproached him that his hysterics and his grand hypnotism were a product of culture. For those who have lived a little in the milieu of the Salpêtrière, it is uncontestable that this reproach was well founded . . .
>
> (Binet and Simon 1910; as translated by Wolf 1964: 770)

Binet and the development of the first valid intelligence test

Binet

Luckily for France's place in the history of psychology, Binet's first experiences with empirical research did not turn him away from psychology, although they almost did. Binet (1857–1911) was the only child of a well-off family with a tradition as medical doctors (this would allow him to pursue his interests without financial concerns). Binet himself was not interested in a medical career. Instead, he first studied law, completing his degree in 1878. While reading for a possible doctorate in the Bibliothèque Nationale in Paris, he became sidetracked by the philosophical books on psychology. He was particularly attracted to the British associationists and above all to John Stuart Mill. In 1880 he published his first article in Ribot's journal *Revue Philosophique* (established in 1876), which got the status of a 'note'. It was a purely theoretical article (about how the mind might make the transition from a single sensation to a double sensation in Weber's two-point threshold experiments; see Chapter 3) without any new experimental data. It would be the first of a long series of journal articles and books.

In 1883 Binet was introduced by a mutual friend to Charles Féré (1852–1907), Charcot's assistant, and he volunteered to do research in the Salpêtrière, which was the start of his investigations on hypnotism together with Féré. After the negative reactions this work received, Binet increasingly distanced himself from the Salpêtrière, also because of the ascent of a strong competitor in Charcot's lab: Pierre Janet (1859–1947). Between 1887 and 1894 Binet would devote more of his time to research in the laboratory of his father-in-law, who was an embryologist. In 1890 he obtained a degree in natural sciences and in 1894 was awarded a PhD from the Faculté de Sciences at the Sorbonne on research with insects. During this period, however, he also published several articles and three books on psychology (Nicolas and Ferrand 2011).

In 1891, on the way back from his summer holidays, Binet had a chance encounter with Henri-Etienne Beaunis (1830–1921), professor of physiology and anatomy, first at the Université de Nancy (where he had defended Bernheim and Liébeault's views of hypnosis), and later at the Sorbonne, where in 1889 he had started a laboratory of physiological psychology together with Louis Liard (1846–1917) under the instigation of Ribot. Although Binet was a shy man, he approached Beaunis and asked whether he could associate with the laboratory. Beaunis seized the opportunity to have a new, dynamic (and cheap) member for his young laboratory, and so Binet started to combine his work in his father-in-law's lab with work in Beaunis' lab, mainly doing memory research. After obtaining his PhD in 1894 he was made director of the laboratory, which he would remain until his early death from a stroke in 1911. In 1894 Binet, with Beaunis, also started the publication of a journal, *L'Année Psychologique* (The psychological year), in which he would publish a lot (filling nearly one-third of the journal up to his death).

Intelligence test

One of Binet's interests was in development of intelligence in young children, which he first studied in small-scale observations of his two little daughters in the late 1880s (and which he published in the *Revue Philosophique*). Binet's involvement further increased when he joined (and was soon president of) *La Société libre pour l'étude de l'enfant* (the free society for the study of the child), a group of scholars and teachers interested in education, founded in 1899 by a colleague at the Sorbonne who was heavily involved in education policies. At the end of the nineteenth century intelligence measurement was a hot topic, not only due to Galton's claims about the heredity of intelligence, but also because primary education became compulsory. In France this happened in 1882.

One of the consequences of compulsory education was what to do with children who did not seem to qualify for regular education, but who were not obviously mentally retarded. The Société insisted on special education for these 'abnormal children', but soon saw itself confronted with the question how to define these (meeting of June 12, 1902). The issue became particularly pressing when in 1904 the Société managed to have a governmental committee established, which would prepare the legislation for such special schools. As Binet wrote:

> But how to examine each child? Which methods to follow? Which observations to use? Which questions to ask? Which tests can be imagined? How will the child be compared to the normal? The Committee did not believe it had to provide an answer: it followed administrative rules, not science.
>
> It seemed extremely important to us to give guidance to future exam committees: these committees must be well oriented from the start. We must avoid that their examiners make decisions whimsically, on the basis of subjective impressions, which cannot

be controlled, . . . It will never be a recommendation, having gone to a school for special needs. We must save those who do not deserve it from this fate.

(Binet and Simon 1904a: 163–4; translated from French).

Binet started to study the measurement of intelligence in earnest. Again, not all reasons for this shift of career seem to have been happy. One of the factors probably driving him was that he had been denied succeeding Ribot as Professor of Psychology in 1902, on the grounds that he did not have a degree in philosophy (Nicolas and Ferrand 2011). In 1905 Binet established a new research centre, *Le Laboratoire-école de la Rue Grange-Aux-Belles* (the laboratory-school on Grange-Aux-Belles Street), specifically devoted to the topic of intelligence testing.

Before 1903 Binet had mainly followed Galton's lead in the study of intelligence and measured perceptual capacities on the basis of the psychophysical methods initiated by Weber and Fechner and on the basis of response times (Chapter 3). In line with prevalent medical beliefs, he also measured head sizes, assuming that low intelligence could be derived from small skulls. None of these measures, however, made clear differences between children with high and low intelligence.

In his renewed efforts, Binet got invaluable input from a medical student, who was soon to become his collaborator, Théodore Simon (1872–1961). Simon did an internship from 1899 till 1901 in the asylum of Vaucluse in Paris. Under Binet's guidance he measured various body parts of the 300 abnormal boys from the asylum and tried to relate them to the boys' intelligence, which would constitute his PhD thesis in medicine (examined in 1900). More important, however, was that the director of the asylum, Docteur E. Blin, in 1902 published an article in which he complained about the gross inconsistencies in the diagnoses of the mentally disabled children referred to him. To bring consistency to the admissions, Blin had started to work with a standardised questionnaire consisting of 20 themes. For instance, under the theme 'Name', he would ask the following questions: 'What's your name?', 'How old are you?', 'What are your first names?', 'In which year were you born?', 'Where do you live?', 'Birthday?', 'Place of birth?', 'County?'. A first study of 250 boys confirmed that there was a relationship between the number of questions the child could answer and his degree of retardation.

Simon and Binet took this questionnaire as the inspiration for their intelligence test and searched for simple tasks that normally developing children of various ages could solve. First, Binet (1904) published an article in which he discussed the findings of a small study in which primary school children had to try to memorise a poem for a short period of time and then were asked to write down as much as they remembered of the poem. He showed how much bigger the difference on this measure was between good and poor pupils (as indicated by the teacher) than a similar attempt by his Belgian colleague Van Biervliet based on the sharpness of vision. In the same year Simon and Binet published an article about other tasks they had tried out with children (Binet and Simon, 1904b), and an article in which they presented the first results on small groups of 'normal' children aged between 7 and 11 years old, and various groups of 'abnormal' children, illustrating the big differences between these groups (Binet and Simon, 1904c). Three years later, they presented the first validated intelligence test with norms for normally developing children (Binet and Simon 1907).

The Binet–Simon test was based on the assumption that developing children can solve problems of increasing difficulty. A sequence of tasks was assembled that allowed the researchers to assess the mental age of a child. By comparing the mental age with the chronological age of a child, it was possible to see whether the child was performing as expected, better or worse. Binet and Simon explicitly aimed for tasks that were fairly independent of what was taught in schools, so that a child's results were little influenced by the quality of the education received. Table 4.1 lists the tasks that were used. Notice how similar they are to contemporary intelligence tasks!

Table 4.1 Tasks used by Binet and Simon (1907) in their intelligence test (a few tasks that would require too much explanation have been omitted)

Age (years)	Action
3 years	Touch nose, eyes, mouth
	Repeat 2 digits
	Repeat a sentence of 6 syllables
	Give family name
4 years	Give gender
	Give the name of a key, a knife and a coin
	Repeat 3 digits
	Compare the length of 2 lines
5 years	Compare 2 weights
	Copy a square
	Repeat a sentence of 10 syllables
	Count 4 coins
6 years	Repeat a sentence of 16 words
	Compare 2 pictures on aesthetic grounds
	Define familiar objects
	Give your age
	Make a distinction between morning and evening
7 years	Indicate missing parts in pictures
	How many fingers on left hand, right, total?
	Copy a written sentence
	Copy a triangle and a diamond
	Repeat 5 digits
	Count 13 coins
8 years	Read a short story and remember 2 elements
	Count money (3 coins of 1 cent and 3 coins of 2 cents).
	Name 4 colours
	Count backwards from 20 to 0
	Write to dictation
9 years	Give the full date (day, month, year)
	Name the days of the week

(continued)

Table 4.1 (*continued*)

Age (years)	Action
	Read a story and remember 6 elements
	Return money when an object of 16 cents is paid with a coin of 20 cents
	Rank 5 weights
10 years	Name the months
	Give the value of the 9 familiar coins that are shown
	Use 3 words in 2 sentences
	Answer 2 lists of comprehension questions
11 years	Indicate absurdities in sentences
	Use 3 words in a single sentence
	Find more than 60 words in 3 minutes
	Give abstract definitions
	Put words in the right order
12 years	Repeat 7 digits
	Give 3 words that rhyme with a given word
	Repeat a sentence of 26 syllables
	Answer questions (e.g. 'Recently my neighbour had many visitors: first a doctor, then a lawyer and a priest. What may be going on?')

Source: Binet & Simon (1907).

Within a few years, Binet and Simon's intelligence test was known all over the world. Stern developed a German version in 1912, Terman published an American version in 1916 (known as the Stanford–Binet test, thereby completely ignoring Simon's contribution), and Kubo standardised a Japanese version in 1918.

Binet and Simon also had an impact on the emergence of developmental psychology. Jean Piaget (1896–1980), a Swiss psychologist who came to study in Paris after Binet's death, started to wonder why children aged 11 had no problem seeing the absurdity in a sentence such as, 'If I wanted to kill myself, I would never do that on a Friday, because that brings bad luck', whereas otherwise intelligent children of 8 years could not do that. This would be the origin of Piaget's theory of cognitive development in children in different stages (see any book on developmental psychology for an account of this theory).

? What do you think?

Did Binet and Simon's IQ test solve all problems of assessing children with special needs? What are its pros and cons? Make a list and keep it with you until we continue the discussion of IQ tests in Chapters 8 and 13.

KEY FIGURE Alfred Binet

- France, 1857–1911.
- Best known for the development of the first valid intelligence test.
- First tried to measure intelligence on the basis of psychophysical measures and measures of the skull.
- Then changed track and, together with Théodore Simon, used meaningful questions. Made sure, however, that the solutions to the questions did not rely too much on information learned in school.
- Test comprised tasks of increasing difficulties, suited for children of different ages.

Source: US National Library of Medicine/Science Photo Library Ltd.

Interim summary

- In France, psychology was seen as part of the humanities as a result of Comte's writings. This was questioned by Ribot, who pointed to the developments in the UK and the German lands.
- Another towering figure in France was Charcot, a neurologist best known in psychology for his research on hysteria. Trusted entirely on his clinical expertise, which turned out to be wrong in the case of hypnosis.
- Binet and Simon's development of the first valid test of intelligence is France's best-known contribution to early psychology.

4.4 Freud and psychoanalysis

At this point it is necessary to interrupt our narrative about how psychology made its way into universities in various countries, because in Vienna another movement took place. This development happened outside academia (more specifically, in the practice of a physician) and, in the proponent's eyes, also outside psychology (as he considered only medical doctors suited for the successful application of his treatment). Still, it would have such a profound effect on psychology that we cannot leave it out of consideration. It was the development of psychoanalysis as a cure of mental disorders by Freud in Vienna, at that time the capital of the Austro-Hungarian Empire. We first discuss the different views of insanity and its treatment in the history of the Western world, then we cover Freud's place within this evolution, and we end by commenting on Freud's research method.

Changes in the treatment of mental disorders

Informal support

Very little is known about the conditions of people with mental problems in early times. Historical writings are mainly confined to strong people (the conquerors) and the few writings we have about the weak mainly consist of sensational events, such as the burning of witches or fathers who killed their disabled babies. However, there are reasonable grounds to assume that people with mental difficulties have mostly been treated with a combination of compassion and contempt (sometimes hostility), given that they were weak and non-productive. The compassion came from the parents and other members of the (extended) family; the contempt from society outside the family. As long as the symptoms were not too bad or dangerous, these people stayed at home and died young, as did the majority of humans in those days. If the family or the relatives could no longer take care of them, they became homeless and part of the larger group of outcasts, who survived by begging and petty crime. Because there was a widespread belief that insanity was due to the devil or a bad ghost, they also risked being seen as a source of disaster.

Informal support meant that the care depended on the persons providing it. In some families it was good; in others it was unacceptable, as can be seen in the following testimonies (Shorter 1997: 1–3):

(a) There is nothing so shocking as madness in the cabin of the . . . peasant. . . . the only way they have to manage is by making a hole in the floor of the cabin, not high enough for the person to stand up in, with a crib over it to prevent his getting up. This hole is about five feet deep, and they give this wretched being his food there, and there he generally dies.

(b) A youth of sixteen, who for years had lain in a pigpen in the hut of his father, a shepherd, had so lost the use of his limbs and his mind that he would lap the food from his bowl with his mouth just like an animal.

(c) If the insane person is peaceful, people generally let him run loose. But if he becomes raging and troublesome, he's chained down in a corner of the stable or in an isolated room, where his food is brought to him daily.

Asylums

From the sixteenth century on, changes in society led to an increased role for the authorities in the treatment of people with a deviation. There was a massive move from the countryside (where people had been serfs for centuries) to the cities, where life became more complex. Labour differentiated. People were required to take up more individual responsibility and they had to interact with an increasing number of other individuals. This required better manners, with more emphasis on self-discipline. The tolerance for deviant behaviour dwindled. As a consequence, the authorities were forced to take action against the outcasts, who were not economically useful and became seen as a disturbance to the established order. Institutions were founded to confine them. In these **asylums** they were treated as prisoners, with a regime of forced labour and religious exercises to re-educate them as good, productive members of society. Other authors have compared the early asylums to farms where the inhabitants were treated as caged animals:

asylum
name given to the institutions for the insane established from the sixteenth century on; first modelled after prisons, later after hospitals for chronic patients

When François-Emmanuel Fodéré arrived at the hospital of Strasbourg in 1814, he found a kind of human stable, constructed with great care and skill . . . These cages had gratings for floors, and did not rest on the ground but were raised about fifteen centimetres. Over these gratings was thrown a little straw upon which the madman lay, naked or nearly so, took his meals, and deposited his excrement.

(Foucault 1961/2006: 68)

From prisoners to patients

Gradually, over the eighteenth century, under the influence of the Enlightenment, the conviction grew that the inhabitants of asylums were not real criminals but ailing patients. Important names in this evolution were William Battie in England, who published the first book on psychiatry, *Treatise on madness* (1758), and Philippe Pinel in France, who liberated the insane of Bicêtre from their chains after the French Revolution. A remaining problem, however, was how to treat the disorders of these patients. Some attempted common-sense 'medical' practices to bring the patients back to their senses, such as cold showers, fast spinning around or cures with leeches. Others turned to educational measures to re-instil morality in the mentally ill. This so-called 'moral treatment' consisted of trying to persuade and influence the patient to behave normally, under the influence of the moral authority of the doctor. In cases of non-adherence, retaliation was swift, with straitjackets, padded cells or other types of confinement. A further problem was the financing of the institutes. Except for patients of wealthy families, who could afford a cure on the basis of rest and tranquillity, living conditions were appalling.

Neurologists

Because the educational approach seemed to lead to (slightly) better results than the medical cures, it was the dominant therapy in the first half of the nineteenth century (Abma 2004). Psychiatrists had a low status. Gradually, however, the biological view of mental illness regained impetus. An important element in this evolution was the discovery of the microbe that caused syphilis, which in those times was a major cause of insanity. Towards the end of the nineteenth century a new group of physicians entered the scene. They called themselves **neurologists** and were particularly interested in the milder forms of mental disturbances, which they called 'nervous disorders' or 'neurasthenia' (weakness of the nerves). They limited asylums to the handling of the worst cases of madness and for the others advocated treatment in private settings including methods such as hypnosis and suggestion. As we saw above, Charcot was a major forerunner of this movement. One of the persons who attended his lectures and went to work with him for a few months in 1885–1886 was Sigmund Freud.

neurologist

name used at the end of the nineteenth century by physicians who were interested in the treatment of milder forms of mental problems outside the asylum; the term was later used to refer to specialists of the nervous system, when the original neurologists merged with the psychiatrists and took up the latter's name

Freud

Sigmund Freud (1856–1939) was born in the Austro-Hungarian Empire. He trained as a physician and then did research on topics such as aphasia and poliomyelitis under the supervision of Ernst Wilhelm von Brücke, a neuro-anatomist. Von Brücke was a strong believer in psychodynamics, a view that considered living organisms as energy systems governed by the principles of physics and chemistry. This view would have a strong impact on Freud's own stand.

Psychoanalysis

psychological treatment

treatment of mental health problems consisting of conversations between the patient and the therapist; initiated by Freud as an alternative to the prevailing medical and educational treatments

Because a university position as professor (more or less with the same status as in the Prussian system) was unlikely, Freud started a private medical practice in 1886 that specialised in neurology, after his stay in Paris. Here, together with his colleague Josef Breuer, he started a new type of treatment based on conversations with patients (remember that previously treatments were either medical or educational). On the basis of this **psychological treatment** (or talking cure, as it was sometimes called),

Freud became convinced that hysterical symptoms (vague pain, insomnia, hysterical paralysis, numbness, lack of appetite or sexual desire) were due to repressed sexual childhood experiences (later, childhood fantasies). These symptoms could be alleviated by the painful process of bringing the unconscious memories into the patient's consciousness and by freeing them from their emotional energy.

Freud was not the first to talk about unconscious mental processes, but nobody before him had given these processes such an explosive emotional power or made them the real drivers of human behaviour. Freud himself considered the insight that human reason was not the real master of a person's action to be a revolution on the same scale as Copernicus's insight that the Earth orbited the Sun and Darwin's insight that man had evolved from animals (as cited in Leahey 2004: 264).

psychoanalysis

name given to Freud's theory and therapy

Psychoanalysis, as Freud's theory and therapy became called, provided the first coherent framework for the treatment of nervous disorders and, therefore, received a warm welcome among the neurologists, the more so because Freud's views were quite compatible with those of Charcot (another of whose students, Pierre Janet, came independently to very similar conclusions). The neurologists with their new, forceful theory replaced the ill-reputed psychiatrists in the asylums (although they took up the latter's title when neurology moved on to confine itself to the examination and treatment of the nervous system itself).

Psychoanalysis also exerted a strong attraction on the developing field of psychology, because it was the first complete theory of human psychological functioning, starkly deviating from the piecemeal approach found in the university laboratories. Many indications can be listed of the rapidly growing impact of psychoanalysis on psychology. In 1908, G. Stanley Hall, the founder of the first psychology laboratory in the USA (see Table 4.2 on page 163), began to give courses on psychoanalysis and in 1909 he invited Freud to Clark University (together with Jung and Ferenczi). The impact of Freud on psychology in the UK was described as follows:

> During the first enthusiasm for psychoanalysis with its startling revelations, the results obtained by the often laborious method of experiment [reported at meetings of the British Psychological Society] seemed dull and even insignificant.
>
> (Edgell 1947: 16)

Throughout this book we will regularly come back to the relationship between psychoanalysis and the other approaches in psychological research.

Freud's research method

Medical case studies

case study

within medicine and clinical psychology, the intensive study of an individual patient within the context of his/her own world and relations, to understand and help the individual patient

Freud's psychoanalytical method was inspired by medical practice and involved case studies, the intensive study of individuals within the context of their own world and their relationships (past and present). The aim of each study was to understand and help the individual patient. The validity of the ideas generated depended on high-quality thought and on cross-checking with the clinical evidence.

Introspection and interpretation by the therapist

Freud's method was also based on introspection: patients talked about their thoughts, dreams and feelings. However, contrary to Wundt's and James's introspection, the literal meaning of what the patients said was of little value, because, according to Freud, the patients did not have access to their own unconscious drives. Freud considered that it to be the therapist's task to be attentive to occasional slips during which the unconscious forces revealed themselves, and to reinterpret the contents of the introspection according to the psychoanalytic theory. The clearest example of this reinterpretation was the distinction Freud drew between the manifest message and the latent message in dream analysis (i.e. what the patients said vs. what they actually meant), as is shown in the following excerpt:

> Another guileless dream of the same patient, which in some respects is a pendant to the above. Her husband asks her: 'Oughtn't we to have the piano tuned?' She replies: 'It's not worth while, the hammers would have to be rebuffed as well.' Again we have the reproduction of an actual event of the preceding day. Her husband had asked her such a question, and she had answered it in such words. But what is the meaning of her dreaming it? She says of the piano that it is a disgusting old box which has a bad tone; it belonged to her husband before they were married, etc., but the key to the true solution lies in the phrase: it isn't worth while. This has its origin in a call paid yesterday to a woman friend. She was asked to take off her coat, but declined, saying: 'Thanks, it isn't worth while, I must go in a moment.' At this point I recall that yesterday, during the analysis, she suddenly took hold of her coat, of which a button had come undone. It was as though she meant to say: 'Please don't look in, it isn't worth while.' Thus box becomes chest, and the interpretation of the dream leads to the years when she was growing out of her childhood, when she began to be dissatisfied with her figure. It leads us back, indeed, to earlier periods, if we take into consideration the disgusting and the bad tone, and remember how often in allusions and in dreams the two small hemispheres of the female body take the place – as a substitute and an antithesis – of the large ones.
>
> (Freud 1900; as translated by Brill)

Finally, Freud's research method was characterised by a surprisingly large input from himself. On the basis of rather little data, a rich and all-embracing theory of human functioning was built. On a continuum from evidence-based to principle-driven research, psychoanalysis clearly was biased towards the latter pole. This was not necessarily bad, as long as the new ideas and insights were helpful. Otherwise, the small empirical base was likely in the end to turn against the theory.

KEY FIGURE Sigmund Freud

- Born in the Austro-Hungarian Empire, 1856–1939.
- Neurologist who started psychological treatment of his patients (talking cure).
- Built a theory and a therapy on the idea that people's actions are controlled by their unconscious (psychoanalysis).
- Used medical case studies as a research method. Evidence derived from introspections by the patients that had to be interpreted by the therapist.

Source: National Library of Medicine/Science Photo Library Ltd.

Interim summary

- Freud was one of the first neurologists, a new group of therapists at the end of the nineteenth century. Before, people with mental disorders had been taken care of first on an informal basis and then – increasingly – in institutions, where they were treated as prisoners or patients. Basic treatment in asylums consisted of containment and attempts to re-educate the patients.

- Freud was the first to actually talk to his patients (psychological treatment). On the basis of these talks he constructed the psychoanalytical theory, which argues that the unconscious mind plays a strong role in the control of people's actions.

- Psychoanalysis had a massive impact, both on neurologists and on psychologists, because it provided a coherent and attractive theory of psychopathology.

4.5 Starting psychology in the UK: finding a place between clerics, philosophers and biologists

In 1870, the French philosopher Ribot was convinced that the UK[2] would take the lead in the establishment of psychology as an academic discipline. As we saw, the British empiricists and associationists were among the most influential psychology authors, with names as Locke, Hume, Mill, Spencer and Bain. Furthermore, there were the contributions of British biologists, above all Darwin with his evolutionary theory. In Ribot's own words (1870: 1, 43–4):

> Since the time of Hobbes and Locke, England has been the country which has done most for psychology. . . .
>
> 'The sceptre of psychology', says Mr. Stuart Mill, 'has decidedly returned to England.' We might go further, and maintain that it has never departed thence. No doubt, psychological studies are now cultivated in England by first-class men, who, by the solidity of their method, and, which is more rare, by the precision of their results, have caused the science to enter upon a new epoch. . . . Since the time of Locke, and even before it, the empirical study of the facts of consciousness has always been in favour among the English; no people have done so much for psychology . . . If, indeed we look at the three or four peoples of modern Europe who only have had a philosophical development, with the exception of Germany, apt at everything, though loving metaphysics above all, we shall see that in Italy experimental psychology is poor, almost nil, because that light, imaginative race, whose life is all outside, have an instinctive repugnance to it; that in France it soon turns to logic, because we have too little taste for patient observation, for exceptions, for accumulated facts, and that we are too fond of compartments, divisions, and subdivisions, order, symmetry, brief and decisive formulas. In England it is natural; it is the simple result of that disposition to the interior life, to that falling back upon one's-self, whence come poetry and romance . . .
>
> (as translated in the American version of Ribot's book in 1874)

The fact that the UK was not able to capitalise on its lead and trailed behind the evolutions in other countries had to do with the organisation of its universities and with resistance from established disciplines against the newcomer.

Universities in the UK

The University of Oxford is the oldest in the UK and one of the oldest in the world, with a birth date that seems impossible to pin down. Religious and secular teaching has existed at Oxford since at least the eleventh century (when Oxford was a residence of rulers such as Edmund Ironside, Canute and Harold I). It received a strong impetus in 1167 when King Henri II banned English students from studying in Paris. The first title of Chancellor was conferred in 1214 and the masters were recognised as members of a university guild in 1231.

As a result of frictions between the masters and the other inhabitants of the town, a number of masters fled to Cambridge in 1209, a similar town with a rich religious life and considerable wealth. At first they lived in lodgings but by 1226 they had set up a guild with a Chancellor, which in 1231 received a charter from Henry III confirming its independence.

For six centuries Oxford and Cambridge were the only universities in England (in 1261 there was a short-lived concession from Henry III to establish a third university in Northampton, which was closed in 1265 after protests from Oxford and Cambridge). There was more dynamism in Scotland, which had three universities by the fifteenth century (the University of St Andrews in 1413; Glasgow University in 1451, and King's College Aberdeen in 1495) and one founded in the sixteenth century (the University of Edinburgh, founded in 1582). Wales got its first university in 1828, when St David's College was opened near Lampeter; in Northern Ireland Queen's College Belfast opened in 1849 (Ireland had already had Trinity College Dublin since 1592).

Oxford and Cambridge were generally considered as conservative universities, heavily dominated first by the Roman Catholic Church and then by the Church of England. Up to the end of the nineteeth century it was impossible to obtain a degree from these universities without swearing an oath of allegiance to the Church of England. As a result, these universities were heavily oriented towards the classics (humanities and mathematics) and unreceptive to natural sciences:

> For social at least as much as for intellectual reasons, a classical education at public school, followed by a sojourn at Oxford or Cambridge, remained the most prestigious educational route well into the twentieth century (though mathematics had long been held to be on a par with classics as a form of mental exercise). The teaching of science did gradually infiltrate these elite institutions – the establishment of a course in the natural sciences at Cambridge in 1850 was a significant landmark, and the endowment by the Duke of Devonshire in 1870 of the Cavendish Laboratory there was another. But in some quarters it continued to be stigmatised as a vocational and slightly grubby activity, not altogether suitable for the proper education of a gentleman.
>
> (Collini 1998: xiii)

> The essential character of new and fertile ideas is often recognised as follows; they run against the ideas of the time and become accepted only after long opposition. . . . The most notable example in this respect was the reception of Newton's new doctrine in England. Forty years after the publication of Newton's immortal work, Descartes' system was still taught at English universities as the only truth. Strange thing! It was not even given to Newton in his lifetime to see his doctrine taught at Cambridge, where he had worked for such a long time. . . . it was not until 1718 that Samuel Clarke managed to slip Newton's ideas into the courses of English professors by inserting them as footnotes to the elementary treatise of Cartesian physics.
>
> (Liebig 1863; translated from German)

More than in other countries, scientific research in England happened outside the universities. First and foremost, there were well-off individuals, who could devote time and money to new inventions and who paid scholars to come and work for them. Second, there were the societies with their fees and endowments, which could afford some staff and sponsor some research. There were also small-scale institutes and centres that did not have university status, but that could finance a small number of scientists. Finally, there were scholars who sponsored their work with the proceeds of the books they published and the articles they wrote for the emerging scientific journals.

Attempts to establish psychology at Cambridge and Oxford

Cattell

The first opportunity to establish a psychology laboratory in the UK was in 1887 when the University of Cambridge was able to attract the American James McKeen Cattell (1860–1944) as lecturer[3], after he had obtained his PhD in Wundt's lab (Rust 2008; Sokal 1972). Two philosophers with interests in psychology were instrumental in bringing Cattell to Cambridge: James Ward (1843–1925) and John Venn (1834–1923). Like many of his colleagues, Ward had made several study visits to Germany and written a number of psychology-related treatises, such as *The relation of physiology to psychology* and *An interpretation of Fechner's Law*. John Venn (best known for his Venn diagrams) had shortly before been presented with some of Galton's instruments to 'measure intelligence' (such as equipment to assess keenness of eyesight, strength of pull and squeeze, head size and breathing capacity) and had started a series of studies along Galton's lines. Cattell was a catch, because not only had he done his PhD on mental testing in Wundt's lab, he also brought considerable equipment with him (being from a wealthy family). Cattell, in turn, was attracted to the UK because of Galton's work in London. However, he found the University of Cambridge less accommodating than he had hoped. As he wrote to his father:

> I have been busied this afternoon trying to find a place for a psychological laboratory. All the buildings are very crowded. Some of the colleges are rich but the university itself is poor, and finds it expensive to house laboratories and museums which have grown rapidly during the past few years. I expect, however, we will be able to get something. I dine with Mr Ward tomorrow to talk it over.
>
> (Cattell 1887; in Sokal 1981)

Finally, Ward found a place for Cattell's equipment in the Cavendish Laboratory of Physics through mediation of a Fellow from his college. In this laboratory, Cattell started a new series of intelligence measurements along Galton's recommendations. Without any prospect of a decent position at the University of Cambridge, he already left in 1888, first to a newly established Professorship in Psychophysics at the University of Pennsylvania and two years later to Columbia University in New York. He took all his laboratory materials with him, giving Cambridge University back its much needed space.

Rivers and Myers

The second attempt to establish a psychology laboratory at the University of Cambridge was made in 1893 by attracting the physician William H.R. Rivers (1864–1922) as psychology lecturer in the physiology department. Rivers had studied in Germany and was at that moment teaching experimental psychology at University College London (see below). In 1897 he was given a room in the Department to start psychological research. However, the Senate of the University would not sponsor it until 1901 (when Rivers received an annual grant of £ 35 to purchase and upkeep equipment). The slow start of the psychology laboratory was also partly caused by the fact that in 1898 Rivers was asked to join in an anthropological expedition to Torres Strait, the part of the ocean between Australia and New Guinea, scattered with islands inhabited by 'primitive tribes'. Rivers's task was to test the then fairly unanimous assumption that savage and semi-civilised races had a higher degree of sense acuteness than Europeans, an assumption for which he could find no evidence.

Rivers's lab would be overhauled in 1912 when it was taken over by his more pro-active and richer (through his wife's family) student Charles Samuel Myers (1873–1946). As Costall (2001: 189) summarised:

> Cambridge, often held to have been a model of scientific enlightenment compared with Oxford, also presented its problems. When Myers became the Director of the new Laboratory of Experimental Psychology in 1913 [sic], this was more an honour Myers bestowed – imposed – upon Cambridge, than the reverse: 'He planned it, to a very large extent in detail he designed it, he himself, his family and his friends, mostly paid for it. With some air of reluctance the University accepted it.'

Once more the start of the renewed lab would be impeded, this time by World War I, which brought Myers to the battle grounds in France, where he treated soldiers for 'shell shock' (a term coined by him). After the war, Myers would become more interested in applied psychology, devoting most of his energy to the new National Institute of Industrial Psychology he established in London:

> On returning to Cambridge after the First World War, Myers was keen to apply psychology to medicine, industry and education. He had become 'increasing disgusted, after my very practical experience during the War, with the old academic atmosphere of conservatism and opposition to psychology' . . . When the University insisted that his Readership should be restricted to *experimental* psychology, his dissatisfaction was complete . . . Myers had already begun to make plans to found a National Institute of Industrial Psychology in London as early as 1918. His new Institute opened in 1921, and, after a year of leave from Cambridge, he resigned, once he had made sure the promised Readership would be handed on to his assistant, Frederic Bartlett.
>
> (Costall 2001: 189)

MYTH BUSTING

Did religion stop the foundation of the first laboratory of Experimental Psychology at the University of Cambridge?

At various sites on the internet you can find the claim that the first attempt to establish a psychological research centre in the UK occurred in 1877 (two years before Wundt!), when James Ward (1843–1925), after study visits to Germany, brought forward the proposal to establish a laboratory for the study of psychophysics at the University of Cambridge. The proposal was rejected by the Senate on the grounds that it 'would insult religion by putting the human soul in a pair of scales' (e.g., **www.psychol.cam.ac.uk/pages/about.html**; or **www.psychol. ucl.ac.uk/info/history.htm**). The origin of this claim seems to be Hearnshaw

(1964) and Sokal (1972), who refer to writings of Myers and Bartlett. In Sokal (1972), however, we read that:

> According to an undocumented legend often repeated, the major reason for the Senate's opposition to the proposal was a mathematician's argument that such a laboratory would 'insult religion by putting the human soul in a pair of scales.'
>
> (Sokal 1972: 145)

So, the information does not seem to be very solid. Indeed, when Whittle (2000) searched for hard evidence in the historical records he was unable to find anything. The first records he could find were requests by Ward and Venn in 1886 and 1888 for £50 and £100, urgently required for the purchase of psychophysical apparatus, presumably to subsidise Cattell. This made Whittle (2000: 25) conjecture that:

> Bartlett (1937) describes the double request, but places it nine years earlier. This has the advantage of suggesting that Cambridge could have had the world's first psychological laboratory, if only the university hadn't been so conservative.

Tongue in cheek (and referring to Bartlett's famous Schema theory, which states that human memory is rarely a literal report of the original events but a fallible reconstruction on the basis of schemas), Whittle (2000: 25) concluded that:

> I could find no discussion of anything to do with these earlier requests. It may well be lurking in sources that I have not searched, but I am left with a distinct suspicion that Myers and Bartlett were demonstrating Bartlett's later thesis on the constructive nature of memory.

There are more reasons to doubt the truth of the claim. In 1877 James Ward was a very junior member of staff (he had won a fellowship only two years earlier and would become Professor of Mental Philosophy and Logic only 20 years later). Furthermore, Ward is unlikely to have had the seed money that usually accompanied demands for new laboratories in the UK (being the impoverished son of a bankrupt merchant). So, although religion was not the strongest promoter of psychology in England, there is no reason to believe that the UK could have had the first laboratory of psychology if only its church had been less dogmatic.

Oxford

While the authorities at the University of Cambridge had to address the repeated demands of psychology to win its place in academia, the University of Oxford was given an easier time. There was just a short period of tension when its graduate, Edward Titchener, in 1892 returned from Wundt's lab with a PhD in psychology and sought a position at the university. He was given a teaching job in biology and luckily after one term got an offer from Cornell University in the United States.

The situation became more serious when one of Rivers's students, William McDougall (1871–1938), was appointed on a Readership funded by the industrialist and inventor Henry Wilde (1833–1919). The Readership had been created to support mental philosophy and for the sake of clarity the incumbent was explicitly forbidden to get sidetracked by experimental research. Still, this is what McDougall did, as is beautifully described in his autobiographical chapter, which gives us a first-hand (albeit partial) glimpse of the times:

By 1904, when the Wilde Readership in Mental Philosophy at Oxford fell vacant, I had begun to realize that I was throwing my seed on stony ground, that my work along the lines I was pursuing could not find a public. I applied for the vacant post and was appointed. The post was in many ways an ideal one for me. The small salary was a welcome addition to my small income. The duties were very light – only two lectures in each of twenty-one weeks a year; and I was at liberty to choose my topics within a very wide field, a liberty of which I took full advantage. I ranged at large over the whole field of psychology conceived in the broadest way. . . . My classes were at first small, except when I lectured on such a sensational topic as hypnotism, with demonstrations; and then my large lecture room was crowded.

But the post had its drawbacks. It was, I think, T. H. Huxley who said that, if he had to devise a punishment for a very wicked scientist, he would condemn him to be a professor of science at Oxford. If I had been recognized as a teacher of science, my punishment would have been light; for by that date science was well established in Oxford. But I was neither fish, flesh, nor fowl. I was neither a scientist nor a philosopher pur sang. I fell between two stools. The scientists suspected me of being a metaphysician; and the philosophers regarded me as representing an impossible and non-existent branch of science. Psychology had no recognized place in the curricula and examinations. For some years I was not even a member of the University; for I could not become a member without first becoming a member of some college; and a man in my position could not, without indelicacy, ask any college to accept him. Further, I was annoyed by the efforts of the founder of the Readership to dislodge me. He was an old manufacturer who had a great admiration for John Locke and a conviction that the mental life cannot be experimentally studied; and he had learned that I had been guilty of efforts along that line.

Still, some of my colleagues were kind, especially the Professor of Physiology (Gotch), who provided me with a good set of rooms in his laboratory where, as a private activity distinct from my work as University Reader, I could carry on research. In these rooms I did both experimental research and teaching, always having a small group of special students, . . .

One of the greatest pleasures of my life fell in the year 1908, namely, a short visit from William James. I had never ceased to admire him greatly; an admiration which had increased when I met him for the first time in Rome in 1906. I felt that his visit was both a great compliment to me and a new evidence of the man's profound kindliness. . . .

During the ten years at Oxford before the War, I carried on work in the laboratory continuously, publishing a few experimental papers. But much of it was unfinished at the outbreak of war and remains unpublished. Among other things I was concerned to devise a series of mental tests that should be, as far as possible, independent of language and of learning, and universally applicable. . . .

But the War came, and I found myself a private in a French army, driving an ambulance and dodging German shells on the Western Front. Early in 1915 the British War Office began to realize the extent of its task, and there was a grave shortage of medical officers. I offered myself, was made a Major in the Royal Army Medical Corps, and was put at once in charge of nervous patients. At this time there was a flood of mental and nervous cases streaming home from the armies on all fronts, and there was little preparation for dealing with them. But it soon became clear that the 'shell-shock' cases required mental treatment. I was put in a position where I could select from this vast stream whatever cases seemed most susceptible to treatment. And soon I was the head of a hospital-section full of 'shell-shock' cases, a most strange, wonderful, and pitiful collection of nervously disordered soldiers, mostly purely functional. One had little time to think out the many theoretical problems. One thing was clear – successful treatment required the exploration and fullest possible laying bare of the causes of the trouble. Hypnosis proved very useful as a method of exploration, but not always indicated or feasible. Sympathetic rapport with the patient was the main thing, not a mysterious 'transference' of a mythical 'father-fixation' of the 'libido'; but, under the circumstances, a very natural and simple human relation. . . .

During the War I had lost my laboratory, which was occupied by students of aviation problems; and after the War the rush of students to the Physiological Department made it impossible for the Department to return the rooms to me. . . .

Then came the invitation to Harvard. It was in every way a very flattering one. The Chair of Psychology at Harvard had not been filled since Münsterberg's death during the War. The tenure of it by James and Münsterberg and the great prestige of the Department of Philosophy and Psychology seemed to justify me in regarding it as the premier post in America, where psychology was so actively cultivated. . . .

(McDougall 1930: 207–12)

McDougall left Oxford for the USA in 1920 and experimental psychology would be almost absent from Oxford University until 1935, when the University received a gift of £10,000 from Mrs Hugh Watts, a student of McDougall's and a friend of the then Wilde Reader William Brown (1881–1952). The gift was to be used for the establishment of an Institute of Experimental Psychology, which resulted in a modest laboratory and a small teaching programme leading to a Diploma.

Developments in London

Foundation of University College London

There is an ongoing discussion about which university qualifies as the third of England: the University of Durham or University College London, because both applications were initiated around the same time and took several years to complete. However, as far as psychology is concerned, there is no question that the title goes to University College London (UCL). This college was founded in 1826 as a neutral (secular) alternative to Oxford and Cambridge, so that Catholics, Dissenters, Jews, non-believers and women could obtain an English degree as well. Its foundation was swiftly followed in 1831 by the establishment of King's College London as an Anglican alternative in the capital. Because the British government was unlikely to give degree-awarding powers to two small institutions in the same city, both colleges formed an official degree-awarding federation in 1836, known as the University of London.

The Grote Chair

Evidently, UCL was much more interested in the natural sciences and more open to the empirical study of the human mind. As for the latter, two elements were of particular importance for the history of psychology: the establishment of a Chair of Logic and the Philosophy of the Human Mind (i.e. a professorship in psychology) and the presence of Galton. With respect to the Chair, there were quite some problems to get it conferred, as there were major disagreements about whether it could be awarded to a minister of religion. In particular, the banker and historian George Grote (1794–1871) opposed the appointment of religion-related persons, blocking several interesting candidates. Eventually his views were overturned, but he had the final say when upon his death in 1871 he endowed £6,000 for the Chair under the explicit condition that it could not be paid to 'a man who either is or has ever been a minister of religion' (Hicks 1928). The person on the Chair at that moment was George Croom Robertson (1842–1892), a Scottish student of Alexander Bain.

Sully and the laboratory of psychology

Upon Robertson's death, the Grote Chair (as it became called) was conferred to James Sully (1842–1923). Sully, then already aged 50, was a man of independent means, who had some extra income from teaching jobs (he had replaced the ailing Robertson a few times), journalism and textbook writing. He had written books on illusions in perception and memory and a *Teacher's handbook of psychology*, in which he translated the insights from psychology to the educational context.

Sully is remembered in British history of psychology for his efforts to establish the first laboratory of psychology in the UK and for the foundation of the British Society of Psychology (see below). An opportunity to start a laboratory presented itself in 1897 when Sully was told that the German psychologist Hugo Münsterberg (1863–1916) was definitely moving to Harvard University as the successor of William James (he had been there before) and was looking for a buyer of the equipment he had collected at the University of Freiburg. Sully frantically began to lobby for space and money, for which he enlisted the help of Francis Galton, the most eminent scholar of psychology-related matters in London (Valentine 1999). Rivers, who had done teaching jobs at UCL since the early 1890s, was to be appointed as instructor. The arrangement had a set-back when Rivers became lecturer at Cambridge, but Rivers agreed to be instructor of the UCL lab as well (which comprised not much more than a single room with equipment that was used mainly for teaching), so that the UCL laboratory could open officially in 1898, a few months after the opening of Rivers's lab at Cambridge. As Table 4.2 shows, the UK was quite late in this respect.

Table 4.2 The establishment of psychology laboratories throughout the world. For each country we list the first few universities

Country	Year	University
Germany	1879	University of Leipzig (W. Wundt)
	1881	University of Göttingen (G.E. Müller)
	1886	University of Berlin (H. Ebbinghaus)
USA	1883	Johns Hopkins University (G.S. Hall)
	1887	Indiana University (W.L. Bryan)
	1887	University of Pennsylvania (J.M. Cattell)
Denmark	1886	University of Copenhagen (A. Lehmann)
Russia	1886	Kazan University (V. Bechterev)
	1895	University of St Petersburg (V. Bechterev)
Japan	1888	University of Tokyo (Y. Motora)
	1906	University of Kyoto (M. Matsumoto)

(continued)

Table 4.2 (*continued*)

Country	Year	University
	1922	Kwansei Gakuin University, Kobe (M. Imada)
Canada	1889	University of Toronto (J.M. Baldwin)
	1910	McGill University (W. Dunlop)
France	1889	Sorbonne (M. Liard and H. Beaunis)
	1896	University of Rennes (B. Bourdon)
	1906	University of Montpellier (M. Foucault)
Italy	1889	University of Rome (G. Sergi)
	1896	Reggio Emilia Hospital (G.C. Ferrari and A. Tamburini)
Belgium	1891	Ghent University (J.J. Van Biervliet)
	1892	University of Louvain/Leuven (A. Thiéry)
	1897	University of Brussels (G. Dwelshauvers)
Netherlands	1892	University of Groningen (G. Heymans)
	1907	University of Amsterdam (T. De Boer)
	1915	University of Utrecht (F. Roels)
Switzerland	1892	University of Geneva (T. Flournoy)
Austria	1894	University of Graz (A. Meinong)
Poland	1897	University of Cracow (W. Heinrich)
UK	1897	University of Cambridge (W.H. Rivers)
	1898	University College London (J. Sully)
	1901	Bedford College London (B. Edgell)
Argentina	1898	University of Buenos Aires (H. Pinero)
Brazil	1899	University of Rio de Janeiro (M. de Madeiros)
Spain	1902	University of Madrid (L. Simarro)
	1928	University of Madrid (G. Rodriguez Lafora)
	1928	University of Barcelona (E. Mira-López)
Japan	1903	Tokyo University (Y. Motora)
	1906	University of Kyoto (M. Matsumoto);
Hungary	1905	University of Budapest (P. Ranschburg)
Chile	1908	University of Chile (G. Mann)
New Zealand	1908	Victoria College (T. Hunter)
India	1915	Calcutta University (N.N. Sengupta)
Mexico	1916	Mexico National University (E. Aragon)
China	1917	University of Peking (C. Daqi and C. Yuanpei)
Finland	1922	University of Turku (E. Kaila)
Australia	1923	University of Sydney (H.T. Lovell)
Brazil	1923	Rio de Janeiro (W. Radecki)
Greece	1926	University of Athens (T. Voreas)
Sweden	1948	University of Uppsala (R. Anderberg)

The following was written about the UCL laboratory in its first annual report (as cited in Valentine 1999: 214):

> The work consisted of the experimental investigation of such points as the following:- the discovery of the spots of the skin of the fore-arm sensitive to pressure, and to hot and to cold objects respectively: the estimation of length of line by sight and by touch: the discrimination of lifted weights: the estimation of the pitch of tones: the estimation of very short time-intervals. The students themselves were the subjects of these experiments, and they appeared to be greatly interested in the researches. As Dr Rivers was unfortunately unable to continue teaching, Mr E. T. Dixon of Cambridge conducted the class during the first term of the 1898–9 session. There were seven students, two of whom were Medical graduates. The Laboratory is now located in its own room. The Committee are very desirous of purchasing additional apparatus and of securing the services of a permanent instructor. In order that this plan may be carried out, more funds are needed. . . . [The committee] are the more anxious to do this as there is reason to hope that the University of London is disposed to include the Subject of Experimental Psychology in the Schedule for the Final B.Sc. Examination.

In 1900 William McDougall was appointed to a part-time readership in Sully's department, but after four years moved to Oxford (as we have seen above).

Galton and research into individual differences

The laboratory of experimental psychology was not UCL's main contribution to early psychology, however. This came from Galton's efforts to study the heredity of features. For these studies, which often failed to yield the desired clear evidence, Galton needed statistical measures that allowed him to draw valid conclusions. As a result, Galton (who was a self-financed, independent researcher) became involved with a group of young mathematicians, the most important of who was Karl Pearson (1857–1936). After Pearson was appointed at UCL as Professor of Applied Mathematics and Mechanics in 1884, Galton became more involved in the college (although he had been educated at King's College London). The connection was further strengthened when five years later another of Galton's students, Raphael Weldon (1860–1906), was appointed as Professor of Zoology. Together the three men established the journal *Biometrika,* which would become the leading journal for the development of statistical methods in the life sciences.

Because of these developments, London has been the place where most modern statistical techniques were discovered. One of these techniques was the correlation coefficient developed by Pearson. The correlation coefficient made it possible to measure the degree to which two variables were related and whether the relationship was strong enough to be reliable. Such a coefficient was desperately needed because the data Galton gathered to research heredity turned out to be much less impressive than he had hoped. Indeed, one of the first high-profile applications of Pearson's correlation coefficient concerned the relationship between the intelligence measures advocated by Galton and everyday indications of aptitude. Wissler (1901), a student of Cattell at Columbia University, correlated the intelligence measurements Cattell had gathered with the school results and the academic grades of the participants. To everybody's dismay, Wissler observed that there was no reliable relationship between the psychological test results, the physical test results, and the mark the participants obtained in school or college (although the latter correlated with themselves to a considerable degree). Consequently, Wissler had to conclude that the intelligence measurements used by Galton, Cattell and so many others were useless to predict academic performance. Within a few months Binet wrote a French summary of Wissler's findings in *L'Année Psychologique,* adding that he had obtained similar findings, and wondering whether the lack of correlation was due to the simple tests used or to the fact that there had not been enough variability in the children tested.

UCL's standing in correlational research was further strengthened when in 1907 Charles Spearman (1863–1945; known from the Spearman correlation) was appointed as Reader. Spearman was an officer in the British army, who as a mature student had gone to study psychology under Wilhelm Wundt. By the time of his appointment at UCL, Spearman had already published articles on the rudiments of factor analysis (a statistical technique to interpret correlations between several variables; see Chapter 11) and a two-factor theory of intelligence, in which he claimed that performance on an intelligence test was influenced by a general intelligence factor and a factor specific to the test. He concluded this from the observation that children who scored low/high on one valid task of intelligence in general also scored low/high on other valid tasks, indicating that the solutions of the various tasks were affected by a single underlying factor, which Spearman called 'general intelligence'. In 1911 Spearman was promoted to the Grote Professorship and steered the UCL Psychology Department firmly into the study of individual differences based on correlational research, a topic for which the Department would remain renowned for decades to come. Ironically, the relationship between Spearman and Pearson never was amicable.

Scotland

Scotland, with its four universities, had its own dynamism. Two figures above all had an influence on the developments of psychology in the UK: Alexander Bain and G.F. Stout.

Bain

We met Alexander Bain (1818–1903) in Chapter 3, when we discussed his textbooks. Bain was a philosopher and educationalist at the University of Aberdeen with a strong interest in biology and experimental research. He not only provided the template of the psychology handbooks to be written. After prolonged stays in London between 1848 and 1860, during which he was in close contact with John Stuart Mill and George Grote, he was also often consulted about psychology-related matters in the UK.

Bain further took an initiative that would provide nineteenth-century English-speaking psychologists and philosophers of mind with a research outlet in their own language. Together with George Croom Robertson he launched the journal *Mind,* the first issue of which appeared in 1876. This issue contained the following articles, among others:

- 'The comparative psychology of man' (by Herbert Spencer)
- 'Physiological psychology in Germany' (by James Sully)
- 'Consistency and real inference' (by John Venn).

The second issue included an article by Wundt ('Central innervation and consciousness'); the third issue had an article by Helmholtz ('The origin and meaning of geometrical axioms'). In the fourth issue James Ward published his article on the interpretation of Fechner's law, which would be important for his appointment at Cambridge, and so on.

A particularly interesting article, whose impact would become clear only much later, was published in 1887 by Joseph Jacobs, a student of Galton's who would move to New York and become a well-known folklore researcher (Fine 1987). Jacobs started from the observation that everyone can repeat the name *Bo* after hearing it once, whereas few could catch the name of the then Greek statesman M. *Papamichalopoulos* without the need for repetition. This made Jacobs wonder how many spoken items people could repeat. First he used nonsense syllables like cral – forg – mul – tal – nop, but soon came to prefer letters and digits. He noticed that schoolgirls could repeat on average 6.1 nonsense syllables, 7.3 letters and 9.3 digits, and that performance increased with age: girls of 11–12 years could repeat 5.3 nonsense syllables, whereas girls of 19–20 years could repeat 7 such syllables. Furthermore, the scores of the children in the top half of the class were higher than those of the children in the lower half. Jacobs (1887: 78) described how the relationship with intelligence was tested further:

> The only difficulty is the very small extent of variability: in order to get a wider range, and also to test the obvious deduction to be made from these figures, it was suggested by Mr. Francis Galton that experiments should be tried on idiots, and he kindly undertook the inquiry in conjunction with Prof. Bain and Mr. Sully. The detailed results are given below. At Earlswood the average span was as low as 4, and much the same at Darenth. 'Idiots' differ so much as to make it, indeed, hardly possible to speak of average results; but it appears that few, if any, attain to the normal span, and that a good number of those who can 'speak' at all are unable to reproduce more than 2 numerals.

At last, there was a simple task that made a clear difference between individuals of high and low intelligence! One of the persons, who read Jacobs' article, was Alfred Binet, who referred to it in an early paper but surprisingly not in his articles together with Simon on the intelligence test, even though the intelligence test relied on memory span testing to a considerable degree (see Table 4.1).

Stout

A second figure of importance in early Scottish psychology was George Frederick Stout (1860–1944), better known as G.F. Stout. He studied at Cambridge with James Ward, where he became a Fellow of St John's College (1884–1896) and wrote the first edition of his high-impact book *Analytic psychology*. In 1896 the University of Aberdeen appointed him to a new lectureship in Comparative Psychology. In 1903 Stout moved to St Andrews as Professor of Logic and Metaphysics, where he stayed until his retirement in 1936. In this period he published several editions of the *Manual of psychology* (first published in 1898), which would be a standard textbook for generations of students taking psychology courses in the UK. Stout was also editor of *Mind* from 1891 to 1920. Like many of his contemporaries, he was more a philosopher than an empirical psychologist. Only after 1926 was the term 'experimental psychology' included in the *Manual* under the instigation of a new collaborator at St Andrews, and apparently not much to Stout's excitement.

Psychological societies

Because so much science in the UK took place outside universities, British scholars had a tendency to found a Learned Society as soon as the interest was strong enough (see also Chapter 2). These Societies had regular meetings and usually published some kind of journal or proceedings to disseminate their findings. The same happened to psychology.

The Psychological Society of Great Britain

As early as 1875 a Psychological Society of Great Britain was set up by the aging lawyer, publisher and politician Edward William Cox (1809–1879). In line with the prevailing interests, the society was not centred on investigations of ordinary human functioning but on research about the powers and virtues of extraordinary phenomena such as hypnotism, spiritualism and other paranormal events (Richards 2001). In particular, spiritualism was high on Cox's agenda. Spiritualism refers to the belief that the spirits of the dead can be contacted by mediums. The movement started in the USA in 1848 when two young adolescent girls began to hear rapping sounds which they believed to be messages from the deceased. Their case was investigated by the Quaker abolitionists, who decided it was genuine. The girls were taken to lecture halls and private meetings, and from there the enthusiasm rapidly spread across America and the rest of the English-speaking world.

The Psychological Society of Great Britain was not completely confined to spiritualism, however. Members also discussed topics such as memory, sleep, the hereditary transmission of endowments and qualities, and character expressed in handwriting (Richards 2001: 37). After four years of existence, the meetings ended when Cox died in 1879.

The British Psychological Society

A new attempt to invigorate British psychology was made by James Sully in 1901 when he convened a group of ten academics, intellectuals and educationalists at UCL to start a Psychological Society (in 1906 changed into the British Psychological Society), which still exists. Among the ten were W.H.R. Rivers and William McDougall. Wary about the strong pull to paranormal phenomena for such a society and the implications this would have for the status of the fledging psychological laboratories at British universities, strong entrance criteria were imposed (Lovie 2001). Only those who were recognised teachers in some branch of psychology or who had published work of recognisable value were eligible to become members. To further increase the standing of the Society, letters of invitation were sent to all scholars in the UK who fitted the criteria. Among those who accepted were James Ward and G.F. Stout. Galton refused, but could be tempted in 1905 when he was offered an Honorary Fellowship.

Table 4.3 includes some of the papers read at the first meetings of the Society. They clearly illustrate the scientific ambitions of the Society. Another interesting

spiritualism

belief that the spirits of the dead can be contacted by mediums; flourished in English-speaking countries at the end of the nineteenth and the beginning of the twentieth century

Table 4.3 Some of the papers read at the British Psychological Society. From 1910, the first papers on Freud and psychoanalysis started to appear

Year	Paper read at the British Psychological Society
1902	'The evolution of laughter'
	'Fechner's paradoxical experiment'
	'Pathological changes in immediate memory and association'
	'Psychophysical parallelism'

Table 4.3 (*continued*)

Year	Paper read at the British Psychological Society
1903	'Bilateral cortical lesion, causing deafness and aphasia'
	'Various types of insanity'
	'The functions of the frontal lobes'
1904	'Subconsciousness'
	'Bearing of modern experimental work on the problem of the unity of the mind'
	'Theories of consonance and dissonance'
	'Visual acuity in different races of man'
	'The illusion of horizontal and vertical lines with momentary and prolonged exposure'
1905	'The brain of the chimpanzee Sally'
	'Relation of intelligence to instinct and to rational thought'
	'The rhythmical sense of primitive people'
1906	'The fundamental forms of mental interaction'
1907	'A suggested physiological basis for the distinction between sensation and revived image'
	'Some points of psychosocial interest suggested by a case of experimental nerve division'
1909	'On the grouping of afferent impulses in the spinal cord'
	'The influence of alcohol on muscular and mental efficiency'
	'Observations on contrast in smoothly graded disks'
	'Character'
	'An objective study of mathematical intelligence'
	'Statistical methods'
1910	'Instinct and intelligence'
	'The nature and development of attention'
	'The aesthetic appreciation of simple colour combinations'
	'The psychology of Freud and his school'
	'A possible factor in the monocular appreciation of spatial depth'
	'The calculation of correlations'
1913	'Are intensity differences of sensation quantitative?'
	'Can there be anything obscure or implicit in a mental state?'
	'An analysis of some personal dreams, with special reference to Freud's interpretation'
	'The psychological system of Sigmund Freud, as set forth in Chapter VII of *Traumdeutung*'
	'Wonder, fascination and curiosity'

Source: Edgell (1947).

observation is that Freud's psychoanalysis started to appear in 1910 and would rapidly expand. A catalyst in this respect was the handling of shell-shock cases in World War I. Those involved in the treatment all received a training that was heavily inspired by psychoanalysis.

A conundrum for the Society was how to reconcile its entrance requirements with the need to have sufficient members. The initial conditions made it impossible to attract many members, given the paucity of psychological research laboratories in the UK. Therefore, at the end of World War I Charles Myers tried to have the criteria relaxed, so that scholars working on psychology-related topics in medicine, industry and education could join as well (recall that around this time Myers founded his own company and was thinking of leaving Cambridge). After a few attempts he managed to get his proposals approved by the members. The outcome was an explosion of the number of members in 1919 from fewer than 100 to more than 400 (partly due to Myers's network of connections built during the war). The number of publications of the Society also increased. Previously the Society only published the *British Journal of Psychology,* which had been initiated by Ward and Rivers in 1904 and had been acquired by the Society when Charles Myers became editor in 1914.

Interim summary

- Psychology had a hard time becoming an academic discipline in the UK. This largely had to do with the fact that the universities did not encourage the new discipline. Although there is no evidence for active opposition, every bit of progress required substantial effort.

- In England James Sully from University College London was the driving force, although the University of Cambridge managed to have the first laboratory of experimental psychology under the direction of W.H.R. Rivers. Another main source of inspiration was Galton's work on individual differences.

- In Scotland the most active college was the University of Aberdeen where Alexander Bain was professor and G.F. Stout got his first appointment as lecturer.

- To fill the void left by universities, intellectuals interested in psychology twice founded a Learned Society. The first attempt collapsed with the death of the initiator; the second one, started by Sully at UCL, was more successful and still exists today.

- The UK also had some impact because it was home to two early journals of psychology: *Mind* and the *British Journal of Psychology,* both of which still exist.

4.6 *Focus on:* What about the five schools of psychology?

Maybe you took an introductory psychology course before you started reading this book. In that case, you may have wondered why in the present chapter we did not use the classical division of early psychology into five schools: structuralism, functionalism, Gestalt psychology, behaviourism and psychoanalysis. After all, isn't it received wisdom that psychology started with structuralism in Wundt's laboratory, which was brought to America by Titchener, where it had to fight first against functionalism and later against behaviourism, while it remained unchallenged in Europe until the rise of the Gestalt psychology? Meanwhile, psychoanalysis steadily grew as a kind of a non-scientific 'outsider'.

To be honest, this was very much the organisation we had in mind before we started to research the present chapter. Gradually, however, we realised that if you look at the original materials, such as the articles published in journals or the papers read at meetings (e.g. Table 4.3), there are surprisingly few traces of the supposedly heroic fights between the schools. Most of the time, the articles and the talks dealt with concrete topics that were tackled with a variety of research methods. Also, there was much more applied research than acknowledged by the five-schools view.

Further research revealed how the picture of the five big, quarrelling schools gradually emerged in the introductory and history books of the first half of the twentieth century. The term 'school of thought' was commonly used in philosophical writings to refer to famous thinkers and their disciples. Occasionally the term also referred to places where a few high-impact thinkers either collaborated or succeeded each other rapidly. The first psychologists, often educated as philosophers, took over this practice. So, you find several references to schools in James's *Principles of psychology*. He writes about Charcot's school, the analytic school of psychology, the school of Herbart in Germany, the Lockian school, the empirical school, the modern dualistic or spiritualistic or common-sense school, the Scotch school, the transcendentalist school, and so on.

Over time the number of schools diminished as the impact of the original thinkers shrank, until only two names were left around the beginning of the twentieth century: the structuralist school vs. the functionalist school. This had partly to do with the discussions between Titchener and James, with the question to what extent psychology had to be fundamental or applied, with the fact that Titchener claimed to be Wundt's true heir in America (Zehr 2000), with the fact that the most influential historian of early times, Edwin Boring (1886–1968), was a student of Titchener, and with the way in which Watson (1913) depicted the existing situation when he tried to convert psychology to behaviourism (Chapter 5).

A further bias in early history writing was that most authors were academics who looked down upon applied research (Cerullo 1988). This was certainly the case for Boring, the man with the unfortunate family name who wrote the extremely popular book *A history of experimental psychology* (1st edition 1929; 2nd revised edition 1950). Although the title explicitly referred to fundamental, academic psychology, the story depicted in the book was rapidly generalised to the entire field of psychology. It also introduced a Hegelian approach to the history of psychology. According to the philosopher Georg Hegel (1770–1831), thinking consists of three stages: first you have a thesis (a proposition), then an antithesis (a reaction against the proposition), followed by a synthesis (a compromise between the thesis and the antithesis). Boring believed in controversy as the driving force of science and, therefore, he tended to magnify existing discussions to true fights between schools involving a string of theses and antitheses (structure vs. function, elements vs. gestalts, introspection vs. behaviourist experimentation, consciousness vs. unconscious drives). This approach had the advantage that Boring (and many history teachers after him) could position himself as the great conciliator, the synthesis-maker.

According to Costall (2006), the Hegelian approach is part of the reason why current textbooks still love to refer to the five basic schools of psychology. Indeed, there is an almost irresistible Hegelian sequence that can be used to 'summarise' the history of psychology. It looks as follows:

1. *Thesis*: psychology, as instituted in the universities, began as the study of mind, based, almost exclusively, on the unreliable method of introspection (structuralism, functionalism, Gestalt psychology).

2. *Antithesis*: in reaction to the blatant unreliability of the introspective method, behaviourism then redefined psychology as the study of behaviour, based primarily on the objective method of experimentation (see Chapter 5).

3. *Synthesis*: in reaction to the limited research agenda and the theoretical bankruptcy of behaviourism, the 'cognitive revolution', in turn, restored the mind as the proper subject of psychology (but now with the benefit of the rigorous experimental methods developed within behaviourism).

What is often overlooked is that such sequences tremendously simplify the past. Richards (2009: 219) made the following attempt to summarise early British psychology in terms of schools:

> *Cambridge School*. Usually used to refer to the main group of psychologists based in Cambridge University during the 1900–40 period. These included C.S. Myers, W.H.R. Rivers and F. Bartlett. The major difference from the *London School* . . . is seen as being less interest [sic] in psychometrics and statistics, as well as a greater concern with social and applied issues. The Cambridge School is routinely juxtaposed with the London School as representing the poles of early twentieth-century English academic Psychological thought, although this grossly distorts the picture since Manchester, Liverpool, Reading, and possibly Bristol, schools could also be identified. The Scottish universities were also pursuing their own agendas to some extent but are rarely referred to as 'schools'. . . .

Ironically, the danger of misinterpreting the term 'schools' was addressed by another influential American author, Robert Sessions Woodworth (1869–1962), who contributed much to their popularity by publishing a much-used textbook (eight editions) entitled *Contemporary schools of psychology*. This book described the various existing schools, as seen by Woodworth, and dealt with functional and structural psychology, associationism old and new, behaviourism, Gestalt psychology, psychoanalysis and related schools, and hormic and holistic psychologies (notice that Woodworth still made more distinctions than the traditional five schools). Then suddenly, at the end of the book, there is the following afterthought:

> In view of all the divergent movements that we have surveyed, all these 'warring schools' of contemporary psychology, the reader may easily carry away the impression that we psychologists are anything but a harmonious body of scientific workers. Looked at from outside, our fraternity has seemed to be a house divided against itself . . . You would get a very different impression from attending one of the International Congresses of Psychology or a meeting of one of the national societies such as the American Psychological Association. You would hear papers read on various psychological topics, with very little mention of any of the schools and with discussions of the usual scientific type, free from acrimony though not of course from the give and take of doubt and criticism . . .
>
> Another reason for the continued unity of psychology is found in the fact that only a minority of psychologists have become active adherents of any of the schools. Some may lean toward one school and some toward another, but on the whole the psychologists of the present time are proceeding on their way in the middle of the road.

So, the division of early psychology into five competing schools looks more like a projection of twentieth-century authors onto early psychology rather than a true depiction of what really happened in the various countries. Therefore, we decided not to use this framework for the organisation of our chapter.

Interim summary

- The beginnings of psychology are often depicted by making a distinction between five quarrelling schools (structuralism, functionalism, Gestalt psychology, behaviourism and psychoanalysis).
- However, a look at the original sources does not warrant this view as a summary of the core developments within psychology. It rather seems to be a re-interpretation of the original meaning of the philosophical term 'school', in order to depict the history of psychology in simplifying theses, antitheses and syntheses.

? What do you think?

Would you describe your lecturers as belonging to different 'schools'? What do you think of the following opinion by a present-day popular textbook writer who was asked about the recent developments in psychology?

How has the field of psychological science changed since I wrote the first edition of my introductory text back in the late 1980s? The first thing that stands out to me is that we have seen a revival of 'schools of thought' or theoretical perspectives that inspire passion in their advocates. When I wrote my overview of the history of psychology for the first edition of my text, it ended with the cognitive revolution, a development that was followed by 20–25 years of theoretical stagnation. Since that first edition, however, I have felt compelled to add coverage of the rise of cross-cultural psychology, evolutionary psychology, and positive psychology. Each of these emerging theoretical perspectives could be characterized as somewhat rebellious movements with zealous champions that have called for profound changes in the field's focus and research priorities. I think that all three of these perspectives have had a refreshing and nourishing impact on psychology

(Weiten 2010; in *APS Observer*, 23, issue 4).

Recommended literature

Original sources

Many of the early writings that have been described in this chapter are freely available on the internet (use a search engine!). The best site to start with is **psychclassics. yorku.ca**, from which we quoted extensively.

If you speak German, Projekt Gutenberg – DE is another good place (**http://gutenberg.spiegel.de/**)

If you speak French, you certainly must have a look at the first issues of *L'Année Psychologique*, the journal Binet founded and in which he published his first intelligence test with Simon: (**http://www.persee.fr/web/revues/ home/prescript/revue/psy**)

An increasing number of early books have also become fully available at Google Books (**www.books.google.com**)

Textbooks

As for textbooks, there are many good books on the history of psychology, which are much more detailed than that covered here. To have good coverage of the early attempts to establish psychology as an academic discipline (rather than a long introduction to the philosophical antecedents), look for books with the words 'history' and 'modern psychology' in the title. Another good read still is Boring's *History of experimental psychology* (either the 1929 or 1950 edition). For the British situation, a good introduction is provided by the various chapters in Bunn, Lovie and Richards (eds) (2001) *Psychology in Britain* (Leicester: BPS Books). Most countries have their own history book(s), which may be worthwhile tracing if you are not from the UK.

References

Abma, R. (2004) 'Madness and mental health.' In J. Jansz and P. van Drunen (eds) *A social history of psychology*. Oxford: Blackwell, pp. 93–128.

Binet, A. (1904) 'A propos de la mesure de l'intelligence', *L'Année Psychologique*, **11**: 69–82 (available at www.persee.fr/web/revues/home/prescript/revue/psy).

Binet, A. & Simon, T. (1904a) 'Sur la nécessité d'établir un diagnostic scientifique des états inférieurs de l'intelligence', *L'Année Psychologique*, **11**: 163–90 (available at www.persee.fr/web/revues/ home/prescript/revue/psy).

Binet, A. & Simon, T. (1904b) 'Méthodes nouvelles pour le diagnostic du niveau intellectuel des anormaux', *L'Année Psychologique*, **11**: 191–244 (available at www.persee.fr/web/revues/ home/prescript/revue/psy).

Binet, A. & Simon, T. (1904c) 'Application des méthodes nouvelles au diagnostic du niveau intellectuel chez des enfants normaux en anormaux d'hospice et d'école primaire', *L'Année Psychologique*, **11**: 245–336 (available at www.persee.fr/web/revues/ home/prescript/revue/psy).

Binet, A. & Simon, T. (1907) 'Le développement de l'intelligence chez les enfants', *L'Année Psychologique*, **14**: 1–94 (available at www .persee.fr/web/revues/home/prescript/revue/psy).

Boring, E.G. (1950) *A history of experimental psychology* (2nd edn). New York: Appleton-Century-Crofts.

Cattell, J.M. (1888) 'The psychological laboratory at Leipsic', *Mind*, **13**: 37–51 (at psychclassics.yorku.ca).

Cerullo, J.J. (1988) 'E.G. Boring: Reflections on a discipline builder', *The American Journal of Psychology*, **101**: 561–75.

Collini, S. (1998) *Introduction to C.P. Snow's The two cultures*. Cambridge: Cambridge University Press.

Costall, A. (2001) 'Pear and his peers'. In G.C. Bunn, A.D. Lovie & G.D. Richards (eds) *Psychology in Britain*. Leicester: BPS Books, pp. 188–204.

Costall, A. (2006) '"Introspectionism" and the mythical origins of scientific psychology', *Consciousness and Cognition*, **15**: 634–54.

Delboeuf, J.R.L. (1873) *Etude psychophysique: recherches théoriques et expérimentales sur la mesure des sensations et spécialement des sensations de lumière et de fatigue*. Bruxelles: l'Académie Royale de sciences, des lettres et des beaux-arts de Belgique.

Donders, F.C. (1868) 'Over de snelheid van psychische processen': Translated by Koster, W.G. (1968). 'On the speed of mental processes', *Acta Psychologica*, **30**: 412–31.

Edgell, B. (1947) 'The British Psychological Society', *British Journal of Psychology*, **37**: 113–32 (reprinted in 2001, *British Journal of Psychology*, **92**: 3–22).

Fancher, R.E. (1996) *Pioneers of psychology* (3rd edn). New York: Norton & Company.

Fechner, G.T. (1860) *Elemente der Psychophysik*. Leipzig: Breitkopf & Härtel.

Fine, G.A. (1987) 'Joseph Jacobs: A sociological folklorist', *Folklore*, **98**: 183–93.

Foucault, M. (1961/2006) *The history of madness*. Oxford: Routledge (original title: *Folie et déraison. Histoire de la folie à l'âge classique*. Paris: Librairie Plon).

Freud, S. (1900/1913) *The interpretation of dreams* (English translation by A.A. Brill). New York: Macmillan (at psychclassics.yorku.ca).

Fuchs, A.H. (2000) 'Teaching the introductory course in psychology circa 1900', *American Psychologist*, **55**: 492–5.

Griffith, C.R. (1921) 'Some neglected aspects of a history of psychology', *Psychological Monographs*, **30**: 17–29 (available at psychclassics.yorku.ca).

Guillin, V. (2004) 'Théodule Ribot's ambiguous positivism: Philosophical and epistemological strategies in the founding of French scientific psychology', *Journal of the History of the Behavioral Sciences*, **40**: 165–81.

Hearnshaw, L. (1964) *A short history of British psychology, 1840–1948*. London: Methuen.

Hicks, G.D. (1928) 'A century of philosophy at University College, London', *Journal of Philosophical Studies*, **3**: 468–82.

Jacobs, J. (1887) 'Experiments on "Prehension"', *Mind*, **12**: 75–9.

Jahoda, G. (2007) *A history of social psychology*. Cambridge: Cambridge University Press.

James, W. (1890) *The principles of psychology* (2 vols). New York: Henry Holt (at psychclassics.yorku.ca).

Leahey, T.H. (2004) *A history of psychology* (6th edn). Upper Saddle River, NJ: Pearson Prentice Hall.

Liebig, J. von (1863) *Ueber Francis Bacon von Verulam und die Methode der Naturforschung*. Munich.

Lovie, S. (2001) 'Three steps to heaven: How the British Psychological Society attained its place in the sun'. In G.C. Bunn, A.D. Lovie & G.D. Richards (eds) *Psychology in Britain*. Leicester: BPS Books, pp. 95–114.

Mandler, G. (2007) *A history of modern experimental psychology*. Cambridge, MA: MIT Press.

McDougall, W. (1930) *William McDougall*. In C. Murchison (ed.) *A History of Psychology in Autobiography*, Vol. 1 (pp. 191–223). Worcester, MA: Clark University Press.

Nicolas, S. (2004) *L'hypnose: L'école de la Salpêtrière face à l'école de Nancy*. Paris: L'Harmattan.

Nicolas, S. & Ferrand, L. (1999) 'Wundt's laboratory at Leipzig in 1891', *History of Psychology*, 2: 194–203.

Nicolas, S. & Ferrand, L. (2011) 'La psychologie cognitive d'Alfred Binet', *L'Année Psychologique*, **111**: 87–116.

Pickren, W.E. & Rutherford, A. (2010) *A history of modern psychology in context*. Hoboken, NJ: John Wiley & Sons.

Pomerantaz, J.R. and Kubovy, M. (1986) 'Theoretical approaches in organization', in Boff, J.P. Kaufman, L. and Thomas, J.P. (eds) *Handbook of perception and human performance*. New York, NY: Wiley.

Porter, R. (2006) 'Medical science'. In R. Porter (ed.), *The Cambridge history of medicine*. Cambridge: Cambridge University Press.

Ribot, T.A. (1870) *La psychologie anglaise contemporaine*. Paris: Librairie philosophique de Ladrange.

Richards, G. (2001) 'Edward Cox, the Psychological Society of Great Britain (1875–1879) and the meaning of institutional failure'. In G.C. Bunn, A.D. Lovie & G.D. Richards (eds) *Psychology in Britain*. Leicester: BPS Books, pp. 33–53.

Richards, G. (2009) *Psychology: The key concepts*. London: Routledge.

Rosenthal, R. (1963) 'On the social psychology of the psychological experiment: The experimenter's hypothesis as unintended determinant of experimental results', *American Scientist*, **51**: 268–83.

Rosenthal, R. (1966) *Experimenter effects in behavioral research*. New York: AppletonCentury-Crofts.

Rust, J. (2008) First psychometric laboratory: Cambridge 1886–1889. At www.psychometrics.ppsis.cam.ac.uk/page/217/first-psychometric-laboratory.htm.

Shorter, E. (1997) *A history of psychiatry: from the era of the asylum to the age of Prozac*. Malden, MA: John Wiley & Sons.

Sokal, M.M. (1972) 'Psychology at Victorian Cambridge – The unofficial laboratory of 1887–1888', *Proceedings of the American Philosophical Society*, **116**: 145–7.

Sokal, M.M. (1981) *An education in psychology: James McKeen Cattell's Journal and Letters from Germany and England, 1880–1888*. Cambridge, MA: MIT Press.

Valentine, E.R. (1999) 'The founding of the psychological laboratory, University College London: "Dear Galton . . . Yours truly, J Sully"', *History of Psychology*, 2: 204–18.

Watson, J.B. (1913) 'Psychology as the behaviorist views it', *Psychological Review*, 20: 158–77.

Weiten, W. (2010) Interview. *APS Observers,* **23**(4).

Whittle, P. (2000) 'W.H.R. Rivers and the early history of psychology at Cambridge'. In A. Saito (ed.) *Bartlett, culture and cognition*. Hove, UK: Psychology Press, pp. 21–35.

Wissler, C. (1901) 'The correlation of mental and physical tests', *Psychological Review Monograph Supplements*, 3(6).

Wolf, T.H. (1964) 'Alfred Binet: A time of crisis', *American Psychologist,* 19: 762–71.

Wolff, G. (1732) *Psychologia empirica*. Frankfurt-Leipzig.

Wundt, W.M. (1896/1897) *Outlines of psychology* (English translation by C.H. Judd). Leipzig: Wilhelm Engelmann (at psychclassics.yorku.ca).

Zehr, D. (2000) 'Portrayals of Wundt and Titchener in introductory psychology texts: a content analysis', *Teaching of Psychology*, **27**: 122–5.

5 Strengthening the scientific standing of psychology
Behaviourism and cognitive psychology

This chapter will cover ...

Questions to consider

?

Historical issues addressed in this chapter

- When did psychology as an independent discipline start in the USA?
- What did people expect from psychology around that time?
- When did behaviourism start?
- Why was Watson's influence limited? Who succeeded him?
- When did cognitive psychology start? What were key events in its initial development?

Conceptual issues addressed in this chapter

- Why did the centre of gravity in psychological research shift from Europe to the USA?
- In what ways is psychological research influenced by the wider society in which it occurs?
- To what extent was original psychological research inspired by eugenics?
- To what extent was the 'new psychology' a break with the past?
- How did animal research inspire psychologists?
- What did behaviourists see as the essential elements of scientific research?
- What inspired psychologists to include cognitions in their research?
- In what ways has the history of psychology been influenced by the invention of the computer?
- What were the specific features of cognitive psychology?
- How revolutionary were the transitions to behaviourism and cognitive psychology?

Introduction

> It is appropriate to begin the history of modern psychology in 1892 because in that year the American Psychological Association (APA) was founded. Our attention from now on will be fixed on American psychology, for although Germany granted the earliest degrees in psychology, it was in America that psychology became a profession . . . for better or worse, modern psychology is primarily American psychology. American movements and theories have been adopted overseas – so much so that a 1980 German text in social psychology was filled with American references and made no mention of Wundt or Völkerpsychologie.
>
> (Leahey 2004: 330)

In this chapter we discuss the efforts made by the academic psychological laboratories to become recognised as scientific laboratories, with the same status as other science laboratories. Because this struggle was particularly outspoken in the USA and because the USA began to rule the discipline in the twentieth century, we limit our discussion to this nation. While Europe was crippled by two devastating wars, the USA became an economic superpower that in addition invested heavily in all types of science. This does not mean that nothing relevant to psychology happened in other parts of the world, but for the present chapter these developments were rather marginal.

US dominance was not only due to the sheer amount of research done, but also to the high quality of the textbooks produced. In Chapter 4 we saw how James's *Principles* eclipsed Wundt's psychology books (available in English through translations) because of its clarity and accessibility. Very much the same was true of the later textbooks. One particularly successful author in the early years was Robert S. Woodworth, who sold over 400,000 copies of his introductory text *Psychology* between 1922 and 1939 and who in 1938 published a most authoritative book, *Experimental psychology*, reviewing the complete literature of laboratory research on topics ranging from psychophysics to the psychology of thinking (Benjafield 2005). Increasingly, lecturers throughout the world either used these books in their courses or relied on them to write their own syllabuses. Therefore, in the twentieth century the history of psychology became very much the American history of psychology.

? What do you think?

Because of the dominance of the English language in the textbook market, it may be argued that the European history of psychology is largely the history as seen from the Anglo-Saxon part of the world. Do you agree? Which other sources do you have at your disposal to learn about the history of psychology (or the history of science for that matter)?

As will become clear, however, not all was benevolent for the psychology researchers in the USA. In the first two parts of this chapter we discuss the developments that culminated in behaviourism; in the third part we look at the changes that resulted in the rise of cognitive psychology.

5.1 The perception of psychology in the USA at the beginning of the twentieth century

The expansion of psychology around the start of the twentieth century

In Chapter 4 we talked about the creation of psychology laboratories and what a success this was in the USA. By 1900 there were already 41 of them. This can be contrasted to the situation in the UK, where only a handful of professorships of psychology were created before World War II.

According to Benjamin (2000), the psychology laboratories were part of the 100-year American love affair with science and technology, starting around the mid-1800s. In that period the USA turned from a land of isolated groups of rural settlers into a nation-state dominated by large cities with extensive communications and exchanges (in 1880 only 25 per cent of the population lived in cities; by 1900, 40 per cent did so). Psychology profited from these developments.

As well as the laboratories, in 1892 the American Psychological Association (APA) was founded, giving psychology researchers a forum to meet and discuss their findings, and two journals were established that would dominate the field and that still exist today. In 1887, G. Stanley Hall founded the *American Journal of Psychology*, and in 1894, J.M. Baldwin and J. McKeen Cattell started the *Psychological Review*.

The first American psychology: functionalism

As psychology in the USA expanded, it got moulded by the expectations and preoccupations of American society. One of these inputs was a strong interest in Darwin's evolutionary theory (Green 2009). This interest was partly inherited from the UK, but also appealed directly to the American citizens because of their struggle to establish a new nation. 'Survival of the fittest' had a very personal touch for many immigrants.

Natural selection involved two elements: inheritance and adaptation to the environment. As for the inheritance part, the USA was one of the first countries where eugenics had a strong impact. Eugenics is a social philosophy claiming that the fate of a nation can be improved by selective breeding of its inhabitants. It started with Galton, who saw this as a logical consequence of Darwin's evolutionary theory. However, whereas Galton predominantly preached positive eugenics (improve society by encouraging people with desirable features to have more children), others after him diverged towards negative eugenics (improve society by preventing people with undesirable features from entering the country and/or having children). Several US states adopted legislation aimed at preventing marriage or at compulsory sterilisation of certain individuals (e.g. mentally retarded people). For instance, in 1913, Iowa supported the establishment of sterilisation laws aimed at 'the prevention of the procreation of criminals, rapists, idiots, feeble minded, imbeciles, lunatics, drunkards, drug fiends, epileptics, syphilitics, moral and sexual perverts, and diseased and degenerate persons' (as cited in Jansz & Van Drunen 2004: 28).

eugenics
social philosophy claiming that the fate of a nation can be improved by selective breeding of the inhabitants

At the same time, the Americans believed in the importance of the environment. Being a country of immigrants, they were convinced that human characteristics and achievements were not solely due to inheritance but depended on the environment as well. Among other things, this meant that one could change and control human actions for the better, a conviction that was shared by the dominant Protestant religion.

Finally, there was mistrust of intellectualism, knowledge for the sake of knowledge. America was a nation of common-sense businessmen, not interested in abstract science (which was left to Europe), but in practical accomplishments that at the same time made money, revealed God's glory, and advanced the American dream. Or as Richards (1996: 27) phrased it:

> Psychological expertise would enable [the Americans] to educate the young efficiently, diagnose and deal with harmful deviancy and pathology, inform their policies towards, and treatment of, various social groups and subject populations, and enable them to direct those they governed into the most fitting walks of life, as well as improving industrial efficiency by a better understanding of phenomena such as fatigue and attention.

If psychology were to prosper, it had to subscribe to American values, which it readily did (except for Titchener). In Chapter 4 we saw how an increasing number of American psychologists started to call themselves functionalists and to take distance from the European tradition, which they identified with the introspective study of consciousness and structuralism. As Sokal (2006) concluded, the Americans interested in becoming psychologists made the trek to Germany less to learn about psychological ideas and more to acquire the prestige of a European degree, to gain professional credentials, and to receive practical instruction in the use of instruments.

Part of the attraction of the functionalist approach to the Americans was also that Wundt's experimental research programme on the basis of reaction times ran into problems in the 1880s (Green 2009). When Wundt started his laboratory in 1879, it was centred on mental chronometry (Chapters 3 and 4). Wundt had continued the work of Donders on response times in simple reaction tasks and extended Donders's theory from three stages (simple reaction, input selection, output selection) to five (Robinson 2001). Wundt assumed that the durations of the stages were fixed (as was the case in physics and physiology) and could be determined by precise measurement. However, even though the research was based on highly motivated participants (his PhD students and himself), there were large individual differences in the estimates, making it impossible to derive a scientific law from them. Arguably this is one of the reasons why Wundt, in his later years, turned to introspection and the historical method (Chapter 4). The Americans, however, saw the differences between the participants as evidence for Darwin's theory. Rather than a nuisance, the individual differences pointed to inherited variability.

Psychology and its position within universities

The above description about the establishment of psychological laboratories and the turn to functionalism is the story you find in the history books of psychology up to the 1980s. It is part of the celebratory narrative, the tale of how scientific psychology conquered the world. At the same time, however, it is very self-centred, the view seen from within psychology. From the outside, psychology's fate looked less glamorous, certainly in the early decades.

For a start, most psychology laboratories were set up within philosophical and theological institutes. Saying that the other members of staff always greeted the newcomers with enthusiasm and generosity would be stretching the truth, as has been described endearingly by Benjamin (2000). He recounted the experiences of Harry Kirke Wolfe who tried to establish his own laboratory at the University of Nebraska. Wolfe received a doctorate with Wundt in 1886 and started his laboratory at Nebraska in 1889 with very minimal equipment that he built himself, borrowed from other departments, or purchased using funds from his library book budget. The next year he applied for $500 to further equip the laboratory. In the application he used phrases like: 'I cannot emphasize too strongly the necessity of providing some facilities for experimental work . . . It is possible to build up an experimental dept. in Psychology with little outlay . . . No field of scientific research offers such excellent opportunities for original work; chiefly because the soil is new' (as cited in Benjamin 2000: 320–1).

Unfortunately, Wolfe did not get his money, so he had to spend even more of his book budget. The year after, Wolfe applied again using stronger appeals and drawing links between psychology and agricultural sciences (a stronghold at Nebraska), alas to no avail. All he got was a written warning about spending book money for other purposes! (Still, this reception did not stop Nebraska from being listed as the fifth university in the USA to found its own laboratory of experimental psychology.)

On other occasions experimental psychologists were told not to stray too far from good old psychology as developed in philosophical writings. In 1894, the president of Princeton University urged psychologists attending a meeting of the American Psychological Association to retain the close ties that psychology had with philosophy and to not let psychology fall 'to the level of a mere science' (as cited in Fuchs 2000: 492). Similarly, George Trumbull Ladd, the second president of the APA, reviewed William James's *Principles of psychology* (1890) and criticised it for reducing psychology to an unattainable 'cerebral psychology', because James excessively related mental phenomena to activities of the brain (Fuchs 2000: 493).

A very similar story could be told about the reactions of the 'hard' scientists at the universities. For reasons which will be outlined in later chapters, many of them have never been able to see psychology and the other behavioural and social sciences as full members of the club. For them, psychology always had the flavour of a 'wannabe science'.

What do you think?

What do you think of the assessment of psychology as a 'wannabe science'? And what do you think of the advice 'not to let psychology fall to the level of a mere science'? What do these two opinions tell you about the world views of their authors? Can you relate this to the topics discussed in Chapters 2–4?

Trying to win over the public

If psychologists had a hard time convincing the hugely expanding and specialising universities of their importance, these efforts were dwarfed by the uphill struggle they faced to convince the public at large. In the second half of the nineteenth century, lay society associated psychology with phrenology, mesmerism, spiritualism and other paranormal subjects. In this respect, there were no differences between America and Europe.

Phrenology

phrenology
view that mental functions are localised in the brain and that the capacity of a function corresponds to the size of the brain part devoted to it; gave rise to personality assessment by means of analysing bumps on the skull; initiated by Gall and Spurzheim at the beginning of the nineteenth century

Phrenology started with the work of the German physician Franz Joseph Gall (1758–1828). Gall was one of the first to hypothesise that different functions were controlled by different parts of the brain. In addition, he conjectured that well-developed functions were supported by parts of the brain with a larger volume. By measuring the skull, it was thus possible to predict the strengths and weaknesses of a person. Gall called this technique *cranioscopy*, a term that was later changed by his associate, Johann Caspar Spurzheim (1776–1832), into phrenology, and applied specifically to the prediction of character, personality and propensity to crime.

Phrenology gave rise to personality assessment on the basis of scalp analysis (by locating the bumps and the troughs on the head). As such, phrenology was part of a much wider and earlier belief that an individual's personality could be deduced from his or her physical appearance, in particular from the head and the face (Chapter 3). Gall initially made a distinction between 27 independent mental faculties, including the instinct of reproduction, love of offspring, self-defence and courage, cleverness, pride and arrogance, caution and forethought, memory of words, sense of language and speech, kindness, morality and compassion, and religion. Later Spurzheim added eight more (Figure 5.1).

Because of their teachings, Gall and Spurzheim ran into difficulties with the Roman Catholic Church in Vienna (which opposed the idea that the divine soul could be fractioned into different faculties) and in 1807 moved to Paris (after two years of travelling through Europe). They parted company in 1812, arguably because Gall did not feel at ease with Spurzheim's increasingly strong claims for the diagnostic value of phrenology. Spurzheim exported phrenology to Britain (where Queen Victoria and the young Galton made use of it) and to the USA, where it found particularly fertile soil in the hands of the Fowler brothers. This is how Leahey (2004: 312) describes their impact:

> They minimized the scientific content of phrenology, maximized the practical applications, and set up an office in New York where clients could have their characters read for a fee. They wrote endlessly of the benefits of phrenology and published a phrenological journal that endured from the 1840s to 1911. They traveled around the country, especially the frontier areas, giving lectures and challenging skeptics. Like the great magician Houdini, they accepted any kind of test of their abilities, including blindfolded examinations of volunteers' skulls. What made the Fowlers' phrenology so popular was its appeal to the American character. It eschewed metaphysics for practical application. It pretended to tell employers what people to hire and to advise men which wives to take.
>
> (Leahey 2004: 312)

Mesmerism

In Chapter 4 we saw how mesmerism at the end of the eighteenth century took root in continental Europe after Mesmer claimed he could cure patients by restoring their 'animal magnetism'. Mesmerism became popular in America after the Parisian Charles Poyen in the 1830–40s gave a series of lectures. These included demonstrations with a lady, Cynthia Ann Gleason, highly susceptible to somnambulism (Schmit 2005). The audience was invited to check the power of the trance (e.g. by testing whether Gleason could be awoken from it). Intriguingly, Gleason even seemed able to look inside the bodies of others and diagnose illnesses in persons presented to her, in line with claims made shortly before that people in a trance could be clairvoyant.

Poyen rapidly had a string of followers who took up the practice. Books, periodicals, manuals and pamphlets were published to meet the growing demand. Again, the Fowler Brothers were involved, who saw cross-overs between phrenology and mesmerism. Demonstrations of mesmeric powers were presented as 'psychological experiments', to be surveyed by honourable gentlemen from the audience.

Spiritualism

A third movement that preoccupied the Americans was spiritualism, the belief that the spirits of the dead could be contacted by mediums. It started in the mid nineteenth century when two young adolescent girls (the Fox sisters) began to hear rapping sounds which they believed to be messages from the deceased (Chapter 4). Belief in spiritualism spread rapidly, the more so because the raging Civil War claimed many lives.

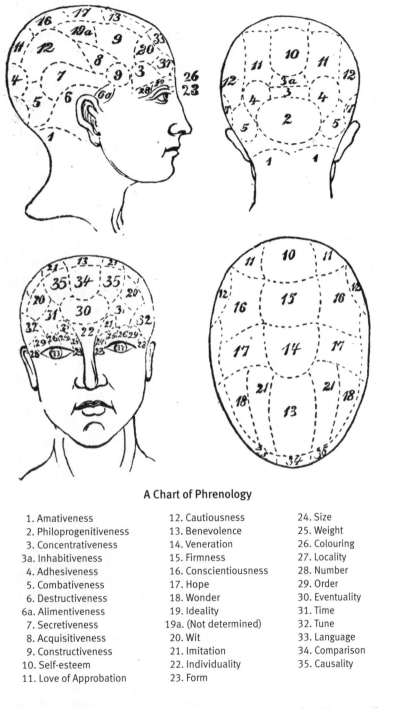

A Chart of Phrenology

1. Amativeness	12. Cautiousness	24. Size
2. Philoprogenitiveness	13. Benevolence	25. Weight
3. Concentrativeness	14. Veneration	26. Colouring
3a. Inhabitiveness	15. Firmness	27. Locality
4. Adhesiveness	16. Conscientiousness	28. Number
5. Combativeness	17. Hope	29. Order
6. Destructiveness	18. Wonder	30. Eventuality
6a. Alimentiveness	19. Ideality	31. Time
7. Secretiveness	19a. (Not determined)	32. Tune
8. Acquisitiveness	20. Wit	33. Language
9. Constructiveness	21. Imitation	34. Comparison
10. Self-esteem	22. Individuality	35. Causality
11. Love of Approbation	23. Form	

Figure 5.1 A drawing of the head with an indication of the various faculties according to Spurzheim (1834).

By the end of the nineteenth century, spiritual sessions were a common feature in social and cultural life and scholars were invited to investigate them. In particular, the first psychologists were called upon to examine the scientific value of these phenomena. William James was one of them and rapidly developed a keen interest in 'psychical research', to the despair of most of his psychology colleagues (Coon 1992). James's successor at Harvard's laboratory of psychology, Hugo Münsterberg (1863–1916), described in one of his writings how he was asked weekly to explore or comment on some mystical or spiritualistic phenomenon. He generally (but not always) refused, because it was 'not . . . part of scientific psychology to examine the so-called mystical occurrences' (Münsterberg 1910; cited in Coon 1992: 145).

Informing the public about the 'new psychology'

In an attempt to turn the tide, the 'new psychologists' (as they called themselves) published hundreds of articles about the new, scientific psychology in popular magazines. Benjamin (2000) described one attempt in *McClure's magazine,* in which an assistant of Münsterberg announced that a psychology laboratory resembled any other science laboratory with a lot of equipment for precise measurement. The psychologists also held thousands of popular speeches, 'reaching out to the public'. Unfortunately, their impact was limited, because the topics they talked about failed to capture the public's imagination to the same degree as phrenology, mesmerism and spiritualism (but see Dennis (2011), for a more positive assessment). The lay audience arguably felt as convinced about the burning necessity of scientific psychology as the parents of James McKeen Cattell after reading the following letter from their 24-year-old son at Wundt's laboratory:

> I spend four mornings and two afternoon's [sic] working in Wundt's laboratory . . . . Our work is interesting. If I should explain it to you you might not find it of vast importance, but we discover new facts and must ourselves invent the methods we use. We work in a new field, where others will follow us, who must use or correct our results. We are trying to measure the time it takes to perform the simplest mental acts – as for example to distinguish whether a color is blue or red. As this time seems to be not more than one hundredth of a second, you can imagine this is no easy task.
>
> (Cattell 1886; cited in Benjamin 2000: 320)

> **? What do you think?**
>
> Is the perception of psychology among the public nowadays different from the perception in the USA at the start of the twentieth century? If yes, what has changed? If no, why haven't psychologists been able to change it?

This, then, was the environment the fledgling psychology research faculty found itself in. It can be argued that within the wider American society the first laboratories were not the glowing beacons of psychology's victory march towards the guild of sciences, as psychology historians liked to describe them, but rather a few speckles of penicillin in a colony of bacteria. According to some psychologists, the precarious position of scientific psychology was due not only to the public's perception but also to the fact that psychology's scientific message lacked strength, as can be read in the following excerpt:

> [They] decided either to give up psychology or else to make it a natural science. They saw their brother-scientists making progress in medicine, in chemistry, in physics.

Every new discovery in those fields was of prime importance; every new element isolated in one laboratory could be isolated in some other laboratory; each new element was immediately taken up in the warp and woof of science as a whole. One need only mention wireless, radium, insulin, thyroxin, to verify this. Elements so isolated and methods so formulated immediately began to function in human achievement.

(Watson 1924; as cited in Mackenzie 1977: 14)

The dissenters took inspiration from research on the behaviour of animals, as we will see below.

Interim summary

- Scientific psychology expanded rapidly in the USA: many laboratories were established at universities, the APA was founded, and two important journals were initiated.

- Meanwhile psychology changed to address concerns prevalent in American society (adaptation to the environment, practical usefulness). This led to functionalism.

- At the same time, the position of the psychology laboratories was precarious. They were mostly part of philosophical institutes (rather than science faculties), and the public at large did not associate psychology with science but with phrenology, mesmerism and spiritualism. This created pressure to enhance the scientific status of psychology.

5.2 Making a science of behaviour

Inspiration from animal research

Researching the preservation of races in the struggle for life

In Chapters 3 and 4 we saw how Galton endorsed Darwin's evolutionary ideas and tried to test them by examining the heredity of human intelligence. Another central person in the dissemination of the evolutionary theory was Herbert Spencer (1820–1903), who in 1864 coined the phrase 'survival of the fittest'. Spencer wrote an essay on evolution two years before Darwin published his *Origin of species*. In this text he defended the view that life started from very simple, homogeneous organisms and constantly became more complex and better integrated. After the publication of *the Origin*, he integrated Darwin's ideas into his own, claiming that evolution had a direction and an equilibrium endpoint (which more or less coincided with the English upper-class view). He also adopted an idea initially proposed by Jean-Baptiste Lamarck (1744–1829) that organisms could pass on newly learned skills to their offspring (remember from Chapter 1 that nothing was known of the genetic inheritance mechanisms at that time; in Chapter 3 we saw how Galton thought that the skin colour of rabbits could be passed on through blood).

As a result of Darwin's and Spencer's writings, many learned individuals became interested in animal behaviour and started to interpret it in terms of the struggle for life. They looked for similarities between human and animal behaviour to place the different species on the evolution scale, and they searched for evidence of intelligent behaviour that had been passed on from generation to generation.

Early research: trying to understand the animal's mind

In the beginning much of the evidence gathered was anecdotal and based on the interpretation of the underlying reasoning by the animal. An important name in this enterprise was the Briton George Romanes (1848–1894). According to him, the approach combined observations of behaviour with inference of the animal's adaptive capacities. These capacities were considered to be the result of a mind that resembled that of humans. In other words, the mental processes in animals were thought to be of the same sort as you would expect to find after introspection of your own consciousness. Or as Romanes described the method:

> [I]f I contemplate my own mind, I have an immediate cognizance of a certain row of thoughts and feelings, which are the most ultimate things – and, indeed, the only things – of which I am cognizant. But if I contemplate Mind in other persons or organisms, I can have no such immediate cognizance of their thoughts and feelings; I can only infer the existence of such thoughts and feelings from the activities of the persons or organisms which appear to manifest them . . . That is to say, starting from what I know subjectively of the operations of my own individual mind, and of the activities which in my own organism these operations seem to prompt, I proceed by analogy to infer from the observable activities displayed by other organisms, the fact that certain mental operations underlie or accompany these activities.
>
> (Romanes 1884; as cited by Mackenzie 1977: 56–7)

An example of the approach is provided by Mr Bidie's observation published in the scientific journal *Nature*. Mr Bidie had a heavily pregnant cat that he had to leave behind when he went on a journey. During his absence two youngsters trespassed his quarters and repeatedly teased the cat. Upon his return Mr Bidie chased the youngsters and shortly afterwards the cat moved her kittens from a concealed nest to his dressing room. According to Mr Bidie, '[the cat's] train of reasoning seems to have been the following "now that my master has returned, there is no risk of the kittens being injured . . . so I will take them out for my protector to see and admire"' (Bidie 1879; as cited in Galef 1998).

The above example is typical of most of the research done on animal behaviour in the second half of the nineteenth century. On the basis of anecdotal evidence authors claimed that animals had reasoning capacities similar to those of humans. This is a typical instance of **anthropomorphic interpretation**, the attribution of human motives and human-like intelligence to other living creatures.

anthropomorphic interpretation
interpreting behaviour of non-human living creatures by attributing human motives and human-like intelligence to them

Thorndike's puzzle box

A different approach was taken by Edward Lee Thorndike (1874–1949). As mentioned in Chapter 4, Thorndike was attracted to psychology after reading James's *Principles*. He went to study with James, who advised him to investigate learning in children (as part of the aim of increasing the functionality of scientific psychology). Unfortunately for James and Thorndike, they ran into difficulties when they tried to recruit participants. Eventually Thorndike proposed the study of instinctive and intelligent behaviour in chickens. The proposal was accepted by the Harvard authorities, as long as Thorndike kept the animals outside the university. So, Thorndike was forced to keep them in his apartment. After he ran into difficulties with his landlady, James had no other option than to house the chickens in the basement of his own house (Benjafield 2005: 139–40). Thorndike eventually left Harvard when he was invited to Columbia by James McKeen Cattell and there he finished his famous research with the puzzle box.

A first change Thorndike introduced was that he did not rely on anecdotal evidence, but on careful observation of animals put in controlled environments. The second change was that he based his conclusions on the animals' behaviour, not on what supposedly went on in their minds. He put hungry animals (chickens, rats, dogs and in particular cats) in puzzle boxes he constructed himself (even though he was not the most skilled carpenter, as can be seen in Figure 5.2). Outside the box, food was presented which the animal could reach if it managed to solve the puzzle and open the door (e.g. by moving a lever, pulley or treadle).

Thorndike noted how long it took the animal to get out of the box. He observed that the time rapidly decreased on successive trials (Figure 5.3), because the animal did not repeat the behaviours that had failed before but focused on the behaviours that had been successful. Thorndike called this the law of effect. Behaviours that are followed by positive consequences are strengthened and repeated; behaviours that are not followed by such consequences are not repeated.

Thorndike further wanted to see whether the animal had any 'knowledge' of the contingency involved. To this end, he had cats observe other cats solve the puzzle. Afterwards he put these 'expert' cats in the box and examined whether they solved the puzzle faster than naïve cats that had not observed the required behaviour. Given that this was not the case, Thorndike concluded that the learning consisted of making an association between the situation of being in the box and performing the appropriate act. The learning did not involve the animal solving the problem by associating ideas of actions and rewards. The cat did not have insight into the contingencies. Thorndike called this type of learning instrumental conditioning.

law of effect

behavioural law introduced by Thorndike to refer to the fact that behaviours followed by positive consequences are strengthened and more likely to be repeated

instrumental conditioning

name introduced by Thorndike to refer to learning on the basis of the law of effect; called operant conditioning by Skinner

Figure 5.2 One of the puzzle boxes made by Thorndike.
Source: Robert Mearns Yerkes Papers/Yale Pictorial Records and Collections.

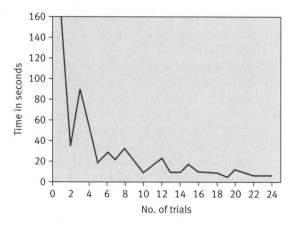

Figure 5.3 Time needed by a cat to escape from one of Thorndike's puzzle boxes in successive trials.

Source: Thorndike, E.L. (1911) *Animal Intelligence: Experimental Studies*, Fig. 2, p. 39, © 1911 by Transaction Publishers. Reprinted by permission of the publisher.

This is how Thorndike summarised his findings:

> The cat does not look over the situation, much less think it over, and then decide what to do. It bursts out at once into the activities which instinct and experience have settled on as suitable reactions to the situation 'confinement when hungry with food outside.' The one impulse, out of many accidental ones, which leads to pleasure, becomes strengthened and stamped in thereby, and more and more firmly associated with the sense-impression of that box's interior.
>
> (Thorndike 1898; as cited in Benjafield 2005: 140)

Incidentally, it must be noted that Thorndike's claim against social learning in animals has since been proven wrong; imitative learning happens in all kinds of species, as we will see in Chapter 12.

comparative psychology
study of behaviour of animals, usually with the intention to shed light on human functioning within the framework of the evolutionary theory

Thorndike's work had an enormous impact on animal research, because his approach was much more in line with the research methods in the natural sciences than the previous anecdotal and anthropomorphic attempts. For this reason, 1898, the year in which Thorndike published his PhD thesis on animal learning, is celebrated as the birthday of **comparative psychology**, even though after his PhD Thorndike returned to his first love, educational psychology.

KEY FIGURE Edward Thorndike

- American psychologist (1874–1949).
- Is seen as the father of comparative psychology because he was the first to study animal psychology in an objective way (as part of his PhD). He did so by placing an animal in a controlled environment and drawing conclusions on the basis of the animal's behaviour.
- Introduced the terms 'instrumental conditioning' and 'the law of effect'.
- After his PhD, turned to educational issues and, therefore, is also celebrated as the father of educational psychology.

Source: Humanities and Social Services Library/New York Public Library/Science Photo Library Ltd.

Pavlov's research on classical conditioning

Thorndike's lead in studying the behaviour of animals without trying to explain it in terms of conscious thoughts and feelings was further increased when researchers became informed of Pavlov's work in Russia (an English account of which was published in 1909 in the journal *Psychological Bulletin*).

Ivan Pavlov (1849–1936) was a physiologist who studied the digestive system of animals (mainly dogs). He devised a procedure that allowed him to continuously measure the secretion of fluids by the digestive organs. This gave him a much more detailed picture of what was going on than the previous attempts, based on vivisections at different times after the meal. In his research Pavlov was inspired by the Russian physiologist I.M. Sechenov, who argued that mental life could be understood in terms of physiological reflexes. Pavlov observed that many digestive processes indeed consisted of reflexes. When food was placed on the animal's tongue, the salivary glands automatically started to emit dribble and the stomach started to excrete gastric juices.

Shortly after 1900 (when he was already more than 50 years old and about to win the Nobel prize for medicine) Pavlov started to become interested in a curious phenomenon: after a few experiences of food delivery, the animal started to secrete digestive fluids *before* the food arrived in the mouth, namely as soon as the animal saw the preparations of the experiment taking place. Pavlov decided to investigate this 'psychic reflex' methodically under strictly controlled circumstances. That was the beginning of the research on classical conditioning, which showed that a neutral stimulus (e.g. a tone) which is presented shortly before a stimulus (food) that automatically elicits a reflex response (salivation) after a few pairings starts to elicit the response as well.

classical conditioning
form of learning discovered by Pavlov in which an association is made between two events in the environment; usually studied with a stimulus that elicits a reflex-like response (e.g. food in mouth → salivation) to which a second, initially neutral stimulus is coupled

---

KEY FIGURE Ivan Petrovich Pavlov

- Russian physiologist (1849–1936).
- Studied digestive system in animals (won a Nobel prize in 1904). Introduced techniques that allowed him to continuously measure the secretion of fluids by the organs.
- After 1900 became interested in the question of why organs started to secrete fluids before the food was presented. This would be the start of his research on classical conditioning.
- Was part of a Russian school which held that psychology could be reduced to physiology: thinking consisted of reflexes.
- Had a big impact on the development of behaviourism.

Source: Ria Novosti/Science Photo Library Ltd.

Pavlov's research, just like Thorndike's, brought research on animal behaviour into the realm of the natural sciences (the story goes that Pavlov resented people calling him a psychologist). The potential of this change in research method was summarised as follows by a young researcher in a popular magazine:

The possibility of learning more about the mental life of animals becomes a probability when we consider that our knowledge of the mental processes of infants, children and defective individuals is obtained almost entirely without the aid of language. The moment we take this broader point of view, that the behavior of man expresses his psychology, and are willing to admit that we can scientifically study his behavior, it follows at once that we can build up an animal psychology, because we can study the behavior of animals just as scientifically as we can study the behavior of man.

The study of behavior thus becomes a broad science; normal adult human psychology forms only a part of its subject matter. The psychology of infants, of children, of the feeble-minded, of primitive peoples, of animals, all form a part of the world to be observed by the psychologist.

(Watson 1907: 421–2)

A few years later this young man, John B. Watson (1878–1958), would publish a pamphlet that would become a decisive moment in the history of psychology.

Interim summary

- The evolutionary theory led to an increased interest in animal behaviour.
- Initially animal behaviour was studied by focusing on anecdotes of intelligent behaviour. These were explained by assuming the same reasoning processes in animals as in humans (anthropomorphic interpretation).
- Thorndike introduced a different approach. Animals were put into a controlled environment (a puzzle box) and conclusions were drawn on the basis of the animals' behaviour (instrumental conditioning resulting in the law of effect).
- The focus on the animal's behaviour (rather than its mind) was further strengthened by Pavlov's work on classical conditioning.
- Together the changes resulted in a research method that much more resembled the methods used in the natural sciences. Watson started to make the claim that the method would also be good for the study of human functioning.

The 1913 behaviourist manifesto

In 1907, Watson was poached by Baldwin, a famous developmental psychologist and one of the founders of *Psychological Review* (see above), to become professor at the Johns Hopkins University. Within weeks after Watson's arrival, however, Baldwin was forced from his Chair because of a scandal involving a brothel, which left Watson in charge of both the department and the journal. (Baldwin would go to the University of Toronto and there found the first psychology laboratory of Canada and, at that time, the British Empire.)

behaviourism

movement in psychology arguing that observable behaviours are the most important aspect of human functioning to be understood; denies to various extents the relevance of information processing going on in the mind; particularly strong in the USA in the first half of the twentieth century

Watson used his position as editor of *Psychological Review* to promote the case for animal research. In 1913, he published a scathing article against the lack of scientific rigour in the ongoing investigations in most psychological laboratories. This article would become the beginning of behaviourism. Because of its importance, both in terms of the impact on the history of psychology and in terms of how psychology came to define its subject and its research methods, we will discuss the article in some detail. (Incidentally, the article is well worth reading in its entirety. It is meant to convince people, so it is very accessible.)

The article (available at **psychclassics.yorku.ca**) begins with the following statement:

Psychology as the behaviorist views it is a purely objective experimental branch of natural science. Its theoretical goal is the prediction and control of behavior. Introspection forms no essential part of its methods, nor is the scientific value of its data dependent upon the readiness with which they lend themselves to interpretation in terms of consciousness. The behaviorist, in his efforts to get a unitary scheme of animal response, recognizes no dividing line between man and brute.

In this statement we clearly see the transition from introspection into one's own mind to the observation of others' behaviour. This was a defining insight in the growth of psychological research. Even though Wundt and the other early psychologists made use of experimental methods, they still ran the studies on themselves as participants.

An element that played a role in the shift from introspection to observation was the impact of evolutionary theory on American psychology. Survival in a context of natural selection primarily depends on how the animal acts, not on what it 'thinks'. Thoughts were the playground of philosophers; biologists had to predict behaviours. Another element that contributed to the shift was that introspection, as described by Titchener in his handbooks, turned out to be a very counterintuitive and difficult procedure for students to use in their practicals. They found it much easier simply to observe what others were doing.

Watson's manifesto continued as follows:

It has been maintained by its followers generally that psychology is a study of the science of the phenomena of consciousness. It has taken as its problem, on the one hand, the analysis of complex mental states (or processes) into simple elementary constituents, and on the other the construction of complex states when the elementary constituents are given . . . It is agreed that introspection is the method par excellence by means of which mental states may be manipulated for purposes of psychology. On this assumption, behavior data (including under this term everything which goes under the name of comparative psychology) have no value per se. They possess significance only in so far as they may throw light upon conscious states.

Here we see Watson turning his bile on Titchener's structuralism, which as we have seen in Chapter 4, was easiest to attack, given its isolated position. This attack continued for several more paragraphs, including sentences such as:

I do not wish unduly to criticize psychology. It has failed significantly, I believe, during the fifty-odd years of its existence as an experimental discipline to make its place in the world as an undisputed natural science. Psychology, as it is generally thought of, has something esoteric in its methods. If you fail to reproduce my findings, it is not due to some fault in your apparatus or in the control of your stimulus, but it is due to the fact that your introspection is untrained . . .

The time seems to have come when psychology must discard all reference to consciousness; when it need no longer delude itself into thinking that it is making mental states the object of observation.

? What do you think?

Can you see how Watson's text influenced the views writers of introductory books in the twentieth century had about psychology before behaviourism? Rather than consulting the original materials, authors simply took over Watson's criticisms of structuralism and introspection.

Next, Watson turned his attention to functionalism and wrote:

> My psychological quarrel is not with the systematic and structural psychologist alone. The last fifteen years have seen the growth of what is called functional psychology. This type of psychology decries the use of elements in the static sense of the structuralists. It throws emphasis upon the biological significance of conscious processes instead of upon the analysis of conscious states into introspectively isolable elements. I have done my best to understand the difference between functional psychology and structural psychology. Instead of clarity, confusion grows upon me.

Then, Watson formulated the alternative:

> This leads me to the point where I should like to make the argument constructive. I believe we can write a psychology [as just described] . . . and never go back upon our definition: never use the terms consciousness, mental states, mind, content, introspectively verifiable, imagery, and the like. I believe that we can do it in a few years . . . It can be done in terms of stimulus and response, in terms of habit formation, habit integration and the like. Furthermore, I believe that it is really worth while to make this attempt now.

In order to become a real science, psychology had to focus on observable behaviour (just as Thorndike had done) and ignore everything that referred to consciousness, thinking, feelings, motives, plans, purposes, images, knowledge or the self. This meant that some topics could not be addressed with the behaviourist method:

> The situation is somewhat different when we come to a study of the more complex forms of behavior, such as imagination, judgment, reasoning, and conception. At present the only statements we have of them are in content terms. Our minds have been so warped by the fifty-odd years which have been devoted to the study of states of consciousness that we can envisage these problems only in one way. We should meet the situation squarely and say that we are not able to carry forward investigations along all of these lines by the behavior methods which are in use at the present time . . . As our methods become better developed it will be possible to undertake investigations of more and more complex forms of behavior. Problems which are now laid aside will again become imperative, but they can be viewed as they arise from a new angle and in more concrete settings.

Although Watson in his manifesto left an opening for later research on information processing in the mind, in subsequent writings he hardened his stance and came to deny the importance/existence of any process that was not observable.

Interim summary

- In 1913 Watson used his position as editor of *Psychological Review* to launch the behaviourist manifesto.
- Psychology was defined as a purely objective experimental branch of natural science, based on the prediction and control of behaviour.
- In the manifesto Watson argued that previous research on introspection into consciousness had failed significantly.
- In the manifesto Watson left an opening for later study of more complex behaviour (such as imagination and reasoning). In his later writings he came to deny the importance of such behaviour.

KEY FIGURE John B. Watson

Source: Bettman/Corbis.

- American psychologist (1878–1958).
- Did a PhD in 1903 on animal psychology. Was influenced by Thorndike's approach and saw this as the approach that would bring all of psychology into the realm of the natural sciences.
- Moved to Johns Hopkins University in 1907 and became editor of the prestigious journal *Psychological Review*.
- Used his position as editor in 1913 to publish the behaviourist manifesto.
- Became the main promoter of behaviourism through the publications of books and articles. Tried to show, together with Rosalie Rayner, that phobias originated on the basis of classical conditioning. Demonstrated this by making a toddler – Little Albert – afraid of a white rat by associating the presence of the rat with a horrendous noise (Watson and Rayner 1920).
- Had an extramarital affair with Rosalie Rayner, which forced him to leave the university in 1920. Kept on publishing on behaviourism until 1930.
- Behaviourist work was continued primarily by Hull, Skinner and Tolman, who agreed on the method, but came up with different views about the relationship between stimuli and responses.

The influence of the philosophy of science

Positivism

Watson's attempt to increase the scientific standing of psychology was embedded within a wider movement to make science the cornerstone of human progress. Impressed by the success of technology, physics and chemistry, scientific inventions were seen as the way forward. Indeed, the nations that invested most in them (USA, Prussia, the Netherlands, the UK) saw their power and status grow more than the countries that did not do so. As we have seen already a number of times, this movement, which saw science as the motor of progress, was known as positivism.

The appeal of positivism to people like Watson was not due to a close reading of Comte (which would have led to some unpleasant surprises, as we have seen in the previous chapters), Mill, Spencer and other philosophers, but to the triumphant writings of scientists and scientifically-minded authors, who used the scientific achievements to try to convince society that scientific knowledge was superior to humanist knowledge (Chapter 2). In a nutshell, their messages were:

1. Because science is based on observation and experimentation, its findings are always true.

2. Scientific theories are summaries of the empirical findings. Therefore, they are always true as well.

3. Because scientific knowledge is infallible, it should be the motor of all progress.

The attraction of positivism to Watson and other early behaviourists is summarised well in the following quote:

> The word positivism became a key-word of the nineteenth century and after. The name of Comte became a symbol, like the names of Darwin or Voltaire; a symbol which by

1870 carried a power far beyond the intellectual influence of the lectures which he gave or the books which he published. No philosopher, he was the only French philosopher of that century to make [an] impact in Britain and Germany. His name stood for a very coherent idea, a very plain and intelligible attitude to life – experimental science the only way to truth. Apart from all the structures built upon it, his name was powerful in conditioning attitudes to truth. He did not invent positivism. But he was widely believed to have invented it, and was the man who tried to make it the key which opened all doors to the only truths said to matter for life and society. The notion of positivism stood for an attitude destined long to outlive the Comtean positivism of the later nineteenth century. Of this attitude Comte was the hero, even for minds who gained nothing from his books.

During the third quarter of the nineteenth century some men believed that science, that is the natural sciences, could solve all problems, even the problems of men; that man and society could be brought under universal laws like the law of gravitation; that we live under a determined process which no free act can stop or check or change. For two, even three decades the idea was magnetic. Science, queen Science, goddess Science, could do all.

(Chadwick 1990: 233)

Given the positivist tenet that the natural sciences were the most successful development in human reasoning, philosophers and scientists started to examine what exactly was the core of the scientific approach, so that other knowledge areas could adopt this method as well. Their subject matter became known as the philosophy of science (Chapter 9).

philosophy of science
branch of philosophy that studies the foundations of scientific research, to better understand the position of scientific research relative to other forms of information acquisition and generation

One principle that had caught everyone's attention since Newton's *Principia mathematica* was the importance of mathematical laws to describe reality. A true science was a science that had its knowledge described as mathematical equations (Chapters 2 and 3). However, this turned out not to be enough. An early example of an attempt to build a Newtonian theory of psychology on the basis of mathematical equations was provided by the Irish-Scottish philosopher Francis Hutcheson (1694–1746). In 1725 he published a treatise in which he introduced 'mathematical calculations in subjects of morality' (Jahoda 2007: 28). He produced an algebraic set of formulae designed to compute the morality of actions. For instance, the Moral Importance (M) of agents was a function of their Benevolence (B) multiplied by their Abilities (A), or $M = B \times A$. A similar attempt was made by the German scholar Johann Freidrich Herbart in 1816 when he published the *Lehrbuch zur psychologie* in which he presented his main ideas in mathematical terms. Neither theory had the impact of Newton's *Principia*, however. So, what was missing?

The requirement of operational definitions

From the writings about the philosophy of science, the behaviourists distilled three ideas that were important for the further development of scientific psychology and behavioural sciences in general. The first was that you had to be able to represent the elements of a mathematical law as numbers. There was no point in trying to establish a mathematical relationship between two variables, if you could not express them numerically. In addition, the numbers had to represent the essence of the variable. The way to do so was to represent the variables in terms of how they had been measured (e.g. weight expressed in kilograms). Such a definition became known as an operational definition. It was first formulated by the Harvard physicist and Nobel

operational definition
definition of a variable in terms of how the variable has been measured; allows description of the variable in quantitative form

laureate Percy Williams Bridgman in 1927 and introduced to psychologists by his university colleague Stanley Smith Stevens in 1935.

The importance of operational definitions can easily be demonstrated with Newton's law. One of these laws states that F = ma (the force on an object is equal to its mass multiplied by its acceleration). Such a law only becomes useful if you are able to measure the force, the mass and the acceleration, and express them in units. This is the reason Hutcheson failed. It was not enough to state that the Moral Importance (M) of people was a function of their Benevolence (B) multiplied by their Abilities (A). For a scientific theory, Hutchinson also had to make clear how these variables could be measured and expressed in numbers.

The need for operational definitions explained to psychologists why psychophysics had been so successful (Chapter 3). Here they were able to describe both the stimulus intensity and the resulting sensation in numerical form, so that it was possible to search for the best-fitting mathematical equation between them. The immediate challenge for the behaviourists, therefore, was to achieve something similar for their learning theories. The person who took this approach the furthest was Clark L. Hull (1884–1952), who sought to explain all learning and motivation by the use of mathematical equations with variables that were operationally defined. For instance, an equation from his book *Principles of behavior* (1943) was:

$$_sE_R = {_sH_R} \times D \times V \times K$$

in which

$_sE_R$ = the excitatory potential of the stimulus to elicit the response,

$_sH_R$ = the habit strength between the stimulus and the response,

D = the drive level of the animal/human,

V = the stimulus intensity,

K = the reward incentive.

All variables had an operational definition and could be expressed in numbers, so that it was possible to predict the precise behaviour of an animal in a particular situation. At the same time, it became clear that the predictions were limited to the controlled situation in which the animal functioned, and could not easily be extrapolated beyond the laboratory.

Independent and dependent variables

The second idea the behaviourists took from the philosophers of science was that a distinction had to be made between independent variables and dependent variables. Independent variables were characteristics of the environment and/or the participant that might have an impact on the behaviour and that could be manipulated by the researcher (e.g. the number of T-junctions in a maze). Dependent variables were behaviour features that could be measured to see whether the independent variable had an effect (e.g. the time the rat needed to find the food in the maze). On the basis of this distinction, psychological research could be defined as the study of the impact of a Stimulus (the independent variable) on the Response (the dependent variable). As a consequence, behaviourism also became known as S-R-psychology.

The need for verification

verification

principle that up to the
1950s formed the core
of the scientific method:
a proposition was
meaningful (scientific)
if its truth could be
empirically verified

Finally, a third idea the behaviourists took from the philosophy of science was the necessity of verification in science. Statements were only useful if they could be verified by empirical observation. The requirement of verification ruled out religious statements, such as 'God loves everyone', but according to the behaviourists also ruled out introspective statements such as 'to me this stimulus looks like a combination of . . .'. Verification meant that researchers had to present their evidence in such a way that it could be verified by others (see also Chapter 9).

The incorporation of the above principles considerably increased the objectivity of research in psychology, although the requirement of mathematically expressed laws turned out to be less important than originally thought by the behaviourists.

Interim summary

- Behaviourism was part of a wider movement within Western society to make science the cornerstone of human progress.
- The philosophers of science tried to define the qualities of a true science. In addition to the ideal of mathematical laws, behaviourists took three ideas from them:
  - operational definitions are necessary
  - there is a distinction between independent variables and dependent variables (this was translated into S-R associations)
  - science relies on verification.

? What do you think?

If you did a course in research methods, you would immediately see the lasting influence of these insights on the way psychology students are taught to do research. If you have your textbook of research methods with you, look up the different insights and what your present-day book says about them.

Further developments in behaviourism: Skinner versus Tolman

In an ironic twist of fate, Watson's scientific career ended in more or less the same way as it started. Remember that his career got a major boost when Baldwin was forced to leave Johns Hopkins University. In October 1920, Watson in turn had to leave Johns Hopkins as a result of an extramarital affair with a graduate student (Rosalie Rayner, with whom he had published the famous study of Little Albert). Watson took up a job in advertising, where his income apparently was many times higher than what he had earned at university.

Skinner and radical behaviourism

Watson's legacy was continued by three heavyweight successors (in addition to hundreds of lesser-known researchers all over the world). The first of them was Clark Hull, whom we described above. The second was Burrhus Frederic Skinner (1904–1990), who is particularly well known for his research on operant conditioning and for his radical behaviourism. Operant conditioning is another name for instrumental conditioning (coined by Skinner) and examines the ways in which behaviour changes as a function of the reinforcement or punishment that follows. Radical behaviourism is a strong version of behaviourism, which holds that an organism is nothing but a place where stimuli provoke behaviours on the basis of S-R associations.

radical behaviourism

strong version of behaviourism, defended by Skinner, which denies the relevance of information processing in the mind and holds that all human behaviour can be understood on the basis of S-R associations

Skinner denied the relevance of information processing in the mind, as stressed by the cognitive psychologists (see below). All that happened was the direct activation of responses on the basis of stimulus input. Below are some quotes from a popular text he wrote on behaviourism, illustrating the point (Skinner 1974; see also Malone & Cruchon 2001):

> The brain is said to use data, make hypotheses, make choices, and so on, as the mind was once said to have done. In a behaviorist account it is the person who does these things. (p. 86)
>
> In all these roles it has been possible to avoid the problems of dualism by substituting 'brain' for 'mind' . . . Both the mind and the brain are not far from the ancient notion of a homunculus – an inner person who behaves in precisely the ways necessary to explain the behavior of the outer person in whom he dwells . . . A much simpler solution is to identify the mind with the person. (p. 130)
>
> We do not need to describe contingencies of reinforcement in order to be affected by them . . . Certainly for thousands of years people spoke grammatically without knowing that there were rules of grammar. (p. 141)
>
> It is often said that a science of behavior studies the human organism but neglects the person or self. What it neglects is a vestige of animism . . . traces of the doctrine survive when we speak of a personality, or an ego . . . of an I who says he knows what he is going to do and uses his body to do it . . . (p. 184)
>
> A person is not an originating agent; he is a locus, a point at which many genetic and environmental conditions come together. (p. 185)

One of Skinner's views was that humans have much less control over their actions than they assume. They simply respond to events in the environment and do not take initiative themselves. It can even be questioned whether they are responsible for their actions. This is how Pickren and Rutherford (2010: 225) summarised Skinner's position:

> How can we have good government and a society in which war, poverty, environmental degradation, and other threats to human welfare are reduced or even eliminated? The answer, Skinner suggested, was to give up our antiquated, sentimental belief in free will. Personal freedom, he argued, was an illusion. What mattered was to more effectively manage the contingencies present in the environment that each of us live in and that control everyday actions on individual and global scales all the time. He exhorted his readers to give up their unscientific, outdated belief in 'autonomous man' and to embrace that all of our behaviour is shaped not by an interior sense of freedom or dignity but by the contingencies in our environment that reward and punish us. His position generated intense controversy and vehement ad hominem attacks.

Skinner's strong stance, though it was in line with Watson, eventually did behaviourism more harm than good. As we will see further on, however, Skinner's views about the lack of free will in humans are still very much alive today and continue to inspire discussions about human functioning.

Tolman and purposive behaviourism

In introductory books behaviourism is often identified with Skinner's radical behaviourism (and, at the same time, dismissed). However, as we have indicated a few times already, it is important to dissociate the ideas of an individual from those of the larger movement. Although Skinner was the best-known behaviourist, this does not imply that his views were shared by everybody who felt attracted to behaviourism. Hull, for instance, allowed some scope for internal mental processes in the form of internal r-s connections (giving rise to S-r-s-R sequences) and the third main neobehaviourist, Edward C. Tolman (1886–1959), actually doubted Skinner's interpretation of operant conditioning.

According to Tolman, operant conditioning could not be understood in simple S-R terms and he devised several experiments to show this. Here we describe only one study, actually carried out by a student of Tolman, Hugh Blodgett, in 1929 (i.e. years before Skinner's radical behaviourism became influential).

In Skinner's view, animals acquired behaviours because the association between an environmental cue and a particular behaviour was strengthened by subsequent reinforcement. So, a rat learned to find its way through a maze because a particular turning at each intersection was followed by food (strengthening the link between the intersection and that turn) whereas others were not. If this reasoning were true, Tolman (1948) argued, then rats who were not reinforced should not learn. However, this was not what Blodgett observed. He had three conditions: (1) a condition in which hungry rats were placed in a maze that contained food at the end of the maze (Figure 5.4), (2) a condition in which hungry rats were placed in the same maze, but

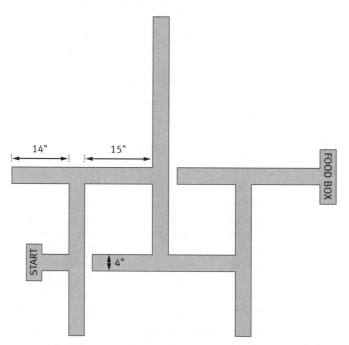

Figure 5.4 The maze used by Blodgett in 1929 to show the phenomenon of latent learning.

According to Tolman (1948) rats that were not reinforced by food at the end of the maze, still learned the layout of the maze (i.e. they built a cognitive map of the maze), because as soon as they got food at the end, they ran as fast as a group of rats that had been reinforced on each trial (see Figure 5.5).

Source: 'Cognitive maps in rats and men', *Psychological Review*, 55, 189–209 (Tolman, E.C. 1948), originally from Blodgett, H.C. (1929) 'The effect of the introduction of reward upon the maze performance of rats', *University of California Publications in Psychology*, 4, 8, p. 117.

the food was only introduced on day 3, and (3) a condition in which food was introduced on day 7.

Blodgett observed that the rats in condition (1) showed a fast learning curve. That is, on successive trials they made fewer errors running towards the food. The rats in condition (2) did not run straight towards the end of the maze on the first two days (when they did not find food there), but showed a very different behaviour on day 4 (after having found food on day 3): now they ran straight to the food location, making no more errors than the rats which had found food (and hence been reinforced) from the first day on. The group that found food on the seventh day showed the same massive and instantaneous learning on day 8 (Figure 5.5). According to Tolman, this showed that the rats' learning was not due to the fact that the presence of food had reinforced taking the correct turns, but that the rats had learned the layout of the maze and were able to use this knowledge when they had a reason to do so. This is how Tolman described the outcome of the finding:

> It will be observed that the experimental groups as long as they were not finding food did not appear to learn much. (Their error curves did not drop.) But on the days immediately succeeding their first finding of the food their error curves did drop astoundingly. It appeared, in short, that during the non-rewarded trials these animals had been learning much more than they had exhibited. This learning, which did not manifest itself until after the food had been introduced, Blodgett called 'latent learning'. Interpreting these results anthropomorphically, we would say that as long as the animals were not getting any food at the end of the maze they continued to take their time in going through it – they continued to enter many blinds. Once, however, they knew they were to get food, they demonstrated that during these preceding non-rewarded

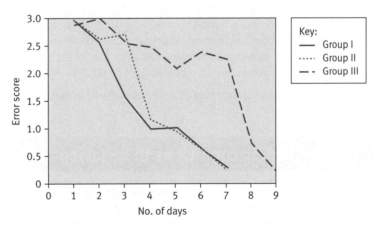

Figure 5.5 The number of errors made by three groups of rats in the study of Blodgett (1929).

The first group always found food at the end of the maze. They showed the usual learning curve. The second group was not fed on the first 2 days and found food on day 3 and each subsequent day. They showed extremely fast learning from day 3 to day 4. The third group was fed from day 7 on. They showed fast learning from day 7 to day 8 and immediately caught up with the performance level of group 1. This finding is difficult to explain within Skinner's radical behaviourism.

Source: 'Cognitive maps in rats and men', *Psychological Review*, 55, 189–209 (Tolman, E.C. 1948), originally from Blodgett, H.C. (1929) 'The effect of the introduction of reward upon the maze performance of rats', *University of California Publications in Psychology*, 4, 8, p. 120.

trials they had learned where many of the blinds were. They had been building up a 'map', and could utilize the latter as soon as they were motivated to do so.

(Tolman 1948: 194–5)

For Tolman, the fact that the animals in Blodgett's study immediately knew where to go to as soon as they had found food once demonstrated that they had learned the layout of the maze during the trials in which no food was given. Together with Blodgett, he called this *latent learning*, the acquisition of knowledge that is not demonstrated in observable behaviour. More specifically, Tolman argued, the rats acquired a cognitive map of the maze. As soon as they knew where food would be given, they were able to make use of this cognitive map to select the correct alleys.

On the basis of these and other findings Tolman stated that animal and human behaviour was motivated by goals: only when the rats were provided with a goal did they make use of their knowledge. Therefore, Tolman's approach is sometimes called purposive behaviourism. Tolman agreed with Watson and Skinner that psychology should be based on observable behaviour and not seek to understand the animal's 'mind' or 'consciousness', but at the same time he did not see why he should be asked to assume that nothing more than the formation of S-R associations happened in the mind. For him, goals could be studied objectively.

purposive behaviourism

version of behaviourism, defended by Tolman, which saw behaviour as goal-related (means to an end); agreed with other behaviourists that psychology should be based on observable behaviour

Interim summary

- After Watson's departure from academic life, behaviourism was continued by three heavyweight neo-behaviourists: Hull, Skinner and Tolman.
  - Hull: mathematical equations with operationally defined variables that allow detailed predictions of behaviour in specified circumstances
  - Skinner: radical behaviourism (there is no information processing in the mind; all human actions are the result of S-R connections)
  - Tolman: purposive behaviourism (behaviour is motivated by goals; the goal-directedness can be studied in an objective way).

5.3 Adding cognitions to behaviour

Tolman's views turned out to be more influential than either Hull's or Skinner's. Although Watson was perfectly right when he asserted that overt behaviours were easier to study than covert cognitions and feelings, later researchers came to believe that the difficulty of investigating what happened in the 'black box' between stimuli and responses did not imply that nothing occurred there at all, as Skinner claimed.

Shortly after World War II voices against behaviourism grew louder and a new movement became visible, which eventually took the name of *cognitive psychology*. Probably the best account of the movement's beginning is given by Gardner (1987). This is how the book begins:

In September of 1948 on the campus of the California Institute of Technology, a group of eminent scientists representing several disciplines met for a conference on 'Cerebral

Mechanisms in Behavior' . . . This conference had been designed to facilitate discussions about a classic issue: the way in which the nervous system controls behavior. And yet the discussions ranged far more widely than the official topic had implied. For example, the opening speaker, mathematician John von Neumann, forged a striking comparison between the electronic computer (then a discovery so new that it smacked of science fiction) and the brain (which had been around for a while). The next speaker, mathematician and neurophysiologist Warren McCulloch, used his provocative title ('Why the Mind Is in the Head') to launch a far-ranging discussion on how the brain processes information – like von Neumann, he wanted to exploit certain parallels between the nervous system and 'logical devices' in order to figure out why we perceive the world the way we do.

Less steeped in the latest technological innovations but more versed in the problems of explaining human behavior, the next speaker, psychologist Karl Lashley, gave the most iconoclastic and most memorable address. Speaking on 'The Problem of Serial Order in Behavior,' he challenged the doctrine (or dogma) that had dominated psychological analysis for the past several decades and laid out a whole new agenda for research.

(Gardner 1987: 10–11)

What was going on and what were the main forces leading to the 1948 meeting described in Gardner's excerpt?

Mathematical and technological advances questioning the behaviourist tenets

As explained in Gardner's text, the most important factors in the developments of the 1940s were technological advances outside the psychological laboratories. Before and during World War II the new spearhead of technology became information handling. There was an increasing need for communication over large distances (e.g. radio and television transmission); the war required the cracking of increasingly sophisticated encryption codes; and engineers became frustrated by the fact that machines, which had led to the industrial revolution, could perform only a single operation, and they were looking for ways to make them more flexible by programming them. So, whereas (radical) behaviourism denied information processing inside the human head, the scientific world outside became very much centred on information handling in machines.

Information can be represented as logical operations

By the beginning of the twentieth century it became clear among mathematicians that any mathematical operation, and indeed any type of information, could be expressed by means of logical operations involving the values 0 and 1, known as Boolean operations after their British inventor George Boole (1815–1864). In a matter of years it was realised that electrical circuits could be modelled to enable Boolean operations, so that those circuits were effectively able to represent and compute all types of information. Furthermore, such an accomplishment was possible for every type of machine that could perform Boolean operations, independently of the way in which the code was put into operation, as was shown by the British mathematician Alan Turing.

Turing proved in 1936 that extremely basic machines working on the basis of Boolean logic would be able to simulate the performance of much more complex

Turing machine

basic (hypothetical) machine operating on the basis of Boolean logic and able to simulate the processing of more complex machines operating according to these principles

and powerful machines working on the same principles, if given enough time. Such a basic machine became known as a **Turing machine** (the machine was not actually built, as the whole argument could be made theoretically).

By the end of World War II, the first practical applications of the new computers became visible. These computers could both store information and transform it (by means of algorithms). This is what von Neumann referred to in Gardner's text above. He was involved in building one of the first operational computers.

? What do you think?

Computers work on a binary code (bits and bytes). How is this related to Boolean logic?

The brain can do Boolean operations

In 1943 a neurophysiologist, Warren McCulloch, and a logician, Walter Pitts, published an article in which they argued that the human brain could be thought of as a Boolean device as well. They showed that under certain assumptions the operations of a neuron and its connections with other neurons could be modelled in terms of Boolean logic. This meant that in principle the human brain was capable of storing and transforming information in the same way as computers. Both computers and brains could be considered as (complex) Turing machines that performed Boolean operations on stored information. McCulloch was the second speaker at the workshop described by Gardner.

Strings of S-R connections cannot be used to represent human thinking

Once it was realised that a Turing machine on the basis of Boolean logic could simulate all types of information processing, including human thinking and language, researchers started to examine whether the same was true for the S-R models postulated by the behaviourists (in particular, Hull). These models accepted only a subset of operations, in particular those in which each element depended on its association with the preceding element (if you want the technical term, these are known as Markov chains).

Karl Lashley (the third speaker at the workshop) was the first researcher to question the viability of the behaviourist S-R models. For instance, he pointed out that in speech words unfold with such rapidity that it is unlikely that each word can be based upon an S-R association with the previous one. In addition, the speech errors made by individuals often include the anticipation of words that have not yet occurred in the sequence (as in the speech-error in 'you hissed my mistory lecture', where we see an exchange of the m- and the h- sounds, although 'history' supposedly is not yet activated at the moment 'missed' is pronounced).

A few years later, the case was made that human grammar indeed required a Turing machine and could not be captured by a model with S-R connections (or more generally a Markov chain). So, if computers were programmed along the models proposed by the behaviourists, they would never be able to produce the same language as humans did. Only a computer that functioned as a Turing machine could do so.

Interim summary

After World War II experimental psychologists came to include mental processing in their models. This was due to the following developments:

- Mathematicians proved that all information could be represented by a Turing machine, working on the basis of binary units and Boolean operations.
- This information is to a large extent independent of the device on which it is implemented (i.e. it can easily be transposed on another device).
- Neurophysiologists presented evidence that the brain could be considered as a Turing machine.
- It was argued that the S-R chains proposed by the behaviourists were not powerful enough to be Turing machines and hence to simulate human behaviour.

KEY FIGURES

Key figures in the discovery that information processing can be thought of as device-independent representations consisting of binary units (bits) to which Boolean operations are applied:

- **George Boole:** British mathematician (1815–1864) who developed Boolean algebra consisting of binary digits and the logical operations AND, OR, NOT and XOR.
- **Alfred Whitehead and Bertrand Russell:** British-American mathematician (1861–1947) and British philosopher (1872–1970) who in 1910–1913 published a series of books showing that the roots of mathematics lie in logic.
- **Alan Turing:** British mathematician (1912–1954) who proved that any machine working on the basis of Boolean algebra is able to perform any mathematical and logical operation (Turing machine).
- **Claude Shannon** (1916–2001): American engineer called 'the father of information theory', who showed that all information can be represented in binary code and that the application of Boolean algebra can construct and resolve any relationship.
- **Warren McCulloch** (1899–1969): American neurophysiologist, famous for his suggestion that the brain can be seen as a Turing machine. Started neural network research.

The liberating metaphor of the computer

Soon, the 1948 California workshop was followed by a string of other meetings to discuss the possibilities of the new insights. These grouped mathematicians, engineers, physiologists, psychologists and philosophers, who all took as their point of departure the analogy of human psychological functioning with computer functioning. Leahey (2004: 418–21) mentions three further ways in which the availability of computers changed research for psychologists.

A new explanation of the purposiveness of behaviour

A problem that had faced psychologists from the start was how to account for the fact that people appear to have clear goals in their life which they deliberately choose and which direct their behaviour. This seemed to require the existence of a **homunculus**, a

homunculus
word (meaning 'little man') used to refer to the difficulty of explaining goal-oriented behaviour without making use of an ultimate intelligent (humanlike) control centre

little man sitting in the brain taking decisions and having a free will to steer behaviour. Even at a lower level, it seemed difficult to avoid the homunculus problem. For instance, when Tolman referred to a cognitive map in rats, he was accused by Skinner of failing to explain who was supposedly reading the map and deciding when to use the knowledge of the map. The homunculus problem has been known since the days of Descartes and is often referred to as the 'ghost in the machine' (remember that Descartes saw the human body as a machine). For Descartes, and many after him, this was the reason why they made a distinction between the body and the soul (Chapter 2).

Computers, however, showed intelligent functioning that could be described as goal-directed. So, why did they not require a homunculus? The answer to this question turned out to be information feedback. When a system is given an end-state, it can reach this state autonomously if it receives feedback about the discrepancy between the current situation and the end-state. Information feedback was already known long before the computer was invented (it was part of the first steam machines), but its power had never been fully realised until during World War II, when the American mathematician Norbert Wiener became involved in the attempts to build guided missiles.

The potential of information feedback can easily be illustrated by the role of a thermostat in a heating system: when the temperature is below the indicated level, it sends a signal to switch on the boiler; when the temperature is above the indicated level, it sends a signal to switch off the boiler. From the outside it looks as if the thermostat has a purpose (to keep the temperature in the room at a certain level). However, all that is happening is an automatic information-processing mechanism on the basis of information feedback.

Although informational feedback did not solve the whole homunculus problem (who sets the end-state?), it drastically increased the similarity between man and machine. It allowed psychologists to tackle information-processing issues without being attacked for describing a system that required a homunculus to keep an eye on the goal and to decide which action to take.

Simulation of human thinking

Computers provided psychologists with a second tool: they could start to simulate the hypothesised psychological processes in computer programs, with the ideal being a computer program that would pass the Turing test. This is a test described by Alan Turing and involves a human interacting from a distance with another human and a machine. When the human can no longer decide which of the two partners is the machine, then the machine has passed the Turing test. That is, its performance has reached the human level. (Incidentally, for a machine to pass the test, it would sometimes have to deliberately introduce an error to confuse the interrogator; otherwise, its superior performance – for instance in calculations – would easily betray the machine.) The comparison of human and computer functioning gave rise to a new research field, artificial intelligence (AI).

Psychologists as software engineers

Finally, computers also gave psychological researchers a better idea of their role relative to that of other scientists. They were the programmers working on the software of humans. This could be done to a large extent independently of the electronic circuits in the machine (the anatomy) and knowledge of the way information is coded, stored and retrieved (the physiology). In addition, psychologists could think

information feedback

mechanism in which the current performance level is compared to the desired end-state and the discrepancy is used to bring the performance closer to the end-state aimed for; important for psychology because it explained a great deal of goal-directed behaviour that previously seemed to require a homunculus explanation

Turing test

test described by Alan Turing, which involves a human interacting with a machine and another human without being able to discriminate the machine from the human; machines that pass the Turing test are seen as the goal of artificial intelligence of information transformation in terms of algorithms that were run on the input. Algorithms are lists of instructions that convert a given input, via a fully defined series of intermediate steps, into the desired output. An example would be an algorithm that turns input speech into a written record of what is said.

algorithm

list of instructions that converts a given input, via a fully defined series of intermediate steps, into the desired output

The role of psychologists as human software engineers can clearly be seen in the following excerpt from the first textbook on cognitive psychology:

> The task of a psychologist trying to understand human cognition is analogous to that of a man trying to discover how a computer has been programmed. In particular, if the program seems to store and reuse information, he would like to know by what 'routines' or 'procedures' this is done.
>
> (Neisser 1967: 6)

What do you think?

When you are surfing on the internet, do you ever think of the mechanical operations that present the information on your screen or that execute the operations summoned by your mouse clicks? Do you need to know this when you want to teach someone how to use the internet?

Interim summary

The existence of computers provided psychologists with a new metaphor to understand the mind and the nature of their own research.

- The computer made it easier to understand how an organism can seem to be goal-directed, without there being a homunculus who sets the goals and checks the progress.
- Computers allowed psychologists to simulate human functioning (artificial intelligence).
- Computers needed programmers who dealt with the information processing, independently of the ways in which the processes were carried out in the machine.

The emergence of cognitive psychology

Because of the above developments, behaviourism came under increasing pressure. Its framework already felt like an uncomfortable straitjacket to many researchers, and now they were given arguments about why it might be wrong. The year 1956 is seen by most people involved as the turning point. In that year there was another workshop assembling the main proponents of the new movement, and several important books and articles were published (see e.g. Miller (2003) for a review).

Miller's article on the limits of short-term memory

One of the decisive 1956 publications was George Miller's article on the limits of human short-term memory (Miller 1956). Up to the publication of that article, new ideas had largely been 'imposed' on psychology from the outside. The people leading the change were mathematicians, engineers, neuroscientists, a political scientist and a linguist. What psychologists missed were psychological experiments that would convince them of the potential of the new movement. Remember that behaviourists insisted on the importance of verifiable evidence based on experiments with operationally defined variables.

In his publication, Miller reviewed the experimental evidence indicating that humans could report only seven (plus or minus two) unrelated items presented at a rate of about one stimulus per second (precursors of this discovery can already be found in the works of Wundt, James, Ebbinghaus, Jacobs and Binet). This finding was the first empirical evidence that the human mind could be considered as a computer with a limited 'working memory'. Psychologists were particularly sensitive to this argument, because in the 1950s the central processing units of the available computers were very limited, so that only simple operations could be performed. Each time the capacity of the central processing unit was increased, the performance of the computer became much better and more complex operations could be handled. So, the thought of the human brain as a computer with a limited capacity had a strong appeal to psychologists and provided them with new ideas of how to investigate the human mind.

Neisser's (1967) *Cognitive psychology*

Another important moment in the new movement was the publication of a book with the title *Cognitive psychology* by Ulric Neisser in 1967. This book not only summarised the evidence in favour of information processing in the mind, but also helped to establish the name of the new movement. The word cognition itself was defined as follows:

> As used here, the term 'cognition' refers to all the processes by which the sensory input is transformed, reduced, elaborated, stored, recovered, and used. It is concerned with these processes even when they operate in the absence of relevant stimulation, as in images and hallucinations . . . given such a sweeping definition, it is apparent that cognition is involved in everything a human being might possibly do; that every psychological phenomenon is a cognitive phenomenon.
>
> (Neisser 1967: 4)

cognitive psychology

movement in psychology arguing that observable behaviours are the result of information processing in the mind; started in the 1950s and currently the dominant form of mainstream psychology

By the mid-1970s academic psychologists identified themselves predominantly with cognitive psychology and not with behaviourism. Although the name cognitive psychology originally referred to research on information processing, as described below, it soon became a kind of catch-all term to represent all psychologists who did experimental research and included mental representations in their theorising. Psychologists who were still known as behaviourists mostly did research on learning in animals, where the behaviourist models did a good job of predicting the animal's behaviour under well-controlled circumstances, although in this research area the need for the inclusion of cognitive processes in the models became increasingly felt as well (e.g. Bouton 2007).

Interim summary

Major steps in the emergence of cognitive psychology:

- Miller's 1956 article on the limits of short-term memory, showing that the human brain could be conceptualised as a computer with a limited capacity.
- Neisser's 1967 book *Cognitive psychology*: review of the evidence and important for establishing the name.

KEY FIGURES

Figures behind the cognitive revolution

- **Norbert Wiener:** American mathematician (1894–1964) who documented the importance of information feedback in information processing systems.

- **Karl Lashley:** American behaviourist (1890–1958), who was one of the first to realise that psychological processes could not be described by a chain of S-R connections. (Also known for his work on brain localisation.)

- **Herbert Simon** (1916–2001) and **Alan Newell** (1927–1992): American political scientist and computer scientist who pioneered the field of artificial intelligence. They were the first to show that computers could be used for something other than number crunching (they created a general problem-solver program).

- **Noam Chomsky:** American linguist (born in 1928) who showed that an S-R chain (Markov chain) is incapable of producing human-like language.

- **George A. Miller:** American psychologist (born in 1920) who strongly promoted the cognitive revolution; wrote an influential article on the limitations of short-term memory and was instrumental in translating Chomsky's insights to psychology.

- **Donald Broadbent:** British psychologist (1926–1993) working in the British (non-behaviourist) tradition, who was one of the first to use flow diagrams to document the different transformations information had to undergo from input to output. Very influential model of selective attention (filter theory), which stimulated much early research.

- **Ulric Neisser** (1928–2012): wrote the first proper textbook on cognitive psychology.

Specific features of cognitive psychology

The fledgling cognitive psychology differed in two important ways from its predecessors. First, it accepted a separate level of mental representations to which algorithms were applied. Second, it introduced more complex information manipulations than the simple associations that had formed the basis of human knowledge since the days of empiricism and associationism (see Chapter 3). Cognitive psychology also differed from pre-behaviourist psychology (but not from behaviourism) by its insistence on verifiable predictions and experimental tests of the hypothesised mechanisms.

Information processing on the basis of mental representations

mental representation

information pattern in the mind representing knowledge obtained through observation or the application of an algorithm; forms a realm separate from the brain and could in principle be copied to another brain (or, in a more extreme version, to a Turing machine)

Remember that mathematicians had discovered that information could be represented and manipulated by means of logical operations involving binary representations (0s and 1s). That is, information could be thought of as bits (decisions between two equally plausible alternatives), completely divorced from the system on which it was implemented. The sequence 1011001 coded the same piece of information, irrespective of how the 0s and 1s were made real, and could be copied onto every machine capable of representing 0s and 1s. This made it possible to think of information as a separate realm, independent of the transmission device and also separate from the outside world. According to Gardner, this was the most important advance of cognitive psychology:

To my mind, the major accomplishment of cognitive science has been the clear demonstration of the validity of positing a level of **mental representation**: a set of constructs that can be invoked for the explanation of cognitive phenomena, ranging from visual perception to story comprehension.

(Gardner 1987: 383)

Mental representations not only became a layer different from the outside world and the brain; psychologists also started to examine how information could be transformed by means of algorithms. They spoke of information that was encoded, transformed, integrated with previously stored information and, in turn, saved. This dynamic aspect of information handling was called information processing, and cognitive psychologists started to make models of how this processing could be achieved (i.e. which procedures or routines were involved). Two approaches were taken.

The first approach was to make use of information-processing diagrams, so-called boxes-and-arrows diagrams. In these diagrams, the boxes stood for (temporary) stores of information, and the arrows for cognitive processes that transformed the information. As it happened, one of the first influential diagrams did not come from the USA, but from the UK, where the behaviourist tradition had been much weaker (see below). In 1958 the British researcher Donald Broadbent presented a flowchart of how he thought selective attention worked. Selective attention refers to the fact that humans are able to respond to a single stimulus and at the same time ignore distraction stimuli.

Broadbent's model (Figure 5.6) included several components. First, it assumed that all stimuli were briefly stored in a short-term store. Due to capacity limitations, not all of these stimuli could be further processed; a choice had to be made. This was done by a selective filter. The selected information was further processed on the basis of past experiences and, if necessary, the filter was directed to a different sensory channel (e.g. when the information was no longer interesting enough).

The second approach taken by cognitive psychologists was to write a computer program that actually performed the various transformations assumed to occur. In the case of Broadbent's model, for instance, one would try to make a computer program that responded in the same way as humans do to multiple, competing input streams. This approach was much more demanding, but at the same time much

information processing

encoding mental representations, transforming them by means of algorithms, and integrating them with existing knowledge; forms the core of cognitive psychology

boxes-and-arrows diagram

flowchart outlining the different information stores (boxes) and information transformations (arrows) involved in the execution of a particular task with observable input and output; used by cognitive psychologists to detail the information-processing involved in the task

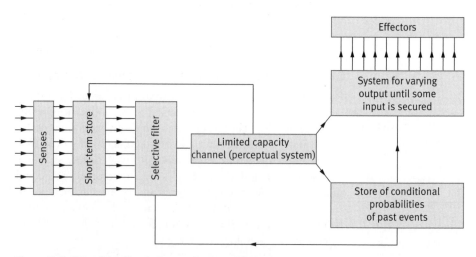

Figure 5.6 One of the first boxes-and-arrows diagrams.
Source: Broadbent (1958).

more insightful. Boxes-and-arrows models were an interesting starting point but left unspecified much of how the information was stored and transformed. They were similar to an engineer's drawing plans, not to a functioning machine.

By trying to implement the various routines and procedures, psychologists had to be much more specific about the precise mechanisms involved, and the model guaranteed that the proposed solution worked as predicted (e.g. would Broadbent's boxes-and-arrows model really work if you tried to implement it in a computer, and would it perform the same as humans?). This was the challenge artificial intelligence tried to meet. Another term that is often used for this approach is the building of computational models, computer models that resemble human performance.

computational model

computer program simulating the human information processing assumed to be involved in the execution of a particular task; requires researchers to be much more precise about what is going on than in a boxes-and-arrows diagram

More complex procedures were needed than foreseen and top-down processes had to be introduced

While trying to make their computer programs work, psychologists were soon confronted by the fact that they had seriously underestimated the complexity of the information processing involved. This became particularly clear in language understanding. For instance, many cognitive psychologists and computer scientists assumed that one of the first straightforward applications of artificial intelligence would be the automatic translation of texts. After all, if you feed a computer with English sentences, a dictionary and a grammar, it must not be too difficult to turn them into correct sentences in whatever other language you choose. However, this turned out not to be the case.

One problem faced by researchers was that the meaning of words often depends on the meaning of the surrounding words (their context). Many words have more than one meaning and use (e.g. bank, coach, swallow) and the meanings of synonyms often differ slightly (e.g. believe, think), so that they are not completely interchangeable. Another problem was that it is often difficult to compute the syntactic structure of sentences and that ambiguities frequently have to be solved on the basis of the plausibility of the different interpretations. To correctly interpret the sentence 'John saw the mountains flying to New York', you must know that John can fly but the mountains cannot.

It soon became clear to everyone involved in machine translation that humans add a lot of background information to the language input they receive, in order to come to the correct interpretation. As long as the computational models were not able to do the same, the quality of the translation remained appalling for all but the simplest sentences. This was a far cry from the conviction in the early days that human knowledge was nothing but associations between elementary sensations (shared by empiricists, structuralists and behaviourists).

One of the new elements the cognitive psychologists had to introduce in their information-processing models was the existence of top-down processes. These refer to the fact that information from higher processing stages is fed back to previous processing stages and influences processing at these stages. Information in the human mind does not flow unidirectionally from the input to the output (bottom-up), but requires multiple interactions between the different processing components to solve ambiguities and direct the interpretation in the right direction. Needless to say, the top-down processes were inspired by the information-feedback mechanisms discovered during World War II (see above).

Incidentally, the extent of the challenge faced by cognitive psychologists and computer scientists to build machine translators can be gauged by looking at the quality

top-down process

process by which information from a higher processing stage is fed back to previous processing stages and influences the processing at these stages; found to be a helpful (and even essential) element in many computational models of current-day software (more than 50 years after the introduction of cognitive psychology and artificial intelligence). What happens if we enter a sentence with a few ambiguities into such a program, translate it in another language and then back to English? Will the program pass the Turing test? Below, you can find out what happened when we asked Google Language Tools to translate an English sentence into a few other languages and then back to English (**translate.google.com**):

Original sentence: 'I believe the coach on the bank should be moved.'
Back translation from Arabic: 'I think it should be moved coach in the West.'
Back translation from German: 'I think the coach should be moved to the bank.'
Back translation from Korean: 'I believe that the bank will be moving in the coach.'
Back translation from Spanish: 'I think the coach on the bench should be moved.'

? What do you think?

Can you imagine the psychologists' excitement when they discovered all these new tools? At the same time, the computer metaphor pushed aside other research topics such as interest in emotions and motivation. What do you think: can we study the human mind without taking into account motivation and emotion?

Verifiable predictions and experimental tests of the hypothesised processes

To investigate information processing in humans, cognitive psychology gratefully relied on the experimental expertise gathered by the behaviourists. They noticed that other sciences also investigated imperceptible processes and did so by examining the influences of these processes on perceptible phenomena. For instance, astronomers tried to unravel the origin of the universe by looking at the movements of the stellar bodies relative to one another. Similarly, in the biological and physical sciences entities often had to be postulated that could not (yet) be perceived (e.g. the existence of DNA in cells, or the existence of neutrinos in the universe). Usually, when the technology improved sufficiently, these theoretical entities could be laid bare. So, there was nothing wrong with postulating non-observable information algorithms, as long as their impact could be verified in a valid way.

The approach can be illustrated with research motivated by Broadbent's model of selective attention, discussed in Figure 5.6. This model predicted the existence of a memory store in which all stimuli are briefly kept, including the ones not attended to by the filter. This assumption seemed to be contradicted by the fact that when people see an array consisting of several elements (e.g. letters) flashed for a short period of time they only manage to see some four elements, a finding already reported by Wilhelm Wundt in 1912.

George Sperling (1960) decided to examine this contradiction. He reasoned that the small number of stimuli reported by the participants might be due to the fact that the traces in the short-term store rapidly fade while the participant is naming the elements, so that only a few can be named before the memory trace is lost. If this is true, Sperling reasoned, then it must be possible to show that people can perceive more stimuli if they are not required to name all of them. To investigate this, Sperling used displays with 12 letters, distributed over three rows, as in the following example:

Q	F	O	I
A	G	N	P
T	L	E	M

Participants did not have to name 'as many letters as they had seen', but they got a tone immediately after the brief stimulus display, telling them which line they had to report. If the tone was high, they had to report the top row; if it was medium they had to report the middle row; and if it was low they had to report the bottom row. With this technique Sperling observed that participants could report each of the rows requested, as was predicted by Broadbent's model with its full information storage for a brief period of time. To further test the latter part of the model, Sperling introduced a short time delay between the display of the stimulus and the presentation of the tone. As predicted, he noticed that the ability of the participants to report the letters sharply declined as the time between the display and the tone increased. Within a second all memory traces in the visual store were lost.

Sperling's research illustrates how cognitive psychologists combined the various advances made in the first half of the twentieth century to identify and examine cognitive functioning in a much more refined and convincing way. At last, it became possible to look into the functioning of the mind on the basis of the performance of participants under highly controlled circumstances. In the next chapter we will see how this research was supplemented by increasingly sophisticated techniques to directly look at the brain during various tasks.

Interim summary

Specific features of cognitive psychology are:

- The acceptance of a separate level of mental representations, to which transformation algorithms apply.
- Information processing on the mental representations captured by boxes-and-arrows diagrams and computational models.
- Models designed to lead to predictions that can be verified in experiments making use of performance measures.

5.4 *Focus on*: Has behaviourism been replaced by cognitive psychology just like behaviourism defeated structuralism and functionalism?

In many introductory books of psychology the history of psychology is summarised as follows. When psychological research started, everyone used introspection to examine consciousness. Gradually this research turned into a crisis because knowledge did not advance adequately and the findings required ever more complicated theories to explain them. Then came the 'behaviourist revolution' which slashed the importance of introspection and consciousness and replaced them by experimentation and observable behaviours. After a few decades this approach fell into a crisis as well, because its theories grew more complicated without really explaining the essence of human psychological functioning. At that moment, behaviourism was overthrown by cognitive psychology in the 'cognitive revolution'. Some authors even have exact dates for the revolutions: 1913 for behaviourism and 1956 for cognitive psychology.

Continuity despite the 'behaviourist revolution'

Seeing the introduction of behaviourism and cognitive psychology as scientific revolutions helps us to understand why topics that were at the forefront of research at one moment, no longer were a few years later, and why scientists often do not refer in a positive way to research done in a certain epoch. However, like all approaches, this view to some extent distorts reality. It maximises the differences that exist between time periods and minimises the continuity that is present (Leahey 1992). For instance, with respect to the behaviourist revolution, it overlooks the experimental work done since the time of Wundt and the advances in applied psychology (e.g. in intelligence research and in the development of psychological therapies). It also ignores the fact that behaviourism was never an all-dominating paradigm.

In Europe and Canada behaviourism did not have the same impact as in the USA. One of the frontrunners of the 'cognitive revolution', George Miller, recounted a talk he gave at the University of Cambridge in 1963 in which he 'lambasted the hell out of the behaviorists' to a puzzled audience, because, as he was told after the talk, there were only three behaviourists in the UK, none of whom was present (Baars 1986: 212). The absence of behaviourist thinking in the UK can easily be supported by the texts published in the heyday of behaviourism. For instance, this is what the director of a major British psychology institute, Kenneth Craik, wrote in 1943 about the function of the mind:

> If the organism carries a small-scale model of external reality and its own possible actions within its head, it is able to try out various alternatives, conclude which is the best of them, react to future situations before they arise, utilize the knowledge of past events in dealing with the present and future, and in every way react to a much fuller, safer and more competent manner to emergencies which face it.
>
> (Craik 1943; as cited in Mandler 2007: 169)

Craik's text clearly is a cognitive text, despite the fact that it was published more than five years before the 'seminal' 1948 workshop described above. Many similar non-behaviourist writings can be found in other parts of Europe and Canada, where the texts of the Gestalt psychologists were read and commented. A case can even be made that the escape of the Gestalt psychologists from Germany to the USA in the wake of World War II was one of the factors contributing to the growth of cognitive psychology in the USA (see Mandler (2007) for a discussion of this possibility).

Even in the USA in the heyday of behaviourism there were many examples of research that did not fit well within the strong behaviourist claims. We already mentioned Tolman, who was very interested in the writings of the Gestalt psychologists and went to study in Germany. Another example was J. Ridley Stroop, who in 1935 published his article on the Stroop effect, which has since become one of the main techniques used in cognitive psychology. Similarly, there is little evidence for strong behaviourist research traditions in developmental or social psychology. Here, behaviourists had an impact through their methodological innovations much more than by their theoretical views.

Continuity despite the 'cognitive revolution'

Very much the same story can be written about the cognitive revolution. In many fields and universities it did not have to 'replace' behaviourism, as behaviourism was not a dominant force there. At the same time, in the research traditions where the behaviourist approach had proven fruitful, researchers felt little need to replace their theories founded on observable behaviour by new ones built on hypothetical cognitions. This was the case for the psychology of learning based on operant and classical conditioning. Here many authors felt that cognitive theories risked throwing the field back to the pre-Thorndike years of anthropomorphic interpretation. According to them, behaviouristic methodology has strengths that must not be lost in the 'cognitive revolution'.

Chiesa (1994) lists the following elements radical behaviourism still has to offer to psychology:

1. Cognitive psychology sees humans too much as 'agents' of the behaviour, rather than as 'hosts'. As a result, cognitive psychologists tend to overlook the fact that much behaviour is the result of environmental factors. Cognitive psychologists think too much in terms of causes and effects, whereas behaviourists see behaviour as the tuning of an organism to correlations that are present in the environment. 'The distinction between the person as agent and the person as host is not a trivial one, because if the person is the agent of creation, then it is the person who must be analyzed, dissected, and investigated . . . . However, if the person is viewed as host, and . . . seen as the confluence of reinforcement history (experience) and present circumstances, then it is history and present circumstances that can more easily be analyzed, dissected, and investigated.' (Chiesa 1994: 30–31).

2. Radical behaviourism promotes an inductive scientific method, rather than a hypothetico-deductive method. Cognitive theorists too rapidly postulate unobservable processes and representations, which bias their perception. They do not proceed from careful observation to theory formulation, but have a tendency to postulate wild guesses and see how these subsequently work out in falsification tests. 'If . . . the aim of science is to formulate general empirical laws based on observation, this will determine an inductive approach that attempts to generalize *from* data.' 'The model diverts attention from specific properties of behavior in the context in which it occurs, obscuring relations *actually* taking place by focusing on relations *assumed* to be taking place.' (Chiesa 1994: 58, 153; see also De Houwer 2011).

3. Radical behaviourism sees the environmental influences on behaviour as direct and not mediated by invisible cognitive or physiological factors (which detract the scientists' attention from the real relationship). 'A reflex, for example, in the Skinnerian system describes a particular kind of correlation between stimulus and response.' (Chiesa 1994: 134)

4. Cognitive psychologists are too much interested in the average data of groups, whereas radical behaviourism is interested in the behaviour of individuals, with their unique history of interactions with their environment. 'Starting from the biological rather than statistical viewpoint, radical behaviorists do not rely on the concepts of average and normal distribution and do not derive statements about effects of independent variables from statistical tests of significance. Psychology adopted and adapted methods that were developed for making statements about populations, statements that cannot be applied to individuals and that are useful where the behavior of individuals is of no interest. Maintaining the biological tradition, radical behaviorists developed methods that accept and incorporate

notions of individuality. In this way, they derive statements that can be applied to the behavior of individuals.' '. . . to Quetelet the mean in any distribution of human phenomena was not merely a descriptive tool but a statement of the ideal and extremes in all things were undesirable deviations. This view differs from the biological concept of variation in that variation to a biologist is far from being an error of nature, an undesirable deviation from an ideal, fixed point. It is the raw material for selection and evolution. Concepts like average and ideal do not enter into a Darwinian, biological formulation, but they continue, in the tradition of Quetelet, to form part of the background to psychology's treatment of its data.' 'Psychologists neglect personal history. They take an ahistorical strategy, focussing on hypothetical structures inside the organism and thus in the current situation . . . history is not a term frequently used by psychologists.'

(Chiesa 1994: 72, 74, 120)

What do you think?

What do you think of Chiesa's recommendations? Do they strike you as reasonable and does this mean that radical behaviourism tends to be depicted too negatively?

For the reasons just outlined, there are still psychological researchers who place themselves firmly within the behaviourist tradition and who are convinced that the negative way in which behaviourism is depicted in mainstream psychology is to the detriment of psychological research rather than to its advancement. They point out, for instance, that the description of Tolman's research on the cognitive map is heavily biased in textbooks and presented as definite evidence against Skinner's views, whereas in reality the true findings can be accounted for within the radical behaviourist framework (e.g. Jensen 2006).

Current research on structuralist and functionalist questions

We could go even further and ask ourselves whether the research favoured by structuralists and functionalists really has been 'defeated' by behaviourism and cognitive psychology. Are there no psychologists interested in consciousness and the usefulness of introspection for its study any more? Are there no more psychologists interested in evolutionary theory and the way in which human behaviour has been shaped by survival advantages? As it happens, both traditions are still very active research topics. Researchers are still tackling the questions of what consciousness is and what can be concluded from introspection (e.g., Fox, Ericsson & Best 2011; Jack & Roepstorff 2002; Lamme 2010; Locke 2009; Marti *et al.* 2010). There is even a journal entirely devoted to these topics, the *Journal of Consciousness Studies*, addressing issues such as 'How does the mind relate to the brain?', 'Can computers ever be conscious?' and 'What do we mean by subjectivity and the self?'. Similarly, the way in which evolution has shaped human behaviour is a very active research theme again, as we will see in Chapter 12, with its own name: 'evolutionary psychology' (Buss 2008; Workman & Reader 2008). Although none of these researchers would call themselves structuralists or functionalists, they continue the type of research that was central to these schools.

Conclusion

All in all, the above examples illustrate once more that although the idea of revolutions, such as the behaviourist and cognitive revolution, is appealing and eye-opening, it is good to keep in mind that this term belies the breadth of reality and that there has been more continuity and knowledge accumulation in psychological research than is suggested by words such as 'revolution' and 'schools'. These words hide the fact that scientific research can be done in different ways, which are not necessarily incompatible but may reinforce and correct each other. For instance, we saw that radical behaviourism favours a strong inductive approach (from data to theory), whereas cognitive psychology believes more in the hypothetico-deductive approach (the postulation of hypotheses, which are tested empirically). This is one of the big conceptual issues in psychological research, which will recur several times in later chapters, where we will see that radical behaviourism is not the only approach questioning cognitive psychology's reliance on hypothesis testing.

Interim summary

- Behaviourism and cognitive psychology are often depicted as revolutions that radically altered psychological research.

- This is only true to some extent, because neither behaviourism nor cognitive psychology has been all-encompassing. This view also hides the fact that various approaches in psychology are not entirely incompatible with each other and represent different ideas of how scientific research should be done.

Recommended literature

We relied heavily on the original resources that are freely available on the internet (in particular at psychclassics.yorku.ca and books.google.com). Two other very useful sources are: Baars, B.J. (1986) *The cognitive revolution in psychology* (New York: Guilford Press) and Gardner, H. (1987) *The mind's new science: A history of the cognitive revolution* (New York: Basic Books). These books contain a discussion about the rise of behaviourism in addition to the start of cognitive psychology.

Further worthwhile reading is the special issues of the *American Psychologist*, published in 1992 (Vol. 47(2) on the occasion of the 100th birthday of the American Psychological Association) and in 2000 (Vol. 55(3) at the start of the new millennium). For the rest, all the history books recommended in Chapter 4 contain chapters on behaviourism and cognitive psychology.

References

Baars, B.J. (1986) *The cognitive revolution in psychology*. New York: Guilford Press.

Benjafield, J.G. (2005) *A history of psychology*. Oxford: Oxford University Press.

Benjamin, L.T., Jr. (2000) 'The psychology laboratory at the turn of the 20th century', *American Psychologist*, 55: 318–21.

Blodgett, H.C. (1929) 'The effect of the introduction of reward upon the maze performance of rats'. *University of California Publications in Psychology*, 4: 113–34.

Bouton, M.E. (2007) *Learning and behavior: A contemporary synthesis*. Sunderland, MA: Sinauer Associates.

Bridgman, P.W. (1927) *The logic of modern physics*. Chicago: University of Chicago Press.

Broadbent, D.E. (1958) *Perception and communication*. Elmsford, NY: Pergamon Press.

Buss, D.M. (2008) *Evolutionary psychology: The new science of the mind*. Harlow, UK: Pearson Education.

Chadwick, O. (1990) *The secularization of the European mind in the nineteenth century*. Cambridge: Cambridge University Press.

Chiesa, M. (1994) *Radical behaviorism: The philosophy and the science*. Sarasota, FL: Authors Cooperative, Publishers.

Coon, D.J. (1992) 'Testing the limits of sense and science: American experimental psychologists combat spiritualism 1880–1920', *American Psychologist,* **47**: 143–51.

De Houwer, J. (2011) 'Why the cognitive approach in psychology would profit from a functional approach and vice versa', *Perspectives on Psychological Science,* **6**: 202–9.

Dennis, P.M. (2011) 'Press coverage of the new psychology by the New York Times during the progressive era', *History of Psychology,* **14**: 113–36.

Fox, M.C., Ericsson, K.A. & Best, R. (2011) 'Do procedures for verbal reporting of thinking have to be reactive? A meta-analysis and recommendations for best reporting methods', *Psychological Bulletin,* **137**: 316–44.

Fuchs, A.H. (2000) 'Teaching the introductory course in Psychology circa 1900', *American Psychologist,* **55**: 492–5.

Galef, B.G. (1998) 'Edward Thorndike: Revolutionary psychologist, ambiguous biologist', *American Psychologist,* **53**: 1128–34.

Gardner, H. (1987) *The mind's new science: A history of the cognitive revolution.* New York: Basic Books.

Green, C.D. (2009) 'Darwinian theory, functionalism, and the first American psychological revolution', *American Psychologist,* **64**: 75–83.

Jack, A.I. & Roepstorff, A. (2002) 'Introspection and cognitive brain mapping: From stimulus-response to script-report', *Trends in Cognitive Sciences,* **6**: 333–9.

Jahoda, G. (2007) *A history of social psychology.* Cambridge: Cambridge University Press.

Jansz, J. & Van Drunen, P. (eds) (2004) *A social history of psychology.* Oxford: Blackwell.

Jensen, R. (2006) 'Behaviorism, latent learning, and cognitive maps: Needed revisions in introductory psychology textbooks', *Behavior Analyst,* **29**: 187–209.

Lamme, V.A.F. (2010) 'How neuroscience will change our view on consciousness (plus subsequent commentaries)', *Cognitive Neuroscience,* **1**: 204–40.

Leahey, T.H. (1992) 'The mythical revolutions of American psychology', *American Psychologist,* **47**: 308–18.

Leahey, T.H. (2004) *A history of psychology* (6th edn). Upper Saddle River, NJ: Pearson Prentice Hall.

Locke, E.A. (2009) 'It's time we brought introspection out of the closet', *Perspectives on Psychological Science,* **4**: 24–5.

Mackenzie, D.B. (1977) *Behaviorism and the limits of scientific method.* London: Routledge & Kegan Paul.

Malone, J.C. & Cruchon, N.M. (2001) 'Radical behaviorism and the rest of psychology: A review/précis of Skinner's *About Behaviorism*', *Behavior and Philosophy,* **29**: 31–57.

Mandler, G. (2007) *A history of modern experimental psychology.* Cambridge, MA: MIT Press.

Marti, S., Sackur, J., Sigman, M. & Dehaene, S. (2010) 'Mapping introspection's blind spot: Reconstruction of dual-task phenomenology using quantified introspection', *Cognition,* **115**: 303–13.

McCulloch, W.S. & Pitts, W.H. (1943) 'A logical calculus of the ideas immanent in nervous activity', *Bulletin of Mathematical Biophysics,* **5**: 115–33.

Miller, G.A. (1956) 'The magical number seven, plus or minus two', *Psychological Review,* **63**: 81–97.

Miller, G.A. (2003) 'The cognitive revolution: A historical perspective', *Trends in Cognitive Sciences,* **7**: 141–4.

Neisser, U. (1967) *Cognitive psychology.* New York: Appleton-Century-Crofts.

Pickren, W. & Rutherford, A. (2010) *A history of modern psychology in context.* Hoboken, NJ: John Wiley & Sons.

Richards, G. (1996) *Putting psychology in its place: An introduction from a critical historical perspective.* London: Routledge.

Robinson, D.K. (2001) 'Reaction-time experiments in Wundt's Institute and beyond'. In R.W. Rieber & D.K. Robinson (eds), *Wilhelm Wundt in history: The making of a scientific psychology.* New York: Kluwer/Plenum, pp. 161–204.

Schimit, D. (2005) 'Re-visioning antebellum American psychology: The dissemination of mesmerism, 1836–1854', *History of Psychology,* **8**: 403–34.

Skinner, B.F. (1974) *About behaviorism.* New York: Knopf.

Sokal, M.M. (2006) 'The origins of the new psychology in the United States', *Physis: Rivista internazionale di storia della scienza,* **43**: 273–300.

Sperling, G. (1960) 'The information available in brief visual presentations', *Psychological Monographs,* **74**: 1–29.

Spurzheim, J.G. (1834) *Phrenology of the doctrine of the mental phenomenon* (3rd edn). Boston: Marsh, Caper and Lyon.

Stevens, S.S. (1935) 'The operational definition of psychological concepts', *Psychological Review,* **42**: 517–27.

Stroop, J.R. (1935) 'Studies of interference in serial verbal reactions', *Journal of Experimental Psychology,* **18**: 643–62 (reprinted 1992 in *Journal of Experimental Psychology: General,* **121**: 15–23).

Thorndike, E.L. (1911) *Animal intelligence.* New York: Macmillan.

Tolman, E.C. (1948) 'Cognitive maps in rats and men', *Psychological Review,* **55**: 189–209 (available at psychclassics.yorku.ca).

Watson, J.B. (1907) 'Studying the mind of animals', *The World Today,* **12**: 421–6 (available at psychclassics.yorku.ca).

Watson, J.B. (1913) 'Psychology as the behaviorist views it', *Psychological Review,* **20**: 158–77 (available at psychclassics.yorku.ca).

Watson, J.B. & Rayner, R. (1920) 'Conditioned emotional reactions', *Journal of Experimental Psychology,* **3**: 1–14 (available at psychclassics.yorku.ca).

Workman, L. & Reader, W. (2008) *Evolutionary psychology: An introduction* (2nd edn). Cambridge: Cambridge University Press.

6 The input from brain research

Questions to consider

Historical issues addressed in this chapter

- What was assumed in Ancient Egypt about the function of the brain?
- What were the main beliefs about brain functioning in Ancient Greece?
- Why is the nineteenth century a critical century in neuroscience?
- Which developments in neuropsychology and neuroscience took place in the twentieth century?
- Which methods to study the brain were developed in the twentieth century?

Conceptual issues addressed in this chapter

- How could Aristotle be so wrong about the seat of the soul?
- Why were the ventricles thought to be so important for communication between the soul and the body?
- Why were psychologists attracted to the notion of the reflex arc to explain brain functioning?
- Why was it necessary to have good staining techniques before the organisation of brain tissue could be understood?
- Why were the World Wars important for the development of brain research?
- What does knowledge about the localisation of brain functions tell us about the nature of the functions?
- What are the commonalities and differences between cognitive neuropsychology, cognitive neuroscience and cognitive neuropsychiatry?

Introduction

A 25-year-old male presented himself to the Psychiatry Outpatients Department with symptoms of restlessness, irritability and episodic anger outburst, delusions of reference and persecution, auditory and visual hallucinations (hearing divine voices and seeing snakes/fires, etc.) and disturbed sleep for a period of about one year. On exploration, it became clear that he had a history of severe headache off and on, for which he was treated at his local hospital with analgesics . . .

X-rays of the right upper limb showed multiple calcified spots. A CT scan revealed multiple calcified brain lesions with surrounding oedema . . . Histopathological examination confirmed the diagnosis of cysticercosis. Cysticercosis is a condition that has been known about since the Hippocratic era and is the commonest infection of the human central nervous system. It is an infection brought about by the larvea of *T. solium*, the pork tape worm. The tape worms are acquired by ingesting undercooked pork containing cysticerci. . . . The ingested tape worm eggs, activated by gastric and duodenal secretions, develop into invasive larvae in the small intestines. They then migrate across the intestinal wall and are carried by the bloodstream to the sites where they settle and mature into cysticerci. The process can take place anywhere in the body but it is more prevalent in the subcutaneous tissue, muscle and the central nervous system. This process takes approximately two months. Epilepsy is the most common presentation of neurocysticercosis (cysticercosis in the brain); psychosis may be seen in up to 5 per cent of patients affected.

(based on Mahajan *et al.* 2004)

In Chapters 1–5 we discussed the start of psychology as a scientific discipline. In particular we considered the contributions of philosophy and the general turn of society towards science. At the same time, there was another stream of input, consisting of the growing insights into the workings of the brain and its consequences for mental life. This is the topic of the present chapter (as illustrated by the case study opening this chapter).

The chapter consists of six sections. First, we discuss the views about the seat of the soul and the role of the brain in Ancient Egypt and Greece. Next, we review the few developments that were made before the nineteenth century. In section 6.3 we talk about five discoveries in the nineteenth century that are generally seen as the major breakthroughs towards the current understanding of the brain. Sections 6.4 and 6.5 deal with developments in twentieth-century psychology, in particular the appearance of (cognitive) neuropsychology and cognitive neuroscience. As usual, we end with a 'Focus on' section, this time on cognitive neuropsychiatry.

What do you think?

Do you know someone who had a brain examination or took part in a brain study? What was the reason? What was the outcome? What did the study comprise?

6.1 Ideas in Ancient Egypt and Ancient Greece

Beliefs of the Ancient Egyptians

The Edwin Smith papyrus

In 1862 an American collector, Edwin Smith, bought a papyrus scroll in the Egyptian city of Luxor (Figure 6.1). Over half a century later, it would be deciphered by the Egyptologist James Breasted (1930). What was recorded on the manuscript perplexed the medical world (Changeux 1997; Gross 1998). In the text, written around 1,700 BCE but probably a copy of an older papyrus from 3,000 BCE, a series of 48 cases were described dealing with the consequences of head and neck injuries. Each case included a title, details of the examination, a diagnosis and an indication of the treatment. The diagnosis consisted of one of three conclusions: 'this is an ailment that I will treat', 'this is an ailment that I will try to treat' or 'this is an ailment that I will not treat'.

Figure 6.1 Cases 47 and 48 in the Edwin Smith Surgical Papyrus.

Source: Plates XVII and XVIIA from Breasted (1930), Vol. 1. Courtesy of the Oriental Institute of the University of Chicago.

The following is what the papyrus said about case 6:

Title: Instructions concerning a gaping wound in his head, penetrating to the bone, smashing his skull, (and) rending open the brain of his skull.

Examination: If thou examinest a man having a gaping wound in his head, penetrating to the bone, smashing his skull, (and) rending open the brain of his skull, thou shouldst palpate his wound. Shouldst thou find that smash which is in his skull [like] those corrugations which form in molten copper, (and) something therein throbbing (and) fluttering under thy fingers, like the weak place of an infant's crown before it becomes whole – when it has happened there is no throbbing (and) fluttering under thy fingers until the brain of his (the patient's) skull is rent open – (and) he discharges blood from both his nostrils, (and) he suffers with stiffness in his neck . . .

Diagnosis: [Thou shouldst say concerning him]: 'An ailment not to be treated.'

Treatment: Thou shouldst anoint that wound with grease. Thou shalt not bind it; thou shalt not apply two strips upon it: until thou knowest that he has reached a decisive point.
(Breasted (1930) retrieved on 23 October, 2007 from http://www.neurosurgery.org/cybermuseum/pre20th/epapyrus.html)

Edwin Smith papyrus

papyrus from Ancient Egypt that contains short descriptions of the symptoms and treatment of different forms of brain injury; named after the person who bought the papyrus in Egypt and had it analysed

This case includes the first known description of the brain's exterior. In case 8 we read about a smash in the skull, that was accompanied by a deviation of the eyes and the fact that the patient 'shuffled' while walking. The latter bewildered the author, because he repeated four times that this happened, despite the fact that 'the wound was in the skull'. He could not understand why a wound to the head could affect the functioning of the legs.

The Edwin Smith papyrus, as the manuscript became known, illustrates how physicians treating wounded soldiers quite early became convinced of the importance of the head (brain) in controlling behaviour.

Beliefs in the wider society

The existence of the Edwin Smith papyrus did not imply that the knowledge contained in it was widespread. As a matter of fact, in Ancient Egypt most scholars were convinced that the heart was the seat of the soul. This can easily be concluded from the finding that many efforts were made to conserve the heart (and other internal organs) at mummification, whereas the brain was picked out through the nostrils by means of hooks. As Gross (1998: 7) concluded: 'Dead Pharaohs were prepared for their next life with everything but a brain.'

What do you think?

Is the communication between medical/psychological practitioners and lecturers nowadays better than it was in Ancient Egypt? Or is it still possible that lecturers teach knowledge to students which practitioners know is wrong? How much experience do your lecturers and textbook writers have with real cases?

The roles of the heart and the brain in Ancient Greece

Plato

The discussion over whether the soul was in the heart or in the brain continued in Ancient Greece. Hippocrates placed the soul in the brain, as did Plato, although the latter also saw a function for the heart. According to Plato, the soul was divided into three parts. The highest part, responsible for reasoning, was situated in the brain. It came directly from the soul of the universe, was immortal, separated from the body, and it controlled the body. The second part of the soul dealt with sensation, was mortal and situated in the heart. To avoid it polluting the divine soul, a neck separated the two. Finally, the lower part of the soul dealt with appetite and was placed in the liver, far away from the other two.

Aristotle

In contrast, Aristotle was convinced that the heart was the seat of the soul. He gave a series of arguments for this conclusion, summarised in Table 6.1. The function of the brain in Aristotle's view was to counterbalance the heat of the heart. The heart and the brain formed a functional unit in which the brain, which was cold, tempered the heat and seething of the heart. The human brain relative to the body was larger than that of other animals because man's heart was hotter and richer and needed a stronger counterbalance for good performance.

Galen

According to Gross (1998), Aristotle's views would have been different if he had been interested in medicine and in particular in the study of the effects of brain damage, which is the reason why many physicians did not follow him on this particular topic. A decisive moment in demonstrating the importance of the brain for sensation and movement control came when Galen (*c.* 130–*c.* 200 CE), six centuries

Table 6.1 Aristotle's arguments for the heart as the centre of sensation and movement

Heart	Brain
1. Affected by emotion.	1. Not affected.
2. All animals have a heart.	2. Only vertebrates and cephalopods have one, and yet other animals have sensations.
3. Source of blood which is necessary for sensation.	3. Bloodless and therefore without sensation.
4. Warm, characteristic of higher life.	4. Cold.
5. Connected with all the sense organs and muscles, via the blood vessels.	5. Not connected with the sense organs or the connection is irrelevant.
6. Essential for life.	6. Not so.
7. Formed first, and last to stop working.	7. Formed second.
8. Sensitive.	8. Insensitive: if the brain of a living animal is laid bare, it may be cut without any signs of pain.
9. In a central location, appropriate for its central role.	9. Not so.

Source: Gross (1998) *Brain, vision, memory: Tales in the history of neuroscience*. Table from p. 21. Copyright © Massachusetts Institute of Technology, by permission of the MIT Press.

after Aristotle, started to experiment on animals. In one of his experiments Galen found that a pig stopped squealing, but kept breathing, immediately after he severed nerves in the throat, thus demonstrating that the voice came from the brain and not from the heart. This finding was subsequently repeated in several more experiments of a similar nature. Galen also dissected brains and published drawings of them. For a long time, researchers were puzzled about the poor quality of these drawings, until it was realised that they were based on ox brains, which Galen resized to fit into a human skull.

Another problem Galen had to solve was how the brain communicated with the rest of the body. The heart was connected to all parts of the body through the blood in the veins, but how did the brain communicate? It was known that white cables – nerves – connected the brain with the body, but there did not seem to be any liquid flowing through them.

animal spirits

spirits that were thought by Galen to travel over the nerves between the ventricles in the brain and the body

ventricles

apertures in the middle of the brain, which for a long time were thought to contain perceptions, memories and thoughts; seat of the animal spirits

It is important to understand that Galen, in line with thinkers before him, did not think the brain itself was important for reason or emotion but for the soul residing inside the brain. The soul lived in the solid parts and produced and stored **animal spirits** in the apertures in the middle of the brain, called the **ventricles**. By means of these spirits the soul communicated with the rest of the body. The spirits travelled between the soul and the organs via the nerves, which were assumed to be hollow tubes. Because of the higher importance attached to the ventricles, they were depicted with much more accuracy and detail in Galen's plates than the brain itself. The convolutions on the surface of the brain were drawn like intestines rather than the way they really looked.

What do you think?

Why would someone like Galen assume that the brains of humans look the same as those of oxes? Have a look at the pictures: what differences do you see? (left: human brain; right: brain of an ox.)

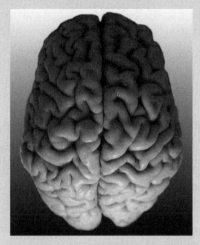 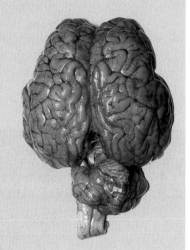

Source: (left) Heidi Cartwright/Wellcome Images; (right) Daniel Templeton/Alamy Images.

Interim summary

- The Edwin Smith papyrus illustrates that practising physicians rapidly made a link between injuries to the brain and mental and behavioural consequences.

- In the Ancient Egyptian and Greek societies at large, however, the link between the heart and intelligence was stronger (e.g. mummification, Aristotle; but see Hippocrates and Plato).

- Galen's experiments clearly established the primacy of the brain and the nerves, rather than the heart and the veins, for the control of movement (e.g. in the squealing of pigs).

- Galen thought that the soul was located in the solid parts of the brain and commanded animal spirits in the ventricles, which travelled through the nerves to the body parts to be influenced.

KEY FIGURE Galen

- Greek physician (*c.* 130–*c.* 200 CE) working in Rome after 162 (Latin name: Galenus).

- Previously worked for 3–4 years as a physician in a gladiator school, where he gained much experience with treating injuries, which he called 'windows into the body'.

- Performed operations on humans and animals; also did vivisections on the latter to study the functions of various body parts.

- Established the primacy of the brain for sensation and movement. Located the soul in the solid parts of the brain and animal spirits in the ventricles. The animal spirits travelled to the body via the nerves.
- Wrote extensively, so that he is a link with the medical knowledge of Ancient Greece.
- Works translated in Arabic in the ninth century and in Latin in the sixteenth century (by Vesalius). Legacy continued until the eighteenth/nineteenth centuries.

6.2 Further insights into the anatomy and functioning of the nervous system in the Renaissance and the seventeenth and eighteenth centuries

Research about the brain came to a complete standstill in the Middle Ages and only really took off again in the nineteenth century. Below we discuss the few developments that happened in the era in between.

Developments in the Renaissance

The continuing primacy of the ventricles

Galen's views remained the norm until well into the eighteenth century. When Andreas Vesalius (1514–1564) resumed dissections and extended them to humans, he persisted in Galen's preoccupation with the correct drawing of the ventricles and did not care much about the convolutions of the brain, which he carried on depicting as intestines (the upper part of Figure 6.2).

Differentiation between the ventricles

Vesalius further established for certain that there were three ventricles (this was not clear from Galen's writings, probably because there is a difference in this respect between the ox brain and the human brain). Gradually, the function of the three ventricles became differentiated. The front ventricle was assumed to receive information from the senses and, therefore, was called the common sense. It also included fantasy and imagination. The second ventricle, in the middle of the head, comprised thought and judgement. Finally the third ventricle, at the back of the head, contained memory. This can clearly be seen in the pictures shown in Figure 6.3, respectively from the German prior Gregor Reisch (1467–1525) and the Italian polymath Leonardo da Vinci (1452–1519).

? What do you think?

Do you see the correspondence between the ideas about the roles of the ventricles and the saying 'to have something at the back of the mind'?

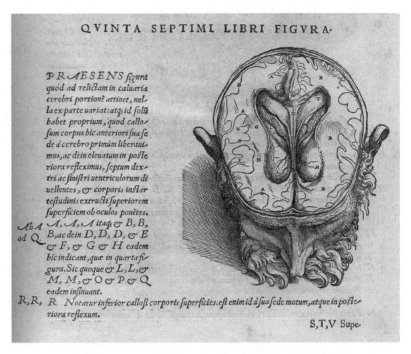

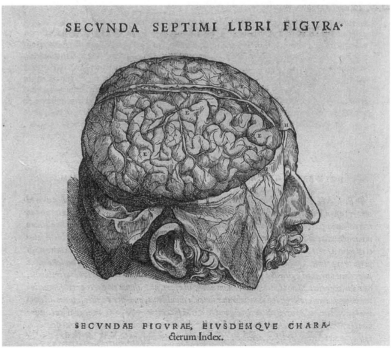

Figure 6.2 Dissections of the brain by Vesalius in 1543.

Notice how the ventricles receive more attention and detail than the brain. In many drawings the convolutions on the outside of the brain were drawn like intestines rather than the way the brain really looks (lower part, also from Vesalius). This bias is in line with the conviction that the ventricles contained the animal spirits.

Source: Vesalius: *De corporis humani fabrica libri septem*. Wellcome Library, London/Wellcome Images.

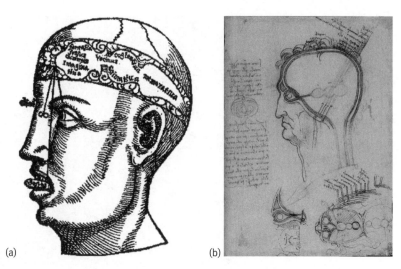

(a)   (b)

Figure 6.3 The three ventricles of the brain as depicted by (a) Gregor Reisch in 1503 and (b) Leonardo da Vinci around 1490.

Source: (a) © 2007 by the Massachusetts Institute of Technology/MIT Journals; (b) Interfoto/Sammlung Rauch/Mary Evans Picture Library.

Speech problems can be caused by brain injury

With the rediscovery of Galen's texts, researchers also regained interest in the relationship between brain injuries and behaviour. A particularly influential publication was the book *Observationes medicae de capite humano* (Medical observations on the human head), published in 1585 by the German physician Johann Schenk von Grafenberg. In this book von Grafenberg reported clinical observations of brain injuries ranging from the ancient writings to new cases from contemporaries. On the basis of these studies Schenk von Grafenberg concluded, among other things, that after brain damage patients sometimes could no longer speak even though their tongue was not paralysed. Rather, what seemed to happen was that the memory of words had disappeared or at least could no longer be accessed.

Developments in the seventeenth and eighteenth centuries

The brain instead of the ventricles

Gradually the investigators turned their focus to the solid parts of the brain rather than the ventricles. In the seventeenth century they started to pay attention to the difference between the outer layer of the cerebral hemispheres (the parts of the brain with the convolutions), which looked greyish, and the layer underneath, which had a white appearance. The former became known as the rind or the cortex; the latter as the white matter. One of the first researchers to implicate the grey part of the brain in the functions of memory and will was the British anatomist Thomas Willis, who published an influential book *Cerebri anatome* in 1664. At the same time, an increasing number of scholars started to doubt the existence of spirits in the nerves. Instead, they hypothesised that fluids flowed in them.

> **? What do you think?**
>
> The influence of the new ideas about the functioning of the brain on the general culture can also be traced in the language. Ever heard of 'the grey cells'?

A problem with the new view, however, was that the brain seemed to be numb. How then could it be involved in sensation and movement? If you exposed the grey matter and touched it, the animal did not seem to be disturbed. However, if you touched the white matter or went into the ventricles, the animal screamed, sometimes showed involuntary movements, and often died. This point against the involvement of the grey matter was strongly made, for instance, by the influential German/Swiss anatomist Albrecht von Haller in a series of book volumes around 1750.

Increased interest in reflexes

A topic that also started to gain momentum in the seventeenth–eighteenth centuries was the insight that some behaviours were elicited automatically, without voluntary intervention. When you step on something sharp, you at once withdraw your foot. Galen had already noticed that sometimes animals performed involuntary acts, which he ascribed to 'sympathy' between the various body parts, so that one could respond sympathetically to another's distress. This view still has an impact on our language, because a part of the autonomic (vegetative) nervous system became known as the sympathetic nervous system.

René Descartes was interested in reflexive movements as well, because they fitted within his mechanistic view of the body (Chapter 2). He discussed the idea in 1633 (Figure 6.4) and argued that a reflex consisted of a sensory impression which rushed to the brain and subsequently was reflected back (as in a mirror) into a motor command to bring about the required action. The event occurred unconsciously, independently of the will.

In 1784 the Czech physiologist Jiří Procháska published a book in which he argued that reflexes were not controlled by the brain but involved the spinal cord and the

Figure 6.4 Drawing from Descartes illustrating the withdrawal reflex when a foot risks being burnt by the fire.

Notice that there is only one nerve tract, carrying the sensory signal to the brain and bringing the motor command back.

Source: The withdrawal arc by Descartes, Stock Montage Inc. Reproduced with permission.

structures just above it. As we will see below, this was the start of one of the great breakthroughs of the nineteenth century.

A proposed treatment for brain injury

It is important to remember that the greater insights into the workings of the nervous system for a long time did not lead to improvements in the treatment of brain injuries, as is exemplified by the following remedy recommended in the seventeenth century to the Archduchess of Austria, who suffered from an apoplexy (stroke):

> A most secret and certain remedy against the apoplexy is to take a lion's dung, powdered, two parts, pour spirit of wine till it be covered three fingers breath, let them stand in a vial stopped three days. Strain it and keep it for use. Then take a crow, not quite pinfeathered, and a young turtle, burn them apart in an oven, powder them, pour on the above said spirit of wine, let them stand in infusion for three days. Then take berries of a linden tree, an ounce and a half. Let them be steeped in the aforesaid spirit, then add as much of the best wine and six ounces of sugar candy, boil them in a pot till the sugar be melted. Put it up. Let the patient take a spoonful of it in wine, often in a day, for a whole month. In the paroxysm give a spoonful with Aqua Tiliae, and with the same water, rub the forehead, neck, temples and nostrils.
>
> (Bonnet 1684; as cited in Prins & Bastiaanse 2006: 772)

? What do you think?

An element often present in folk medicine (i.e. remedies for maladies proposed by people who do not systematically examine the effectiveness of the recommended treatments) is the use of revolting substances, as if the 'evil' should be repelled from the body. Can you see how this applies to the treatment presented here? What other elements do you typically find in folk remedies?

Interim summary

Advances in the understanding of the brain in the Renaissance and the seventeenth and eighteenth centuries:

- In the Renaissance, Vesalius and peers followed Galen's belief that the soul was located in the solid parts of the brain and commanded animal spirits that resided in the ventricles and travelled through the nerves to the other body parts.
- There was also a renewed interest in the behavioural consequences of brain injury.
- In the seventeenth–eighteenth centuries there was a gradually increasing focus on the brain itself. A distinction was made between the grey and the white matter in the cerebral hemispheres.
- There was also growing interest in the reflex, as a type of response that seemed to escape voluntary control.
- The new insights did not (yet) lead to improved treatment.

6.3 The breakthroughs of the nineteenth century

A series of five breakthroughs in the nineteenth century irrevocably altered the model of brain functioning and made modern neurophysiology possible (Clarke & Jacyna 1987). They were:

1. the discovery of the cerebrospinal axis
2. the growing impact of the reflex
3. the localisation of brain functions
4. the discovery of the nerve cell
5. the disentangling of the communication between neurons.

Below, we discuss the findings one by one. While you read them, keep in mind that their timelines largely overlap and that the discoveries occurred shortly before (and sometimes after) psychology was founded as an independent discipline. Think of the ways in which these developments increased the likelihood of the scientific study of the human mind.

The discovery of the cerebrospinal axis

The body remains functioning when the cerebral hemispheres are disconnected

The first breakthrough in the nineteenth century was the discovery of the role of the cerebrospinal axis in the regulation of physical functions. The received wisdom since Galen was that only the brain was the origin of nerve signals. The spinal cord, in line with the nerves, was seen as a transmission channel of the spirits or – later – the brain fluid. This view started to be questioned when researchers began to realise that a body remained functioning in a vegetative state when the cerebral hemispheres were taken away or disconnected from the structures at the top end of the spinal cord (nowadays called the subcortical structures). So, there were many bodily functions that did not seem to require the cerebral hemispheres. In addition, the work of Procháska (see above) strongly pointed towards the possibility that reflexes were mediated by the spinal cord and not by the cerebral hemispheres.

Clarke and Jacyna (1987: 30–1) summarised the outcome of this change of view as follows:

> Ideas of the structure of the cerebrospinal axis underwent a revolution between 1800 and 1840. Quite literally, an inversion of previous modes of conceiving the axis took place: instead of proceeding from above downwards and seeing the spinal cord as a process of the brain, anatomists began to go from below upwards and to describe the brain as the culmination of the spinal cord.

The new view of the precedence of the spinal cord and the subcortical structures in the control of physical functions agreed with the finding that some animal species had a spinal cord but no brain, whereas the reverse was never observed. It looked as if the spinal cord had evolutionary precedence over the brain and that the brain had grown increasingly larger in mammals (with humans as the apex).

reflex arc

notion introduced in the nineteenth century to describe the processes underlying a reflex: a signal is picked up by sensory receptors, transmitted to the spinal cord through an afferent nerve, transferred to interneurons, which activate motor neurons that send a motor command over an efferent nerve to initiate the withdrawal movement

> ### ? What do you think?
>
> Ideas about the evolutionary precedence of the spinal cord over the brain only made sense after the publication of the *Origin of species*. Can you explain why?

Growing focus on reflexes

The reflex arc

Researchers also started to pay more attention to the nature and function of reflexes in brain functioning. An important figure in this respect was the British physician and physiologist Marshall Hall (1790–1857). He introduced the notion of the reflex arc to refer to the mechanisms involved in involuntary movements elicited by sensory stimuli (Figure 6.5). Hall profited from the discovery made shortly before that there exist two different types of nerves: one set that carries information from the senses to the spinal cord and the brain (afferent nerves), and another set that carries motor information from the brain and the spinal cord to the muscles (efferent nerves). Previously it had been thought that the nerves worked in both directions (see Descartes' drawing in Figure 6.4).

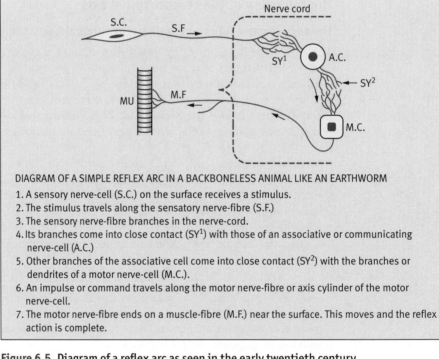

DIAGRAM OF A SIMPLE REFLEX ARC IN A BACKBONELESS ANIMAL LIKE AN EARTHWORM

1. A sensory nerve-cell (S.C.) on the surface receives a stimulus.
2. The stimulus travels along the sensatory nerve-fibre (S.F.)
3. The sensory nerve-fibre branches in the nerve-cord.
4. Its branches come into close contact (SY^1) with those of an associative or communicating nerve-cell (A.C.)
5. Other branches of the associative cell come into close contact (SY^2) with the branches or dendrites of a motor nerve-cell (M.C.).
6. An impulse or command travels along the motor nerve-fibre or axis cylinder of the motor nerve-cell.
7. The motor nerve-fibre ends on a muscle-fibre (M.F.) near the surface. This moves and the reflex action is complete.

Figure 6.5 Diagram of a reflex arc as seen in the early twentieth century.

Signals are picked up by a sensory nerve-cell, travel along a 'sensatory' nerve-fibre to the nerve cord (or spinal cord). There the signal is transmitted to a communicating nerve-cell, from which it activates a motor nerve-cell. Next, it travels over the motor nerve-fibre to the muscle, and finally initiates the reflex reaction. Notice that the distinction between the afferent sensory nerve-fibre and the efferent motor nerve-fibre was not known until the early 1800s. Before, scientists thought there was only one fibre in which the signals travelled back and forth (see Figure 6.4).

Source: Thomson (1922).

Hall further extended the reflex concept from a simple physiological phenomenon to a biological principle that formed one of the pillars of nervous activity. He insisted that all muscular function other than that owing to volition, respiration, cardiac activity and irritability depended on reflexes controlled by the spinal cord. In the first decades of the twentieth century the British physiologist Charles Scott Sherrington would describe the precise mechanisms of the spinal reflex, for which he was awarded the Nobel Prize for Medicine in 1932.

The reflex arc as the basis of mental functioning

Some time later, researchers extended Hall's reflex arc from the spinal cord to the complete brain. For them, the reflex was no longer one mode of action in the nervous system among others, but the basal unit from which the remaining nervous functions evolved. One of the scholars who took this view was the Russian physiologist Ivan Sechenov. In 1863 he published a theoretical treatise under the title *Reflexes of the brain,* in which he claimed that all higher functions of the brain were of a reflex nature. Sechenov's treatise was important because it influenced Pavlov, who was a student of his. As we saw in Chapter 5, Pavlov was studying the reflex mechanisms in the digestive system, when he noticed that the dogs started to secrete digestive fluids before food arrived in their mouth. This was the start of research on classical conditioning, which Pavlov saw as a psychic reflex.

The idea of the reflex arc as the basis of psychological functioning also reached the first psychologists in the United States. For instance, in the *Principles* (1890, Vol. 1, Chapter 3) William James asked the following question:

> The conception of reflex action is surely one of the best conquests of physiological theory; why not be radical with it? Why not say that just as the spinal cord is a machine with few reflexes, so the hemispheres are a machine with many, and that that is all the difference? The principle of continuity would press us to accept this view.
>
> (James 1890, Vol. 1: 129)

James himself did not go as far as to accept that all thoughts consisted of reflexes, because in his view this would be incompatible with the existence of human consciousness and free will (see Chapter 7), but the excerpt clearly shows that from the very beginning of American psychology the reflex arc was considered as a model of brain functioning.

A similar ambivalence towards the reflex arc can be seen in John Dewey's 1896 article 'The reflex arc concept in psychology' published in the *Psychological Review*. In this article Dewey criticised the reflex concept as too elementaristic and mechanistic, but he proposed a version that remained quite close to the original (in Dewey's version the stimulus and the response mutually influenced each other). As we saw in Chapter 5, none of James's or Dewey's hesitations were shared by Watson when he introduced behaviourism as the science of the S-R reflex arc, or by Skinner in his radical behaviourism.

Localisation of brain functions

The brain equipotentiality theory

Another major discussion taking place in the nineteenth century was whether different psychological functions were localised in different parts of the brain or whether the whole brain was involved in all of them. Before, it had been widely assumed that the brain was a single organ, without further subdivisions (although a few scattered

brain equipotentiality theory

theory saying that all parts of the brain have equal significance and are involved in each task; first thought to apply to the complete brain; since the nineteenth century limited to the cerebral hemispheres

localisation theory

theory saying that brain processes are localised, meaning that only part of the brain underlies a particular mental function

reports can be found of physicians who noticed that certain symptoms were more likely after some brain injuries than after others).

The view that the brain functions as a whole with all parts having an equal significance is known as the **brain equipotentiality theory**. A series of findings in the nineteenth century convinced an increasing number of investigators that this theory was wrong and had to be replaced by the **localisation theory**, which states that mental functions are localised in specific parts of the brain. Proponents of the localisation theory were hampered because their opponents constantly associated them with the phrenologists Franz Joseph Gall (1758–1828) and Johann Spurzheim (1776–1832; see Chapter 5). In this section we review some of the early evidence for brain localisation; later we will describe more recent evidence on the basis of brain imaging techniques.

Language production is controlled by the front parts of the brain

In 1825 the French professor of clinical medicine and a student of Gall, Jean-Baptiste Bouillaud, presented evidence which according to him proved that speech was controlled by the front parts of the brain, the parts of the left and the right brain half touching the forehead (Figure 6.6). In a paper read to his colleagues he reviewed the data from 14 autopsies. Eight patients with speech problems all had lesions in the frontal lobes of the brain, whereas these lobes appeared to be intact in the six other patients without speech disorder. In 1848 he presented a large number of new cases to support his theory.

Bouillaud's message was strongly opposed by his fellow countryman, Marie Jean Pierre Flourens, who was one of the great brain physiologists of his time. On the basis of ablation and stimulation studies, Flourens agreed that the big structures of the nervous system had divergent functions. For instance, he concluded that the spinal cord was vital for the conduction of brain signals, that the cerebellum was

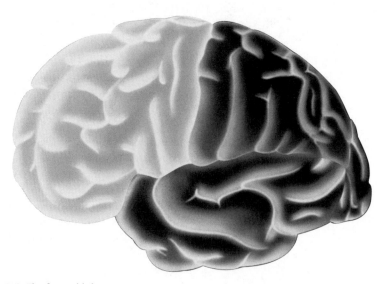

Figure 6.6 The frontal lobes.

This picture shows the frontal lobe of the left brain half. The right hemisphere also has a frontal lobe. In 1825 Bouillaud claimed that speech production was controlled by the two frontal lobes, because patients with speech problems all had an injury here, whereas people without speech problems had injuries in other parts of the brain. In 1861 Broca claimed that only the left frontal lobe controlled language production.

Source: BSIP, JACOPIN/Science Photo Library Ltd.

involved in movement, and that a structure above the spinal cord – the medulla – was vital for vegetative functioning (when this structure was severed, the animal died at once). Finally, he argued that perception, memory and will were controlled by the cerebral hemispheres. Importantly, however, he strongly defended the equipotentiality of the cerebral hemispheres. These consisted of a single organ. If a small part of them was removed, there was no isolated function lost (as long as the lesion was not too large, so that the remaining tissue could take over).

A similar stance about the equipotentiality of the cerebral hemispheres was taken by the German physiologist, Johannes Peter Müller, who wrote that:

> the mind is a substance independent of the brain and hence . . . a change in the structure of the brain cannot produce a change in the mental principle itself, but can only modify its actions . . . The loss of portions of the cerebral substance . . . cannot deprive the mind of certain masses of ideas, but diminishes the brightness and clearness of conceptions generally.
>
> (Müller 1838; as cited in Tizard 1959: 134)

CASE STUDY: Broca's and Wernicke's aphasias

Samples of speech in aphasic patients asked to describe the Cookie Theft Picture

Source: *The assessment of aphasia and related disorders*, Lea and Febiger (Goodglass, H. and Kaplan, E. 1983), from *Boston Diagnostic Aphasia Examination*, 3rd edn (BDAE-3) with Kaplan, E. and Barresi, B., 2001, Austin, TX: Copyright 2001 by PRO-ED, Inc. Reprinted with permission.

Patient with Broca's aphasia

'Well . . . see . . . girl eating no . . . cookie . . . no . . . ah . . . school no . . . stool . . . ah . . . tip over . . . and ah . . . cookie jar . . . ah . . . lid . . . no . . . see . . . water all over . . . spilled over . . . yuck . . . Mother . . . daydreaming.'

Patient with Wernicke's aphasia

'Well this . . . mother is away here working her work out o'here to get her better, but when she's looking, the two boys looking in the other part. One their small tile into her time here. She's working another time because she is getting, too.'

Source: Goodglass (1983) and Helm-Estabrooks *et al*. (1981: 425); as cited in Andrewes (2002: 310).

Language production is controlled by the left frontal lobe

In April 1861, however, Paul Broca, professor of pathology in Paris, repeated and extended Bouillaud's work and presented evidence to the Société d'Anthropologie that speech production was controlled by the frontal lobes. A patient with a long-standing, severe speech problem had just died. The autopsy showed widespread damage to his left frontal lobe. In subsequent years, Broca provided more cases showing the importance of the frontal lobes for language production. In 1865 he went further and claimed that only a region in the frontal lobe of the *left* hemisphere was involved. This region has since been called Broca's area (Figure 6.7).

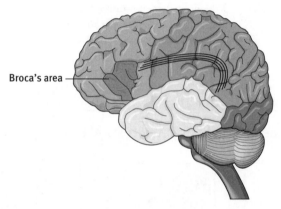

Figure 6.7 Broca's area.

Damage to the coloured part of the brain often leads to speech problems. This part is called Broca's area, after the man who first described it. In most people, it is situated in the left hemisphere. For some people, it is situated in the right hemisphere (in about 5% of right-handers and about 25% of left-handers).

Source: Adapted from Geschwind (1972: 78). Courtesy of the estate of Bunji Tagawa.

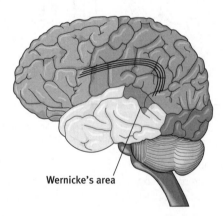

Figure 6.8 Wernicke's area.

Damage to the coloured part of the brain leads to problems with speech understanding. This part is called Wernicke's area, after the man who first described it. It mostly is in the left hemisphere, but can occasionally be in the right hemisphere.

Source: Adapted from Geschwind (1972: 78). Courtesy of the estate of Bunji Tagawa.

Language understanding and the posterior part of the brain

Stimulated by Broca's findings, the German-Polish physician Karl Wernicke in 1874 presented evidence that language problems could also occur after damage to the rear part of the left hemisphere (Figure 6.8). These problems, however, had nothing to do with speaking, but rather with the understanding of language. The patients at first sight gave the impression of fluent speakers, until you tried to make sense of what they were saying; there was no meaning in their language.

Just how innovative were Broca and Wernicke?

Having your name given to a specific condition, effect or theory is about the highest honour a scientist can receive. Such eponyms, as they are called, seem to be the recognition of the unique contribution made by the researcher. However, historical research makes it increasingly clear that eponyms are subject to the same attribution biases and errors as we highlighted in the 'Focus on' section of Chapter 1 (Draaisma 2009), partly because eponyms are often conferred decades after the initial discoveries. So, what do we know about the two major eponymous brain disorders: Broca's and Wernicke's aphasia?

The French physician and academic, Paul Broca (1824–1880), is generally considered as the father of neuropsychology, because he was the first to show the localisation of speech production in a region of the left hemisphere frontal lobe. What is usually overlooked, however, is that Broca's conclusion was made in two different papers four years apart (1861 and 1865) and that each paper followed a similar claim made by another researcher.

In 1861 the French physician, Ernest Aubertin, read a paper before the Société d'Anthropologie, in which he presented further evidence for Bouillaud's claim of speech localisation in the frontal lobes. As could be expected, Aubertin's paper was met with great scepticism, also because Aubertin was Bouillaud's son-in-law. One of the members present at the exchange was Paul Broca. When a patient of his with severe speech problems died shortly afterwards, he seized the opportunity to test Aubertin's claim and indeed found that the damage was situated in the frontal lobe. A few days later, Broca presented his evidence to the Société, thereby 'stealing Aubertin's thunder' (Fancher 1996: 89).

Although the patient's lesion was clearly in the left brain, Broca did not make much of this asymmetry, seeing it as a coincidence. In line with the predominant 'law of symmetry', Broca (and all his colleagues) assumed that a function as important as human language would be controlled by both brain halves. In 1863, however, Broca gave a lecture in which he presented eight cases of aphasia that all had their lesions on the left side. Finally, in 1865 he published a paper in which he reluctantly came to the conclusion that all evidence pointed to involvement of the left hemisphere only. Immediately, he was accused by Gustave Dax of having stolen the idea from his father, Marc Dax, who in 1836 had presented a paper on the left hemisphere dominance for speech control at a medical congress in Montpellier. Gustave Dax had submitted a paper of his father's findings to the Académie de Médecine in Paris shortly before Broca presented his evidence in 1863. Gustave Dax did not receive a response to this submission, and in 1865 published his father's paper himself. Broca published his own assessment six weeks later (Schiller 1979; Cubelli & Montagna 1994; Buckingham 2006). Broca repeatedly acknowledged Auburtin's input (Thomas 2007), but never mentioned being inspired by Dax.

According to Cubelli and De Bastiani (2011), Broca remains the father of neuropsychology, but mostly because he was the first to make the explicit connection between brain lesions and psychological dysfunction, not because he was the first to defend localisation or to propose brain lateralisation.

In 1874 Carl Wernicke (1848–1905) published a book *Der aphasische symptomenkomplex: Eine psychologische studie auf anatomischer basis* (The aphasia symptom complex: A psychological study based on anatomy), which would become a classic in neuropsychology, introducing a theory of language processing and presenting evidence for what became known as Wernicke's aphasia. At that time, Wernicke was only 26 years old and had been working on speech problems for less than a year. Whitaker and Etlinger (1993) argued that this was only possible because Wernicke had profited greatly from the input of Theodor Meynert, a psychiatrist under whose supervision he worked and whose contribution was extensively acknowledged in the book. Eling (2006a) assessed the evidence for Whitaker and Etlinger's claim, but found it unconvincing. The personal contacts between Meynert and Wernicke seem to have been too patchy and Meynert never developed a theory of aphasia close to what Wernicke wrote.

At the same time Eling (2005, 2006b) noticed that Wernicke's work did not come out of the blue, but was heavily inspired by books published shortly before. As Eling (2005: 301) concluded: 'before Wernicke published his model for the representation of language in the brain in 1874, not only Baginsky [a German researcher] but also other authors – in England, the Netherlands and France – have used concepts such as functional centres and connections. Apparently, Wernicke unjustly received credit for formulating the first connectionist model for language representation in the brain.'

These examples once again demonstrate how difficult it is to attribute a scientific finding to a single person, even when history bestows the honour of an eponym to a researcher.

The discovery of the nerve cell

The fourth big breakthrough in the nineteenth century was the finding that the grey matter of the cerebral hemispheres consisted of billions of cells and that the white matter and the nerves were the 'tails' (later called axons) of these cells. Two technical innovations were needed for this development.

The availability of better microscopes

First, microscopes of sufficient quality had to be built and used correctly. These only become available in the nineteenth century. Before, the magnification was not strong enough and there were major distortions in the images obtained, leading the British researcher Everard Home in 1798 to come to the conclusion that:

It is scarcely necessary to mention, that parts of an animal body are not fitted for being examined by glasses of a great magnifying power; and, wherever they are shown one hundred times larger than their natural size, no dependence can be placed upon their appearance.

(Home 1798; as cited in Clarke & Jacyna 1987: 59)

Technical innovations in the beginning of the nineteenth century, however, hugely increased the quality of the microscopes, so that researchers (including Home) within a few decades could confidently conclude that the brain, just like all other tissue, was composed of minute 'globules'.

New techniques to stain the brain tissue

The second innovation needed to understand the functional units of the brain was a way to colour the brain cells with all their fine details. There was little to be noticed about the organisation of brain tissue as long as the researchers had to look at the raw material. A major step forward was realised by the Italian physician Camillo Golgi in 1873 when he used silver to colour the brain tissue. This technique made the neurons stand out against the surrounding cells and revealed that they not only consisted of globules (cell bodies) but in addition comprised a highly interconnected network of branches (Figure 6.9).

Disentangling communication in the nervous system

Individual neurons instead of a continuous network

The big question among brain physiologists after Golgi's discovery of the network of globules and branches was whether the network was a continuous structure or whether it consisted of individual cells. Golgi strongly argued in favour of the former,

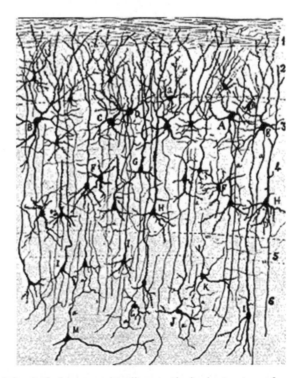

Figure 6.9 Staining techniques used to discover the basic structure of neurons.

After he was able to stain nerve cells, Golgi discovered that the grey matter of the brain consisted of a network of branches and globules. Golgi was convinced that the network formed a single unit; Ramón y Cajal argued that it consisted of separate neurons communicating with each other.

Source: Clarke & Jacyna (1987). Reproduced with permission.

neuron

brain cell; basic unit of the
nervous system; contains
a cell body, dendrites and
an axon

and it would take nearly half a century before it became generally accepted that the network was composed of individual cells, called neurons, which communicated with each other without being attached to one another (Shepherd 1991). An important name in this development was the Spanish researcher Santiago Ramón y Cajal. Golgi and Ramón y Cajal would share the Nobel Prize for Medicine in 1906.

Once it was accepted that the nervous system consisted of billions of independent neurons, the next challenge was to explain how they stored and exchanged information. Remember that for centuries the natural philosophers had been mystified by how the nerves were able to transmit information from and to the brain (soul). First they thought that animal spirits rushed through hollow tubes, and when this was no longer tenable, they proposed brain fluids. However, the latter explanation had difficulty accounting for the speed of neural transmission (which easily exceeds 100 km per hour). In addition, there was the problem that no-one was able to show the presence of fluid in the nerves.

Electricity within neurons

A new idea emerging at the end of the eighteenth century was that communication in the nervous system might resemble the transmission of electrical signals. Around 1650 the first electricity generator was built, followed in 1745 by the first usable device to store electricity, the so-called Leyden jar (invented in the Dutch University of Leyden, hence the name). With the help of a generator and a Leyden jar scientists could study the characteristics of electrical currents. Physiologists were struck by the similarities between electrical signals and what happened in the nerves (a signal was transmitted at a high speed and at the end made something happen). Could it be that brain activity was electrical activity?

The first to find clear empirical evidence for the involvement of electricity in the nervous system was the Italian physician Luigi Galvani. In 1786, while operating on frogs, he noticed that a dissected leg of a frog contracted each time his assistant touched a bare nerve with his scalpel and the electricity generator nearby produced a spark. Galvani decided to test the phenomenon more in detail and in 1791 published a text on his findings. Although in hindsight he misinterpreted quite a lot of findings, it was undeniable that body movement could be generated by an electric current applied to a nerve. This is how a colleague described the reception of Galvani's findings:

> The storm among physicists, physiologists and physicians, which the appearance of the commentary created, can only be compared to the one that appeared on the political horizon of Europe at that time [1791]. It can be said that wherever frogs were to be found, and where two different kinds of metal could be procured, everyone wished to see the mutilated limbs of frogs re-animated in this remarkable manner; the physiologists believed that at last the dream handed down from their ancestors of a vital power was within their grasp; the physicians, whom Galvani somewhat thoughtlessly encouraged to attempt the treatment of all manner of nervous disorders, such as sciatica, tetanus, and epilepsy, began to believe that no cure was impossible, and it was considered certain that in the future no one in a trance could be buried alive, provided only that he were galvanized!
>
> (du Bois-Reymond 1848; as translated by Clarke & Jacyna 1987: 169)

The next question, of course, was how the brain could generate electricity. In the worst-case scenario, all Galvani had shown was that a frog's leg contracted if you sent electricity through it. He had not shown that brain signals were electrical signals, a criticism made most poignantly by Galvani's Italian colleague Alessandro Volta (as part of his endeavour to refute that Galvani stumbled across the first battery, a device to produce electricity on the basis of chemical reactions). It would take another 50 years before Emil du Bois-Reymond, a Prussian physicist with Swiss roots, would make enough headway to firmly establish that nerve signals indeed involved electricity. He was able to do so with the use of electric fishes (fishes that are capable of discharging electricity on prey and predators) and much improved techniques to measure small electrical signals.

Another question was whether nerves were like real electrical wires or whether the electrical signal generated was based on chemical processes within the nerve. Were the nerves simple, passive transmitters of electrical signals generated in the brain or did they actively continue a chemical process initiated at the level of the brain (or the spinal cord)? This was the background against which von Helmholtz in 1852 decided to measure the speed of signal transmission in the nerve. If nerves were like electric wires, the signal speed should be astronomically high (close to the speed of light). Alternatively, if the signal was based on chemical processes, as von Helmholtz assumed, it would be much slower. As we saw in Chapter 3, the latter was the case: the speed of the nerves in the leg of a frog was only some 30 metres per second (or 108 km per hour).

In the twentieth century the exact mechanisms of signal transmission in the nerves would be unravelled (Figure 6.10), largely on the basis of the neurons of the giant squid, which were so big that they could be seen with the naked eye.

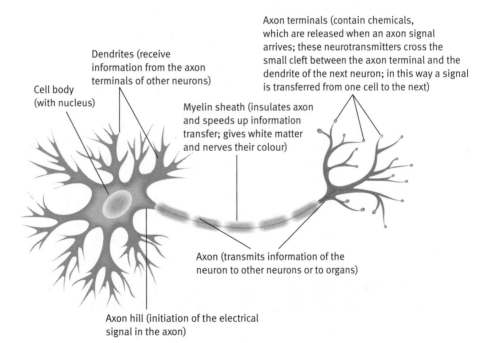

Figure 6.10 Functioning of neurons.

Neurons receive chemical signals from other cells via their dendrites. These signals are grouped in the axon hill from which an electrical signal starts when a threshold is exceeded. The electrical signal travels through the axon, on the basis of chemical changes in the axon, and causes neurotransmitters to be released in the terminals. These neurotransmitters are the signals for the next cell. Most axons have a myelin sheath which is white; hence the colour of the nerves and the white matter in the brain.

Source: Brysbaert (2006). Reproduced with permission from Academia Press.

Communication between neurons: the synapse

In the twentieth century the communication between neurons also became understood. Although a small part of this communication is electrical, the bulk is achieved chemically, by means of neurotransmitters. Towards their end, the axons branch out in a multitude of terminals, called synapses, which contain chemicals and lie close to the dendrites (and bodies) of other cells. When the electrical signal reaches a synapse, it induces chemicals to be released, which make contact with the next cell. These chemicals are called **neurotransmitters** and they can be influenced by chemical substances, which opened the door to the creation of medicines that either block or increase the availability of neurotransmitters and that have an impact on brain-related disorders, from epilepsy to depression (see Chapter 12).

neurotransmitter

chemical substance used to communicate between neurons; is released from the synapse when a signal arrives through the axon; can be affected by drugs

Interim summary

Five big breakthroughs in the nineteenth century

- Understanding that the spinal cord was an integral part of the central nervous system and was involved in the control of many bodily functions.

- Discovery that many processes in the central nervous system were reflexes that did not need voluntary initiation; question to what extent higher cognitive functions could be considered as reflexes as well (e.g. Pavlov, behaviourism).

- Intense discussions between proponents of brain equipotentiality and adherents of brain localisation; initially the former were dominant; increasingly, however, evidence for the latter position was found.

- Discovery that the brain consisted of a network of individual neurons that communicated with each another; required good microscopes and techniques to stain neurons.

- Discovery that the neurons store and transfer information by means of electro-chemical signals; electrical information mainly involved in intra-cell communication, chemical information transfer important for communication between neurons.

KEY FIGURES

Understanding the workings of the nervous system

- **Galen** (*c.* 130–*c.* 200): ventricles and animal spirits; legacy until well into the eighteenth century.
- **Andreas Vesalius** (1514–1564): translated Galen's anatomical works in Latin and extended them by new dissections, including on humans.
- **René Descartes** (1596–1650): proposed the idea of automatic, reflexive reactions that did not involve the will.
- **Thomas Willis** (1621–1675): published an influential atlas of the brain in which he attached more importance to the solid brain parts.
- **Luigi Galvani** (1737–1798): discovered that electricity is involved in signal transmission in the nerves.

- **Jiří Procháska** (1749–1820): importance of the spinal cord and the subcortical structures for the control of reflexes.
- **Franz Joseph Gall** (1758–1828) and **Johann Gaspar Spurzheim** (1776–1832): proposed idea of localisation of functions in the brain, against the equipotentiality idea. Nowadays mostly associated with phrenology.
- **Marshal Hall** (1790–1857): stressed the importance of reflexive actions and initiated the term 'reflex arc'.
- **Marie Jean Pierre Flourens** (1794–1867) and **Johannes Peter Müller** (1801–1858): strong defenders of the brain equipotentiality theory on the basis of empirical studies.
- **Jean-Baptiste Bouillaud** (1796–1881): localisation of language in the frontal lobes; first empirical evidence for localisation of function in the brain.
- **Paul Broca** (1824–1880): localisation of speech in the left frontal lobe.
- **Camillo Golgi** (1843–1926): staining technique that made neurons visible.
- **Carl Wernicke** (1848–1905): localisation of language understanding in the rear part of the left hemisphere.
- **Santiago Ramón y Cajal** (1852–1934): established the neuron doctrine, which says that the brain consists of individual neurons that communicate with each other.
- **Charles Scott Sherrington** (1857–1952): described the mechanisms of the spinal reflex.

6.4 The emergence of neuropsychology in the twentieth century

Much of the research discussed in section 6.3 was based on animals (remember that the workings of the neuron were largely unravelled by examining the nervous 'system' of the giant squid). This was highly informative because there is a great similarity between brain functioning in humans and animals. Research on animals continued at an ever faster speed in the twentieth century. However, in the rest of this chapter we will focus on research into the human brain, in particular on the relationship between brain functioning and mental and behavioural performance.

Localisation studies in the World Wars

Localisation studies continued in the twentieth century. In particular the World Wars resulted in new insights. The invention of high-velocity bullets had the unforeseen consequence that brain wounds were more focused than before, allowing researchers to get a sharper image of function loss after damage to small parts of the brain.

Vision problems after gun-shot wounds at the back of the head

One of the most famous series of case studies in World War I was published by the British neurologist, Gordon Holmes (1876–1965). He examined the consequences of small-scale wounds at the back of the head. Here is the first case study he reported in his 1918 article:

CASE 1. – Private R—, 15104, was wounded on September 26, 1916, by a shrapnel ball which penetrated his steel helmet. He was unconscious for an hour or so, and stated that he was completely blind till the next day. He never noticed any subjective visual phenomena. He was admitted to a Base Hospital on the day following the infliction of the wound.

Wound. – There was a small penetrating wound from which softened brain extruded, immediately to the right of the middle line of the skull and 1 inch (2–5 cm) above the inion. A radiograph revealed much depressed bone, but no foreign body. An operation was performed next day, and several fragments of bone as well as clots and pulped brain tissue were removed from the occipital pole. The recovery was rapid and uneventful. His visual fields were taken by a perimeter and a screen scotometer six days after the infliction of the wound, and again a week later. There was then a large left homonymous paracentral scotoma to an object $7mm^2$ which reached the fixation point and extended outwards from it to about 25°. Its mesial border coincided with the vertical above the fixation point, but receded from it below this. Peripheral vision was unaffected, and the colour fields were normal in the right halves, but there was no perception of either red or green to the left of the middle line (Figure 6.11).

(Holmes 1918: 354–5)

World War II and prosopagnosia

Similar observations were made in World War II. A particularly important paper here was that of the German physician, Joachim Bodamer (1947), describing soldiers who lost their ability to recognise faces as a consequence of an injury to the rear of the brain. The author called this condition *prosopagnosia*. Subsequent literature searches

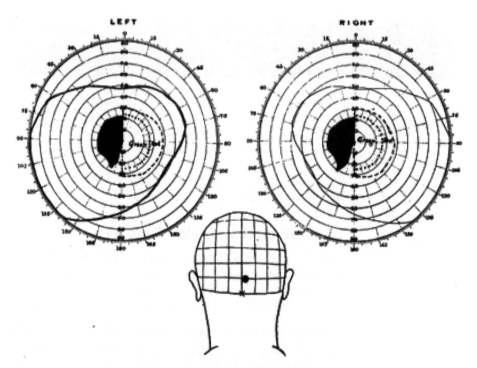

Figure 6.11 The first figure given in Holmes (1918) about the consequences of gun-shot wounds.

The soldier got a shrapnel ball at the back of the head (exact position in the lower part of the figure). As a result, he lost vision in the left half of his central visual field (the black areas in the upper figures, representing vision in the left and the right eye).

Source: Holmes (1918) 'Disturbances of vision by cerebral lesions', *British Journal of Opthalmology*, **2**: 355, at www. pubmedcentral.nih.gov/articlerender.fcgi?artid=513514. Copyright 1918 with permission from the BMJ Publishing Group Ltd.

revealed that similar cases had been described by French, British and German neurologists in the second half of the nineteenth century (Ellis & Florence 1990). The following are excerpts from Bodamer's text:

CASE 1: S (24 years old)

On 11.9.44 S went into a special hospital for brain injuries . . . After the injury, S was completely blind for several weeks. His sight returned gradually, in defined phases . . . But all impression of colour was missing – he could distinguish only light and dark, black and white. . . .

He said he had had difficulties with objects for a long time after his injury but he had gradually got to know objects again – he made mistakes now only with those objects he had not seen since his injury . . .

Also S had . . . a disorder of the recognition of faces and, in a wider sense, of expressions . . . S recognized a face as such, i.e. as different from other things, but could not assign the face to its owner. He could identify all the features of a face, but all faces appeared equally 'sober' and 'tasteless' to him . . .

25.11.44. S is told to look at own face in the mirror. At first he mistakes it for a picture but corrects himself. He stares for a long time as though a totally strange object is before him, then reports he sees a face and describes its individual features . . .

30.12.44. A picture of a long-haired dog, from the front, sitting [is shown]: S identifies it as human but with 'funny' hair.

(Bodamer 1947; as translated in Ellis & Florence 1990)

The start of neuropsychology

The mission of neuropsychology

Increasingly, in the second half of the twentieth century psychologists rather than physicians became involved in studying the behavioural consequences of brain injury. They started to call themselves **neuropsychologists** and established their own journals and societies (e.g. the first issue of the journal *Neuropsychologia* was published in 1963). Initially, their research was a continuation of the existing research and aimed at gaining further insight in the localisation of different functions in the brain. They also wanted to get a more detailed picture of the consequences of brain injury for higher mental functions, such as perception, language and action.

This is how the mission statement of the first issue of *Neuropsychologia* read:

At Mond See in Austria, in 1951, a small group of European neurologists and psychologists met to discuss disorders of higher mental function associated with injury or disease of the brain. The specific themes of the Conference were disorders of spatial perception and psychic symptoms associated with lesions of the third ventricle . . .

The papers given at these conferences have never been published, the aim being above all to stimulate discussion and to provoke the expression of widely different points of view. None the less, in view of the fact that a certain unity of subject matter and approach has emerged which goes beyond the limits of the individual disciplines (neurology, psychology, neurophysiology) involved, the members of the group believe that the time is now ripe for the launching of a new journal, dedicated to the idea of 'neuropsychology' . . .

Under the term 'neuropsychology', we have in mind a particular area of neurology of common interest to neurologists, psychiatrists, psychologists and neurophysiologists. This interest is focused mainly, though not of course exclusively, on the cerebral cortex. Among topics of particular concern to us are disorders of language, perception and action.

(Editorial, *Neuropsychologia*, 1963, Vol. 1: 1)

neuropsychology

branch of psychological research and practice that looks at the relationship between brain and behaviour; research traditionally focused on understanding the consequences of brain damage and localising the affected tissue; practice aimed at assessing the behavioural and mental consequences of the injury and administering the rehabilitation programme

Neuropsychology was presented as a new link between psychologists and the medical world (in addition to the links that already existed through clinical psychology and counselling). The assessment and treatment of the effects of brain damage became a joint enterprise of physicians and psychologists.

A change of focus: cognitive neuropsychology

Dissent among neuropsychologists

In the 1970 and 1980s, a number of neuropsychologists became dissatisfied with the way in which the subject matter was investigated. They had two grievances. First, the localisation issue turned out to be difficult to address on the basis of human brain injuries. All that could be done was to establish a correlation between symptoms measured while the patient was alive and brain damage observed much later, after the patient had died. Furthermore, the damage caused by brain injuries and strokes is usually widespread and not limited to one specific brain structure, making it difficult to decide which part of the damage was at the origin of the symptoms.

What do you think?

Another reason why the traditional neuropsychologists gave up the localisation issue was the development of better techniques to localise brain functions. Can you think of examples?

The second reason why neuropsychologists felt dissatisfaction was that the results of the examinations rarely went beyond a list of symptoms displayed by various patients (case studies). There was little theory behind the enterprise, little effort to link the various findings and draw implications for normal, healthy functioning. What neuropsychology had to do, the dissenters argued, was to use observations from patients with brain damage to test and amend the information-processing models proposed by the cognitive psychologists (Chapter 5). Instead of looking for anatomical localisations, neuropsychologists should investigate the functional implications of injuries: which cognitive processes were affected by the brain damage?

A new name

To emphasise the difference between the new type of research and the traditional neuropsychological approach, a new name was coined: cognitive neuropsychology. It referred to research dealing with the consequences of brain injuries for the information-processing models proposed by the cognitive psychologists. This is how one of the textbooks described the need for cognitive neuropsychology:

cognitive neuropsychology

part of neuropsychology aimed at understanding and treating the behavioural consequences of brain damage within the information processing models proposed by cognitive psychologists

For 100 years, it has been well known that the study of the cognitive problems of patients suffering from neurological diseases can produce strikingly counterintuitive observations . . . However, in general, neuropsychology has had little impact on the study of normal function.

With any knowledge of the history of clinical neuropsychology, it is easy to understand why this neglect occurred. The standard of description of the psychological impairments of patients was low, often being little more than the bald statement of the clinical opinion of the investigator. There was frequently a dramatic contrast between the vagueness of the psychological account of the disorder and the precision with which anatomical investigation of the lesion that had given rise to it was carried out post-mortem.

(Shallice 1988: 3)

By relating the consequences of brain damage to the theories of normal functioning, the cognitive neuropsychologists explicitly aimed to increase the impact of their research within the departments of psychology.

Deep dyslexia

A landmark publication in the history of cognitive neuropsychology was a book on deep dyslexia, edited by Coltheart, Patterson and Marshall (1980). Dyslexia refers to reading problems, which can either be due to developmental factors (making it hard for children to learn to read) or to brain damage (disrupting the performance of previously fluent readers). Deep dyslexia is a condition of strongly impaired reading after brain injury with a very particular symptom: sometimes, when patients try to identify a word, they do not read the word itself but a semantically related word. For instance, when asked to read the word storm, they might say thunder; or the stimulus word uncle might be read as nephew. When first discovered, this phenomenon baffled psychologists: how can the meaning of written words become activated when the patient is not capable of recognising the words?

To explain the semantic reading mistake, Morton and Patterson (1980) postulated a distinction between a logogen system and a cognitive system (Figure 6.12). The logogen system could be compared to a mental dictionary; it contained all the words known to a patient (later the name 'lexicon' was used for this system). The logogen system did not contain information about the meaning of the words; this was stored in a central cognitive system with which the logogen system interacted. Written words

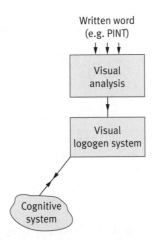

Figure 6.12 Figure illustrating the distinction between the logogen and the cognitive system made by Morton and Patterson (1980).

According to Morton and Patterson, a distinction had to be made between processing the word forms and processing the word meanings. To read the written word PINT, first the sequence of letters must be recognised as a known word form (this happens in the visual logogen system). Only then can the meaning of the word become activated in the cognitive system.

Source: Based on Morton and Patterson (1980). Reproduced with permission. (See also Figure 6.13.)

were recognised by first activating their entry in the visual logogen system and then by activating the corresponding meaning in the cognitive system.

Morton and Patterson (1980) argued that there were three different logogen systems: a visual logogen system for the recognition of written words, an auditory logogen system for the recognition of spoken words, and an output logogen system for the production of speech (Figure 6.13). Within the full model there were three routes for a normal reader to read aloud a written word. The first route directly converted the letters into sounds; this one was called the grapheme phoneme conversion route. It allowed readers to name non-words, such as *dom* and *pham*. The second route consisted of a direct connection between the visual logogen system and the output logogen system. The existence of such a route predicted that there would be patients who were able to name words with irregular pronunciations (e.g. *yacht*, *pint*) without knowing their meaning. Such patients have subsequently been described (see Coltheart 2004). Finally, the third route to name written words was one via the visual logogen system, through the cognitive system, to the logogen output system. In this route the visual logogen activated its meaning and on the basis of this meaning candidate output logogens were activated.

According to Morton and Patterson (1980), the third route was the origin of the semantically related errors observed in deep-dyslexia patients. In these patients the grapheme phoneme conversion route and the direct route between the visual logogen system and the output logogen system were severed (Figure 6.13). All they had left was the route mediated by the cognitive system. Because this route was not very accurate,

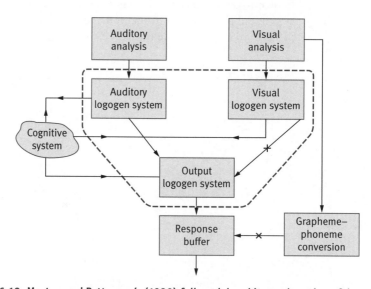

Figure 6.13 Morton and Patterson's (1980) full model and its explanation of deep dyslexia.

In this model for the naming of spoken and written words, three different logogens are distinguished, together with a grapheme phoneme conversion system for the naming of unknown words and non-words. For a normal reader, there are three routes to name a written word. For a patient with deep dyslexia, two of these routes are severed and the only remaining route is the one via the cognitive system. This route gives rise to the semantically related errors observed in these patients.

Source: Based on Morton and Patterson (1980). Reproduced with permission.

A workshop on deep dyslexia in 1979 is seen as the start of cognitive neuropsychology. In this photo you see (from left to right): A. Marcel, T. Shallice, P. Kossanyi, E. Saffran, J. Morton, L. Bogyo, O. Marin, M. Schwartz, A. Allport, E. Adreewsky, K. Patterson, S. Sasanuma, M. Coltheart, F. Newcombe and J. Marshall. Also present but not in the photo were E. Warrington and G. Deloche. (With thanks to K. Patterson for the photo and to A.W. Ellis for pointing the authors to its existence).

they failed to read a lot of words altogether and other words gave rise to semantically related responses. For instance, the input word storm activated the meanings associated with storms and tempests, but these meanings were not specific enough to activate the correct output logogen storm and instead a related word (thunder) was activated.

By integrating neuropsychological research in the mainstream of cognitive research, the cognitive neuropsychologists not only advanced the cognitive information processing models, but also ensured that the findings from the clinic became central to psychological thinking and teaching.

Interim summary

Neuropsychology

- Examination of bullet wounds in the World Wars provided physicians with more detailed knowledge about the behavioural consequences of brain injuries. Two famous examples were the partial loss of vision after gun-shot wounds above the neck, and the inability to recognise faces (prosopagnosia).

- Research and treatment of the consequences of brain damage were increasingly taken over by psychologists, who called themselves neuropsychologists.

- In the 1970s and 1980s a number of neuropsychologists started to study the implications of brain damage for the information-processing models proposed by cognitive psychologists; this was the start of cognitive neuropsychology.

- One of the first topics addressed by the new approach was deep dyslexia.

6.5 Brain imaging and the turn to neuroscience

For a long time the evidence about the neurophysiology of the brain and the localisation of functions was based on post-mortem analyses. Needless to say, such analyses revealed very little about the actual functioning of the living brain. In the twentieth century, however, scientists increasingly managed to extract information from a working brain. One of the first techniques used was single-cell recording. In this technique electrodes were planted in individual brain cells and recorded when the cells fired. By presenting different types of stimuli, researchers could determine in which processes each cell took part. Unfortunately, because this technique involved brain surgery and the insertion of electrodes in the brain, its use in humans was very limited. Eventually, however, brain imaging techniques became available that did not require the researchers to touch the brain. These are called **non-invasive techniques**. Below we summarise the most important and give a flavour of some of the results they have provided.

non-invasive techniques

methods in neuroscience that allow the study of the workings of the brain without surgery or the use of irreversible interventions

Measuring electrical signals from groups of cells

EEG recording

In 1928 the German physician and psychologist Hans Berger published an article that would dramatically change brain research. He reasoned that if brain activity was electrical activity, he might be able to pick up some signals if he put electrodes

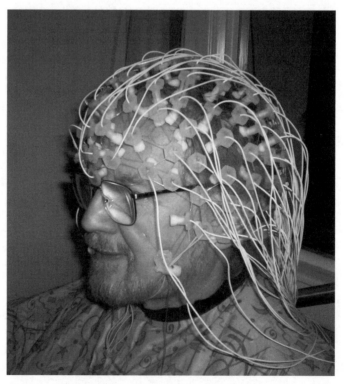

Making an EEG recording.
Source: Harry Whittaker.

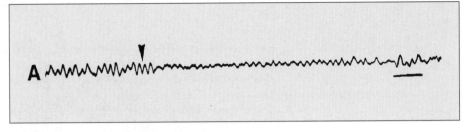

Figure 6.14 EEG recording of Hans Berger.

This shows one of Berger's first recordings. First the participant was awake but resting with his eyes closed. The EEG consists of an alpha wave (a slow, regular wave of 10 cycles per second; the underlined segment represents half a second). At the point indicated by the arrow, the hand of the participant was touched. Immediately the recording becomes irregular, with lower amplitude and a faster rhythm, a pattern Berger called a beta wave. After some time without stimulation, the alpha wave returns.

Source: Berger (1969; as cited in Changeux 1997).

on the human scalp (there was some evidence that brain activity could be measured on the exposed brain surface of animals). Berger indeed found very weak signals that seemed to oscillate at a frequency of some 10 cycles per second, at least when the person was at rest with their eyes closed. As soon as the person opened their eyes or was touched on the skin, the regular signal disappeared and was replaced by smaller and faster oscillations, which disappeared again when the person closed their eyes and returned to rest (Figure 6.14).

Berger called the printout of the electrical brain activity as a function of time an electroencephalogram, better known under its abbreviation EEG. He further called the slow, regular waves at rest alpha waves, and the fast, irregular waves under situations of alertness beta waves. These waves are the result of the firing of millions of neurons underneath the skull. If the neurons fire at a slow pace in synchrony, the waves are large; if they fire rapidly and independently, the waves become small and fast. The former is the case under rest conditions, the latter under conditions of information processing and alertness.

One of the first applications of the EEG measurement was the demonstration that epileptic seizures involved uncontrolled electrical discharges (Figure 6.15). Another application was the discovery of different sleep stages.

Event Related Potentials and magnetoencephalography

As the accuracy of the EEG recordings grew, two further applications became available. The first was the measurement of changes in the electrical signal as a function of specific stimuli. In this type of research, two types of stimuli are presented repeatedly and researchers examine in what respects the brain response to one type of stimulus differs from that to the other. This research is called Event Related Potential (ERP) research, because the electrical responses to individual events are registered and compared.

Figure 6.16 illustrates the ERP technique. The left part shows the EEG recordings on trials when nothing was presented; the right part shows the recordings on trials when an auditory click was presented. When the average is calculated across different trials, a smooth curve is obtained with peaks and troughs. This is the ERP signal. It can be used to determine how fast the brain responds to various types of signals and how the response differs as a function of the stimulus.

EEG

electroencephalogram: outcome of measurement of electrical brain activity by means of sensors placed on the scalp; routinely used in hospitals for the detection of epilepsy

Event Related Potential (ERP)

signal obtained by averaging the EEG signals to stimuli that are repeated a number of times; allows researchers to look for differences in the signal as a function of characteristics of the stimulus

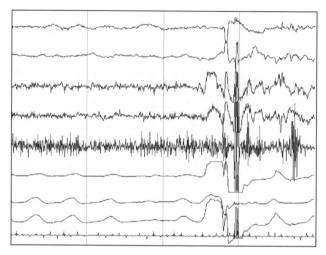

Figure 6.15 EEG recording during an epileptic seizure.

This recording shows that an epileptic seizure is often accompanied by a strong electrical discharge, making lots of neurons fire in an uncontrolled manner. Each line represents the recording of a different electrode placed at a different location on the head.

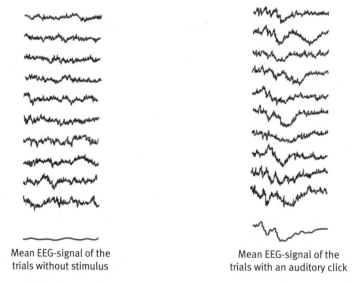

Mean EEG-signal of the
trials without stimulus

Mean EEG-signal of the
trials with an auditory click

Figure 6.16 Calculating an ERP signal.

This figure shows the EEG signal of an electrode on 10 trials without stimulus (left column) and 10 trials when an auditory click was presented (right column). By taking the mean of the trials, the random noise in the signal (the jitter) is averaged out and the remaining smooth curve is the ERP signal.

Source: Brysbaert (2006). Reproduced with permission from Academia Press.

The second new use of EEG recordings was the fact that one could try to localise the source of the electrical signal. In a recording up to 128 different electrodes are placed on the head. Not all of these electrodes return an equally strong signal. Depending on the distribution of signals, it is possible to have an estimate of the part of the brain that was at the origin of the signal. Unfortunately, because of the limit to the number of electrodes that can be placed on the head (and because of the small errors involved in the placement itself), localisation on the basis of EEG recordings is not very accurate.

A much better resolution can be obtained if, instead of measuring the electrical activity on the scalp, researchers measure the magnetic field around the head. The electrical signals in the brain produce magnetic fields, which can be picked up by sensitive sensors. This forms the basis of **magnetoencephalography** (MEG), a technique which is still in its early stages but which is expected to have a very significant impact.

magneto-encephalography (MEG)
measurement of the electrical brain activity by means of measurement of the magnetic field around the head; is one of the most promising brain imaging techniques, because it has the potential of both a high temporal and spatial resolution

Measuring blood flow in the brain

Brain activity is very energy demanding. It is estimated that the brain requires some 20% of the blood in the body and 25% of the oxygen to function properly. A short interruption in the blood flow to the brain results in massive and irreversible damage.

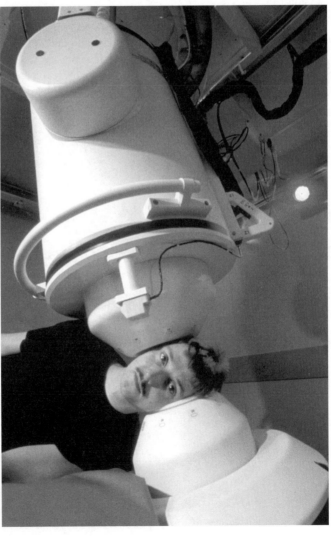

An MEG unit.

Source: Dr Jurgen Scriba/Science Photo Library Ltd.

positron emission tomography (PET)
brain imaging technique based on measurement of a radioactive tracer injected into the bloodstream

fMRI
brain imaging technique based on the measurement of blood with oxygen vs. blood without oxygen; currently the most popular imaging technique because of its high spatial resolution (allows good localisation); has rather low temporal resolution (cannot trace what is happening at a speed of hundreds of registrations per second)

By looking at the blood flow it is thus possible to know which brain regions are particularly active during a task.

PET and fMRI

There are several ways to determine the blood flow, depending on how precise the measurement has to be. One of the first techniques consisted of injecting a radioactive tracer into the blood circulation and detecting the radioactive signal. The more blood a certain region requires, the more tracer goes to that area. This was the basis of PET (positron emission tomography), a technique that now is used infrequently because of the need to use radioactive material and because the precision of the measurement is limited.

Another technique is to measure the magnetic resonance of the blood. This differs between blood with oxygen and blood without oxygen. Measurement of the magnetic resonance makes it possible to determine which regions of the brain are using a lot of oxygen (and thus are very active). Further advantages of the technique, which is called fMRI (functional magnetic resonance imaging), are that more accurate measurements can be made and that the investigation takes place without the need for an injection. A limitation of the technique is that at present the oxygen use can only be registered at a rate of a few times per second, so that researchers cannot measure the detailed processing that is going on (e.g. an ERP signal is based on 1,000 measurements per second).

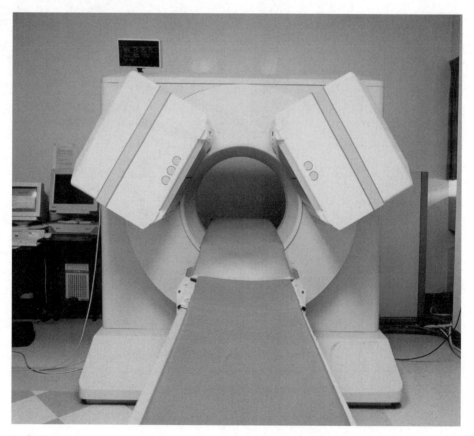

An fMRI scanner.
Source: Raymond Koch/Photonica/Getty Images.

An example of an fMRI study is a study in which people are put in the scanner and asked to generate as many words as possible that start with a particular letter (e.g. S). Given that this task deals with word generation, we can assume that Broca's area will be involved (Figure 6.7). In addition, we can assume that for the majority of people the area will be in the left hemisphere. However, for some people it will be in the right hemisphere. The latter is more likely in left-handed people than in right-handed people, as it is known from neuropsychological research that some 25% of left-handers have their speech area in the right hemisphere compared with fewer than 5% of the right-handers.

The upper part of Figure 6.17 displays the fMRI output of four participants who showed the typical pattern of brain activity in the word-generation task; they had their language production neatly lateralised to the left hemisphere. The lower part of the figure shows the data of two left-handers, who turned out to rely on their right hemisphere for word generation. So, the localisation of Broca's area can easily be picked up with an fMRI scanner and the word generation task.

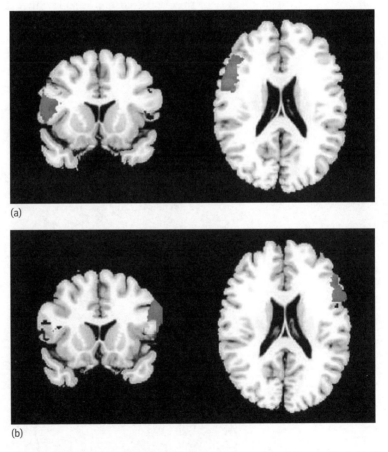

(a)

(b)

Figure 6.17 fMRI signal of people generating words that start with a particular letter.

The upper part shows the brain activity in the majority of people; the lower part shows the activity in people with right-brain dominance. The left side in each part gives a view from behind, the right side a view from above.

Source: Hunter *et al.* (2008). 'Visual half-field experiments are a good measure of cerebral language dominance if used properly: Evidence from fMRI', *Neuropsychologia*, 1, 316–25. With permission from Elsevier.

Measuring effects of 'virtual lesions'

TMS

Whereas the previous techniques allow researchers to measure how active different brain regions are during the performance of specific tasks, a final technique allows them to interfere temporarily with the activity in a restricted brain area. Because brain activity is electrical activity, it is possible to interfere with it by inducing a weak electric current in the neurons. Interference with the electrical activity of neurons in a restricted brain area is the basic mechanism behind transcranial magnetic stimulation (TMS). A coil is placed on the head of the person and a focused electric current is sent to the grey matter underneath. If the current is sent to the region in the brain that controls arm movements, for instance, the participant will feel an involuntary trembling in the arm on the other side of the body. If the current is sent to the location of the shrapnel wound described in Figure 6.11, then the person will experience unstructured light sensations (phosphenes) in the corresponding part of the visual field.

The intensity of the electric current is so low that the interference with the brain activity is too small to elicit involuntary actions, but is strong enough to interfere

transcranial magnetic stimulation (TMS)

stimulation of a brain region by means of a coil placed on the head; allows temporary interference with the processing of a small part of the brain

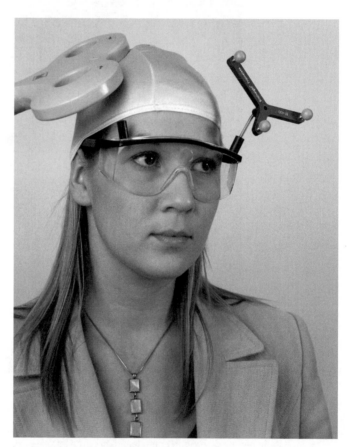

TMS is delivered by a coil. The resulting electric current briefly interferes with the activity of the neurons underneath the coil.

Source: University of Durham/Simon Fraser/Science Photo Library Ltd.

slightly with the ongoing activity. This can be picked up by looking at the speed at which the activity is performed (e.g. the time needed to respond to a stimulus). With the use of TMS, psychologists can establish which brain areas are needed for the completion of particular cognitive processes, just like cognitive neuropsychologists are able to test cognitive theories on the basis of brain injuries. The advantages of TMS over lesion research are that the effects are transitory and that the interference can be limited to a restricted brain area.

TMS is complementary to fMRI, because fMRI only allows researchers to see a correlation between activity in certain brain regions and performance on a particular task. It does not tell researchers whether the brain activity is necessary for the behaviour. Such a conclusion is only possible with TMS. By interfering with the activity of an area, the researchers can examine whether the region is critical for good task performance. The usual line of investigation in brain imaging studies, therefore, is first to use fMRI to identify a potentially interesting brain area and then to turn to TMS to confirm the critical involvement of the area in performance.

What do you think?

If you were given the opportunity to conduct research with one of the above techniques, which one would you prefer? Why? Do you have reasons for not wanting to do this type of research? Which technique do you object to?

The birth of cognitive neuroscience

Cognitive neuroscience: testing the cognitive information-processing models with brain imaging techniques

The availability of techniques to measure human brain activity while participants are performing mental operations opened a completely new field of research for psychologists. Just as neuropsychological information was used to test cognitive models of information processing (see above), so did psychologists increasingly rely on brain imaging data to test their theories. This branch of research became known as cognitive neuroscience, the scientific study of the biological mechanisms underlying cognition.

cognitive neuroscience
the scientific study of the biological mechanisms underlying cognition; largely based on brain imaging techniques, TMS and the measurement of electrical activity

Is cognitive neuroscience more than high-tech localisation?

Not everyone is convinced, however, that brain imaging and TMS allow the researcher to really say something about the information-processing models proposed by cognitive psychologists. According to some authors (e.g. Uttal 2001; Coltheart 2006), the findings of fMRI are more comparable to the localisation efforts of traditional neuropsychology (sometimes mockingly referred to as 'blob spotting') than to the testing of cognitive models done in cognitive neuropsychology. This criticism has probably been formulated most cogently by Uttal (2001):

> Even if we could associate precisely defined cognitive functions in particular areas of the brain (and this seems highly unlikely), it would tell us very little if anything about how the brain computes, represents, encodes, or instantiates psychological processes.
> (Uttal 2001: 217)

Kihlstrom (2007) went even further and argued that the conclusions based on brain imaging have a strong resemblance to the claims made by the nineteenth-century phrenologists. He took social cognition (i.e. knowledge about oneself and others) as an example. First, he noticed that many of the faculties identified by Spurzheim had to do with social functioning (see the blue parts of Figure 6.18). Then he pointed out how similar a modern picture based on brain imaging looks (Figure 6.19). Placing the two pictures next to one another, Kihlstrom wondered how much more information the modern brain imaging pictures have provided for the understanding of social cognition than Spurzheim's picture from 1834.

In defence of cognitive neuroscience

Needless to say, cognitive neuroscientists strongly disagree with the claim that their studies are unable to provide anything more than information about the localisation of brain activity (e.g. Henson 2005). They point to the deep influence cognitive neuroscience has had on psychological thinking. These are some of the arguments.

First, there is a difference between empirically showing the brain regions involved in a particular task and speculating about them. Though the overlap between Figures 6.18 and 6.19 may be striking, Spurzheim's broad claims were based on speculation

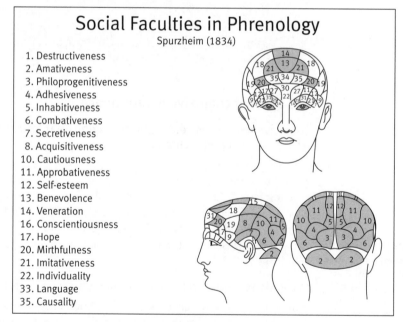

Figure 6.18 Faculties of social functioning.

According to some authors, localisation based on brain imaging is nothing more than an improved version of phrenology, without real impact on our insight of underlying mechanisms. They claim the information provided by cognitive neuroscience comes closer to that provided by traditional neuropsychology than that provided by cognitive neuropsychology. This figure shows the parts of the brain that were involved in social cognition according to Spurzheim (1834). Compare this with the parts of the brain involved in social cognition according to the latest brain imaging results.

Source: Gross (1998) *Brain, vision, memory: Tales in the history of neuroscience.* Figure from p. 54. Copyright © Massachusetts Institute of Technology, by permission of the MIT Press.

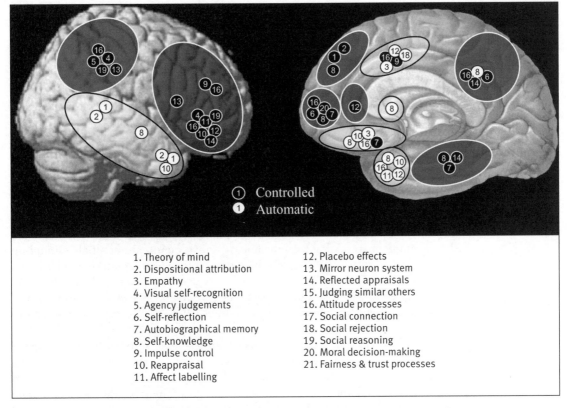

1. Theory of mind
2. Dispositional attribution
3. Empathy
4. Visual self-recognition
5. Agency judgements
6. Self-reflection
7. Autobiographical memory
8. Self-knowledge
9. Impulse control
10. Reappraisal
11. Affect labelling
12. Placebo effects
13. Mirror neuron system
14. Reflected appraisals
15. Judging similar others
16. Attitude processes
17. Social connection
18. Social rejection
19. Social reasoning
20. Moral decision-making
21. Fairness & trust processes

Figure 6.19 Localisation of social cognition functions on the basis of brain imaging studies.

For instance, the regions numbered 6 are the ones that are particularly active when people reflect about themselves. Kihlstrom (2007) wondered how much more informative this picture is than Spurzheim's picture shown in Figure 6.19.

Source: Lieberman (2007). Reproduced with permission.

and scattered brain injury findings, whereas Figure 6.19 is the result of a detailed analysis of activity in well-controlled tasks. As a result, the amount of reliable information is much higher in Figure 6.19 than in Figure 6.18.

Second, localisation of the brain activity while a person is performing a task does provide information about the processes involved. For instance, in Chapter 7 we will see that the brain regions normally involved in moving the feet are activated when participants see a picture of a person kicking something or are asked to read the word 'kick'. This strongly suggests that activation of movement commands is part of the understanding of actions and words referring to actions. This information (and the ensuing changes in theories of how people understand concepts) would not have been there without brain imaging.

Third, on the basis of brain imaging data it is now recognised that, although the brain is compartmentalised into regions with specialised functions (as defended by the localisers), all tasks (even the simplest) require the interaction of several areas distributed over distant parts of the brain (see Figures 7.3 and 7.5 for examples). This too was not realised before the start of cognitive neuroscience. In addition, although brain areas are specialised, they are involved in several tasks with different stimuli. For instance, it has been found that the Broca's area is involved not only in speech production but also in language understanding and music perception, possibly because it plays a role in grammar processing.

The overlap of functions in brain areas and the cooperation of different, distant parts of the brain were not known in the traditional localisation theories or indeed in the early days of cognitive neuroscience. These are genuine insights resulting from brain imaging studies. It might even be argued that the discussion about equipotentiality vs. localisation has been settled to a large extent by these two findings. Different parts of the brain are indeed specialised in the processing of different types of information, but task performance requires extensive interactions between various areas all over the cerebral hemispheres. There is also evidence that the extent of a brain region is not fixed but depends on practice. For instance, it has been found that music-related brain areas are substantially more developed in professional musicians than in non-musicians (Peretz & Zatorre 2005).

As we will see in Chapter 7, the discussion between cognitive psychologists and cognitive neuroscientists about the value of cognitive neuroscience research is more than a simple methodological squabble. It touches upon an essential assumption underlying cognitive psychology research, namely the idea that information processing forms a realm independent of the machinery upon which it is realised (remember from Chapter 5 how the computer metaphor gave cognitive psychologists the idea of hardware-independent cognitive representations). If one accepts hardware-independent information processing, trying to understand the human mind by localising the brain parts involved is like trying to understand computer software by examining the electronic parts implicated. This critique addresses one of the core conceptual issues in psychology, namely the question of how the mind and the brain are related to each other. In the next chapter, we review the various positions about this issue, at the end of which we will return to the debate between the cognitive neuropsychologists and cognitive neuroscientists.

What do you think?

Do we know anything more about how people think when we know which precise brain parts are involved?

Interim summary

Advances in studies of the working brain

- Single-cell recording allows researchers to find out to which type of information individual neurons respond; it is an invasive technique, however.
- EEG recordings allow researchers to pick up the summed electrical activity of groups of cells non-invasively. They allow researchers to detect cases of epilepsy and to discover different stages in sleep.
- ERP studies are based on EEG recordings and allow researchers to find out how the brain response changes as a function of different types of stimuli.
- MEG scanning also measures the electrical activity of groups of neurons and allows researchers to add localisation to the ERP studies.

- PET scanning allows researchers to see which brain areas require extra blood during the performance of tasks by tracing a radioactive substance injected into the blood.

- fMRI scanning also allows researchers to localise brain activity on the basis of oxygen use. Produces more detailed images than PET and does not require an injection of substance into the participants.

- TMS allows researchers to interfere briefly with the activity of a small region of the grey matter and to examine the effects of this interference on the time needed to complete a particular task. Makes it possible to ascertain that the brain region is crucial for performance.

- The above techniques have allowed researchers to measure brain activity while participants are performing mental tasks. This created a new research field, known as cognitive neuroscience.

- Not everyone is convinced that brain imaging techniques allow researchers to examine the detailed cognitive processes involved in correct task performance.

6.6   *Focus on*: Can delusions be investigated with the cognitive neuropsychological approach?

Cognitive neuropsychiatry as a new research area

In the previous sections we saw how neuropsychology and neuroscience shifted from the question 'where in the brain do different processes take place?' to the question 'how does brain functioning constrain cognitive theories of information processing?' To stress the change of focus, the new disciplines called themselves cognitive neuropsychology and cognitive neuroscience.

At the end of the twentieth century a group of researchers argued that a similar approach could be used in the study of faulty thinking in mental disorders, in particular with respect to delusions. Delusions are strong erroneous beliefs that are not supported by empirical evidence. They are present in approximately 75% of people diagnosed with schizophrenia, but also happen sometimes after brain injury and even seem to be experienced by some 5–10% of the general population at least once in their life. For instance, in a large-scale longitudinal study over two years, Hanssen *et al.* (2005) reported that 2% of their interviewees in the general population experienced one or more delusions.

The most common delusions in acutely hospitalised psychiatric patients are (Appelbaum *et al.* 1999):

- persecutory (e.g. someone is trying to harm me) (51%)

- body/mind control (e.g. my thoughts are controlled by an alien) (27%)

- grandiose (e.g. I have achieved something big but nobody realises it) (23%)

- religious (e.g. I am in direct contact with an important religious figure) (18%).

cognitive neuropsychiatry

subfield that tries to understand consequences of mental disorders in terms of breakdowns in the cognitive models of normal psychological functioning

The new subfield that tries to understand delusions (and other consequences of mental disorders) in terms of breakdowns within the cognitive models of normal psychological functioning is called **cognitive neuropsychiatry**. We illustrate the approach with the Capgras delusion.

The case study of Joseph Capgras

On a summer day in 1918, Mme M. went to a Parisian police station to alert the authorities that her children had been imprisoned by a gang. She urgently asked the police officers to help her. Upon further questioning she added that in several other places in Paris people had been kidnapped as well and were being kept in underground prisons. It soon turned out that Mme M. had a long history of mental problems. In 1906, after the death of her twins, she had delusions of grandeur, thinking she was the illegitimate daughter of an extremely wealthy man from South America. In 1914, she suddenly stopped recognising her daughter and was convinced that the child had been replaced by a double. She also thought that her husband in reality might be a look-alike.

Instead of being helped to free her children, Mme M. was brought to a psychiatric emergency clinic and from there to a psychiatric institute. She was taken into care by a psychiatrist called Joseph Capgras (1873–1950). He was a famous French psychiatrist, specialising in delusions. So, none of the beliefs of grandeur and persecution really surprised him (as indicated above, they are quite common among psychotic patients). However, he was struck by the strength of this woman's conviction that her child and her husband had been replaced by imposters. She still recognised them, but they did not feel 'real' to her. They had lost all their warmth and familiarity, hence her conviction that they were look-alikes and that her real relatives had been kidnapped (and maybe killed). In 1923 Capgras wrote an article on this delusion, together with his collaborator Reboul-Lachau.

A Freudian interpretation of the delusion

The following year Capgras published two more papers on the case. However, by this time he had retracted his original interpretation that the delusion was the result of a discrepancy between rationally recognising the family member and no longer feeling any sense of familiarity. Instead, he advanced a psychoanalytic explanation in line with the growing dominance of Freudian thinking in (French) psychiatry. Capgras now proposed that the source of the delusion was an incestuous desire for the father. This led to ambivalence in the feelings for other relatives, resulting in a mixture of love and hate. If the conflict escalated too much, it was 'solved' by making a dissociation between the real, beloved person, who was absent, and the look-alike that could be hated.

Arguably, in his revision Capgras was influenced by the similarity of Mme M. with the Paul Schreber case, which Freud analysed in 1911. Paul Schreber had been a judge in Dresden, who in his autobiography described his descent into paranoia and wrote how he was surrounded by '*flüchtig hingemachte Männer*' (evanescent, makeshift men). On the basis of Schreber's writings, Freud linked the paranoia to anxieties surrounding homosexuality and questions of paternity, caused by a 'father complex'. Capgras may have seen an analogy between the evanescent men in Schreber's world and the imposters of Mme M., from which he deduced that Mme M.'s delusion could be attributed to a 'father complex' as well.

It soon turned out that the delusion described by Capgras was not a unique case (although rather rare) and the term *Capgras delusion* became used to refer to the condition, together with Capgras's revised Freudian interpretation. The interpretation seemed to make sense, because patients only complained about family members being replaced by doubles.

The cognitive neuropsychiatry alternative

Cognitive neuropsychiatrists grew interested in the Capgras delusion when it became clear that the delusion sometimes started after a brain injury. Ellis and Lewis, for instance, described the following case:

> A recent well-publicized UK court case of Capgras delusion involved a teacher named A.D. who, following a car crash, developed the belief that his wife had died in the incident and that the woman living with him was an impostor, someone with whom he is now uncomfortable. He still insists that his real wife died in the accident and he successfully sued the driver of the other vehicle for the distress caused. In court a consultant psychiatrist explained that Mr D. was suffering from Capgras delusion.
>
> (Ellis & Lewis 2001: 149)

Apart from the Capgras delusion, the man did not seem to have other symptoms of an underlying Freudian conflict.

The Capgras delusion further attracted interest because cognitive models of face processing had pointed to the conclusion that face recognition involved two different routes. This conclusion was based on neuropsychological research of prosopagnosia (see above). Bauer (1984) showed pictures of famous people and family members to a 39-year-old male college graduate who had been involved in a serious motorcycle accident, leaving him unable to recognise faces, including his own. On each trial of Bauer's experiment, a picture was shown and five names were read to the patient. The patient had to indicate which of the names represented the picture. At the same time, his skin conductance was measured. This is a variable that is influenced by the autonomous (i.e. involuntary) nervous system and that in people without face-processing difficulties shows an increased activity when a familiar person is encountered.

As expected, the patient was unable to match the names to the faces. However, on many trials the skin conductance response increased when in the series of names the correct name was mentioned. So, it seemed as if the patient (on an unconscious, emotion-related level) did recognise the face. Bauer's finding was subsequently repeated in several other experiments: individuals with prosopagnosia do not recognise faces consciously, but show an unconscious emotional reaction when they are confronted with a familiar face.

Relating the prosopagnosia findings to the Capgras delusion, Ellis and Young (1990) put forward the hypothesis that what might be happening in the Capgras delusion is that the unconscious, emotion-based, face processing route has been severed. Such a disconnection would result in the patients still recognising the person at a conscious, rational level but failing to experience the emotional response associated with the person (Figure 6.20). To test the hypothesis, Ellis et al. (1997) measured the skin conductance of five patients with Capgras delusion and five control patients to known and unknown faces. As expected, the control patients showed enhanced skin conductance responses when a known face was presented than when an unknown face was presented, but the Capgras patients did not, giving credence to the hypothesis.

? What do you think?

Have cognitive psychiatrists been too fast in trying to reject the Freudian interpretation of the Capgras delusion? What evidence would you use to support your claim?

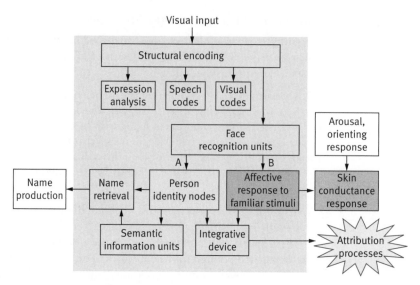

Figure 6.20 A cognitive model to explain face recognition and the occurrence of prosopagnosia and Capgras delusion.

There are two routes in which faces are recognised: one leads to the conscious recognition of the person (via a person identity node) and one leads to an unconscious emotional response (an affective response). A disruption in the first route (A) leads to prosopagnosia; a disruption in the second route (B) leads to a Capgras delusion.

Source: Based on Ellis and Lewis (2001). Reproduced with permission.

The research on the Capgras delusion is an example of the growing interactions between cognitive psychology and psychiatry. Just as in cognitive neuropsychology and cognitive neuroscience, researchers are seeing merit in combining psychological models of information processing with biological processes (for more examples, see Halligan & Marshall 1996; Coltheart 2007). This is a theme to which we will return in Chapter 12.

Interim summary

Cognitive neuropsychiatry

- Cognitive neuropsychiatry states that symptoms of mental disorders (such as delusions) can be understood as the result of errors in the cognitive information-processing model that accounts for normal psychological functioning.

- The Capgras delusion refers to a situation in which a person still recognises close relatives, but is convinced that they have been replaced by look-alikes.

- The Freudian interpretation of the delusion refers to conflicting feelings towards the relatives, which result in a dissociation between the absent loved persons and the present hated look-alikes.

- Cognitive neuropsychiatry argues that the condition results from blocked information transfer in an unconscious, emotion-related processing route that under normal circumstances elicits an emotional response each time we encounter a familiar person. As a result, the relatives feel strange, even though we recognise them.

Recommended literature

Most handbooks of neuropsychology contain a chapter on the history of the discipline. In addition, an increasing number of the original publications are becoming available on the internet. Interesting books on the history of neurophysiology are Finger, S. (1994) *Origins of neuroscience: A history of explorations into brain function* (Oxford: Oxford University Press), Gross, C.G. (1998) *Brain, vision, memory: Tales in the history of neuroscience* (Cambridge, MA: The MIT Press) and Clarke, E. & Jacyna, L.S. (1987) *Nineteenth-century origins of neuroscientific concepts* (Berteley, CA: University of California Press). A classic textbook of cognitive neuropsychology is Ellis, A.W. & Young, A.W. (1988) *Human cognitive neuropsychology* (Hove, UK: Psychology Press). Good books about cognitive neuroscience are Gazzaniga, M.S. (2008) *Cognitive neuroscience: The biology of the mind* (New York: W.W. Norton & Co.) and Ward, J. (2010) *The student's guide to cognitive neuroscience* (2nd edition) (Hove, UK: Psychology Press).

References

Andrewes, D.G. (2002) *Neuropsychology: From theory to practice*. Hove: Psychology Press.

Appelbaum, P.S., Robbins, P.C. & Roth, L.H. (1999) 'Dimensional approach to delusions: Comparisons across types and diagnoses', *American Journal of Psychiatry*, **156**: 1938–43.

Bauer, R.M. (1984) 'Autonomic recognition of names and faces in prosopagnosia: A neuropsychological application of the guilty knowledge test', *Neuropsychologia*, **22**: 457–69.

Berger, H. (1969) 'Hans Berger on the electroencephalogram of man: The fourteen original reports on the human electroencephalogram', *EEG & Clinical Neurophysiology*, Supp. 28.

Breasted, J.H. (1930) *The Edwin Smith surgical papyrus*. Chicago: University of Chicago Press (2 vols).

Brysbaert, M. (2006) *Psychologie*. Gent, Belgium: Academia Press.

Buckingham, H.W. (2006) 'The Marc Dax (1770–1837)/Paul Broca (1824–1880) controversy over priority in science: Left hemisphere specificity for seat of articulate language and for lesions that cause aphemia', *Clinical Linguistics & Phonetics*, **20**: 613–19.

Capgras, J. & Reboul-Lachaux, J. (1923) 'L'Illusion des "sosies" dans un délire systématisé chronique', *Bulletin de la Société de Médecine Mentale*, **11**: 6–16. (Translated into English in Ellis, H.D., Whitley, J. & Luauté, J.-P. (1994) 'Delusional misidentification. The three original papers on the Capgras, Frégoli and intermetamorphosis delusions', *History of Psychiatry*, **5**: 117–46. If you read Dutch, also available in Draaisma, D. (2006) *Ontregelde geesten*. Groningen: Historische Uitgeverij.)

Changeux, J.P. (1997) *Neuronal man: The biology of mind* (translated by Laurence Garey). Princeton, NJ: Princeton University Press.

Clarke, E. & Jacyna, L.S. (1987) *Nineteenth-century origins of neuroscientific concepts*. Berkeley: University of California Press.

Coltheart, M. (2004) 'Are there lexicons?' *Quarterly Journal of Experimental Psychology*, **57A**: 1153–71.

Coltheart, M. (2006) 'What has functional neuroimaging told us about the mind (so far)?', *Cortex*, **42**: 323–31.

Coltheart, M. (2007) 'The 33rd Sir Frederick Bartlett Lecture: Cognitive neuropsychiatry and delusional belief', *Quarterly Journal of Experimental Psychology*, **60**: 1041–62.

Coltheart, M., Patterson, K. & Marshall, J.C. (eds) (1980) *Deep dyslexia*. London: Routledge & Kegan Paul.

Cubelli, R. & De Bastiani, P. (2011) '150 years after Leborgne: Whis is Paul Broca so important in the history of neuropsychology?' *Cortex*, **47**: 146–7.

Cubelli, R. & Montagna, C.G. (1994) 'A reappraisal of the controversy of Dax and Broca', *Journal of the History of the Neurosciences*, **3**: 215–26.

Dewey, J. (1896) 'The reflex arc concept in psychology', *Psychological Review*, **3**: 357–70 (at psychclassics.yorku.ca).

Draaisma, D. (2009) *Disturbances of the mind*. Cambridge: Cambridge University Press.

Eling, P. (2005) 'Baginsky on aphasia', *Journal of Neurolinguistics*, **18**: 301–15.

Eling, P. (2006a) 'Meynert on Wernicke's aphasia', *Cortex*, **42**: 811–6.

Eling, P. (2006b) 'The psycholinguistic approach to aphasia of Chajim Steintha', *Aphasiology*, **20**: 1072–84.

Ellis, H.D. & Florence, M. (1990) 'Bodamer's (1947) paper on prosopagnosia', *Cognitive Neuropsychology*, **7**: 81–105.

Ellis, H.D. & Lewis, M.B. (2001) 'Capgras delusion: A window on face recognition', *Trends in Cognitive Sciences*, **5**: 149–56.

Ellis, H.D. & Young, A.W. (1990) 'Accounting for delusional misidentifications', *British Journal of Psychology*, 157: 239–48.

Ellis, H.D., Young, A.W., Quayle, A.H. & de Pauw, K.W. (1997) 'Reduced autonomic responses to faces in Capgras delusion', *Proceedings of the Royal Society London: Biological Sciences*, 264: 1085–92.

Fancher, R.E. (1996) *Pioneers of psychology* (3rd edn). New York: Norton.

Geschwind, N. (1972) 'Language and the brain', *Scientific American*, 226: 76–83.

Goodglass, H. (1983) 'Linguistic aspects of aphasia', *Trends in Neuroscience*, June: 241–3.

Goodglass, H. & Kaplan, E. (1983) *The assessment of aphasia and related disorders*. Philadelphia: Lea & Febiger.

Gross, C.G. (1998) *Brain, vision, memory: Tales in the history of neuroscience*. Cambridge, MA: The MIT Press.

Halligan, P.W. & Marshall, J.C. (1996) *Method in madness: Case studies in cognitive neuropsychiatry*. Hove, UK: Psychology Press.

Hanssen, M., Bak, M., Bijl, R., Vollebergh, W. *et al.* (2005) 'The incidence and outcome of subclinical psychotic experiences in the general population', *British Journal of Clinical Psychology*, 44: 181–91.

Helm-Estabrooks, N., Fitzpatrick, P.M. & Barresi, B. (1981) 'Response of an agrammatic patient to a syntax stimulation program for aphasia', *Journal of Hearing and Speech Disorders*, 46: 422–7.

Henson, R. (2005) 'What can functional neuroimaging tell the experimental psychologist?' *The Quarterly Journal of Experimental Psychology*, 58A: 193–233.

Holmes, G.M. (1918) 'Disturbance of vision by cerebral lesions', *British Journal of Ophthalmology*, 2: 353–84.

Hunter, Z.R., Brysbaert, M. & Knecht, S. (2007) 'Foveal word reading requires interhemispheric communication', *Journal of Cognitive Neuroscience*, 19: 1373–87.

James, W. (1890) *The principles of psychology*. New York: Henry Holt.

Kihlstrom, J.F. (2007) *Social neuroscience: The footprints of Phineas Gage*. At http://socrates.berkeley.edu/~kihlstrm/SocialNeuroscience07.htm.

Lieberman, M.D. (2007) 'Social cognitive neuroscience: A review of the core processes', *Annual Review of Psychology*, 58: 259–89.

Mahajan, S.K., Machhan, P.C., Sood, B.R., Kuman, S. *et al.* (2004) 'Neurocysticercosis presenting with psychosis', *Journal of the Association of Physicians in India*, 52: 663–66.

Morton, J. & Patterson, K. (1980) 'A new attempt at an interpretation, or, an attempt at a new interpretation'. In M. Coltheart, K. Patterson & J. C. Marshall (eds), *Deep dyslexia*. London: Routledge & Kegan Paul.

Müller, J.P. (1838) *Elements of physiology* (translated by W. Baly). London: Taylor and Walton.

Peretz, I. & Zatorre, R.J. (2005) 'Brain organization for music processing', *Annual Review of Psychology*, 56: 89–114.

Prins, R. & Bastiaanse, R. (2006) 'The early history of aphasiology: From the Egyptian surgeons (c. 1700 BC) to Broca (1861)', *Aphasiology*, 20: 762–91.

Schiller, F. (1979) *Paul Broca: Founder of French anthropology, explorer of the brain*. Berkeley: University of California Press.

Shallice, T. (1988) *From neuropsychology to mental structure*. Cambridge: Cambridge University Press.

Shepherd, G.M. (1991) *Foundations of the neuron doctrine*. New York: Oxford University Press.

Spurzheim, J.G. (1834) *Phrenology of the doctrine of the mental phenomenon* (3rd edn). Boston: Marsh, Caper and Lyon.

Thomas, R.K. (2007) 'Recurring errors among recent history of psychology textbooks', *American Journal of Psychology*, 120: 477–95.

Thomson, J.A. (1922) *The outline of science: A plain story simply told*. New York: G.P. Putnam's Sons.

Tizard, B. (1959) 'Theories of brain localization from Flourens to Lashley', *Medical History*, 3: 132–45.

Uttal, W.R. (2001) *The new phrenology: The limits of localizing cognitive processes*. Cambridge, MA: MIT Press.

Whitaker, H.A. & Etlinger, S.C. (1993) 'Theodor Meynert's contribution to classical 19th century aphasia studies', *Brain and Language*, 45: 560–71.

7 The mind–brain problem, free will and consciousness

Questions to consider

Introduction

> The Astonishing Hypothesis is that 'You,' your joys and your sorrows, your memories and your ambitions, your sense of personal identity and free will, are in fact no more than the behavior of a vast assembly of nerve cells and their associated molecules. As Lewis Carroll's Alice might have phrased it: 'You're nothing but a pack of neurons.'
>
> (Crick 1995: 3)

The above citation comes from a book by the British scientist and co-discoverer of the structure of DNA, Francis Crick (1916–2004). In this book Crick argued that the spectacular advance of modern science made the concepts of the soul and consciousness redundant. In his view, we should no longer be satisfied with the religious guesses of yesterday, however charming they may be.

The present chapter also deals with the question of how we can reconcile the biological workings of the brain with the feeling we all have of being more than a mere pack of nerve cells. Throughout history, humans have been impressed by their ability to reflect about themselves and the world around them. Asked what they consider to be the essence of their life, most people refer to their self, the feeling they have of being an individual

self

the feeling of being an individual with private experiences, feelings and beliefs, who interacts in a coherent and purposeful way with the environment with private experiences, feelings and beliefs, who interacts in a coherent and purposeful way with the environment. The existence of such a feeling begs the question, where does the self come from? What gives us the power to experience ourselves as consistent entities with goals and values? Even stronger, what gives us the power to think, to have a mind? This is arguably the biggest conceptual issue in psychology. How do the brain and the mind relate to each other? This issue is known as the mind–brain problem.

mind–brain problem
issue of how the mind is related to the brain; three main views: dualism, materialism and functionalism

Three different views of the interaction between mind and brain will be discussed in the sections below. The first is the oldest and intuitively the most appealing. It says that the mind (or the soul) is something independent of the body. This view is called *dualism*. The second approach states that the mind is nothing but a by-product of the biological processes taking place in a particular brain. This view is called *materialism*. Finally, the third approach says that the mind is indeed realised in a brain, but that it could be copied to any other brain, just like information on a computer can be copied to other machines. This is the *functionalist* view.

After a discussion of the three views, we will continue with a review of present-day research about consciousness and end by looking at the evidence suggesting that unconscious processing is the automatic pilot that guides us through life and that may help us to reach better decisions.

As with all the topics in this book, we can only paint the broad brushstrokes of what are much richer themes with heated discussions (albeit more among philosophers of the mind than among psychologists). We have made a selection of the big historical developments and the contemporary ideas that have particular appeal to psychologists, accepting that for many of the players involved our discussion this may do injustice to the richness of their proposals. Indeed, reading a book on philosophy of mind sometimes looks like opening a catalogue of-isms (substance dualism, property dualism, epiphenomenalism, philosophical behaviourism, methodological behaviourism, physicalism, eliminativism, fictionalism, computationalism, . . .). We have opted to keep these -isms to a bare minimum, because it is our experience that they are powerful magnets for exam questions and, as a result, tend to draw attention to the details of the discussions rather than to the main themes.

Interim summary

- The mind–brain problem refers to the relationship between the mind and brain.
- Three main approaches are discussed in this chapter:
  - dualism: mind and brain are two independent entities
  - materialism: the mind is a by-product of the biological workings of the brain
  - functionalism: the mind is realised in the brain, but the information can be copied to another machine with the same structure.

? What do you think?

Before you continue reading it may be good to ask yourself what your opinion of the mind–brain problem is. Which approach appeals most to you? Why? Is this the first time you have thought about this question?

7.1 Dualism: the mind is independent of the brain

When scholars refer to the mind, they mean the faculties humans (and animals) have to perceive, feel, think, remember and want. The oldest and intuitively most appealing view of the mind is that it is something completely different from the body (in particular the brain). The mind and the body are two different realms. This view is known as dualism.

mind

aggregate of faculties humans (and animals) have to perceive, feel, think, remember and want

dualism

view of the mind–body relation according to which the mind is immaterial and completely independent of the body; central within religions and also in Descartes' philosophy

Dualism in religion and traditional philosophy

Religion

Dualism is central to religions. They are grounded in the belief that people possess a divine soul created by God, which temporarily lives in the body, and which leaves the corpse upon its death. The soul is what gives people their purpose and values in life. It usually aims for the good, but can be tempted and seduced by evil forces. This belief gave rise to the so-called demonologist view of psychopathology, the conviction that mental disorders are due to possession by bad spirits. Indeed for a long time it seemed more acceptable that mental disorders were due to evil ghosts than to physiological malfunctions.

Plato and Descartes

Dualism was also central in the philosophies of Plato and Descartes. Plato (Chapter 1) maintained that the soul exists before, and survives the body. Human souls were made of the leftovers of the soul of the cosmos and travelled between the cosmos and the human bodies they temporarily inhabited. Because human souls were part of the cosmos-soul, they had knowledge of the perfect realm that contained the eternal, ideal forms of which the worldly objects were but imperfect reflections filled with error. By focusing on the innate knowledge of their immortal soul, humans could get access to the true ideas.

A very similar view was defended by Descartes, who was strongly influenced by Plato and the teachings of the Roman Catholic Church. According to Descartes, humans were composed of a divine soul in a sophisticated body (sometimes referred to as 'the ghost in the machine'). The soul was immaterial and formed the thinking part of the person. Just like Plato, Descartes believed that the soul brought divine information to humans and, therefore, that people had innate knowledge, which they could recover through deductive reasoning.

Because Descartes was the first modern philosopher to address the relationship between the body and the mind, and because he strongly defended the dualist view, current-day philosophers use the term *Cartesian dualism* to refer to theories in which the mind is seen as radically different from the body and as independent of the biological processes in the brain. Dualism in philosophical writings does not make reference to the mind's fate after the body's death, however, though this issue is central to religious writings.

? What do you think?

Do you think that humans are born with some forms of innate knowledge? And is heavenly or divine information the only possible source of such knowledge?

Dualism in early psychology and lay thinking

Dualism in early psychology

For reasons that will be outlined below, in the second half of the nineteenth century a growing number of scientists began to question the dualistic view. They felt increasingly uncomfortable with the emphasis religions placed on the immortality of the soul, the connection of the soul to a divine entity, and its independence of the body. At the same time, they were unwilling to reduce the human mind to nothing but brain tissue, so that in practice most defended some kind of implicit dualistic view. Lyons (2001) gives several examples of such ambivalence among early psychologists, as can be seen in the following citation from a much used textbook, *A manual of psychology*, authored by G.F. Stout (1924):

> It thus appears that even if the being which is a mind is also supposed to be a body, yet the mental aspect of its nature is so distinct from its bodily aspect that each requires separate and independent investigation. Knowledge concerning the mind does not of itself include or conduct to knowledge concerning the body as such. Knowledge concerning the body does not of itself involve or conduct to knowledge concerning the mind as such. Hence Physiology and Psychology are radically distinct sciences, each dealing with its own subject matter.
>
> (Stout 1924; as cited in Lyons 2001: 18)

The distinction between the body and the mind was additionally attractive to early psychologists because it provided them with their own study area that could not be invaded and taken over by brain scientists. It also resulted in the development of research methods that differed from those of the neurophysiologists.

Dualism in lay thinking

The Australian philosopher David Chalmers (1996: 125) argues that dualism nowadays still is the fundamental attitude people have about the relationship between the mind and the brain. Very few people spontaneously say that the mind is a biological brain process, even though they readily accept that such processes form the basis of mental operations. They feel more comfortable with statements like 'The mind arises from the brain', showing that, deep down, the mind is experienced as something different from the brain. There is a gap between the mind and the body. What could be the origin of this feeling?

? What do you think?

Chalmers claims that dualism is the fundamental attitude people have about the relationship between the mind and the brain. Does this agree with your own feelings? Does your intuition tell you that your thinking forms a separate reality from your body?

Dualism puts consciousness at the centre of human functioning and seems to give humans free will

Dualism has an intuitive appeal because it puts conscious information processing at the centre of our functioning and it gives us the feeling of being in control of our actions.

In dualist models consciousness is the core of human existence

Dualism not only makes a clear distinction between the mind (soul) and the brain, in general it also gives priority to the mind. Our conscious, deliberate thinking is at the centre of our existence and controls our actions. Because of this conscious control, we experience ourselves and the world around us as rich and coherent. We see ourselves as individuals with particular appearances and traits, who respond in a reasonably consistent way, are guided by goals and values, and have a strong feeling of continuity. Similarly, our experience of the world around us is rich, meaningful and much more than simply knowing what is there and what it is for. Our private experiences are so rich that we often feel we cannot fully describe them to someone else (see the notion of qualia later in this chapter).

Our self-perception and the explicit experiences we have of the world around us are part of what is usually referred to as our consciousness, a word that has different meanings within different theories but that in general refers to the private, first-person experiences we live through (our 'I'). It contains all the mental states and psychological functions we are aware of, such as thoughts, beliefs, desires, feelings and intentions.

Dualism puts consciousness at the centre of the person, because the mind (or the soul) is the acting unit and the mind coincides with consciousness. The actions of an individual are guided by the private, first-person experience of that individual.

consciousness

word referring to the private, first-person experiences an individual lives through; contains all the mental states a person is aware of; part of the mind that can be examined with introspection

Dualism and free will

Because in the dualist view consciousness is the centre of the mind, nothing happens unless it is licensed by the mind. This seems to put humans in control over their actions and decisions (see below for some qualifications, however). Humans can choose their course of action from a number of alternatives, a phenomenon that is referred to as free will. Individuals with free will are motivated by intentions they set themselves. They try to achieve goals and they are guided by reason. They have an open future and can decide which path of action to take. Having free will also means that individuals are responsible for their actions: they could have chosen to behave otherwise.

According to Walter (2001), three conditions must be met before an action can be ascribed to free will:

free will

situation in which individuals can choose their course of action; choice is the outcome of an informed deliberation

- The agent must have been able to do otherwise. Free will only exists when there is a choice.
- The act must originate in the agent, not in some external force.
- The act must be the outcome of rational deliberation (acts that are erratic and unpredictable are not seen as free).

? What do you think?

Can you think of an instance in which you decided to do something different from everyone else? And can you think of an instance in which you did something without really wanting to do it? How do these relate to your free will?

Problems with dualism

Although dualism strongly agrees with human intuitions (and we mostly rely on it in our everyday social functioning), it has come under severe attack since the second half of the nineteenth century, to such an extent that it is no longer a viable approach within the philosophy of mind. It also has been banned from models of cognitive functioning (although Chalmers (1996) argues that this is usually done by sweeping the mind–brain problem under the carpet rather than by explicitly denying dualism). Several factors contributed to the downfall of dualism. We discuss the most important.

The interaction problem

A first problem for dualism was how to explain the mechanisms by which an independent mind (or soul) can influence the body. This 'interaction problem' had already arisen in Descartes' day, when the 25-year-old Princess Elizabeth of Bohemia sent Descartes the following question: 'How can the soul of man, being only a thinking substance, determine his bodily spirits to perform voluntary actions?' (Lyons 2001: 25). Because the soul cannot be perceived, Descartes thought of it as an immaterial substance that did not occupy volume in the material world. The soul had no length, no width, no depth. How, then, could such an immaterial soul steer the human body into action? Similarly, how can a non-physical, spiritual mind control physical brain processes? Descartes and the dualists after him have never found a satisfactory answer to this problem.

The existence of unconscious control processes

A second factor that was difficult to account for in dualism was the discovery that many mental functions seemed to happen outside consciousness. John Locke (1690) was the first to raise the issue. He wondered what happened to the mind when humans were asleep. If consciousness was the defining feature of human existence, as claimed by Descartes ('I think, therefore I am'), did this imply that human existence was interrupted during sleep? Locke thought not.

A similar problem was raised by the German mathematician and diplomat Gottfried Wilhelm Leibniz (1646–1716). He too thought that the human mind could not be limited to conscious thinking, because 'there is in us an infinity of perceptions . . . of which we are unaware because the impressions are either too minute and too numerous, or else too unvarying, so that they are not sufficiently distinctive on their own' (Leibniz 1765; as translated by Nicholls & Liebscher 2010: 6–7). Leibniz disagreed with Descartes that the universe could be thought of as a machine. Instead he compared it to a living organism. The building blocks were not material particles, but energy-laden and soul-invested units, which Leibniz called monads. He made a distinction between four types of monads (Fancher 1996):

1. *Simple monads* formed the bodies of all matter (organic and inorganic). They had some type of unconscious and unorganised perception, and they were motivated by a tendency to keep in line with the existing, pre-established harmony of the universe.

2. *Sentient monads* were present in all living organisms, but not in inorganic material. They had capacities for feeling pleasure and pain, and for the voluntary focusing of attention. However, they lacked the ability to reason about their experiences.

3. *Rational monads* corresponded to the conscious minds of humans. They possessed the capacity of apperception, the faculty not only to perceive but also to reflect upon what is perceived. Apperception according to Leibniz was not entirely based on empirical evidence, but also on innate truths. The latter could be inferred from the fact that humans sometimes felt absolutely sure about a phenomenon (e.g. a mathematical or geometric law). Such certainty could never be based on perception alone; it was innate knowledge demonstrated by perception.

4. The *supreme monad* controlled and motivated all other monads. This in Leibniz's eyes was the omniscient and omnipotent God of Christian religion.

Crucially, for Leibniz human consciousness was not aware of the activity of the simple monads and, to a large extent, of the sentient monads. Still, these monads could motivate human behaviour, as illustrated in the following fragment:

> [Simple and sentient monads resemble] so many little springs trying to unwind and so driving our machine along. . . . That is why we are never indifferent, even when we appear to be most so, as for instance when to turn left or right at the end of a lane. For the choice that we make arises from these insensible stimuli, which, mingled with the actions of objects and our bodily interiors, make us find one direction of movement more comfortable than the other.
>
> (Leibniz 1765; as translated in Fancher 1996: 70)

Influenced by Leibniz, Kant at some point also started to wonder how much wider human knowledge was than the part people were conscious of:

> There is something imposing and, it seems to me, profoundly true in the thought of Leibniz: the soul embraces the universe only with its faculty of representation, though only an infinitesimally tiny part of these representations is clear.
>
> (Kant 1755–1770; as translated in Nicholls & Liebscher 2010: 10)

Kant thought of the unconscious representations as dark representations ('dunkele Vorstellungen') and devoted a complete section to them in his 1798 book *Anthropology from a pragmatic point of view*. At the same time, Kant seems to have been puzzled (bothered?) by the door to the 'dark' he had opened and he left the unconscious representations out of his 'more serious' philosophical writings, because he could not integrate them within his overall philosophical system trying to reconcile realism with idealism (Chapter 3).

Leibniz's and Kant's thoughts, however, were music in the ears of the German Romanticists (Chapter 2). They saw these ideas as evidence for the argument that rational thinking was but the tip of human potential and that the most interesting part of the mind was active below the level of consciousness. They urged their readers to strive for unconscious artistic productivity and intuitive aesthetic sense. Goethe (1749–1832), for instance, liked to be described as a philosopher (or even a scientist) working on the basis of 'unconscious naivety' (*unbewuβe Naivetät*). Others started to associate the unconscious part of the mind with sexual and sometimes destructive desires. This was true for Schopenhauer (1788–1860), Nietzsche (1844–1900) and Freud (1856–1939).

The prospect that a large part of mental life may be unconscious also found its way to the UK. For instance, this is what was written about the Scottish philosopher William Hamilton in 1858:

> Sir William Hamilton . . . thinks that in order to explain certain phenomena of memory, and of association of ideas, it is necessary, as far as we are able, to take account

of the unconscious modifications of the mind. It is a curious speculation, and as it is rather novel in our country, though we are assured, familiar to the Germans, we shall take a glance at it.

. . . the mind 'contains certain systems of knowledge, or certain habits of action which it is wholly unconscious of possessing in its ordinary state, but which are revealed to consciousness in certain extraordinary exaltations of its powers.' For evidence of this, we are referred to the class of cases . . . where knowledge is revived in fever, delirium or somnambulism, which apparently had become extinct.

(Blackwood's Edinburgh Magazine, October 1858, pp. 506–7; at books.google.com).

The study of unconscious processing gained further momentum from the nineteenth-century neurophysiologic discovery that reflexes and bodily functions were controlled by the spinal cord and subcortical structures, not by the cerebral hemispheres (Chapter 6). A lot seemed to happen in a person without their conscious control. Needless to say, the more mental processes started to escape conscious control, the less central became the position of consciousness in human functioning.

The disappearance of mystery forces in the scientific world

Another reason why dualism lost its appeal was that it needed the existence of an immaterial, mysterious, animistic 'soul'. Scientists had bad experiences with such entities, which to them looked more like relics from the pre-scientific world with its animistic explanations than building blocks of a sound scientific theory. There were two prime examples of such mysterious 'substances' that had been postulated in science before but which in the end turned out to be materialistic phenomena that could be measured and manipulated by the scientists.

phlogiston

substance that was believed to make materials flammable before the chemical processes of combustion were understood

The first substance was phlogiston. This had been invoked in the seventeenth century to explain why some materials easily caught fire (wood, certain types of gas), whereas others did not catch fire at all (stone, water). The idea was that flammable materials contained a substance, called phlogiston, which was released during burning. Materials without the substance were not combustible. Experimentation, however, called the phlogiston theory into question. For instance, it was found that materials sometimes weighed more after being burned than before. This was difficult to reconcile with the idea that phlogiston provided the fuel for the flames. It was also found that fire depended on the availability of oxygen. These findings gradually brought researchers to the insight that fire and heat were by-products of particular chemical changes involving the elements carbon, oxygen, hydrogen and nitrogen (although a bit of sulphur helps as well). The process needed a certain temperature (flash point) to get going, but afterwards it was self-perpetuating as long as the base elements were present.

Once the combustion processes were known, the phenomenon of fire was understood and could be controlled. It became possible to determine how flammable new chemical compounds would be. It was even possible to develop fire-repellents, materials that were impenetrable to flames (and did not weigh too much). Researchers also started to realise that the processes involved in combustion showed similarities to what happened in respiration. As a result, fire lost its mystery.

vital force

animistic substance thought to be present in living matter before the chemical and biological differences between living and non-living matter were understood

The second mystery substance that in the end turned out not to exist was the vital force. This force had been postulated to explain why some organisms were living and others not. Living matter was supposed to have a 'vital force', which non-living matter lacked. Like many other animistic explanations, the vital force stayed nearly unquestioned until the seventeenth century. A defining moment in its demise was the realisation that it was possible to make living (organic) matter out of non-living (inorganic) components. This finding was reported in 1828 by the German chemist Friedrich Wöhler, who synthesised urea (an organic substance found in urine) from the inorganic compounds potassium cyanate and ammonium sulphate. Suddenly it became clear that the distinction between organic and inorganic matter was not as sharp as had always been assumed. The main difference turned out to be the central role of the chemical element carbon in organic material.

Wöhler's finding was but the first in a long series of discoveries that disentangled the essence of living matter. Another important insight was that all living things were composed of cells that grew out of previous cells. This discovery was made possible by the invention and optimisation of the microscope. Once the cell was isolated as the basic unit, researchers started to unravel the processes taking place in it. Among other things, they discovered that the instructions to build the cell were stored in the DNA of the cell nucleus and that DNA consisted of a sequence of four bases. Currently researchers think they are on the brink of creating a new life form by inserting a newly designed sequence of DNA bases into the nucleus of existing cells. They are adamant that the resulting organism will be a living organism, capable of reproducing itself.

Given that mysteries like phlogiston and the vital force in the end turned out to be chemical and biological processes that could be manipulated, an increasing number of scholars began to claim that something similar would happen to the mind. Once all the brain processes were understood, what humans experienced as their mind would simply turn out to be a by-product of the working brain, just as fire was a by-product of certain chemical reactions and the vital force was a consequence of a particular arrangement of molecules. At some point it would be discovered what biochemical processes were involved in the human mind and the mystery would be solved. This belief gave rise to materialism, which we discuss in the next section.

Interim summary

- The mind refers to a person's faculties to perceive, feel, think, remember and want.

- In religions the mind is often equated with an immaterial, divine soul. This is an example of dualism. A similar view was defended by Descartes and, therefore, in philosophy is often called Cartesian dualism.

- Dualism is an intuitively attractive model of the mind–brain relationship because it gives humans free will (i.e. control over their actions and decisions) and it readily accounts for the existence of consciousness in humans. The latter refers to the rich and coherent, private, first-person experience people have about themselves and the world around them.

- Dualism does have problems explaining how an immaterial mind can influence the body, and how it is possible that so much information processing in humans occurs unconsciously. It also does not agree with a scientific world view, where there is no place for mysterious and animistic substances.

7.2 Materialism: the mind is the brain

The alternative: materialism

The idea of an independent, incorporeal mind (soul) as the core of a human being struck British empiricists in the eighteenth and the nineteenth centuries as quite implausible, although they had to be careful not to upset the church too much. After one of them, David Hume (1711–1776), openly declared that he saw no good reason why one should believe in a soul (and in God), he was prevented from getting an academic post in the UK (Jahoda 2007: 29) and had to make a living as a tutor and secretary to embassies, despite the fact that his writings were (and still are) among the best of their time.

materialism

view about the relationship between the mind and brain that considers the mind as the brain in operation

The idea of the mind as nothing other than a brain in operation really took off towards the end of the nineteenth century. This view is usually called materialism. As we saw in Chapter 6, the end of the nineteenth century was when it was discovered that many brain processes were reflexes. It was also the time when Darwin's evolutionary theory started to have a considerable impact on philosophy and psychology (Chapters 3 and 12). Materialism says that there is no distinction between the mind and the brain (as defended by dualism), although there are divergences between philosophers in the views about what exactly this entails for the mind. In the writings below, we use a strong definition as was done by Lyons (2001), namely that materialism implies that the specific cells of a person's brain and their connections constitute the person's mind. That is, the mind of a person cannot exist without his or her brain. This definition makes a clear distinction between materialism and functionalism (as we will see below).

Within psychology, the rise of materialism was one of the reasons why behaviourists wanted to get away from the study of 'consciousness' (Chapter 5). Although psychologists were still at a loss to explain how human consciousness could be the emanation of biological processes, it was not done to keep defending the idea of a non-materialistic mind. Even Boring, who as a student of Titchener started his career studying the structure of consciousness (Chapter 4), wrote in the 1930s that:

> While there is no possibility of disproving or proving dualism, the exposition of the present book is based on the assumption that it is scientifically more useful to consider that all psychological data are of the same kind and that consciousness is a physiological event.
>
> (Boring 1933: 14)

The consequences for consciousness and free will

The replacement of dualism by materialism was not without consequences for the ideas of consciousness and free will. Whereas dualism put them at the centre of human functioning, materialism did not require either of them. Below we give examples of the most extreme positions this led to. Crick's book (cited at the beginning of this chapter) is another example.

Consciousness is folk psychology

The Canadian philosopher Paul Churchland (1981) argued that consciousness as the centre of the human mind and the controller of human actions was not only an illusion but also a dangerous idea, because it gave individuals a misunderstanding of what makes them tick. For Churchland, consciousness and the associated opinions

folk psychology

collection of beliefs lay people have about psychological functioning; no efforts made to verify them empirically or to check them for their internal coherence

were examples of folk psychology, unsubstantiated convictions of lay people, similar to 'folk medicine' and 'folk science', which are also incoherent collections of beliefs and superstitions that are void of empirical verification. This is how Churchland introduced his view:

> Eliminative materialism is the thesis that our commonsense conception of psychological phenomena constitutes a radically false theory, a theory so fundamentally defective that both the principles and the ontology of that theory will eventually be displaced, rather than smoothly reduced, by completed neuroscience. Our mutual understanding and even our introspection may then be reconstituted within the conceptual framework of completed neuroscience, a theory we may expect to be more powerful by far than the common-sense psychology it displaces, and more substantially integrated within physical science generally.
>
> (Churchland 1981: 67)

It is not so difficult to find examples of strongly held opinions in most people's consciousness that turn out to be wrong when they are properly tested. For instance, most people are adamant that they would help other people in need and that they would never deliberately harm someone else. Darley and Latané (1968) examined the first claim and found that people quite often fail to assist others in emergency situations. One of the most counterintuitive findings was that the chances of helping someone decreased in proportion to the number of people who witnessed the situation. Apparently, when there are other people who could intervene, we feel less compelled to do it ourselves, a phenomenon the authors called the bystander effect. Another finding is that people are less likely to help others who differ from them (e.g. in race, clothing or language), as predicted by the Darwinist account that we are more likely to help someone who shares many genes with us.

Milgram (1963) examined the claim that we would not harm others. He invited ordinary participants to a laboratory where they were introduced to another person (supposedly another participant but actually a colleague of the experimenter). The other person had to learn a particular task and would be punished by electric shocks of increasing intensity each time he made an error. The shock was to be administered by the participant. The colleague (who had gone to another room and interacted with the participant via an intercom) made many mistakes and so the participant was forced to administer ever-increasing shock intensities. The control panel clearly indicated the induced pain and the associated risks. Beforehand, psychologists and psychiatrists predicted that every participant would stop as soon as the intensity became too high. However, as is now well known, this was not what Milgram observed. Even though the experimenter did not insist too much, all participants gave much higher shock intensities than they had thought themselves capable of, and 65% went up to the highest level, which was clearly indicated as lethal.

The above findings agree with Churchland's (and the other materialists') claim that the conscious human mind is not the controller of human behaviour, but a delusion that can have damaging consequences.

Is there still room for free will?

If our conscious mind is not the controller of our actions, does this then also imply that we have no free will, that our actions are basically governed by our biological make-up? A view very close to this has been defended by the British biologist Richard Dawkins (1976/2006). According to Dawkins, the evolutionary theory was misunderstood in the first century after its introduction by Darwin. Whereas everyone assumed natural selection was about the survival of individuals (in their offspring) and species, the selection actually concerns the survival of DNA molecules. Dawkins points out that the contribution of individuals to their offspring rapidly dilutes after a few generations, making it impossible that something 'biological' of an individual is preserved. Similarly, he points out that throughout history life forms have come and gone, to be replaced by others that were better adapted to the (changed) circumstances. So, species do not survive either. The only things that have remained constant throughout are the genes that make up the living organisms. They are the true survivors, and they have managed to mobilise a whole range of survival machines that keep them alive and enable them to multiply.

The overlap in genetic material among the many species on earth is indeed remarkable. For instance, the similarity in genetic material between mice and humans is estimated to be around 85%. If anything comes close to eternity, Dawkins argues, it is the genes. The present-day genes are very similar to the genes of a million years ago and in all likelihood will have a high resemblance to the genes found on earth in a million years' time. In Dawkins's view, humans are nothing more than survival machines for the genes they carry around, on a par with mice, bacteria and plants, which are also survival machines for very similar genes. In his own words:

> We are survival machines, but 'we' does not mean just people. It embraces all animals, plants, bacteria, and viruses. The total number of survival machines on earth is very difficult to count and even the total number of species is unknown. Taking just insects alone, the number of living species has been estimated at around three million, and the number of individual insects may be a million million million. Different sorts of survival machine appear very varied on the outside and in their internal organs. An octopus is nothing like a mouse, and both are quite different from an oak tree. Yet in their fundamental chemistry they are rather uniform, and, in particular, the replicators that they bear, the genes, are basically the same kind of molecule in all of us – from bacteria to elephants. We are all survival machines for the same kind of replicator – molecules called DNA.
>
> (Dawkins 1976/2006, introduction of Chapter 3)

If one day humans fail, that will be bad for the genes in them, but other carriers with very similar genes will take over and continue the journey of the genes.

Needless to say, a vision of humans as mere survival machines for the genes they contain is a far cry from the dualist conjecture of the conscious mind being the control centre of humans and characterised by free will. This shift of emphasis is exemplified in the terminology used to describe humans in a materialistic world. They are variously described as survival machines, slaves, robots or automata.

? What do you think?

How does it feel to assume that your life is nothing but a means to continue the existence of the genes that made you? How do you reconcile this with the efforts you are currently making to become a psychologist and the joy you experience in learning new things?

Problems with materialism

The fact that many researchers preferred materialism over dualism does not imply that the materialistic approach is problem-free. We discuss two issues.

How can different experiences be compared?

identity problem
the difficulty the materialistic theory of the mind–brain relationship has to explain how two events can be experienced as the same despite the fact that their realisation in the brain differs

A first criticism addressed to materialism was how to account for the identity problem. The identity problem refers to the difficulty of explaining how two events can be experienced as the same if their encodings differ. If two brains have their own distinctive ways of encoding an event, how can they appreciate that both encodings refer to the same event? How is it possible for two humans to communicate with each other if their brain codes differ? Even worse, if experiences completely depend on the way in which they have been realised in a specific brain at a specific time, how can people realise that two codes with some time in between refer to the same stimulus? Given the complexity and the flexibility of the human brain (involving over 100 billion neurons and trillions of connections), it is next to impossible for two experiences of a particular input to be encoded in exactly the same way. How then can the brain know these codes refer to the same stimulus?

How can we build a mind as the by-product of a brain?

A second limitation of materialism is that nobody has a convincing idea of how the human mind could be a by-product of the biological processes in the brain. Claiming that the mind is nothing but the brain is one thing; showing how this can be achieved is another. Dupuy (2009) argued that the first cybernetic attempts in the 1940 and 1950s to make artificial intelligence were based on the materialistic idea. Researchers were convinced that if they built a brain-like computer they would automatically get an intelligent machine, returning a particular input into a desired output on the basis of self-learning. There was no need for them to define the meaning of the input or to detail the operations to be performed:

> . . . cybernetics proposed another conceptual approach . . . Like eliminative materialism, it banished from its language all talk of reasons, all talk of mental representations having semantic content, and so on. . . . It recognized no intermediate level of symbolic computation operating on representations. . . . It redefined meaning by purging it of all traces of subjectivity. Having redefined meaning in this way, it was able to reach it from the far bank of physical causation in a single bound. Since physical causality is computable, and since computation can be implemented in matter, this leap also linked computation with meaning. Had cybernetics succeeded in realizing its ambitions, it would have successfully accomplished the very enterprise – the mechanization of the mind.
>
> (Dupuy 2009: 14)

However, the cybernetic attempts along these lines resulted in failure:

> The ideas of cybernetics were good ones. By this I . . . mean . . . that they constituted a coherent model that was perfectly suited to the objective that cognitive science continues to share with cybernetics, which is to say the mechanization of the mind. Those who dedicate themselves to this purpose today may find it useful to immerse themselves once again in these pioneering debates. If any further reason is needed to convince them of this, it would be the following . . . : cybernetics ended in failure. It was a historical failure, one that was all the more bitter as its advertised ambitions were enormous; a conceptual failure, all the less comprehensible in view of the fact that it had marshalled very great intellectual advantages on its side.
>
> (Dupuy 2009: 15)

At the same time, another type of machine turned out to be much more successful. This consisted of rather simple computers (Turing machines) that were able to store information in binary code (memory units turned on or off) and that could execute algorithms on this information on the basis of sequences of instructions given. In addition, the instructions could be run on each and every computer compatible with them, indicating that there was a distinction between the machine (the hardware) and the information processed by the machine (the software). This was an important eye-opener, giving rise to functionalism.

Interim summary

- Materialism holds that there is no distinction between the mind and the brain, and that the mind is a direct consequence of the brain in operation. To make the distinction with functionalism clear, we take this to imply that the mind is linked to the specific brain in which it has been realised.

- According to the strongest versions of materialism, there is no consciousness or free will. Consciousness is an illusion, a form of folk psychology, and humans are comparable to robots or machines. According to Dawkins, they are the slaves of their genes.

- A first problem with materialism was that it seemed unable to account for the identity problem: how can different exposures to the same event be experienced as the same if they are not encoded similarly? A second problem was that attempts to simulate the human mind as a by-product of biological or mechanical processes were not successful, whereas computers running sequences of instructions on stored information started to thrive.

7.3 Operational computers: the new eye-opener leading to functionalism

Because humans using the materialistic approach were increasingly compared to robots, controlled by their biology, it was normal for philosophers of mind to keep a close eye on the developments in artificial intelligence. One particular finding in this discipline had far-reaching consequences for ideas about the human mind.

Information transcends its medium

Something few researchers had foreseen at the outset of cybernetics was that the efforts to make machines intelligent would confront them with the discovery that information can be thought of as a realm separate from the medium upon which it is realised. Whereas cybernetics at first tried to make individual machines function like human minds (as described in Dupuy's excerpt above), in line with materialism, real advancement consisted of rather simple machines on which information could be manipulated in binary form. In addition, although this information had to be processed on a computer and, therefore, depended on the functioning of the machine, it could easily be copied to other computers or even to completely different devices.

This contradicted a basic tenet of materialism, namely that information is linked to the machine (brain) upon which it is realised.

As we saw in Chapter 5, mathematicians and logicians in the nineteenth and twentieth centuries ventured that all intelligence could be represented by binary symbols (zeros and ones) upon which Boolean transformations (algorithms) operate. Every medium capable of doing so could process the same information and was a so-called Turing machine. This is how Turing described the insight:

> The idea of a digital computer is an old one. Charles Babbage, Lucasian Professor of Mathematics at Cambridge from 1828 to 1839, planned such a machine, called the Analytical Engine, but it was never completed . . . The fact that Babbage's Analytical Engine was to be entirely mechanical will help us to rid ourselves of a superstition. Importance is often attached to the fact that modern digital computers are electrical, and that the nervous system also is electrical. Since Babbage's machine was not electrical, and since all digital computers are in a sense equivalent, we see that this use of electricity cannot be of theoretical importance.
>
> (Turing 1950: 439)

Engineers found out that the Boolean approach could easily be applied to computers and was the fastest (only?) way to make machines intelligent. At the same time, the building of operational, digital computers showed that information could transcend the medium upon which it was realised. This insight was not only a big breakthrough for computer scientists (because it meant that computer programs could be developed for many different types of machines at the same time), but it also had major implications for the way in which the mind was conceived. In Chapter 5 we saw how it led to the emergence of cognitive psychology. Here we discuss the impact on the philosophy of mind.

A solution to the identity problem

The first outcome of the understanding that information forms a device-independent realm was that it provided an answer to the identity problem. Because information in operational computers was independent of the precise ways in which it had been realised (as long as it retained the binary symbols and the Boolean transformations), the physical changes by which computers code zeros and ones and worked with them did not really matter. Similarly, the minute physiological changes that accompany a particular human experience may not be important, as long as they preserve the information code. The same information can be realised and communicated in multiple ways.

Functionalism in philosophy

functionalism

in philosophy, view about the relationship between the mind and brain that considers the mind as a separate layer of information implemented on a Turing machine; predicts that the mind can be copied onto another Turing machine

The conclusion that not the exact implementation but the functional organisation determines the nature of the information gave rise to a school in philosophy called functionalism (also sometimes called machine functionalism), not to be confused with functionalism in psychology (Chapter 4). Just as functionalists in psychology around 1900 studied the functions of the mind rather than the nature of the mind, so functionalists in philosophy from the 1970s onwards examined the functions of information, rather than the precise ways in which the information was realised. To understand what hunger is, they argued, it is not necessary to know what neurophysiological mechanisms make the phenomenon possible, but what they do to the organism.

This is how one of the most famous proponents, the American philosopher Jerry Fodor, summarised the movement:

> In the past 15 years a philosophy of mind called functionalism that is neither dualist nor materialist has emerged from philosophical reflection on developments in artificial intelligence, computational theory, linguistics, cybernetics and psychology. All these fields, which are collectively known as the cognitive sciences, have in common a certain level of abstraction and a concern with systems that process information. Functionalism, which seeks to provide a philosophical account of this level of abstraction, recognizes the possibility that systems as diverse as human beings, calculating machines and disembodied spirits could all have mental states. In the functionalist view the psychology of a system depends not on the stuff it is made of (living cells, metal or spiritual energy) but on how the stuff is put together.
>
> (Fodor 1981: 124)

Beam me up, Scotty

The British philosopher Derek Parfit presented an interesting thought experiment that illustrates the difference between functionalism on the one hand and Cartesian dualism and materialism on the other. A thought experiment is a hypothetical scenario that helps us understand things. In Parfit's case, it is even a very easy thought experiment, because most of us already seen it 'in action' in the science fiction series *Star Trek*. The actors in this series can be transported from their ship, the *Enterprise,* to nearby planets and back by teleportation, operated by the transport chief Montgomery 'Scotty' Scott (hence, the catchphrase at the beginning of this paragraph). The teleportation works by disassembling the particles of the person's body at the place of departure and reinstating them at the location of destiny.

thought experiment
hypothetical scenario that helps with the understanding of a philosophical argument

Now, the interesting question about such teleportation is what it would do to the mind. In Descartes' approach, we would probably have to predict that the mind would not survive such a process. Given that the mind (soul) does not come from biological brain processes and forms an independent, non-material entity, it cannot be teleported with the rest. So, teleportation would result in the reinstatement of the body without the accompanying mind. In contrast, within the functionalist framework, teleportation should work fine (as it did in the TV series). The mind is nothing but the information stored within the physiological network of the brain and, if the latter is restored, the mind should be back as well.

In the materialist view the mind would survive the teleportation without any loss of information only when exactly the same brain is reinstated. Because the mind depends on the specific brain operations that give rise to it, only a reinstatement of the original particles in their initial positions would result in a flawless transportation of the mind. In contrast, within the functional view, the mind will be transported as soon as the information code can be implemented on the new brain. Because we have seen teleportation 'work' so often in *Star Trek*, we may have overlooked its implications for the mind–brain problem.

Information as the saviour of free will?

Information allows humans to rebel against the genes

Given that information in the cybernetic world can be considered as independent of the matter on which it is realised, does this mean that information escapes the control of the genes? Is it possible that humans escaped the tyranny of the biological make-up, because they assembled matter-independent information? One of the most outspoken scholars defending this position is the Canadian psychologist Keith Stanovich in his book *The robot's rebellion: Finding meaning in the age of Darwin*. This is his view:

> People who do not like the idea of genetic determinism do in fact have an escape route. However, the escape route is not to be found in denying the known facts about the heritability of human behavioral traits, or in denying their evolutionary origins . . .
>
> The first step in conceptualizing the escape route involves focusing on the startling fact . . . that the interests of replicators [genes] and vehicles [survival machines] do not always coincide. When a conflict occurs, short-leashed response systems will prime the response that serves the genes' interests (replication) rather than those of the vehicle. However, as humans, we are concerned with our own personal interests, not those of the subpersonal organic replicators that are our genes. The presence of our analytic processing systems makes it possible to install the mental software . . . that maximizes the fulfillment of our own interests as people. This mindware ensures a mental set to give primacy to the person's fulfillment (to side in favor of the vehicle and against the replicators when their interests do not coincide). That mental set is the proclivity for rational thought.
>
> (Stanovich 2004: 81–2)

In other words, the fact that humans can encode, store, retrieve and manipulate information enables them to pursue intentions that need not coincide with those of the genes. As Stanovich sees it, the robots have a potential to rebel, if they are willing to use rational thought aimed at their own personal interests.

Memes

Not everybody is convinced, however, that information is liberating humankind. Dawkins (1976) was probably the first person to spot that information shows many similarities with DNA molecules. According to him, DNA need not be the only replicator in the universe. There may be others, which also work on the principles of variation (the introduction of spontaneous small changes when existing material is copied), selection (of the changes that fit well within the environment) and replication (of the successful variations).

Dawkins argues that the build-up of information by humans fulfils all the principles of Darwinism. A few variations find a storage facility and a way to get copied. During the copying small changes are introduced. Many of these changes are uninteresting and fail to be reproduced. However, the few ideas that fit well in the environment copy themselves copiously and spread throughout the territory. Dawkins calls the individual ideas that make up information and try to replicate themselves, memes.

meme
information unit proposed by Dawkins that reproduces itself according to the principles of the evolutionary theory (variation, selection and replication)

Although Dawkins did not write this explicitly, the picture of memes he paints is not one of a medium that liberates people, but rather one of a medium that also uses humans as 'survival machines'. So, it might be that humans are not only 'programmed' to spread genes, but also to spread information in the form of memes. The main difference between genes and memes at present is that the former have managed to harness many organisms, so that they can survive the extinction of a species, whereas the latter (still) largely depend on the human race for their growth and distribution. Such a view would predict that memes will push for the development of forms of information multiplication other than humans (e.g. by means of computers, robots and neural networks).

What do you think?

One prediction of the meme theory is that memes need not be helpful to get copied. Some memes may even be harmful to humankind and will still get copied. An example of an unhelpful meme that gets copied endlessly is a chain letter; an example of a harmful meme is the belief that you have to kill individuals who do not share your opinions (memes). Can you think of other examples?

Telecopying

Needless to say, the above ideas find fruitful soil in science fiction (which to some extent can be compared with thought experiments, as we have seen in the example of Parfit). You may have recognised the theme of the *Terminator* film trilogy in the previous paragraph: intelligent machines taking over from humans and starting to produce/control information. Similarly, it is not so difficult to take the teleportation example a few steps further on the basis of what we have seen. Let us suppose that teleportation does not require that the very same participles disassembled at the point of departure are reinstated at the destination location but that other particles with similar features would do just as well (computer technology allows that). Then, we would not only be able to teleport a person, but also to telecopy them. And if we can do that once, then in principle we can repeat it indefinitely (as long as we have the resources to make the particles). Each copy would have the same information and thus would start off with the same mind. Furthermore, nothing requires the tissue to be biological tissue. If we manage to assemble a silicone network with the same layout as the human brain, then in principle it should be possible to copy human knowledge onto that network. An interesting question at this point is whether such a network also would inherit the human mind, complete with consciousness and (the illusion of) free will.

Problems with functionalism

The functionalist framework agreed perfectly with cognitive psychology and cognitive neuropsychology. Psychology's task was not to understand how the brain functioned or how mental representations were implemented; this was the hardware side. Psychology's challenge was to understand the software that runs on the human brain. Researchers enthusiastically referred to a book published posthumously by David Marr (1945–1980), a neuroscientist who developed one of the first computer models of human vision. Marr (1982) argued that information processing could be studied at three levels. First, at the computational level researchers postulate ideas about how a system can generate output representations from input representations received. Next, at the algorithmic level, they try to specify the algorithms necessary to perform the processes proposed at the computational level. Finally, at the implementation level, they aim to make the algorithms work on a specific physical system. Cognitive psychologists could easily identify themselves with researchers operating at Marr's computational and algorithmic level (leaving the implementation level for the neurophysiologists and the engineers).

Similarly, cognitive neuropsychologists placed themselves squarely in the functionalist camp, as can be seen in the following excerpt:

> One of the fundamental assumptions of cognitive neuropsychology is that the behaviour and experience of brain-damaged patients can provide information about the nature of the independent cognitive modules that underlie normal behaviour and experience. Given this assumption, it is, of course, perfectly possible for fruitful discussions about the nature of cognitive processes to proceed without any consideration of the nature of the associated brain systems.
>
> (Frith 1992: xii)

The challenge posed by cognitive neuroscience

As discussed in Chapter 6, the clear separation between information processing and brain tissue was questioned anew by cognitive neuroscience, which argued that human information processing could be understood by examining the brain parts involved in the operations. As Gazzaniga *et al.* (1998: 20) wrote in one of the first textbooks devoted to the new discipline: 'Any computational theory must be sensitive to the real biology of the nervous system, constrained by how the brain actually works.'

Cognitive (neuro)psychologists were quick to object that such an approach was at odds with the functionalist approach. It was the equivalent of an engineer claiming that the operations of a software package could be understood by studying the computer parts involved in the execution of the program (e.g. Hatfield 2000; Uttal 2001; Coltheart 2004; Harley 2004). As Miller (2010: 718) formulated it: 'A parallel could be drawn regarding social networking carried out via a network of computers. One's (social) network is not one's computer nor its connections to other computers.'

To strengthen their message, the adherents of the functionalist approach questioned whether cognitive neuroscience has had any theoretical impact beyond what is already known to psychologists on the basis of behavioural and neuropsychological data (Coltheart 2006; Kihlstrom 2010). They argued that cognitive neuroscience provides little more than nice pictures about correlations between brain activity and psychological experiences, despite the massive investments and the repeated promises of more profound impact.

> The issue . . . is not whether biology influences mind and behaviour . . . The issue is whether data about the structure and function of the brain can constrain theories advanced at the psychological level of analysis.
>
> (Kihlstrom 2010: 765)

> What we can do (increasingly often and increasingly well) is localize in space a portion of the tissue that seems differently associated with mental events. What we can do is correlate a person's thinking of this or that with localized brain activity . . . But this does not show that the brain is thinking, reflecting or ruminating; it shows that such-and-such parts of person's cortex are active when the person is thinking, reflecting or ruminating.
>
> (Miller 2010: 727)

The fact that cognitive neuroscience has tremendously expanded since its beginnings in the 1990s, according to the critics, is not due to the theoretical progress made by the new approach but to the appeal pictures of brain activity have for humans (readers, researchers, reviewers, assessors). People tend to see pictures of brain activity as more informative than they really are. Skolnick-Weisberg and colleagues (2008), for example, observed that pictures of brain activity made naive adults and students of a neuroscience course less critical about weak explanations of a phenomenon. Similarly, McCabe and Castel (2008) reported that an article of brain imaging results was rated as more convincing by undergraduate students when it was accompanied by a brain image, even when the article included a paragraph with scathing criticism from another researcher.

Beck (2010) listed the following reasons for the non-scientific appeal of brain images:

1. Brain imaging pictures afford a simple message: brain area X is responsible for this particular complicated psychological or social phenomenon.

2. Reductionist, biological explanations have extra appeal, because they seem to give a definite and scientific account (they address the basis of the behaviour). People have greater confidence in a biological marker of a behavioural phenomenon than in the phenomenon itself. Watching a brain area light up when chocolate cravers see chocolate seems to be more convincing than hearing the people talk about their irresistible cravings.

3. Part of the appeal of biological explanations is that people tend to confuse them with innateness, thinking that brain activity is the outcome of fixed, innate wiring rather than the result of a learning process.

4. Brain imaging pictures hide the complicated comparisons and statistical analyses needed to come to the image. They create an illusion of a direct snapshot of the brain in action.

As Beck (2010: 763) wrote: 'It is worth pointing out that the construction of the colorful images we see in journals and magazines is considerably more complicated, and considerably more processed, than the photo-like quality of the images might lead one to believe.' Indeed, brain imaging research has recently been accused of too rapidly accepting associations between brain activity and psychological processing, leading to so-called voodoo correlations. Vul and colleagues (2009) showed that cognitive neuroscience studies of emotion, personality and social cognition frequently report correlations between brain activation and personality measures higher than can be expected on theoretical grounds, and they argued that these were due to statistical artefacts.

According to the critics of cognitive neuroscience, the contribution of the new techniques for psychological understanding will turn out to be very limited, because what matters are the computational and algorithmic levels of information processing, not the implementation level. Given the incompatibility of the basic tenet of cognitive neuroscience with the prevailing functionalist framework used by cognitive (neuro)psychologists, it is perhaps surprising to see that cognitive neuroscience has been so successful in the past decades (including the retraining of many cognitive neuropsychologists). Cognitive neuroscientists argue this is because the brain is a much more varied device than present-day computers. The parts of the brain active in various tasks constrain cognitive theories in ways that cannot be addressed by traditional behavioural experiments. As a result, differences in brain functioning can be used to gain insights in the ongoing information processing. Henson (2005) argued that, in particular, function-to-structure deductions are compelling. According to him, if two conditions produce qualitatively different patterns of activity over the brain, then it can safely be concluded that these conditions differ in at least one function. Less convincing evidence comes from structure-to-function inductions, which involve the claim that if two functions activate the same brain regions they must involve the same functions.

> ### ? What do you think?
>
> Which position strikes you as the most promising avenue for progress in psychological understanding: further theorising about the information processing by the brain, as defended by the scientists who believe in functionalism, or further research into the biological functioning of the brain, as claimed by the cognitive neuroscientists? Are these approaches incompatible? Or can they be combined in fruitful ways? If so, how?

The challenge posed by symbol grounding and survival in a changing environment

The success of digital computers turned the rather unspecified materialistic view (the mind is the brain in operation) into a more concrete functionalist proposal (the mind is the outcome of [Boolean] information processing in the brain). Gradually, however, an important distinction between human and computer functioning became clear. Although the current performance of computers is breathtaking (certainly compared to that at the beginnings of computing a few decades ago), there is one big limitation. Computers do well as long as they stay disconnected to the environment and are fed information by humans. As soon as they have to interact with changing surroundings, they tend to be sluggish and unpractical. The reason is that computers based on Boolean information processing have no inherent knowledge about what information is important in which situation, so that they are obliged to process much more information than humans seem to do (Anderson 2003).

The difficulties in making computers interact with their surroundings have confronted researchers with the fact that humans seem to have a lot of information based on their interactions with the world. Even stronger, researchers have started to realise that information (symbols and algorithms) ultimately must be grounded in an external reality. Boolean logic is great to represent information and to process it (e.g. by combining symbols in new ways), but ultimately the symbols need to refer to some reality. This is known as the symbol grounding problem, the fact that the representations used in computations require a reference to an external reality in order to get a meaning. Harnad (1990) compared the grounding problem to the situation you would encounter when trying to understand a foreign language by means of a dictionary in that language. Each word (symbol) is defined by means of other words (symbols) and as long as you have no grounding for a single symbol, it is impossible for you to start figuring out the language. This is how Glenberg and Robertson (2000: 379) described the importance of the grounding problem for cognitive psychology:

symbol grounding problem

the finding that representations (symbols) used in computations require a reference to some external reality in order to get meaning

> Meaning is the most important problem in cognitive psychology. Meaning controls memory and perception. Meaning is the goal of communication. Meaning underlies social activities and culture: To a great degree, what distinguishes human cultures are the meanings they give to natural phenomena, artifacts, and human relations. Yet, rather

than being a hotbed of theoretical and empirical investigation, meaning in cognitive psychology has been coopted by a particular approach: Meaning arises from the syntactic combination of abstract, amodal symbols that are arbitrarily related to what they signify.

The solution to the symbol grounding problem has been sought in the interactions humans have with the world through their bodies. These interactions provide humans with sensory and motor representations in which symbols can be grounded. According to Anderson (2003) the importance of the interactions with the surroundings was overlooked when Descartes associated the human mind with what sets humans apart from the rest of the universe, *including animals*. As a result, the day-to-day physical interactions with the world became excluded from what constituted the human mind. The alternative is embodied cognition, the conviction that the interactions between the human body and the environment form the grounding of human cognition.

embodied cognition

the conviction that the interactions between the human body and the environment form the grounding (meaning) of human cognition

Anderson (2003) lists four sources of embodied information:

1. The human physiology. Humans can do some actions in some situations, but others not, because of bodily limitations. As Glenberg and Robertson (2000) argued, confronted with the same challenge (e.g. crossing a river) effective actions are quite different for a mole, a bird and a human. Similarly, grown-ups can use a chair to fend off an aggressive dog, whereas toddlers cannot.

2. Evolutionary history. Not all actions are equally effective for survival and reproduction. By natural selection, the meaning of a particular situation for a particular animal becomes associated with a set of actions that enhance successful coping with the situation.

3. Practical activities during reasoning. Very often, when confronted with a problem, humans do not keep on reasoning until they have found the best solution. They try out various actions that seem sensible to bring the solution closer. This constant interaction between action and thinking grounds cognitive representations.

4. Socio-cultural situatedness. For humans (and presumably other higher mammals), the actions allowed by objects depend on the social context. Whereas a chair invites sitting on it, this is not true for a chair in a museum or the throne of a king (or a tribal chief). Living in a group strongly constrains the type of actions that can be performed, and it is important to make use of this information.

The symbol grounding problem and the existence of embodied cognition have confronted scholars with the fact that the human mind is more than a simple Turing machine. Knowledge in the real world is not completely independent of the substrate on which it is realised, because such knowledge is not agile enough to function in the world. Instead, the human mind is shaped intimately by the underlying body and its interactions with the physical world. As you may notice, this brings the human mind back closer to the materialistic view as we defined it than to the functionalist view.

Interim summary

- Computer science has shown that information may transcend the medium on which it is realised. It can be copied from one Turing machine to another.

- This insight provides a solution to the identity problem, the fact that it is unlikely that two identical thoughts are physiologically realised in exactly the same way.

Interim summary (continued)

- This insight also led to functionalism in the philosophy of mind, the conviction that philosophers of mind had to investigate the functions of information, and not the precise ways in which the information was realised in the brain.

- Functionalism (and materialism) can explain how the mind is not lost in the thought experiment of teleportation, unlike dualism.

- Some authors see the fact that information is a realm separate from the machine upon which it is implemented as a way in which humans can reclaim their free will; others claim it simply implies that humans are not only slaves of their genes but also slaves of the information realm (composed of memes).

- Cognitive psychology and cognitive neuropsychology were realisations of functionalism in psychological research. They are currently questioned by the rapid expansion of cognitive neuroscience, which postulates a closer link between information processing and brain functioning. A further challenge for functionalism lies in the fact that digital computers cannot survive independently because they rely on humans for symbol grounding and to remain functional in a changing environment. This suggests that the human mind is more intimately connected to the brain and body upon which it is realised than is postulated by functionalism.

7.4 Consciousness

As we saw in the previous section, since the 1940s the comparison of human and computer functioning has played a main role in the philosophy of mind. For instance, functionalism claimed to have demystified the human mind as nothing but a by-product of information stored and manipulated in a Turing machine. Others doubt whether the real mystery has been solved yet, and point to the continuing differences between information processing in computers and in humans (such as symbol grounding and embodied cognition).

A central theme in these discussions is that of consciousness: humans are thought to be 'conscious' of their information processing in ways computers are not. Because of its importance, we devote a separate section to this concept, starting with the question of what scholars understand by 'consciousness'.

Block (1995) called it a mongrel concept, because the same word is used to refer to different aspects. This leads to contradictions and misunderstandings:

> We reason about 'consciousness' using some premises that apply to one of the phenomena that fall under 'consciousness', other premises that apply to other 'consciousnesses' and we end up with trouble. There are many parallels in the history of science. Aristotle used 'velocity' sometimes to mean average velocity and sometimes to mean instantaneous velocity; his failure to see the distinction caused confusion . . .
>
> (Block 1995: 227)

Block (1995) proposed to make a distinction between two types of consciousness: access consciousness and phenomenological consciousness. To illustrate the difference, he referred to blindsight. This is a condition in which patients (after damage to their primary visual cortex) are unable to see anything in part of their visual field. However, when the experimenter flashes stimuli in the blind area and asks patients to guess what was presented, they can do so better than expected by chance. For instance, De Gelder et al. (1999) tested patient GY, who reported seeing nothing in the right visual half-field as a result of damage to his left occipital lobe at the age of eight. De Gelder and colleagues presented short videos of a female face displaying a happy, sad, angry or fearful expression in the blind half-field and asked the patient to guess which emotion had been expressed on each trial. GY turned out to be correct in 52% of the trials (whereas performance due to guessing alone was 25%). Clearly there was visual processing going on without the patient being aware of it. However, this information could not be reported by the patient, used for reasoning, or acted upon intentionally.

Information that has an effect but is not available for reporting or intentional use is said by Block (1995) not to have access consciousness. It is inaccessible for intentional, deliberate processing. Phenomenological consciousness is more difficult to define, but refers to the richness of human experiences. Individuals have the feeling that their conscious experiences are deeper than can be described. They have the impression that it is impossible to convey their experiences to other people in a way that fully does justice to the richness of the experience. Whatever unconscious representation blindsight people have of their affected part of the visual field, it does not seem to have the phenomenological richness associated with conscious experiences.

access consciousness

access conscious information can be reported by the patient, used for reasoning and acted upon intentionally

phenomenological consciousness

refers to the fact that human experiences possess subjective qualities that seem to defy description; experiences have a meaning that goes beyond formal report (semantics instead of syntax)

Access consciousness

Above we described the phenomenon of blindsight as an indication of unconscious processing. In the past decades many more examples of such processing have been documented, also in healthy persons.

Masked priming

Scientific research on consciousness began when researchers discovered empirical evidence for the existence of unconscious processing. One of the first experiments showing that humans can be influenced by stimuli they do not perceive consciously was published by Kunst-Wilson and Zajonc (1980). The experiment consisted of two phases. In the first phase, participants were asked to watch a screen and try to discern what was presented. Ten irregular polygons were presented five times for one millisecond, too short a time to be seen by the participants (all they saw were light flashes). In the second phase, participants were shown two polygons and had to decide which one they thought they had seen in phase 1, and which one they liked most. One of the polygon pairs had been presented in the first phase, while the other was new. Figure 7.1 shows the findings. As expected, the participants could not indicate which polygon had been presented in the first phase (because they were not aware of having seen them). However, the participants more often than predicted by chance preferred the polygon shown in the first phase. This was the first strong evidence that emotional responses could be based on unconscious information processing.

Shortly after the study by Kunst-Wilson and Zajonc (1980), Marcel (1983) presented evidence that cognitive processing could be unconscious as well. He made use of a technique known as semantic priming. In this technique two stimuli are presented immediately after one another: the prime and the target. The usual finding is that the target is recognised faster when it succeeds a semantically related prime

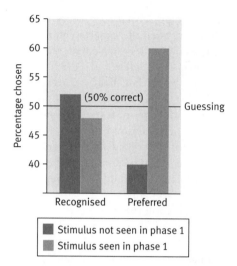

Figure 7.1 The effect of stimuli that cannot be perceived consciously.

When participants in a first phase are exposed to stimuli they cannot perceive consciously, they are unable in the next phase to indicate which stimulus of a pair was presented in the first phase and which one is new, but they show a reliable preference for the stimuli they were exposed to in the first phase. This was the first evidence for unconscious stimulus processing.

Source: Kunst-Wilson, W.R. and Zajonc, R.B. (1980) 'Affective discrimination that cannot be recognized', *Science*, 207, 557–558. Reprinted with permission from AAAS.

than when it succeeds an unrelated, neutral prime. So, the target word *boy* is recognised faster after the prime word *girl* than after the prime word *goal*. In Marcel's experiments, target word recognition time was measured by means of a lexical decision task. In this task participants have to decide on each trial whether a presented string of letters is a word (e.g. boy) or not (e.g. doy). The target stimuli (both words and non-words) were preceded by primes to which the participants did not have to respond. In a first condition, Marcel presented the primes long enough for them to be clearly visible. In this condition, as expected he found a nice semantic priming effect (left part of Figure 7.2). That is, participants indicated faster that *boy* was an existing English word if it had been preceded by the prime *girl* than if it had been preceded by the prime *goal*. In a second condition, Marcel limited the presentation time of the primes to a few milliseconds, so that participants could no longer see them consciously. Still he found a priming effect that was nearly as strong as the effect with the clearly visible primes (right part of Figure 7.2). This indicated that the prime word did not have to be perceived consciously in order to be processed and to influence the subsequent recognition of the target word.

Marcel's pioneering work has been followed by thousands of experiments showing visual information processing of primes participants were not aware of. The easiest way to make primes 'invisible' is to present them between other stimuli, so-called masks. In a typical experiment, the prime would be preceded by a meaningless string of letters or symbols (e.g., *RPSDT* or #&<=@) and followed by the target word. Because the surrounding stimuli mask the prime, the technique is called masked priming. If you are somewhat familiar with psychological research, you will not be surprised to hear that a lively debate exists about the extent to which masked primes really are unconscious (e.g., Holender 1986; Greenwald *et al.* 1996; Merikle *et al.* 2001).

masked priming

experimental technique to investigate unconscious information processing, consisting of briefly presenting a prime between a forward meaningless mask and a subsequent target, and examining the effect of the prime on the processing of the target

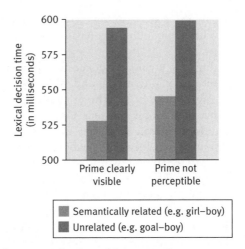

Figure 7.2 Evidence for unconscious cognitive processing.

Target words are recognised faster when they are preceded by a semantically related prime than when they are preceded by an unrelated prime. This is so both when the primes are clearly visible and when they are presented too briefly to be seen consciously.

Source: Marcel (1983). Reproduced with permission.

Implicit memory

Other strong evidence for unconscious processing in humans comes from research on implicit learning and implicit memory (e.g. Schacter 1987). Traditionally, memory studies relied on conscious recollection of information presented before. This research showed strong individual differences and confirmed that some individuals were unable to learn and remember new information. These were patients suffering from amnesia. Gradually, however, it was discovered that, although amnesic patients could not consciously recollect information, they often showed performance benefits of information presented before, when they were not asked to remember the recently presented information but invited to perform a task that was related to the previously presented information.

The first experimental demonstration of implicit learning and retention of information was published by Milner (1962) who examined the famous amnesic patient H.M. (1926–2008). After an operation to treat epilepsy, H.M. lost all ability to learn new information (e.g. Corkin 2002). The psychologist examining him, Brenda Milner, tried out all types of tests with no avail, until she examined whether H.M. could learn new actions. She asked H.M. to copy a star while watching his hand in a mirror, which is a very demanding task (try it out using the star shown below!).

Type of star used in the mirror drawing experiment with H.M. H.M. was asked to draw a line between the lines starting from the S, while looking at the star in a mirror.

H.M. was asked to do this three days in a row. Although on the second and the third day he did not remember having done the task before, his performance improved day after day.

Further strong evidence for the existence of implicit memory came from research by Warrington and Weiskrantz in the 1960s and 1970s (e.g. Warrington & Weiskrantz 1978). They also investigated amnesic patients, but looked at tasks other than motor learning. One of these tasks involved patients learning a list of words. Sometime later they were asked to recall the words or to try to fill in the missing parts in word fragments, such as _ss_ss__. The patients could not consciously recall any word from the list, but they were more likely to successfully complete the fragment if the word had been part of the previously learned list (assassin) than if it had not.

Schacter (1987: 502) noted that, although the evidence with amnesic patients put implicit memory on the map, writings about 'unconscious memory' are much older. He identified Leibniz as the first person to realise the importance of memory without awareness. Indeed, Leibniz wrote in 1704 that: '. . . often we have an extraordinary facility for conceiving certain things, because we formerly conceived them, without remembering them'. Another early scholar pointing to the existence of memory traces without awareness was the French philosopher Maine de Biran (1766–1824). In 1804 he published a treatise (with the translated title *The influence of habit on the faculty of thinking*), in which he pointed to the importance of habits in human thought and behaviour. According to Maine de Biran, after sufficient repetition habits are executed automatically and unconsciously without awareness of the acts themselves or of the episodes in which they were learned. These habits were stored in dedicated memories: a mechanical memory for repeated movements, and a sensitive memory for repeated feelings.

Libet's study on the initiation of movement

In 1985 the American neurophysiologist Benjamin Libet (1916–2007) published a famous study in which he showed that not only perception and memory to a large extent escape conscious control, but that the same is true for action control. According to Libet, the initiation of an action, even a deliberate one, happens outside consciousness, because a lot of preparation is needed.

Libet based his claim on a fairly simple but straightforward experiment (as has been the case for many classic findings in scientific research). He asked participants to deliberately make a finger movement from time to time. Participants saw an analogue clock face in front of them with a light going round the face every 2.56 seconds. Participants were asked to indicate after each trial when they had decided to initiate the movement by telling the experimenter at what position the light had been at the moment they made their decision. Libet measured two extra things: (1) the time at which the movement was initiated, and (2) the electrical brain activity of the participants. The latter was registered because it had been shown in the 1960s that voluntary movements are preceded by a readiness-potential in the brain, a change in the EEG signal very similar to the Event Related Potentials discussed in Chapter 6 (Figure 6.16).

What everyone expected would happen was that the participants would first decide to make a movement, then after some delay would show a readiness-potential in their EEG, and after some more delay would initiate the movement. However, this was not what Libet observed. His data clearly showed that the brain signalled its readiness for the response (as seen by the onset of the readiness-potential) well before the participant had the conscious impression of starting the movement! Rather than consciousness deciding it would make a movement, it looked as if consciousness was informed by the brain that a movement was about to be initiated. Figure 7.3 shows the timeline of the events. Later studies have confirmed Libet's findings and shown that the time estimates may even be too conservative. Using fMRI, Soon and colleagues (2008) were able to predict upcoming 'voluntary' responses by brain activity up to 10 seconds before the actual movement.

What Libet's (1985) experiment and subsequent replications showed was that under the conditions tested, consciousness did not control the initiation of the movement, as the participants thought, but that it was notified by the unconscious part of the brain when everything was ready for a movement. In other words, there was no free will involved in the initiation of the movement. In a later publication Libet (1999) conceded that free will might still play a role, because it could stop a programmed movement once it was ready to be launched.

Wegner (2004) was more critical about the involvement of free will in the control of actions. According to him, our feeling of doing things is an 'illusion of conscious will'. What happens is that the human mind is programmed to attribute actions to its own initiative as soon as three conditions are met:

1. a thought appears in consciousness just prior to an action,

2. the thought is consistent with the action, and

3. there is no salient alternative cause of the action.

As soon as these three conditions are met, the conscious human mind will claim authorship for the action, even though in reality unconscious processes were the origin both of the action and the thought.

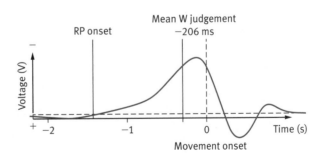

Figure 7.3 Depiction of Libet's findings (1985)

There is evidence of an increase in EEG activity more than 1 s before the actual movement took place (at time 0). The conscious experience of intending the movement occurred 206 ms before the actual movement. By that time, however, the increase in EEG signal had already been going on for nearly 1 s. This means that the conscious decision to start the movement could not be at the origin of the increased EEG activity. The brain was already planning the movement long before the person thought they initiated the movement.

Source: Based on Haggard (2005).

The global workspace model

Since the seminal studies discussed above, many more instances of unconscious processing have been documented, to such an extent that unconscious information processing nowadays is generally accepted in cognitive psychology. This should not surprise us. Unconscious information processing is a mystery within a dualist vision, where the conscious human mind controls everything, but is perfectly acceptable within a materialistic or functionalistic view. There is nothing untoward in sense receptors that fire automatically when they are activated by an appropriate stimulus, or in motor neurons that are mobilised for an upcoming movement. There is also nothing strange in signals being passed through the various nerves and brain centres and activating representations that are related to the original stimulus. What is difficult to explain within materialism and functionalism is why this processing from a certain point onward gives rise to a conscious experience of the event. So, with respect to Marcel's experiment there is no problem explaining how briefly presented primes are processed by the brain. What is more difficult to grasp, however, is why from a certain presentation time onward, the participant has a clear, conscious, vivid image of the word that is presented.

A metaphor that is increasingly used within cognitive psychology to understand the role of consciousness is that of a theatre (e.g. Baars 1997). According to this metaphor, the brain can be compared to a big theatre where many processes are needed in the background for the play to take place (preparation of the decors, costumes, new players ready to come on stage, etc.). These processes work to a large extent independently, but they need to be informed about what is going on in the play, in order to synchronise their activities with those of the central event. This is the role of consciousness: making information available to the global workspace, so that the activities of the automatic processes can be tuned to each other.

global workspace model model that explains the role of consciousness by analogy to a theatre: consciousness is meant to make some information available to the whole brain (i.e. the play), so that the various background processes can align their functioning to what is going on centrally

The French neuroscientist Dehaene and his colleagues (2001) presented brain imaging evidence for the global workspace model. They measured brain activity to visual stimuli that were presented either too briefly to be consciously perceptible or long enough to be clearly visible. When the stimuli were presented below the consciousness threshold, some activity was noticed in areas at the back of the brain that are normally associated with object and word recognition (Figure 7.4a). However, as soon as the participants started to see the words consciously, a large network distributed all over the brain became active (Figure 7.4b), making the stimulus available everywhere in the cerebral hemispheres.

Lamme (2006) argued that sensory information is brought into consciousness by means of a continuous exchange of information between different brain areas. Incoming information not only activates bottom-up processes from the perceptual input regions to the higher cortical regions but also activates top-down processes back from the higher cortical areas to the perceptual input areas. This sustained information exchange between brain areas allows the organism to become aware of the stimulus. The bottom-up processes only allow the organism to respond automatically to a stimulus, without being conscious of the stimulus.

This is how Lamme described the process related to the perception of visual stimuli:

> When a new image hits the retina, it is processed through successive levels of visual cortex, by means of feedforward connections, working at an astonishing speed . . . Thus, the feedforward sweep enables a rapid extraction of complex and meaningful features

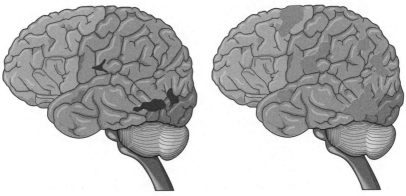

(a) Briefly presented visual stimuli   (b) Consciously visible stimuli

Figure 7.4 Brain activity for unconscious and conscious visible stimuli.

(a) Brain activity (measured with fMRI) when stimuli are presented too briefly to be consciously perceptible; the activity is largely limited to those brain areas that are responsible for visual object identification.

(b) Brain activity when the stimuli are clearly visible; now the object recognition areas are supplemented by activity in a large network that is distributed all over the cerebral hemispheres.

Source: Based on Dehaene *et al.* (2001).

from the visual scene, and lays down potential motor responses to act on the incoming information.

Are we conscious of the features extracted by the feedforward sweep? Do we see a face when a face-selective neuron becomes active? It seems not. Many studies, in both humans and monkeys, indicate that no matter what area of the brain is reached by the feedforward sweep, this in itself is not producing (reportable) conscious experience. What seems necessary for conscious experience is that neurons in visual areas engage in so-called recurrent (or re-entrant or resonant) processing, where high- and low-level areas interact. This would enable the widespread exchange of information between areas processing different attributes of the visual scene, and thus support perceptual grouping.

(Lamme 2006: 495–7)

Is unconscious processing dangerous?

When the first experimental evidence for unconscious information processing was published, it received quite a lot of attention in the media, because many people tended to be wary of information processing beyond their conscious control. This was partly due to Freud's claims that the unconscious is a dark force, aiming at instant gratification of its sexual and aggressive desires without regard for social or ethical considerations, which constantly tries to control humans and has to be restrained by the ego. Another reason why people did not like the idea of unconscious processing was that several urban legends existed about the powers of unconscious information processing. One of these legends was that it is possible to manipulate people's actions through subliminal advertising. Another was that unconscious messages, intermixed in music or sea sounds, can be used to heal. Still another was that hidden backward messages in songs can take control of the listeners and, for instance, incite them to commit murder or suicide.

Psychologists have been unable to find empirical support for any of the above strong claims (see Greenwald 1992; Loftus & Klinger 1992; Mayer & Merckelbach 1999; Kreiner *et al.* 2003). For instance, Greenwald *et al.* (1991) examined the effects of 'subliminal messages' (i.e. messages below the consciousness threshold) in records that otherwise sounded like normal soothing sounds. According to the makers, some records were good for improving memory; others were good for improving self-esteem. Greenwald *et al.* gave half of their participants a record to improve their memory and half a record to increase their self-esteem (this was clearly indicated on the record). Participants listened for a month at least once a day to the records. At the end of the study, they completed questionnaires about their memory performance and their self-esteem (they had done the same at the beginning of the study).

As predicted by the makers of the tapes, the participants who had listened to the self-esteem enhancing records reported higher self-esteem, and the participants who had listened to the memory enhancing records reported better memory skills. However, unknown to the participants, Greenwald *et al.* had changed the labels of half of the records, so that half of the participants who thought they were listening to self-esteem enhancing messages actually heard memory enhancing messages. Similarly, half of the participants who thought they were listening to memory enhancing messages were really exposed to self-esteem enhancing messages. Greenwald *et al.* found no difference whatsoever between the type of the actual records used; they only obtained an effect of the type of message the participants thought they had been listening to. On the basis of these findings, Greenwald *et al.* concluded that the positive effects participants reported were due to a placebo effect (participants expected to do better after the treatment), and not to the actual 'messages' they had been hearing. This finding agrees with the limited results of therapies based on subliminal messages.

What is possible, however, is to subtly increase the activation of certain goals and feelings with subliminal primes (e.g. Dijksterhuis *et al.* 2005; Meerman *et al.* 2011). Just as non-visible prime words can activate target words, so it is possible to use non-conspicuous cues in the environment to make participants more likely to perform certain actions. For instance, Johnston (2002) showed that participants took more ice in a consumer test, when the person before them (a colleague of the experimenter) had taken a large sample than if the person had taken a small sample. None of the participants was aware of this influence. Similarly, Lowery *et al.* (2007) showed that they could increase the academic performance of students by increasing their self-confidence and motivation to perform well. The authors had half of their participants look at subliminally presented words that either primed for intelligence (intelligent, smart, brilliant, bright) or that were neutral (smock, birch, bring, tale). Subsequently, the participants took part in a practice exam. Those who had seen the intelligence-related words performed better in the exam than those who had been exposed to the neutral words. Interestingly, the effect persisted in a true exam a few days later, possibly as a result of the better results on the practice exam.

With respect to the above findings, it is important that they are not peculiar to unconscious processing. Exactly the same priming effects are found when participants perceive the information consciously, for instance as part of a word searching task with the words hidden in a letter matrix (e.g. Bargh *et al.* 2001). The similarity between conscious and unconscious priming is in line with the conjecture of the global workspace model that unconscious processing is the same type of information processing as conscious processing. It is processing that happens in the background, assists adequate performance, enters consciousness when important enough, and occasionally influences the line of thought or action (see also Baumeister *et al.* 2011). There is no evidence, however, that it has dangerous, mythical powers.

Phenomenological consciousness

Phenomenological consciousness refers to the fact that conscious human experiences possess subjective qualities that defy description. Conscious experiences have elements that escape formal report and make it impossible to fully communicate them to others. Authors have proposed various thought experiments to illustrate what they mean by this. Two famous thought experiments are those of the Chinese room and Mary.

The Chinese room and Mary thought experiments

Chinese room

thought experiment proposed by Searle to illustrate the difference between information processing in humans and information processing in computers

The Chinese room thought experiment was conceived by the American philosopher John Searle (1980) to illustrate the difference between information processing in computers and in humans (recall that functionalists see them as the same). Suppose you don't know any Chinese and you are locked up in a room where you regularly receive a Chinese character through a slot and have to supply another character in return. In order for you to be able to select the right answer, you have a book full of rules that, for each character you receive, tells you which character to return. Gradually you become more and more practised in the task, so that you can return the required character rapidly. Also, now and then you receive a batch of additional rules, which allow you to process a larger number of symbols. Could we then say that you have come to master Chinese, because you are able always to provide the right answer to each question you get (and hence would be able to fool a Chinese speaker in a Turing test; see Chapter 5)?

Another thought experiment to illustrate the difference between information processing in computers and the human mind is the Mary thought experiment, proposed by the Australian philosopher Frank Jackson:

Mary is a brilliant scientist who is, for whatever reason, forced to investigate the world from a black and white room via a black and white television monitor. She specializes in the neurophysiology of vision and acquires, let us suppose, all the physical information there is to obtain about what goes on when we see ripe tomatoes, or the sky, and use terms like 'red', 'blue', and so on. She discovers, for example, just which wavelength combinations from the sky stimulate the retina, and exactly how this produces via the central nervous system the contraction of the vocal chords and expulsion of air from the lungs that results in the uttering of the sentence 'The sky is blue' . . .

What will happen when Mary is released from her black and white room or is given a color television monitor? Will she learn anything or not? It seems just obvious that she will learn something about the world and our visual experience of it. But then it is inescapable that her previous knowledge was incomplete. But she had all the physical information. Ergo there is more to have than that . . .

(Jackson 1982: 130)

Qualia

Searle and Jackson proposed their thought experiments to make clear that the operations of a computer do not by themselves lead to the experience of consciousness as we humans know it. A processing entirely based on the application of rules (algorithms) on shapes (symbols) stays devoid of meaning. It resembles a language with words and syntactic rules, but without meaning (semantics).

The absence of meaning in computer processing is very unlike human thinking, where the symbols have extensive and rich meanings, grounded in the interactions with the world. When we read about a tree, we have a rich image of what this word stands for, where we can expect to find it, what characteristics it has, what actions it affords, and so on. Philosophers refer to these quality-feelings of conscious thoughts as **qualia**. Block (2004) defined qualia as follows:

> Qualia include the ways things look, sound and smell, the way it feels to have a pain, and more generally, what it's like to have experiential mental states. . . . Qualia are experiential properties of sensations, feelings, perceptions and, more controversially, thoughts and desires as well.

qualia

qualities of conscious thoughts that give the thoughts a rich and vivid meaning, grounded in interactions with the world

---

? What do you think?

To illustrate the importance of qualia in consciousness, Nagel (1974) suggested you try to imagine what it is like to be a bat. How does the experience of the environment differ between you and a bat as a consequence of differences in qualia?

---

zombie thought experiment

thought experiment proposed by Chalmers to illustrate that consciousness is more than the working of the brain or the implementation of information on a Turing machine because it involves a subjective component with qualia

Zombies and the hard problem

Because of qualia, philosophers like Searle and Jackson argue that seeing human consciousness as information processing in a Turing machine overlooks a fundamental property of human thinking and cannot be a full account of the human mind.

Another thought experiment suggesting that functionalism may not have solved the complete mystery of the human mind was presented by the Australian philosopher, David Chalmers (1996), and is known as the **zombie thought experiment**. Chalmers argued that we can perfectly imagine a twin of ourselves, who is molecule for molecule identical to us, but who lacks conscious experience with qualia. Chalmers called this twin a zombie. Usually zombies refer to reanimated corpses (or corpses made undead), but in Chalmers's view the only difference between the zombie and us is that it does not have the consciousness we have. All the rest, including the appearance and the behaviours, is identical to what we are and do. Our zombie would respond in exactly the same way as we do, but it would lack the qualia that make up our phenomenal world. When it is stabbed, it would show the same overt reactions as we do (groan, grimace, try to defend itself), but it would feel no pain. We could even imagine a zombie world, a world physically identical to ours, but in which there are no phenomenological experiences.

The fact that we can imagine a world that is physically and functionally identical to ours, but lacks phenomenological consciousness, Chalmers argues, means that we cannot reduce consciousness to functionalism. Consciousness is something more, and trying to grasp this something is what Chalmers calls the hard problem. According to Chalmers, trying to explain why we have phenomenological experiences with qualia is the problem cognitive psychologists skirt when they draw their flow diagrams, write their computational models, or talk about access consciousness. They limit their efforts to the so-called easy problems of detailing the processes and functions of cognitive functioning, without worrying about what makes our minds different from those of zombies.

hard problem

name given by Chalmers to refer to the difficulty of explaining in what respects consciousness is more than accounted for on the basis of functionalism

---

What do you think?

Not everyone agrees with Chalmers that there is a hard problem with consciousness. In their view, the hard problem is similar to the 'problems' posed by phlogiston and vital force. That is, they are problems because an unnecessary entity is postulated. Also, the zombie thought experiment need not prove anything. Maybe humans are zombies with the illusion of qualia? What do you think? Would a fully implemented artificial brain have qualia like humans do? Or could we all be zombies with delusional self-images?

KEY FIGURES

Philosophy of science

- **Descartes:** Cartesian dualism (mind is immaterial and independent of the body, a 'ghost in a machine').
- **Paul and Patricia Churchland:** defenders of an extreme version of materialism, claiming that the mind is nothing but brain processing and that phenomenological consciousness is an illusion.
- **Richard Dawkins:** humans are survival machines for genes and memes.
- **Alan Turing:** information forms an independent realm that can be copied from one Turing machine to another.
- **Jerry Fodor:** strong supporter of functionalism in the philosophy of science.
- **Derek Parfit:** the *Star Trek* thought experiment.
- **Keith Stanovich:** matter-independent information provides humans with a chance to rebel against their genes.
- **Benjamin Libet:** impression of free will in the initiation of action is an illusion.

- **Bernard Baars:** global workspace model.
- **John Searle:** Chinese room thought experiment (importance of qualia).
- **Frank Jackson:** Mary thought experiment (importance of qualia).
- **David Chalmers:** zombie thought experiment and formulation of the 'hard problem' in the explanation of consciousness (importance of qualia).

Embodied cognition as the source of qualia?

Claims about the importance of qualia in human experiences received a major boost from research on symbol grounding and embodied cognition. Maybe human experiences feel so rich because they are effectively grounded in our bodily interactions with the world? Cognitive neuroscience has found compelling evidence for this possibility. After it became clear from brain imaging that vast, interconnected networks in the brain become active during even the simplest tasks, researchers started to notice that the brain areas normally activated when people perceive visual stimuli or perform motor actions also become active when people think about these stimuli or actions, or read words related to them.

Figure 7.5 shows the brain areas that became active when participants read the words 'kick', 'pick' and 'lick'. As expected, these areas included Broca's area (Figure 6.7) and Wernicke's area (Figure 6.8). However, in addition, the word 'kick' activated the brain region that is normally active when the participants move their legs. Similarly, the word 'pick' activated the brain region related to the control of hand movements, and the word 'lick' activated the brain region related to the control of tongue movements.

The fact that perceptual and motor areas become co-activated when we say or hear perceptually or motor-related words arguably is the reason why conscious experiences are so rich that they cannot be fully communicated to others by means

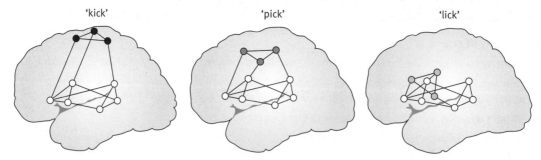

Figure 7.5 Schematic illustration of the cortical systems for language and action.

These regions not only involve Broca's area (Figure 6.7) and Wernicke's area (Figure 6.8), but also brain regions that are active when respectively a leg movement is made ('kick'), a hand movement is made ('pick'), or a tongue movement is made ('lick'). This suggests that the motor information related to the actions becomes co-activated as part of the meaning of the word. This may provide an explanation of why conscious experiences are characterised by qualia.

Source: Adapted from Pulvermüller, F. (2005) 'Brain mechanisms linking language and action', *Nature Reviews Neuroscience*, 6, (7), July, 576–82, Fig. 1. Schematic illustration of the cortical systems for language and action, adapted by permission from Macmillan Publishers Ltd.

of words (symbols). The word 'tree' has a phenomenally vivid meaning for an individual, because it activates memories of actual experiences with trees (both perceptual and motor). The fact that consciousness is able to bind information from different parts of the brain makes it possible to interconnect everything. The human brain does not normally manipulate meaningless symbols; upon encountering a familiar symbol it co-activates a big chunk of our previous experiences with that particular stimulus. Therefore, we immediately understand which sentences make sense (e.g. 'After wading barefoot in the lake, Erik used his shirt to dry his feet') and which do not ('After wading barefoot in the lake, Erik used his glasses to dry his feet'), even though both types of sentences are equivalent at the symbolic level (Glenberg & Robertson 2000).

Interestingly, evidence is accumulating that bodily grounding is involved in not only the understanding of words closely related to human interactions with the environment. Lakoff and Johnson (1980, 1999) argued that a lot of human thinking is metaphorical thinking, in which the knowledge of one domain is mapped onto another domain in such a way that the new domain inherits the complete inferential structure of the source domain. Lakoff and Johnson (1980) give the example of 'an argument', which according to them is understood through the metaphor of war. As a result, all thinking about arguments is imbued with knowledge of wars (and fighting). This is how Lakoff and Johnson (1980: 4) formulated their insight:

> It is important to see that we don't just talk about arguments in terms of war. We can actually win or lose arguments. We see the person we are arguing with as an opponent. We attack his positions and defend our own. We gain and lose ground. We plan and use strategies. If we find a position indefensible, we can abandon it and take a new line of attack . . . It is in this sense that the Argument is War metaphor is one that we live by in this culture; it structures the actions we perform in arguing.

Similarly, Miles and colleagues (2010) argued that the human capacity to subjectively travel through time can be understood by a metaphorical 'arrow of time' integrating temporal and spatial information (past = back, future = forward). They asked participants to describe a typical day of their life four years ago and to describe how a typical day in their life would look like four years in the future. Meanwhile the posture of the participants, who were standing, was measured. As expected on the basis of embodied cognition, the participants were leaning more forward when describing the future than when describing the past.

? What do you think?

Embodied cognition, just like cognitive neuroscience, emphasises the physical experiences of the thinking individual much more than traditional cognitive (neuro)psychology did. Previously we discussed how this undermines the functionalist view of the mind–brain relationship and seems to point more in the direction of materialism. What do you think? Is there a way to combine embodied cognition with functionalism? Or is embodied cognition a nail in the coffin of functionalism?

Interim summary

- Information as currently implemented in computers does not seem to possess the phenomenological richness of human consciousness. Block proposed to make a distinction between access consciousness and phenomenological consciousness.

- There is a lot of empirical evidence that processing is going on in humans without them being consciously aware of it. We discussed the phenomena of masked priming, implicit memory, and Libet's experiment on the voluntary initiation of movement.

- Unconscious processing strongly resembles conscious processing; the main differences seem to be that it is less rich and integrated than conscious processing and that humans cannot deliberately act on it.

- A model of access consciousness is the global workspace model, which compares the human mind to a theatre. A lot of activity is going on behind the scenes, but the activity on the scene must be visible to all, in order to synchronise the various activities. This is the function of consciousness.

- The phenomenological richness of human conscious experiences seems to require the existence of qualia. This has been illustrated by three thought experiments: the Chinese room, Mary, and the zombie world.

- Because of the differences between human consciousness and information processing in computers, Chalmers claims that the hard problem of phenomenological consciousness has not yet been solved. Others disagree and argue that it will be solved when a solution to the symbol grounding problem is found.

- A possible solution to the symbol grounding problem is to assume that human cognitive representations (symbols) derive their meaning from the interactions between the human body and the environment (both the physical and social environment). Cognitive neuroscience has found evidence in line with this view of embodied cognition.

7.5 *Focus on*: Can automatic processing help us to make better decisions?

In the myth-busting box, we saw that automatic, unconscious processing is not the dangerous entity Freud imagined. As a matter of fact, researchers are starting to consider it more and more as a kind of 'automatic pilot' that keeps us alive (as far as the vegetative functions such as breathing and heart beating are concerned, even in a very literal sense!) and in good shape. It is the type of background processing that is required for us to function properly. Researchers increasingly call this type 1 thinking, as opposed to the conscious type 2 thinking.

Type 1 thinking

The automatic system involves all types of information processing that do not require focused attention and that produce an output without any apparent effort or awareness. It is based on innate knowledge that has been inherited from previous generations as a result of natural selection (e.g. caution for snakes, automatic

associative learning

learning of simple associations (correlations) between all types of events; thought to be the basis of automatic, type 1 thinking

attention capture by angry voices or approaching noises) and on knowledge that has been acquired on the basis of associative learning. The latter refers to the learning of simple associations (correlations) between events. It not only includes associations between elements that we have deliberately memorised, but also associations between stimuli co-occurring in the environment (which we have picked up through classical conditioning; e.g. certain smells and the availability of food), and associations between stimuli and actions (learned on the basis of operant conditioning; e.g. being given a present and saying 'thank you'). The automatic processing system forms the basis of our motor skills, but also of our practical, everyday functioning and the knowledge we typically call intuition or gut feeling (Lieberman 2000).

Type 2 thinking

In humans, automatic type 1 thinking is supplemented by a second form of reasoning that is controlled, serial and conscious. This type of thinking allows us to go beyond what is physically present in the environment. We can think of people and events that are absent, and we can try out hypothetical, counterintuitive solutions and evaluate what outcomes they would produce. As such, it is the core of scientific thinking (see Chapter 9). It is also related to the intelligence of people as measured by IQ tests or school results.

Table 7.1 provides an overview of the main differences that have been postulated between type 1 and type 2 thinking.

A focus on type 2 thinking

In the first decades of cognitive psychology most research was geared towards type 2 thinking. For instance, a lot of effort went into the questions regarding how good people are at reasoning and problem solving. Do people follow the rules of logic when they reason? Are they thinking like intuitive scientists? Do they take all evidence into consideration when making a decision? Are their evaluations and explanations of events error-free and unbiased?

Table 7.1 Characteristics associated with automatic (type 1) and controlled (type 2) thinking

System 1	System 2
Unconscious/implicit	Conscious/explicit
Automatic	Controllable
Evolved early	Evolved late
Shared with other animals	Uniquely human
Independent of language	Related to language
Pragmatic/contextualised	Logical/abstract
High processing capacity, parallel	Constrained by working memory, sequential
Driven by learning and innate modules	Permits hypothetical thinking
Independent of general intelligence	Correlated with general intelligence

Source: Adapted from Evans, J.S.B.T. (2002) 'Logic and human reasoning: An assessment of the deduction paradigm', *Psychological Bulletin*, 128, 978–96.

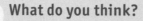

What do you think?

How good are people at reasoning? Do you approach a problem like an intuitive scientist? If yes, what exactly does your approach involve and why is this scientific? If no, in what ways does your approach differ from the scientific method as discussed in Chapter 2?

Out of this research came the conclusion that without formal training people do not reason like intuitive scientists. They do not strictly follow the strategies that in science have proven to lead to the most reliable knowledge (Chapters 2, 5 and 9). Instead, they spontaneously make use of heuristics, rules of thumb that do not require as much effort as a full-blown scientific evaluation and that most of the time result in good decisions, but that occasionally go wrong.

A typical example of this type of research makes use of the following problem (from Swinkels 2003):

Dr. Swinkels's cousin, Rudy, is a bit on the peculiar side. He has unusual tastes in movies and art, he is married to a performer, and he has tattoos on various parts of his body. In his spare time Rudy takes yoga classes and likes to collect 78 rpm records. An outgoing and rather boisterous person, he has been known to act on a dare on more than one occasion. What do you think Rudy's occupation most likely is?

(A) Farmer   (B) Trapeze Artist

What do you think?

Which occupation is most likely in Swinkels's example? Why?

A scientific approach to the Swinkels problem would require knowledge of (1) the probability of each of the occupations and (2) the predictive value of the different traits for each of the occupations. So, if farmers make up 5% of the population and if the features described in the story are present in 10% of farmers, one can conclude that 0.5% of the population (i.e. one person in every 200) will be a farmer and show the characteristics described in the example. Similarly, if 0.0001% of the population is a trapeze artist (these people tend to be rather rare) and 60% of trapeze artists show the characteristics described, one can conclude that 0.00006% of the population (i.e. roughly one person in every 17,000) will be a trapeze artist and show the described characteristics. In other words, chances are much higher that Dr Swinkels's cousin is a farmer than he is a trapeze artist.

As you may have experienced, the above type of reasoning is not what the participants in Swinkels's (2003) study did. They simply reasoned that more elements of the story agreed with the stereotypical image of a trapeze artist than with the stereotypical image of a farmer, and they predominantly – but wrongly – opted for the trapeze artist alternative as the most probable one.

**heuristic-based
thinkers**

those who think based
on heuristics, rules of
thumb that do not require
as much effort as the
scientific method and that
most of the time result in
good decisions, but that
are subject to a number
of biases

On the basis of studies like the one just described, cognitive psychologists came to see humans as suboptimal, heuristic-based thinkers cursed with a list of biases towards reasoning errors (e.g. Kahneman & Tversky 1974, 1979; Nisbett & Wilson 1977; Nisbett & Ross 1980). Good psychology students were taught about these pitfalls and warned to avoid them. Within this research, type 1 thinking did not figure predominantly, and was seen as the main origin of the reasoning biases. For instance, the reasoning error in the Swinkels example could be attributed to an unwarranted reliance on associative learning between personality characteristics and occupations (giving too much weight to the correspondence of the features described and the prototypical image of a trapeze artist).

The revival of system 1 thinking

In the last decade, however, some researchers have started to re-appreciate system 1 thinking. Automatic thinking is not always inferior to controlled thinking, and may even turn out to be superior. To understand when this could be so, it is important to keep in mind that type 1 thinking consists of the automatic detection of correlations between the events in everyday life (including books, films, stories told, etc.). As a result, some stimuli become associated with an automatic approach response and others with an automatic avoidance response. These automatic evaluations can activate the wrong answer in 'artificial' situations, such as the Swinkels example, but they should be reliable in often-experienced, everyday situations.

An example of a theory that defends the superiority of type 1 thinking in certain everyday situations is the so-called *theory of unconscious thought* proposed by Dijksterhuis and colleagues (e.g. Dijksterhuis & Nordgren 2006). In this theory, three main differences are postulated between conscious and unconscious thought:

1. Unconscious thinking, unlike conscious thinking, is completely determined by the stimuli. They automatically activate stored associations, without the interference of hypothetical thinking. On the negative side, this means that important considerations may be overlooked in unconscious thinking (such as the probability of the different occupations in Swinkels's experiment). On the positive side, it means that the response will be in line with what has worked in the past.

2. Conscious thinking is able to follow strict rules, whereas unconscious thought only results in a gist or a hunch. To know the answer to the problem 13×14 you need conscious thought. However, on the basis of unconscious thinking you can rapidly decide that it will not be equal to 4,000,000 without having to do the detailed calculations.

3. The main limit of conscious thought is that it has a low capacity. Without making use of systematic data analysis and written notes, conscious processing can only take into account the contribution of some four, rather easy-to-understand variables. As soon as a problem becomes more complex, the processing effort increases so rapidly that it exceeds the capacities of most individuals. In contrast, unconscious thinking can take into account the simultaneous contribution of a large number of influences. The outcome will still be a hunch, but no less accurate than for a simple problem.

To test the theory of unconscious thought, Dijksterhuis and colleagues (2006) presented their participants with vignettes of real life choices. For instance, the participants had to decide which car or apartment to buy. One of the alternatives was significantly worse than the other, though not on all attributes. There were two different conditions:

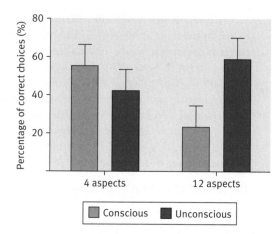

Figure 7.6 Conscious deliberation in decision making is not always the best strategy.

This figure shows the percentage of participants who chose the most desirable car as a function of the complexity of the decision and the mode of thought. When the choice was relatively easy, a careful comparison of the two alternatives produced the best results. In contrast, when the complexity of the choice exceeded the limited capacity of conscious processing, it was better not to think about the problem for some time, and to trust the hunch of unconscious thought.

Source: Dijksterhuis, A. *et al.* (2006) 'On making the right choice: The deliberation-without-attention effect', *Science*, 311, 1005–7. Reprinted with permission from AAAS Science by Moss King.

information was given about 4 attributes (easy condition) or about 12 attributes (difficult condition). Participants either had to make an immediate decision based on conscious thinking, or they first had to complete a distracter task that prevented them from further thought about the choice. If the theory of unconscious thought was correct, Dijksterhuis and colleagues predicted an interaction between the mode of thinking and the difficulty of the problem, as they indeed observed (Figure 7.6). Participants made better decisions if they were allowed to think consciously about the easy alternatives, whereas they performed better if the complex alternatives could be put aside for some time and mulled over by the unconscious brain.

On the basis of their findings, Dijksterhuis *et al.* advised 'sleeping on' complex problems, so that unconscious thought can evaluate the alternatives and contribute to the final decision. Although originally they particularly emphasised the importance of unconscious thought, in later publications they acknowledged that the best strategy to solve complex problems is a combination of conscious and unconscious thought: a solution must both look right after scrutinising it, and feel right after having slept on it (Nordgren *et al.* 2011).

Interim summary

- There is increasing evidence for two thinking systems: one that is automatic and based on associative learning (type 1), and one that is controlled, explicit and based on hypothetical thinking (type 2).
- For a long time, cognitive psychology was only interested in type 2 thinking, which was seen as heuristic-based and prone to reasoning errors; type 1 thinking was largely overlooked and considered as the origin of some of the reasoning errors.

- Currently there is a redressing of the balance, because it is now realised that system 1 thinking forms the basis of much of everyday interaction and intuitive thinking.

- According to the theory of unconscious thought, it is possible to evaluate information without consciousness. Such evaluation is less susceptible to the capacity limitations of conscious thought. It does not lead to precise conclusions, but to rough estimates of the desirability of the alternatives, and can be used in combination with conscious thought when complex decisions must be made.

Recommended literature

The argument in the first three sections of this chapter has been inspired by the line of thought developed in Lyons, W. (2001) *Matters of the mind* (New York: Routledge). If you are interested in a broader review of philosophy of mind, a good introduction is Ravenscroft, I. (2005) *Philosophy of mind: A beginner's guide* (Oxford: Oxford University Press). An interesting book on consciousness is Dietrich, A. (2007) *Introduction to consciousness* (Basingstoke: Palgrave Macmillan). If you are interested in free will, we strongly recommend Kane, R. (2005) *A contemporary introduction to free will* (Oxford: Oxford University Press). This book contains many counterintuitive, thought-provoking ideas that unfortunately were too detailed for the present chapter.

References

Anderson, M.L. (2003) 'Embodied cognition: A field guide', *Artificial Intelligence, 149*: 91–130.

Baars, B.J. (1997) *In the theater of consciousness: The workspace of the mind.* New York: Oxford University Press.

Bargh, J.A., Gollwitzer, P.M., Lee-Chai, A., Barndollar, K. *et al.* (2001) 'The automated will: Nonconscious activation and pursuit of behavioral goals', *Journal of Personality and Social Psychology, 81*: 1014–27.

Baumeister, R.F., Masicampo, E.J. & Vohs, K.D. (2011) 'Do conscious thoughts cause behavior?', *Annual Review of Psychology, 62*: 331–61.

Beck, D.M. (2010) 'The appeal of the brain in the popular press', *Perspectives on Psychological Science, 5*: 762–6.

Blackwood's Edinburgh Magazine (1858), October, pp. 506–7. At http://books.google.be/books?id=sggHA QAAIAAJ&pg=PA506&dq=hamilton+%22phenome na+of+memory%22+intitle:Edinburgh+intitle:Magaz ine&hl=nl&sa=X&ei=lJyET7DUI9CeOtSp3M0I&ve d=0CDcQ6AEwAA#v=onepage&q&f=false.

Block, N. (1995) 'On a confusion about a function of consciousness', *Behavioral and Brain Sciences, 18*: 227–87.

Block, N. (2004) 'Qualia'. In R. Gregory (ed.), *Oxford companion to the mind* (2nd edn). Oxford: Oxford University Press.

Boring, E.G. (1933) *The physical dimensions of consciousness.* New York: Appleton-Century.

Chalmers, D.J. (1996) *The conscious mind: In search of a fundamental theory.* New York: Oxford University Press.

Churchland, P. (1981) 'Eliminative materialism and the propositional attitudes', *Journal of Philosophy, 78*: 67–90.

Coltheart, M. (2004) 'Brain imaging, connectionism and cognitive neuropsychology', *Cognitive Neuropsychology, 21*: 21–5.

Coltheart, M. (2006) 'What has functional neuroimaging told us about the mind (so far)?' *Cortex, 42*: 323–31.

Corkin, S. (2002) 'What's new with the amnesic patient H.M.?' *Nature Reviews Neuroscience, 3*: 153–60.

Crick, F. (1995) *The astonishing hypothesis: The scientific search for the soul.* London: Touchstone Books.

Darley, J.M. & Latané, B. (1968) 'Bystander intervention in emergencies: Diffusion of responsibility', *Journal of Personality and Social Psychology, 8*: 377–83.

Dawkins, R. (1976/2006) *The selfish gene: 30th anniversary edition – with a new introduction by the author.* Oxford: Oxford University Press.

De Gelder, B., Vroomen, J., Pourtois, G. & Weiskrantz, L. (1999) 'Non-conscious recognition of affect in the absence of striate cortex', *Neuroreport, 10*: 3759–63.

Dehaene, S., Naccache, L., Cohen, L., Le Bihan, D. *et al.* (2001) 'Cerebral mechanisms of word masking and unconscious repetition priming', *Nature Neuroscience,* **4**: 752–8.

Dijksterhuis, A. & Nordgren, L.F. (2006) 'A theory of unconscious thought', *Perspectives on Psychological Science,* **1**: 95–109.

Dijksterhuis, A., Bos, M.W., Nordgren, L.F. & van Baaren, R.B. (2006) 'On making the right choice: The deliberation-without-attention effect', *Science,* **311**: 1005–7.

Dijksterhuis, A., Smith, P.K., van Baaren, R.B. & Wigboldus, D.H.J. (2005) 'The unconscious consumer: Effects of environment on consumer behavior', *Journal of Consumer Psychology,* **15**: 193–202.

Dupuy, J.P. (2009) *On the origins of cognitive science: The mechanization of the mind.* Cambridge, MA: MIT Press.

Evans, J.S.B.T. (2002) 'Logic and human reasoning: An assessment of the deduction paradigm', *Psychological Bulletin,* **128**: 978–96.

Fancher, R.E. (1996) *Pioneers of psychology* (3rd edn). New York: Norton.

Fodor, J.A. (1981) 'The mind–body problem', *Scientific American,* **244**(1): 124–32.

Frith, C. (1992) *The cognitive neuropsychology of schizophrenia.* Hove: Erlbaum.

Gazzaniga, M.S., Ivry, R. & Mangun, G.R. (1998) *Fundamentals of cognitive neuroscience.* New York: W.W. Norton.

Glenberg, A.M. & Robertson, D.A. (2000) 'Symbol grounding and meaning: A comparison of high-dimensional and embodied theories of meaning', *Journal of Memory and Language,* **43**: 379–401.

Greenwald, A.G. (1992) 'New look 3: Unconscious cognition reclaimed', *American Psychologist,* **47**: 766–79.

Greenwald, A.G., Draine, S.C. & Abrams, R.L. (1996) 'Three cognitive markers of unconscious semantic activation', *Science,* **273**: 1699–702.

Greenwald, A.G., Spangenberg, E.R., Pratkanis, A.R. & Eskenazi, J. (1991) 'Double-blind tests of subliminal self-help audiotapes', *Psychological Science,* **2**: 119–22.

Haggard, P. (2005) 'Conscious intention and motor cognition', *Trends in Cognitive Sciences,* **6**: 290–5.

Harley, T.A. (2004) 'Does cognitive neuropsychology have a future?' *Cognitive Neuropsychology,* **21**: 2–16.

Harnad, S. (1990) 'The symbol grounding problem', *Physica D,* **42**: 335–46.

Hatfield, G. (2000) 'The brain's "new" science: Psychology, neurophysiology, and constraint', *Philosophy of Science,* **67**: S388–S403.

Henson, R. (2005) 'What can functional neuroimaging tell the experimental psycholohist?' *The Quarterly Journal of Experimental Psychology,* **58A**: 193–233.

Holender, D. (1986) 'Semantic activation without conscious identification in dichotic listening, parafoveal vision, and visual masking: A survey and appraisal', *Behavioral and Brain Sciences,* **9**: 1–23.

Jackson, F. (1982) 'Epiphenomenal qualia', *Philosophical Quarterly,* **32**: 127–36.

Jahoda, G. (2007) *A history of social psychology.* Cambridge: Cambridge University Press.

Johnston, L. (2002) 'Behavioral mimicry and stigmatization', *Social Cognition,* **20**: 18–35.

Kahneman, D. & Tversky, A. (1974) 'Judgment under uncertainty: Heuristics and biases', *Science,* **185**: 1124–31.

Kahneman, D. & Tversky, A. (1979) 'Prospect theory: Analysis of decision under risk', *Econometrica,* **47**: 263–91.

Kihlstrom, J.F. (2010) 'Social neuroscience: The footprints of Phineas Gage', *Social Cognition,* **28**: 757–83.

Kreiner, D.S., Altis, N.A. & Voss, C.W. (2003) 'A test of the effect of reverse speech on priming', *Journal of Psychology,* **137**: 224–32.

Kunst-Wilson, W.R. & Zajonc, R.B. (1980) 'Affective discrimination of stimuli that cannot be recognized', *Science,* **207**: 557–8.

Lakoff, G. & Johnson, M. (1980) *Metaphors we live by.* Chicago, IL: University of Chicago Press.

Lakoff, G. & Johnson, M. (1999) *Philosophy in the flesh: The embodied mind and its challenge to Western thought.* New York: Basic Books.

Lamme, V.A.F. (2006) 'Towards a true neural stance on consciousness', *Trends in Cognitive Sciences,* **10**: 494–501.

Leibniz, G.W. (1765) *Nouveaux essais sur l'entendement human* (New essays on human understanding). First appeared in Raspe, R.E. (ed.) (1765) *Oeuvre philosophiques, latines et françaises, de feu Mr. de Leibniz, tirées de ses manuscrits, qui se conservent dans la bibliothèque royale à Hanovre.* Amsterdam and Leipzig.

Libet, B. (1985) 'Unconscious cerebral initiative and the role of conscious will in voluntary action', *Behavioral and Brain Sciences,* **8**: 529–39.

Libet, B. (1999) 'Do we have free will?' *Journal of Consciousness Studies,* **6**: 47–55.

Lieberman, M.D. (2000) 'Intuition: A social cognitive neuroscience approach', *Psychological Bulletin,* **126**: 109–37.

Locke, J. (1690) *Essay concerning human understanding.* London.

Loftus, E.F. & Klinger, M.R. (1992) 'Is the unconscious smart or dumb?' *American Psychologist,* **47**: 761–5.

Lowery, B.S., Eisenberger, N.I., Hardin, C.D. & Sinclair, S. (2007) 'Long-term effects of subliminal priming on academic performance', *Basic and Applied Social Psychology,* **29**: 151–7.

Lyons, W. (2001) *Matters of the mind*. New York: Routledge.

Marcel, A.J. (1983) 'Conscious and unconscious perception: Experiments on visual masking and word recognition', *Cognitive Psychology*, 15: 197–237.

Marr, D. (1982) *Vision*. San Francisco: Freeman.

Mayer, B. & Merckelbach, H. (1999) 'Unconscious processes, subliminal stimulation, and anxiety', *Clinical Psychology Review*, 19: 571–90.

McCabe, D.P. & Castel, A.D. (2008) 'Seeing is believing: The effect of brain images on judgments of scientific reasoning', *Cognition*, 107: 343–52.

Meerman, E.E., Verkuil, B. & Brosschot, J.F. (2011) 'Decreasing pain tolerance outside of awareness', *Journal of Psychosomatic Research*, 70: 250–7.

Merikle, P.M., Smilek, D. & Eastwood, J.D. (2001) 'Perception without awareness: Perspectives from cognitive psychology', *Cognition*, 79: 115–34.

Miles, L.K., Nind, L.K. & Macrae, C.N. (2010) 'Moving through time', *Psychological Science*, 21: 222–3.

Milgram, S. (1963) 'Behavioral study of obedience', *Journal of Abnormal and Social Psychology*, 67: 371–8.

Miller, G.A. (2010) 'Mistreating psychology in the decades of the brain', *Perspectives on Psychological Science*, 5: 716–43.

Milner, B. (1962) 'Les troubles de la mémoire accompagnant les lesions hippocampiques bilatérales'. In *Physiologie de l'hippocampe*. Paris: Centre National de la Recherche Scientifique.

Nagel, T. (1974) 'What is it like to be a bat?' *Philosophical Review*, 4: 435–50.

Nicholls, A. & Liebscher, M. (2010) *Thinking the unconscious: Nineteenth-century German thought*. Cambridge: Cambridge University Press.

Nisbett, R. & Ross, L. (1980) *Human inference: Strategies and shortcomings of social judgment*. Englewood Cliffs, NJ: Prentice-Hall.

Nisbett, R. & Wilson, T. (1977) 'Telling more than we can know: Verbal reports on mental processes', *Psychological Review*, 84: 231–59.

Nordgren, L.F., Bos, M.W. & Dijksterhuis, A. (2011) 'The best of both worlds: Integrating conscious and unconscious thought best solves complex decisions', *Journal of Experimental Social Psychology*, 47: 509–11.

Pulvermüller, F. (2005) 'Brain mechanisms linking language and action', *Nature Reviews Neuroscience*, 6: 576–82.

Schacter, D.L. (1987) 'Implicit memory: History and current status', *Journal of Experimental Psychology: Learning, Memory, and Cognition*, 13: 501–18.

Searle, J. (1980) 'Minds, brains, and programs', *Behavioral and Brain Sciences*, 3: 417–57.

Skolnick-Weisberg, D., Keil, F.C., Goodstein, J., Rawson, E. *et al.* (2008) 'The seductive allure of neuroscience explanations', *Journal of Cognitive Neuroscience*, 20: 470–7.

Soon, S.C., Brass, M., Heinze, H.J. & Haynes, J.D. (2008) 'Unconscious determinants of free decisions in the human brain', *Nature Neuroscience*, 11: 543–5.

Stanovich, K.E. (2004) *The robot's rebellion: Finding meaning in the age of Darwin*. Chicago: University of Chicago Press.

Swinkels, A. (2003) 'An effective exercise for teaching cognitive heuristics', *Teaching of Psychology*, 30: 120–2.

Turing, A. (1950) 'Computing machinery and intelligence', *Mind*, 59: 434–60.

Uttal, W.R. (2001) *The new phrenology: The limits of localizing cognitive processes*. Cambridge, MA: MIT Press.

Vul, E., Harris, C., Winkielman, P. & Pashler, H. (2009) 'Puzzlingly high correlations in fMRI studies of emotion, personality, and social cognition', *Perspectives on Psychological Science*, 4: 274–90.

Walter, H. (2001) *Neurophilosophy of free will*. Cambridge, MA: MIT Press.

Warrington, E.K. & Weiskrantz, L. (1978) 'Further analysis of the prior learning effect in amnesic patients', *Neuropsychologia*, 16: 169–76.

Wegner, D.M. (2004) 'Précis of "The illusion of conscious will"', *Behavioral and Brain Sciences*, 27: 649–59.

8 How did psychology affect everyday life?
The history of applied psychology

Questions to consider

Historical issues addressed in this chapter

- When were the first psychological clinics established? What opposition existed?
- Why was research about shell-shock so important in the early years of applied psychology?
- When did client-centred therapy start? In what respect was the time ripe for such a development?
- Which events increased the status of clinical psychology during and after World War II?
- When did psychoactive drugs become available? What impact did they have?
- When were the first achievement tests used?
- What triggered the start of the research on work and organisation at the beginning of the twentieth century?
- How have the views on work motivation changed over the twentieth century?

Conceptual issues addressed in this chapter

- To what extent has psychological research changed the way people see each other?
- Is it possible to do research about the efficacy of psychotherapy?
- What has the welfare state to do with the development of clinical psychology?
- What are tests used for?
- Why should a test be reliable and valid?
- Why do psychologists need tests?
- What needs to be done to have a useful test?
- Why is Western society becoming increasingly individualised?
- Why have text writers a tendency to idealise classic experiments? What is the outcome of this practice?

Introduction

> What every educator, every jail-warden, every doctor, every clergyman, every asylum-superintendent, asks of psychology is practical rules. Such men care little or nothing about the ultimate philosophical grounds of mental phenomena, but they do care immensely about improving the ideas, dispositions, and conduct of the particular individuals in their charge.
>
> (James 1892: 148)

Another way of looking at the history of psychology is to see what impact it has had on society. In his book *Modernizing the mind: Psychological knowledge and the remaking of society*, the American sociologist Steven C. Ward (2002) argues that the discipline of psychology, over the course of the twentieth century, grew from a marginal academic field to a discipline that has done more than any other to transform the routines and experiences of everyday life. In his own words:

> Today, psychological knowledge is present in such diverse places as the discourse of TV talk shows, the organization and production in factories and the self-esteem workshops in public schools. Its practitioners and representatives are found not only at traditional centers of knowledge production, such as universities and research laboratories, but also in courtrooms, at disaster scenes, in advertising agencies, in sports training camps and corporate education centers. In fact, it can be argued that psychological knowledge is so pervasive that to think and feel in the early twenty-first century inevitably means utilizing and activating its terminology, classifications and modes of understanding.
>
> (Ward 2002: 1)

A similar conclusion was reached by the Dutch authors Jansz and Van Drunen (2004). Both they and Ward talked about the *psychologisation* of society to refer to the growing impact of psychological theories and findings on everyday life in our society. We will discuss the socio-political issues of this psychologisation in Chapter 13. Here we deal with the knowledge itself. What did psychology have to offer?

A noteworthy observation is that most of psychology's influences on society have to do with applied aspects of psychological knowledge, the application of psychological knowledge and research methods to solve problems in other areas. This is interesting because for a long time **applied psychology** hardly figured in the history books of psychology, as if it were a branch of secondary importance (see our discussion of the schools of psychology in Chapter 4). Applied psychology is rapidly expanding nowadays (e.g. in the areas of health, sport, law, business management and product design). However, as in the other chapters, we must limit our coverage. Only three areas with histories going back to the late nineteenth century will be discussed. First, we review the developments in clinical psychology. Next, we discuss why psychological testing became so popular, and we end by tracing the history of the psychology of work and organisation.

applied psychology
the application of psychological knowledge and research methods to solve practical problems

8.1 Changes in the treatment of mental health problems

In Chapter 4 we looked at the history of mental health care up to the twentieth century. We ended with the appearance of neurologists at the end of the nineteenth century signalling the beginning of a new era in the treatment of psychopathology. Neurologists were physicians who treated milder forms of mental disorders in private settings using methods such as communication, hypnosis and suggestion. They were the initiators of psychotherapy and had a strong influence on their medical colleagues in the asylums, the psychiatrists, who took over their ideas. The best-known neurologist was Freud, partly inspired by developments in France (e.g. Charcot).

Evolutions before World War II

Mental health problems must be treated by practitioners with a medical degree

Although psychologists are keen to present Freud as the person who introduced the psychological treatment of mental health problems, they usually fail to mention that Freud saw himself in the first place as a medical doctor and psychoanalysis as a medical treatment. Likewise, psychiatrists in various countries lobbied to have psychoanalysis acknowledged as a medical treatment and, therefore, confined to practitioners with a medical degree (e.g. Ward 2002: 48–51). Psychologists were not allowed to provide unsupervised therapies in official settings and their private practices were not covered by health insurance. As a result, psychologists involved in mental health care had a subordinate function (reporting to the psychiatrist) and were mainly hired to administer psychological tests (see below).

The first clinical psychology centres

Treatment centres run by psychologists started in the USA and were university-related. The facility that is considered to be the first psychology health centre was opened by Lightner Witmer in 1896 at the University of Pennsylvania. Tellingly, it was aimed at helping behavioural and learning problems in school children, building upon the growing impact of educational psychology (Chapter 13) and keeping away from what happened in psychiatric clinics.

In subsequent years the growth of psychology clinics was slow (in 1914 there were only 19 of them in the USA) and up to World War II were limited to dealing with problems in school children (McReynolds 1987). The founding of clinical psychology centres was further impeded by the lack of support from the academic psychologists. This was partly because the psychology departments at the universities were dominated by experimental psychologists, who wanted to promote psychology as a science (Chapters 5 and 10), and partly because the academics did not want to upset their medical colleagues, whose help they needed for the expansion of their departments (Chapter 13). Even in 1921, the American Psychological Association (APA) made it publicly known that its objective was the advancement of psychology as a science, not as a profession (Abma 2004: 108). Although Witmer was a founding member of the APA, he withdrew from it bitterly in the early 1900s (McReynolds 1987).

In the meantime mental health problems and psychoanalysis became popular courses in psychology. In 1907, Witmer used the term **clinical psychology** to refer to the branch of psychology applying psychological knowledge to the assessment and treatment of mental disorders. These were his words:

clinical psychology
branch of psychology applying psychological knowledge to the assessment and treatment of mental disorders

> Although clinical psychology is clearly related to medicine, it is quite as closely related to sociology and to pedagogy . . . An abundance of material for scientific study fails to be utilized, because the interest of psychologists is elsewhere engaged, and those in constant touch with the actual phenomena do not possess the training necessary to make the experience and observation of scientific value . . . While the field of clinical psychology is to some extent occupied by the physician, especially by the psychiatrist, and while I expect to rely in a great measure upon the educator and social worker for the more important contributions to this branch of psychology, it is nevertheless true that none of these has quite the training necessary for this kind of work. For that matter, neither has the psychologist, unless he has acquired this training from sources other than the usual course of instruction in psychology . . . The phraseology of 'clinical

psychology' and 'psychological clinic' will doubtless strike many as an odd juxtaposition of terms relating to quite disparate subjects . . . I have borrowed the word 'clinical' from medicine, because it is the best term I can find to indicate the character of the method which I deem necessary for this work.

(Witmer, 1907; as cited in McReynolds 1987: 852)

The first clinical psychology centre in the UK was set up in 1920 in a private house in Tavistock Square, London. It was named the Institute for Medical Psychology (later renamed the Tavistock Clinic). This is how Wooldridge (1994: 140) described it:

> The clinic, the first of its kind in the country, aimed at treating patients who suffered from hysteria, abnormal fears and obsession, neurasthenia, and behaviour disorders. Its general approach was eclectic, embracing all the known methods of psychotherapy, such as various forms of suggestion, re-education and mental analysis, but it laid particular emphasis on Freudian psychoanalysis.

As was the case for Witmer's centre, the Tavistock Clinic had a particular interest in child psychology. Its first patient was a child.

The impact of World War II

An urgent need for psychological advice and treatment

World War I had taught the military that the new fighting techniques (with more devastating weapons and less physical contact) put heavy mental strain on the soldiers. A phenomenon that became documented was shell-shock, an anxiety response that prevented soldiers and officers from functioning properly despite the usual disciplinary actions. This finding gave rise to two developments. First, there was a need for increased psychological testing to predict who would be prone to shell-shock and hence should not be employed by the paid armed forces. Second, there was increased pressure to treat personnel who suffered from shell-shock. As a result, when the USA decided to join World War II, they also decided to properly staff the military psychiatric service. Because the demand vastly outstripped the number of available psychiatrists, a crash course in the treatment of mental disorders was offered to all medical officers, and clinical psychologists were taken on board, both for testing and treatment. Given that after World War II the USA became involved in other wars (e.g. Korea 1950–1953, Vietnam 1965–1975), the service remained.

shell-shock

anxiety response on battlefield that prevents soldiers from functioning properly; was one of the first topics addressed by applied psychology

The beginning of client-centred therapy

The rising demand for psychological help also provided a rich environment for new developments in therapy. Psychoanalysis required a long series of treatment sessions and was not experienced by all therapists as effective. In 1942, Carl Rogers published *Counseling and psychotherapy*, in which he proposed client-centred therapy as an alternative. In this therapy, the clients searched for solutions to their current problems by talking them through with a listening, understanding and supporting therapist. This is how Rogers (1942: 3) introduced it:

> There are a great many professional individuals who spend a large portion of their time in interviewing, bringing about a constructive change of attitude on the part of their clients through individual and face-to-face contacts. Whether such an individual calls himself a psychologist, a college counselor, a marital advisor, a psychiatrist, a social worker, a high-school guidance counselor, an industrial personnel worker, or by some other name, his approach to the attitudes of his client is of concern to us in this book . . .

There are various names which may be attached to such interviewing processes. They may be termed treatment interviews, which is a simple and descriptive term. Most frequently they are termed counseling, a word in increasingly common use, particularly in educational circles. Or such contacts, with their curative and remedial aim, may be classed as psychotherapy, the term most frequently used by social workers, psychologists, and psychiatrists in clinics. These terms will be used more or less interchangeably in these chapters, and will be so used because they all seem to refer to the same basic method – a series of direct contacts with the individual which aims to offer him assistance in changing his attitudes and behavior.

In the light of the power struggle between psychiatrists and psychologists about the right to give psychotherapy, it is interesting to see how cleverly Rogers downplayed the requirement of a medical degree for his 'treatment interviews'. What characterised a good counsellor in Rogers's eyes was not knowledge of physical diseases and their cures, but:

- unconditional positive regard: the counsellor supports the client unconditionally and non-judgementally,
- empathic understanding: the counsellor ensures that he/she understands the client's thoughts, feelings and meaning from the client's point of view,
- congruence: the counsellor is genuine in his/her support and understanding, it is not a mere implementation of a therapeutic technique.

After World War II: antipsychiatry, scientific input and psychoactive drugs

Three major developments after World War II further strengthened the status of clinical psychologists. The first was unease with the way in which patients were treated by psychiatrists in asylums. The second was the input from scientific research into psychotherapy. The third was the fact that psychiatrists increasingly turned to medicines for the treatment of mental disorders.

KEY FIGURE Carl Rogers

- American psychologist (1902–1987).
- Best known for his client-centred therapy in which people search for solutions to their current problems by talking them through with a listening, understanding and supporting therapist or counsellor.
- Rogers's therapeutic approach was based on a personality theory, which stressed that humans are driven by a positive force to move forward and to realise themselves, a force Rogers called self-actualisation. This was a reaction to Freud's negative view of humans (who saw individuals as being in a never-ending struggle between unconscious factions).

Source: Roger Ressmeyer/ CORBIS.

- Rogers was also one of the founders of humanistic psychology in the 1950s, a movement that emphasised the fact that humans are individuals, unique beings who should be recognised and treated as such by mental health practitioners. The humanistic approach was presented as the third way, a counterweight for psychoanalysis (which reduced humans to unconscious drives and wishes), and behaviourism (which reduced persons to behaviours controlled by environmental contingencies).

Antipsychiatry

As part of a wider cultural movement against the establishment in the 1960–1970s, the treatment of patients in mental hospitals began to be questioned. It was seen not only as ineffective, but also as dangerous and demeaning for the patients. In the previous decades, psychiatry had experimented with a number of controversial and invasive biological treatments, such as lobotomy and electric shocks, which had adverse consequences.

Lobotomy consisted of cutting the nerve tracts between the frontal lobes and the thalamus. It had been proposed by the Portuguese neurologist Egas Monitz as an efficient treatment of violent behaviour and it was applied on a massive scale in the USA (in 1949 Monitz received the Nobel Prize for the procedure). However, gradually it became clear that the procedure resulted in massive side-effects, as described by Hoffman (1949):

> These patients are not only no longer distressed by their mental conflicts but also seem to have little capacity for any emotional experiences – pleasurable or otherwise. They are described by the nurses and the doctors, over and over, as dull, apathetic, listless, without drive or initiative, flat, lethargic, placid and unconcerned, childlike, docile, needing pushing, passive, lacking in spontaneity, without aim or purpose, preoccupied and dependent.

Electric shocks consisted of applying electrical shocks to the brain, resulting in a massive discharge of neurons. Although this procedure has been shown to be effective for the treatment of otherwise incurable depression (UK ECT Review Group 2003), its use in mental hospitals for a long time was much wider and without empirical support.

The use of electric shocks and lobotomy to subdue unruly psychiatric patients became known to the public after the publication of the cult novel *One flew over the cuckoo's nest* by Ken Kesey in 1962 (based on his experiences as an orderly at a mental health institute). The novel was subsequently turned into an equally successful play and film.

Lobotomy, electric shocks and other demeaning treatments (such as the use of straitjackets and isolation cells to discipline patients) exposed psychiatry to anti-establishment protests in the 1960s–1970s. This resulted in the **antipsychiatry movement**, a pressure group that called the usefulness of psychiatry into question. Psychiatry was not seen as a profession helping patients with mental health problems, but as a way of controlling patients and expelling them from society (see the discussion of Foucault in Chapter 13). This criticism did not only come from outside. Within universities it was driven by the publications of a number of psychiatrists who felt unhappy with the prevailing treatments (Rissmiller & Rissmiller 2006). For example, in 1960 the American psychiatrist Thomas Szasz published *The myth of mental illness*, in which he argued that most psychiatric disorders were not incurable mental diseases, but transient problems with life and difficulties fitting in with society. He argued that this should be reflected in treatment. A similar case was made by the Scottish psychiatrist Ronald Laing (e.g. Laing 1960).

Another milestone in the realisation that the existing psychiatric institutions did not help patients with mental problems came with the publication of the article 'On being sane in insane places' in 1973 by the psychologist David Rosenhan. In this study, eight healthy volunteers (including Rosenhan and a few other psychologists) went to mental hospitals complaining that they heard voices saying 'empty', 'hollow' and

antipsychiatry movement

a pressure group started in the 1960s that called into question the usefulness of the prevailing psychiatric treatments 'thud'. All 'patients' were admitted and essentially left to their own devices. Even though the complaint about the voices was the only symptom ever mentioned and the pseudopatients immediately ceased simulating any more symptoms of abnormality once they were admitted, they were institutionalised for between 7 and 52 days and eventually discharged with the diagnosis 'schizophrenia in remission' (meaning that they were thought to be schizophrenic, but at that moment did not display symptoms). None of the staff noticed that the patients behaved 'normally', although the nurses did mention in their reports that the patients' behaviour was exemplary (i.e. not disruptive).

On the basis of incidents like the ones just described, the antipsychiatry movement contended that the treatment of mental disorders had to change. For a start, there had to be much more respect for the rights and the dignity of the patients. Second, hospitalisation had to be as short as possible and geared towards reintegration in society. And, finally, many more initiatives had to be taken to prevent hospitalisation and to treat people with mental problems outside clinics. All of these recommendations went in the direction of the positions defended by clinical psychologists (e.g. Rogers's client-centred approach) and, as a result, improved the standing of clinical psychologists within mental health organisations.

What do you think?

The idea put forward by the antipsychiatry movement (treating people with mental problems in society, outside clinics) very much resembles the informal care that existed before the state started to intervene with its asylums (Chapter 4).
In what respects does the new care differ from the old, informal care? Does it make any difference to you whether you work as a psychologist in a mental health centre or whether you take care of a relative with a mental health problem? Why?

Input from science

efficacy of therapies
measure to indicate how much improvement a therapy brings to patients

Another evolution after World War II that improved the standing of clinical psychologists was the fact that researchers started to evaluate the **efficacy of therapies**. It was no longer enough to believe the founders' claims about the usefulness of their therapies; value had to be shown empirically. In this respect, one of the first studies turned out to be a severe wake-up call. Hans Eysenck (1952/1992) reviewed the available evidence about the effectiveness of talking cures for non-psychotic patients (i.e. patients without hallucinations and delusions). He compared the improvement of persons who were given psychotherapy with the improvement of persons who did not see a therapist but were put on a waiting list (and remained in contact with their general practitioner). Eysenck observed that in both groups about two-thirds of the patients were significantly better two years later. The therapy group did not outperform the control group, indicating that the effect of the therapy had been minimal or even absent. All progress could be explained by a general improvement in the condition of the patients since the moment they sought therapeutic help. On the basis of this finding Eysenck concluded that:

> . . . certain conclusions are possible from these data. They fail to prove that psychotherapy, Freudian or otherwise, facilitates the recovery of neurotic patients. They show that roughly two-thirds of a group of neurotic patients will recover or improve to a

marked extent within about two years of the onset of their illness, whether they are treated by means of psychotherapy or not. This figure appears to be remarkably stable from one investigation to another, regardless of type of patient treated, standard of recovery employed, or method of therapy used. From the point of view of the neurotic, these figures are encouraging; from the point of view of the psychotherapist, they can hardly be called very favorable to his claims.

(Eysenck 1952/1992: 661–2)

Although Eysenck (1952/1992) could have concluded from his findings that all forms of psychotherapy were worthless, his message was more subtle. He argued that the therapies in the 1950s were ineffective, because they were not based on scientific research. If therapists wanted their therapies to be helpful, they had to systematically examine which techniques worked and which did not, and adapt their approach as a function of the feedback. Indeed, Eysenck would later become a strong supporter of therapies grounded in psychological research, such as behaviour therapy (based on the principles of operant and classical conditioning; see Eysenck 1976) and cognitive therapy (based on research in cognitive psychology about debilitating thoughts and convictions).

Eysenck's (1952/1992) study also led to much more research on the effectiveness of therapies, both existing ones and new ones. Thankfully for the mental health sector, these new results were considerably more reassuring: more clients who were given psychotherapy recovered than clients who were denied psychotherapy; they also improved more rapidly (see e.g. Wampold *et al.* 1997). As all this research was done by psychologists, it once again raised the status of clinical psychologists in the mental health services.

The availability of medicines for mental disorders

Another reason why clinical psychologists became more involved in psychotherapies was that the psychiatrists lowered their resistance to treatment by non-medical practitioners. This was partly because of the influence of psychology pressure groups, but also because psychiatrists increasingly turned towards medicines as the preferred treatment for mental health problems. Given that only medical practitioners were allowed to prescribe medicines, this gave psychiatrists a new edge over psychologists.

psychoactive drugs
medicines prescribed for
mental disorders

The first psychoactive drugs, medicines that relieve the symptoms of mental disorders, were discovered by chance, as side-effects of existing medicines. The emergence of these drugs can be traced back to antihistamines synthesised in the 1940s (i.e. medicines for allergic reactions). From these, in 1950 chlorpromazine was developed, which turned out to be a sedative (i.e. it made animals and people calm). It was tested in a French hospital on patients with debilitating psychotic episodes and turned out to be unexpectedly effective for most of them, significantly diminishing their delusions and hallucinations. In a few years, chlorpromazine swept across the mental hospitals, and pharmaceutical companies tried to improve on it which, among other things, gave rise to new applications. One of the derivatives of chlorpromazine, for instance, turned out to be an antidepressant.

Together with the altered views of society, the psychoactive drugs radically changed the treatment of mental disorders. First, they contributed to non-residential therapies, greatly reducing the number of patients who had to be hospitalised for long periods. Second, they lowered the threshold for treatment of mental health problems. In most developed countries psychoactive drugs nowadays account for 15% of all medicines taken (a number that is still rising), with antidepressants and anti-anxiety medicines figuring among the top 10 of the medications taken.

Social management and individualisation

social management

management and control of deviant individuals and individuals in need by official social services

welfare state

socio-political system in which individuals insure themselves against setbacks via taxes, which are used by the state to provide welfare services

The growing impact of clinical psychology over the twentieth century was also linked to the enhanced role of social management in society. As we saw in Chapter 4, from the sixteenth century onwards authorities increasingly replaced the family and relatives for the control of individuals who did not adhere to the existing norms and for the care of those who could not maintain themselves. This process continued in the twentieth century, giving rise to the so-called welfare state, a situation in which individuals insured themselves against setbacks via taxes, with the state providing welfare services.

The reliance on public services, including mental health organisations, grew not only because people wanted to have professional help, but also because social structures became looser. Due to increased social mobility, social relationships were more and more limited to work contacts as people moved away from their families, and people often found themselves in situations in which they did not trust their acquaintances enough to confide in them. At the same time, people developed a growing awareness of their individuality and defined themselves increasingly in terms of their own qualities, achievements and emotions rather than on the basis of the groups they belonged to. The greater focus on the self further increased the likelihood that people would want to talk to a professional counsellor about their functioning. As we saw in Chapter 3, both evolutions (looser social relations and a greater focus on the self) are summarised in the sociological literature under the name *individualisation*.

CASE STUDY: Working in the health care unit of a prison

When I finished my BSc in Psychology, I applied for a position of prison officer working on a health care unit that caters for women with varying mental health needs. I always had a passion for forensic psychology and in my final year of university elected to study various units pertaining to this subject. Post graduation I wanted to gain practical experience working with mentally disordered offenders and saw the Prison Service as a perfect opportunity to achieve this. To my delight, I got recruited. This was two years ago.

Now I work as part of a multidisciplinary team caring for women with all manner of mental health needs in the prison environment. We aim to help these women reintegrate themselves into the generic prison population or where necessary arrange for their transfer to medium or high security psychiatric hospitals.

All things tend to be very different in practice than they are in theory. This was exactly what I found when I was first exposed to individuals who were diagnosed with the mental illnesses I had read so much about. At times this proved to be incredibly stressful and upsetting. Dealing with repeated acts of serious self-harm, restraining violent patients or even just listening to women recount tales of an abusive past or talk about their crimes can be mentally and physically draining.

However, the experiences have been invaluable and far surpass any negative aspects. In prison many of these women were provided with the treatment and care that had not been afforded to them in the community. It may be a cliché but by working in this type of environment you really do feel like you are making a positive difference to the lives of many.

In the meantime I have also started a Masters in Forensic Mental Health with the intention of exploring the subject further at a doctoral level.

(C.J., personal communication, 24 April 2008)

Increased knowledge about psychology in the population

A final reason why clinical psychology became increasingly pervasive in society towards the beginning of the twenty-first century was that this type of knowledge had become integrated into mainstream education and became part of everyday interactions. As for the former, an increasing number of degree programmes involving communication with clients started to pay attention to psychological ideas and findings. The majority of teachers, nurses, social workers, clergy and secretaries nowadays take at least one introductory psychology course as part of their education. As Jansz put it:

> . . . as important was the gradual adoption of psychological methods and more generally, a psychologized perspective, by other professionals. Almost without exception, psychology was introduced as part of the training in the 'helping' professions. In particular, the basic technique of 'counseling', developed . . . by the psychologist Carl Rogers, became a widely used tool among professionals of various disciplines. Focusing on the articulation of clients' needs and encouraging a supportive and advisory, rather than directing, role of professionals, it fitted perfectly with the change from an authoritarian, disciplinary style of intervention to more subtle ways of influencing behavior.
>
> (Jansz & Van Drunen 2004: 39)

At the same time, psychological research findings have become part of general knowledge. People who today read newspapers and magazines have a weekly supply of the newest psychological findings; psychology and psychological problems are discussed in television talk shows; and psychology has become by far the most popular topic of self-study. Even everyday conversations are full of words borrowed from psychology: people are said to be nervous, unconscious, extrovert, intelligent, depressed, self-conscious, neurotic, emotionally stable, dependent, etc. This does not mean that all the information is correct and that everyone has a coherent picture of what is known in psychology. It does mean, however, that knowledge of basic psychological findings and psychological vocabulary slowly but surely has become public property, as indicated by Ward (2002) at the beginning of this chapter.

Interim summary

Twentieth-century changes in the treatment of mental health problems

- Before World War I psychologists were largely excluded from treatment; their main task was administering psychological tests; there were a few university-related centres.
- Because of the increased need for advice and treatment during World War II, psychologists became involved in treatment.
- After World War II, the position of psychologists in the treatment of mental disorders was further strengthened by
  - the antipsychiatry movement
  - scientific research on the efficacy of psychotherapies

- the fact that psychiatrists became more involved with the prescription of psychoactive drugs
  - the increase of social management and individualisation in society.
- Knowledge of psychology also became of public interest.

8.2 Psychological testing

The need for tests in society

Throughout recorded history, people have used tests in three types of situations: to establish a person's honesty, to select the best person and to diagnose illness.

Authenticity tests to expose dishonesty

authenticity test

test to determine whether a person is who he/she pretends to be and to ascertain guilt or innocence

Humans can deceive. They can present themselves differently from whom and what they are. To counteract this tendency, social groups have devised a long tradition of techniques to see through lies and to reveal the underlying truth. These techniques were called **authenticity tests**, tests to establish whether individuals were who they claimed to be. An early example of such a test can be found in Homer's epic poem, *The odyssey* (written around 700 BCE). In this poem Queen Penelope set two authenticity tests to find out whether the person who turned up after 20 years' absence was indeed her husband Odysseus. One of the tests was to string a particular bow and shoot an arrow through 12 axe handles, a feat only Odysseus could accomplish.

Authenticity tests were also used to ascertain guilt and innocence. One such test was trial by ordeal. For instance, in Europe between 500 and 1200 CE the innocence of people was sometimes determined by throwing them into a river with their hands and feet bound. The assumption was that God would reveal his judgement by letting the innocent drown and making the guilty float (the latter was believed to be particularly true for witches).

Qualifying tests to measure aptitude and competence

qualifying test

test to find the best person for a task

Authenticity tests were only useful when someone was suspected of wrongdoing. Another situation asking for tests occurred when the best person for a task had to be designated. Then, a so-called **qualifying test** was required. This happened, for instance, in the legendary, medieval world of King Arthur. Only the person who was able to draw the magic sword Excalibur from the rock would be the rightful king.

Tests to diagnose disease

diagnostic tests

tests to determine which condition a person has

A final use of tests was to determine which adverse condition people had. These are the so-called **diagnostic tests**. For instance, papyri from Ancient Egypt minutely described the symptoms that pointed to various diseases. Similarly, Byzantine doctors (*c.* 300–*c.* 1450 CE) had an extensive system to assess illnesses on the basis of a visual analysis of the patient's urine (a technique known as uroscopy, not to be confused with the current-day chemical analysis of urine, known as urinalysis). This technique was passed on to the Arabs and people in medieval Western Europe.

What is a test?

Although most people have an implicit understanding of what a test is, the American sociologist Alan Hanson claims that few are aware of the fact that tests actually involve three basic conditions (Hanson 1993):

1. A test contains the condition of intent: tests are planned, arranged and given by someone with a purpose in mind; they are never random events.

2. A test is not administered to collect information about performance on the test itself, but as an indication of some other condition: for instance, uroscopy was not meant to collect information about the urine, but to make statements about possible illnesses in the person.

3. A test involves a difference in status between the test giver and the test taker: the test giver draws conclusions on the basis of the test which the test taker has to undergo. Usually test givers represent organisations, whereas the test takers are individuals. (The importance of this aspect will become clearer in Chapter 13.)

Psychologists and tests

From the outset psychologists were adamant that they could provide society with good tests about mental functioning. They could make authenticity tests (e.g. for lie detection), qualifying tests (e.g. for personnel selection), and diagnostic tests (e.g. for the assessment of learning difficulties) that went far beyond what was available. These tests would be based on scientific research, inspired by the belief that human nature depended on invariable laws, which science could discover and bring into use. (You may have noticed that none of the pre-scientific, historical examples given above has stood the test of time.) Psychology would do for mental functioning what medical science was doing for physical functioning: provide practitioners with scientifically validated tests they could rely on.

The need for reliable and valid assessment

A first major achievement of psychologists was that they were able to define what good tests were and how this could be assessed in an objective way. Two issues were of importance: reliability and validity.

Reliability

reliability

in test research, the degree to which the outcome of a test is the same if the test is repeated under unchanged circumstances or if an equivalent test is used

By reliability, psychologists mean that the assessment will be the same if it is repeated under unchanged circumstances. For instance, reliable scales imply that you get the same weight if you step on them twice with a few seconds in between or if you weigh yourself on two different scales. Similarly, a reliable psychological assessment means that you will get the same outcome if the assessment is repeated without any intervention or if the assessment is repeated by another professional.

The reliability of a test can be measured by calculating the correlation between two different measurements. For instance, a group of people is given a test twice with a few weeks in between. Then, a mathematical formula is used to express the relationship between the measures. This results in a correlation coefficient, which can in theory vary from −1.00 (when the measurements are each other's opposite), to 0.00 (when the two measurements are not related to each other), to +1.00 (when the measurements indicate the same ordering of participants). In practice, the correlation coefficient in reliability research will be between 0.00 (a useless test) and +1.00 (a perfect test). This is illustrated in Figure 8.1. Over the years, test construction has become so

(a) Scenario 1: A perfect test

	Score 1	Score 2	
person 1	15	15	
person 2	20	20	
person 3	18	18	
person 4	10	10	
person 5	16	16	
correlation coefficient = 1.00			

(b) Scenario 2: A good test

	Score 1	Score 2	
person 1	15	13	
person 2	20	22	
person 3	18	14	
person 4	10	11	
person 5	16	16	
correlation coefficient = 0.82			

(c) Scenario 3: A bad test

	Score 1	Score 2	
person 1	15	14	
person 2	20	11	
person 3	18	20	
person 4	10	14	
person 5	16	22	
correlation coefficient = 0.03			

(d) Scenario 4: A weird test

	Score 1	Score 2	
person 1	15	15	
person 2	20	10	
person 3	18	16	
person 4	10	20	
person 5	16	18	
correlation coefficient = −0.83			

Figure 8.1 The reliabilities of tests expressed as correlation coefficients.

Five people take the same test twice in 3 weeks. The first scenario depicts the ideal situation. Each person gets exactly the same score on the second test-taking as on the first test-taking. This is expressed by the correlation coefficient of +1.00. Scenario 2 depicts a more realistic situation: there are some small differences in the scores, but participants who scored highly the first time also score highly the second time, and people who scored low the first time score low the second time. This is expressed in the correlation coefficient of +0.82. Scenario 3 points to a very bad test: there is no relationship whatsoever between the scores obtained on the first test-taking and the scores obtained on the second test-taking. This is captured by the correlation coefficient of +0.03. Finally, scenario 4 illustrates a situation that would be very alarming: the participants who performed worst on the first test-taking score best on the second test-taking and vice versa. This is represented by the correlation coefficient of −0.83. Such a situation never occurs in reliability research, because it would imply that the first test-taking had a profound impact on those who took it.

professionalised that only test–retest correlation coefficients higher than +0.80 are still acceptable.

The concept of test reliability was introduced in 1904 by the British psychologist Charles Spearman, shortly after his colleague Karl Pearson developed the first useful technique to calculate correlations. Spearman's work was picked up by the American psychologist Edward L. Thorndike, who at that time was writing his highly influential book *An introduction to the theory of mental and social measurements*. From there it spread rapidly throughout the group of psychologists interested in test construction.

Validity

validity

in test research, the degree to which a test measures what it claims to measure; determined by correlating the test results with an external criterion

A valid assessment means that the assessment measures what it claims to measure. Validity implies reliability but goes beyond that. For instance, you can imagine that Byzantine physicians were quite reliable in establishing the colour of urine, but that very often there was no correlation between the colour of the urine and the disease they diagnosed. A similar situation would be present if you tried to predict people's intelligence by measuring the strength of their hand grip. Although you can get reliable measurements of grip strength (which remain stable on repeated tests), knowing this value for a particular person would tell you nothing about that person's intelligence. People with a strong hand grip can have low, average or high intelligence. Similarly, people with a weak grip can have all possible levels of intelligence. So, knowledge about the grip strength of a person gives you no information about the person's intelligence. It is not a valid measure of intelligence. Indeed, as we saw in Chapter 4, many of the first attempts to measure intelligence turned out to be invalid (see the efforts of Galton and Van Biervliet, and the first attempts of Binet).

Validity concerns were present from the very beginning of test construction. For instance, Binet and Simon (Chapter 4) made sure that the items of their intelligence test could be answered by all children up to a certain age (and not, for example, by 5-year-olds but no longer by 11-year-olds). This age-differentiation criterion was based on the assumption that intelligence increases with age through childhood and that this should be reflected in the performance on the items. In addition, the scores on the intelligence tests were compared with the judgements of teachers (or the school results) to see whether they showed the expected relationship with school performance.

Most of the early validation attempts were done in an unorganised way, however, with every test constructor using his or her own home-made method. This changed at the end of the 1940s when the American Psychological Association supported a task force to streamline the various attempts and to write a proper manual on how to establish the validity of psychological tests (which was published in 1954).

Clinical impressions and unstructured interviews do not score high on reliability and validity

A second important finding by psychologists was that the intuitively most appealing way to obtain information about other people, a face-to-face interview, did not score high on reliability and validity. We start with one of the first studies on this topic and then continue with some more recent theorising.

Differences between raters

Hollingworth (1922) ran a study in which 12 experienced sales managers interviewed 57 applicants for 'positions involving personal salesmanship of a well-known service'. The managers were free to discuss anything they pleased with the applicants during the interviews. After the interviews, the sales managers were asked to rank the candidates as a function of their suitability for the job (1 = best candidate, 57 = worst candidate). Table 8.1 shows the results Hollingworth obtained for the first

Table 8.1 Ranks assigned to applicants by interviewers

Lack of agreement of sales managers concerning the suitability of candidates for a sales position. Managers were asked to rank the candidates on the basis of an unstructured interview with them (1 = best candidate; 57 = worst candidate).

Applicant	Sales managers											
	1	2	3	4	5	6	7	8	9	10	11	12
A	33	46	6	56	26	32	12	38	23	22	22	9
B	36	50	43	17	51	47	38	20	38	55	39	9
C	53	10	6	21	16	9	20	2	57	28	1	26
D	44	25	13	48	7	8	43	11	17	12	20	9
E	54	41	33	19	28	48	8	10	56	8	19	26
F	18	13	13	8	11	15	15	31	32	18	25	9
G	33	2	13	16	28	46	19	32	55	4	16	9
H	13	40	6	24	51	49	10	52	54	29	21	53
I	2	36	6	23	11	7	23	17	6	5	6	9
J	43	11	13	11	37	40	36	46	25	15	29	1

Source: Hollingworth (1922: p. 65).

10 candidates. In this figure you can clearly see the disagreement between the different managers with respect to the suitability of the various candidates. (If you are interested, the correlations between the various managers varied from +0.62 between managers 3 and 11 to −0.48 between managers 7 and 9! The mean correlation coefficient over all managers was a meagre +0.15.)

This is what Hollingworth concluded on the basis of his findings:

> The facts shown by the table are instructive enough. Almost any given applicant is likely to receive ratings placing him at any point in the scale, from first position to last. Applicant C, for example, is given position 1 by one judge, 57 by another, 2 by a third, and 53 by a fourth judge; in general he occupies positions all along the scale of 'suitability.' Much the same result is to be observed with all of the applicants. Occasionally an applicant is found whom all the judges tend to judge more or less favorably. Thus applicant 1 may be said to be favorably rated, on the whole, although even here the positions assigned him range all the way from 2 to 36. . . .
>
> When it is borne in mind that these judges were not casual people who were enlisted in the investigation, but expert sales managers, experienced interviewers and directors of personnel, and that the position (salesmanship) for which they were rating the applicants was precisely in the line of work in which they had developed expertness and acquired positions of responsibility, the inference is clear. However much the interview may be improved by better methods of inquiry and report, in its traditional form it is highly unreliable. No better evidence is required than the spectacle of two different expert interviewers, one rejecting an applicant as the most unsuitable of the group of fifty-seven, another selecting him as the choice specimen of the lot.

(Hollingworth 1922: 64–6)

Subsequent research confirmed Hollingworth's finding about the low reliability of unstructured interviews and extended it to validity issues. It has been shown over and over again that on the basis of unstructured interviews there is little correlation between scores given by personnel managers at job interviews and subsequent performance levels (McDaniel *et al.* 1994); there is little correlation between how positively students are evaluated on university intake interviews and their subsequent exam results (Hell *et al.* 2007); and there is little correlation between the impression inmates make on probation panels and their subsequent risk of reoffending (Monahan 1981). Binet around 1900 had already reported that teachers were not able to assess a pupil's intelligence on the basis of an interview (as mentioned in Hollingworth 1922).

First impression and the implicit personality theory

It took psychologists quite some time to find out why decisions on the basis of interviews turned out to be so unreliable and invalid. A major breakthrough came when it was shown that the decisions on the basis of interviews largely depended on the first impression candidates make. This impression is based on the so-called **implicit personality theory** of the assessors, a mixture of stereotypes and individuation information every person has and uses to make predictions about how others will behave (Kunda & Thagard 1996; Schneider 1973). Stereotypes are simplistic views about groups of people based on categories such as gender, race, age, place of birth, profession and appearance. For instance, when you hear that your new roommate will be a Spanish exchange student called Manolo, this activates a number of expectations about what type of person he will be and how he will act. Stereotypes are mostly acquired through observational learning, on the basis of how various groups are treated and how they are represented on television and in the other media. For instance, it has been shown over and over again that physically attractive people are considered to be more interesting and competent than less attractive people (e.g. Eagly *et al.* 1991; Hosoda *et al.* 2003). Along the same lines, it has been observed that overweight people make a less positive first impression, which they must overcome in subsequent contacts (Puhl & Brownell 2001).

implicit personality theory

mixture of stereotypes and individuating information about the associations of personal characteristics that people use to make predictions about how others will behave in social relations

Individuation information refers to everything known about a person as an individual. The more contact one has with a particular person, the more the individuating information replaces the stereotypical views, which are particularly strong on first encounters.

Dougherty *et al.* (1994) showed that if recruiters are not careful, job interviews are to a large extent coloured by first impressions. Candidates who make a positive first impression on the interviewer receive easier questions, with which they have more chance of making a good impression than candidates who make a less favourable first impression. Other research has shown that candidates can improve the first impression they make by paying attention to their appearance and their behaviour (as shown in Figure 8.2). This phenomenon is known as *impression management* (Barrick *et al.* 2009). Such impression management again reduces the validity of an unstructured interview, because fundamentally nothing has changed; the candidate has just learned to make a better first impression on the interviewer.

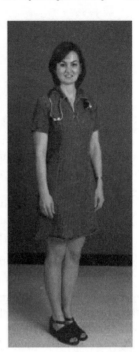

Figure 8.2 Which doctor would you prefer to look after you?

Patients in an Accident and Emergency unit were shown a card with pictures of different physicians and asked who they wanted to look after them: 80% of the patients preferred to be treated by a doctor in a white coat. This was particularly true when the pictures were of female physicians. This figure shows four pictures of the same person that were used on the different cards.

Source: Rehman *et al.* (2005). Reproduced with permission.

? What do you think?

Sometimes people find it hard to believe that their first impression has such a strong influence on their expectations and judgements of others. One situation you may be familiar with, however, is when you first see a person for some time and then hear them talk. Have you ever experienced surprise because the voice was so different from what you expected? The reverse is also true. Often people are astonished when they see a photograph of a radio presenter they know well. They had imagined them completely differently. Can you find other examples of how you automatically seem to activate expectations of people on the basis of small bits of information? For instance, with whom would you prefer to collaborate: Michael or Hubert? And why?

Psychological tests as the alternative

Having found ways to measure the quality of a test and having found that face-to-face interactions with unknown people did not score well, psychologists set out to develop and scrutinise better alternatives.

Structured vs. unstructured interviews

On the basis of their initial experiences, psychologists realised that they had to take away the variability due to assessors and contexts if they wanted to improve the reliability of their assessments. Reliability was adversely affected by factors that varied randomly from observation to observation. For instance, given that the type of questions asked in job interviews depended on the first impression the candidate made, one way to increase the reliability of the procedure was to ask a standard set of questions of each candidate, so that all applicants could be judged on the same core of information. Such a procedure became known as a **structured interview**, as opposed to an unstructured interview, in which the questions depended on the answers the applicants gave. Research later indeed confirmed that structured interviews were a more reliable and valid way of assessing job applicants than unstructured interviews (McDaniel *et al.* 1994; Schmidt & Hunter 1998).

structured interview

interview in which all interviewees receive the same set of questions

Standardised tests

A still better way to limit the influence of biasing factors was to develop and use **standardised psychological tests**. These were tests that psychologists had examined for reliability and validity, for which they had information about the expected performance, and which were administered in a uniform way (so that the performance was not affected by the test giver). Many of these insights were present in a rudimentary form when psychologists started to develop their first tests at the beginning of the twentieth century, but required decades of test development and test research before they were fully understood and implemented. As a consequence, the quality of the tests improved throughout the twentieth century and in all likelihood will continue to do so for some time to come (as psychologists are still working on further improvements of many tests currently used). Below, we discuss the main developments in three of the most frequently used standardised tests: intelligence tests, achievement tests and personality tests.

standardised psychological test

test that psychologists have examined for reliability and validity, for which they have information about the expected performance, and which is administered in a uniform way

Intelligence and achievement tests

IQ tests

In Chapter 4 we saw how Binet and Simon designed the first valid intelligence test. It was no coincidence that the test was proposed around the time when primary school education became compulsory. Suddenly schools were confronted by the fact that not all children were doing well, even though many of them did not show obvious signs of mental limitations. It was not clear whether these children performed badly because they were 'feeble-minded' or because they did not get enough support at home, hence the need for an intelligence test and its enormous popularity once it became available.

Although the IQ test was primarily meant for schools, its aim was not to duplicate school exams. It was not intended as an evaluation of what had been learned, but as an indication of the potential to learn, independent of the circumstances in which the test-taker had grown up. Although the latter seems quite obvious to us now, it took psychologists many years to realise that information-related questions very often showed cultural biases, which advantaged some groups of participants over others. These biases became painfully visible when IQ tests were administered on a very large scale to army recruits in World War I (which the USA entered in 1917) and to

IQ test

test which is supposed to measure the intelligence of a person; focuses on learning potential; results correlate with school performance and suitability for intellectually demanding occupations immigrants. There was a massive difference in test scores between white people with an English-speaking background and those with another background. Although at first this was used as an argument to limit the immigration of people with a non-English background, it gradually became clear that part of the difference was due to the questions used. For instance, in one test participants were given a picture of a tennis court without a net and asked what was missing. Needless to say, those who had never heard of tennis (and there were many of them at the beginning of the twentieth century) failed this particular question. Awareness of cultural biases resulted in increased efforts to make the IQ tests culture-neutral.

Another development in the construction of IQ tests was the finding that intelligence did not consist of a single ability, but of a group of abilities (see any textbook on intelligence for this). This led to a greater diversity of tasks in the IQ tests (most of Binet's tasks had to do with verbal material). The researcher who arguably was the most instrumental in this change was the American psychologist David Wechsler, who developed the *Wechsler adult intelligence scale* in 1939. In this test he measured at the same time so-called verbal intelligence and performance intelligence, the latter being measured with tasks such as picture completion, block design and matrix reasoning. By comparing the verbal IQ with the performance IQ, psychologists could see whether the test-taker had a particular weakness in language functions or in performance functions. The distinction between verbal and performance intelligence was retained in the later tests Wechsler developed for children and preschool children, and encouraged the use of a larger diversity of tasks in other intelligence tests as well.

Achievement tests

achievement test

standardised test which measures the knowledge of a particular topic or set of topics

Quite soon (American) test developers saw that the approach of IQ tests could be combined with that of traditional exams to make so-called standardised **achievement tests**. Seven years after Lewis Terman finished the *Stanford–Binet intelligence test* (the first truly standardised intelligence test in the USA, published in 1916), he was co-author of the *Stanford achievement test*. Achievement tests probed the participants' knowledge of a preset series of topics, to measure the intellectual progress of the participants and their suitability for intellectually demanding positions. To increase their reliability, the tests mostly made use of multiple-choice questions (i.e. for each question a limited number of possible answers is given and the candidate has to indicate which one is correct).

Achievement tests rapidly conquered the educational system. They became the instrument of choice to compare the performance of pupils. In many countries they also started to play a role in the entrance to universities and government positions. For instance, in the USA the scholastic aptitude test was introduced in 1926 and is still administered (under a different name) to almost two million students every year. These students see their university options affected by the results they obtain. Similarly, future employees of the European Union have to pass an entry exam that largely consists of an achievement test.

Achievement tests also became part of the quality control set up by political administrations. For instance, in 1989 the British government not only introduced minimum standards of what had to be taught in primary and secondary schools in England and Wales, it also introduced a system of nationwide achievement tests to assess pupils' performance regularly in the different schools (the so-called Standard Attainment Tests or SATs).

What do you think?

Discuss the importance of reliability and validity for achievement tests. Can you see why parents in England and Wales would be upset if it turned out that the SATs were unreliable or invalid?

Achievement tests were also used to compare whole nations. Table 8.2 shows the results of one such evaluation, looking at science education in different countries. All participants sat the same science achievement test and, on the basis of their results, average scores per country were calculated. Each time the results of such a comparison are published, they are followed by lengthy discussions in governments and in the media about the relative position of their own country and what can be done to improve it (or retain it).

Table 8.2 Standardised achievement tests
Standardised achievement tests are used to compare the performance of schools across countries. This table shows the results of 15-year-olds on a science test administered in different countries, ranked from highest to lowest.

Country	Mean score	Country	Mean score	Country	Mean score
Finland	563	Ireland	508	Israel	454
Hong Kong – China	542	Hungary	504	Chile	438
Canada	534	Sweden	503	Serbia	436
Chinese Taipei	532	Poland	498	Bulgaria	434
Estonia	531	Denmark	496	Uruguay	428
Japan	531	France	495	Turkey	424
New Zealand	530	Croatia	493	Jordan	422
Australia	527	Iceland	491	Thailand	421
Netherlands	525	Latvia	490	Romania	418
Liechtenstein	522	United States	489	Montenegro	412
Korea	522	Slovak Republic	488	Mexico	410
Slovenia	519	Spain	488	Indonesia	393
Germany	516	Lithuania	488	Argentina	391
United Kingdom	515	Norway	487	Brazil	390
Czech Republic	513	Luxembourg	486	Colombia	388
Switzerland	512	Russian Federation	479	Tunisia	386
Macao – China	511	Italy	475	Azerbaijan	382
Austria	511	Portugal	474	Qatar	349
Belgium	510	Greece	473	Kyrgyzstan	322

Source: Based on Figure 2.11b, 'Multiple comparisons of mean performance on the science scale', p. 56, *PISA 2006 Science competencies for tomorrow's world*, 1. OECD 2007. Reproduced with permission.

Achievement tests in China

It may be good to know that the Western society is not the only society that uses achievement tests for entry to highly esteemed positions. Nor, for that matter, was it the first. Some 2,000 years ago the Chinese Han Dynasty (206 BCE–220 CE) used a standardised test battery to select and promote civil servants in an objective way. The administration of these tests became better and better organised (involving a hierarchy of local, regional and national testing centres) to reach the maximum number of candidates. Only those who passed the final (national) set of tests were eligible for office.

There is good evidence that the Western world learned about achievement tests through the Chinese (Kaplan & Saccuzzo 2005: 12). Reports by British missionaries and diplomats in the nineteenth century encouraged the English East India Company to use the Chinese system for the selection of their personnel. From there the practice spread to the British government, the governments of mainland Europe and the USA. Standardised achievement tests still are a central element in Chinese education and the civil service.

Personality tests

personality test

test to measure relatively stable and distinctive patterns of behaviour that characterise individuals and their reactions to the environment

Personality tests are another widely used type of test. They are meant to probe relatively stable and distinctive patterns of behaviour that characterise individuals and their reactions to the environment.

The Woodworth Personal Data Sheet

One of the first personality tests was the *Woodworth Personal Data Sheet*, published by Robert S. Woodworth in 1920 to identify soldiers who would be susceptible to shell-shock (remember that this became a problem in World War I). The test consisted of 116 questions, including:

- Does the sight of blood make you sick or dizzy?
- Are you happy most of the time?
- Do you sometimes wish you had never been born?
- Do you drink whisky every day?
- Do you wet the bed at night?

There were two features of Woodworth's questionnaire that soon turned out to need improvement. First, the questions were mainly based on Woodworth's clinical judgement without properly testing whether they did indeed make a distinction between soldiers who would develop shell-shock and those who would not (although Woodworth did reject questions that in a pre-test had been endorsed by 25% or more of a normal sample in the scored direction). The second feature was that the test started from the assumption that participants would answer all questions honestly, even though the available response alternatives often differed in social desirability.

Going beyond face validity

Woodworth's approach of using his own judgement to decide which questions were informative rapidly turned out to be insufficient. A study by Langner (1962) illustrates this point. Langner also wanted to develop a test that would indicate who was likely to develop psychiatric impairment. He started from a total of 120 questions that looked interesting to him. However, unlike Woodworth, he tested the usefulness of the questions by administering them to a group of 72 participants without psychiatric symptoms and a group of 139 hospitalised psychiatric patients and outpatients. Only 21 questions made a clear difference between the two groups and were retained in the test. Subsequently, these questions were administered to a community sample of 1,660 adult residents to determine from which score onward there was an increased risk of psychiatric problems. So, rather than deciding which questions looked all right, Langner gathered empirical evidence about the usefulness of his questions. He not only took into account the face validity of the test (whether the questions looked valid to him and his colleagues), but also empirically tested this validity. Such evidence-based validation rapidly became the norm for psychology tests.

face validity

estimating the validity of a test by estimating to what extent the items of the test agree with one's own beliefs; is not evidence-based

The problem of social desirability

Another problem that became clear with the publication of Woodworth's Personal Data Sheet was that often the aim of the questions was clear and that participants could adapt their answers as a function of what they thought was socially desirable. One big difference between IQ tests and personality tests is that in the former case the results depend on the test-taker's abilities, whereas in the latter case candidates can choose whatever answer they prefer, even when it does not (really) apply to them. Social desirability refers to the bias people have to present themselves in a manner they think will be viewed favourably by others (in particular, the psychologist who gives the test). This is especially the case in high-stakes situations, where the outcome of the test has implications for the candidate's future (as in job applications; see Ones *et al.* (1996) and Morgeson *et al.* (2007) for the issue of social desirability in this situation).

social desirability

bias people have to present themselves in a manner they think will be viewed favourably by others

Psychologists have explored various ways to circumvent the problem of social desirability. These include making the questions subtler, including a scale to measure the bias in the test-taker, and using formats other than self-report questionnaires. The first two measures were included in the Minnesota Multiphasic Personality Inventory (MMPI), published in 1943 and arguably the first high-profile personality questionnaire used in clinical settings. This test consisted of 566 items selected from an original pool of 1,000. They had to be marked 'true' or 'false' by the test-taker. In the validation process, the test was administered to eight different groups of 50 psychiatric patients each (including 'hypochondriacs', 'depressives' and 'schizophrenics') and a group of 700 control participants. On the basis of the answers of the various groups, items were selected that made a distinction between them and were included in a scale for the different clinical profiles (e.g. hypochondria, depression, schizophrenia). In addition, three so-called validity scales were compiled. Two of these validity scales addressed whether the participants were presenting themselves too favourably, for instance by not wanting to acknowledge minor flaws that are present in virtually everybody (e.g. 'I sometimes lose control of myself'). The third validity scale included items that were virtually never endorsed (e.g. 'I am aware of a special presence that others cannot perceive') and, therefore, could indicate whether someone wanted to make a particularly negative impression.

The validation efforts and the measures to come to grips with the social desirability problem illustrate why psychological tests are more than simply 'collecting a few questions' and why they are capable of returning more information than can be obtained on the basis of a simple interview.

Measuring personality differences in the non-pathological range

Personality tests were not only used to distinguish between the normal and the pathological range. They also became used to distinguish between people in the normal range. Particularly influential in this respect was the trait theory of personality. According to this theory, people differ from one another on the basis of a limited number of **personality traits,** or relatively enduring ways in which they interact with their environment.

The search for personality traits started in the 1930s when the American psychologist Gordon Allport tried to discover the structure that underlies the adjectives people use to describe each other (e.g. 'my left-hand neighbour is polite, helpful and modest, whereas my right-hand neighbour is rude, obstructive and boastful of his wealth'). Allport started from a total of 4,504 adjectives in the English language and set out to see how this number could be reduced. Some adjectives were close synonyms or had largely overlapping meanings (e.g. friendly, cordial, welcoming, amiable, warm). These could be grouped. Other adjectives were opposites (e.g. friendly vs. unfriendly, warm vs. cold). These could be placed at opposite ends of bipolar traits. Allport's main problem, however, was how to do this grouping in an objective way, so that it went beyond his own personal judgement.

Although Allport made some headway (Allport & Odbert 1936), the real breakthrough came when the British psychologist Raymond Cattell joined him for some time at Harvard University. Cattell was a specialist in a new statistical technique to find relationships between stimuli, called factor analysis (see Chapter 11), and he managed to achieve what had eluded Allport. Using a series of studies, he claimed that each person could be described adequately on the basis of 16 bipolar traits, such as reserved–warm, serious–lively, expedient–conscientious, shy–bold and trusting–vigilant. Cattell developed a questionnaire to measure these traits, called the *Sixteen Personality Factors Questionnaire* (Cattell 1956, see Figure 8.3).

personality trait

basic dimension used to describe differences in personality between people; is often bipolar with opposites at the extremes (e.g. introvert vs. extrovert)

A simplified version of the Sixteen Personality Factors Questionnaire
Indicate your position on each scale by placing a mark on each line indicating your position between the extremes.

Reserved	-------------------------------------	Warm
Reasoning: Concrete	-------------------------------------	Abstract
Emotionally reactive	-------------------------------------	Emotionally stable
Deferential	-------------------------------------	Dominant
Serious	-------------------------------------	Lively
Expedient	-------------------------------------	Rule-conscious
Shy	-------------------------------------	Socially bold
Utilitarian	-------------------------------------	Sensitive
Trusting	-------------------------------------	Vigilant
Grounded	-------------------------------------	Abstracted
Forthright	-------------------------------------	Private
Self-assured	-------------------------------------	Apprehensive
Traditional	-------------------------------------	Open to change
Group-oriented	-------------------------------------	Self-reliant
Tolerate disorder	-------------------------------------	Perfectionistic
Relaxed	-------------------------------------	Tense

Figure 8.3 An example of a personality test

Score yourself and a friend by placing marks on each line to indicate your positions on each bipolar trait (e.g. where do you see yourself and your friend on the continuum going from reserved to warm?). Ask your friend to do the same, and compare your answers.

Source: Simplified version of Cattell's Sixteen Personality Factors Questionnaire based on the bipolar traits identified by Cattell (the personality test itself is protected by copyright).

Cattell's conclusions were opposed by Hans J. Eysenck, who argued that Cattell's 16 traits were not independent dimensions and that people only differed on three traits: introversion–extroversion, neuroticism–emotional stability and psychoticism (without antipole). These were measured with the *Eysenck Personality Questionnaire* (Eysenck & Eysenck 1975; Eysenck *et al.* 1985). Further analyses of the data obtained with the different personality questionnaires suggested that Cattell had indeed overestimated the number of personality traits needed to accurately describe people, but that Eysenck had underestimated them. In the early 1980s researchers more or less settled on a total of five fundamental traits, called the Big Five (e.g. Goldberg 1990). They are:

- openness to experience
- conscientiousness
- extroversion
- agreeableness
- neuroticism.

Since 1980, a large number of personality questionnaires have been developed based on this categorisation (which can easily be remembered by using the acronym OCEAN). For instance, in personnel selection it has repeatedly been found that employees who score low on conscientiousness ('I rarely plan my work', 'I tend not to be very organised', 'I rarely check the quality of my work') do not get the best appraisals from their supervisors.

What do you think?

Make a list of the occasions on which you were given psychological tests (IQ, achievement, personality, other). Did you perceive these tests as informative? How would you as a psychologist make use of these tests?

KEY FIGURES Development of personality tests

- **Robert S. Woodworth** (1869–1962)
  - American psychologist and author of very influential textbooks of psychology in the first half of the twentieth century.
  - Author of one of the first personality tests, the Woodworth Personal Data Sheet (measured vulnerability to shell-shock).
- **Gordon W. Allport** (1897–1967)
  - American psychologist who initiated the trait approach in personality research.
  - Sought to find the minimum number of dimensions (traits) needed to describe the personalities of people by analysing the relevant adjectives in the English language.
- **Raymond B. Cattell** (1905–1998)
  - British-born psychologist working in the USA.
  - Used factor analysis to find the minimum number of dimensions needed to describe the personality of people on the basis of adjectives.

- Settled on 16 dimensions that were measured with the 16 Personality Factors Questionnaire.
- Also used factor analysis to look at the structure of intelligence as measured with IQ tests (leading to a distinction between fluid intelligence and crystallised intelligence).

- **Hans J. Eysenck** (1916–1997)
  - German-born psychologist working in the UK.
  - Argued that personalities were adequately described on the basis of three dimensions: introversion–extroversion, neuroticism–emotional stability and psychoticism.
  - Also known for his strong support of behaviour therapy after having shown that the psychotherapies of the 1950s were ineffective.

Hans J. Eysenck
Source: Popperfoto/
Getty Images.

- Various test researchers at the beginning of the 1980s
  - Came to the conclusion that five dimensions are needed to describe personality: openness, conscientiousness, extroversion, agreeableness and neuroticism.

Tests have become increasingly popular due to the individualisation of society

Since their inception the number of psychological tests administered has steadily increased (Hanson 1993). There are several reasons for this. One is that psychological tests are the best way we have to make assessments and predictions about human functioning, even if they are not infallible. Another is that society increasingly turned to science-based evidence to make decisions (Chapters 9 and 13), if only so as not to be found legally liable in case the decision was called into question. Finally, the growing individualisation of society also enhanced the need for information about individuals.

Growing individualisation

As we saw in Chapter 3, individualisation involves looser social relations and a greater focus on the self. This process started several centuries ago (arguably when more and more people left their villages and moved to the emerging cities), but further intensified in the twentieth century. At the beginning of that century, more people agreed with statements like 'Children must stay with their parents until they are married' and 'I respect the decisions taken by my family' than at the end of the century. Conversely, more people at the end of the twentieth century agreed with statements like 'If a social group hinders my development, it is better to leave the group' and 'I want to be judged on the basis of my own achievements'.

Within an individualised society, members are more interested in what distinguishes them from others than in what they have in common. Applied to achievement and personality, they are more interested in what is unique to them than in what they share with others. Personality research has followed this shift. Whereas at the beginning of the twentieth century personality theories were about what defined humans in general (e.g. Freud's and Rogers's theories), towards the end of the century research became dominated by individual differences, as measured by ability and personality tests.

An intriguing question is why Western society has become increasingly individualised and whether such a shift is true for other cultures as well. In addition to the views presented in Chapter 3, another possibility was raised by Kagitcibasi (2002). According to her, researchers in the 1970s thought collectivism depended on the fear parents had that their children would not take care of them in their old age. As a result, children were not encouraged to show initiative and independence. They were expected to obey their parents and stay in close contact with them. However, after the welfare state became established, the elderly were able to rely less on their children, for example because they received a retirement pension. Consequently, the younger generation was given more freedom and was able to become more autonomous and to optimise their individual potential. This tendency may have been reinforced by the dominance of the countries where the individualisation happened first (the UK, the USA).

What do you think?

Does Kagitcibasi's account agree with your feelings? Also have a look at the other factors mentioned in Chapter 3.

Interim summary

Psychological testing

- Psychologists needed reliable and valid assessments. These were not provided by unstructured interviews, due to problems with first impressions and the implicit personality theories people have.

- Standardised tests were proposed as an alternative. These tests were administered to a test group in a uniform way, so that the users knew how new test-takers scored relative to the test group. In addition, the reliability and validity became empirically verified.

- IQ tests allowed psychologists to assess an individual's intellectual potential. Achievement tests allowed them to test the acquired knowledge about a particular topic in a reliable and valid way.

- Good personality tests required empirical validation (i.e. they had to go beyond face validity) and measures to tackle the problem of social desirability.

- In the non-pathological range, most personality tests are self-report questionnaires that measure traits. At the moment most researchers believe that the personality can be described accurately on the basis of five traits (the Big Five). Previously, Cattell defended a minimum of 16 and Eysenck a minimum of 3.

- Tests have become popular partly because of the increased individualisation of society.

8.3 The psychology of work and organisation

An aspect of life that changed beyond recognition in the twentieth century was the type of work people did and the ways in which they interacted at work. Again psychology had a strong involvement in this evolution, not only because an increasing number of psychologists were part of it (e.g. as human resource managers), but also because the different players, from the lowest to the highest level, were inspired by psychological findings. In the previous section we talked about the increased use of standardised tests in personnel selection. In this section we will see how ideas of work motivation changed and how psychology contributed.

Industrial psychology at the beginning of the twentieth century

The industrial revolution in the eighteenth and nineteenth centuries (see Chapters 2 and 3) introduced a separation between work and family. Whereas before, family life and work responsibilities had been closely intertwined on the small farms and in the housebound craftsmen's businesses, the new factories broke up that bond. In addition, the growing size and complexity of companies meant that many workers no longer turned out finished products, but were a link in a much longer production chain.

For most of the nineteenth century and the first half of the twentieth century, employees were considered as 'the hands of the factory'. They were thought to be motivated by physiological needs (to eat, drink, have shelter) and money was seen as their only incentive. Industrial psychology, as it became known at the beginning of the twentieth century, was geared towards improving the efficiency of the work processes and selecting the best applicant for the job. Typical research topics were the minimum number of breaks needed by workers, the most efficient lighting level, or the best organisation of the workplace. In this endeavour, industrial psychology was inspired by the American engineer and inventor Frederick W. Taylor (1856–1915), who improved the productivity of companies by dividing production into a sequence of stages and searching for ways to speed up the stages (this was done, among other things, by measuring the time needed to finish various operations). Taylor (1911) called this approach *scientific management*. Complex tasks (such as building a machine) were split into a sequence of simple actions that could be performed rapidly and easily. This led to the well-known assembly line.

industrial psychology
first theory about how work should be organised; strongly influenced by Taylor's scientific management: employees were the hands of the company that would accept any work if remunerated enough; tasks had to be made simple so that everyone could do them without much practice

In Taylor's view, there was a distinction between thought and action: the management thought and the employee carried out the orders. The management's aim was to simplify the various actions, so that there was no problem finding suitable candidates for the jobs. Wages were set in such a way that the individual worker was motivated to work as hard as possible (e.g. by using a bonus system). One of Taylor's convictions was that a lack of individual monitoring and rewarding encouraged the forming of 'gangs', which tended to oppose productivity, because they feared higher productivity would lead to higher performance standards and eventually loss of jobs. Taylor's basic philosophy was that employees would have no problems performing simple, routine jobs in isolation, if they were paid enough. This formed the foundation for the first views of work and organisation, usually indicated with the name **industrial psychology**.

The Hawthorne studies and the human relations movement

Between 1924 and 1932 a number of studies were run at the Hawthorne plant of the Western Electric Company near Chicago, which would have a profound influence on the psychology of work and organisation. They started off as technical optimisation studies, fully in line with the prevailing scientific management approach. One of the factors the researchers examined was the lighting level for the assemblage of tele-phone relays. Another study looked at the effect of changes in working hours.

Although the studies were not particularly well designed or well performed (Adair 1984; Kompier 2006; also see below), they led one of the researchers, Elton Mayo, to draw a very far-reaching conclusion. On the basis of the studies, Mayo (1945) decided that it was not so much the physical circumstances or the pay that determined pro-ductivity, but the extent to which the workers found themselves valued and esteemed. The various changes the authors introduced had a limited impact, while at the same time the employees involved in the studies outperformed their colleagues. On the basis of these findings, Mayo concluded that performance was higher because the participants knew they were part of a study and because they had a say in the course of the study.

Mayo used the findings in the Hawthorne plant to argue that industrial psychol-ogy was wrong in its emphasis on the physical environment and pay. What counted in the workplace were an employee's social relations and the fact he/she belonged to a group. Informal groups in a company had a strong influence on the workers' well-being and productivity, and good companies looked after these groups. This was the start of the **human relations movement**. Companies were encouraged to acknowledge the humanity of their employees (rather than seeing them as disposable equipment) and make them feel part of a social organisation (e.g. by supporting informal group activities).

human relations movement

second main theory of how work should be organised; stressed the humanity of the employees and the importance of social relations

The human relations movement also pointed to the importance of the ways in which supervisors interacted with their subordinates. They took inspiration from Kurt Lewin's research on attitude changes in youth groups (e.g. Lewin *et al*. 1939). In particular, Lewin had looked at the consequences of three types of leadership: auto-cratic (imposing commands), democratic (leading through negotiations), and laissez-faire (giving no leadership). Lewin and his colleagues concluded that there was more originality, group-mindedness and friendliness in the democratic groups, whereas there was more aggression, hostility, scapegoating and discontent in the laissez-faire and autocratic groups. This message agreed with the wider change that was taking place in Western culture from a 'command society' to a 'negotiating society' (Van Drunen *et al*. 2004: 157).

What do you think?

The citation below suggests that virtual informal groups are becoming increasingly important in companies. Do you agree? How do they complement face-to-face gatherings? What are their advantages? And can something that is written and visible to everyone be informal?

This year London became the biggest city on Facebook, and more than 1.8 million people now identify it as their primary geographic network – about a quarter of London's official real world population.

Businesses, too, are increasingly finding that their workers are gathering in ad hoc groups on the site.

'It's a bit like an electronic smoking room, but one that's spread across the whole company,' says Giles Deards, a spokesman for BT, where about 8,000 work-ers are registered on the company's Facebook network. The group was set up by employees rather than corporate bosses, but workers are not blocked from logging on to social networking sites while in the office.

'It's not an official network; it was set up by staff to discuss issues. We've had some surprisingly liberal conversations on there, but that's because people have taken an adult and responsible approach to it.'

(B. Johnson, *The Guardian,* 15 December 2007.
Copyright Guardian News & Media Ltd 2007)

Human resource management

human resource management

third main theory of how work should be organised; stressed the desire for self-actualisation in employees; employees will perform best if given autonomy and authority

In the 1980s a new approach replaced the human relations movement: human resource management. It stressed more than before that a company's main assets were its employees, who had to be retained and nurtured. The emergence of the human resource management approach was embedded within other major societal changes, such as a change in the type of work that had to be done, and an overall increase in the level of affluence among employees. Most of the monotonous jobs that had made up the bulk of factory work at the beginning of the twentieth century were taken over by robots and computers and were replaced by more intellectually demanding jobs in the service sector. In addition, for many of the new jobs, the

Table 8.3 Evolution of the psychology of work and organisation

A comparison of industrial psychology and human resource management shows how much ideas about the relations between organisations and their employees changed over the twentieth century.

Industrial psychology	Human resource management
Technology comes first.	Social and technical systems are optimised together.
People are extensions of machines.	People complement machines.
People are expendable spare parts.	People are resources to be developed.
Tasks are narrow and individual: skills are simple.	Related tasks make an optimum grouping; skills are multiple and broad.
Controls are external – for example by supervisors, staff, procedures, books.	Individuals are self-controlled; work groups and departments are self-regulating.
Organisation chart has many levels; management style is autocratic.	Organisation chart is flat; management is participative.
Atmosphere is competitive and characterised by gamesmanship.	Atmosphere is collaborative and cooperative.
Only the organisation's purposes are considered.	Individual and social purposes, as well as the organisation's, are considered.
Employees are alienated: 'It's only a job.'	Employees are committed: 'It's my job!'
Organisation is characterised by low risk-taking.	Organisation is innovative: new ideas are encouraged.

Source: Weisbord (1985) reproduced by permission from Elsevier. Adapted and reproduced with permission from Trist, E. (1981) 'The evolution of socio-technical systems – A conceptual framework and an action research program', Toronto, Canada: Ontario Ministry of Labour, Ontario Quality of Working Life Centre, Occ. paper 2. Copyright © Queen's Printer for Ontario, 1981.

relationship between productivity and salary became less straightforward than it had been for manufacturing goods.

Influenced by Rogers and humanistic psychology, psychologists started to consider employees as individuals who sought self-actualisation in their work. It became acceptable to give autonomy and authority to workers and to trust them in terms of discipline. Employees became seen as people who would respond positively to challenges if these contributed to their needs for self-actualisation and autonomy. Management did not have to impose control but give the employees enough trust and responsibility so that they controlled themselves.

Weisbord (1985) published a table that nicely summarises the changes between industrial psychology and human resource management (Table 8.3). With some exaggeration, this table can be considered as the legacy of what the psychology of work and organisation achieved in the twentieth century.

Interim summary

The psychology of work and organisation

- At the beginning of the twentieth century, industrial psychology was under the influence of scientific management which considered workers as dispensable 'hands of the factory', motivated solely by money to address physiological needs.

- Based on the Hawthorne studies, Mayo pointed to the importance of social and psychological factors for the well-being and motivation of employees. This was the start of the human relations movement (e.g. the importance of democratic leadership).

- In the 1980s, human resource management stressed that the employees were the central asset of a company. Workers should not be controlled but given autonomy and responsibility so that they come to self-discipline. Work is no longer a chore, but an opportunity that can help self-actualisation.

8.4 *Focus on*: The lure of idealising classic studies

Without doubt, the Hawthorne studies have played a major role in the history of the psychology of work and organisation. As such, this study is part of all introductory books covering this area of research. It even figures in many general introductions to psychology and educational science, because it shows how knowledge of taking part in a study can have a profound effect on the participants' behaviour (this is known as the 'Hawthorne effect'). However, it is becoming increasingly clear that the Hawthorne studies were of a much lower quality than most people believe. There are even questions as to whether anything relevant was found in the Hawthorne studies at all!

What actually happened at the Hawthorne plant

The discussion below is based on Kompier (2006). A very similar message can be found in Adair (1984) and other critical reviews. Kompier first described what actually happened in the Hawthorne research (references are omitted):

The Western Electric Factory was the supplier of telephone equipment to the last American Bell System. The Hawthorne plant was its main factory. At the start of the studies, it offered employment to some 29 000 men and women, many of them immigrants. The Hawthorne research consisted of the following six, partly overlapping, studies: (i) three illumination experiments (November 1924–April 1927), (ii) the first relay assembly test room (April 1927–February 1933), (iii) the second relay assembly group (August 1928–March 1929), (iv) the mica splitting test room (October 1928– September 1930), (v) the interview program (September 1928–early 1931), and (vi) the bank wiring observation room study (November 1931–May 1932).

(Kompier 2006: 403)

Next Kompier described how the Harvard business professor, Elton Mayo, became known as the main interpreter of the Hawthorne studies (in many later accounts referred to as 'the director of the studies'), even though for the first years he was not involved at all (his first visit to the factory was in 1928) and the bulk of his publications were based on five reports by the real researchers. By the time he published his book *The social problems of an industrial civilization* (1933; see Mayo 1945), the study was not only suspended because of the economic recession but most of the participants involved in the study had been laid off as well.

More importantly, Mayo gave a much embellished version of what actually happened. Kompier (2006: 403–4) listed the following flaws in the first relay assembly study from 1927 to 1933:

● The group consisted of five young women operators and a sixth lay-out operator who distributed the materials among the operators; her income was dependent on the output of the five operators.

● Two operators had initially been selected because they were 'thoroughly experienced' and 'willing and cooperative' and not soon to be married; next, these two operators invited the three other operators.

● The two independent variables (rest pauses and duration of work) were manipulated in a very complicated order, depending on unmotivated decisions by the experimenters and influenced by economic circumstances (e.g. breaks were introduced in period 4, removed in period 12, and then reinstated); in addition, at a certain point in time an additional variable was introduced, consisting of a piecework system based on the average output of the experimental group and not, as before, on the output of the entire department.

● No control group was established.

● At the beginning of period 8 (January 1928) operators 1a and 2a were removed from the experimental group because they were too busy 'talking and fooling'.

In particular the last event illustrates how differently the study was reported by Mayo than it was perceived by those participating in it. Whereas the researcher involved wrote that an obstructive minority had been rejected, Mayo noted that operators 1a and 2a 'dropped out' and were 'permitted to withdraw'. There is good evidence that the former was the correct interpretation, because Mayo himself had previously written of operator 2a in a letter: 'One girl, formerly in the test group, was reported to have "gone Bolshevik" and had been dropped.' Although the two girls had been warned repeatedly and threatened with disciplinary action, they 'did not display that wholehearted cooperation desired by the investigators' (as cited in Kompier 2006: 404).

The above problems are only part of those identified by Kompier. His list made up several pages, making him conclude that the scientific worth of the studies was next to nil and that their impact was solely due to the myth Mayo managed to spread. If the studies were submitted to a journal nowadays, they would be rejected outright because of the many methodological flaws.

Why did the low quality of the Hawthorne studies not prevent them from being taught to students?

Another issue Kompier pondered is why these studies keep being cited and praised in introductory books, despite the fact that the devastating methodological problems have been described many times before. He suggested five reasons:

1. *The story is too good not to be true.* The story that employees worked harder because they received human attention is too seductive not to include in an introductory psychology book. In this respect, the Hawthorne effect resembles an urban legend. Once you have heard the story, you never forget it.

2. *The original researchers published biased and selective reports; later generations simply referred to them without checking the evidence.* A lot of scientific writing is based on secondary sources. Once a 'good story' gets into the literature, it is likely to be quoted without consultation of the original sources (which sometimes are difficult to get hold of, especially if they are old studies).

3. *The underlying message is correct.* The Hawthorne studies also keep being cited because the basic message of the human relations movement – that social and psychological factors are important in the workspace – was correct. The Hawthorne studies should not have been used to promote the human relations movement (and certainly no longer can be, now that we know what really happened!), but this does not detract from the message of the human relations movement that scientific management was flawed in its conceptions of workers' motivation. As such, the Hawthorne message seems to have been 'confirmed' by the subsequent findings and developments.

4. *The story is good for psychologists.* The Hawthorne message (attention and social influences are important on the work floor; supervisors should learn social skills) suits the psychologists' interests. Therefore, they love to teach the story to students.

5. *The story is also good for management.* Finally, Mayo's message that social factors prevail over the physical environment was also good news for the management level. The roles of management are to ensure worker productivity and to control the social processes in the factory, and Mayo reassured the managers that these are indeed important responsibilities. As a result, the Hawthorne studies became included in management books as well.

Because of the above features, a second take-home message of the Hawthorne studies is that you must remain sceptical when you read a glowing text about a 'classic' study that without a shred of doubt seemed to prove a particular point or theory. Writers of scientific textbooks have a tendency to idealise 'old' studies that became turning points in history. They want to present a straightforward and convincing story and as a result are not sufficiently critical when it comes to describing the classics.

Other examples of idealised reporting of 'classic' studies

We wish we could tell you that the Hawthorne studies are a one-off as far as idealised reporting is concerned, but it is becoming clear that such reporting is widespread. Further examples in psychology are the ways in which introductory books write about Rayner and Watson's classic study on the conditioning of fear in Little Albert (Albert was not so easy to condition and was also less afraid of other furry things than often reported; Harris 1979), the case study of the murder of Kitty Genovese (there were not 38 witnesses who saw the murder happen and who could have intervened; Manning *et al.* 2007), the first study 'showing' a positive effect of psychotherapy on the survival rates of cancer patients (the effect could not be replicated; Coyne & Palmer 2007), the influence of the number of words for 'snow' on the perception of the colour white in Eskimos (no such study took place; Martin 1986), the apparatus used by Pavlov in his salivation experiments with dogs (Pavlov rarely used a bell [it scared the dogs] and the picture usually given to illustrate Pavlov's dog shows apparatus used by someone else; Goodwin 1991), and the remarkable case study of what happened to Phineas Gage after his frontal lobes were pierced by a rod (there is actually very little known of what happened to him; Kotowicz 2007). Allchin (2003) reported similar biases in the reporting of studies in biology and medicine.

Given the above examples, it is important to keep in mind that scientific issues have rarely been settled by a single study and that the so-called 'classics' are often idealised crystallisations and hindsight reinterpretations on the basis of much additional research (see also our discussion of Mendel's findings in Chapter 1). Sometimes it is better not to see textbook descriptions of classic studies as reports of what actually happened but as portrayals of 'what ought to have happened' given what we know (believe) now.

The danger of establishing a pseudohistory of science

pseudohistory of science

text that looks like a history of science, but that contains systematic errors because of a desire to present the research as more impressive and important than it was and to depict the scientist as a genius who has to battle against the lack of understanding and appreciation by the peers

Allchin (2004) is less lenient in his appraisal of idealised classic studies in introductory books. He calls them examples of a pseudohistory of science. Although the heroic stories of the discoveries are meant to convey enthusiasm for science and are based on historical events, they are flawed and promote false ideas about how science works (such as: science is faultless, science is entirely fact-driven, discoveries come out of the blue and are met with disbelief, big discoveries are simple findings).

What do you think?

Have you ever read a historical text about a scientific subject? Was this one that presented the materials matter-of-factly, or one that tried to engage you by making the findings more surprising, sensational, important or unbelievable than they probably were? What is better: that people read a popularised history, even though it includes elements of pseudoscience, or that they read no history at all?

Figure 8.4 summaries the features Allchin discerns in the pseudohistory of science. They may help you to spot them in the literature. In the next chapter we will have more to say about how science works and what status it has.

Warning Signs of Pseudohistory

romanticism
flawless personalities
monumental, single-handed discoveries
'Eureka'-type insight
'crucial' experiments only
sense of the inevitable (plot trajectory)
rhetoric of truth-versus-ignorance
absence of any error
unproblematic interpretation of evidence
general oversimplification or idealization
ideology-laden conclusions
author with a narrow agenda

Context is missing:
- no cultural or social setting
- no human contingency
- no antecedent ideas
- no alternative ideas
- uncritical acceptance of new concept

Figure 8.4 Warning signs identified by Allchin (2004) that may help you to identify and avoid pseudohistory.

Source: Allchin (2004). Reproduced with permission.

Interim summary

The weak methodology of the Hawthorne studies

- The Hawthorne studies were not well done, because many aspects were changed simultaneously, so that the authors could not conclude for sure which factor was the origin of the effects they observed.
- Still, strong conclusions were drawn on the basis of the findings.
- These conclusions have been perpetuated in textbooks, because:
  - writers do not read the original sources (certainly if these are difficult to obtain)
  - the story is too good not to be true
  - the basic message of the human relations movement was correct
  - the story strengthened the positions of psychologists and managers.
- The idealised depiction of the Hawthorne studies is an example of the pseudohistory of science, an attempt to excite enthusiasm for science by narrating simplified and heroic stories that promote false ideas of how science works.

Recommended literature

The present chapter was inspired by three books: Jansz, J. & Van Drunen, P. (eds) (2004) *A social history of psychology* (Oxford: Blackwell Publishing); Ward, S.C. (2002) *Modernizing the mind: Psychological knowledge and the remaking of society* (Westport, CT: Praeger Publishers); and Hanson, F.A. (1993) *Testing testing: Social consequences of the examined life* (Berkeley: University of California Press).

If you are interested in the history of clinical psychology, a good book is Reisman, J.M. (1991) *A history of clinical psychology* (2nd edn) (London: Taylor & Francis). Also try to find a text on the history of the mental health services in your country. For the UK this can be Rogers, A. & Pilgrim, D. (2001) *Mental health policy in Britain: A critical introduction* (2nd edn) (Basingstoke: Palgrave Macmillan).

If you are interested in test research, two good books are Gregory, R.J. (2010) *Psychological testing: History,* *principles, and applications* (6th edn) (Boston: Pearson Education); and Kaplan, R.M. & Saccuzzo, D.P. (2005) *Psychological testing: Principles, applications, and issues* (6th edn) (Belmont, CA: Thomson Wadsworth).

A good book on the psychology of work and organisation is Arnold, J. & Randall, R. *et al.* (2010) *Work psychology: Understanding human behaviour in the workplace* (5th edn) (Harlow: Pearson Education).

References

Abma, R. (2004) 'Madness and mental health.' In J. Jansz & P. van Drunen (eds), *A social history of psychology*. Oxford: Blackwell, pp. 93–128.

Adair, J.G. (1984) 'The Hawthorne effect: A reconsideration of the methodological artifact', *Journal of Applied Psychology,* 69: 334–45.

Allchin, D. (2003) 'Scientific myth-conceptions', *Science Education,* 87: 329–51.

Allchin, D. (2004) 'Pseudohistory and pseudoscience', *Science & Education,* 13: 179–95.

Allport, G.W. & Odbert, H.S. (1936) 'Trait-names, a psycho-lexical study', *Psychological Monographs,* 47(1).

Barrick, M.R., Shaffer, J.A. & DeGrassi, S.W. (2009) 'What you see may not be what you get: Relationships among self-presentation tactics and ratings of interview and job performance', *Journal of Applied Psychology,* 94: 1394–411.

Cattell, R.B. (1956) 'Validation and intensification of the Sixteen Personality Factor Questionnaire', *Journal of Clinical Psychology,* 12: 205–14.

Coyne, J.C. & Palmer, S.C. (2007) 'Does anyone read the classic studies they cite? Reflections on claims that psychotherapy promotes the survival of cancer patients', *The European Health Psychologist,* 9: 46–9.

Dougherty, T.W., Turban, D.B. & Callender, J.C. (1994) 'Confirming first impression in the employment interview: A field study of interviewer behavior', *Journal of Applied Psychology,* 79: 659–65.

Eagly, A.H., Ashmore, R.D., Makhijani, M.G. & Longo, L.C. (1991) 'What is beautiful is good, but . . . : A meta-analytic review of research on the physical attractiveness stereotype', *Psychological Bulletin,* 110: 109–28.

Eysenck, H.J. (1952/1992) 'The effects of psychotherapy: An evaluation', *Journal of Consulting Psychology,* 16: 319–24. Reprinted in *Journal of Consulting and Clinical Psychology,* 60: 659–63.

Eysenck, H.J. (1976) 'Learning theory model of neurosis: New approach', *Behaviour Research and Therapy,* 14: 251–67.

Eysenck, H.J. & Eysenck, M.W. (1975) *Manual of the Eysenck personality questionnaire.* San Diego: Educational and Industrial Testing Service.

Eysenck, H.J., Eysenck, S.B.G. & Barrett, P. (1985) 'A revised version of the psychoticism scale', *Personality and Individual Differences,* 6: 21–9.

Foucault, M. (1976) *Surveiller et punir: Naissance de la prison.* Paris: Gallimard. [English translation: Foucault, M. (1979) *Discipline and punish: The birth of the prison.* New York: Vintage.]

Goldberg, L.R. (1990) 'An alternative "description of personality": The big-five factor structure', *Journal of Personality and Social Psychology,* 59: 1216–29.

Goodwin, C.J. (1991) 'Misportraying Pavlov's apparatus', *The American Journal of Psychology,* 104: 135–41.

Hanson, F.A. (1993) *Testing testing: social consequences of the examined life.* Berkeley: University of California Press.

Harris, B. (1979) 'Whatever happened to Little Albert?', *American Psychologist,* 34: 151–60.

Hell, B., Trapmann, S., Weigand, S. & Schuler, H. (2007) 'The validity of admission interviews – a meta-analysis', *Psychologische Rundschau,* 58: 93–102.

Hoffman, J.L. (1949) 'Clinical observations concerning schizophrenic patients treated by prefrontal leukotomy', *New England Journal of Medicine,* 241: 233–6.

Hollingworth, H.L. (1922) *Judging human character.* New York: Appleton & Company.

Hosoda, M., Stone-Romero, E.F. & Coats, G. (2003) 'The effects of physical attractiveness on job-related outcomes: A meta-analysis of experimental studies', *Personnel Psychology,* 56: 431–62.

James, W. (1892) 'A plea for psychology as a "natural science"', *The Philosophical Review,* 1: 146–53.

Jansz, J. & Van Drunen, P. (eds) (2004) *A social history of psychology.* Oxford: Blackwell Publishing.

Johnson, B. (2007) 'Twenty-eight people ask Hugh MacLeod to be their friend each day. What's so special about him? Answer: he may be Britain's most successful Facebooker'. *The Guardian,* 15 December, p. 3.

Kagitcibasi, C. (2002) 'A model of family change in cultural context'. In *Online Readings in Psychology and Culture.* At www.wwu.edu/culture/kagitcibasi.htm.

Kaplan, R.M. & Saccuzzo, D.P. (2005) *Psychological testing: Principles, applications, and issues* (6th edn). Belmont, CA: Thomson Wadsworth.

Kompier, M.A.J. (2006) 'The "Hawthorne effect" is a myth, but what keeps the story going?', *Scandinavian Journal of Work Environment & Health,* 32: 402–12.

Kotowicz, Z. (2007) 'The strange case of Phineas Gage', *History of the Human Sciences,* 20: 115–31.

Kunda, Z. & Thagard, P. (1996) 'Forming impressions from stereotypes, traits, and behaviors: A parallel-constraint-satisfaction theory', *Psychological Review,* 103: 284–308.

Laing, R.D. (1960) *The divided self: An existential study in sanity and madness.* Harmondsworth: Penguin.

Langner, T.S. (1962) 'A twenty-two item screening score of psychiatric symptoms indicating impairment', *Journal of Health and Human Behavior,* 3: 269–76.

Lewin, K., Lippitt, R. & White, R. (1939) 'Patterns of aggressive behaviour in experimentally created "social climates"', *Journal of Social Psychology,* 10: 271–99.

Manning, R., Levine, M. & Collins, A. (2007) 'The Kitty Genovese murder and the social psychology of helping: The parable of the 38 witnesses', *American Psychologist,* 62: 555–62.

Martin, L. (1986) '"Eskimo words for snow": A case study in the genesis and decay of an anthropological example', *American Anthropologist,* 88: 418–23.

Mayo, E. (1945) *The social problems of an industrial civilization.* Cambridge, MA: Harvard University Press.

McDaniel, M.A., Whetzel, D.L., Schmidt, F.L. & Maurer, S.D. (1994) 'The validity of employment interviews: A comprehensive review and meta-analysis', *Journal of Applied Psychology,* 79: 599–616.

McReynolds, P. (1987) 'Lightner Witmer: Little-known founder of clinical psychology', *American Psychologist,* 42: 849–58.

Monahan, J. (1981) *The clinical prediction of violent behavior.* Washington, DC: Government Printing Office.

Morgeson, F.P., Campion, A., Dipboye, R.L., Hollenbeck, J.R. *et al.* (2007) 'Reconsidering the use of personality tests in personnel selection contexts', *Personnel Psychology,* 60: 683–729.

OECD (2007) 'Multiple comparisons of mean performance on the science scale', *PISA 2006: Science competencies for tomorrow's world,* 1.

Ones, D.S., Viswesvaran, C. & Reiss, A.D. (1996) 'Role of social desirability in personality testing for personnel selection: The red herring', *Journal of Applied Psychology,* 81: 660–79.

Puhl, R. & Brownell, K.D. (2001) 'Bias, discrimination, and obesity', *Obesity Research,* 9: 788–805.

Rehman, S.U., Nietert, P.J., Cope, D.W. & Kilpatrick, A.O. (2005) 'What to wear today? Effects of doctor's attire on the trust and confidence of patients', *The American Journal of Medicine,* 118: 1279–86.

Richards, G. (2002) *Putting psychology in its place: A critical historical overview* (2nd edn). London: Routledge.

Rissmiller, D.J. & Rissmiller, J.H. (2006) 'Evolution of the antipsychiatry movement into mental health consumerism', *Psychiatric Services,* 57: 863–6.

Rogers, C.R. (1942) *Counseling and psychotherapy.* Boston, MA: Houghton Mifflin.

Rosenhan, D.L. (1973) 'On being sane in insane places', *Science,* 179: 250–8.

Schmidt, F.L. & Hunter, J.E. (1998) 'The validity and utility of selection methods in personnel psychology: Practical and theoretical implications of 85 years of research findings', *Psychological Bulletin,* 124: 262–74.

Schneider, D.J. (1973) 'Implicit personality theory: Review', *Psychological Bulletin,* 79: 294–309.

Szasz, T.S. (1960) 'The myth of mental illness', *American Psychologist,* 15: 113–18.

Taylor, F.W. (1911) *Scientific management.* New York: Harper & Brothers.

UK ECT Review Group (2003) 'Efficacy and safety of electroconvulsive therapy in depressive disorders: A systematic review and meta-analysis', *The Lancet,* 361: 799–808.

Van Drunen, P., Van Strien, P.J. & Haas, E. (2004) 'Work and organization.' In J. Jansz and P. Van Drunen (eds) (2004) *A social history of psychology.* Oxford: Blackwell Publishing.

Wampold, B.E., Mondin, G. W., Moody, M., Stich, F. *et al.* (1997) 'A meta-analysis of outcome studies comparing bona fide psychotherapies: Empirically, "all must have prizes"', *Psychological Bulletin,* 122: 203–15.

Ward, S.C. (2002) *Modernizing the mind: Psychological knowledge and the remaking of society.* Westport, CT: Praeger.

Weisbord, M.R. (1985) 'Participative work design: A personal odyssey', *Organizational Dynamics,* 13: 4–20. (Table adapted from Trist, E. (1981) *The evolution of socio-technical systems – A conceptual framework and an action research program.* Toronto: Ontario Ministry of Labour.)

Wooldridge, A. (1994) *Measuring the mind: Education and psychology in England, c. 1860 – c. 1990.* Cambridge: Cambridge University Press.

9 What is science?

This chapter will cover . . .

Questions to consider

?

Historical issues addressed in this chapter

- When did the shift from an emphasis on deductive reasoning to an emphasis on inductive reasoning take place? Who were the big names in this transition?
- What impact did World War II have on the philosophy of science?

Conceptual issues addressed in this chapter

- How certain is scientific information?
- Is science a cumulative process, in which knowledge constantly increases?
- Is passive observation the only way of gaining knowledge, according to the empiricists?
- What did the logical positivists claim was the essence of science?
- Is it possible to define a set of criteria that demarcate science (i.e. set scientific knowledge apart from other types of knowledge)?
- What are the shortcomings of the verification principle?
- What was the new insight of Popper about the nature of science?
- What does this mean for the status of scientific theories?
- Why did Popper at a certain moment talk about sophisticated falsificationism?
- What new insight did Kuhn propose? What did his theory look like?
- Why did Lakatos make a distinction between a degenerative research programme and a progressive research programme?
- How did Kuhn's theory inspire the postmodernists?
- In what ways does pragmatism offer an interesting new approach? Why has it been ignored most of the time by the philosophers of science?

Introduction

Are we living in a sci-fi novel where scientists have taken over the world, and democracy is replaced by a tyranny of men and women in white coats?

It seems that every policy and initiative, from climate change to child obesity, now has to be based on what 'the science tells us'. So the new Intergovernment Panel on Climate Change report is hailed as 'a pocket guide for policy-makers' that will tell governments what harsh measures they must impose to cut our carbon emissions, whether voters like it or not.

Discussions no longer start with a political leader telling us 'This is what I believe in.' Instead a little news report will inform us how 'research shows . . .' that some problem or other is getting worse. And where such supposedly scientific research leads, politicians follow.

> Scientists have not really staged a coup. Instead, political leaders lacking ideas or authority of their own are hiding behind scientists, trying to use the status of science to give them something to stand on, rather as tobacco companies once used doctors to advertise cigarettes. And once 'The Science' has spoken on, say, climate change, we are told there is no room for further debate.
>
> (*The Times*, 20 November 2007)

In previous chapters we described the growth of the scientific approach. The time has come to analyse what science stands for. Is it true that 'once science has spoken, there is no room for further debate', as the author of the cited newspaper article disparagingly claims? Do we have to slavishly follow the white coats?

As we saw in Chapter 2, the idea of infallible scientific knowledge was promoted by scientists and positivists at the end of the nineteenth century in their competition with the humanities (cf. the two cultures). Science had proven its worth by producing 'such a wonderful revolution in human affairs' (Draper 1847) and had to be the driver of all future progress. Because science was based on observation and experiment, rather than opinion and dogma, its conclusions were safe and trustworthy. This contrasted with 'the little advance in knowledge produced for two thousand years by the mathematicians and metaphysicians of the humanities' (Draper 1847).

Upon further scrutiny, science's claim of superiority was based on four principles (Gauch 2003):

1. *Realism*. There is a physical world with independent objects, which can be understood by human intellect.

2. *Objectivity*. Knowledge of the physical reality does not depend on the observer. Consequently, 'objective' agreement among people is possible, irrespective of their worldviews. Science aims to uncover this knowledge so that it becomes public, verifiable and useable.

3. *Truth*. Scientific statements are true when they correspond to the physical reality.

4. *Rationality*. Truth is guaranteed because scientific statements are based on sound method. Scientific statements are not arbitrary guesses, but justified conclusions grounded on convincing evidence and good reasoning, and expressed with the right level of confidence.

Given the importance of the scientific method for the guarantee of truth, it is perhaps surprising that few researchers seem to know the specifics of the method. Indeed, the Nobel laureate and biologist Peter Medawar (1969) described how many successful scientists tend to show an expression of both solemnity and shifty-eyedness when asked to describe what their scientific method is: solemn, because they feel they ought to give a weighty answer, shifty-eyed because they have no clue about what to say. According to Medawar this may be because working scientists are too preoccupied with *doing* research to have time to contemplate *how* they do it. Apprentices simply take over the methods of their masters, without giving them much thought. As we will see in this chapter, another reason why scientists are not overly knowledgeable of their research method may be that the advanced writings on this topic tend to be much less reassuring than the message conveyed to the public.

We start this chapter with a recapitulation of the main developments before the twentieth century (see also Chapters 1 to 3). Then we discuss the attempts of the logical positivists at the beginning of the twentieth century to define the specificity of science (as opposed to philosophy and pseudo-science). In the third section we describe how these views were criticised in the middle of the twentieth century and how it was accepted that scientific research proceeds more by venturing possibly wrong ideas, which are subsequently tested. Next, we review evidence showing that research is influenced by the social norms of the research community and how these norms may change. We end with the pragmatic proposal that currently is gaining currency, and with the implications this has for our attitude towards science.

You will notice that in this chapter we include very few psychology examples. This is deliberate, because we want to discuss the ideas about the so-called hard sciences (e.g. physics, astronomy, chemistry) before we apply them to psychology (see Chapter 10). Also, remember that in Chapter 2 we asked you to write down your ideas about science and the scientific method. This is the right time to dig up that sheet of paper and see how far your intuitions got you!

9.1   Thoughts about information acquisition from Ancient Greece to the end of the nineteenth century

Thoughts before the scientific revolution

Plato, Aristotle and the sceptics

Plato was one of the first philosophers to have an explicit opinion of how knowledge is acquired. In Chapter 1 we saw that he defended a strong rationalist view of knowledge acquisition: to understand the Universe, it was more important to rely on reason than on the senses. Human perception was fallible and the observable world was only a shadow of the Real World. In contrast, the human Soul had innate knowledge of the Universe, which could be harnessed.

Aristotle saw more scope for observation and made a distinction between deductive reasoning and inductive reasoning. However, he too was clear that true, theoretical knowledge started from axioms or first principles, from which new knowledge was deduced via so-called demonstrations. Perception was a source of information, but not knowledge itself. The real ideal was knowledge as exemplified by mathematics and geometry. Aristotle was the first to formulate the **correspondence theory of truth**: truth is a property of a statement and is achieved when the statement corresponds with the physical reality. There is an outside reality which governs human existence and which the human mind tries to understand.

A third view originating from Ancient Greece has not been mentioned so far, namely the possibility that humans might not be able to understand the physical reality. This view is known as scepticism and was first proposed by Pyrrho of Ellis (c. 360–275 BCE). Scepticism does not deny the existence of a physical reality, but denies that we can have reliable knowledge of it. Therefore, humans must suspend judgement on all matters of reality. Scepticism influenced Western thought through the book *Outlines of Pyrrhonism* written by the Greek philosopher and physician Sextus Empiricus around 200 CE. This was one of the books translated towards the end of the sixteenth century. It was known to many actors involved in the scientific

correspondence theory of truth

a statement is true when it corresponds with reality. Assumes that there is a physical reality which has priority and which the human mind tries to understand. First formulated by Aristotle

scepticism

philosophical view that does not deny the existence of a physical reality, but denies that humans can have reliable knowledge of it; first formulated by Pyrrho of Ellis revolution, who tried to refute it or, in the case of Berkeley, used it to go one step further and claim that there might be no physical reality at all, just human thoughts (see Chapter 3 on idealism).

Augustine

As the Catholic Church took over education in the Middle Ages, its views became dominant. These came mostly from Augustine (354–430 CE), who adopted Aristotle's logic and sought to reconcile it with Christian theology. This is how Gauch (2003: 50) summarised Augustine's influence:

> For Augustine, the foremost standard of rationality and truth was not Euclid's geometry. Rather, it was Christian theology, revealed by God in the Holy Scripture. Theology had the benefit of revelation from God, the All-Knowing Knower. Accordingly, theology replaced geometry as queen of the sciences and the standard of truth. But Augustine's view of how humans acquire even ordinary scientific knowledge relied heavily on divine illumination . . . His theory of divine illumination claimed that whatever one held to be true . . . one knew as such because God's light, the light of Truth, shone upon the mind.

According to Augustine true knowledge was knowledge based on God's revelations. Augustine's writings would remain dominant until well into the seventeenth century. They were first questioned by a group of scholars at the Universities of Paris and Oxford in the twelfth and thirteenth centuries, but this group had little influence outside the academic world of their universities (see the 'Focus on' section of Chapter 2).

Interaction between theory and experiment: the scientific revolution

Galilei's thought experiments

Galilei is usually credited as the person who convinced the world of the importance of observation and experimentation for the acquisition of knowledge. After all, was he not the one who showed the truth of Copernicus's heliocentric theory with his telescope and who ran the first experiments to decide between theories? As for the latter, a nice illustration can be found in Galilei's final book *Two new sciences* (published in 1638 in the Netherlands because Galilei had been put under house arrest by the Roman Catholic Church; see Chapter 2). In this book Galilei described how he set out to test whether the velocity of a rolling ball was constant, as claimed by Aristotle, or accelerating, as Galilei thought. He took a board 12 cubits long and half a cubit wide (about 5.5 m by 23 cm) and cut a groove, as straight and smooth as possible, down the centre. He inclined the plane and rolled brass balls down it, timing their descent with a water clock – a large vessel that emptied through a thin tube into a glass. After each run he weighed the water that had run out – his measurement of elapsed time – and compared it with the distance the ball had travelled. On some trials the ball would roll for 3 cubits, on others it would roll for the full length of 12 cubits. Galilei observed that the time required for 12 cubits was not four times longer than the time required for 3 cubits, as predicted by Aristotle, but only about twice as long, in line with his own predictions. On the basis of many measurements with the board, Galilei formulated the law of falling bodies, which stated that the distance travelled was proportional to the square of the time travelled ($d \sim t^2$).

Questioning the picture of Galilei as the first experimentalist, Gower (1997) documented how Galilei in reality was a transition figure steeped in the Aristotelian tradition. His 1638 book was not a work in which Galilei presented a new law on the basis of empirical evidence, but a treatise in which Galilei derived a new law from Euclidian geometry on the basis of demonstration, which he subsequently illustrated with a few empirical observations. Galilei also referred more often to thought experiments than real experiments in his writings. Thought experiments were experiments his readers could easily relate to, because they depended on reason and imagination rather than on the use of unknown equipment.

> By using [thought experiments] in an ingenious and convincing manner, Galileo was able to broaden the scope and the concept of experience without compromising its validity. They enabled everyone, using common experience and simple reasoning, to know facts about motion which had not previously been known. And these facts would be both necessary and universal. For example, we can know that, contrary to what was commonly believed, even the heaviest of objects must be travelling only very slowly when they begin falling, for common experience tells us that, when using such an object to drive a stake into the ground, very little will be achieved by dropping it onto the head of the stake from the height of an inch or so, and this must be because, despite its weight, it is travelling only slowly when it hits the stake. In the light of this thought experiment we can know, without needing to perform any real experiment, that all heavy objects must travel slowly when they begin falling.
>
> (Gower 1997: 31–2)

Galilei may have derived his law of motion from real experiments, but he did not use them to convince his readers, because he did not consider them as decisive and he knew that his audience would not buy them either. True knowledge was knowledge resonating with human understanding (i.e. demonstrated knowledge).

? What do you think?

Many people believe psychological findings only when these resonate with their own intuitions. Could this be the current version of 'demonstrated knowledge'? Or do you disagree with the claim that people only accept findings from psychological research if they agree with their own feelings? Give arguments for your position.

Bacon: induction

In Chapter 2 we saw how Francis Bacon promoted the use of systematic observation and inductive reasoning as the road to new knowledge (Bacon 1620). Instead of demonstrated knowledge or divinely revealed knowledge, an inductionist approach had to be followed. Particularly relevant for the present discussion is how Bacon thought research should start off. When investigating a new topic, Bacon recommended beginning with the collection of a large number of facts in a mechanical way, without theoretical prejudice, and to put them into tables for a better understanding.

> . . . after having collected and prepared an abundance and store of natural history, . . . still the understanding is as incapable of acting on such materials of itself, with the aid of memory alone, . . . [W]e put its forces in due order and array, by means of proper

and well arranged, and, as it were, living tables of discovery of these matters, which are the subject of investigation, and the mind then apply itself to the ready prepared and digested aid which such tables afford.

(Bacon 1620: *Aphorisms*, CI–CII)

When deriving conclusions from the tables, Bacon warned readers not to jump to conclusions:

Nor can we suffer the understanding to jump and fly from particulars to remote and most general axioms . . . , and thus prove and make out their intermediate axioms according to the supposed unshaken truth of the former. This, however, has always been done to the present time from the natural bent of the understanding, educated too, and accustomed to this very method, by the syllogistic mode of demonstration. But we can then only augur well for the sciences, when the assent shall proceed by a true scale and successive steps, without interruption or breach, from particulars to the lesser axioms, thence to the intermediate . . . , and lastly, to the most general.

(*Aphorism*, CIV)

Bacon also warned readers not to search exclusively for positive evidence, but to make use of three types of tables. The first comprised of 'Essence and Presence', all instances in which the phenomenon under investigation was present. The second table contained 'Deviation or Absence in Proximity'. It provided a list of instances matched to the first table in which the phenomenon was absent, even though the circumstances were very similar. By putting the second table next to the first, one could see which instances were critical for the phenomenon. For instance, Bacon noticed that whereas the rays of the sun contain heat, the same was not true for the rays of the moon. On the basis of these matched instances, he concluded that light was not critical for heat. Finally, Bacon advised to make a third table of 'Degrees or Comparison', including instances in which the phenomenon was present in different degrees. This again allowed searching for critical characteristics.

In forming axioms, we must invent a different form of induction from that hitherto in use . . . The induction which proceeds by simple enumeration is puerile, leads to uncertain conclusions, and is exposed to danger from one contradictory instance, deciding generally from too small a number of facts, and those only the most obvious. But a really useful induction for the discovery and demonstration of the arts and sciences, should separate nature by proper rejections and exclusions, and then conclude for the affirmative, after collecting a sufficient number of negatives.

(*Aphorism*, CV)

When an examination was done this way (a large-scale, exploratory collection of facts, followed by careful tabulation and by inductive reasoning on the basis of positive, negative and degree instances), Bacon was adamant that it would lead to true, scientific information about the world.

Bacon's recommendations were later ridiculed by von Leibig (1863), who claimed he knew of no successful researcher working in such an imagination-less way. What was the point of fact collection if there was no question or goal behind it? In von Liebig's view there was as much similarity between Bacon's proposals and true scientific research as between the noise produced by a child striking on a drum and real music. Science started from the researcher's imagination, not from blind data collection. In Bacon's defence, it should be recalled that Bacon's full views of the scientific method were much richer and closer to von Liebig's (as we saw in Chapter 2). The first phase of exploratory data collection and tabulation only led to what Bacon called the rudiments of interpretation or the first vintage. Once this vintage was collected, researchers were urged to verify their interpretations by means of further, targeted experimental histories. Indeed, in some of his writings Bacon noted that truth could not be obtained by simply observing Nature; it had to be extracted from her.

What do you think?

Gilles (1996) argued that Bacon's purely inductive approach is gaining new momentum in the current age of massive digital data storage together with the availability of automatic search algorithms. This makes it possible to scan vast databases of stored information for hidden patterns. Do you agree? Which information could be discovered in this way? Do you know of an example?

Newton

Arguably the greatest scientist of the scientific revolution (certainly in Anglo-Saxon writings) is Isaac Newton. As Newton devoted some paragraphs to the scientific method, it is interesting to have a look at them. What did the master recommend? As it happens, his advice was deeply ambivalent about the roles of theory and observation (Gower 1997), to such an extent that it can be used as an illustration of both Aristotle's deductive approach and Bacon's inductive approach. This can be seen in the following two excerpts:

> . . . for by the propositions mathematically demonstrated in the former Books, in the third I derive from the celestial phenomena the forces of gravity with which bodies tend to the sun and the several planets. Then from these forces, by other propositions which are also mathematical, I deduce the motions of the planets, the comets, the moon, and the sea. I wish we could derive the rest of the phenomena of Nature by the same kind of reasoning . . .

> In experimental philosophy we are to look upon propositions inferred by general induction from phenomena as accurately or very nearly true, notwithstanding any contrary hypotheses that may be imagined, till such time as other phenomena occur, by which they may either be made more accurate, or liable to exceptions.

These are two excerpts from the *Principia mathematica*, in which Newton proposed his laws of physics. The first excerpt was part of the original 1687 edition; the second excerpt was added in the third, 1726 edition of the book (Gower 1997). In the 40 years in between, Newton seems to have shifted his preference from deduction (mainly emphasised when he formulated the laws of physics) to induction (particularly important in his works on the diffraction of light and the nature of colour, as published in his 1704 book *Opticks*).

A further puzzling paragraph in the *Principia* is the following:

> But hitherto I have not been able to discover the cause of those properties of gravity from phenomena, and I frame no hypothesis; for whatever is not deduced from the phenomena is to be called an hypothesis; and hypotheses, whether metaphysical or physical, whether of occult qualities or mechanical, have no place in experimental philosophy. In this philosophy particular propositions are inferred from the phenomena, and afterwards rendered general by induction.

This paragraph deals with the thorniest issue of Newton's laws of physics. Newton had proposed mathematical equations describing and predicting the movements in the Universe, but in doing so, he had accepted phenomena he could not explain (gravity, forces having an impact on distant object such as planets). Newton was heavily criticised for this, among others by Leibniz (1646–1716), who objected that the conclusion of every body being attracted to every other body by gravitational force was not 'deduced from the phenomena', as Newton claimed, but postulated. Indeed, Newton (and Galilei before him) had significantly redefined the nature of science. Whereas for Aristotle and his followers science was about finding (final) causes, Newton was satisfied with a mere mathematical description of observations even if the equations included ill-defined variables.

Another reason why Newton wrote the passage about hypotheses may have been in response to the many remarks made by other men of science about possible alternative 'hypotheses' for the phenomena he described (Cajori 1934). Indeed, Newton was extremely sensitive to criticism and resented having to enter into discussion about matters he considered beyond doubt. This is how (Cajori 1934: 671) summarised his interpretation of Newton's passage:

> 'I frame no hypotheses' . . . is . . . an expression frequently quoted to indicate [Newton's] contempt for reckless speculation and his absolute reliance upon observation and experiment. No doubt readers of Newton's *Principia*, of his early published papers on light, and of his *Opticks,* will be puzzled by this absolute declaration, . . . for surely Newton himself framed many hypotheses – as many, perhaps, as any other scientist of note. How is this statement of his position to be reconciled with his actual practice?
> . . . An examination of the various passages in Newton's writings, relating to the use of hypotheses, discloses the rule that experimental facts must invariably take precedence over any hypothesis in conflict with them. Secondly, hypotheses which seem incapable of verification by experiment are to be viewed with suspicion. In any event, one should observe the distinction between exact experimental results and mere suggestions derived from hypotheses.

Gower (1997: 79) came to a similar conclusion about the essence of Newton's scientific method:

> Newton's achievement so far as scientific method is concerned, then, was to identify and use a method which gave scope for emphasis upon the use of mathematical results, as in the *Principia*, and for emphasis upon experimental evidence, as in the *Opticks*. The method is called 'deduction from the phenomena' in the *Principia*, 'experimental philosophy' in the *Opticks*, but its essential features are the same in both treatises. It uses nothing other than deductive reasoning from basic principles or from 'Phenomena', these principles and these 'Phenomena' being established by . . . induction.

So, in Newton's eyes the scientific method was not so different from Aristotle's demonstrations based on deduction, except for the fact that the first principles had to be based on observation, experimentation and inductive reasoning (i.e. Phenomena), rather than on self-evident axioms. Indeed, reading the preface to the *Principia* from this point of view shows how much Newton saw science as the application of deduction (mathematics) to matters of practical certainty as revealed through observation and experiment:

> The ancients considered mechanics in a twofold respect; as rational, which proceeds accurately by demonstration, and practical. To practical mechanics all the manual arts belong, from which mechanics took its name. But as artificers do not work with

perfect accuracy, it comes to pass that mechanics is so distinguished from geometry that what is perfectly accurate is called geometrical; what is less so, is called mechanical. However, the errors are not in the art, but in the artificers. He that works with less accuracy is an imperfect mechanic; and if any could work with perfect accuracy, he would be the most perfect mechanic of all, for the description of right lines and circles, upon which geometry is founded, belongs to mechanics. Geometry does not teach us to draw these lines, but requires them to be drawn, for it requires that the learner should first be taught to describe these accurately before he enters upon geometry, then it shows how by these operations problems may be solved. To describe right lines and circles are problems, but not geometrical problems. The solution of these problems is required by mechanics, and by geometry the use of them, when so solved, is shown; and it is the glory of geometry that from those few principles, brought from without, it is able to produce so many things. Therefore geometry is founded in mechanical practice, and is nothing but that part of universal mechanics which accurately proposes and demonstrates the art of measuring.

(Newton 1687, *Principia*)

KEY CONCEPTS Deductive vs. inductive reasoning

Deductive reasoning

- Is a form of reasoning in which one starts from known statements and deduces new conclusions.
- The conclusions are guaranteed to be true if the known statements are true and if the correct logical rules are followed.
- Usually presented in the form of a syllogism, a logical argument consisting of two premises and a conclusion. For instance,
  - all children younger than 6 months do not yet talk
  - Hattie is a child younger than 6 months
  - therefore Hattie does not yet talk.
- This is the type of reasoning stressed in rationalism, according to which reality can be known by reasoning from innate knowledge (e.g. Plato and Descartes).
- Is used in science to formulate hypotheses on the basis of existing theories, so that the theories can be tested.
- Is the type of reasoning used in daily life to make predictions about specific instances on the basis of general information:
  - if I want to get full marks for coursework essays, I have to submit them before the deadline
  - I want to get full marks for my next essay
  - therefore, I have to submit my next essay before the deadline.

Inductive reasoning

- Is a form of reasoning in which likely conclusions are drawn on the basis of a series of convergent observations.
- The conclusion is not necessarily true. As a matter of fact, certainly in the beginning conclusions are often guesses that turn out to be wrong and have to be replaced.

- Is mostly used:
  - to generalise from a limited number of observations to a general conclusion (e.g. concluding that sparrows are brown on the basis of the sparrows we have seen thus far)
  - to detect correlations between events (e.g. noticing that there are more sparrows in the garden after we put food in the feeder)
  - to make causal inferences (e.g. concluding that there are more sparrows in the garden after we put food in the feeder, *because* the sparrows are hungry and want to get some of the food).
- Is used in daily life to bring order to our many experiences by noticing the similarities and correlations between events, so that general principles can be formulated and mechanisms hypothesised about how these principles operate (see the sparrow example above).
- Is the type of reasoning stressed in empiricism, according to which knowledge is achieved on the basis of experiences and observations.
- Is used in science to work out explanations for observed phenomena (reasoning from effects to causes).

Probabilistic reasoning and the ascent of hypotheses

Inductive reasoning and probable truths

As we saw above and in Chapter 2, inductive reasoning was disapproved of up to (and including) the scientific revolution because it did not guarantee true conclusions. Only deduction was legitimate, as proven by the success of mathematics and geometry. Indeed, we saw how the first natural philosophers, like Galilei and Newton, struggled to convince their readership that the conclusions they drew were not 'mere' products of observation and induction. Even John Locke, the empiricist philosopher, made a distinction between scientific knowledge (which required absolute certainty) and 'judgement' (probable opinion, on which most of natural philosophy was built). Bacon's endorsement of induction was bolder, but he was seen foremost as a philosopher/politician by his peers rather than as a man of science. Also, the research he did often diverged considerably from the recommendations he offered to others, as pointed out by von Liebig (1863).

However, there was little denying that inductive reasoning was exactly what the new scientists were doing: backwards reasoning from observed effects to probable causes. One of the first to explicitly defend the virtues of inductive logic was the Dutch mathematician, astronomer and physicist Christiaan Huygens (1629–1695).[1] In the preface to his 1690 book *Treatise on light* he wrote:

> There will be seen in [this book] demonstrations of those kinds which do not produce as great a certitude as those of Geometry, and which even differ much therefrom, since whereas the Geometers prove their Propositions by fixed and incontestable Principles, here the Principles are verified by the conclusions to be drawn from them; the nature of these things not allowing of this being done otherwise.
>
> It is always possible to attain thereby to a degree of probability which very often is scarcely less than complete proof. To wit, when things which have been demonstrated by the Principles that have been assumed correspond perfectly to the phenomena which experiment has brought under observation; especially when there are a great number

of them, and further, principally, when one can imagine and foresee new phenomena which ought to follow from the hypotheses which one employs, and when one finds that therein the fact corresponds to our prevision.

Two critical assertions in Huygens's text were that:

- It was possible to verify principles from their effects with a degree of probability that was scarcely less than complete proof, when a great number of (observable) phenomena in line with the principles were collected.
- Truth was particularly guaranteed when the principles in addition allowed researchers to make new predictions and to verify them.

A similar positive message about scientific probabilistic reasoning was defended by Leibniz, who compared it to legal practice (as Bacon had done before him). In science, just as in legal affairs, the aim was not absolute truth but truth beyond reasonable doubt, and scientific evidence could be more or less reliable depending on the skills of the experimenters examining and testing the testimony of nature (just as evidence in court depended on the skills of the Lawyers examining the witnesses).

Definition of probability

Induction did not lead to necessary truths but to 'highly probable conclusions'. This, of course, required a definition of probability. Two definitions were proposed. The first involved mathematics and derived from an analysis of betting games. When a game has several possible outcomes, it is possible to calculate the probability of each outcome. For instance, if you throw an unbiased die, you can expect each side to have a 1 in 6 chance of being on top. If you throw two dice, you have 1 chance in 9 of throwing a 4.

Probabilities of outcomes are rather easy to calculate when the underlying mechanism is known (e.g. dice being thrown). However, researchers were confronted with the so-called 'inverse probability' problem: determining how probable a theory was, given a series of observations. An important figure in this tradition was the British Presbyterian minister and mathematician Thomas Bayes (1702–1761). In the final years of his life he developed a theorem that showed how the inverse probability could be calculated on the basis of the *a priori* probability of the theory, the probability of observing the effect given the theory, and the probability of observing the effect in general. The treatise almost got lost because it was only published after Bayes's death.

The French marquis Pierre-Simon de Laplace (1749–1827) was another main figure in probabilistic reasoning. He provided a simple equation to calculate the probability of a scientific law given that it had been replicated n times in succession. This equalled: $(n + 1) / (n + 2)$. So, the probability of the statement 'every morning the sun rises' being true grows as follows with each successive observation of a sunrise:

$$\text{1st morning: } (0+1)/(0+2) = 0.50$$

$$\text{2nd morning: } (1+1)/(1+2) = 0.67$$

$$\text{3rd morning: } (2+1)/(2+2) = 0.75$$

$$\text{4th morning: } (3+1)/(3+2) = 0.80$$

$$\text{5th morning: } (4+1)/(4+2) = 0.83$$

$$\ldots$$

$$\text{100th morning: } (100+1)/(100+2) = 0.99$$

What do you think?

Calculations of the inverse probability critically depend on the assumption that the world remains the same. Taleb (2007) illustrated this dramatically by picturing a Christmas turkey one week before Christmas contemplating its life and trying to predict the future on the basis of its experiences so far. Can you think of other instances in which circumstances altered so dramatically that existing regularities were overthrown?

It soon became clear that the mathematical treatment of probability did not solve all problems, because it required researchers to enter subjective estimates into the equations. For instance, Bayes's theorem required researchers to have information about the *a priori* probability of the theory and the observed phenomenon in general. This information was not provided by the theorem but had to be 'estimated' by the researcher. Because of this prerequisite, a second definition of probability gained prominence. It said that in practice the probability of a scientific theory depended on the researcher's degree of belief in the theory. At the end of the day, the main criterion defining the probability of a scientific theory was how certain scientists felt about it. According to Gower (1997) this definition was first raised by the French polymath Jean d'Alembert (1717–1783). Shapin (1996: 94) observed that because of this definition science was infused by social class. Certainly for the early men of science in Britain, only gentlemen were trustworthy enough to do research:

> That is to say, for such practitioners the disciplining of experience importantly implicated a map of the social order. Experience suitable for philosophical inference had to emerge from those sorts of people fit reliably and sincerely to have it, to report it, or, if it was not their own, to evaluate others' reports of experience. Undisciplined experience was of no use.

An increased appreciation of hypotheses

As the appreciation of inductive reasoning for the advancement of knowledge grew, hypotheses also received a more positive evaluation than had been the case with Newton. A nice illustration of this change is given in the book *Preliminary discourse on the study of natural philosophy* by the British astronomer and physicist John Herschel (1792–1871). In this book Herschel wrote that although scientific reasoning started from observation, it became increasingly more abstract:

> As particular inductions and laws of the first degree of generality are obtained from the consideration of individual facts, so Theories result from a consideration of these laws, and of the proximate causes brought into view in the previous process, regarded all together as constituting a new set of phenomena, the creatures of reason rather than of sense, and each representing under general language innumerable particular facts. In raising these higher inductions, therefore, more scope is given to the exercise of pure reason than in slowly groping out our first results. The mind is more disencumbered of matter, and moves as it were in its own element. What is now before it, it perceives more intimately, and less through the medium of sense, or at least not in the same manner as when actually at work on the immediate objects of sense.

(Herschel 1831: 190)

Tellingly, at this point Herschel did not continue by saying that such reasoning was deductive, as Galilei and Newton would have done, but by arguing that observation-independent scientific reasoning led to truth if done carefully:

> But it must not be therefore supposed that, in the formation of theories, we are abandoned to the unrestrained exercise of imagination, or at liberty to lay down arbitrary principles, or assume the existence of mere fanciful causes. The liberty of speculation which we possess in the domains of theory is not like the wild licence of the slave broke loose from his fetters, but rather like that of the freeman who has learned the lessons of self-restraint in the school of just subordination.
>
> (Herschel 1831: 190–1)

Because scientific theories were to some extent speculative, Herschel acknowledged that it was possible to have different views of the same phenomenon.

> Now, nothing is more common in physics than to find two, or even many, theories maintained as to the origin of a natural phenomenon. For instance, in the case of heat itself, one considers it as a really existing material fluid, of such exceeding subtlety as to penetrate all bodies, and even to be capable of combining with them chemically; while another regards it as nothing but a rapid vibratory or rotatory motion in the ultimate particles of the bodies heated.
>
> (Herschel 1831: 195)

The temporary co-existence of rivalling theories was not bad, because a choice could be made between them by formulating hypotheses and seeing which hypotheses accounted best for the findings:

> Now, are we to be deterred from framing hypotheses and constructing theories, because we meet with such dilemmas, and find ourselves frequently beyond our depth? Undoubtedly not. . . . Hypotheses, with respect to theories, are what presumed proximate causes are with respect to particular inductions: they afford us motives for searching into analogies; grounds of citation to bring before us all the cases which seem to bear upon them, for examination. A well imagined hypothesis, if it have been suggested by a fair inductive consideration of general laws, can hardly fail at least of enabling us to generalize a step farther, and group together several such laws under a more universal expression. But this is taking a very limited view of the value and importance of hypotheses: it may happen (and it has happened in the case of the undulatory doctrine of light) that such a weight of analogy and probability may become accumulated on the side of an hypothesis, that we are compelled to admit one of two things; either that it is an actual statement of what really passes in nature, or that the reality, whatever it be, must run so close a parallel with it, as to admit of some mode of expression common to both, at least in so far as the phenomena actually known are concerned. Now, this is a very great step, not only for its own sake, as leading us to a high point in philosophical speculation, but for its applications; because whatever conclusions we deduce from an hypothesis so supported must have at least a strong presumption in their favour: and we may be thus led to the trial of many curious experiments, and to the imagining of many useful and important contrivances, which we should never otherwise have thought of, and which, at all events, if verified in practice, are real additions to our stock of knowledge and to the arts of life.
>
> (Herschel 1831: 196–7)

The idea that hypotheses were worthwhile conjectures, even if wrong, can also be found in the writings of the British Anglican priest and polymath William

Whewell (1794–1866). In the book *Novum organum renovatum* (1858),[2] he wrote (Section II):

> To discover a Conception of the mind which will justly represent a train of observed facts is, in some measure, a process of conjecture . . . [T]he business of conjecture is commonly conducted by calling up before our minds several suppositions, and selecting that one which most agrees with what we know of observed facts. Hence he who has to discover the laws of nature may have to invent many suppositions before he hits upon the right one . . . A facility in devising hypotheses, therefore, is so far from being a fault in the intellectual character of a discoverer, that it is, in truth, a faculty indispensable to his task. . . . To try wrong answers is, with most persons, the only way to hit upon right ones. The character of the true philosopher is, not that he never conjectures hazardously, but that his conjectures are clearly conceived, and brought into rigid contact with the facts.

Theories influence observations

A final insight formulated before the twentieth century was that the distinction between observations and ideas (including first principles, deductive demonstrations and scientific hypotheses) was not as clear as traditionally assumed by philosophers. Fact and theory depended on each other.

Whewell

The person credited with the insight that observation and theory influence each other is Whewell, who we just met. His text *On the fundamental antithesis of philosophy* (1844) began by summarising the classical distinction between deductive reasoning leading to necessary truths and inductive reasoning resulting in truths from experience.

> Necessary truths are established, as has already been said, by demonstration, proceeding from definitions and axioms, according to exact and rigorous inferences of reason. Truths of experience are collected from what we see, also according to inferences of reason, but proceeding in a less exact and rigorous mode of proof. The former depend upon the relations of the ideas which we have in our minds: the latter depend upon the appearances or phenomena, which present themselves to our senses. Necessary truths are formed from our thoughts, the elements of the world within us; experiential truths are collected from things, the elements of the world without us. The truths of experience, as they appear to us in the external world, we call Facts; and when we are able to find among our ideas a train which will conform themselves to the apparent facts, we call this a Theory.
>
> (paragraph 6)

Whewell called the distinction between thoughts and things, theory and fact 'the fundamental antithesis of philosophy':

> This distinction and opposition, thus expressed in various forms; as Necessary and Experiential Truth, Ideas and Senses, Thoughts and Things, Theory and Fact, may be termed the Fundamental Antithesis of Philosophy; for almost all the discussions of philosophers have been employed in asserting or denying, explaining or obscuring this antithesis.
>
> (paragraph 7)

Then Whewell gave his reasons for why he thought the fundamental antithesis of philosophy was wrong:

> We can have no knowledge without the union, no philosophy without the separation, of the two elements. We can have no knowledge, except we have both impressions on

our senses from the world without, and thoughts from our minds within . . . The two elements, sensations and ideas, are both requisite to the existence of our knowledge, as both matter and form are requisite to the existence of a body. . . .

But though philosophy considers these elements of knowledge separately, they cannot really be separated, any more than can matter and form. We cannot exhibit matter without form, or form without matter; and just as little can we exhibit sensations without ideas, or ideas without sensations; . . .

(paragraphs 8 & 9)

Because fact and theory could not be separated, Whewell argued that it was an illusion to think they referred to neatly distinguished entities:

Not only cannot these elements be separately exhibited, but they cannot be separately conceived and described. The description of them must always imply their relation; and the names by which they are denoted will consequently always bear a relative significance. And thus the terms which denote the fundamental antithesis of philosophy cannot be applied absolutely and exclusively in any case. We may illustrate this by a consideration of some of the common modes of expressing the antithesis of which we speak. The terms Theory and Fact are often emphatically used as opposed to each other: and they are rightly so used. But yet it is impossible to say absolutely in any case, this is a Fact and not a Theory; this is a Theory and not a Fact, meaning by Theory, true Theory. Is it a fact or a theory that the stars appear to revolve round the pole? Is it a fact or a theory that the earth is a globe revolving round its axis? Is it a fact or a theory that the earth revolves round the sun? Is it a fact or a theory that the sun attracts the earth? Is it a fact or a theory that a loadstone attracts a needle? In all these cases, some persons would answer one way and some persons another. . . . We see then, that in these cases we cannot apply absolutely and exclusively either of the terms, Fact or Theory. Theory and Fact are the elements which correspond to our Ideas and our Senses. The Facts are facts so far as the Ideas have been combined with the sensations and absorbed in them: the Theories are Theories so far as the Ideas are kept distinct from the sensations, and so far as it is considered as still a question whether they can be made to agree with them. A true Theory is a fact, a Fact is a familiar theory.

(paragraph 10)

Comte

Much less known is that the founder of positivism August Comte also acknowledged the influence of theory on observation. This is what he wrote in his *Cours de philosophie positive*:

All good intellects have repeated, since Bacon's time, that there can be no real knowledge but that which is based on observed facts. This is incontestable, in our present advanced stage . . . If it is true that every theory must be based upon observed facts, it is equally true that facts can not be observed without the guidance of some theory. Without such guidance, our facts would be desultory and fruitless; we could not retain them: for the most part we could not even perceive them.

(Comte 1830: 8–9; as translated by Martineau 1858)

Idealisation of scientific knowledge

Much of the doubts about the status of scientific knowledge, which figured so prominently in the scientific revolution and the centuries after, were forgotten towards the end of the nineteenth century, when the writings of positivists dominated. After all, wasn't it clear that Galilei and Newton had been right all along? And wasn't it clear that scientific knowledge considerably improved the lives and powers of those who possessed it? Wasn't the advancement of science proof that the initial uncertainties had been part of science's struggle to detach itself from the humanistic tradition of deduction from authority, religion and dogma? Science's victory march was used as an argument to sweep the more critical passages on the scientific method under the carpet. The doubts were rarely read, let alone taught to future scientists or communicated to the wider public. As a result, they became obsolete, gathering dust in libraries.

Interim summary

Thoughts before the twentieth century

- To a great extent, the rise of the scientific approach can be summarised as a shift in balance from deductive reasoning to inductive reasoning. Before the scientific revolution it was generally accepted that only deductive reasoning led to necessary truth (Plato, Aristotle).

- The men of science at first tried to convince their audience that the new way of thinking was very close to traditional deductive reasoning and demonstration (Galilei, early Newton).

- Gradually natural philosophers started to argue that inductive reasoning could lead to conclusions as probable as truth, when facts were collected in large numbers and without prejudice, when effects could be replicated, and when theories led to new verifiable predictions (Bacon, Huygens, Newton in his later years, Bayes, Laplace, Herschel).

- Whewell and Comte further pointed out that there is no clear distinction between observation and idea, between fact and theory. They are closely interconnected and influenced by the other.

- As a result of the successes of science, most of the initial doubts about whether inductive reasoning could lead to true conclusions were swept under the carpet towards the end of the nineteenth century.

9.2 The first twentieth-century attempt at demarcation: observation, induction and verification

Philosophy of science and the demarcation of science

In the early twentieth century a group of philosophers and scientists decided to revisit the specificity of the scientific method. By that time, science's power within Western culture was beyond doubt, magnifying the contrast between the achievements of science and the philosophical doubts about whether inductive reasoning could lead to truth. What was unique to science, making it so influential? Where had philosophy gone wrong? What was the difference between scientific reasoning and non-scientific thinking? Could the scientific method be identified and applied to other domains of knowledge?

The demonstration of science's power was not the only reason why scholars re-addressed the issue of the scientific method. There also was the astonishing finding in the nineteenth century that Euclidean geometry was not the only possible geometry. Ever since the Ancient Greeks, geometry had been the ideal of scientific knowledge, together with mathematics. Here was a field of true knowledge, derived from a very limited set of self-evident axioms by means of pure deductive reasoning. In the nineteenth century, however, it became apparent that Euclid's axioms were not the only ones. Several alternative geometries were proposed, such as hyperbolic geometry, elliptic geometry and Riemannian geometry. Needless to say, this development further diminished the status of deduction.

A final reason why philosophers thought the issue of the scientific method could be settled in the twentieth century consisted of the major advances in knowledge about logical reasoning made in the preceding decades. Maybe now the time had come to decide what science was and to find its **demarcation** criteria, the lines that would define science and its borders.

The new branch of philosophy dealing with questions related to the status and the uniqueness of science became known as the **philosophy of science**.

Logical positivism

The Vienna Circle

The new movement came to prominence in the 1920s when the physicist Moritz Schlick (1882–1936) arranged regular meetings of a group of scholars in Vienna. They were called the Wiener Kreis (Vienna Circle). Well-known members, in addition to Schlick, were Otto Neurath (1882–1945), Hans Hahn (1879–1934) and Rudolf Carnap (1891–1970). Other attendants (who were not officially members but took part in some of the meetings) were Ludwig Wittgenstein (1889–1951) and Karl Popper (1902–1994). In the years leading up to World War II the group became dispersed and many members moved to the USA and the UK, where they continued and extended their work. In addition, they already had close contacts with like-minded philosophers in these countries (e.g. Alfred Ayer and Bertrand Russell in the UK).

The movement became known by the name **logical positivism** (although the British philosophers and Schlick preferred the name 'logical empiricism'). The 'positivism' part referred to the high esteem of the scientific approach shared with Comte's nineteenth-century movement, in particular related to the assumption that scientific knowledge was true knowledge. 'Logical' referred to the preoccupation with language and meaning. The first meetings of the group were largely devoted to a discussion of Wittgenstein's book *Tractatus logico-philosophicus* (first published under a different title in German in 1921; English translation 1922). In this book Wittgenstein argued that language had a logical structure, which limited what could be said and thought about the world. He further claimed that language was a faithful depiction of physical reality and, therefore, that the physical reality could be known by analysing the logical structure of language. Given that the Vienna Circle wanted to demarcate the meaning of the concept 'science', this seemed to be an interesting starting point. What set science apart from other ways of knowledge acquisition and generation? Which set of criteria could distinguish science from non-science (such as religion, voodoo, astrology), so that the scientific standing of new disciplines could be appraised and advice be given to those disciplines about how to become more 'scientific'? Could the definition of science be made universal (i.e. hold for all sciences) and ahistorical (i.e. applicable to all times)?

---

demarcation

setting and marking the boundaries of a concept; used, for instance, in the philosophy of science to denote attempts to define the specificity of science

philosophy of science

branch of philosophy that studies the foundations of scientific research, to better understand the position of scientific research relative to other forms of information acquisition and generation

logical positivism

philosophical movement in the first half of the twentieth century, claiming that philosophy should stop thinking about metaphysics, and instead try to understand the essence of the scientific approach; central tenet was the verification principle

The 1929 manifesto

The outcome of the discussions was a manifesto published in 1929: *Wissenschaftliche Weltauffassung. Der Wiener Kreis* [The scientific conception of the world. The Vienna Circle]. The following conclusions could be distilled from the text (and were further refined in later publications by various members):

1. Truth divides into two types: empirical truths and logical truths.
2. Empirical truths make claims about the world and are established through empirical verification (observation and experiment).
3. Logical truths are based on deductive logic and are influenced by linguistic conventions.
4. Statements not belonging to one of the categories above are meaningless.

It is easy to see how the manifesto built on existing ideas (the distinction between induction and deduction, the need for empirical verification) and entered new ones (the influence of language). The most partisan part arguably was the last declaration, that propositions not based on empirical verification or deductive reasoning were meaningless (i.e. could not be decided as true or false). These included large parts of the humanities (religion, metaphysics, arts, . . .).

According to the logical positivists, science proceeded by means of a cycle consisting of observation, induction and verification. The first step was careful observation of what happened. The next step of the scientific cycle was the translation of individual observations into general conclusions on the basis of inductive reasoning. The ideal here was the formulation of a mathematical law, as had been done by Newton for physics. Such a mathematical law made it possible to have a detailed understanding of what was going on. Finally, the general conclusion (or scientific law) based on observation and induction had to be verified. In particular, the last step, empirical verification, was seen as the demarcation criterion of science: a statement was scientific if and only if it could be verified as true or false through objective, value-free observation. This criterion became known as the verification principle and its requirement for valid knowledge as **verificationism**.

Next to induction, the logical positivists also accepted deductive reasoning as a way of making meaningful statements. However, this type of reasoning could only be used to deduce conclusions from what was already known; it did not generate new knowledge. If the reasoning resulted in new knowledge, the ensuing statement had to be verified anew.

verificationism
adherence to the principle that a proposition is meaningful only if it can be verified as true or false; with respect to science states that a proposition is scientific only if it can be verified through objective, value-free observation

Problems with the verification criterion

The impact of logical positivism was not in the first place due to the new insights it produced (as we have seen, most ideas had already been proposed), but to the questions and criticisms it raised. Below we summarise the most important.

Verification is logically impossible

A first problem the verification criterion encountered had been well-known since Aristotle. Indeed, it was the reason why inductive reasoning had been mistrusted for centuries. It was the fact that it is logically impossible to prove the truth of a conclusion on the basis of repeated observations. In order to move from observation to a general conclusion, one needs inductive reasoning, and inductive reasoning does not lead to conclusions that are guaranteed to be true according to the rules of logic.

A beautiful illustration of the danger associated with inductive reasoning is provided by the saying 'all swans are white'. For centuries Europeans were 100% sure of the truth of this saying, because all the swans they encountered were white. As a result, many languages had the expression 'black swan' to refer to something impossible. Imagine then the surprise when the Dutch explorer, Willem de Vlamingh, in 1697 came across black swans on his discovery voyage to Australia! Here we had a cherished 'truth' based on observation, which in the end turned out to be wrong.

In 1620 Bacon wrote, 'The induction which proceeds by simple enumeration is puerile, leads to uncertain conclusions, and is exposed to danger from one contradictory instance, deciding generally from too small a number of facts, and those only the most obvious' (see above). In what respect was the verification criterion immune to this criticism?

Scientific theories are full of non-observable variables

A further problem the verification criterion encountered was that many scientific theories include non-observable variables. This can easily be illustrated with one of Newton's laws. His second law of motion reads $F = ma$ (force equals mass times acceleration). None of these variables is observable in the sense that they can be directly perceived with the human senses. So, does this mean that Newton's second law is meaningless?

To solve this problem, logical positivists had to accept that not all variables in scientific theories needed to be directly observable, as long as they involved dimensions that could be measured in relatively simple ways: mass could be measured as weight (e.g. in grams), or acceleration as the rate of change of velocity over time (which ultimately boiled down to measuring distances and times). As long as it was possible to calculate the values of non-observable variables, logical positivists argued, it was acceptable to include such variables in scientific theories. Bridgman (1927) proposed the term *operational definition* to denote this requirement (as you may recall from Chapter 5). If you could express variables in numbers by referring to the ways in which you measured them, the resulting law was fine. Otherwise, it was unverifiable and, hence, meaningless. An example of the latter was Hutcheson's 'law' of moral importance discussed in Chapter 5. This 'law' stated that moral importance equalled benevolence times abilities ($M = B \times A$), but did not indicate how variables could be expressed in quantities.

How should we define 'observable'?

Although the criterion that non-observable variables in scientific theories should have an operational definition solved some of the problems, it was not watertight. Some variables require complex, indirect methods to be revealed. Does this still count as an operational definition? Any dividing line between observable and non-observable ultimately turned out to be an arbitrary distinction, as was eventually also recognised by Carnap, one of the founders of logical positivism:

> There is no question here of who is using the term 'observable' in a right or proper way. There is a continuum which starts with direct sensory observations and proceeds to enormously complex, indirect methods of observation. Obviously no sharp line can be drawn across this continuum; it is a matter of degree. A philosopher is sure that the sound of his wife's voice, coming from across the room, is an observable. But suppose he listens to her on the telephone. Is her voice an observable or isn't it? A physicist would certainly say that when he looks at something through an ordinary microscope,

he is observing it directly. Is this also the case when he looks into an electron microscope? Does he observe the path of a particle when he sees the track it makes in a bubble chamber? In general, the physicist speaks of observables in a very wide sense compared with the narrow sense of the philosopher, but, in both cases, the line separating observable from nonobservable is highly arbitrary.

(Carnap 1966, Chapter 23)

The uncertain nature of 'observable' had already played tricks with Galilei, as can be seen in the following excerpt from a letter written by Horky to Kepler, describing one of Galilei's demonstrations with his telescope. In 1610 Galilei had taken his telescope to the house of one of his opponents, Magini, to demonstrate its potential to 24 professors of all faculties. This is how Horky described the event (as mentioned in Feyerabend 1993: 88):

I never slept on the 24th or 25th April, day or night, but I tested the instrument of Galileo's in a thousand ways, both on things here below and on those above. *Below it works wonderfully*; in the heavens it deceives one, as some fixed stars [. . .] are seen double. I have as witnesses most excellent men and noble doctors . . . and all have admitted the instrument to deceive. . . . This silenced Galileo and on the 26th he sadly left quite early in the morning . . . not even thanking Magini for his splendid meal.

Because we now 'know' that Galilei was right, it is easy to forget how shaky much of his empirical evidence looked to his audience.

Non-observables may become observable

The fuzzy border between observable and non-observable was further evidenced by the finding that, over time, many initially hypothesised, non-observable phenomena became observable, because of technical improvements and because the theory allowed the scientists to know what they were looking for (so that they could focus their efforts much more). Probably the most notorious example in this respect is that of the atom. Towards the end of the nineteenth century, leading scientists such as Ernst Mach and Wilhelm Ostwald refused to see atomic theory as a true description of reality, because atoms were unobservable. Therefore, they claimed, atoms had no place in science and should at best be treated as fictions that were helpful to generate new ideas. Although atoms are still invisible in a literal sense (they are too small to be seen with visible light), in the twentieth century it became possible to observe them indirectly with an electron microscope by scanning atoms with an electrons laser.

So, what is unobservable at one point in time may become observable at another point. However, this raises the question of how to make a distinction between hypothesised non-observables that turn out to be empirically verifiable and hypothesised non-observables that turn out not to exist. An illustration of the latter is provided by the 'discovery' of phosphohistidine. In 1963, highly respected American biochemist Paul Boyer published an article in the top journal *Science*, in which he claimed that at last he had found the missing, non-observable substance required according to the prevailing theory for the final stage of the chemical reactions that provide cells with energy (see Allchin 2002 for more details). Chemists had been searching for this substance for more than a decade. Boyer called the substance phosphohistidine and described not only how he had observed it using the latest techniques, but also how he had made sure that it indeed fulfilled some of the roles that were ascribed by the theory to the substance. Phosphohistidine had a huge influence on chemistry for the next 20 years, but in the end turned out to be a red herring. In 1981, Boyer admitted he had been wrong. By that time he had already started to work on a new theory of energy provision in cells that no longer required the intractable intermediate (and for which he was awarded the Nobel Prize for Chemistry in 1997).

Boyer's experiences clearly illustrate the limits of the verification principle in scientific practice. At some point in time, researchers assumed the existence of a substance that could not (yet) be verified. After the substance was empirically 'verified', it turned out not to exist or at least not to have the properties researchers thought it had.

Verifiable observations are no guarantee of correct understanding

The limits of observation, inductive reasoning and verification as the only sources of scientific understanding were further illustrated by the many occasions on which erroneous scientific conclusions had been drawn from empirically verified 'facts'. A well-known example comes from Galilei (which also illustrates that not every scientific claim Galilei made turned out to be true). In one of his writings, Galilei proposed a method to determine the magnitude of the stars (as cited in Chalmers 1999: 25). His method was simple and straightforward. He positioned himself relative to a cord so that the cord just blocked a particular star out of sight. On the basis of the thickness of the cord and the distance of his eye from the cord, Galilei calculated the visual angle subtended by the cord and therefore, so he thought, the visual angle of the star. Based on these observations Galilei calculated the magnitudes of the various stars. What he did not realise, however, was that the apparent size of a star in the sky is largely due to atmospheric scatter (so that stars seem much bigger than they actually are) and that the distances from stars to the Earth vary widely. As a result, Galilei's estimates of the diameters of the stars turned out to be worthless once they were compared to the measurements corrected for these errors. Still, they were based on observable facts that could easily be verified by others.

Positivism as naive idolatry of science?

All in all, rather than solving the demarcation problem of science, the logical positivists testified to the difficulty or maybe the impossibility of doing so. As a result, the term positivism in the twentieth century gained a negative connotation (which suited the humanities). Positivism became associated with the naive (and wrong) conviction that science always resulted in true knowledge and could solve all problems. If it was impossible to define what science was and to prove that its method guaranteed true knowledge, how then could one claim that scientific knowledge was superior to other types of knowledge and that it should have priority in decision making?

Another descendant of logical positivism's failure: a new look at the meaning of words

The demarcation problem not only called positivism into question, it also led to a completely different understanding of language. No-one illustrated this better than Wittgenstein. Above we saw how his book *Tractatus logico-philosophicus* was a source of inspiration for the Vienna Circle. In this book Wittgenstein argued that language was a faithful depiction of the state of affairs in the world and so the world could be known by analysing the logical structure of language. By analysing the meaning of the words and their interrelations, one could get insights into the physical reality.

However, the impossibility of conclusively defining science made Wittgenstein realise that the same was true for many other words in the language. Try to find a set of criteria that fully define the words 'games' (including mind games), 'sports', and their distinction. Wittgenstein understood that, except for artificial categories made by man or society (e.g. 'king' or 'bachelor'), words only loosely referred to the entities they represented. They did not fully define them (as also exemplified by the fuzzy boundary between 'observable' and 'non-observable' we saw above). The meaning of words was determined by their use in a social context, which Wittgenstein called language games. As a result, the meaning of words depended on the circumstances in which they were used. They did not have fixed meanings, objectively depicting the physical reality, as Wittgenstein originally thought.

These insights were posthumously published in Wittgenstein's book *Philosophical investigations* (1953). The transition from the *Tractatus* to the *Investigations* is testimony of the deep changes epistemology went through in the first half of the twentieth century.

What do you think?

Did the verification criterion of logical positivism strike you as reasonable when you first read about it? If so, were you surprised by the criticisms? If not, why did the logical positivists make this mistake? What do you think will happen in future in this area?

Interim summary

Logical positivism

- Logical positivism tried to reconcile the practical success of sciences with the methodological concerns formulated by philosophers.
- It tried to define demarcation criteria for science that would be universal and ahistorical, and that could be applied to other knowledge areas.
- The movement found prominence with the publication of the 1929 manifesto of the Vienna Circle.
- The most important demarcation criterion put forward for empirical truths was empirical verification.
- Almost immediately, however, the criterion met with a series of objections:
  - verification does not solve the induction problem
  - scientific theories are full of variables that cannot be observed directly
  - there are no demarcation criteria that unambiguously define 'observable'
  - sometimes things are not observable until one knows how to search for them
  - verifiable observations do not guarantee a correct understanding.
- Because of the many criticisms, logical positivism failed, which gave positivism a negative connotation of naive belief in the power and the truthfulness of scientific research.

9.3 The second twentieth-century attempt at demarcation: falsification

The more the logical positivists tried to defend observation, induction and verification as the basis of scientific knowledge, the more it became clear that these criteria did not capture the essence of scientific progress. An alternative view was in the making. This came from Karl Popper (1902–1994), an Austrian-born scholar who was educated in the heyday of the Vienna Circle (and attended several of their meetings as a student). Popper published his first important work *Logik der forschung* (The logic of scientific discovery) in 1934. Because of the political situation, he moved to New Zealand in 1937 and to the UK in 1946, where he remained.

Preliminary: perception is more than sensing stimuli

Before we introduce Popper's proposals, we will make a short detour and go back to Comte's and Whewell's understanding that human observation is not theory-independent. This insight made a deep impression on Popper and it is important for you to have a good grasp of it before we embark on Popper's alternative.

Perception requires interpretation

When the logical positivists claimed that science was special because it was based on facts, they assumed that facts could be perceived prior to and independently of any theoretical framework, and that the perception of facts was the same for all careful observers. Unfortunately, there is considerable evidence that this is not the case. As every introductory psychology textbook will tell you, perception involves the interpretation of sensations. To illustrate this, look **at** Figure 9.1.

Figure 9.1 very much resembles the fragmented reality researchers are confronted with when they try to understand a phenomenon on the basis of the facts they observe. Each black blob represents an isolated observation. Different groups of researchers try to understand the different blobs. For instance, a group of a few hundred (thousand?) scientists is working on the second blob of the first line in Figure 9.1, trying to understand

Figure 9.1 An illustration of the fragmented reality researchers are confronted with when they observe facts.

Source: Edith Brysbaert.

Figure 9.2 **An illustration of how a general theory of a phenomenon may alter the way in which scientists are able to examine the 'facts' (blobs).**
Source: Edith Brysbaert.

its functioning by carefully observing what happens and using experiments to verify whether their understanding is correct. Another group of scientists is trying to understand the blob below. Both groups may inform each other of their findings, although there is no real need to do so, as both phenomena are thought to be independent.

Now suppose someone comes along with a theory of what the overall framework might be, how the different components fit within a larger organisation, as shown in Figure 9.2. At that moment, the situation alters dramatically for the scientists. Although the facts are still the same, they suddenly have a completely different meaning, because they are part of a much wider organisation.

A theory changes the perception of the facts

What Figure 9.2 illustrates is that the understanding of a scientific phenomenon involves more than simply sensing the isolated facts. It involves an element of interpretation to understand what the different facts mean and how they relate to each other. Once such an interpretation has been found, the meaning of the originally observed facts changes spectacularly. Look back at Figure 9.1: is it possible for you now not to see the girl any more, and to see the figure as you saw it at first?

If you think the situation depicted in the Figures 9.1 and 9.2 is exaggerated, just think of the efforts astronomers had to make in order to come up with a model of the universe that would explain the observable movements of the Sun, the Moon, the planets and the stars! Also think of how the perception of the world changed, once it was realised that the Earth was not flat but round. Or how the field of chemistry changed, once the periodic table was discovered.

A theory enables scientists to focus on the important facts

A theory not only changes the perception of the facts, it also allows scientists to search in a more directed way. It helps them to sort out the avalanche of facts and to decide which facts are important and which are not. Figure 9.2, for instance, shows that not all blobs are equally important for the overall interpretation and, therefore, a better understanding of some blobs is more crucial than the understanding of others.

Without a theory, scientists do not know which observations are important and which are not. For instance, in the nineteenth century much energy was invested in determining the exact weights of the chemical elements. This was done because researchers believed that the relative weights of the elements would provide them with information about the structure of the elements. In particular, it had been observed that the weights of the chemical elements tended to be multiples of the weight of hydrogen, the lightest element. Therefore, it was hypothesised that all matter consisted of combinations of hydrogen atoms (for example, oxygen was about eight times heavier than hydrogen, suggesting that oxygen consisted of eight hydrogen atoms). Once it was realised that the different chemical elements have their own composition, it became clear that their relative weights were not at all important and researchers could drop this particular line of investigation.

The above examples illustrate just how difficult it is to maintain that facts are perceived prior to and independently of background knowledge (theory). What humans observe depends on what they know (or think they know). The more observers know about a particular phenomenon, the richer their perceptions. Botanists see more in meadows and marshlands than people without knowledge of plants; radiologists see more in X-rays than people without such training. The same is true for scientists, as became known in the nineteenth century. The impact of theory on observation was downplayed by the positivists, but taken up again by Popper.

Popper: falsification instead of verification

Science constantly questions its explanations

Popper fully accepted the importance of theories in scientific thinking. What distinguishes science from non-science, he argued, is not that the former is based on facts (observations, verifications) and the latter on ideas (dogma, prejudices). Both proceed by constant interactions between observation and interpretation. However, what sets science apart is that it constantly questions its explanations, whereas non-scientific movements have no such inclination.

Popper was particularly intrigued by the difference between physics and Freudian psychoanalysis. Both claimed to be a science. However, studies in physics were primarily aimed at suspected weaknesses of the theories (remember that physics at the turn of the twentieth century went from Newton's physics to Einstein's relativity and subsequently to quantum physics). In contrast, studies in psychoanalysis mainly consisted of trying to find corroborating evidence for the theory.

Although physics arguably had a sounder basis (given that Newton's ideas had been successful for over 200 years, whereas Freud's were still very much in the making), its researchers predominantly tried to achieve progress by making sure that no errors had been overlooked. Psychoanalysts, on the other hand, tried to make progress by gathering observations in favour of their view. Popper noticed a similarity between this approach and the approach advocated by religions and sects. As Chalmers (1999: 59) wrote:

> Popper himself tells the story of how he became disenchanted with the idea that science is special because it can be derived from the facts, the more facts the better. He became suspicious of the way in which he saw Freudians and Marxists supporting their theories by interpreting a wide range of instances . . . in terms of their theory and claiming them to be supported on this account. It seemed to Popper that these theories could never go wrong because they were sufficiently flexible to accommodate any instances of human behaviour or historical change as compatible with their theory. Consequently, although giving the appearance of being powerful theories confirmed by a wide range of facts, they could in fact explain nothing because they could rule out nothing.

Falsification instead of verification

Because of the problems related to verification, Popper argued that what distinguishes scientific from non-scientific theories is that scientific theories are falsifiable. According to **falsificationism**, statements that cannot be falsified because they make no clear predictions are not scientific. This is, for example, the case for statements like: 'You may feel better tomorrow' and 'God shows his love in multiple ways'. These are not falsifiable, because all possible outcomes are in line with them.

A theory is falsifiable if it rules out a range of outcomes, or if there is agreement about observations that would be inconsistent with the theory and, therefore, refute the theory. A statement like 'It rains more on Wednesdays than on Thursdays' is falsifiable, because failing to observe a difference in rainfall between Wednesdays and Thursdays invalidates the statement.

Popper pointed to the logical superiority of falsification over verification. Whereas it is impossible to prove the truth of an inductive conclusion, it is easy to prove the falseness of an inductive conclusion. All you need is one counterexample. Whereas the truth of the saying 'all swans are white' was not proved by the observation of thousands of white swans in the Western world, the observation of a single black swan in Australia sufficed to demonstrate the falseness of the statement. Therefore, Popper stressed, hypothesis testing should not be directed at trying to confirm a theory (which is futile, or puerile, in Bacon's words), but at seeing whether the theory could be falsified. If researchers repeatedly tried to reject a theory and failed to do so, they had strong evidence about the correctness of the theory. On the other hand, as soon as a test falsified the theory, they knew the interpretation was a false trail.

falsificationism

view within the philosophy of science that statements are scientific only if they can be falsified empirically

> **? What do you think?**
>
> If you've taken a course on statistics, you know that a statistical test consists of trying to reject the null hypothesis. Can you see how this fits in with falsificationism?

In later writings Popper pointed to the need not only for falsifiability, but also for a commitment by the proponents to put their ideas to the test effectively. Many statements in psychoanalysis and astrology could in principle be put to the falsification test but Popper saw little enthusiasm in their advocates to do so. All they tried to do was find evidence in favour of their statements.

hypothetico-deductive method

model introduced by Popper to understand the scientific method; on the basis of observation, induction and educated guesswork, a theory of a phenomenon is formulated; the correctness of the theory is evaluated by the formulation of a testable prediction (hypothesis) on the basis of deductive reasoning; the prediction is subsequently put to a falsification test, which provides new observational data for further theorising

> **? What do you think?**
>
> Is the horoscope below falsifiable? And is it ever likely to be falsified?
> 'You will be feeling more like your old self today, as the influence of the earth element increases, making things a lot more settled.'

The hypothetico-deductive method

To further illuminate the role of falsification in scientific reasoning, Popper introduced the **hypothetico-deductive method** (which, he argued, went back to Whewell and can also be found in some preliminary form in many other authors). According to this method, scientific progress involves a combination of inductive and deductive reasoning (Figure 9.3). On the basis of observation, induction and educated

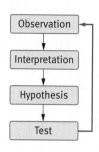

Figure 9.3 The different steps of the hypothetico-deductive method.

The step from observation to interpretation is based on inductive reasoning, the step from interpretation to hypothesis on deductive reasoning. The observation and test stages make sure that the scientific explanations are empirically grounded. According to Popper, the hypothesis must be directed at a possible falsification of the interpretation/theory.

guesswork, an interpretation (theory) of a phenomenon is formulated. To check the correctness of the interpretation, the researcher uses deductive reasoning to generate a testable prediction. This prediction (hypothesis) is next put to the test by means of an experiment. The result of such a test provides new observational data for further theorising and new predictions, and so on. The novel element Popper introduced was that hypothesis testing must be based on falsification instead of verification.

An example of the use of the hypothetico-deductive method is the way in which the French chemist Louis Pasteur (1822–1895) in the nineteenth century discovered why wine, beer and milk turn sour. Through inductive reasoning he came to the tentative conclusion that this might be due to organisms introduced in the liquids from the environment, contrary to the prevailing explanation that the souring was a result of spontaneous changes in the liquid. Pasteur hypothesised that if his interpretation was correct he should be able to prevent the souring by putting a filter between the liquid and the air, which blocked organisms from entering the liquid. Finding such a filter would falsify the spontaneous account and would add evidence to Pasteur's alternative interpretation. Pasteur was able to show that an air filter did indeed prevent the souring of wine and beer, but not (quite) the souring of milk (which in addition needed to be boiled to kill the germs already present in it).

Degrees of falsifiability

A further distinction Popper made was that not all falsification tests had the same status. There were different degrees of falsifiability, and the degree to which a statement or theory exposed itself to falsifiability was informative. The more falsifiable a theory was, the higher its scientific status. Consider the following two statements:

1. Wine sours because of organisms.

2. Wine sours because of bacteria coming from the air.

Because of its higher specificity, the second statement is more prone to falsification than the first and, therefore, according to Popper has a higher scientific standing. The clearer and the more precise a theory, the higher its status if it stands repeated falsification tests. Another important variable is the scope of a theory: the more facts a theory explains, the better it is.

Popper was particularly impressed by Eddington's test of Einstein's theory of general relativity. Einstein had predicted that rays of light would bend as they passed close to a massive object. Eddington decided to make use of a solar eclipse in 1919 to test this prediction (see Figures 9.4a and b). Expeditions were sent to two different places where the observation conditions were best. One was led by Eddington himself to the island of Principe off the West African coast, and one was to northern Brazil. Each expedition was to take pictures of the sky during the eclipse and also on a night when the stars were at exactly the same position relative to the Earth without the interfering presence of the Sun (Eddington had to wait for several months before these conditions were met at his site). Although the results were less clear-cut than Eddington had hoped for (Coles 2001), they still convinced nearly all researchers involved that the data were in agreement with Einstein's predictions and significantly different from what was predicted by Newtonian physics. There was a significant difference between the perceived location of the stars during the eclipse and the perceived location without the interfering sun. In addition, the magnitude of the deviation was within measurement error of the deviation predicted by Einstein.

This, Popper argued, was science at its best: an extremely falsifiable theory was put to the test. There were hundreds of reasons to expect no difference in the perceived location of the stars at the time of the eclipse and at the time of the reference measurement; there was only one reason to expect the predicted difference, namely that Einstein's theory and his calculations were right. Without Einstein's theory the odds of finding the expected deviation were next to nil.

Figure 9.4a How a solar eclipse looks.

The white part around the occluded sun is called the corona.

Source: © UC Regents/Lick Observatory. Reproduced with permission.

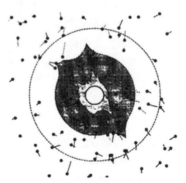

Figure 9.4b Changes in star positions during the eclipse in 1922 in Australia.

How the position of the stars, as viewed from Earth, differs on the day of a solar eclipse and on a comparison night. The eclipsed Sun is represented by the circle in the middle of the diagram. Stars too close to the Sun cannot be seen because of the corona. The recorded displacements of the other stars are represented by lines. The differences observed were only predicted by Einstein's relativity theory. Therefore it was a strong test of the theory, as the chances of the theory being falsified were much higher than its chances of being confirmed.

Implications of Popper's proposals for science's status

Science proceeds by trial and error

Because theories in Popper's view were generated with no guarantee of correctness, Popper was the first philosopher of science to wholeheartedly accept that scientific explanations could be wrong, even when they initially seemed to be in line with the collected evidence (i.e. have passed the first few falsification tests). As a matter of fact, he argued that scientists were never fully sure of the correctness of their scientific explanations, given that these were based on inductive reasoning. All the scientists could say was that a particular theory thus far had passed the various falsification tests and, therefore, was likely to be correct. They also had a lot of information about explanations that were wrong, because these did not pass the falsification test. Theories can be proven false, but cannot be proven true; they are just the best available, the ones that (thus far) have passed the tests.

Because there is no guarantee that scientific explanations are correct, Popper argued that progress in science is best seen as a process of trial and error, in which many possible explanations are ventured and only the fittest survive. On the positive side, the ruthless falsification ensures that scientists are less likely to stick to wrong opinions than people who do not critically evaluate their opinions. At some point in time, a wrong scientific theory will hit on a falsification test it cannot pass and will have to be replaced by a (hopefully) better theory. In this respect, science learns from its mistakes. On the negative side, however, falsificationism implies that scientists can give wrong advice if they base their advice on wrong theories that have not yet been falsified.

What do you think?

Popper's view of science as a trial and error enterprise puts scientific advice in another light. Apply this to the scientific advice below, given by the behaviourist John Watson about how to educate children. He gave this advice in the full conviction that it was right, because it was in line with the latest findings of behaviourism. Try to evaluate the advice within a Popperian framework and within the framework of the logical positivists. In what respects will your evaluations differ?

> Never hug and kiss [children], never let them sit in your lap. If you must, kiss them once on the forehead when they say goodnight. Shake hands with them in the morning.

> (Watson 1928; as cited in Birnbaum 1955)

Falsification goes against human intuition: the confirmation bias

The fact that it took philosophers so long to discover the power of the falsification test may be related to the finding that falsification is a very counterintuitive way of thinking. When confronted with a statement, humans have a tendency to assess the validity of the statement by searching for corroborating evidence rather than trying to make sure there is no possibility to refute the statement.

The tendency to use verification instead of falsification, and the power of falsification over verification, are beautifully illustrated by an experiment published in 1960 by the British psychologist Peter Wason. He presented participants with cards on which a series

Can psychological research be the origin of popular myths about psychology?

Lilienfeld *et al*. (2010) published a book about 50 great myths of popular psychology. In this book, they picture the most common misconceptions about human behaviour. When reading the book, it is striking to see how many of these misconceptions (arguably more than half) have their origins in psychological research. The sequence of events is as follows. A researcher proposes a counterintuitive hypothesis for which there is some evidence. Falsification tests subsequently show that the hypothesis was wrong after all. However, in the meantime the hypothesis managed to find its way to the larger public, where it is exaggerated and continues to be presented as truth.

These are some of the myths listed by Lilienfeld *et al*. with a scientific origin:

1. Most people use only 10% of their brain power.
2. Subliminal messages can persuade people to purchase products.
3. Playing Mozart's music to infants boosts their intelligence.
4. Adolescence is inevitably a time of psychological turmoil.
5. Most people experience a midlife crisis in their 40s or early 50s.
6. When dying, people pass through a universal series of psychological stages.
7. Hypnosis is useful for retrieving memories of forgotten events.
8. Individuals commonly repress the memories of traumatic events.
9. Intelligence tests are biased against certain groups of people.
10. The defining feature of dyslexia is reversing letters.
11. Individuals can learn information, like new languages, while asleep.

The fact that research can be the origin of popular myths is a further reminder that not all hypotheses proposed in scientific research turn out to be true. Only after repeated falsification attempts can researchers have some certainty about the validity of their conjectures. In this respect, it is ironic that Lilienfeld *et al*. (2010) end their book with new 'psychological findings that are difficult to believe but true' (because they are based on scientific findings). Among the findings reported by Lilienfeld and colleagues, quite a few still seem to have the status of interesting hypotheses that require a fair bit of falsification testing, such as:

1. People asked to hold a pencil with their teeth find cartoons funnier than do people asked to hold a pencil with their lips.
2. An unusually large number of people live in places with names similar to their first name (e.g. George living in Georgia).
3. People's handshakes reveal their personality traits.
4. Dogs resemble their owners.

Before long these new 'truths' may enter popular discourse in some exaggerated form, while further research indicates that the evidence for them is not quite as strong as originally thought . . .

of three numbers was printed, for instance '2, 4, 6'. Wason told the participants that they could ask as many questions as they thought necessary to find out the rule according to which the numbers had been generated. The rule Wason had in mind was 'each number is larger than the previous one'. This rule could easily be found by generating theories and trying to falsify them. For instance, a participant's initial theory could be that the experimenter added 2 to each number. This theory could be falsified by asking the experimenter whether the sequence '1, 2, 3' was a valid sequence. If this sequence was valid, then the participant knew for sure that his or her initial theory was false and had to be replaced by another theory. On the other hand, if the sequence '1, 2, 3' turned out not to be valid, then the participant had further evidence for the initial theory and could try out another falsification (e.g. by asking 'is 6, 4, 2 a valid sequence?'; see the illustration box).

ILLUSTRATION How falsification can be used to find out which rule generated the sequence 2, 4, 6

Trying to find the rule that generated the sequence 2, 4, 6

Initial theory: 'Each number is generated by adding 2 to the previous number'.

Try to falsify the theory. One way of reasoning could be: 'If the theory is correct, then the sequence 1, 2, 3 should be invalid (as each number is generated by adding 1 to the previous number)'. Test this.

Two possible outcomes:

- *1, 2, 3 turns out to be valid*. Then the initial theory is wrong and a new theory must be generated (e.g. that each number is generated by adding the same amount to the previous number; this new theory can be falsified by asking whether 1, 2, 5 is a valid sequence).

- *1, 2, 3 turns out to be invalid*. This is in line with the initial theory that 2 has to be added to each number and a new attempt to falsify the theory must be made (e.g. by asking whether 6, 4, 2 is valid; this allows the participant to test whether subtracting 2 from the previous number is permitted).

As you can imagine, Wason did not observe many participants using falsification (only 21% found the correct rule). The majority of participants started from the theory 'add 2 to each number' and asked questions to verify this theory, such as 'is 1, 3, 5 a valid sequence?' and 'is 14, 16, 18 a valid sequence?'. In other words, the participants asked questions to which they expected a yes answer. They did not ask questions that would have required the experimenter to say no. The tendency people have to search for evidence that confirms their opinions is known in psychology as the confirmation bias. Notice how this bias prevented the participants from finding the correct rule. After a few trials they said they knew the answer and that it was 'add 2 to the previous number' (because all the evidence they had gathered was in line with this rule).

confirmation bias

tendency people have to search for evidence that confirms their opinion; goes against falsificationism

---

? What do you think?

Try to find evidence in favour of the opinion 'smoking is good for your health'. Can you see how such selective evidence-gathering may strengthen health-hazardous opinions in people who use the confirmation bias? How could you use falsification to test the correctness of this opinion?

In one go, Wason's experiment illustrated the weakness of verification (which resulted in the confirmation bias) and the strength of falsification to unearth the truth. If participants thoroughly tried to falsify each rule they came up with and if at some point they generated the correct rule, they were bound to find the solution Wason had in mind at the outset of the experiment. This was in line with Popper's recommendation of how scientists should work: they should generate bold theories as speculative and tentative conjectures, and then ruthlessly put them to the test on the basis of experiment and observation.

At the same time, because falsification was so important for scientific progress and so counterintuitive, for the first time philosophy of science made an important contribution to the education of science. Here was a novel insight to teach to new scientists and to use in the evaluation of new branches of knowledge claiming to be scientific. Unfortunately, as is true for many discoveries, the application of the falsification criterion turned out to be more complicated than at first thought.

Sophisticated falsificationism

Do not give in too easily

Popper's approach was soon perceived by the philosophers of science as more fruitful to the understanding of scientific progress than logical positivism. However, it had its problems too. In particular the idea that theories should be rejected as soon as they were falsified did not seem to be in line with the way in which scientists worked. Scientists did not throw away a theory as soon as some data contradicted it. First, they investigated whether the data were sound, so that they did not reject a theory on flawed grounds. Second, if they were convinced of the soundness of the evidence, they examined whether the theory could be amended so that it incorporated the new finding. Most of the time theories contain several variables that can be adapted to accommodate a deviating finding.

A particularly compelling example of how a deviating observation may lead to a modification of the existing theory concerns the problems the motion of Uranus caused for Newton's laws of physics. In the nineteenth century it became undeniable that Uranus's path deviated too much from Newton's laws to be acceptable. According to falsificationism, this should have been the signal to give up the theory and look for something new. An alternative, however, was proposed by Leverrier in France and Adams in the UK. They put forward the suggestion that Newton's laws could be saved if there was another planet in the neighbourhood of Uranus that influenced its orbit. The astronomers started to calculate where the new planet should be and how big it should be. On the basis of these calculations it was possible to inspect the designated part of the sky more thoroughly. This eventually led to the discovery of Neptune.

Episodes like the one above illustrate that science is more than simply rejecting falsified bold conjectures and replacing them with equally bold alternative conjectures. Often it is better to adapt an existing, good theory so that it is no longer contradicted by the available empirical evidence. If scientists had always given up their theories as soon as they were confronted with some negative evidence, they arguably would have none left! Even Popper eventually agreed that scientists should not give up their theories too easily:

> I have always stressed the need for some dogmatism: the dogmatic scientist has an important role to play. If we give into criticism too easily, we shall never find out where the real power of our theories lies.

(Popper 1970: 55)

Modifications of theories in the light of counterevidence

If modifications of existing theories are allowed, the next question, of course, is which modifications are acceptable and which are not. Popper himself pointed out that a modification must under no condition make the theory less falsifiable. As a matter of fact, the theory should become more falsifiable as a result of the modification. The postulation of a new planet to save Newtonian physics in the light of the disturbing evidence from Uranus's motion was an acceptable modification, because it led to a new falsifiable prediction, namely that a certain planet should be observed in a certain region of the universe. In contrast, modifications that were not testable or that made a theory less falsifiable were unacceptable to Popper. He called them ad hoc modifications.

ad hoc modifications

modifications to a theory that according to Popper make the theory less falsifiable; decrease the scientific value of the theory

A clear example of an ad hoc modification was the response of the adherents of the phlogiston theory when it was discovered that some materials weighed more after being burnt than before. Remember from Chapter 7 that the phlogiston theory for some time 'explained' why certain materials were highly flammable and others not. The idea was that highly flammable materials contained a lot of an invisible substance, phlogiston, which was released during the fire. This theory predicted that materials should weigh less after being burnt than before, which was contradicted for some materials by a series of careful observations. In order to save the phlogiston theory, some adherents ventured the possibility that phlogiston could have a negative weight for some materials, so that these materials became heavier when the phlogiston was released. According to this view, phlogiston was not only invisible but also could not be weighed! This increased lack of falsifiability is a tell-tale sign of unscientific thinking.

Unfortunately, the situation about allowable and unallowable modifications was not as simple as suggested by Popper. Researchers could go a long way to modifying their theories with falsifiable amendments without making any scientific progress. This was illustrated by the following hypothetical scenario from Lakatos, obviously inspired by the events surrounding the discovery of Neptune:

> The story is about an imaginary case of planetary misbehaviour. A physicist of the pre-Einsteinian era takes Newton's mechanics and his law of gravitation (N), the accepted initial conditions, I, and calculates, with their help, the path of a newly discovered small planet, *p*. But the planet deviates from the calculated path. Does our Newtonian physicist consider that the deviation was forbidden by Newton's theory and therefore that, once established, it refutes the theory N? No. He suggests that there must be a hitherto unknown planet *p'* which perturbs the path of *p*. He calculates the mass, orbit, etc., of this hypothetical planet and then asks an experimental astronomer to test his hypothesis. The planet *p'* is so small that even the biggest available telescopes cannot possibly observe it: the experimental astronomer applies for a research grant to build yet a bigger one. In three years' time the new telescope is ready. Were the unknown planet *p'*; to be discovered, it would be hailed as a new victory of Newtonian science. But it is not. Does our scientist abandon Newton's theory and his idea of the perturbing planet? No. He suggests that a cloud of cosmic dust hides the planet from us. He calculates the location and properties of this cloud and asks for a research grant . . .
>
> (Lakatos 1970: 100–1)

Measuring skulls

If the above hypothetical example looks far-fetched to you, see what happened when the great nineteenth-century French scholar Paul Broca (see Chapter 6) encountered data that did not agree with his ideas. Broca was heavily involved in attempts to investigate whether the major differences observed in the brains of people were associated with individual differences in functioning. (The brains of individuals differ as much in their appearance as, for instance, faces. Brain imagers who work with a limited number of patients know after some time who a particular brain image is from by simply looking at it, just as we can identify people by looking at their faces.)

One rather straightforward and generally accepted hypothesis was that there would be a positive correlation between the size of a brain and the intelligence of the person: the larger the brain, the more intelligent the person. And indeed the pattern of carefully measured specimens initially seemed to bear out the prediction. For instance, an analysis of brains of high-performing individuals showed that famous people like Cromwell, Byron and Cuvier had brains weighing more than 1,800 g, well above the male average. Other measurements showed that males had larger brains than females, that adult people had larger brains than the elderly, and that Europeans had larger brains than natives from Africa and America (you can find a review of these findings in the first volume of the *Journal de Médecine Mentale* (1861), in an article entitled 'Du volume et de la forme du cerveau').

However, in 1862 Broca was given a collection of 60 skulls excavated from a cemetery in a poor Basque village in Spain. As can be seen in Figure 9.5, the highly unexpected finding was that these people had consistently larger brains than the Parisians! Here is how Broca responded to this finding (translated from Broca 1863: 11–13):

> The average skull capacity of the Basque people is . . . larger than that of the total group of the Parisians. Only inferior to the skulls from the Morgue, it surpasses . . . the capacity of the skulls of the aristocrats from the Middle Ages . . . and even that of the skulls of the bourgeoisie from the nineteenth century.
>
> What could be the reasons for this unexpected result? The skulls in all samples have been collected without selection, so that the relative proportion of skulls of the two sexes should be more or less the same in all samples. A comparison of the Parisian samples has shown the influence of the social class on the volume of the head. The skull of a modern bourgeois is more voluminous than that of a proletarian; it is also more voluminous than that of an aristocrat from the Middle Ages; this would establish that

	NOMBRE de crânes.	CAPACITÉ moyenne.
Crânes de la Cité	116	1,427.57
Crânes des Innocents	117	1,409.23
Crânes du (Sépult^{es}. partic^{ss}	90	1,484.23
xixe siècle (Fosse commune	35	1,403.14
Les deux séries précédentes	125	1,461.53
Crânes de la Morgue	17	1,517.29
Tous les crânes parisiens réunis	384	1,437.24
Crânes des Basques	60	1,486.88

Figure 9.5 Original table from Broca (1863).

This shows the larger brain capacities in 60 Basque skulls than in 384 Parisian skulls (there were five different sources for the latter). The mean size of the Basque people was 1,487 cm^3; that of the Parisians 1,437 cm^3. Only one small Parisian sample (coming from the Morgue) outperformed the Basques.

in the same race, the progress in civilization, comfort and education coincides with a growth of the brain. But this evidently cannot be the reason of the great capacity of the skulls in the Basque people. Those skulls come from a poor village cemetery, from a backward and ignorant populace that vegetated in the darkness . . .

The substantial capacity of the skulls is, therefore, a natural characteristic of this race. However, M. Broca is far from concluding on the basis of this that the Basque people would be more intelligent than the people from Paris. As a matter of fact, the intelligence does not depend solely on the volume of the encephalon; it also depends on the relative development of the different regions of the brain. The brains of the Basque people are, on average, larger than ours; but this would only be an indication of superiority if they had the same shape, if, for instance, the frontal region were in absolute or in relative terms as developed as ours. So, M. Broca has measured separately the main parts of the head, and he has discovered that *the anterior skull is, in absolute terms, smaller in Basque people than in Parisian people*. It is the considerable development of the occipital region that gives the Basque skulls their big capacity. (Italics in original)

So, rather than giving up his theory in the face of falsifying evidence, Broca introduced a modification to salvage the theory: the Basque people had larger skulls, not because they were more intelligent (or because intelligence was not correlated with brain size), but because the brain parts unrelated to intelligence were larger. Notice that this modification would have been acceptable for Popper as it was based on empirical evidence and increased the falsifiability of the theory. All that was needed was to set up a study to test the new claim (which, as far as we know, never happened).

It is important to realise that Broca is by no means an exception. Everyone reading primary scientific literature (i.e. original research reports) will be familiar with this type of wriggling by authors who are confronted with evidence that does not fit their theory, and who propose all types of modifications without testing them.

Why researchers do not like to give up theories

The reason why scientists in general do not like to give up their theories is not so much that they have to admit they were wrong (although this is sometimes a problem for the researcher who initially proposed the theory), but that rejecting a theory means the scientists have to start all over again. They have to search for a new, plausible theory that explains everything the previous theory explained plus the novel, contradictory finding. This, arguably, is one of the hardest challenges in science.

Remember the Wason task we discussed above. There we said that: 'If participants thoroughly tried to falsify each rule they came up with and *if at some point they generated the correct rule,* they were bound to find the solution.' The condition in italics is the bottleneck: someone has to come up with the correct idea, before falsificationism leads to progress. Falsificationism by itself does not lead to the correct explanation; it only eliminates wrong ideas. As long as no-one ventures the right interpretation, falsificationism is a dead end. This is what Einstein meant when he wrote: 'A theory can be proved by an experiment; but no path leads from experiment to the birth of a theory' (as cited in Andrews 1987: 264). For that reason, scientists need convincing evidence before they are willing to give up their favourite theories.

Although Popper's insights of falsificationism and the unacceptability of ad hoc modifications were important steps forward, they did not explain why most of the time researchers tend to cling on to their theories in the light of counter-evidence and why at other times they are willing to give up a theory in search for a new conjecture. A model that does a better job in this respect was proposed in the 1960s by Thomas Kuhn.

Interim summary

Popper's falsification alternative to logical positivism

- Science is better considered as the formulation of theories (on the basis of inductive reasoning and educated guessing) that scientists subsequently try to falsify by deriving hypotheses which are put to the falsification test; this is the hypothetico-deductive method.

- There is no guarantee that an initially proposed theory is correct; therefore, science proceeds by trial and error.

- Science differs from non-science because (1) the theories can be falsified and (2) there is a willingness to do so.

- Falsification is a better criterion than verification, because it is logically possible to falsify a statement based on inductive reasoning.

- The more falsifiable a theory is (depending on its level of detail and scope), the better the theory is.

- Falsification is counterintuitive because people have a bias towards trying to confirm their opinions rather than trying to reject them.

- Limitations of falsificationism:

  - Popper's insistence on replacing falsified theories by bold alternatives as soon as they are contradicted by empirical observations does not agree with scientific practice and would also seem to be too radical.

  - When researchers are confronted with conflicting evidence, they first try to modify the existing theory so that it can account for the contradictory finding.

  - According to Popper, modifications are acceptable as long as they do not make the theory less falsifiable; otherwise, they are unacceptable ad hoc modifications.

  - Problem: researchers regularly propose modifications they do not test and that are not taken up by other researchers. Is this still science?

9.4 Science is a succession of paradigms

Thomas Kuhn (1922–1996) was an American physicist who, after taking his PhD, first turned to the history of science and then to the philosophy of science. His best-known publication is *The structure of scientific revolutions* (first published in 1962; second, revised edition in 1970). Kuhn agreed with Popper about the priority of theory over observation. In his view too, science did not in the first place proceed from fact to theory, but on the basis of conjectures that were mercilessly tested. Even more than Popper, he stressed that all observations and theoretical concepts were dependent on the language of the adopted theory/conjecture. He also emphasised the pressures that are present in the science community to keep individual scientists within the confines of the prevailing research tradition. Only certain research questions are considered to be of interest by the majority of researchers; in addition, these questions must be examined in well-specified ways. Researchers that do not adhere to these conventions are seen as mavericks and are ostracised, as we will see below.

Kuhn's theory of scientific progress

pre-science → normal science → crisis → revolution → new normal science
→ new crisis → . . .

Figure 9.6 Different stages in Kuhn's theory of scientific progress.

The general layout of Kuhn's theory

Pre-science

Figure 9.6 shows the general layout of Kuhn's theory. In his view, each research discipline starts with an unorganised amalgam of facts, observations and models to explain small-scale phenomena (i.e. the situation illustrated in Figure 9.1). Figure 9.7 shows another example of this situation. Researchers try to understand isolated facts (the black lines) without having an idea of the wider framework. As a consequence, their explanations often contradict each other (e.g. the explanation of one fact is incompatible with that of another fact). They also do not agree about the methods to use.

The creation of a paradigm

At some point in time, a general framework (theory) is proposed (Figure 9.8). This not only informs the researchers about the interrelations of the various blobs, but they also gain an idea of the methods that must be used to properly investigate the different facts. In Kuhn's terms, at that moment the researchers share a paradigm, a set of common views of what the discipline is about and how the problems must be approached. This is the start of science. The paradigm will determine:

paradigm

notion introduced by Kuhn to refer to the fact that scientists share a set of common views of what the discipline is about and how problems must be investigated

1. what is to be observed and scrutinised,

2. which questions should be asked,

3. how the questions are to be structured, and

4. how the results of scientific investigations should be interpreted.

Figure 9.7 Pre-science stage of Kuhn's theory.

Researchers have a collection of facts, observations and models to explain these facts. There is not yet a general theory that integrates the different findings within an overall framework. There is also no agreement yet about the precise research methods to be used.

Source: Adapted from Fisher (1968). Reproduced with permission.

Figure 9.8 Normal science stages of Kuhn's theory.

When researchers start to use a common theoretical framework to investigate the different facts (i.e. that the lines represent a swan), according to Kuhn they have a paradigm. This paradigm determines which facts should be examined, how this should be done, and what types of explanations are allowed.

Source: From Isa Brysbaert, based on Fisher (1968).

Normal science

Once the researchers share a paradigm, the discipline finds itself doing normal science. This involves attempts to falsify the theory, to see how strong the theory is. If there is a consistent deviation between the theory and a line of findings, a modification or extension is introduced to capture the intractable fact without changing the core of the paradigm (as indicated above). Although there is no explicit ban, researchers are not expected by their colleagues to question the paradigm and to come up with incommensurable, bold conjectures. If they do so, they will find themselves ostracised, which will result in difficulties in obtaining money for their research and having their papers published.

Kuhn also called the stage of normal science puzzle-solving, because researchers work on familiar topics using well-known techniques and practices. They have confidence that they will be able to solve the puzzle using the available tools. They are guided (governed) by the rules of the paradigm.

Crisis and revolution

Inevitably, according to Kuhn, the phase of normal science will yield results that cannot be accounted for by the paradigm. At first, these findings are seen as anomalies, unexplained observations, rather than falsifications, and researchers will question the quality of the findings or look for ways in which they can be explained with the use of modifications to the existing theory. Again, inevitably (in Kuhn's view) the anomalies will multiply and become more severe. They will require an increased use of ad hoc modifications and changes to the theory that other researchers do not find interesting enough to test (like Broca's proposal about the magnitude of the different brain regions). Because of the proliferation of ill-substantiated modifications, the original framework will become increasingly incoherent and cluttered, resulting in a state of affairs very similar to the pre-science situation. Scientific progress stalls and confidence in the paradigm is undermined. In Kuhn's term, the discipline finds itself in a state of crisis.

At the time of a crisis, a scientific discipline is more open to bold, alternative conjectures that question the core of the paradigm. These alternatives must provide the same level of detail and falsifiability as the existing paradigm and, in addition, provide a better interpretation for the deviating findings. In particular, scientists are looking for a conjecture that allows the discipline to make progress again, to yield new predictions that can be falsified and stand the test.

A particularly interesting distinction in this respect was introduced by the Hungarian born mathematician, Imre Lakatos (1970). He called a paradigm that does not allow its adherents to make new predictions and that requires a growing number of post hoc modifications to explain conflicting findings, a degenerative research programme. In contrast, a paradigm that allows the formulation of novel, hitherto unexpected facts he labelled a progressive research programme. Dienes (2008: 48) used the following colourful description to illustrate the difference between the two types of programmes: 'In a progressive programme, theory keeps ahead of the data; in a degenerating programme, theory lags behind the data, desperately trying to adjust itself to keep up.'

Kuhn called the replacement of a paradigm in crisis by an incompatible, new paradigm that makes new predictions and that repeatedly stands the falsification test, a scientific revolution. During a scientific revolution, a *paradigm shift* takes place, in which the old paradigm (the degenerative research programme) is replaced by a new paradigm (the progressive research programme). This is a time of intense scientific progress. Suddenly, a lot of facts which were previously not understood start to make sense. It is a time of enormous scientific excitement (because of the major breakthroughs that are made in rapid succession), unlike the everyday ebb and flow that characterises normal science.

To give you an idea of what happens during a scientific revolution, have a look at Figure 9.9. It contains the same facts as Figures 9.7 and 9.8. However, because of the shift in paradigm, the meaning of the facts has changed emphatically. What

degenerative research programme

notion introduced by Lakatos to indicate a paradigm that does not allow researchers to make new predictions and that requires an increasing number of ad hoc modifications to account for the empirical findings

progressive research programme

notion introduced by Lakatos to indicate a paradigm that allows researchers to make new, hitherto unexpected predictions that can be tested empirically

Figure 9.9 Crisis stage in Kuhn's theory.

During the crisis phase in Kuhn's theory, a paradigm in crisis is replaced by an incompatible, new paradigm that enables the prediction of new, hitherto unexpected facts, which subsequently stand the falsification test (i.e. the lines do not come from a swan but a squirrel). Kuhn called this a paradigm shift.

Source: From Isa Brysbaert, based on Fisher (1968).

researchers previously believed to be a head (metaphorically speaking) suddenly turns out to be a tail! No wonder the scientists did not understand the facts within the previous paradigm and had to revert to increasingly degenerative modifications of their theory.

Examples of scientific revolutions

Astronomy provides several examples of degenerative theories that were replaced by incompatible new ones. The most famous, of course, is that of the Copernican revolution, when geocentrism was replaced by heliocentrism (see Chapter 2). Another example around the same time was the replacement of circular orbits by ellipsoid orbits. Copernicus had started his model of the universe by assuming that all movements of the celestial bodies were circular. This required him to work with epicycles, to explain the observed movements of the sun and the known planets (the 'wandering stars'; Figure 9.10). Each time a significant deviation was noticed between the predicted movements and the observed movements, a new epicycle had to be added post hoc (i.e. after the deviation had been observed). In the end, Copernicus needed more than 30 of them (which he claimed was still less than the geocentric model of Ptolemy and Aristotle).

At the beginning of the seventeenth century the German astronomer Johannes Kepler proposed a theory according to which the orbit of a planet around the Sun was ellipsoid rather than circular, with the sun in one of the foci of the ellipse (Figure 9.11). This model was not only simpler; it also allowed for new predictions about the speed of the planets.

Incidentally, both examples of Copernicus and Kepler illustrate that scientific revolutions do not always happen overnight, as the name may suggest. As we saw in Chapter 2, Copernicus first wrote about his model in 1514, more than a century before Galilei started to defend it! Similarly, Kepler published his ideas about the

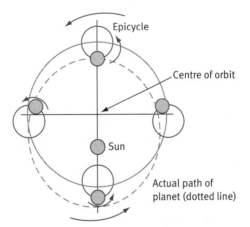

Figure 9.10 The use of epicycles to explain the movement of a planet around the Sun in Copernicus's model of the universe.

To approach the observed path of the planet, Copernicus had to assume (1) that the Sun was not at the centre of the orbit of the planet, and (2) that the planet not only moved in a circle around the Sun, but in addition in a circle around the first circle, a so-called epicycle. Because in some cases the predictions still did not fully match the observations, a further epicycle on the first epicycle was required.

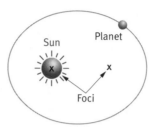

Figure 9.11 Kepler's alternative model.

Based on the idea that the orbit around the Sun is an ellipse with the sun in one of the foci. This model not only was much simpler, it also gave a better account of the speed of the planet.

orbits of the planets in 1619, but they were largely ignored for the first 50 years (by, among others, Galilei and Descartes). To some extent this is understandable. Only when the discipline is in crisis do scientists start to look for alternative explanations. Either these have to be newly found as a result of the crisis, or they are based on a search through the archives for ideas that for a long time have been overlooked (because they were not in line with the then prevailing paradigm).

Still related to scientific revolutions, it is important to keep in mind that they consist of a paradigm shift, a shift of the theoretical backbone of a discipline. A scientific revolution means that many existing research topics lose their appeal (either because their mystery has been solved or because it becomes clear that the research on them was misguided). They are replaced by new topics that follow from the novel paradigm and that often require different research methods. When only a minor part of the paradigm needs to be replaced by an alternative explanation, Kuhn did not consider this to be a revolution. Others, however, have been less restrictive in their use of the word paradigm (see, for instance, Chapter 11, where the opening quote talks of a 'paradigm war' in psychology). In particular psychology seems to have been quite generous with the term, using it for nearly every major change in theory and approach, making the anthropologist Geertz (2000) jest that in psychology paradigm shifts come along not by the century but by the decade or even by the month (Driver-Linn 2003).

What do you think?

In Chapter 5 we saw the emergence of behaviourism and cognitive psychology. Were these scientific revolutions involving a paradigm shift? Can you think of arguments in favour of this belief? And what are the counter-arguments? (Remember that you always must try to falsify statements, rather than give in to the confirmation bias.)

Return to normal science

Once the paradigm shift has taken place, the new paradigm takes over and forms the new background against which research occurs. After the rapid changes and excitement of the revolution, the situation returns to normal and the scientists go back to their usual activity of puzzle-solving. They will defend the new paradigm and the associated research methods with the same vigour as they defended the previous paradigm.

The pressure exerted by a research community in a period of normal science on its members to stay within the limits of the shared paradigm can be illustrated by the ways in which novices (students) are introduced into the field. They are taught a set of 'objective' and 'generally accepted' (i.e. unquestionable) research techniques and facts, which they study from textbooks hiding the paradigm shifts of the past. The latter is achieved either by reinterpreting the past so that it fits within the current paradigm or by placing the start of the discipline at the moment of the most recent revolution. Everything that happened before is then conveniently summarised as well-meant but ultimately naive precursors of the current, 'real' science. In this way, the illusion of science as a cumulative enterprise of ever increasing knowledge is maintained. As Gould (1996: 25) noted, 'Most scientists don't care a fig about history; . . . they do regard the past as a mere repository of error – at best a source of moral instruction in pitfalls along paths to progress.' Normal science continues until the anomalies once more become too numerous and too severe to remain acceptable, propelling the discipline into its next crisis . . .

What do you think?

Go back to the Preface, where we defined conceptual issues. Can you see now how the conceptual issues are closely intertwined with the paradigm in a research discipline (the implicit set of rules about what is worthwhile to investigate and how this has to be done)?

On the relativity of paradigms and the science wars

Paradigms are ever changing

A disturbing aspect of Kuhn's theory was that each paradigm is considered to be a temporary set of ideas, bound to turn into a crisis and to be replaced by an alternative paradigm. This means that current scientific knowledge cannot be considered as absolute truth but must be seen as a transition phase from the previous paradigm to the next. The squirrel in Figure 9.9 is not the final interpretation. At some point in the future it will be replaced by yet another organisation, which itself will only last for some time, and so it will go on.

The unbearable lightness of science

A second disturbing factor about Kuhn's theory was that Kuhn was rather unclear about whether a revolution meant progress or simply a change of paradigm. Whereas scientists felt affinity with the former view (bad theories are replaced by better ones), philosophers of science were more intrigued by the second possibility. What if science was nothing but an endless parade of paradigms, each throwing a different, limited light on what is essentially a multifaceted reality? This would completely rob science of its aura of objectivity and remove it from its supposed superiority over other forms of knowledge!

Kuhn's demonstrations that scientific disciplines depend on paradigms and that all disciplines have known major paradigm shifts were in stark contrast with the positivists' claims that science was always right and, therefore, should be the motor of all progress. Science had been wrong in the past and there was no guarantee that it was right this time. This eye-opener released the floods of resentment that had built up against science's position in several segments of society. After all, science had no other security to offer than the arrogance and self-confidence of the scientists. The claim that science, and only science, offered true knowledge of the world was difficult to uphold given that there was no warranty of the current paradigm being the right one.

Kuhn's analysis rekindled the controversy between realism and idealism. As you may remember from Chapter 3, realism says that:

realism

view within philosophy that human knowledge tries to reveal real things in the world; the truth of knowledge is determined by the correspondence of the knowledge with the real world

- concepts used in human knowledge refer to a physical reality which has priority (e.g. is more important for survival),
- knowledge is discovered rather than created, and
- truth is determined by the correspondence between knowledge and the physical world.

In contrast, idealism holds that:

idealism

view within philosophy that human knowledge is a construction of the mind and does not necessarily correspond to an outside world; the truth of knowledge depends on coherence with the rest of the knowledge in the social group

- the world as we know it is a construction of the mind,
- human knowledge is a subjective or social construction that does not necessarily correspond to an outside world,
- all knowledge is affected by language and culture, and
- the truth of statements depends on their coherence with the rest of the knowledge.

The discussion of idealism vs. realism was first raised explicitly by the Irish philosopher George Berkeley (1685–1753). He reasoned that if one assumes that all knowledge is based on observation (as empiricists do), then there is no guarantee of an outside physical reality corresponding to the knowledge. The only thing that is real for people is perception itself. As we saw in Chapter 3, philosophers (including Kant, the Scottish common-sense philosopher) tried to refute the argument, but were not fully successful.

Kuhn's analysis of research paradigms reinvigorated the debate in the second half of the twentieth century. Whereas scientists claimed they were discovering the physical reality (realism), Kuhn's scrutiny suggested that all they were doing was creating a set of stories about their perceptions (idealism), shrouded in a secretive language (jargon) and adorned with an unjustified air of objectivity, which in a hundred years' time would be looked upon as another outmoded paradigm based on wrong assumptions. After all, there were plenty of examples of superseded scientific 'facts' that in the past had been defended with the same zeal as contemporary scientists push their new 'data'. Nothing guaranteed that the prevailing paradigms in the different sciences were the right ones. Kuhn's theory predicted they are not (and never will be). Or as Feyerabend (1975) put it in his anarchistic theory of knowledge: scientific claims may be no different from other kinds of opinions, such as those provided by ancient myths or religions. Science has no inherent authority and the respect for science in current Western society is nothing more than the reverence people in the Middle Ages felt for the Catholic Church.

The science wars

postmodernist

in the philosophy of science, someone who questions the special status of science and sees scientific explanations as stories told by a particular group of scientists

Events culminated in a frontal attack against science by a number of philosophers and sociologists, who are referred to as postmodernists (although several names are used in the literature, referring to different positions taken). Postmodernism refers to a general cultural movement adopting a sceptical attitude to many of the principles and assumptions that underpinned modernity, such as uncritical belief in the benefits of capitalism, science and technology, which replaced the traditional ways of life (Sim 1998). Important names of postmodernists in the philosophy of science are the Austrian-British philosopher Paul Feyerabend (1924–1994) and the French philosophers Jean-François Lyotard (1924–1998), Michel Foucault (1926–1984) and Bruno Latour (born in 1947). They particularly called into question the claim of realism on which science was based.

According to the postmodernists, the analyses of Popper and in particular Kuhn showed that scientific knowledge had less to do with realism than with the opinions shared by the group of scientists. According to them, so-called scientific knowledge was a social construction by the scientific community, affected by their language and culture. The truth of scientific statements did not depend on how well the statements represented reality, but on how coherent they were with the rest of the paradigm shared by the group. Scientific knowledge was not superior to other types of knowledge; scientists had simply managed to acquire a lot of power in Western society by forming alliances with other strong groups, and they had been able to impose their views on other segments of society (see also Chapter 13).

The ensuing debate between scientists and postmodernists is sometimes referred to in the philosophy of science as the science wars (which is a good term to use to search for further information on the internet), although very few scientists seem to be aware of these wars (in line with their general indifference towards the efforts to define the essence of the scientific method, as we saw at the beginning of this chapter). For them, the scientific achievements of the past 400 years are so overwhelming that it is inconceivable that anyone would doubt them. As Sokal (1996) wrote, paraphrasing the eighteenth-century philosopher David Hume: 'anyone who believes the laws of physics are mere social conventions is invited to try transgressing those conventions from the windows of my apartment. (I live on the twenty-first floor.)'

social construction

notion used by postmodernists to indicate that scientific knowledge is not objective knowledge discovering the workings of an external reality, but a story told by a particular scientific community on the basis of its language and culture

science wars

notion used by the postmodernists to refer to their attacks against the special status of science and their unmasking of scientific knowledge as a social construction

? What do you think?

What do you think of the postmodernist ideas about science? Is it possible that all scientific knowledge is nothing but a social construction? If so, is there any point in 'harassing' students with compulsory science courses? And what does this mean for psychology?

Interim summary

Kuhn's theory

- A discipline needs a general theory to become scientific (otherwise it is a pre-science). This theory forms a paradigm against which observations are made, questions posed and answers interpreted.

- During periods of normal science, scientists solve puzzles within the existing paradigm. They defend the paradigm and ostracise colleagues who question it. Modifications of the theory in the light of contradictory findings must stay within the paradigm. Otherwise the finding is an unexplained anomaly.

Interim summary (continued)

- During a period of normal science, anomalies accumulate and modifications become increasingly ad hoc. This triggers a crisis.

- During a crisis, scientists are more open to an alternative, incommensurable theory, if the latter provides the same level of explanation and in addition allows the formulation of new predictions that stand the falsification test. If such an alternative is found, a paradigm shift takes place, which Kuhn calls a scientific revolution.

- Because of these scientific revolutions, scientific progress is not steady and cumulative. During the revolution progress is very fast; at the end of a period of normal science, progress is very slow or non-existent.

- The cycle of periods of normal science followed by scientific revolutions is never-ending.

- Paradigm shifts in Kuhn's theory do not imply that the old paradigm is replaced by a better one; it is just replaced by another one.

- This means that all scientific knowledge is relative and time-dependent, because it is based on a paradigm that is bound to be replaced in the future.

- The awareness that scientific knowledge is relative has elicited strong criticism from the postmodernists. In their view science is in no way superior to other types of knowledge, because it consists of social constructions made up by the scientists. Scientists have more power because they have formed strong alliances with other powerful groups.

9.5 The pragmatic alternative

In Chapter 3 we saw how Kant and Reid struggled to refute idealism. The science wars of the twentieth century illustrate just how difficult this is. Both realism and idealism have strong arguments in their favour, making it impossible to convince die-hard proponents. Looking at the various arguments made by Kant and Reid, the one that seems to have had the most impact is that of the constraints the physical world imposes on human actions (an argument already found in the Ancient Greek responses to scepticism). This is what Reid called 'common sense'.

Peirce and pragmatism

The American philosopher Charles Peirce (1839–1914) took the idea of common sense one step further and argued that success in coping with the physical reality could be taken as the criterion to decide how worthwhile knowledge was. If you asked scientists which scientific insights were valuable and likely to be carried on in subsequent research, they may be more likely to refer to ideas that allowed them to make a practical difference than to 'true' ideas (whatever 'true' may mean).

Peirce's position is known as **pragmatism**. Its basic tenet is that knowledge arises from the interactions of the individual with the world. Knowledge is not a passive mirror of reality (as defended by realism), nor a subjective construction (as claimed by idealism). It is information about how to cope with the world. Truth within this view depends on the success one has in engaging with the world, on

pragmatism

view within philosophy that human knowledge is information about how to cope with the world; the truth of knowledge depends on the success one has in engaging with the world, on what works what works. The truth of a theory (as opposed to its rival) is only of interest if it makes a practical difference. Because the world constantly changes, the truth is not fixed either.

Why pragmatism was overlooked for a long time in the philosophy of science

Despite the fact that the pragmatic approach was formulated at the end of the nineteenth century, well before the advent of logical positivism, it did not have much impact on the latter or on subsequent developments within the philosophy of science (e.g. Chalmers (1999) does not mention it in his bestselling book on the philosophy of science). One reason why the logical positivists were not impressed by the pragmatic alternative was that it did not seek to draw a distinction between scientific knowledge and non-scientific knowledge (recall the demarcation criteria). Peirce (1877) made a distinction between four ways of gathering knowledge, of which the scientific method was only one. The other three were:

1. *The method of tenacity.* People hold assumptions and beliefs because they have been around for a long time. Peirce (1877) considered this to be the most primitive form of knowledge. It is the origin of culture-specific customs passed on from generation to generation through observational learning.

2. *The method of authority.* People form opinions by consulting 'experts'. This is usually associated with the influence various religions have on human thinking. However, it also applies to the automatic adoption of scientific advice, or to situations in which scientists rely on the conclusions of other scientists without checking them.

3. *The a priori method.* People use their own reason and logic to reach conclusions. This includes deductive reasoning, but also the type of knowledge that is important in disciplines such as art history, literary criticism, philosophy and theology, where people express opinions and theories without feeling a need to verify them empirically. This type of knowledge also includes intuitive knowledge (defined as hunches people have about what may work in a particular situation without knowing the reasoning that resulted in the hunch).

According to Peirce, there was no clear difference between the scientific method and the three other methods of knowledge acquisition. All knowledge that helped to cope with the world was useful, wherever it came from (science, tradition, religion, philosophy).

Another reason it took a long time for Peirce's views to have a real impact on the philosophy of science was that they seemed less coherent and watertight than the usual writings on logic and epistemology. For instance, pragmatism's definition of truth ('what works') seemed to be much weaker than the traditional definitions based on logic. Indeed, in response to the criticism he received, in 1905 Peirce to some extent distanced himself from his earlier views. Peirce's impact was further compromised because for most of his life he was not connected to a university (he actually had a rather tragic life, which can easily be researched on the internet). His influence was mainly due to a friend of his, William James (yes, him!), and a PhD student he had during a short stint at Johns Hopkins University, John Dewey. Both men were more effective in the launch of functionalist psychology in the USA than in the launch of pragmatism in the philosophy of science, even though towards the ends of their lives they identified themselves predominantly with the latter. In addition, the three proponents did not have exactly the same ideas of what pragmatism was, making the message less straightforward and convincing than it could have been.

Renewed interest in pragmatism

The science wars with their revitalised debate of idealism vs. realism created new momentum for the pragmatic alternative, because it does not require a stance for or against the existence of an independent physical reality (Rochberg-Halton 1987; Bem & Looren de Jong 2006), even though it remains true that for many philosophers pragmatism is not as securely established as the other approaches. Indeed, Talisse and Aikin (2011: 1) started their book *The pragmatism reader: From Peirce to the present* with the observation that:

> Although the term *pragmatism* is frequently used to characterize some or other highly specific thesis or program, pragmatism is not and never was a school of thought unified around a distinctive doctrine. In fact, the first pragmatists – Charles Peirce, William James, and John Dewey – were divided over what, precisely; pragmatism is.

As we will see in the coming chapters, the most interesting aspect of pragmatism for psychologists is the proposal that practical utility is an important aspect to judge the worth of new knowledge, even when there is no guarantee that the insight is true according to the correspondence theory (i.e. matches an entity in a physical reality with priority over human action). Indeed, the existence of a physical reality corresponding to human thought is a thornier issue in psychology (studying the workings of the human mind) than in sciences studying the workings of the world.

KEY FIGURES in the philosophy of science

- **Francis Bacon** (1561–1626)
  - British scholar and politician.
  - Among the first to promote the use of observation and experimental histories as the basis of knowledge acquisition, rather than reliance on tradition and authority.
- **William Whewell** (1794–1866)
  - British priest and polymath.
  - Argued that theories affect observations.
  - Also acknowledged that hypotheses were possibly wrong conjectures.
- **Charles Peirce** (1839–1914)
  - American philosopher.
  - Founder of pragmatism (together with James and Dewey).
  - Maintained that only knowledge of practical value to cope with the world was true.
  - Neglected for most of the twentieth century because pragmatism did not make a distinction between scientific and non-scientific knowledge; currently there is increasing interest in his views.
- **Wiener Kreis** (Vienna Circle; 1924–1936)
  - Group of philosophers and scientists in Vienna (Austria) who tried to define the essence of the scientific method.
  - Known as the proponents of 'logical positivism', which saw the scientific method as based on verification through observation (verificationism); also requirement of operational definition of variables.

- **Karl Popper** (1902–1994)
  - Born in Vienna; attended meetings of the Wiener Kreis.
  - Left Austria because of the growth of Nazism, first to New Zealand, and then to England, where he became professor at the University of London.
  - Argued that science is theory-driven: scientists conjecture explanations which they subsequently try to falsify. This is the so-called hypothetico-deductive method. As a result, science proceeds by trial and error.
  - Stressed the importance of falsification over verification.
  - Modifications to theories are only allowed if they make the theory more falsifiable.

Karl Popper
Photo by Hutton Archive/
Getty Images.

- **Thomas Kuhn** (1922–1986)
  - American physicist who first became interested in the history of science and then in the philosophy of science.
  - Stressed that science is a social activity, because researchers in a scientific discipline share a paradigm they impose on newcomers.
  - An established science continuously goes through a cycle of normal science → crisis → revolution → normal science . . .
  - During a revolution, a paradigm shift takes place.
  - Because scientific research depends on a paradigm that will change in the future, scientific findings are relative.

Thomas Kuhn
Photo by Bill Pierce/Time &
Life Pictures/Getty Images.

- **Postmodernists** (end of the twentieth century)
  - Group of philosophers (first in Austria and France, then also in other countries) who, following Kuhn, argued that scientific theories were social constructions, no different from other types of knowledge.

Interim summary

- A strong component of the discussion within the philosophy of science is the extent to which human perception and understanding correspond to a physical reality. This is known as the realism vs. idealism debate.
- Another view is that knowledge of reality is derived from successfully coping with the world. Ideas that work are retained; ideas that do not make a practical difference get lost. This is the pragmatic view.
- The pragmatic view has been ignored for a long time, because it does not give a special status to scientific knowledge, but currently seems to be gaining momentum.

9.6 *Focus on*: How to respond to scientific findings?

In our experience, students at the end of a lecture/course on the philosophy of science usually feel bewildered (as we have been as well). What to make now of scientific findings? Can they be trusted or not? Which side to take: that of scientists or that of postmodernists? For what it is worth, here is the conclusion we distilled from our readings and experience, even though it is likely to be contested by both sides.

Two extreme views of the status of science

In the preceding sections we have seen two extreme views of the status of science. On the one hand, there is the claim that science is objective, because it is based on observable facts and on theories that have been verified and that survived falsification tests. On the other hand, critics argue that science consists of time-dependent personal views, because the perception of facts is biased by the scientists' theoretical background (paradigm), which will change in the future.

The first message is still largely promoted in scientific education (science textbooks and classroom discussions). According to McComas (1998), the idealisation of science initiated by the positivists remains widespread in our times. He extracted 15 'myths of science' that continue to be propagated. They are:

1. Scientific hypotheses become theories that in turn become laws (which have the highest status of scientific truth).
2. Scientific laws are absolute (i.e. they are always true).
3. A hypothesis is an educated guess (rather than a bold conjecture).
4. A general and universal scientific method exists (in line with the universal and ahistorical demarcation criteria sought by the logical positivists).
5. Evidence accumulated carefully results in sure knowledge.
6. Science and its method provide absolute proof.
7. Science is procedural more than creative (see also Chapter 10).
8. Science and its methods can answer all questions.
9. Scientists are particularly objective.
10. Experiments are the principal route to scientific knowledge.
11. Scientific conclusions are reviewed for accuracy (before they are published).
12. Acceptance of new scientific knowledge is straightforward.
13. Scientific models represent reality.
14. Science and technology are the same.
15. Science is a solitary pursuit (again see Chapter 10).

The postmodernist view of science is popular among those who want to curtail science's influence in society. It is used, for instance, to argue against the need of compulsory science education in primary and secondary schools.

In search of middle ground

The first step

A first step towards middle ground is to accept that facts have an objective basis even if there is a subjective component in their perception. As argued over and over again, human actions are constrained in a number of ways by a physical reality. Also, it cannot be denied that science has been quite successful in its interactions with the environment (cf. the pragmatic criterion). Therefore, it seems wise to accept that the perception of facts has both an objective and a subjective component. Just as it cannot be denied that the observations of facts are coloured by the theoretical framework within which they are studied, it seems better to accept that these observations correspond to 'something' in the world. It is not true that scientists have consistently found what they expected to find. Throughout history, empirical observations have imposed themselves on scientists and forced them to revise their ideas. More than once, their perceptions have baffled scientists because they were so much at odds with the existing expectations.

When Galilei first observed moons around Jupiter with his telescope (Chapter 2), this was not because he expected to find them there. Neither did his critics, when they were invited to have a look through the telescope. Similarly, the Danish scholar Ørsted had no biasing prejudices when in 1820 he suddenly observed that the needle of his compass deflected each time he switched on an electric battery (this was the origin of the research showing a close relationship between electricity and magnetism). Researchers have a name for this type of accidental discovery while they are looking for something entirely different; they call it *serendipity*.

Accidental discoveries illustrate that perceptions have an origin outside the perceiver and at times can enforce themselves. They are more than theory-laden projections by the scientists. Observations may be misinterpreted, but they will never be completely at odds with the events that are at their origin. As such, the constant coupling of scientific statements to observations is an assurance that statements will not be completely unsubstantiated (as may be the case with unchecked, principle-driven claims), even if there is no guarantee of their full correctness.

The second step

A second step towards middle ground is the acceptance that scientific claims must be treated with caution, certainly when they are new. They are not unquestionable. We have seen a multitude of reasons why a particular claim may be wrong, why scientific progress should be considered as a process of trial and error rather than a steady accumulation of sure facts. Therefore, it is crucial to remain critical about claims made by scientists. It is not true that once science has spoken there is no more room for debate (as suggested in the excerpt that opened this chapter).

The danger of erroneous scientific claims is particularly high for newly proposed ideas that have not been through repeated falsification tests. As is true for other products of human creativity, only a small percentage of all scientific ideas put forward survive the first few years of their existence, either because they are shown to be wrong or because they do not seem to have any practical relevance. Ioannidis (2005), for instance, studied the fate of high-impact clinical intervention studies claiming to have found significant effects, published between 1990 and 2003. Of the 45 such studies, only 20 (44%) were replicated. Seven (16%) were contradicted by subsequent research and 7 more (16%) were found to have much smaller effects than originally reported. The remaining 11 studies had not (yet) been replicated. Arguably, the fate of less cited scientific findings is even worse.

Replication by other, independent researchers is critical (though not enough) to establish the usefulness of a scientific finding. As Feyerabend (1993: 19) observed, individual researchers go to great lengths to promote their cherished positions, including the use of rhetoric and power. Scientists are more eager to use the falsification test for others' theories than for their own (when the confirmation bias seems to be stronger).

The advice for critical thinking is reasonably well known to people who take scientific courses. After all, they are urged to look for possible falsifications. However, in general this advice is limited to questioning the validity of the empirical findings within the existing paradigm (how sound are the data and how justified is the scientist to draw his or her conclusions on the basis of the data that were obtained?). What the present chapter adds is that we should always keep in mind that a finding may be wrong because the existing paradigm misconceives the perception of the issue.

Conclusion

There is no fail-safe advice to be given about how to avoid misleading scientific claims. One helpful rule of thumb is to look at the time period since the claim has been introduced and the amount of research that has gone into it thus far. Most people are particularly impressed by the latest research, but in general this is the most risky part of science. The more falsification tests a statement has passed, the surer we can be of its validity (always keeping in mind that it is impossible to achieve 100% certainty). In this respect, researchers talk about the importance of converging evidence, evidence from a long series of different falsification attempts, each aimed at a potential weakness of the statement.

Of all the research that is done and the theoretical modifications that are introduced, only a fraction survives the first 10 years. Although some of the forgotten ideas may later turn out to be missed critical insights (like Kepler's), the vast majority are overlooked because they were false starts or simply not important enough. The short life span of many newly proposed scientific ideas is also the reason why scientific textbooks and lectures should not be limited to the research of the last few years (Sternberg 1999). They should first of all pay attention to the well-established, 'classic' findings and interpretations.

Interim summary

- The strong relative view of scientific knowledge is based on the assumption that the perception of facts is fully dependent on the perceiver's background knowledge.

- If one accepts that the perception of facts has an objective component, grounded in reality, then the constant coupling of ideas to observations by means of verification and falsification is a guarantee that the ideas will not be completely in contradiction with the reality as it can be observed.

- The observation that science proceeds by trial and error and happens within a paradigm that may turn out to be wrong should warn people always to remain critical about scientific claims. A helpful rule of thumb in this respect is to always look at how many falsification tests the claim has stood.

Recommended literature

An interesting introduction to the philosophy of science is Chalmers, A.F. (1999) *What is this thing called science?* (Maidenhead, UK: Open University Press).

Gauch, H.G. (2003) *Scientific method in practice* (Cambridge: Cambridge University Press) is another remarkable book, because it has been written by a scientist taking the postmodernists criticisms seriously and examining the consequences for science education.

Gower, B. (1997) *Scientific method: An historical and philosophical introduction* (London: Routledge) gives particularly useful information about developments before the twentieth century.

Dienes, Z. (2008) *Understanding psychology as a science: An introduction to scientific and statistical inference* (Basingstoke: Palgrave Macmillan) provides information particularly related to psychology.

References

Allchin, D. (2002) 'To err and win a Nobel Prize: Paul Boyer, ATP synthase and the emergence of bioenergetics', *Journal of the History of Biology*, 35: 149–72.

Andrews, R. (1987) *The Routledge dictionary of quotations*. London: Routledge.

Bacon, F. (1620) *Novum organum scientiarum*.

Bem, S. & Looren de Jong, H. (2006) *Theoretical issues in psychology: An introduction.* London: Sage Publications.

Birnbaum, L.C. (1955) 'Behaviorism in the 1920's', *American Quarterly,* 7: 15–30.

Bridgman, P.W. (1927) *The logic of modern physics.* Chicago: University of Chicago Press.

Broca, P. (1863) 'Sur les caractères des cranes basques', *Extrait des Bulletins de la Société d'anthropologie de Paris.* At books.google.com.

Cajori, F. (ed.) (1934) *Sir Isaac Newton's Mathematical Principles of natural philosophy and his system of the world.* Berkeley: University of California Press.

Carnap, R. (1966) *Philosophical foundations of physics: An introduction to the philosophy of science.* New York: Basic Books.

Chalmers, A.F. (1999) *What is this thing called science?* (3rd edn). Maidenhead, UK: Open University Press.

Coles, P. (2001) 'Einstein, Eddington and the 1919 eclipse', *Historical Development of Modern Cosmology,* ASP Conference Series, 252.

Dienes, Z. (2008) *Understanding psychology as a science: An introduction to scientific and statistical inference.* Basingstoke: Palgrave Macmillan.

Draper, J.W. (1847) *A textbook on natural philosophy for the use of schools and colleges.* New York: Harper & Brothers.

Driver-Linn, E. (2003) 'Where is psychology going? Structural fault lines revealed by psychologists' use of Kuhn', *American Psychologist,* 58: 269–78.

Feyerabend, P.K. (1975/1993) *Against method: Outline of an anarchistic theory of knowledge.* London: New Left Books.

Fisher, G.H. (1968) 'Ambiguity of form – old and new', *Perception & Psychophysics,* 4(3): 189–92.

Gauch, H.G. (2003) *Scientific method in practice.* Cambridge: Cambridge University Press.

Geertz, C. (2000) *Available light: Anthropological reflections on philosophical topics.* Princeton, NJ: Princeton University Press.

Gilles, D. (1996) *Artificial intelligence and scientific method.* Oxford: Oxford University Press.

Gould, S.J. (1996) *The mismeasure of man* (2nd edn). New York: Norton & Company.

Gower, B. (1997) *Scientific method: An historical and philosophical introduction.* London: Routledge.

Herschel, J.F.W. (1831) *A preliminary discourse on the study of natural philosophy.* London.

Ioannidis, J.P.A. (2005) 'Contradicted and initially stronger effects in highly cited clinical research', *Journal of the American Medical Association,* 294: 218–28.

Kuhn, T.S. (1962/1970) *The structure of scientific revolutions.* Chicago: University of Chicago Press.

Lakatos, I. (1970) 'Falsification and the methodology of scientific research programs.' In I. Lakatos & A. Musgrave (eds), *Criticism and the growth of knowledge.* New York: Cambridge University Press.

Liebig, J. von (1863) *Ueber Francis Bacon von Verulam und die Methode der Naturforschung.* Munich.

Lilienfeld, S.O., Lynn, S.J., Ruscio, J. & Beyerstein, B.L. (2010) *50 great myths of popular psychology: Shattering widespread misconceptions about human behaviour.* Chichester: Wiley-Blackwell.

Martineau, H. (1858) *The positive philosophy of Auguste Compte.* New York: Calvin Blanchard.

McComas, W.F. (ed.) (1998) *The nature of science in science education.* Dortrecht: Kluwer Academic Publishers.

Medawar, P.B. (1969) *Induction and intuition in scientific thought.* London: Methuen. As cited in R. Rosenthal & R.L. Rosnow (2008) *Essentials of behavioral research: Methods and data analysis* (3rd edn). Boston: McGraw-Hill.

Peirce, C.S. (1877) 'The fixation of belief', *Popular Science Monthly,* **12** (November): 1–15.

Popper, K.R. (1970) 'Normal science and its dangers.' In I. Lakatos & A. Musgrave (eds), *Criticism and growth of knowledge.* New York: Cambridge University Press.

Rochberg-Halton, E. (1987) 'Why pragmatism now?' *Sociological Theory,* 5: 194–200.

Shapin, S. (1996) *The scientific revolution.* Chicago: University of Chicago Press.

Sim, S. (ed.) (1998) *The Routledge companion to postmodernism* (2nd edn). London: Routledge.

Sokal, A.D. (1996b) 'A physicist experiments with cultural studies', *Lingua Franca,* May/June, 62–4. (Also available at www.physics.nyu.edu/sokal.)

Sternberg, R.J. (1999) 'Twenty tips for teaching introductory psychology.' In B. Perlman, L.I. McCann & S.H. McFadden (eds), *Lessons learned: Practical advice for the teaching of psychology* (vol. 1). Washington, DC: American Psychological Society, pp. 99–104.

Taleb, N.N. (2007) *The black swan: The impact of the highly improbable.* New York: Random House.

Talisse, R.B. & Aikin, S.F. (eds) (2011) *The pragmatism reader: From Peirce to the present.* Princeton, NJ: Princeton University Press.

Wason, P.C. (1960) 'On the failure to eliminate hypotheses in a conceptual task', *Quarterly Journal of Experimental Psychology,* 12: 129–40.

Wittgenstein, L. (1953) *Philosophical investigations.* (trans. G.E.M. Anscombe). Oxford: Basil Blackwell.

10 Is psychology a science?

This chapter will cover . . .

Questions to consider

?

Historical issues addressed in this chapter

- When did the hermeneutic approach in psychology start?
- Who were the main contributors to this approach?

Conceptual issues addressed in this chapter

- Why did psychologists claim their endeavour was a continuation of previous philosophical efforts to understand human functioning?
- Why did psychologists stress the use of the scientific method? What consequences did this have for their education programmes?
- Why do people have difficulty in seeing psychology as a science?
- What is the difference between scientific psychology and hermeneutic psychology?
- Does psychology have an unbiased image of men and women?
- What makes a good history of psychology?

Introduction

On various internet sites you can find the story 'How to identify professors'. Below we give an abbreviated version.

Chemistry professor: Wears a white lab coat. This may actually be clean but does not have to be. Physical chemistry professors have a brand new coat that has never been in the lab; polymer chemists have strange glop on their coat, and freshman chemistry professors have acid holes.

Physics professor: Wears blue jeans and a flannel shirt. May sometimes forget to wear shirt altogether. If a professor is wearing blue jeans and suspenders, ten to one he is a physicist. Physics profs often have German accents, but this is not a distinguishing characteristic.

Biology professor: Sometimes wears a lab coat, though usually this is the sign of a biochemist. Marine biologists walk around in hip boots for no explainable reason, even in the middle of winter. They are apt to wear grey slacks and smell like fish, as opposed to most biologists, who smell strongly of formalin. Microbiology instructors go around in spotless white coats, refuse to drink beer on tap, and wipe all their silverware before using it.

Psychology Professor: Psychologists are not real scientists, and can be easily identified by their screams of protest whenever anyone questions whether psychology is a science. Psychologists have beady little eyes and don't laugh at jokes about psychology. If you are not sure whether a person is a scientist or a comparative religion instructor, he is probably a psychologist.

Funny stories like the one above reflect (and reinforce) stereotypes but often include a true core. In Chapter 5 we saw how behaviourists and cognitive psychologists struggled to have their investigations acknowledged as scientific research. And presently many introductory classes to psychology still start by stressing that psychology is a true science as well (as if, otherwise, students might finish their course without properly realising this). So, why do academic psychologists feel the need to emphasise that psychology is a science and why does the public at large have a problem believing this? In what respects does psychology resemble and differ from physics, chemistry and biology?

Now that we have seen what science is (Chapter 9), we can address the question to what extent psychology is a science. We start by reviewing the reasons why psychology is claimed to be science. Then, we discuss the reasons why people do not perceive it as such. We end with a discussion of the movements in psychology that have criticised the exclusive reliance on scientific research methods, and ask whether this implies that the history of psychology ought to be given by neutral historians.

10.1   Reasons why psychology is claimed to be a science

The foundation of psychology as an academic discipline was legitimised on two pillars

Psychology has a long, respectful past and uses the scientific method

In his book *Modernizing the mind*, the American sociologist Steven Ward (2002; see also Chapters 8 and 13) made the case that a new branch of knowledge can establish itself and survive only if it succeeds in convincing the ruling powers of the need for such knowledge as well as reassuring them that it is no threat to their prosperity. This requires rhetoric and alliance formation with powerful groups, as much as (and in Ward's view, even more than) intellectual substance. The founders of psychology promoted it as a new academic discipline by stressing two messages:

1. Psychology was the continuation of the old and respectful tradition of mental and moral philosophy, going back at least to Aristotle.

2. The new element was that the scientific method, so successful in other disciplines, would be applied to the study of the human mind. Because of the use of this method, psychology made a bridge to the natural sciences and derived status from them.

There are many examples of the rhetoric with respect to the first claim. For instance, the German psychologist Hermann Ebbinghaus wrote in 1908 that 'Psychology has a long past but only a short history'. Similarly, James McKeen Cattell asserted in his 1895 presidential address to the American Psychological Association that (cited in Ward 2002: 36):

> While the recent progress of our science has been great, we do not admit that psychology is a new science . . . If science is to date from the year of 'the master of those who know', then we may take pride in the beginnings of psychology whose foundations were more securely laid by Aristotle than those of any other science.

A nice example of how the new, scientific method was promoted can be found in the book *Psychology,* published by John Dewey in 1887. In this book Dewey stated that psychological investigation had languished for too long under the metaphysical philosophy associated with the American mental philosophers and that it was time psychology had a treatment of its own. In his own words, 'how shall we make our psychology scientific and up to the times, free from metaphysics – which, however good in its place, is out of place in a psychology? (Dewey 1887: iv).

The adherence to the scientific method was further communicated by putting the start of the discipline at 1879, the year when the first scientific laboratory of psychology was established by Wundt in Leipzig. As we saw in Chapter 4, the teaching of psychology was considerably older.

Consequences for the psychology curriculum

Because psychology was promoted on the basis of its long past and its sound method, both 'history of psychology' and 'research methods' were major components of the curriculum. Students were taught how to run proper studies in laboratories and had to buy syllabuses or books on research methods. Similarly, students had to study the history of psychology. Shortly after 1910, the first textbooks on the history of psychology appeared, the best known of which is that of Baldwin, published in 1913 (which you can find on the internet). Remember this was only some 20 years after the foundation of the very first psychology laboratory in the USA! Little surprise, then, that these history books hardly dealt with the new discipline. They were reviews of person-related ideas and insights from philosophy and religion, which were rephrased as precursors of psychological thought. These books were self-legitimisation as much as essential stepping stones for a good psychology education.

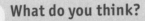

What do you think?

An intriguing observation is that the importance of history courses in psychology seems to be questioned more now than a century ago. Could this be because psychology as an independent branch of learning has become more self-confident? Or is it because nowadays much more is known about psychology than 100 years ago, so that more topics are competing for a limited number of time slots? What's your view about the role of history courses in a psychology education: essential or self-glorification?

Science is defined by its method rather than by its subject matter

Every topic studied with the scientific method is a science

To be accepted as a science, psychologists – together with sociologists – had to make the case that what differentiated sciences from non-sciences was the way in which problems were investigated, and not the type of problems addressed. Chemistry at the end of the nineteenth century was a highly successful science not because of its topics, but because it had embraced the scientific method. Indeed, before it did so, it was an obscure and secretive subject practised by a group of alchemists who failed to make any noticeable progress. Only when people like Robert Boyle in the seventeenth century began to experiment and publish their findings did chemistry start to flourish.

The founders of psychology claimed that a similar feat would be achieved by psychologists if they were given the means to start the scientific study of the human mind (Chapters 3–5). Although few people spontaneously associated the study of mental life with scientific research (certainly not in the nineteenth century!), the first academic psychologists maintained that there was nothing inherent in the subject matter that prevented it from being studied using the scientific method.

Methodolatry

Because of its emphasis on method in the definition of science, academic psychology invested heavily in developing appropriate research designs and analysis techniques. It is not a coincidence that since the beginning of the twentieth century psychologists have been at the forefront of investigations into increasingly powerful research designs and statistical analyses of complicated datasets. Psychologists had to be the top of the class as far as research methods and statistics were concerned! Even recently this was apparent when psychological researchers in the 1990s started to collaborate with their medical colleagues in cognitive neuroscience. A recurrent complaint among the psychologists (although rarely recorded on paper) was the low level of methodological sophistication in their medical collaborators, making the findings vulnerable to a long line of validity threats.

It has been argued by several authors that psychology throughout its existence has overplayed the role of research methods at the expense of theory building (see Chapter 9 for the importance of theories in science). This, for instance, was the conclusion the eminent American psychologist Sigmund Koch (he would later become its president) drew after he was asked by the American Psychological Association to analyse the status of psychology in the mid-twentieth century:

> Ever since its stipulation into existence as an independent science, psychology has been far more concerned with being a science than with courageous and self-determining confrontation with its historically constituted subject matter. Its history has been largely a matter of emulating the methods, forms, symbols of the established sciences, especially physics.
>
> (Koch 1961: 629–30)

A similar criticism can be heard from Noam Chomsky, the linguist who in the 1960s formulated a theory of language processing that would form the inspiration for thousands of scientific studies in cognitive psychology (see Chapter 5):

> Take the phrase 'behavioral sciences.' It's a very curious phrase. I mean it's a bit like calling the natural sciences 'meter-reading sciences.' In fact a physicist's data often consists of things like meter readings, but nobody calls physics 'meter-reading science.' Similarly, the data of a psychologist is behavior in a broad sense. But to call a field 'behavioral science' is to say it's a science of behavior in the sense in which physics is a science of meter reading.
>
> (Chomsky, in Baars 1986: 346–7)

This was also the conclusion Baars himself reached:

> Almost every mature science shows a tension between experimentalists and theoreticians. Experimental scientists often complain that the theoreticians ignore inconvenient evidence, whereas theoreticians tend to believe that experimentalists cannot see the larger picture. This tension can be healthy and creative, providing that there is also good communication . . .

But in psychology, only one-half of this dialectic existed. There simply was no credible theory. In the absence of accepted theory, it was never clear which experiments had important implications.

(Baars 1986: 161–2)

> **? What do you think?**
>
> The last sentence of the excerpt from Baars may be quite detrimental for psychology, because 'in the absence of accepted theory' may be interpreted as meaning that psychology still is in the pre-science phase of Kuhn's framework. Remember from Chapter 9 that this is the stage in which isolated phenomena are investigated without being integrated within a coherent, larger framework (a paradigm). It is the phase in which a discipline is not yet a science, according to Kuhn. What do you think? Does psychology have a paradigm? Or is it still a loose amalgam of isolated observations?
>
> Would your answer be any different if you knew that Kuhn (1962/1970) in his book on paradigms mentioned psychology as an example of a discipline in pre-science phase?

methodolatry or **methodologism**

tendency to see methodological rigour as the only requirement for scientific research, at the expense of theory formation

The bias towards methodological rigour rather than theory formation has been called **methodolatry** or **methodologism** (e.g. Teo 2005). Instead of searching for a theoretical framework that united them, the founders of psychology assumed that as long as they followed the rules of scientific methodology they would contribute to progress in the discipline.

The shadow of positivism

One reason why psychologists tended to stress valid testing rather than theory formation was that they tried too hard to be good scientists. Remember that the first decades of psychology were the heyday of positivism. There probably were no keener or more obedient students of this movement than the experimental psychologists (in particular the behaviourists). Just have a look at how well they followed the core advice on how to do proper science:

1. science proceeds from facts to knowledge on the basis of observation, inductive reasoning and verification,

2. non-observables must be excluded, unless they have an operational definition,

3. theories are limited to descriptions of the observed facts, preferentially in the form of a mathematical law; by no means must they include speculation.

> **? What do you think?**
>
> Do you agree with the criticism that a psychology degree is more about learning the right research methods rather than useful theories? Or has the situation changed in the last 30–50 years?

The scientific method has not let psychologists down

In the preceding chapters and sections we saw how psychology started as the outcome of the growing impact of scientific thinking in Western society. In the nineteenth century this led to an increasing number of scholars becoming convinced that there was a future in the application of the scientific method to the human mind. At that time, this was a matter of faith, rather than a guaranteed success. The fact that after nearly a century and a half, the majority of academic psychologists still subscribe to this choice is a sign that they have not regretted it. Looking through a variety of sources suggests that the factors below are the main reasons why psychologists keep on using the scientific method.

Systematicity and cumulativeness of knowledge

Science, more than any other method of knowledge acquisition, stresses the requirement that knowledge builds on existing knowledge. New findings and explanations must be coherent with existing information. Therefore, previous knowledge should be available and new knowledge must be made public. Remember from Chapter 1 how in preliterate society knowledge was local and diffuse, so that contradictions were abundant and went unnoticed. In contrast, science is meant to be cumulative: researchers consult what has been found before with respect to a particular topic, so that they can build on it and avoid previous pitfalls. An analogy often used in this respect (among others, by Newton) is that of a scientist 'standing as a dwarf on the shoulders of giants'.

As we saw in Chapter 9, there are limits to the cumulative nature of science, because the accumulation of knowledge depends on the prevailing paradigm, which may change. However, the records of previous attempts should remain available and a proper literature search is seen as a prerequisite of good science. In particular, the historians of a discipline should be able to go beyond the current paradigm and see the continuities and discontinuities in thinking.

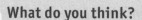

? What do you think?

Breeuwsma (2008) argues that textbooks have a tendency to exaggerate the extent of knowledge continuity and cumulativeness. He gives an example from psychology. In the fourth edition of a much used textbook of psychology (2002), the following introductory sentences can be found: 'You and I stand at a moment in time preceded by Aristotle, Descartes, Darwin, and millions less known. Psychology today is the accumulated and sifted ideas of all people before us who have attempted to fathom the mysteries of the human mind.' Quite acceptable, you may think, except for the fact that in the previous edition of the same book (1999), the first sentence read: 'You and I stand at a moment in time preceded by Aristotle, Descartes, Freud, and millions less known.' What happened here? Why was Freud replaced by Darwin? And more importantly, what does this tell us about textbooks?

The use of well-defined methods

Information must be gathered in line with agreed methods that are clearly outlined. There is systematicity in the collection of observations. The methods used must be accepted by the existing research community and be described in such detail that the observation can be replicated by others. As we saw in Chapter 9, this does not preclude research methods comprising an element of relativity (due to the paradigm on which they are based), but they can be repeated by others if they follow the instructions.

Clarity

The findings are stated in such a way that they are interpreted in the same way by different readers. As you may have noticed from some of the quotations in the present book, this requirement was not always met in philosophical writings (cf. the interpretation problems related to Plato, Aristotle and even Wundt).

Prediction

Science, again much more than any other method of information generation, stresses the importance of prediction. It is not enough to explain phenomena post hoc (after they have happened); a scientist must be able to predict what will happen in the future (under well-controlled circumstances). Such prediction enables control of the event.

Knowledge is revisable

Scientific knowledge is open, and can be revised at all times. As we saw in Chapter 9, trying to falsify existing convictions is central to science, to make sure that no wrong beliefs are perpetuated. Knowledge is not person-bound. Opinions are not held on to because of the person who formulated them. They are adhered to because they are not contradicted by the available evidence. This does not mean that all revisions happen instantaneously (remember the fate of anomalies in periods of normal science; Chapter 9), but knowledge that consistently fails to pass the falsification test will eventually lead to a revision of the theory, even if that includes a paradigm shift.

Comparison with pseudoscience

pseudoscience

branch of knowledge that pretends to be scientific but that violates the scientific method on essential aspects, such as lack of openness to testing by others and reliance on confirmation rather than falsification

Another way to illustrate the importance of the scientific method for psychology researchers is to compare it with the methods prevalent in **pseudoscience**, a branch of knowledge that pretends to be scientific but violates the scientific method on essential aspects, such as:

1. the use of vague, exaggerated or untestable claims,
2. a tendency to invoke ad hoc hypotheses as a means to immunise claims from falsification,
3. personalisation of issues (intuitions of leaders rather than data),
4. over-reliance on confirmation rather than falsification,
5. excessive reliance on anecdotal and testimonial evidence to substantiate claims,
6. lack of openness to testing by other experts and scrutiny by peer review,
7. a tendency to place the burden of proof on sceptics, not proponents, of claims,
8. failure to connect with the existing scientific knowledge (sometimes replaced by an accusation of being excluded),
9. use of misleading language (e.g. maintaining ideas that are known to be false).

? What do you think?

Can you think of examples of pseudoscience?

Acceptable progress thus far

Another reason why psychological research remains largely scientific is that psychologists themselves are not unhappy with the progress they have made in the past 150 years. They have evidence that standardised tests are better predictors of future performance than unstructured interviews (Chapter 8); they know that people in many situations do not behave in the way that they think they do (Chapters 7 and 11); and experimental research allows psychologists to investigate phenomena that otherwise would be inaccessible. As we saw in Chapter 7, many phenomena occur outside a person's conscious awareness (for instance, the processes involved in text reading). These cannot be examined by introspection but require careful performance monitoring in controlled situations (e.g. by measuring the speed of word recognition). The 'experimental histories', as Francis Bacon called them (Chapter 2), have enabled psychologists to gain a much better understanding of how people achieve good performance in a wide variety of tasks and why performance sometimes goes awry (see the section on cognitive neuropsychology in Chapter 6).

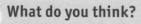

What do you think?

A straightforward objection to the last criterion (acceptable progress) is that psychologists may very well be biased in their perception of the progress they have made (e.g. on the basis of the confirmation bias; Chapter 9). How does this agree with your impression? On the basis of what you have learned thus far, do you think psychology has made genuine progress in understanding the human mind in the past century? Or do you agree with the philosopher Wittgenstein who said more than 50 years ago that in psychology there are experimental methods and conceptual confusion?

Relationships to other sciences

By looking at cross-references it is possible to position psychological research relative to the other research disciplines. Is psychology an isolated discipline that does not feed insights into other disciplines and that does not take into account information from other sciences either? How often do researchers from other disciplines refer to findings in psychology and how often do psychologists refer to findings from other disciplines?

Boyack *et al.* (2005) analysed citation data from more than one million journal articles appearing in over 7,000 scientific journals in the year 2000, to see how often researchers in the different disciplines mention each other's findings. Their results are summarised in Figure 10.1. In this figure, journals which often make cross-references are close together. Journals which rarely refer to one another are further apart. Disciplines near the perimeter are more isolated than those near the centre. The findings of Boyack *et al.* can best be summarised by quoting their conclusion:

> The order of major fields in follows an intuitive pattern as one moves clockwise around the map: Mathematics, Physics, Chemistry, Earth Sciences (including Biological, Plant, and Animal Sciences), Medicine, Psychology, and Social Sciences . . . The fine structure of the map is also revealing. Engineering disciplines are near Physics and Chemistry.

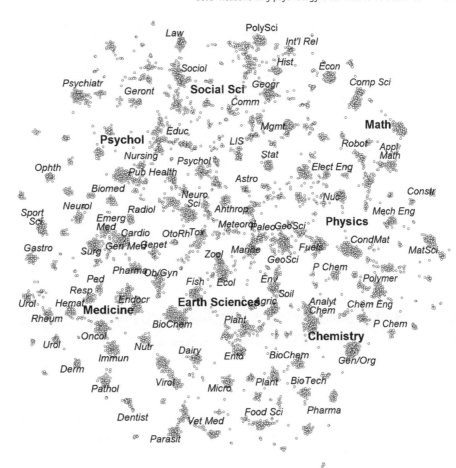

Figure 10.1 Map of science generated on the basis of the number of citations between the different scientific disciplines.

Each dot represents one scientific journal. Large font-size labels identify major areas of science. Small labels denote the disciplinary topics of clusters of journals.

Source: Boyack *et al.* (2005). Reproduced with permission.

> Interfacial disciplines appear to be reasonably placed. For example, Public Health lies between Medicine and Psychology . . .
>
> In general, the more insular fields lie toward the outside of the map, and those with more interdisciplinary linkages are toward the center . . . Social Sciences are tied to Psychology through various specialties in Psychology; Medicine is tied to Psychology directly and through Neurology; Biochemistry links directly to Medicine and Chemistry; . . .
>
> (2005: 366)

A particularly interesting feature that comes out of Boyack *et al.*'s (2005) analysis is that psychology does not form an isolated island only referring to itself. As a matter of fact, it is one of the seven major areas of research (next to maths, physics, chemistry, earth sciences, medicine and social sciences), forming a hub for a series of other disciplines related to human functioning, with strong links to two other major areas (medicine and social sciences). This agrees with the claim that psychological research is well embedded within the sciences.

Interim summary

Reasons why psychology is claimed to be a science

- The founders have defined psychology as the study of the human mind with the scientific method.

- They further argued that whether or not a discipline is a science depends on the research methods used and not on the topic investigated: psychology used the scientific method and, therefore, was a science.

- The scientific method has proven to be a fruitful approach and is fully integrated within mainstream psychological research.

- Psychological research is fully integrated within other scientific research. It is one of the seven major areas with strong links to two other major areas. It forms a hub for a series of less central sciences related to human functioning.

10.2 Reasons why psychology is not seen as a science

In the previous section we explored the arguments behind the scientific status of psychology. We now address the arguments questioning this status.

There is little overlap between the stereotypical view of a scientist and the stereotypical view of a psychologist

It has been shown repeatedly in social psychology that the perception of unfamiliar groups is largely driven by social stereotypes. These are automatically activated, unsophisticated opinions of other groups (Bargh & Chartrand 1999) that strongly affect the first impression people have when they encounter members of these groups. Social stereotypes can be overruled by controlled thinking or when one has enough individuation information about a group or an individual due to regular contact, but for most people they will be the basis upon which their judgements are made.

So, the first aspect to look at is how much overlap there is between the stereotypical views of a psychologist and a scientist. If the overlap is small, then the first impression about a psychologist will not be that of a scientist, no matter how often psychologists repeat their message that psychology is a science.

Stereotypes about science and scientists

What are the stereotypical views about science? A look at the literature (e.g. Kessels *et al.* 2006; Sandoval 2005; Vilchez-Gonzalez & Parales Palacios 2006) suggests the following:

1. science is for males,
2. science is difficult,
3. science affords fewer opportunities to be creative than arts and languages, because only one answer is correct; this answer is found by collecting facts,
4. scientific discoveries are made by chance,

5. knowledge accumulation in science is linear (i.e. there no crises, deadlocks, or paradigm shifts in science),

6. science does not offer much variation in work; the only research methods are observation and experimentation.

In addition, there are stereotypes related to scientists (e.g. Finston *et al.* 1995; McDuffie 2001; Yasar *et al.* 2006). These are that scientists:

1. are middle-aged,

2. are male (often with glasses and unconventional hairstyles),

3. are serious or crazed,

4. work alone,

5. are obsessed with their work, and

6. do not have good writing, verbal or people skills.

When people hear or read about a scientist, the attributes just listed are the ones most likely to be activated. A test sometimes used to study the stereotypical views about scientists is to ask people to draw 'a scientist'. Figure 10.2 shows some of the drawings McDuffie (2001) obtained from teachers (including science teachers!).

Depictions of scientists in books and films

The stereotypical views listed above are the outcome of how scientists are depicted in the wider culture (i.e. the associations that are there to be picked up by the individuals). After a review of the Western literature, Haynes (2003) distilled seven archetypes of scientists that are used as convenient shorthand to include such characters in books and films:

1. the scientist as an evil and dangerous man (this is by far the most frequent picture),

2. the noble scientist as hero or saviour of society,

Figure 10.2 Examples of teachers' sketches of scientists, revealing the stereotypical views people have about these individuals.

Source: McDuffie (2001).

3. the foolish scientist (absentminded and nutty),

4. the inhuman researcher,

5. the scientist as adventurer who travels in space and time,

6. the mad, bad, dangerous scientist, and

7. the helpless scientist, unable to control the outcome of his work.

What do you think?

Stereotypes figure prominently in cartoons (which in turn are important perpetrators of stereotypes). Go to **images.google.com** and type in 'cartoon scientist'. Analyse the first 100 images you get. How well do they agree with the stereotypical views outlined above?

Stereotypes about psychology and psychologists

In the same way, we can look at the stereotypical views that the words 'psychology' and 'psychologist' evoke. These are the opinions automatically associated with psychology:

1. psychology involves an interaction between a therapist and a client (notice the confounding with psychiatry),

2. psychology is interested in abnormal behaviour,

3. psychology aims at helping others,

4. also sometimes reference to the other applications of psychology, in particular school psychology and work psychology, and

5. psychology is easier than the natural sciences.

When asked about psychologists, the following features are most likely to be activated (Barrow 2000; Hartwig 2002; von Sydow 2007):

1. The image of a psychologist is largely dominated by the 'shrink' stereotype (male, psychoanalytically oriented, looking like Freud, with a client – often female – on his couch).

2. Ambivalence between idealisation (warm, intelligent, understanding, almost mystical powers) and very negative images (neurotic, dangerous, manipulative, lack of common sense).

3. Balding, wearing a suit, glasses, sitting with his legs crossed, middle-aged and older.

Figure 10.3 shows some examples of drawings of 'typical' psychologists.

What do you think?

Again go to **images.google.com** and type in 'cartoon psychologist'. Analyse the first 100 images you get. How well do they agree with the stereotypical views outlined above?

Figure 10.3 Drawings of 'typical psychologists'.
Source: Hartwig (2002).

Depiction of psychologists in books and films

Again the stereotypes people have of psychologists are strongly influenced by the roles psychologists are given in the media. If we zoom in on the image of psychotherapists (the image most frequently associated with psychologists), the following four types seem to be used, with the negative depictions outnumbering the positive ones (Gabbard & Gabbard 1999; Orchowski *et al.* 2006):

1. *The oracle.* When portrayed positively, the psychologist has brilliant insight into the psyche (e.g. to solve crimes); when portrayed negatively, the psychologist is a pretentious know-it-all who provides misinformation.

2. *The social agent.* When portrayed positively, helps patients with social problems; when portrayed negatively, coerces patients into unwanted action (e.g. adherence to dull society norms for creative, non-conforming individuals).

3. *The eccentric and the romantic therapist.* When depicted positively, seen as a sign of humanity; when depicted negatively, the result is a dishevelled, clownish and unorganised professional who conducts largely ineffective psychotherapy.

4. *The wounded healer.* When depicted positively, again sign of humanity; when depicted negatively, indication of someone who is unfit for the job.

Lack of overlap between the stereotypical image of a scientist and a psychologist

The fact that a psychologist is spontaneously associated with the image of a practising clinical psychologist means that there is virtually no overlap in the stereotypical images of scientists and psychologists. Whereas the former are essentially depicted as loners obsessed with their investigations, the latter are nearly always seen in interaction with other people. There is some overlap in the negative traits (mad, dangerous, lack of social skills and common sense), but these are more part of the effort to keep the image of one's own group high by attributing negative features to other groups rather than essential characteristics of scientists and psychologists. Finally, there is the – ironic – overlap in the fact that both groups are spontaneously associated with older men (whereas the majority of psychologists are women).

Given the small overlap in the stereotypical views of scientists and psychologists, it should come as no surprise that the general public does not spontaneously associate psychologists with scientists. People find it hard to think of psychologists as loners obsessed with their instruments and investigations.

Psychology researchers vs. psychology practitioners

Professional psychologists largely outnumber psychology researchers

In the previous section we saw that the general population spontaneously associates psychologists with psychology practitioners, in particular clinical psychologists. The fact that the practitioners strongly outnumber the researchers is another feature that distinguishes psychology from sciences such as physics, chemistry and biology. The only real comparison here is with medical practitioners.

Practitioners, both psychological and medical, rarely see themselves as (stereotypical) scientists. They are users of scientific information, but do not consider it as part of their job to generate new knowledge on the basis of the scientific method. Their scientific training helps them to look critically at the evidence presented in favour of an intervention, and to appreciate whether the claims made have sufficient empirical support or are unsubstantiated conjectures. However, practitioners typically have no ambition to be involved in scientific research themselves. Returning to the types of knowledge acquisition differentiated in Chapter 9, they make much more use of the method of tenacity ('this intervention has always been used for this type of problem'), the method of authority ('this intervention is advised by experts') and the a priori method ('this looks like a good intervention to me'), than the scientific method ('this intervention works because I have tested it empirically and shown its effectiveness with a falsification test').

The fact that psychological (and medical) practitioners are users of science rather than scientists means that there is quite some variety in the scientific standards to which they adhere, as has been observed by the sociologist Ward (2002: 223):

> Although groups such as the APA and most experimentalists sought to control strictly the type of people who could be called 'psychologists' and the type of knowledge the discipline was to produce, they were never able to establish a monopoly on what would count as legitimate psychological knowledge. As a result, practitioners peddled all types of intellectual wares under the label of 'psychology' throughout most of the twentieth century.

Interestingly enough, Ward (2002) argues that the differentiation between researchers and practitioners has been a strength of psychology rather than a weakness, because each approach meets different needs in the population, an idea we will return to in Chapter 13.

Psychology practitioners often forget their scientific education

Dawes (1994) has been more critical about the use of scientific information and the adherence to a scientific attitude among clinical psychologists (see also Baker *et al*. 2009). In Dawes's view, after graduation clinical psychologists have a tendency to forget all they have learned and to return to 'clinical intuition', which, he warned, is not much better than that of untrained people:

> . . . the rapid growth and professionalization of my field, psychology, has led it to abandon a commitment it made at the inception of that growth. That commitment was to establish a mental health profession that would be based on research findings, employing insofar as possible well-validated techniques and principles. . . . What was never envisioned was that a body of research and established principles would be available to inform practice, but that the practice would ignore that research and those principles. . . . Instead of relying on research-based knowledge in their practice, too many mental health professionals rely on 'trained clinical intuition.' But there is ample evidence that such intuition does not work well in the mental health profession. (In fact, it is often no different from the intuitions of people who have no training whatsoever.)
>
> (Dawes 1994: vii–viii)

> Two conditions are important for experiential learning [i.e. learning from experience]: one, a clear understanding of what constitutes an incorrect response or error in judgment, and two, immediate, unambiguous and consistent feedback when such errors are made. In the mental health professions neither of these conditions is satisfied.
>
> (Dawes 1994: 111)

Along the same lines, Cummings and O'Donohue (2008) noted that scientific talks rarely dominate at conferences of clinical practitioners. Much more attention is devoted to charismatic leaders who are treated like gurus, in line with the personalisation of issues seen in pseudoscience.

> Although there was utility in elevating our leaders to omniscience to give us validation when otherwise there was none, the tragedy of guru-based practice is that it fosters orthodoxy and stymies progress toward a therapeutically sound foundation. It created a culture that resisted science and isolated itself from an appropriate scientific base that is the evidence, along with the art, for medicine and all healthcare aside from mental healthcare. The schism between practice and science also isolated the science from that which it would study. Most academicians are poor psychotherapists and are unaware of what appropriately should or can be subjected to research and what cannot be.
>
> (Cummings & O'Donohue 2008: 47)

> Amazing as it seems, few psychotherapists are willing to acknowledge that most of the successes of our gurus result from their charisma, a personal and scintillating behavior that cannot be replicated by the rank-and-file practitioner. It is not the technique as much as it is the delivery. However, no one wants to admit that our psycho-religions are products of the charisma of the founder and have less, and sometimes nothing, to do with the efficacy of the method.
>
> (2008: 46)

The schism between practice and science has also been reported for organisational psychology. Rynes, Colbert and Brown (2002) analysed responses from nearly 1,000

American human resource (HR) managers about which techniques work, and found that there were large discrepancies between research findings and practitioners' beliefs, in particular with respect to personnel selection and recruitment. HR managers place far less faith in intelligence and personality tests as predictors of employee performance than is indicated on the basis of HR research (about which they learned during their education). Instead they return to the intuitively more appealing (unstructured) interviews and to reliance on their subjective judgment. Similar results were reported by Sanders *et al.* (2008) for the Netherlands, and Carless *et al.* (2009) for Australia. Complete the questionnaire below to see how good your HR knowledge is.

? What do you think?

How good are your human resource skills?

Circle for each statement whether it is true or false according to research findings.

1. The most important requirement for an effective leader is an outgoing, enthusiastic personality. T / F

2. In order to be evaluated favourably by line managers, the most important competency for HR managers is the ability to manage change. T / F

3. On average, encouraging employees to participate in decision-making is more effective for improving organisational performance than setting performance goals. T / F

4. Most errors in performance appraisals can be eliminated by providing training that describes the kinds of errors managers tend to make and suggesting ways to avoid them. T / F

5. The most valid employment interviews are designed around each candidate's unique background. T / F

6. On average, applicants who answer job advertisements are likely to stay in a job for a shorter time than those referred by other employees. T / F

7. There is very little difference among personality inventories in terms of how well they predict an applicant's likely job performance. T / F

8. On average, conscientiousness is a better predictor of job performance than is intelligence. T / F

9. Companies that screen job applicants for values have higher performance than those that screen for intelligence. T / F

10. Surveys that directly ask employees how important pay is to them are likely to overestimate the true importance of pay in actual decisions. T / F

The research-based answers are: 1-F, 2-T, 3-F, 4-F, 5-F, 6-T, 7-F; 8-F, 9-F, 10-F. If your score is rather low, that is not a problem as the above statements concern counterintuitive research findings. More worrying is that many HR managers, despite their education, still make these mistakes, because in practice they rely more on their intuition (which they claim is experience-based) than on actual findings.

Source: Rynes *et al.* 2002; Sanders *et al.* 2008

Ways in which psychology researchers have tried to distinguish themselves

Because psychology researchers saw the natural-scientific status of psychological research constantly being misunderstood, they repeatedly tried to distinguish their own work from the mainstream image of psychology. One way of doing this was to adopt a different name. Three names have been used: 'the new psychology' (which was apt up to the middle of the twentieth century but now has become obsolete), 'experimental psychology' (to stress the use of experiments as the basis of information acquisition) and 'scientific psychology' (to stress the more general scientific method).

Another way in which researchers distanced themselves from professionals was by the creation of their own societies. Indeed, in many countries you find psychology societies that are predominantly meant for (university) researchers and societies that are predominantly meant for practitioners. These are not always in unison, although they have the shared goal of promoting psychologists' standing in the wider society.

In the USA, for instance, the APA (American Psychological Association) began largely as a gathering of psychology researchers and had little interest in practitioners' needs (see Witmer's experiences in Chapter 8). The disenchantment of the practitioners (in particular the clinical psychologists) with the way in which they were treated reached its height in 1937, when a number of them walked out and founded the Association for Applied Psychology. Only after the APA promised to do more for professionals were they willing to become part of the APA again (this happened in 1945). One of the initiatives set up by the APA to make amends was a task force on how to establish the reliability and validity of psychological tests (see Chapter 8). The APA was keen to demonstrate that it had something to offer to professionals.

The efforts of the APA to serve practitioners were not appreciated by all researchers, who questioned the usefulness of such a society for them. As a result, twice there was a revolt of researchers, leading to the foundation of the Psychonomic Society in 1959 and the American Psychological Society (now called the Association for Psychological Science) in 1988.

A similar tension between professionals and researchers can be seen in the UK, where there is a distinction between the British Psychological Society (established in 1901 mainly by researchers, but increasingly taking on the interests of professional psychologists; see Chapter 4) and the Experimental Psychology Society (founded in 1946 to better meet researchers' needs). At the European level there are also societies primarily aimed at practitioners (e.g. the EFPA [European Federation of Psychologists' Associations]) and societies primarily meant for researchers (e.g. the ESCoP [European Society for Cognitive Psychology]).

Unlike scientific results, psychological findings are easy to understand

Everybody understands worthwhile psychological findings

As we have seen above, science is perceived as difficult, a challenge many people try to avoid. In contrast, psychology is seen as accessible (e.g. Keil *et al.* 2010). The reason for this is more or less as follows: because we are all humans interacting with others, we all have experience with what works and what does not work in our daily life. Psychological research can give us new insights (ideas which we had not thought of before), but if these insights are worthwhile we will have no difficulty relating to them. There will be a resonance between our own intuition and the new knowledge. This line of thinking has both positive and negative consequences.

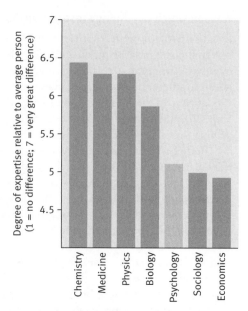

Figure 10.4 Difference in expertise between expert and average person.

When people are asked how much more expertise a college professor or licensed professional has relative to an average person, they make a distinction between the so-called 'hard sciences' (chemistry, medicine, physics, biology) and the 'soft' social sciences (psychology, sociology, economics).

Source: Janda *et al.* (1998), 'Attitudes towards psychology relative to other disciplines', *Professional Psychology: Research and Practice*, 29, 140–43.

A positive consequence is that most people are much more interested in psychological findings than in findings from other sciences. They are not put off by the perceived difficulty. As a result, psychological thinking has had a larger impact on society than many other sciences (see the psychologisation of society in Chapters 8 and 13). People are convinced that every sane and sufficiently intelligent person can understand the really important psychological findings.

A negative consequence is that the public in general does not believe psychologists have much specialised knowledge. Psychological findings that are too difficult to understand are not 'real' psychology, and findings that do not agree with the general opinion are likely to be wrong. For instance, Janda *et al.* (1998) asked a representative sample of 100 residents of Virginia (USA) how large the difference was between what an expert (i.e. a college professor or a licensed professional) knows about his or her field and how much an average person knows about the field. Seven disciplines were examined: biology, chemistry, economics, medicine, psychology, physics and sociology. Figure 10.4 shows the findings. From these, it is clear that the natural sciences (chemistry, medicine, physics, biology) are perceived as having much more expert knowledge than the social sciences (psychology, sociology, economics).

? What do you think?

Philosophers of science from time to time claim that psychology is overly complicated, because it lacks a paradigm (see the citations of Kuhn and Wittgenstein in Chapter 9). Could this be because they spontaneously assume that psychology ought to be simple? Is the knowledge in psychology really more complex, specialised and contradictory than the knowledge in, say, physics, medicine or computer sciences?

Not all psychologists are convinced of the added value of the scientific method

A final reason why psychology has difficulties being seen as a science is that not all psychologists, academics included, are convinced that the turn towards the scientific approach has been the right choice to study the human mind. Remember from Chapters 3 and 4 that before Wundt started his psychology laboratory, there was already a flourishing literature on the human mind. This literature grew out of three sources:

1. an increased philosophical interest in the human mind,
2. interest from teacher education programmes, and
3. interest from religious studies.

The hermeneutic alternative

hermeneutics

approach in psychology according to which the task of the psychologist is to interpret and understand persons on the basis of their personal and socio-cultural history

Not everyone agreed with the positivists that psychology ought to jump on the bandwagon of the natural sciences. According to them, psychology should stay within the humanities and in particular adopt the investigation approach of history. A common name for this approach is hermeneutics (although other names have been used as well throughout history). Hermeneutics is a word from Ancient Greek referring to the interpretation and translation of messages sent by the gods (these messages were usually conveyed by the god Hermes, hence the word). In psychology, hermeneutics refers to the interpretation and understanding of individuals on the basis of their personal and socio-cultural histories. Hermeneutics will, for instance, pay close attention to the motives people give for their actions and the purposes they want to achieve in life.

Throughout the history of psychology, the hermeneutic approach has coexisted with the mainstream natural-scientific approach, often on not very friendly terms (e.g. Park & Auchincloss 2006). Experimental psychologists objected to the fact that the hermeneutic approach kept on questioning the status of psychology as a natural science and, thereby, hindered attempts to have psychology departments accepted as scientific departments at universities. Hermeneutically oriented academics in turn maintained that the experimental approach overlooked essential skills practitioners needed for their profession (see, for instance, Zeldow 2009).

Unravelling how the human mind functions v. understanding what the human mind comprises

The main criticism of the proponents of hermeneutics against the experimental study of the human mind has been that it is too much geared towards unravelling the processes of the mind (answering the question 'how does it work?'), in the same way as natural scientists try to understand the workings of the heart, the behaviour of electrons in an atom, or the operation of a computer. What the experimental psychologists overlooked, according to the hermeneutists, was that understanding a person involves not so much knowing how the person functions, but what the person thinks, believes, feels and wants.

Because the tension between the experimental and the hermeneutic approach has been a central issue throughout the history of psychology, we will devote the rest of this chapter and the next chapter to it. First, in this chapter we give a short review of the hermeneutic approach. Then, in Chapter 11, we have a look at the methods proposed by both traditions.

Interim summary

Reasons why psychology is not seen as a science

- The stereotypical view people have of a psychologist is that of a clinical psychologist treating patients. This view does not overlap with the stereotypical view people have of a scientist as a loner who is obsessed with his work and which he studies in an uncreative way, making use of instruments.

- Professional psychologists largely outnumber psychology researchers, and they are users of scientific knowledge rather than creators of such knowledge. There is even evidence that many practitioners return to their intuition once they have finished their studies.

- People are convinced that they have as much knowledge about psychological issues as psychologists, or at least that they can keep up with psychologists as long as they pay attention to the psychological research that is described in the media.

- Next to the mainstream scientific tradition in academic psychology, there is a hermeneutic approach that is more in agreement with the public's view of psychology as non-scientific.

10.3 The critique of scientific psychology

In the previous section we saw how throughout the history of psychology scientifically oriented psychologists have coexisted with psychologists who questioned the usefulness of the scientific method for the study of mental life. In this section, we explore the evolutions within the hermeneutic movement.

Dilthey: *Naturwissenschaften* vs. *Geisteswissenschaften*

One of the first authors to openly criticise psychology's turn to the natural sciences was the German historian and philosopher Wilhelm Dilthey (1833–1911). In a series of publications in the 1880s and 1890s, he drew a distinction between what he called the *Naturwissenschaften* (natural sciences) and the *Geisteswissenschaften* (mental sciences or human sciences). He noted that the natural sciences sought to distil universal laws from a limited set of observations; their main method was the experiment. In contrast, the mental sciences aimed at understanding and interpreting the individual person by an analysis of his or her personal and socio-cultural history. The main research method here was understanding, in the same way as a historian tries to understand what happened in the past. According to Dilthey, the human mind should be understood, not explained.

The four elements of Dilthey's approach

There were four main elements in Dilthey's approach. First, psychology should be *content-based*. It should not focus on how the brain functions (the form), but on what the mind comprises (the meaning structure of the person). Because psychology was based on understanding the content of the mind, Dilthey argued, it belonged to the *Geisteswissenschaften*, together with history, political science, law, theory, literature and art.

Second, Dilthey argued that the subject matter of psychology was the *human experience in its totality*, including cognition (thoughts), emotion, and volition (motivation to act). Psychology should not aim at dissecting the human mind but at describing the complete mind with its constant interplay of cognition, emotion and volition.

The third element was that a person's life was embedded in a *context*. A person could not be studied in isolation, but had to be seen in his/her socio-cultural and historical context. A similar remark was made by Karl Marx (1818–1883), who urged philosophers and psychologists to study the mind of the individual as part of a society, instead of focusing on abstract individuals apart from history and society.

Finally, the natural-scientific research method with its experimentation and bias towards measurement could never grasp the totality of the mental life within its context. Therefore, the appropriate method for psychology was *understanding*. Dilthey distinguished three different levels of understanding:

1. elementary forms of understanding used to solve the simple problems of life,

2. empathy through which an observer can re-experience someone elses experiences,

3. the hermeneutic level of understanding, by which an observed person can be better understood than the person understands him/herself.

Psychoanalysis and related schools

Freud

Another major source of inspiration for the hermeneutic approach came from Freud's psychoanalysis and the subsequent evolutions. Although Freud saw his efforts as part of the natural-scientific tradition, the approach he recommended was much closer to that of Dilthey than to that of Wundt and his American students (although Stanley Hall, the founder of the first psychological laboratory in the USA, would invite Freud to the USA in 1909 and award him an honorary degree from Clark University). Freud's method was in line with the hermeneutic approach because it aimed at understanding the contents of a person's mind and was based on the interpretation of visible human products (dreams, memories, slips of the tongue, symptoms, art) with the use of psychoanalytic theory.

What do you think?

How does Freud's theory relate to the four elements of Dilthey's approach? Which level of understanding is the most important for Freud?

Related schools

In the twentieth century, Freud's ideas inspired a series of other theorists to come up with alternative theories of what constitutes the core of the human mind and how it develops over time. The best known are:

● **Carl Jung** (1875–1961) He made a distinction between the personal unconscious (forgotten and repressed contents of the individual's mental life) and the collective

unconscious (acts and images shared by all human beings or by a particular culture; manifest themselves in archetypes – e.g. the archetype of an old, wise man
with a white beard). Jung also distinguished several personality types and introduced the characteristic of extroversion versus introversion.

- **Alfred Adler** (1870–1937) He argued that the most important motive for a human
  being was a feeling of inferiority, originating from the sense of dependence and
  helplessness felt by infants. The feeling of inferiority resulted in a striving for superiority and perfection.

- **Erik Erikson** (1902–1994) Erikson is best known for his theory of developmental
  stages. According to this theory the human life comprised eight stages (infant,
  toddler, preschooler, school-age child, adolescent, young adult, middle adult, old
  adult) in each of which a new psychosocial crisis had to be solved (e.g. gaining
  trust in infancy). If the crisis was solved well, it resulted in a psychosocial virtue
  (e.g. hope and faith in infancy). If the crisis was not solved well, it resulted in mal-
  adaptation and malignancy (e.g. withdrawal of the infant).

- **John Bowlby** (1907–1990) He is known for his attachment theory, which states that
  infants seek proximity to a limited number of familiar people (in particular his/her
  mother) and use these people for comfort in stressful times and as a secure basis for
  exploration of the environment. Secure attachment is only possible if the adults are
  sensitive and responsive to the child's communications; it is also adversely affected
  by an abrupt and long-lasting separation. The quality of the emotional attachment
  formed in infancy has a lasting influence on the person's later emotional and social
  development. Bowlby supported falsification tests of his theory, in particular via a
  long-term collaboration with Mary Ainsworth, who devised the 'strange situation'
  test (in which the caregiver temporarily had to leave the child in an unfamiliar environment) to measure the attachment style of the child.

In the second half of the twentieth century, psychoanalysis placed increasing emphasis on the functioning of the ego (dealing with the unconscious drives from the id)
and the relations with others, past and present. The former is known as *ego psychology* and was inspired by Erikson's work. The latter is called *object relations* and
developed partly out of Bowlby's findings.

Rogers and humanistic psychology

Rogers

The psychoanalysts were not the only ones who on the basis of their treatments
formulated theories of human functioning that deviated from the natural-scientific
tenets defended by the experimental psychologists. Shortly before World War II, Carl
Rogers (see Chapter 8) started to question the tenets of the Freudian therapy and promoted an alternative form of therapy. In his client-centred approach, a therapist still
tried to understand the client, but this was done without interpretation on the basis
of psychoanalytic theory. Viewed within Dilthey's scheme of understanding, Rogers
emphasised the empathic form of understanding, whereas Freud chose the hermeneutic level. The therapist in Rogers's view had to share the client's experiences but not
interpret them; his/her role was supportive rather than enlightening.

Just like Bowlby, Rogers combined the hermeneutic approach with the natural-
science approach when he insisted that the efficacy of his therapy be tested (see also
Eysenck's research in Chapter 8). In 1954, he co-edited a book (Rogers & Dymond

1954) in which the results of a four-year programme on the efficacy of the client-centred therapy were examined. In the words of a reviewer:

> Changes in the clients during therapy were measured not against some abstractly defined global criterion or index of success of failure; instead, objective measures were used that would detect changes in certain specific personality variables that could be predicted from the theories of Rogers and operationally defined. These were: changes in self-perception, changes in the total personality make-up as determined by the TAT test, changes in the client's attitude toward others, and changes in scores on an emotional maturity scale.
>
> (Hulett 1955: 369)

The APA thanked Rogers for this initiative by bestowing on him one of its first Distinguished Scientific Contribution Awards in 1956.

What do you think?

In what respects does Rogers's research qualify as science according to the (logical) positivists? And in what respects does it qualify according to Popper?

Maslow

humanistic psychology

psychological movement promoted by Rogers and Maslow as a reaction against psychoanalysis and behaviourism; stressed that people are human, inherently positive, endowed with free will and living within a socio-cultural context

Rogers was, together with Abraham Maslow (1908–1970), one of the founders of humanistic psychology in the 1950s. This movement was promoted as the 'third force', because it offered an alternative to psychoanalysis and behaviourism. In 1966 Maslow published a book, *Psychology of science,* in which he detailed what he thought was wrong with a psychology exclusively built on the 'classic' scientific method. In his words:

> In my own history this clash in scientific world view first took the form of living simultaneously with two psychologies that had little to do with each other. In my career as an experimentalist in the laboratory, I felt quite comfortable and capable with my heritage of scientific orthodoxy . . . Indeed it was John B. Watson's optimistic credo (in *Psychologies* of 1925) that had brought me and many others into the field of psychology. His programmatic writings promised a clear road ahead. I felt – with great exhilaration – that it guaranteed progress . . .
>
> But insofar as I was a psychotherapist, an analysand, a father, a teacher, and a student of personality – that is, insofar as I dealt with whole persons – 'scientific psychology' gradually proved itself to be of little use . . .
>
> It was as if psychologists then lived by two mutually exclusive sets of rules, or as if they spoke two different languages for different purposes. If they were interested in working with animals, or with part-processes in human beings, they could be 'experimental and scientific psychologists.' But if they were interested in whole persons, these laws and methods were not of much help. (Maslow 1966: Chapter 2)

Importantly, Maslow did not conclude from this that science was worthless for the study of the whole person. Rather, he stressed the need for a new type of science, which was not exclusively based on Descartes' mechanistic world view (in which everything is interpreted as a machine). This can be seen in the following quote (Maslow 1966: Preface):

> I have been disturbed not only by the more 'anal' scientists and the dangers of their denial of human values in science, along with the consequent amoral technologizing

of all science. Just as dangerous are some of the critics of orthodox science who find it too skeptical, too cool and nonhuman, and then reject it altogether as a danger to human values. They become 'antiscientific' and even anti-intellectual. This is a real danger among some psychotherapists and clinical psychologists, among artists, among some seriously religious people, among some of the people who are interested in Zen, in Taoism, in existentialism, 'experientialism,' and the like. Their alternative to science is often sheer freakishness and cultishness, uncritical and selfish exaltation of mere personal experiencing, over-reliance on impulsivity (which they confuse with spontaneity), arbitrary whimsicality and emotionality, unskeptical enthusiasm, and finally navel-watching and solipsism. This is a real danger . . . I certainly wish to be understood as trying to enlarge science, not to destroy it.

Maslow's citation is a reminder that the humanities-based, hermeneutic approach must not be confounded with an anti-intellectual stance in which all systematicity is dropped. In the next chapter we will see how qualitative research methods currently try to address the need for systematicity without reduction to a mechanistic world view.

Neglect of individual differences

Another criticism raised against experimental psychology was that it ignored individual differences and tried to understand the functioning of the 'average' person. All participants of an experimental condition were considered to be equal. The American psychologist Gordon Allport (1947) argued that this was a direct consequence of psychology's infatuation with physics and technology: humans were made to fit in a machine model.

As it happened, Allport's criticism struck a chord with the natural-scientific approach as well as with the hermeneutics approach, partly because around that time statistical techniques became available that allowed researchers to measure individual differences. Shortly after Allport's seminal work, quantitative research on individual personality differences was booming, even to such a degree that it nearly oppressed the existing research into what people had in common. In line with the tenets of the natural-scientific approach, however, this research did not treat the participants as individuals with their own thoughts, emotions and motivations. They were considered as types that differed on a limited number of features (traits), and tests were devised to measure these differences (see Chapter 8).

Research methods govern research questions

A further criticism of natural-scientific psychology was that the method determined the research questions to be addressed. Research questions that did not fall within the realm of the natural-scientific approach were not examined and, by consequence, were not thought to be of interest. According to Giorgi (1970), this included all knowledge that could not be characterised as empirical, positivistic, reductionistic, quantitative, deterministic or predictive. The requirement of operationally defined variables meant that a large number of phenomena could not be investigated and, therefore, were excluded from psychology's discourse. As Maslow (1966) observed in the excerpts above, the topics of experimental psychology worked well as long you did not have to respond in a role as psychotherapist, father or teacher.

Books on research methods often make a distinction between facts and values (e.g. Stangor 2006: 8–9). Facts are defined as 'objective statements determined to be accurate through empirical study' (e.g. smoking increases the incidence of cancer and heart disease). In contrast, values are defined as 'personal statements that cannot be considered to be true or false' (e.g. it is important for me to quit smoking; or, I'd better not start drinking alcohol). Values cannot be proved or disproved by science; all science can do is provide facts that help people select their values. Within this perspective it could be argued that the direct impact of experimental psychology on everyday life is limited because many human choices and interactions are centred on values rather than facts.

Psychology has been confined too long to white Western males

Scientific psychology has also been criticised for being interested only in topics and research approaches that were of concern to Western males. The history of psychology indeed for a large part reads as a history of middle-class males in Western Europe and Northern America. This is the result not only of the group's dominance in academic life over the past centuries, but also the fact that white men have largely ignored the contributions of other groups and sometimes even actively suppressed them. For instance, Titchener excluded women from the 'experimental club' he founded to discuss psychological research. This impeded the careers of women researchers such as Mary Whiton Calkins, Margaret Floy Washburn and Christine Ladd-Franklin. The bias against female and non-Western values has respectively been studied in feminist psychology and postcolonial psychology.

We will say more about racism in psychology in Chapter 13. The objections feminist psychologists raised to traditional scientific psychology can be summarised as follows (Gross 2003):

feminist psychology
movement in psychology aimed at understanding women; is particularly concerned with the way in which women are treated in mainstream psychology

postcolonial psychology
movement in psychology addressing the issues of racism and the ways in which dominant groups treat other groups

- Men are taken as the standard/norm from which women deviate.
- Men decide what is worth investigating and how it should be investigated.
- There is a bias to publish the results of studies that show a difference between the genders.
- Results regarding gender differences are regularly interpreted in line with stereotyped expectations.
- Results regarding gender differences are interpreted as due to the individual and not to the social context.

Although not all feminist critiques question the value of the natural-scientific method, they do take issue with the fact that it is seen as the only acceptable research method, and they point out that such an approach is a typical Western white male approach. According to feminist psychologists, the way in which gender differences have been examined and interpreted clearly shows that science is not an objective and value-free enterprise, as claimed by the positivists, but a value-laden approach related to the socio-cultural context in which it occurs. Psychological researchers would do better acknowledging these influences, so that they do not continue the ongoing prejudice and discrimination against women under the guise of impartial scientific inquiry. A summary of this critique can be found in the following excerpt:

> feminist researchers have joined with other voices within philosophy and science . . . to challenge some of the traditional tenets of 'objectivity' in science. There appear to be

two major thrusts to the feminist challenge. The first is the recognition that values are an integral part of science, that they influence all phases of the process, and that they should be acknowledged and made explicit in the same way that we recognize that scientific truths are not independent of time and place . . . The second challenge to traditional scientific thinking goes further and argues more explicitly that the language, objectives, and methods of individual disciplines, and of science itself, particularly as defined by the experimental method, have been shaped by 'masculine' concerns, interests, and personality.

(Lott 1985: 158–9)

What do you think?

Currently there are many more female psychology students than male psychology students. Is this translated into the teaching you get and the type of research you are allowed to do, or are the criticisms raised by feminist psychology still valid today?

The scientific claims of objectivity and universal validity are exaggerated

A final criticism of the natural-scientific approach in psychology has been that it promises more than it can deliver. One promise, for instance, is that evidence-based opinions are guaranteed to be objective and true. In Chapter 9 we saw that this is not so. All scientific research is embedded within a paradigm, which determines the questions asked and the type of answers that are allowed. In addition, the postmodernists have pointed out that scientists are influenced by the society in which they work.

Ward (2002: 87–92) gives some eye-opening examples of the relativity of scientific opinions (see also Chapter 13). These examples are related to the late-nineteenth-century teenage-sex panic that took over the USA after it became an issue that teenagers engage quite regularly in masturbation. Psychologists were more than willing to offer scientific advice to the worrying parents and educators. G. Stanley Hall – student of Wundt, founder of the first psychological laboratory in the USA, first president of the APA, and leading child psychologist of the day – wrote in his influential 1904 two-volume book *Adolescence* that:

Sex asserts its mastery in field after field, and works its havoc in the form of secret vice, debauch, disease, and enfeebled heredity . . . dangerous malady . . . most liable to occur in individuals who lack stamina . . . the very saddest of all the aspects of human weakness . . . bought at the cost of the higher life.

(as cited in Ward 2002: 88)

Hall was by no means the only psychologist giving scientific advice. Another well-known PhD in psychology, trained with Wundt in Germany, was Elwood Worcestor. He was involved in a Boston-based religious and psychotherapy group known as the Emmanuel Movement. His appreciation in 1908 was:

no one can deny that serious moral and nervous affections follow the habitual practice of masturbation, and these are more serious in early life, and when, as is often the case, the victim is temporarily nervous and delicate. The physical symptoms are weakness, pallor, and backache and general debility. The effects on the brain and nervous system are more serious.

(as cited in Ward 2002: 89–90)

Although it is tempting to explain these unsubstantiated pieces of advice as the outcome of a lack of empirical data at the beginning of the twentieth century, the postmodernists warn us that they are much more a testimony of the fact that opinions ventured by scientists are influenced by the socio-historical context in which they live. Psychologists who nowadays are asked to give advice about masturbation are as much influenced by the prevailing morals about sexuality as their colleagues were in the early 1900s. According to the postmodernists, the same is true for advice on autism, ADHD, OCD, global warming, smacking children, testing children from an early age, and so on.

Critical psychology

critical psychology

movement in psychology that criticises mainstream psychology for failing to understand that knowledge does not refer to an outside reality (idealism), that scientific knowledge is not cumulative but consists of social constructions, and that psychological theories and claims have an impact on the world in which people live

The latest development within the hermeneutic approach has been the emergence of a number of positions that became known as critical psychology (or rather critical psychologies, as the different positions do not see themselves as fully compatible; Teo, 2005). Critical psychology is based on the following tenets (e.g. Fox *et al.* 2009).

Idealism instead of realism

As we saw in Chapters 3 and 9, there are two opposing views in philosophy about the nature of human knowledge. On the one hand, there is realism, saying that knowledge corresponds to reality, which must be discovered; its truth depends on the correspondence with the real world. On the other hand, there is idealism, saying that knowledge is a social construction, which does not necessarily correspond to an outside world; the truth of statements depends on their coherence with the rest of knowledge. Critical psychologists argue that scientific psychology (which they usually call 'mainstream psychology') wrongly believes in realism. According to them, human language does not represent things in the world but is meant to facilitate social interaction. For the same reason, mainstream psychology is wrong in the emphasis it puts on the individual in isolation; what matters is the person as a social being.

Science is a social construction

The idealistic world view of critical psychologists also has implications for their perception of science. They agree with the postmodernists (Chapter 9) that science is not a progressive uncovering of reality, but a social construction in which scientific statements are primarily determined by the language and the culture of the scientists. As a result, scientific statements are not fixed 'truths', but ever-changing stories that reflect the socio-political and cultural world of the scientists. Scientific writings must be read like history texts: as one of the possible accounts of what is/was going on. Indeed, one of the first writings in critical psychology was entitled 'Social psychology as history' (Gergen 1973). This implies that, to understand psychology, it is important not to see it in isolation but to examine the context in which it takes part as an academic discipline.

For example, Fox *et al.* (2009) point out that mainstream psychology currently has a strong individualistic approach. The emphasis is on the functioning of the individual, his or her biological and psychological features, and the maintenance of his/her self-esteem in social interactions. By focusing on the individual rather than the group or society, mainstream psychology currently accentuates individualist values at the expense of mutuality and community. This is not because science 'proves' that these values are better, but because these values nowadays dominate Western society. Most powerful institutions encourage people to seek identity and meaning through individual and competitive pursuits instead of through collaborative or community endeavours. Mainstream psychology forms an allegiance with these institutions and simply imposes their values on members of marginalised and less powerful groups:

> Watching television and surfing the Internet, advancing in careers, keeping the lawn green, and shopping for fun are only some of the things many people do that divert attention and energy from constructing more meaningful friendships, participating in community life, or recognizing and working to end injustice. It is no coincidence that a self-focused mindset offers more benefits to those who control corporate capitalism and other members of relatively privileged groups than to the vast numbers who congregate in shopping malls and football stadiums or search for anonymous on-line community.
>
> (Fox *et al*. 2009: 6)

Psychologists have a moral responsibility

Because the (social) reality is constantly changing as a function of what happens, critical psychology urges psychologists to be aware of the fact that their research affects reality. Psychological theories change the perception of people and, as a result, the world in which they live. Psychology research can condone a social injustice and promote its continuation by giving it a 'scientific' justification. Because of concerns about the implications of research, there is usually a larger degree of social and political engagement among critical psychologists than among mainstream psychologists. This, for instance, can be seen in the close ties that exist between the critical psychology movement, feminist psychology and postcolonial psychology. According to critical psychology, psychologists cannot pretend they are studying their subject matter in a detached way from the outside; they are part of the subject matter and have to act accordingly, as shown in the citation below:

> One bottom-line lesson which I feel to be important is really a moral one: the psychologist is not outside the things that he or she studies, not an external 'objective' observer of the human psyche, but an active participant in the collective psychological life of their community, culture and, ultimately, species. This means that what psychologists say and do, the theories, images and models of the psychological that they devise and promote, have real consequences for everybody else. They are in an even weaker position than the physical scientists to disclaim responsibility for what society does with what they produce, for even in producing it they are participating in this collective social psychological process.
>
> (Richards 2002: 5)

We will return to the ways in which psychological research changes society in Chapter 13.

? ### What do you think?

Above we saw that, according to feminist psychology, the ways in which psychology researches gender differences colour the perceptions people have of such differences. Can you find a specific example? And can you think of other examples in which psychological research has had an impact on the way in which people perceive a particular phenomenon?

Conclusion

Ever since psychology carved itself a niche in academia as a science, there has been the feeling that the scientific method does not provide all the information psychologists need. This has been felt in applied contexts, but also in academic psychology. Remember from Chapter 4 that Wundt had already made a distinction between three research methods: experimental methods, introspection and the historical method. Only the first one qualified as scientific according to the behaviourists.

A similar ambiguity towards experimental psychology can be found in James and his successor at Harvard University, Hugo Münsterberg, who published a textbook in 1915 under the title *Psychology: General and applied*. In this book Münsterberg drew a distinction between causal psychology (the natural-scientific approach) and purposive psychology (the hermeneutic approach), which he saw as complementary:

> [In the causal psychology] we shall resolve the personality into the elementary bits of psychical atoms and shall bring every will act into a closed system of causes and effects. But in the purposive part we shall show with the same consistency the true inner unity of the self and the ultimate freedom of the responsible personality. Those two accounts do not exclude each other; they supplement each other, they support each other, they demand each other.
>
> (as cited in Cahan & White 1992)

Also, nowadays introductory textbooks of psychology include a discussion of ideas from the hermeneutic tradition, even though in the introduction they define psychology as a scientific discipline.

Although it is fair to say that the natural-scientific and the hermeneutic approaches in general have not been comfortable with each other, there have been many attempts to find common ground and to see how each could strengthen the other. Unfortunately, those attempts have not been very fruitful, possibly because the two traditions represent the two opposing cultures: science vs. humanities (Chapter 2). For the science-oriented psychologist, the fact that not everything can be addressed with the scientific method is an indication that the available scientific tools are not yet powerful enough or that it is not yet known how to measure certain phenomena properly. For the humanities-oriented psychologist, the fact that not everything can be addressed with the scientific method is a sign that the scientific rationalisation of life and the depiction of the world as a soulless machine miss the most fundamental aspect of (human) life.

On the other hand, there is evidence that the two approaches inspire each other indirectly, through their respective influences on society and because psychologists study both traditions in their education. The psychoanalyst Bornstein (2005) calls this type of implicit influence **unconscious plagiarism**. Table 10.1 lists some of the terms used in cognitive psychology that according to Bornstein have such an overlap with Freudian ideas that they have to be inspired by them. An influence the other way round is the growing discussion within psychoanalysis about the desirability of empirical research on the psychoanalytic tenets (e.g. Luyten *et al.* 2006).

unconscious plagiarism
term used by Bornstein to indicate how the scientific and the hermeneutic approach in psychology have influenced each other without the proponents being aware of it

Table 10.1 Revisions and reinventions of psychoanalytic concepts
Cognitive terms that have a strong resemblance to ideas put forward by Freud more than half a century earlier.

Psychoanalytic concept	Revision or reinvention
Unconscious memory	Implicit memory
Primary process thought	Spreading activation
Object representation	Person schema
Repression	Cognitive avoidance
Preconscious processing	Preattentive processing
Parapraxis	Retrieval error
Abreaction	Redintegration
Repetition compulsion	Nuclear script
Ego	Central executive
Ego defence	Defensive attribution

Source: Bornstein (2005), 'Reconnecting psychoanalysis to mainstream psychology: challenges and opportunities', *Psychoanalytic Psychology*, 22, 323–40.

Interim summary

The critique of experimental psychology

- Dilthey: psychology belongs to the *Geisteswissenschaften* (mental sciences) because:
  - it deals with the *content* of the human mind,
  - it describes the *human experience in its totality* (including cognition, emotion and volition),
  - it sees a person's life within its *context,*
  - only the method of *understanding* can study the full human experience (different levels of understanding).
- Psychoanalysis used the hermeneutic approach because it tried to understand the content of the human mind through interpretation on the basis of the psychoanalytic theories.
- The client-centred approach also stressed the importance of understanding the other in psychotherapeutic relations; in this tradition, however, understanding was defined as empathy and not as an interpretation within a theoretical framework.
- Allport criticised experimental psychology because it ignored individual differences.
- In the natural-scientific approach the interesting research questions are too much defined as a function of what can be examined with the scientific method.
- Experimental psychology is partly the result of the dominance of white Western males in psychological research. Gave rise to feminist and postcolonial psychology.
- The natural-scientific approach ignores the fact that all knowledge is relative, depending on the prevailing research paradigm and influences from society.
- The strongest criticism of experimental psychology currently comes from critical psychology. This movement points to the facts that (1) knowledge is not a mirror

of reality, (2) science is a social construction, and (3) psychologists have a moral responsibility because their research changes the social reality.

● Criticism of experimental psychology has had an influence on mainstream research, but mostly indirectly (through unconscious plagiarism).

10.4   *Focus on*: Can the history of psychology be taught by psychologists?

Traditional vs. new history of psychology

In this chapter we saw how history became part of the curriculum of psychologists, not only because it was essential for their education but also because it legitimised psychology as a young science. This history had a number of characteristics:

● It stemmed from psychologists themselves, who did it 'on the side'.
● It was undertaken out of curiosity, for celebratory reasons, or for didactic purposes.
● It took the contemporary state of psychology as the starting point and saw history as the anticipation of that state (often with hindsight bias of what had been important in the history and what had been false starts).
● Saw psychology as a progressive, cumulative process that over time came closer to the truth.
● Was basically a review of the achievements of the 'great men' of psychology.

In 1989, the American historian Laurel Furumoto called for a different (new) approach to the history of psychology. According to her, the new history:

● investigates the assumptions that gave rise to contemporary psychology,
● tries to understand the historical events within the knowledge that existed at the time of the event,
● has an eye for the influences of the wider society and the relativity of knowledge,
● is done by independent and specialised historians, and
● takes a detached and often critical stance towards psychology.

Vested interests

The advantage of independent history teachers is that they are not associated with one particular approach. A danger associated with psychology teachers is that they may be biased (implicitly or explicitly) towards their own stance. For instance, the fact that this book has been written by two cognitive psychologists could make readers expect that:

● mainstream psychology will be described in a positive way,
● the scientific approach will be presented positively,
● psychological knowledge will be seen as cumulative (we know more now than we ever did before),

- there will be more detailed information about the natural-scientific approach than about the other approaches, and
- there will be a bias towards academic research at the expense of applied psychology.

What do you think?

How is the book doing with respect to the criticisms above? How would the book differ if it was written by authors from the hermeneutic approach?

Because of the vested interests of psychologists, some psychology departments have decided to outsource the teaching of the history of psychology to the history department. Unfortunately, this raises other issues. Just to cite a few:

- The attitude towards psychology is influenced by the attitude a lecturer has towards science in general, and this is true for historians as much as for psychologists.
- Although the wider social influences are important, there remains a sequence of events that have shaped psychology and that must be included in any course. So, historians teaching the history of psychology need to have a good grasp of what happened in the field if they want to teach a relevant course.
- There is no 'true' history of psychology. Many different histories can be written (and have been written). The history of psychology consists of everything that has ever been recorded in relation to psychology (or the study of the human mind in general), including a myriad of ambiguities, inconsistencies and contradictions between different actors and, quite often, within the same actors on different occasions. Every history is a simplified summary of the raw material on the basis of the materials that are easily available and the opinions held within the social groups to which the authors belong. The only distinction one can make is between blatantly biased histories and histories that are perceived by the different actors at a particular time as 'reasonably (un)biased'. Whether or not the narrator is a psychologist is of secondary importance.

What do you think?

How would you tell the story of your life? And how would someone else tell it? Someone you get on with and someone you do not get on with? Your parents? What would be the true story of your life? And how long should it be before it is 'complete'? And would that then still be interesting to anyone?

Psychology: a failed bridge?

In Chapter 2 we described how in 1959 Charles Snow regretted the separation that had grown between people interested in science and people interested in the humanities, which he called 'the two cultures'. In a postscript written four years later he was more optimistic (see the reprint: Snow 1998). In particular he referred to the growing social and behavioural sciences (including psychology), which would form a bridge between the two cultures, because the education would have a grounding both in the humanities and in the natural sciences.

> I am now convinced that this is coming. When it comes, some of the difficulties of communication will at last be softened; for such a culture has, just to do its job, to be on speaking terms with the scientific one.
>
> (Snow 1998: 71)

Our analysis in the present chapter illustrates that the divide between the two cultures may be harder to overcome. Rather than being bridged, it seems to create a split within psychology itself (and the other social/behavioural sciences).

Kagan (2009) also concluded that the social sciences have failed to become a bridge between the natural sciences and humanities, but he argued that they have become a separate, third culture, with their own language and assumptions, further fractioning the cultural landscape and hindering communication between the various groups.

? What do you think?

Do you agree with Kagan (2009) that psychology has become a separate culture with very few connections to either humanities or natural sciences? If so, is this because of an insurmountable disparity between the two cultures or because the total amount of knowledge exceeds human capacities to such an extent that fractioning is unavoidable? What do you think of Sarton's (1937) assertion that only a discipline 'history of science' can bridge the divide, because such a discipline is steeped both in the humanities (history) and in the sciences?

> To complete the integration [between humanists and scientists], each group must learn to understand the other. The educated people in general must obtain some knowledge and appreciation of science; the scientists must receive some historical training, must be taught to look backward as well as forward, and to look with reverence. These good offices may be rendered to both groups by the teaching of the history of science and of the history of civilization focused upon it . . . Between the old humanist and the scientist, there is but one bridge, the history of science . . .
>
> (Sarton 1937: 56–7)

Other possible points of view

Whether or not the history of psychology can be taught by psychologists, it is important for you to realise the relativity of each approach taken in a particular course. To illustrate this, we list a number of ideas about history books we have encountered in our research for this book but that in the end did not (quite) make it. Maybe you want to pursue one of them?

- Psychology has generated no useful knowledge thus far, but has managed to impose itself on society by making clever alliances and by creating problems for which it subsequently pretended to offer solutions. (This is an approach often found in postmodernistically inspired sociological writings; e.g. Achterhuis 1979; Ward 2002.)

- Psychology has had no ideas by itself, but has always borrowed ideas from other disciplines and from developments within society.

- History is a constant recycling of ideas that thrive for some time, become forgotten and are then returned to.
- A history of psychology should focus on the scientists who made the discipline.
- A history should be organised in terms of the main problems and ideas that have been addressed.
- A history should divide the past into periods.
- A history must give due attention to the biographies of the main actors; how their ideas were shaped by their life experiences.
- A history should focus on the distribution of powers in the society and show how dominating groups oppressed the ideas of others.
- A history of psychology should not be limited to the history of Western psychology.
- The history of psychology cannot be understood without a detailed analysis of the changing attitudes towards religion in Western society.

Interim summary

- Each history is relative and conveys only part of the rich raw material that is available.
- In the history of psychology a distinction is often made between the traditional approach (largely seen as a legitimisation of the current state of affairs) and the new approach (more critical, has an eye for the relativity of knowledge, tries to expose the assumptions that gave rise to current opinions).
- An extra problem is that book authors and lecturers may have vested interests, which bias the coverage of the history.
- The history described in the present book is not *the* history of psychology. It is only one of the possible stories, which we hope will not be perceived as being too biased.

Recommended literature

The scientific tradition in psychology is well described in the first chapters of most research books in psychology. We in particular used Christensen, L.B. (2004) *Experimental methodology* (9th edn) (Boston: Pearson Education) and Rosenthal, R. & Rosnow, R.L. (2008) *Essentials of behavioral research: Methods and data analysis* (3rd edn) (Boston: McGraw-Hill).

For the critical part we found much information and many ideas in Teo, T. (2005) *The critique of psychology: From Kant to postcolonial theory* (New York: Springer Science); in Gross, R. (2003) *Themes, issues and debates in psychology* (2nd edn) (Abingdon: Hodder Arnold); and in Fox, D., Prilleltensky, I., & Austin, S. (eds) (2009) *Critical psychology: An introduction* (2nd edn) (Los Angeles: Sage Publications).

References

Achterhuis, H. (1979) *De markt van welzijn en geluk* [The market of well-being and happiness]. The Netherlands: Uitgeverij Ambo.

Allport, G.W. (1947) 'Scientific models and human morals', *Psychological Review,* 54: 182–92.

Baars, B.J. (1986) *The cognitive revolution in psychology.* New York: Guilford Press.

Baker, T.B., McFall, R.M. & Shoham, V. (2009) 'Current status and future prospects of clinical psychology: Toward a scientifically principled approach to mental and behavioral health care', *Psychological Science in the Public Interest*, 9: 67–103.

Bargh, J.A. & Chartrand, T. (1999) 'The unbearable automaticity of being', *American Psychologist*, 54: 462–79.

Barrow, R. (2000) 'Determining stereotypical images of psychologists: the Draw A Psychologist Checklist', *College Student Journal*, 34: 123–33.

Bornstein, R.F. (2005) 'Reconnecting psychoanalysis to mainstream psychology: Challenges and opportunities', *Psychoanalytic Psychology*, 22: 323–40.

Boyack, K.W., Klavans, R. & Börner, K. (2005) 'Mapping the backbone of science', *Scientometrics*, 64: 351–74.

Breeuwsma, G. (2008) 'Het vergeten weten: De teloorgang van klassiekers in de psychologie' [Forgotten knowledge: The decline of classics in psychology]. *De Psycholoog*, 43: 202–9.

Cahan, E.D. & White, S.H. (1992) 'Proposals for a second psychology', *American Psychologist*, 47: 224–35.

Carless, S.A., Rasiah, J. & Irmer B.E. (2009) 'Discrepancy between human resource research and practice: Comparison of industrial/organisational psychologists and human resource practitioners' beliefs', *Australian Psychologist*, 44: 105–11.

Cummings, N.A. & O'Donohue, W.T. (2008) *Eleven blunders that crippled psychotherapy in America*. New York: Routledge.

Dawes, R.B. (1994) *House of cards: Psychology and psychotherapy built on myth*. New York: The Free Press.

Dewey, J. (1887) *Psychology*. New York: Harper & Brothers.

Ebbinghaus, H. (1908/1973) *Psychology: An elementary textbook*. New York: Arno Press.

Finston, K.D., Beaver, J.B. & Cramond, B.L. (1995) 'Development and field test of a checklist for the Draw-a-Scientist test', *School Science and Mathematics*, 95: 195–205.

Fox, D., Prilleltensky, I. & Austin, S. (eds) (2009) *Critical psychology: An introduction* (2nd edn). Los Angeles: Sage Publications.

Furumoto, L. (1989) 'The new history of psychology.' In I. Cohen (ed.), *The G. Stanley Hall Lecture Series* (vol. 9). Washington, DC: APA.

Gabbard, G.O. & Gabbard, K. (1999) *Psychiatry and the cinema* (2nd edn). Washington, DC: American Psychiatric Press.

Gergen, K.J. (1973) 'Social psychology as history', *Journal of Personality and Social Psychology*, 26: 309–20.

Giorgi, A. (1970) *Psychology as a human science*. New York: Harper & Row.

Gross, R. (2003) *Themes, issues and debates in psychology* (2nd edn). Abingdon, UK: Hodder Arnold.

Hartwig, S.G. (2002) 'Surveying psychologists' public image with drawings of a "typical" psychologist', *South Pacific Journal of Psychology*, 14: 69–75.

Haynes, R. (2003) 'From alchemy to artificial intelligence: Stereotypes of the scientist in Western literature', *Public Understanding of Science*, 12: 243–53.

Hulett, J.E. (1955) 'Book review of *Psychotherapy and personality change: Coordinated research studies in the client-centered approach*, by Carl R. Rogers and Rosalind F. Dymond', *American Sociological Review*, 20: 369–70.

Janda, L.H., England, K., Lovejoy, D. & Drury, K. (1998) 'Attitudes toward psychology relative to other disciplines', *Professional Psychology: Research and Practice*, 29: 140–3.

Kagan, J. (2009) *The three cultures: Natural sciences, social sciences, and the humanities in the 21st century*. Cambridge: Cambridge University Press.

Keil, F.C., Lockhart, K.L. & Schlegel, E. (2010) 'A bump on a bump? Emerging intuitions concerning the relative difficulties of the sciences', *Journal of Experimental Psychology: General*, 139: 1–15.

Kessels, U., Rau, M. & Hannover, B. (2006) 'What goes well with physics? Measuring and altering the image of science', *British Journal of Educational Psychology*, 76: 761–80.

Koch, S. (1961) 'Psychological science versus the science–humanism antinomy: Intimations of a significant science of man', *American Psychologist*, 16: 629–39.

Kuhn, T.S. (1962/1970) *The structure of scientific revolutions*. Chicago: Chicago University Press.

Lott, B. (1985) 'The potential enrichment of social personality psychology through feminist research and vice versa', *American Psychologist*, 40: 155–64.

Luyten, P., Blatt, S.J. & Corveleyn, J. (2006) 'Minding the gap between positivism and hermeneutics in psychoanalytic research', *Journal of the American Psychoanalytic Association*, 54: 571–610.

Maslow, A.H. (1966) *Psychology of science*. New York: Harper & Row.

McDuffie, T.E. (2001) 'Scientists – geeks & nerds? Dispelling teachers' stereotypes of scientists', *Science and Children*, 38: 16–19.

Münsterberg, H. (1915) *Psychology: General and applied*. New York: D. Appleton & Co.

Orchowski, L.M., Spickard, B.A. & McNamara, J.R. (2006) 'Cinema and the valuing of psychotherapy: Implications for clinical practice', *Professional Psychology: Research and Practice*, 37: 506–14.

Park, S.W. & Auchincloss, E.L. (2006) 'Psychoanalysis in textbooks of introductory psychology: A review', *Journal of the American Psychoanalytic Association*, 54: 1361–80.

Richards, G. (2002) *Putting psychology in its place: A critical historical overview*. London: Routledge.

Rogers, C.R. & Dymond, R.F. (eds) (1954) *Psychotherapy and personality change: Coordinated research studies in the client-centered approach*. Chicago: The University of Chicago Press.

Rynes, S.L., Colbert, A.E. & Brown, K.G. (2002) 'HR professionals' beliefs about effective human resource practices: Correspondence between research and practice', *Human Resource Management,* **41**: 149–74.

Sanders, K., van Riemsdijk, M. & Groen, B. (2008) 'The gap between research and practice: A replication study on the HR professionals' beliefs about effective human resource practices', *International Journal of Human Research Management,* **19**: 1976–88.

Sandoval, W.A. (2005) 'Understanding students' practical epistemologies and their influence on learning through inquiry', *Science Education,* **89**: 634–56.

Sarton, G. (1937) *The history of science and the new humanism.* Cambridge, MA: Harvard University Press (1988 reprint from Brunswick: Transaction Books).

Snow, C.P. (1959/1998) *The two cultures* (with introduction by Stefan Collini). Cambridge: Cambridge University Press.

Stangor, C. (2006) *Research methods for the behavioral sciences.* Boston, MA: Houghton Mifflin.

Teo, T. (2005) *The critique of psychology: From Kant to postcolonial theory.* New York: Springer Science + Business Media, Inc.

Vilchez-Gonzalez, J.M. & Parales Palacios, F.J. (2006) 'Image of science in cartoons and its relationship with the image in comics', *Physics Education,* **41**: 240–9.

von Sydow, K. (2007) 'The public image of psychologists, psychotherapists, and psychiatrists', *Psychotherapeut,* **52**: 322–33.

Ward, S.C. (2002) *Modernizing the mind: Psychological knowledge and the remaking of society.* Westport, CT: Praeger.

Yasar, S., Baker, D., Robinson-Kurpius, S., Krause, S. & Roberts, C. (2006) 'Development of a survey to assess K-12 teachers' perceptions of engineers and familiarity with teaching design, engineering, and technology', *Journal of Education,* **95**: 205–16.

Zeldow, P.B. (2009) 'In defense of clinical judgment, credentialed clinicians, and reflective practice', *Psychotherapy Theory, Research, Practice, Training,* **46**: 1–10.

11 The contribution of quantitative and qualitative research methods

Questions to consider

Conceptual issues addressed in this chapter

- What are the assumptions upon which quantitative research methods in psychology are based?
- Why do quantitative researchers see a hierarchy of evidence going from descriptive research, via relational research, to experimental research?
- What are the assumptions upon which qualitative research methods in psychology are based?
- Why is discourse analysis more in line with social constructionism than grounded theory?
- What are the arguments psychologists use to defend the idea that qualitative and quantitative research methods cannot coexist?
- What are the arguments psychologists use to defend the idea that qualitative and quantitative research methods complement each other and that progress in psychology is best guaranteed by a combination of both types of methods?
- What implications does the coexistence of quantitative and qualitative methods in psychology have for philosophy of science?

Introduction

Collecting and editing the manuscripts have reminded me of the rapidity of change in our world and our scholarly work. Ten years ago, after I completed one of the first qualitative dissertations done in my college, I was a participant in the great paradigm war between positivists and constructivists – the Quantoids and the Smooshes . . . There were few qualitative sessions at the American Education Research Association (AERA) meetings, and the Educational Researcher was full of salvos fired across the paradigm lines.

It feels to some of us like we won the war. Has qualitative research taken over the high ground and become what Kuhn (1962/1970: 10) called 'normal science'?

(Hatch 1995: xvi)

In Chapter 10 we saw that psychology can be divided into two research lines. On the one hand, there is the mainstream, natural-science oriented approach, on which psychology as an academic discipline was founded. On the other hand, there is the hermeneutic alternative, which argues that the scientific method is unsuitable to study mental life, because the method of the natural sciences makes it impossible to access the richness of the human experience. As the quote above shows, this discussion is not limited to psychology, but can be found in all human and social sciences (e.g. education, social work, management, sport, health, . . .).

In recent years, the discussion has crystallised into the question to what extent the traditional quantitative methods should be supplemented (or replaced) by qualitative research methods. In the quote at the opening of this chapter this is referred to as the 'paradigm war'. Below we will have a look at the various positions and see whether the situation is indeed as grave as suggested in the citation. First, we discuss the essence of the quantitative and the qualitative methods.

11.1   The essence of quantitative research

quantitative research methods

research methods based on quantifiable data; are associated with the natural-science approach based on the hypothetico-deductive model

Quantitative research methods are research methods based on quantifiable data, findings which can be represented as numbers either because their magnitude can be measured or because their frequency of occurrence can be counted. They usually involve statistical analysis and are the methods preferred by the traditional, natural-science oriented psychology researchers. Their application depends on a number of assumptions, which we first outline.

Assumptions underlying quantitative research methods

There is an outside reality that can be discovered

Quantitative psychologists start from the assumption that phenomena in the world have an existence outside people's minds. That is, they believe in realism (Chapter 9). In addition, they defend the idea that humans can discover reality by using the scientific method. This does not mean they subscribe to the positivist view that reality can be known simply by means of observation, induction and verification, and that scientific knowledge is always true. They are well aware of the fact that science is not a linear accumulation of facts but proceeds through trial and error (with theories and paradigms that do not stand the falsification test and that after some time have to be abandoned). However, they are convinced that in the long term the scientific method based on the hypothetico-deductive model (Chapter 9) leads to an understanding of reality; scientific knowledge is cumulative.

The main aim of scientific research is to find universal causal relationships

Researchers who subscribe to quantitative research methods are primarily interested in discovering relationships between causes and effects. They want to know how humans function: how various variables interact and how particular functions are accomplished. In addition, they want to know how general the principles are. Ideally they hope the mechanisms they discover will apply to all humans. If this turns out not to be the case, they search for the causes underlying individual differences and try to integrate them into a wider pattern that covers the entire spectrum.

Trying to avoid confounds and sources of noise

Users of quantitative research methods are extremely vigilant about the possible intrusion of undesired factors into their designs. Because they are looking for 'true' cause–effect relations, they try to avoid the presence of so-called confounding variables, variables that were overlooked but that could be the true causes of the effects observed (see below for an example). As a result, quantitative researchers try to maximally control the circumstances under which they run their studies, even if this leads to artificial situations (i.e. so-called laboratory situations).

Quantitative researchers also try to eliminate the impact of random variables. These are elements that vary randomly from one study to the next and that may lead to findings which are not replicable (because the effect was due to a random variable that only in one particular study had the value causing the effect). These random variables are called noise.

Suspicion about the researcher's input

A source of confounding and noise that is of particular interest to quantitative psychology researchers is the researcher him- or herself. Humans are known to have fallible perceptions and opinions, meaning that they can be a source of bias (confound) or randomness (noise). A biased researcher is a researcher who consistently obtains 'evidence' other people cannot find. This usually consists of evidence in line with the researcher's convictions (see Chapter 9 for the ways in which opinions shape the perception of facts). A random researcher is a researcher who in a study obtains evidence no-one else (including the researcher him/herself) can replicate, because it was a fluke.

To protect themselves against biases and noise, quantitative researchers make use of standardised measurements and instruments. For instance, they will make use of generally accepted questionnaires to measure aspects of people and they will analyse the data with generally accepted statistical tests. In this way, they have more certainty that the findings they obtain can be replicated by others using the same methods.

Progress through falsification

One final feature of the quantitative research approach is that researchers continuously evaluate the truth of their conclusions, theories, hypotheses and instruments. This is part of the falsification element in scientific research. Researchers constantly try to prove each other wrong, which often bewilders non-scientific spectators who cannot understand why scientists rarely seem to agree with one another. As a rule of thumb, an effect will only be accepted as 'probably true' when there is a great deal of converging evidence for it, coming from different measurements and falsification attempts.

Now that we have seen the assumptions underlying quantitative research methods, we can have a closer look at the various techniques that are available. These are usually divided into three broad orientations (e.g. Rosenthal & Rosnow 2008): descriptive research, relational research and experimental research.

Descriptive research

Observation of numerical data

In descriptive research, the focus is on observation, a careful charting of the situation. As we have seen several times in this book, detailed observation is the start of scientific research. Certainly with respect to psychology, this is not a platitude. Just think of how long philosophers thought they could study human functioning without looking at what people were actually doing. The same is true for many everyday conversations, in which people vent opinions based on their hunches. How often do you hear someone say they cannot discuss a particular psychological topic (e.g. the influence of divorce on the well-being of children) because they would first need to have a look at the empirical evidence?

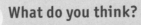

What do you think?

Why do you think many people have little problem discussing psychological topics without first seeing empirical evidence?

Would there be a difference between different types of topics?

Can you answer the above two questions without having data on how many people are willing to discuss various topics without empirical evidence?

Typical for quantitative research is that the data are gathered in a numerical form, either by collecting measurements or by counting frequencies of occurrence. Quantitative researchers will not observe 'violence', but will measure aspects of violence (e.g. the number of incidents reported to the police, the number of incidents reported in diaries or interviews, the amount of violence as rated by participants on a Likert scale, etc.). In Chapter 5 we called this the requirement of operational definitions. In addition, before researchers collect data, they have a good idea of how they will analyse them: what types of measurements they will obtain and what types of statistics they can apply to summarise and evaluate the data.

Large samples and a few data points per participant

Although this is not an absolute rule, the vast majority of descriptive quantitative studies involve the collection of a limited amount of data from a reasonably large group of participants. There are two main reasons why researchers want to include large groups in their studies. The first is that the larger the sample examined, the more representative it becomes of the population (i.e. the more it resembles the population). As indicated above, quantitative researchers usually want to generalise their findings from the sample studied to the population, so that universal conclusions can be reached. Although quantity is only one aspect of representativeness, it is an important one and one that is taught to all psychology students.

The second reason why descriptive quantitative studies usually involve many participants is that large numbers of observations yield more precise statistics. In all likelihood, the mean of a sample is closer to the population mean when it is based on a large sample than when it is based on a small sample. When social services want to know how many teenagers are unhappy, they will feel more confident about an estimate if it is based on a sample of 1,000 respondents than if it is based on a sample of 20 respondents, even when every precaution has been taken to make both samples equally representative. The reason why the mean of 1,000 observations is more reliable than the mean of 20 observations is that the former is likely to be very much the same if the study were repeated with another sample of the same size, whereas there can be a serious difference in estimates based on two different samples of 20 participants only.

Descriptive research usually is only the first step of a quantitative research programme, because researchers want to know what caused the data they observe. How did the figures come about? To discover cause–effect relations, a first move is to find out which events (variables) are related. If a survey indicates that 15% of the teenagers call themselves unhappy, the logical next question is which variables are related to being (un)happy. Do teenagers who call themselves unhappy have less money to spend than teenagers who call themselves happy? Are they less supported by their parents? Do they have fewer friends? This is addressed in relational research.

Relational research

Correlations

The way to find out whether two variables are related according to quantitative psychologists is to collect measures of both variables and to correlate them. There are various statistical techniques to calculate a coefficient that indicates how closely two variables co-vary. These techniques not only provide information about whether or not two variables are correlated, but also provide information about how strong the correlation is (see Chapter 8).

Quantitative researchers point to the importance of calculating and using statistical correlation coefficients to decide which variables are correlated and which are not, because people do not seem to be good at detecting them (at least not at a conscious level; see Chapter 7). For instance, since the seminal publication of Paul Meehl (1954) there has been a continuous stream of studies showing that decisions based on standardised interviews/questionnaires and statistical correlations outperform clinical judgments by psychologists. This is true, for example, for the prediction of academic performance, psychotherapy outcome, success in military training, probation success, business failure and detection of malingering (for reviews, see Grove *et al.* 2000; Aegisdottir *et al.* 2006).

There are two problems involved in the intuitive detection of correlations by humans. The first is the failure to detect genuine correlations. In particular, negative correlations (where the variables vary in opposite directions) seem to be difficult to perceive. The most notorious example in this respect is the time it took before people realised that there was a negative correlation between smoking and longevity (the more you smoke, the younger on average you will die; Figure 11.1).

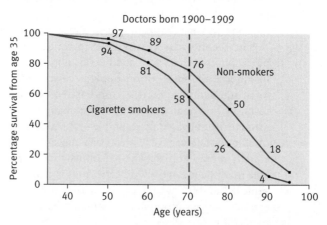

Figure 11.1 The negative correlation between smoking and age at death.

In this study, a cohort of male British medical doctors was followed from the age of 35 years on. The graph shows the survival rate for smokers and non-smokers. Of the smokers, 58% were still alive at the age of 70, against 76% of the non-smokers.

Source: *British Medical Journal*, 'Mortality in relation to smoking: 50 years observations on male British doctors', Doll, R., Peter, R., Boreham, J. and Sutherland, I., Vol. 328, pp. 1519–28, © 2004 with permission of the BMJ Publishing Group.

illusory correlation

perception of a correlation between events for which no independent evidence can be found

The second problem with the detection of correlations by humans is that in some cases people tend to perceive correlations that do not exist. These are called illusory correlations. For instance, in Chapter 10 we mentioned that for many people there is a positive correlation between being a scientist and being a middle-aged man with untidy hair. Similarly, King and Koehler (2000) showed that graphologists tend to conclude that people who write fast have an impulsive personality, whereas people who write slowly have a cautious personality. There are no such correlations to be detected in quantitative data, but people are prone to believing in them because the meanings of the variables are associated: slowness seems to go along with caution and speed with impulsivity. In general, people are prone to illusory correlations when two variables overlap in meaning (e.g. red hair and hot temper) or when the correlation is good for the self-esteem (e.g. members of one's own group are perceived as more interesting than members of other groups).

Factor analysis

Statistical correlations are interesting not only because they allow researchers to assess the relationship between two variables, but also because they make it possible to investigate the pattern of correlations between any number of variables. A statistical technique often used in this respect is factor analysis. We will illustrate the technique with a small example. Suppose you want to know what the correlations are between the marks psychology students obtain in their exams in statistics, research methods, social psychology, and historical and conceptual issues. Are students who are good at stats also good at the three other courses? Or is it the case that someone who gets a high mark on stats obtains a relatively low mark on historical and conceptual issues? Or could it be that the courses are not related to each other, and that knowing the stats score of a student does not help you to make a better prediction about their score on historical and conceptual issues?

To find out, you collect the exam marks of all students at a particular university and you calculate the correlations between the various scores. Suppose Table 11.1 summarises your findings.

Table 11.1 Fictitious example of correlations between exam marks of four courses in a psychology degree
In this table you see that there is a high correlation (0.80) between the exam marks of statistics and research methods, and between social psychology and historical and conceptual issues. In contrast, there are no correlations between statistics and research methods on the one hand and social psychology and historical and conceptual issues on the other hand. This suggests that the exam scores are determined by two independent factors: one for statistics and research methods and one for social psychology and historical and conceptual issues.

	Stats	**ResMeth**	**SocPsy**	**HisConcep**
Stats	1.00	0.80	0.00	0.00
ResMeth	0.80	1.00	0.00	0.00
SocPsy	0.00	0.00	1.00	0.80
HisConcep	0.00	0.00	0.80	1.00

In this figure you see an interesting pattern of findings. There is a high positive correlation (0.80) between the exam marks of statistics and research methods, and between social psychology and historical and conceptual issues. In contrast, there are no correlations between statistics and research methods on the one hand and social psychology and historical and conceptual issues on the other hand. This means, for instance, that a student who scores high on the stats exam in all likelihood will also have a high mark on the research methods exam, and can have a high, medium or low score on social psychology and historical and conceptual issues. Such a pattern suggests that the exam scores are determined by two independent factors: one for statistics and research methods and one for social psychology and historical and conceptual issues.

Now suppose that your correlations looked as shown in Table 11.2. Here you see that there are high positive correlations between all courses. A student who scores highly in the statistics exam also on average scores highly in the three other exams, and a student who scores low in one exam scores low in the other exams as well. This is not in line with the idea that there are two factors underlying the scores. Rather, all scores seem to be due to a single factor, which we could call an intelligence/motivation factor: students who score high on this factor get good marks in all exams, students who score low on this factor score low in all exams.

Factor analysis is a statistical technique calculating how many factors are needed to account for the correlations between the variables measured and how these variables relate to the factors. For instance, for the data of Table 11.1 it would extract two factors, one with statistics and research methods loading on it, and one with social psychology and historical and conceptual issues loading it. For Table 11.2 it would return one factor on which all courses load.

Experimental research

Correlations do not allow researchers to be sure about causes

Relational research makes it possible for quantitative researchers to assess which variables are related and which are not, but does not allow them to be certain about the origin of the correlation (i.e. the underlying cause–effect relation). For instance, several studies have shown that there is a negative correlation between the presence of children and marital satisfaction: couples with children show less marital satisfaction

Table 11.2 Another fictitious example of correlations between the exam marks of four courses in a psychology degree
In this table you see that there are high correlations (0.80) between all four exams. This suggests that the exam scores are determined by a single factor.

	Stats	ResMeth	SocPsy	HisConcep
Stats	1.00	0.80	0.80	0.80
ResMeth	0.80	1.00	0.80	0.80
SocPsy	0.80	0.80	1.00	0.80
HisConcep	0.80	0.80	0.80	1.00

than couples without children (Twenge *et al.* 2003). Although it is tempting to conclude from this correlation that the presence of children does decrease the degree of marital satisfaction experienced by parents (i.e. the children are the cause of the decrease in satisfaction), there is nothing in the correlation itself that allows the researchers to draw this conclusion. There could be tens of other reasons why couples with children rate their marital satisfaction lower than couples without children. Maybe couples without children split up sooner, so that the remaining ones score high on satisfaction? Or it might be that couples who score high on satisfaction do not feel a need for children? Or that people who enjoy their job score high on marital satisfaction and do not feel a need for children?

?

What do you think?

To help you appreciate that correlations often have a more complicated explanation than simply one variable being the cause of the other, try to explain the following correlations.

1. There is a positive correlation between the number of ice-creams sold at the seaside and the number of people who need to be saved from drowning: the more ice-creams sold, the more people need to be saved.

2. There is a positive correlation between the number of churches in a town and the number of murders in that town: the more churches, the more murders.

3. There is a positive correlation between the weight of a person and their net income: the more a person weighs, the higher their income.

Variables responsible for the correlation: (1) temperature, (2) size of the town, (3) age

---

Experiments to determine cause–effect relations

To be able to draw firm conclusions about cause and effect, quantitative psychologists will set up an experiment in which they manipulate the suspected cause and see whether this has an effect on the phenomenon they are examining. For instance, if psychologists suspect that tea helps students to remember texts, they will design an experiment in which half of the participants get a cup of tea and the other half get nothing or something else (e.g. a glass of water) while they are studying. If the experiment is run properly and if the predicted difference between both conditions is observed, the psychologist can be pretty sure that the tea indeed caused the difference in performance.

Controlling for confounding variables

An important aspect of experiments is that only the suspected causes are manipulated and the resulting changes in the phenomenon registered. Everything else must be held constant. The latter stipulation is critical. If researchers want to be sure that the manipulated variable really is the cause of the effect, then they

confounding variable

variable that was not taken into account in the study and that may be the origin of the effect observed

must make sure that no other variables can be the origin of the change detected. As indicated above, this requirement is known as the problem of the confounding variable.

To illustrate the problem of confounding variables we again take the example of a psychologist wanting to know whether a cup of tea helps students to memorise a text. Suppose two groups of participants took part in the experiment. One group (in the morning) studied a text with a cup of tea and after an hour took part in a multiple choice quiz. The second group (in the afternoon) studied the same text and completed the same quiz, but was not given tea. Suppose the group with tea answered 20% more questions correctly than the group without tea. Can the psychologist then conclude that tea is helpful for studying?

As you may have noticed, the problem with the study, as it has been described, is that one group was seen in the morning and the other in the afternoon. Maybe people study better in the morning than in the afternoon: could that be the reason for the difference in performance? The time of test is a confounding variable of the availability of tea and prevents the psychologist from being able to conclude for certain that tea is good for studying. In addition, when you come to think of it, there are other possible confounding variables in the design. Maybe the first group consisted of more motivated participants than the second. Could there be a difference between people who take part in a morning experiment and people who take part in an afternoon experiment?

To address the criticism of possible confounds, experimental psychologists introduce an increasing number of controls (e.g. by testing both groups at the same time, by testing four groups on two different days with the availability of tea counterbalanced over the days, and by randomly allocating the participants over conditions). Unfortunately, each control adds an extra constraint to the situation and puts the testing into an increasingly artificial setting. To counter this problem, quantitative researchers usually run several experiments on the same topic (involving different manipulations, measurements and controls) and look for converging evidence across studies.

Experiments are not always possible

Needless to say, not all issues in psychology can be addressed experimentally. For instance, although it is easy to think of a hypothetical experiment addressing the question of whether the presence of children is the cause of the drop in marital satisfaction, such an experiment could never be run in practice. It would involve the selection of two matched samples of couples, one of which would be forced to have children and the other prevented from having children. Both groups of couples would then be followed for several years to see how their marital satisfaction evolves. If the presence of children is indeed the cause of the drop in marital satisfaction, such a drop should be observed in the sample with children only.

The fact that many psychological experiments are impossible may be one of the reasons why progress in psychology is harder to achieve than in sciences such as physics, chemistry or botany, where researchers are less often confronted with practical and ethical limits.

Analogy with the hierarchy of evidence in medical science

The status of the different approaches in quantitative research can be illustrated by relating them to the so-called hierarchy of evidence in medical science (cf. Greenhalgh 1997). This hierarchy indicates how strong the evidence is for a particular therapy or pathogen (Figure 11.2).

At the bottom of the hierarchy we find case reports, consisting of anecdotal evidence related to individual patients. They have the same status as descriptive research: they may point to interesting phenomena but do not provide much information about the underlying causes.

At the second level we find cross-sectional surveys. They form the first step in relational research. A group of participants is asked to complete a questionnaire about health-related topics. Afterwards the researchers look for correlations between the answers to the various questions (e.g. is the consumption of a certain food related to a higher/lower risk of cancer?). This type of research enables epidemiologists to find potential relationships. However, there is little control of confounding variables (e.g. the relationship between the food and cancer could be due to other lifestyle differences between the people eating the food and those who do not).

In case-control studies (level 3) patients with a particular disease are matched on a series of possible confounding variables (age, gender, socioeconomic status' etc.) with participants who do not have the disease. The medical histories of both groups are compared to search for differences that may be the origin of the ailment observed.

In follow-up studies (level 4) two matched groups, one with the disease/treatment and one without, are followed for a certain period of time, to see how they evolve.

Figure 11.2 The hierarchy of evidence in medical science.

Any difference between the groups is likely to be due to the disease/treatment, as the groups were originally matched on possible confounding variables.

At level 5 we find the randomised controlled trials. These are the equivalent of experimental studies and are often used to assess the efficacy of therapies. Patients are randomly distributed over two conditions, so that both conditions are equivalent in terms of possible confounding variables. Then, one group (determined at random) receives the experimental treatment, whereas the other group receives a placebo treatment that looks exactly like the experimental treatment but without the critical agent (e.g. a pill of the same size and colour as the experimental pill but only consisting of the binding and colouring agents used for the experimental pill). Further controls are introduced to make sure that any effect observed cannot be due to other variables. For instance, the patients and the practitioners do not know which type of pill has been administered, so that the results are not biased by the expectations people have when they know they only received a placebo pill rather than the 'real' pill (such studies are called double-blind studies, because neither the patients nor the treating practitioners know which group the patient is in).

Finally, at the top of the hierarchy we find the meta-analysis. This is a review of all the available evidence concerning a particular treatment or pathogen coming from many different sources. For each study the relevant features and the accompanying effects are collected. On the basis of these figures, an overall estimate of the effect size is calculated. Because the analysis is based on many different studies, coming from different labs and using different procedures, this type of evidence exceeds the limitations of each individual study. In addition, because it is based on a large sample of participants, the conclusions are stable.

> **? What do you think?**
>
> Suppose you want to answer the question 'does watching violence on TV increase the aggression of the viewers?' Which studies could you run at each level of the hierarchy? Can you see how the evidence becomes stronger as you go higher up in the hierarchy?

Strengths of quantitative research methods

Because quantitative research makes use of the scientific method applied to psychological topics, it inherits all the strengths of the method we have discussed in the preceding chapters. The application of powerful statistical analyses enables researchers to detect nearly every pattern of association in large datasets, and the merciless application of the falsification test prevents wrong ideas and weak theories from thriving for too long.

Because the strengths of quantitative research have been extensively discussed before, we will not dwell on them any longer. Instead, we will have a look at the weaknesses of this approach.

Limits of quantitative methods

No interest in the person behind the participant

With some exaggeration, participants in quantitative research can be described as number providers. The research is designed in such a way that each participant returns one or a few numbers, which can be used in statistical analyses. As a consequence, quantitative studies are usually brief. In addition, participants are confronted with researchers who shun close interactions during the data gathering because they fear such interactions might invalidate the study (e.g. by betraying the research question or by biasing the participants in their responses). To make sure that no situation factors could turn into confounding variables, good researchers are taught to act as uninvolved, dispassionate observers.

This is how one critic summarised the way in which participants are treated in quantitative research:

> In the first half of the twentieth century the investigative practice of American psychology came to rely increasingly on the construction of 'collective subjects' for the generation of its knowledge products . . . Three types of these artificial collectivities were distinguished: those that were the result of averaging the performance of individuals subjected to similar experimental conditions, those that were constituted from scores obtained by means of some psychometric testing instrument, and those that were produced by subjecting groups of individuals to different treatment conditions.
>
> (Danziger 1990: 113)

The lack of interest in the person behind the participant is of particular concern when the research concerns real-life situations (e.g. the psychology of health), because in these situations psychologists can learn a lot by listening to the experiences and opinions of the people involved (practitioners, patients, support staff, relatives).

Research is too much driven by what can be measured numerically and tested experimentally

quantitative imperative

a bias only to find measurable topics interesting because quantitative research methods require numerical data

Because quantitative analyses require the data to be represented as numbers, quantitative psychologists have a bias to limit their research to topics that can easily be measured. According to the hermeneutic critique, this has resulted in the **quantitative imperative**, the conviction that you cannot know what you cannot measure.

Furthermore, because experiments provide the strongest information within the quantitative paradigm, much research has been geared towards questions that can be addressed experimentally. The aspects of mental life that cannot be captured by numbers and that cannot be manipulated in an experiment have been considered of secondary importance.

The falsification test lends itself better to destroying ideas than to finding practical solutions to specific problems

Another limitation of quantitative research is that the falsification test, on which the method rests, is primarily geared towards erasing wrong theories rather than generating new ones. It is much easier to set up an experiment showing that someone is wrong than to come up with a new theory that is worthwhile. As a result, it is not unusual to see theories that have been discredited for some time still being 'rejected' on a regular basis in scientific journals, just because it is so easy to set up an experiment to disprove them.

The negative tone underlying falsification tests can easily be illustrated by comparing the ways in which automatic speech recognition (speech recognition by computers) has been approached by quantitative psychologists and engineers. Table 11.3

Table 11.3 Differences between the quantitative and the pragmatic approaches
Some differences between the quantitative psychological approach and the pragmatic engineering approach.

Artificial intelligence/psychology	Engineering
Motivated by long-term goal (exhaustive understanding)	Motivated by short-term goals (so that progress can be measured)
Seeks breakthroughs and radically new perspectives	Tends to proceed by improving existing systems
Tries to solve problems in their most general form (general-purpose system)	Looks for solutions for specific problems
Makes recourse to introspection about human capabilities and about what seems intuitively likely	Designs and tunes systems to work on average; focuses on the desired input–output behaviour and designs algorithms to achieve this

Source: Ward (1998).

summarises the differences as perceived by one of the players (Ward 1998). While the psychologists tried to solve the problem by generating and testing general theories of how humans (and by extension machines) function and spent a lot of time showing each other that their respective theories and ideas were wrong (as indicated by falsification tests), the engineers concentrated on the problem at hand and searched for concrete steps that would bring the solution closer. The psychologists were looking for the truth, the engineers searched for algorithms that would improve the performance of the machine. Ward noticed that over a period of 40 years the latter, pragmatic approach resulted in significantly more progress.

The above example is not meant to question the value of the falsification test for scientific progress (Chapter 9). However, it does remind us that falsification only leads to progress when there are worthwhile proposals to be tested. An exclusive reliance on the falsification test involves the danger that more knowledge is gathered about what is not 'true' than about what works. Falsification tests without equally strong efforts to try to understand what is going on, risk ending up in a situation where rival views are more interested in showing each other they are wrong than in contemplating whether the resulting discussion brings the solution any closer. An informative book in this respect is Eysenck and Keane (2005), because for each topic it nicely summarises the different points of view and the evidence *against* them.

Interim summary

The essence of quantitative research

- Quantitative research methods refer to research methods based on quantifiable data and the following assumptions:
  - there is an objective reality to be discovered
  - the main aim of scientific research is to find universal cause–effect relations
  - to do this, one has to rely on the hypothetico-deductive method and avoid confounds and sources of noise.

- A distinction can be made between descriptive, relational and experimental research:
  - descriptive research: trying to express variables in numbers, usually involves a few measures from a large group of participants
  - relational research: searching for statistical correlations in order to understand relationships between variables; use of factor analysis to find the structure in datasets with many variables
  - experimental research: searching for cause–effect relationships by excluding confounding variables; experiments often not possible
  - status of the different types of research can be understood by analogy with the hierarchy of evidence in medical science.
- Strengths:
  - inherits the strengths of the natural sciences (in particular of the falsification criterion)
  - Application of powerful statistical techniques enables researchers to detect every pattern of association in large datasets.
- Weaknesses:
  - no interest in the person behind the participant
  - research too much driven by what can be measured numerically and tested experimentally
  - the falsification test is not primarily geared towards the generation of new ideas and finding practical solutions to specific problems.

11.2 The essence of qualitative research

qualitative research methods

research methods based on understanding phenomena in their historical and socio-cultural context; are associated with the hermeneutic approach based on understanding the meaning of a situation

Qualitative research methods are directed at understanding phenomena (including people) in their historical and socio-cultural context. They are favoured by the hermeneutic approach in psychology, because they allow researchers to understand the complete situation they find themselves in. In line with our discussion of quantitative research methods, we start with the general assumptions underlying this type of research, before we describe specific techniques and their strengths and weaknesses.

Assumptions underlying qualitative research methods

In psychology there is little or no evidence for a reality outside people's minds

Unlike quantitative psychologists, most qualitative psychologists are not convinced that in psychology there is an objective reality, which can be discovered with the scientific approach. For them the only reality that matters is the reality as perceived and constructed by people. There are differences in the degree to which the various methods question the existence/importance of an objective reality, as we will see below, but they all agree that it is more important to understand people's views rather than their responses to aspects of the environment.

Attempts to control the situation make the setting artificial and impoverished

According to qualitative psychologists, quantitative researchers are misguided in their attempts to try to measure 'reality' in unbiased ways. The attempts to control for confounding variables and noise do not help to make the 'real world' visible, but turn the environment into an artificial setting that robs the participants of their usual ways of interacting and coping in meaningful situations. For instance, when Milgram (1963; Chapter 7) saw participants punish other humans with increasingly harmful electrical shocks in his experiments, he did not observe 'true' obedience, but participants pressing buttons in one particular social environment that was perceived and interpreted by the participants in ways unknown to Milgram.

Similarly, the attempts to restrict and streamline the interactions between the researcher and the participants do not in the first place increase the chances of making the 'true' world visible, but seriously limit the information the researcher can get from the study. Rather than being an uninvolved, distant observer, the investigator should become an active participant and listen to what the participant has to say. He or she should not be guided by fear of drawing wrong conclusions but by a constructive desire to understand the meaning of what is going on.

Qualitative researchers acknowledge that the approach they promote entails the danger of the conclusions being influenced by the researcher, but argue that:

1. This danger is offset by the expected gains due to an understanding of the situation.

2. All conclusions, even those reached on the basis of quantitative research and falsification tests, are relative (because they depend on the prevailing paradigm).

3. The most obvious biases can be avoided by being aware of them and by doing the analysis in such a way that it can be repeated and checked by others.

Immersion and understanding

The point of departure of qualitative psychology is the immersion of the researcher in the situation that is being studied, so that the meaning of the situation can be understood. The researcher will not approach the situation with a preconceived list of variables that need to be scored and that constrain the outcome of the study. Instead, the researcher approaches the situation open-mindedly and sees what comes out. This is how Willig described the essence of the qualitative methodology:

> Qualitative researchers tend to be concerned with meaning. That is, they are interested in how people make sense of the world and how they experience events. They aim to understand 'what it is like' to experience particular conditions (e.g. what it means and how it feels to live with chronic illness or to be unemployed) and how people manage certain situations (e.g. how people negotiate family life or relations with work colleagues). Qualitative researchers tend, therefore, to be concerned with the quality and texture of experience, rather than with the identification of cause–effect relationships. They do not tend to work with 'variables' that are defined by the researcher before the research process begins. This is because qualitative researchers tend to be interested in the meanings attributed to events by the research participants themselves. Using preconceived 'variables' would lead to the imposition of the researcher's meanings and it would preclude the identification of respondents' own ways of making sense of the phenomenon under investigation.

(Willig 2008: 8–9)

Ideographic vs. nomothetic

The emphasis on immersion in and understanding of a particular situation implies that qualitative research methods are not in the first place interested in generalisable knowledge. In principle their analysis is limited to the situation and the participant(s) at hand. This is called an **ideographic approach**, a study of what is relevant to the subject under study, as opposed to a **nomothetic approach**, a search for universal principles that exceed the confines of the study (i.e. the approach that is prominent in quantitative research).

ideographic approach

the conclusions of a study stay limited to the phenomenon under study

nomothetic approach

a study is run in search of universal principles that exceed the confines of the study

Induction rather than deduction

Quantitative researchers often make use of predetermined variables because they have specific hypotheses to test as part of the hypothetico-deductive model they follow. In their research, theories are tested over and over again by deriving hypotheses from them and putting them to a falsification test. Each hypothesis deals with a particular detail of the theory. As a result, most research within the quantitative approach consists of testing details that have been produced on the basis of deductive reasoning (i.e. reasoning from theory to fact, in which one starts from known – or at least assumed – statements and deduces new conclusions).

Qualitative researchers object to this approach because it entails a serious risk of the scientist missing the essentials of the situation. By constantly focusing on details, researchers can easily lose sight of the wider picture. According to the qualitative psychologists, it is much more important to look with an open mind at the complete situation, rather than always homing in on a single detail. Instead of constantly using deductive reasoning, psychologists should pay more attention to inductive reasoning (i.e. reasoning from fact to theory, in which one tries to draw adequate conclusions on the basis of a series of convergent observations). The advice of qualitative psychologists to start an investigation by looking at the complete situation with an open mind and freeing themselves from their preconceptions is called bracketing (cf. Lemon & Taylor 1997).

bracketing

requirement in qualitative research to look at a phenomenon with an open mind and to free oneself from preconceptions

Qualitative research is evidence-based

The above characteristics do not mean that data are less important for qualitative than for quantitative researchers. In qualitative research, too, a study depends on collecting and analysing empirical findings. In addition, these data must be gathered and made available in such a way that the conclusions can be verified by others. It is not the case that qualitative research is based on the researcher's intuitions and opinions. The main difference in data with quantitative research is that the findings typically are not coded in a numerical format. They comprise an organised set of verbal statements that in the researcher's eyes summarises the examined situation. Below we will see three examples of such analysis.

Data collection and analysis

Qualitative researchers stress the importance of 'rich information'. By this they mean information that in the participants' eyes adequately describes the situation. Rather than the researcher defining beforehand what aspects are of importance, the participants determine what will be found.

semi-structured interview

interview in which each interviewee gets a small set of core questions, but for the rest of the time is encouraged to speak freely; achieved by making use of open-ended, non-directive questions

Data collection

The most frequently used technique of data collection is the semi-structured interview. In such an interview, the interviewer uses a limited set of core questions, so that the answers of the participants can be compared, but for the rest of the time encourages participants to speak freely. This is done by using open-ended and non-directive questions. Open-ended questions are questions that invite the interviewees to give a considered reply rather than a yes/no answer (e.g. one would ask 'What do you think of qualitative research methods?' rather than 'Do you think qualitative research methods are good?'). Non-directive questions are questions that do not give the participant an indication of the desired answer (e.g. a qualitative researcher would never ask 'Do you agree that qualitative research methods are useful?').

focus group
technique in which a group of participants freely discuss a limited set of questions

Another technique increasingly used in qualitative research is that of focus groups. In this technique the questions of the semi-structured interview are given as the basis of a discussion by a group of participants rather than by individual participants. This creates a different dynamic to face-to-face interviews and is more likely, for instance, to bring out differences in point of view between the participants.

Transcription

The raw materials of semi-structured interviews usually consist of auditory or visual recordings. These have to be transcribed in written form, so that they can easily be referred to. By making use of standardised codes, the transcription not only contains what was said, but also the non-verbal signals, such as hesitations, gestures and intonations. This part of the research is usually very time-intensive, but ensures the easy availability of the raw materials.

After the transcription, the written records are numbered. The text is torn apart into its constituent parts, which are numbered. Usually, the numbering is very detailed, going down to the level of individual sentences and even single phrases. Before researchers start doing this, it is recommended that they go through the texts/interviews a few times, so that they have a good feel of the topics that are covered.

Data analysis

In a qualitative analysis the investigator rewrites the raw materials as a flow chart of core ideas, based on multiple close readings and guided by the questions emphasised by the different approaches (see below). The analysis requires an adequate classification of the various statements into a number of (recurring) themes and clear ideas of how the components are interconnected. The researcher tries to encompass the data as comprehensively and systematically as possible. The analysis keeps cycling through the materials, until saturation is reached. All the time the researcher remains careful not to overlook elements or to bias the interpretation towards a preconceived theory. Software programs are available to number and rephrase the various statements and integrate them within the coding scheme.

In the remainder of this section, we discuss three main approaches used in qualitative research (see Willig (2008) and Smith (2008) for further details and more techniques). They are: grounded theory, interpretative phenomenological analysis (IPA) and discourse analysis.

grounded theory
qualitative research method that tries to understand what is going on in a particular situation and which, on the basis of a qualitative analysis and induction, tries to come to a theoretical insight grounded in the data

Grounded theory

Grounded theory is the oldest of the techniques described here. It is based on the book *Discovery of grounded theory* (1967) by the Chicago sociologists Glaser and Strauss. Its name derives from the explicit goal of coming to theoretical insights that are grounded in the data. Glaser and Strauss wrote their book as a reaction to the then dominant sociological approach of formulating large, abstract theories without much empirical input.

In a grounded theory analysis, the investigator rewrites the raw materials on the basis of questions such as 'What is going on here?', 'What are the main problems of the participants?', 'How do they try to solve them?' On the basis of these questions, the participants' answers are recoded into a sequence of themes, which are then grouped into higher-order categories. According to Glaser and Strauss (1967) this makes it possible for a theory to emerge from the data through inductive reasoning.

The best way to get a feeling for what is going on in a grounded theory analysis is to look at a case study. The example we describe uses a grounded theory analysis to find out why students procrastinate.

CASE STUDY: An example of grounded theory

Why do students procrastinate?

Schraw *et al.* (2007) examined academic procrastination with the grounded theory. Their goal was to get a complete picture of the phenomenon, starting from the conflicting observations that many people view it as a negative personality trait but at the same time that the majority of students seem to do it. The available quantitative data were largely in line with the negative view, as questionnaire data pointed to negative correlations with health, long-term learning and self-esteem, and positive correlations with anxiety and fear of failure. As a consequence, most researchers conceptualised procrastination as a combination of three components: fear of failure, task aversiveness and laziness.

Schraw *et al.* described the reasons for starting their study as follows:

> The purpose of the present research was to construct a grounded theory of procrastination on the basis of college students' reports about their own procrastination. We did so for several reasons. One is that there is relatively little research on procrastination, even though it is a commonly occurring phenomenon among college students. Second, most of the existing research has reported correlations between self-reported procrastinatory behavior and academic outcomes, such as grades and study time. We hoped to expand on this research by providing a more in-depth descriptive account of academic procrastination. Third, and most important to us, there is no existing theory or process model of procrastination. We conducted the present research to examine the process by which procrastination occurs and to propose a preliminary paradigm model . . . that can be tested in future research.
>
> (Schraw 2007:12–13)

The study involved 67 students over a total of four phases (Table 11.4). In the first phase a combination of focus groups and semi-structured interviews was used to identify the themes students found important with respect to procrastination. The general instructions were:

> I'm going to ask you about academic procrastination. I'm interested in how you define it, factors that affect whether you procrastinate, and whether there are positive or negative consequences. I have a structured interview with some follow-up probes after each question. Please take your time when responding and focus on your own procrastination behavior rather than other students. If you would like to return to a point that you discussed earlier, feel free to do so.
>
> (2007:15)

Answers were sought for the following open-ended questions:

1. How would you describe academic procrastination?
2. What do you do when you procrastinate?

CASE STUDY: *(continued)*

Table 11.4 Phases involved in the Schraw *et al.* (2007) study

Phase	Coding	Semester	Purpose	Participants (*n*)
1	Open	1	Identify codes within categories for further analysis.	26 (20 in focus groups; 6 individual interviews)
2	Axial	2–6	Explore codes in detail; relate codes to one another to construct themes.	18 individual interviews
3	Selective	6 and 7	Construct paradigm model and discuss themes in relation to model; establish story line that integrates paradigm model.	12 individual interviews
4	Selective	8	Test, validate and explicate paradigm model until saturated; identify emergent principles consistent with paradigm model; conduct member checks.	11 individual interviews

Source: Schraw *et al.* (2007), 'Doing the things we do: A grounded theory of academic procrastination', *Journal of Educational Psychology*, 99, 12–25, Table 1, p. 15. Copyright American Psychological Association, reprinted with permission.

3. Are there situations where you are most likely to procrastinate?

4. How do you cope when you do procrastinate?

5. What are some of the positive and negative consequences of procrastination?

Table 11.5 lists the 33 codes that were extracted from phase 1, together with the five categories in which they were classified. In phase 2 structured in-depth interviews were held with students to get a better understanding of each of the five categories. On the basis of these interviews, the structure was refined by inserting macrothemes between the categories and the initial codes (now reduced to 29 themes). Phase 3 was used to further check and polish the structure distilled from phase 2 by means of a new set of structured interviews. Table 11.6 shows the structure resulting from phases 2 and 3.

In phase 4, 11 new students were interviewed individually and asked to respond to the model as displayed in Table 11.6. This step helped to ensure, according to the authors, that the final model was fully saturated, dependable and credible.

On the basis of the model in Table 11.6, Schraw *et al.* (2007) distilled six emergent principles that affected students' procrastination:

1. *Minimum time*: students have busy lives with the following sequence of priorities: personal relationships, work and study. The amount of study time is minimised to maximise the time available for friends and work. Procrastination enables students to delay as much study as possible until the last weeks of the semester. This is done more to safeguard personal time than to avoid failure or indulge laziness.

2. *Optimum efficiency*: a concentrated effort late in the semester increases productivity, creativity and quality of work, and reduces wasted time due to boredom and false starts.

3. *Peak affective experience*: working hard towards a deadline creates a state of 'flow' by increasing motivation and eliminating distractions.

Table 11.5 Codes extracted from phase 1 in the Schraw *et al.* (2007) study

Category	Code
Antecedents of procrastination	1. Lack of personal interest
	2. Lack of task-relevant knowledge
	3. Aversive task
	4. Better use of resources to delay work
	5. Competing interests
	6. Lack of focus
	7. Laziness
	8. Low motivation
	9. Poor instruction
Definitions of procrastination	10. Putting things off that need to be done
	11. Deferring necessary work
	12. Postponing important tasks
Contexts and conditions that affect procrastination	13. Busy with other activities
	14. Grades
	15. Belief that effort doesn't help
	16. Help from others
	17. Low study self-efficacy
	18. Poor study strategies
	19. Teacher doesn't hold students accountable
	20. Poor teaching
	21. Stress
Coping strategies	22. Make a schedule
	23. Manage time
	24. Plan and prioritise
	25. Work with other students
	26. Monitor negative self-talk
	27. Use a variety of study strategies
Consequences	28. Guilt
	29. Less effort put into schoolwork
	30. Greater productivity
	31. Increased stress
	32. Procrastination does not affect quality of work
	33. Increased confidence

Source: Schraw *et al.* (2007), 'Doing the things we do: A grounded theory of academic procrastination', *Journal of Educational Psychology*, 99, 12–25, Table 2, p. 16. Copyright American Psychological Association, reprinted with permission.

CASE STUDY: *(continued)*

Table 11.6 Refined structure resulting from the interviews of phases 2 and 3 in the Schraw *et al.* (2007) study

Category	Macrotheme	Theme
Antecedents of procrastination	1. Task 2. Self 3. Teacher	1. Low background knowledge 2. Task difficulty 3. Interest 4. Organisational skills 5. Clear expectations for course 6. Well-organised course materials 7. Tests and graded assignments
Definitions of procrastination phenomenon	4. Adaptive aspects of procrastination 5. Maladaptive aspects of procrastination	8. Cognitive efficiency 9. Peak work experience 10. Laziness 11. Fear of failure 12. Postponement of work
Contexts and conditions that affect procrastination	6. Unclear directions 7. Deadlines 8. Lack of incentives	13. Ill-defined course content 14. Unclear criteria for grading 15. Lack of due dates for assignments 16. Low intrinsic motivation: high self-efficacy 17. Low impact of procrastination on grades
Coping strategies	9. Cognitive 10. Affective	18. Identifying clear learning goals 19. Planning and organising future work 20. Budgeting resources (time and effort) 21. Reframing 22. Protective self-talk 23. Stress reduction (physical and psychological)
Consequences of procrastination	11. Quality of life 12. Quality of work	24. Cognitive efficiency 25. Improved quality of work 26. Peak work experience 27. Increased efficiency 28. Cognitive incubation 29. Less revision of work

Source: Schraw *et al.* (2007), 'Doing the things we do: A grounded theory of academic procrastination', *Journal of Educational Psychology*, 99, 12–25, Table 3, p. 17. Copyright American Psychological Association, reprinted with permission.

4. *Early assessment of work requirements*: procrastination is often the result of planning. Students at the beginning of term gauge the efforts that will be needed for a particular course and adapt to them. As a result, procrastination tends to increase as students become senior, because they can better assess the demands of the courses.

5. *Open escape routes*: students protect themselves against the negative psychological consequences of procrastination by engaging in three self-handicapping thoughts: (1) it is a necessary evil, (2) I am satisfied with a B rather than an A, and (3) I learn the big ideas and forget the rest.

6. *Rewards*: there are rewards associated with procrastination, such as more rapid feedback, and the sudden and intense release of stress once the deadline is met.

Schraw *et al.* (2007) stressed that their conclusions, which deviated substantially from the available conclusions on the basis of quantitative, correlational research, were interpretative in nature and required further investigation.

Phenomenological analysis

Unease with grounded theory

Although grounded theory was warmly received by the hermeneutically oriented psychologists, it soon turned out to have limitations. The first was that grounded theory largely assumed the existence of an objective reality that was there to be discovered. In this respect, grounded theory stayed close to mainstream psychology based on quantitative research. The findings that emerged from a grounded theory analysis were meant to describe 'reality'.

A second problem was that grounded theory stressed the importance of inductive reasoning (from data to theory) and verification (up to the saturation point). As you may remember from Chapter 9, these were exactly the criteria identified by the logical positivists for good scientific research. Scientists had to begin with careful observations, from which theories would emerge, and the truth of theories could be established by means of empirical verification. Given that these tenets of logical positivism were completely overthrown by the twentieth-century philosophy of science, they are shaky foundations for good research. Even Glaser and Strauss in later writings disagreed as to what extent a grounded theory analysis could be completely theory-neutral, with Strauss being less convinced that data could be gathered and analysed adequately without making use of some pre-existing theoretical framework. One way in which grounded theory has responded to this criticism was by accepting that the outcome of an analysis is not a description of reality, but a social construction by the researcher (see Willig 2008). Other researchers, however, sought a more radical alternative.

A final problem with grounded theory for psychological research was that it did not take into account the fact that the data provided by the participants actually comprised their perceptions and interpretations of what was happening. In this respect, it became clear that grounded theory had found its origin in sociology where the research topics may be less dependent on the participants' views than in psychology.

Inspiration from Husserl

To address the problems with grounded theory, hermeneutically inspired psychologists stressed that the primary aim of qualitative research was to examine what reality looked like for the participants, leaving open the question whether in psychology there is something of an objective, person-independent reality.

A main source of inspiration came from the phenomenology of the Austrian-German philosopher Edmund Husserl (1859–1938). Husserl's phenomenology stressed that psychology should be a reflective study of consciousness as experienced from the first-person point of view. With respect to mainstream psychological research, Husserl warned that it had turned away from the concrete human experience too rapidly. Psychology had been too eager to study the 'objective reality', rather than the world as perceived by people. By developing abstract and unexamined concepts to describe this 'reality', psychological research risked addressing spurious issues because the concepts they used were not properly grounded in experience. In Husserl's eyes it was much better for psychology to return to the experience itself. The human experience was not in the first place a matter of lawful responses to events in the environment, but a system of interrelated meanings, which Husserl called a *Gestalt* or *Lebenswelt* ('lifeworld'; see also Ashworth 2003).

interpretative phenomenological analysis

qualitative research method in psychology that tries to understand how a phenomenon is experienced by the people involved

Husserl's views gave rise to the so-called phenomenological analysis in qualitative research. A widely used variant of such analysis in psychology is the **interpretative phenomenological analysis** (IPA) (Smith 1996, 2008), which we will use in the rest of our discussion.

How does IPA work?

IPA resembles very much the analysis in grounded theory (cf. Willig 2008: 72–3). Both proceed by systematically going through the transcriptions identifying themes that can be clustered into higher-order categories, which capture the essence of the phenomenon under investigation. They are both based on a limited number of single-case studies which are combined to get a more complete picture.

The main difference between IPA and grounded theory is that IPA is centred on how participants make sense of their personal and social world. It attempts to explore the personal experience and is concerned with the participant's personal account, not with an understanding of the phenomenon itself. Therefore, guiding questions are 'How is this perceived by the participant?', 'What meaning does the participant attach to this event?' and 'How does the participant make sense of this situation?'

In addition, IPA acknowledges the input from the researcher, who tries to make sense of the participants trying to make sense of their world. Possible guiding questions in this respect are 'What is the person trying to achieve here?' and 'Is something leaking out here that was not intended?' The researcher's involvement does not mean that the researcher is allowed to introduce obvious biases. As a matter of fact, as in all other qualitative methods, investigators are advised to bracket as much as possible and to approach the new situation open-mindedly. However, because this is not totally possible, IPA accepts that some form of meta-interpretation on the part of the researcher is inevitable.

Reid *et al.* (2005: 20) identified the following key elements of IPA:

● It is an inductive approach going from data to understanding (i.e. it is 'bottom-up' rather than 'top-down'). It does not test hypotheses, and prior assumptions are avoided.

● IPA aims to capture and explore the meanings that participants assign to their experiences. Participants are experts on their own experiences and can offer researchers an understanding of their thoughts and feelings.

● Researchers reduce the complexity of the raw data through rigorous and systematic analysis.

● The analysis is primarily focused on what is specific for the phenomenon studied (cf. the ideographic approach), although it usually also attempts to take into account what is shared by the various participants in the study (i.e. it includes an element of the nomothetic approach).

● The resulting analysis is interpretative (i.e. it does not have the status of fact).

● A successful analysis is transparent (grounded in the data of the study) and plausible (to the participants, co-analysts and readers).

● Researchers should reflect upon their role in the process.

To give you a clearer picture of what an IPA involves, we again include a case study, this time on how the chronic fatigue syndrome is experienced by patients.

CASE STUDY: An example of IPA

How is the chronic fatigue syndrome experienced?

Dickson, Knussen and Flowers (2008) examined the experiences of people living with the chronic fatigue syndrome (CFS). They did semi-structured, in-depth interviews with 14 patients. Each participant was interviewed individually. The researchers had prepared a number of non-directive, open-ended questions which were used in a flexible way. Typical questions included 'Tell me about your experience with CFS', 'What aspects of your life has CFS impacted on most?', 'In what ways?' and 'How have other people reacted to your condition?'

Transcripts were analysed manually for recurrent themes using IPA. When the same themes appeared in at least half of the transcripts, they were categorised as being recurrent (i.e. offered some scope for nomothetic conclusions). Analysis was centred on capturing the meaning of the phenomenon to the participant, taking into account the inevitability of the researchers' interpretative engagement with the transcripts.

Three recurrent, interrelated themes were identified:

1. *Identity crisis, agency and embodiment*. This theme comprised a feeling of personal loss characterised by profound diminishing personal control and agency, as exemplified by the following statement: 'CFS is a dictator. It dictates my everyday life. It determines what I can and cannot do. It controls my body and my mind and every part of my being.'

2. *Scepticism and the self*. This theme referred to difficulties in social interactions because of scepticism about the wider society. It is exemplified in the following excerpt: 'Well, people thought you were a malingerer . . . That you were "at it" and there was this idea that you were just lazy'. This led to a sense of crisis of the self: 'I started to think to myself "Am I just making this up? Is it all in my head?".'

3. *Acceptance, adjustment and coping*. This theme referred to the attempts made by the patients towards acceptance, adjustment and coping with their situation, as shown in the following statement: 'It's all about accepting the illness and learning to deal with it. Accepting it stops you from feeling down in the dumps and it helps you just to take each day as it comes. That helps a lot. You know that you're going to have good days and bad days and that people don't understand what you have, you've just got to get through it.'

Discourse analysis

The linguistic turn in the philosophy of science and in critical psychology

discourse analysis

qualitative research method that aims to discover how social relations between people are determined by the language they use

The final qualitative analysis we discuss is discourse analysis. This analysis investigates the ways in which language constructs social reality. It is a direct consequence of the linguistic turn in the philosophy of science and in critical psychology, which claims that reality is nothing but a social construction based on language and culture (Chapters 9 and 10). In this view, language is the only topic worth investigating because it makes the world in which humans live.

According to Alvesson (2000) the linguistic turn in postmodernist writings influenced the development of qualitative research in three ways:

1. Researchers turned their attention from reality to language and examined the possibilities and impossibilities language brought with it.

2. Researchers became particularly interested in language use in real-world or naturally occurring settings (as opposed to artificial, research-related settings).

3. Finally, there was an enhanced reflexivity on the part of the researchers regarding their own language use. Research reports were no longer seen as dispassionate, transparent accounts of social reality, but as stylised, rhetorical and constructed accounts intended to have an impact.

How are relations between people determined by the language they use, and how do people try to achieve goals by means of their language?

As was the case for grounded analysis and phenomenological analysis, there are several variants of discourse analysis (see e.g. Willig 2008). They all try to determine how participants use discursive resources and what effects this has. How do participants use language to manage social interactions? How do they use language to achieve objectives? In which roles are participants pushed by the language they use and how does this relate to the power balance between them? What can be said by whom, where and when?

A comparison of discourse analysis with grounded theory and phenomenological analysis

To illustrate the specific character of discourse analysis, we make use of a study by Starks and Trinidad (2007), who not only applied discourse analysis but also grounded theory and phenomenological analysis to the same set of raw materials. The materials consisted of interviews with 25 general practitioners (GPs) about prostate cancer screening (PCS). In this situation a difficult choice exists between, on the one hand, recommending a screening (which involves a rather distressing examination in addition to the likelihood of a false alarm and even the unnecessary treatment of a benign ailment) and, on the other hand, not recommending such a screening (involving the risk of the patient developing a lethal cancer).

The GPs were asked a number of open-ended, non-directive questions meant to elicit rich discussions of the problems involved in raising the issue of prostate cancer screening with patients. Starks and Trinidad analysed the transcripts of the interviews along the dimensions advocated by grounded theory, phenomenological analysis and discourse analysis.

Grounded theory was used to build a theory of what was going in discussions between GPs and patients on the desirability of a PCS test and how these visits could be improved. It concerned an analysis of the circumstances leading to such a discussion and how GPs and patients engaged in the discussion. Starks and Trinidad used the 'six Cs' of social processes as guiding principles in the analysis of the transcripts (what are the causes, contexts, contingencies, consequences, covariances and conditions of a discussion about a PCS test?). As part of this analysis, they discovered that an important factor deciding whether a discussion would take place consisted of the limitations imposed by the appointment schedule on the GP (mostly 10 to 15 minutes per patient). Another important variable was the patients' expectations about such screening. GPs were most likely to give full information when patients had not yet made up their mind and showed an interest in the pros and cons of the options. On the basis of the grounded theory analysis, Starks and Trinidad were able to formulate a theory about the logistical, professional and personal constraints that limited the GP's likelihood of giving enough information so that patients could make an informed decision about which action to take in their particular case.

The purpose of *phenomenological analysis* was to understand how GPs experienced an uncertain clinical decision-making process within the larger context of the doctor–patient relationship. For instance, many interviewees expressed their discomfort with the fact that they could not meet their patients' expectations because there are no clear recommendations for prostate cancer screening. A typical comment was: 'It's hard [to have these discussions with patients] because the data stinks, and there's so much misinformation and so much promotion of prostate cancer screening that it puts the primary care physician who wants to be evidence-based in a very difficult position . . . And so, you leave the patient with, this "Well, I have no clue what to do," kind of a handout' (Starks & Trinidad 2007: 1378).

Finally, *discourse analysis* was concerned with the question how the discourse in medicine and public health constructed the roles, identities and interactions between patients and GPs in PCS discussions. For instance, the discourse of medicine strongly pushes GPs into the roles of expert diagnostician, scientist practising evidence-based medicine, and advisor to the patients. This gives GPs a high status and helps them, for instance, when they want to have a PCS test done on a particular patient. However, it also puts them in a difficult position when they want to explain to patients that prostate cancer screening is not always indicated, certainly if at the same time they want to convey the message that regular cancer screenings in general are a good idea. Under these circumstances the GPs often found themselves confronted with the fact that their knowledge was more limited than expected from their role, as can be seen in the following comment: 'What I would really like to have – and I know these exist, so I guess it's mainly my own fault that I don't have it, honestly – is the accepted age-based normal range for PSA [prostate specific antigen testing], and secondly, the likelihood of prostate cancer based on PSA reading and age' (Starks & Trinidad 2007: 1378). [Notice how the GP in this statement tried to affirm his/her role as expert diagnostician, evidence-based scientist and advisor, even in the light of faltering knowledge.]

By analysing the communication between doctors and patients, the discourse analysis aimed to discover what these individuals did while they were communicating, how they created a common reality by means of language, and how their communication coordinated their activities. According to Starks and Trinidad, such an analysis can be used to shed light on why GPs fail to give enough information for patients to make an informed decision.

Table 11.7 summarises the specificities of the three different approaches for the study of Starks and Trinidad.

Table 11.7 Informed Decision Making (IDM) as seen through the different approaches
A comparison of three qualitative research approaches to the question of how general practitioners (GPs) discuss prostate cancer screening with their average-risk patients.

	Grounded theory	Phenomenology	Discourse analysis
Research question	How does IDM about prostate cancer screening happen between GPs and their average-risk patients?	What is the lived experience of GPs as they discuss prostate cancer screening with their patients?	What discourses are used in IDM, and how do they shape GP and patient roles and identities in the doctor–patient relationship?
Purpose	To develop effective training and education for GPs about how to approach prostate cancer screening discussions	To understand GPs' experience of decision making with patients under conditions of clinical uncertainty	To shed light on the reasons for the limited or incomplete adoption of IDM by GPs

Source: Adapted from Starks and Trinidad (2007).

> ## What do you think?
>
> If you had to choose one qualitative approach for a study, which one would you take? Why?

Strengths of qualitative research

Directly focused on understanding situations and solving problems

Qualitative research is directly aimed at understanding a problem and working towards a solution. This is different from the detour quantitative research makes by trying to reach the truth via rejecting false explanations. In this respect, it is no coincidence that the major drive behind qualitative research has come from applied psychology, where psychologists are confronted with specific cases that need to be solved (see the engineers' approach in Table 11.3). In such situations, the search for generalisable, universal principles is often secondary to a focused intervention. A client interacting with a counsellor is not interested in the counsellor compulsively trying to falsify wrong accounts, but is helped by a counsellor who tries to understand what is going on and helps find ways to cope with the situation. Similarly, a company consulting a psychologist about a publicity campaign is more interested in what would work than in hearing what would be ineffective.

Stratton (1997) described how his group became involved in research, paid for by British Airways, into the needs of long-haul air passengers. The research was one of the studies the company repeatedly ran to discover what its customers wanted, so that they could not only improve their service, but also knew how best to advertise and whether there was scope for 'new product development', finding a market for something that did not yet exist. Stratton argued that the last two goals in particular could not easily be studied using quantitative research and would profit from an in-depth qualitative approach.

Generation of new ideas and elaboration of theories

Because qualitative studies involve intensive investigations, they are particularly well suited for finding new ideas. Quantitative studies, in which a specific hypothesis is tested, constrain the situation to such an extent that only a yes/no answer is expected. This type of study is perfect for the deductive part of the hypothetico-deductive method, but does not provide much inspiration for the theory-building part. A qualitative study like Schraw *et al.*'s (2007) on procrastination in students can result in a series of new ideas to be tested. In the same vein, a qualitative study can lead to an extensive elaboration of a theory if it shows that the existing quantitative research has measured only a small part of a much wider phenomenon.

An interesting analogy in this respect was reported by Vandenbroucke (2008). He noticed that the hierarchy of evidence in medical science (Figure 11.2) was a hierarchy to decide whether a treatment or pathogen had the expected effect (i.e. to evaluate a hypothesis). When it came to discovery of new facts or explanations, the hierarchy actually had to be inverted. A new discovery was least likely on the basis of a meta-analysis and most probable as part of a case report.

More perceptive to the needs of the participants

Because qualitative researchers want to understand events as they are perceived by the participants, they will have a much better feeling for the participants' needs.

This decreases the risk of advice that is perceived as unhelpful by the participants. Given that science proceeds by trial and error (see Chapter 9), a potentially erroneous intervention is extra painful if it has not been experienced as helpful by the persons involved.

Limits of qualitative research

Limits of inductive reasoning and verification

Qualitative research stresses the importance of inductive reasoning (from data to theory) and verification (up to the saturation point). As we saw above, these problems were raised in particular with respect to grounded theory. However, they apply to all the methods we discussed. Although qualitative researchers took their inspiration from postmodernist critiques of the scientific method, it cannot be denied that they in fact returned to the very first scientific method recommended by philosophers of science and since successfully criticised by Popper and Kuhn.

Less well suited to decide between theories

Because qualitative methods stress the inductive part of research, they are extremely well suited for charting new grounds and infusing new ideas in a discipline (i.e. theory generation and elaboration). However, they fare less well when it comes to deciding between ideas and theories. Suppose that other researchers find the topic of experiences in the chronic fatigue syndrome interesting and decide to repeat Dickson *et al.* (2008). Should they then start from the findings of Dickson *et al.* or should they bracket themselves and start from scratch? Furthermore, if they find deviating results, what conclusions are they to draw? That their study differed from the original one and that both conclusions have equal value, given that they were never meant to be nomothetic? Suppose 50 groups of researchers ran a study equal to Dickson *et al.*'s. Who would be able to make sense of the various differences reported by the different groups? Or would that be a pointless question, given that each study was ideographic and not meant to be compared with the others?

Qualitative methods are based on introspection

The reason why qualitative methods create difficulties in deciding between competing conclusions is that in the end they go back to introspective opinions, formulated by participants (in face-to-face interviews or in focus groups) and interpreted by researchers. In the absence of an external criterion, it is impossible to decide between conflicting opinions of people.

When evaluating the conclusions of introspective research (both qualitative and quantitative), it may be good to keep in mind that introspection still has the same precarious status it had in the early days of psychology (Chapters 4 and 5). People have no knowledge of many things they do and factors that influence them (Chapter 7). In addition, a century of psychological research has shown that even if people have strong opinions, they do not always agree with their actions. This is not the place to go into this literature, but the quotes below may be a good reminder of what is at issue (they also contain pointers for those who want to explore this literature in more depth).

> Recent developments in the behavioral-, cognitive- and neurosciences indicate that, more often than not, we act in an automatic and unaware fashion, making up reasons only as we go along . . . We are not directly aware of what drives our actions but

infer reasons on the basis of a priori causal theories, confabulating them if we cannot find reasonable explanations . . . So many causal factors escape consciousness that confabulation seems to be the rule rather than the exception . . . Even our moral judgments seem to be based on intuitions that are not, or are only partially, accessible to introspection. The reasons we come up with to justify these judgments are post hoc rationalizations that had no role in their generation . . .

(Sie & Wouters 2008: 3)

. . . the vast adaptive unconscious is dissociated from conscious awareness and can never be directly viewed via introspection. Introspection reveals the contents of consciousness, such as at least some of people's current thoughts and feelings. It cannot, however, no matter how deeply people dig, gain direct access to nonconscious mental processes. Instead, people must attempt to infer the nature of these processes, by taking what they know (e.g. their conscious states) and filling in the gaps of what they do not know (their nonconscious states) by constructing a coherent narrative about themselves.

(Wilson & Dunn 2004: 505)

The researcher's involvement may be a disadvantage in high-stakes situations

Finally, qualitative researchers acknowledge that the outcome of a study to some extent depends on the person who does the study. The researcher has an impact on the interview and colours the analysis. Although such a state of affairs may be acceptable in fundamental research and in some areas of applied psychology (e.g. when the intervention can be tailor-made to the individual client), there are other situations in which psychologists may find themselves vulnerable to criticism. In general, society is not too happy when high-stakes decisions like personnel selection, university admissions or probation judgements differ too much from one psychologist to another. In those situations psychologists have to show that they adhere to standardised instruments that have a high inter-rater reliability and that have proven their validity (Chapters 8 and 13).

Interim summary

The essence of qualitative research

- Qualitative research methods are directed at understanding phenomena in their historical and socio-cultural context. They are based on the following assumptions:
  - in psychology there is little or no evidence for a reality outside people's perception and experience
  - attempts to control the situation make the setting artificial and no longer meaningful
  - researchers must immerse themselves in the situation so that they can understand the meaning of the situation
  - qualitative research is in the first place meant to understand specific situations (ideographic), not to come to general rules (nomothetic)
  - induction is more important than deduction; the researcher must approach the situation open-mindedly and accept input from the participants
  - qualitative research must remain evidence-based, starting from a careful and verifiable collection of data.

- Data collection usually occurs by means of semi-structured interviews with a limited number of participants; increasingly also focus groups are used.
- The data need to be transcribed and analysed up to saturation along the lines proposed by the qualitative method that is used.
- Three methods were described:
  - grounded theory: introduced by sociologists, tries to understand the phenomenon
  - interpretative phenomenological analysis (IPA): inspired by phenomenology (Husserl), tries to understand the ways in which the phenomenon is perceived and experienced by the participants
  - discourse analysis: inspired by postmodernism, tries to understand how language constructs human interactions.
- Strengths:
  - directly focused on understanding situations and solving problems
  - generation of new ideas and elaboration of theories
  - more attention to the participants' needs.
- Weaknesses:
  - based on induction and verification
  - no external criterion to decide between theories
  - based on introspection (with the risk of participants confabulating)
  - input from the researcher may be a problem in high-stake situations.

11.3 How do quantitative and qualitative research methods relate to each other?

Now that we have discussed the two types of research methods, we can ask ourselves how they relate to each other. As you can imagine, the existence of two types of methods related to two different views about the nature of psychology (natural-science oriented vs. humanities oriented) has given rise to a great deal of controversy. The various positions can be divided into two groups. On the one hand, there are psychologists who strongly feel that the two types of research cannot coexist and, therefore, psychology must make a choice. On the other hand, there are psychologists who see the methods as complementary, each with their own weaknesses and strengths, and that psychology gains by combining them. Below we discuss the two stances.

? What do you think?

Before you start reading about the different sides of the controversy it may be interesting for you to establish for yourself where you stand at this moment. After having read the essentials of the quantitative and the qualitative research methods, to what extent do you see them as incompatible or complementary?

The two types of research are incompatible

Incompatibility of the underlying paradigms

Psychologists who stress the incompatibility of quantitative and qualitative research methods emphasise the different world views underlying them: objective reality vs. social construction, natural sciences vs. humanities, hypothetico-deductive research vs. hermeneutics, mainstream psychology vs. critical psychology, and above all positivism vs. postmodernism. According to these authors, the approaches are so contradictory that trying to integrate them results either in an oxymoron or a stealthy attempt to win back lost ground. This is the 'paradigm war' referred to in the opening of this chapter. Below we discuss some examples.

Quantitative psychology's arguments against the need for qualitative psychology

A first argument fervent quantitative psychologists use against qualitative methods is that the hermeneutic and postmodernist movements throw away all the progress that has been made in the past 150 years and catapult psychology back to the early 1800s, before psychology became seen as the scientific study of mental life (Chapters 3–4).

> Psychology would become, as it is in some parts of Europe, an arts-based discipline; its funding would decline; and scientific psychologists would leave to take up appointments in departments of cognitive science or neuroscience . . .
>
> There are some issues which can be solved by finding a middle way, and others where one has to make a choice. My opinion is that we have to reject postmodernism from scientific psychology, if only to have a coherent teaching programme. We cannot have one set of lecturers explaining to students how to study psychology scientifically, and another set of lecturers telling the same students that when studying people, the methods of science are no use. It won't work, and psychology departments won't work.
>
> (Morgan 1998: 481–2)

Another argument against qualitative research methods is that they reject the existence of an objective reality, which is the *raison d'être* of science.

> I began this debate by suggesting that qualitative psychologists pose a threat to traditional notions of psychology as a science. The problem is not that they use single case studies; it is not that they may find no use for statistics; it is not even that they reject the goal of quantitative laws. The real problem is that they reject the notion of something 'out there' which can be studied objectively.
>
> (Morgan 1998: 488)

A final criticism heard from proponents of the quantitative research methods is that qualitative research methods do not provide researchers with new information and devalue psychological research to pop psychology. Again, Morgan (1998) phrased this most cogently:

> [They seem] to be making the claim that the aim of psychology should be to understand people, and that one can only understand people by forming social relationships with them, to which scientific objectivity is a barrier. To this one could reply that we have been forming social relationships with one another for some half a million years, and have indeed got to understand one another quite well at a certain level as a result.
>
> But it is unlikely that qualitative psychology will improve this intuitive understanding unless it brings some new technique to the job, and I have yet to be convinced that the techniques go beyond those of good investigative journalism.

'Forming relationships' with people is the job of everyone; I see no reason to pay researchers to do it. Something a bit different is expected from scientists.

(Morgan 1998: 482)

Qualitative psychology's arguments against the need for quantitative psychology

For each of the arguments put forward by quantitative researchers, a similar argument can be found among ardent qualitative supporters. They too see quantitative and qualitative research as incompatible, but argue that quantitative psychology should be dropped. They question the superiority of scientific knowledge and hold that mainstream psychologists clutch at the scientific method not because it has brought understanding of human functioning, but because it has brought status and money to psychology departments. This has been formulated most eloquently by Stevenson and Cooper (1997) in an otherwise more moderate paper.

> The adoption of a positivist position allows psychology to maintain 'scientific' respectability. Psychology as a discipline and profession therefore has a vested interest in maintaining the dominance of objectivity in relation to the production of psychological knowledge.
>
> The emergence of constructivist approaches creates a particular form of knowledge that appears to challenge the nature of psychology itself by suggesting that knowledge (and therefore psychology) is socially constructed, and that knowledge is associated with power. Perhaps because of the potentially far-reaching consequences for the discipline of adopting a qualitative inquiry position, the legitimacy of qualitative research is frequently questioned.

(Stevenson & Cooper 1997: 159)

Qualitative psychologists further argue that quantitative research is misguided in its search for the 'objective reality': If something like an objective reality existed in psychology, one would have expected quantitative psychology to be more successful after 150 years.

> What about the claimed solidity of traditional psychological knowledge? It has become characteristic of our discipline that different theories, each equally empirically confirmed according to prevailing standards, exist side by side. We are pointing here to more than a mere multiplicity of theories. Rather, they make universal claims about identical objects on the basis of incompatible (or at least mutually problematic) concepts, and we are in no position to be able to decide which of the theories is tenable and which ought to be rejected. (A comparable situation would exist in physics if there were half a dozen permanently competing theories about the free fall of objects.)

(Maiers 1991: 33)

Finally, the hardcore qualitative psychologists argue that if there is no objective reality, quantitative research methods have nothing to tell us about human functioning. All they can do is give us replicable, useless information.

> I am far less sanguine about the predictions of artificial and culturally isolated behaviors often used in testing abstract hypotheses about mental function. The question is not whether such hypotheses are true or false in any ultimate sense but whether the particular predictions have any utility outside the local game of truth. As I see it, a postmodern empiricism would replace the 'truth game' with a search for culturally useful theories and findings with significant cultural meaning.

(Gergen 2001: 808)

Trying to reconcile quantitative and qualitative research methods are attempts to regain lost ground

Psychologists who consider qualitative and quantitative research to be incompatible often mistrust efforts to unite them, because they see these efforts as disguised attempts to regain lost ground. The quantitative researchers consider those efforts as the latest attempt of hermeneutics to grab a slice of the cake after the status of psychoanalysis declined in the second half of the twentieth century. The qualitative researchers fear that the integration attempts by quantitative psychology are meant to seize the qualitative research methods under the umbrella of positivist psychology, oppressing everything that is typical for the qualitative methods, such as the convictions that participants should be studied in rich contexts of history, society and culture, that people should be studied in meaningful situations which form part of their life worlds, and that mental life consists of social constructions on the basis of language and culture. An example of this position can be found in Marecek (2003), who listed four misunderstandings about qualitative methods that are prevalent among quantitative researchers who treat qualitative research methods as just another type of scientific research:

1. Qualitative and quantitative psychology are complementary methods and lead to the same type of understanding.
2. Qualitative research is an adjunct to quantitative research; its findings are an interesting first step but they require further quantitative exploration.
3. Qualitative research only consists of inductive reasoning.
4. Qualitative research is nothing but psychology without numbers.

According to Marecek, if one opts for qualitative research, one should also opt for the values that underlie this approach and not try to tweak the research methods so that they fit in a quantitative framework.

The two types of research complement each other

The other view (e.g. Todd *et al.* 2004) is that qualitative and quantitative research methods can be used in tandem depending on the question one wants to answer. Such a view is found, for instance, in Lee *et al.* (1999: 164), who wrote about the use of qualitative research in organisational and vocational psychology that:

> Summarizing across these major characteristics and themes, [we conclude] that qualitative research is well suited for the purposes of description, interpretation, and explanation. In particular, it can effectively address questions such as 'What is occurring?' and 'How is it occurring?' In contrast, qualitative research is not well suited for issues of prevalence, generalizability, and calibration. For example, it cannot effectively answer a question such as 'How much—of whatever it is—is occurring?' Thus, the kinds of questions that are answered by qualitative and quantitative research methods differ. Perhaps needless to say, organizational and vocational psychologists should apply the method that best fits their theoretical question and analytical situation. In our judgment, qualitative methods simply offer additional and more specialized tools that seem likely to be useful for some of our research.

Similar statements can be found in an increasing number of texts, making it likely that in the future quantitative and qualitative research methods will be used in combination. Psychologists who defend this position are less concerned with the contradictions in the underlying philosophies but focus on what the methods themselves deliver in terms of information. They point out that those who argue for incompatibility exaggerate the differences between the approaches at the expense of the commonalities, and that each method to some extent compensates for weaknesses in the other.

Quantitative research is more than a positivist search for physical laws

Quantitative psychologists are depicted by hardcore qualitative psychologists as positivists in search of scientific laws of behaviour. This description contains three strong statements: (1) quantitative psychology defends a positivist view of the world, (2) quantitative psychology is looking for laws similar to Newton's laws of physics, and (3) quantitative psychology is only interested in behaviour.

The first claim suggests that quantitative psychologists subscribe to positivism. Certainly in the last decades such a claim has a negative connotation, because positivism is taken to mean that only scientific knowledge is worthwhile and that scientific knowledge is never wrong (because it is a constant accumulation of knowledge). As explained in Chapter 9, this view was rejected in the second half of the twentieth century, and claiming that quantitative psychologists still subscribe to it assumes they are unaware of these developments. A more realistic view of the attitude of quantitative psychology towards the merits of the natural science approach is given by Smith (1994):

> What I see as most unfortunate, however, is the tendency, abetted by Gergen, to give up the conception of science—natural or human, historical or ahistorical—as an evidential, public, self-critical social enterprise, an enterprise that has successfully sought progressively more adequate and comprehensive understanding of the phenomena in its domain—an enterprise committed to an ideal of truth, the approach to which can be evaluated pragmatically. I find little justification in the postmodernist literature for the claim that scientific constructions, fallible as they are and always subject to disconfirmation and revision, are simply optional myths on all fours with religious or political dogmas and ideologies.
>
> (Smith 1994: 408)

The second claim, that quantitative psychology is only interested in laws similar to those of physics, is outdated as well. It is true that in its early days scientific psychology was infatuated with physics, like all sciences at that time. However, this is no longer the case. Scientists nowadays make a distinction between deterministic and stochastic processes. A *deterministic process* is a process in which the variability is so small that you can predict the outcome with high accuracy when you know the precursors. In contrast, a *stochastic process* is a process where the variability in the possible determinants and the contribution of the random noise is so big that it becomes impossible to exactly predict the next outcome. All you can do is to estimate the probability with which various outcomes may occur and search for variables that (slightly) change this probability. A typical example is trying to predict which clubs of a sports league will win the next round of matches. Although some clubs may be better than others, and therefore more likely to win their match, there is never certainty, only differences in probability. Psychology deals with stochastic processes, as opposed to Newtonian physics.

The changed nature of quantitative psychological research has been documented nicely by Teigen (2002). He made an analysis of the use of the notion 'law' in the psychological literature of the twentieth century and observed a steady decline. The term was used almost exclusively to refer to ideas of the nineteenth and the early twentieth centuries (such as Weber's law, the law of effect or the Gestalt laws). In the course of the twentieth century psychologists increasingly described regularities as principles, effects, trends or functions. In particular the word 'model' came into vogue.

> More complex regularities in the second half of the century are often called models, a term practically unknown in psychology until the publication of Rosenblueth and Wiener's (1945) seminal article. Subsequently, the popularity of this term has increased sharply from decade to decade; today it can be found in about 10% of all PsycLit journal abstracts . . . The term has the advantage of flexibility, it does not claim universality or definitiveness, and can be embraced by scientists regardless of their position on the realism vs. relativism issue.
>
> (Teigen 2002: 113)

Finally, the claim that quantitative psychology is only interested in behaviour is overstated as well. Some qualitative psychologists have the tendency to equate quantitative research with the collection of numbers in artificial, impoverished and restrained situations that no longer have a meaning for the participants. Usually this is connected to problems with external validity (the degree to which the findings of a study can be generalised to other participants, measurements and contexts) and ecological validity (the degree to which findings in laboratory studies can be generalised to the real world). Most of the time, however, this criticism is not substantiated. It is presented as a truism, something that can be taken for granted. However, a search through the literature does not reveal a string of publications showing that quantitative psychology findings deviate consistently from the way people live in real life. As a matter of fact, there is a rather substantial literature indicating that findings in laboratories are similar to those from field studies (Anderson *et al.* 1999) and that quantitative data based on standardised tests for some topics predict performance better than clinical judgement based on interviews (Meehl 1954; Grove *et al.* 2000: Chapter 8).

A particularly instructive case in this respect was published by Van Strien and Dane (2001). They described a personnel recruitment and selection agency in the mid-twentieth century that operated on the basis of the then dominant phenomenological psychology in the Netherlands (van Hezewijk & Stam 2008). This phenomenological psychology was promoted by the physiologist and psychologist Frederik Buytendijk and maintained that humans could not be understood by means of standardised tests and techniques. Such understanding required a 'meeting of minds', a personal relationship between a 'you' and 'me'. Observations could only result in information after they had been contemplated and understood by the interviewer. Consequently, the bureau recruited personnel on the basis of a day's meeting of minds including the contemplation and understanding of in-depth interviews and observed behaviours on home-made tasks. The agency was one of the leading consultants in the Netherlands, until a collaborator started to analyse the recommendations and correlated them with outcome measures obtained from the companies that had taken on the personnel. The result was a disappointing correlation of +0.15 (Modderaar 1966), hardly better than if the agency had tossed a coin to decide which candidates could be employed (in which case one would expect a correlation of 0.00).

This example illustrates that having the intention to talk about meaningful situations by itself is no guarantee that the outcome will be more useful than numbers obtained under more constrained circumstances (Schmidt and Hunter (1998) report correlations up to +0.58 between test results and performance measures in personnel selection; see also Hanson and Morton-Bourgon (2009) for a comparison of recidivism risk assessment based on test scores vs. clinical judgment). An interesting development in this respect will be to see whether findings based on current-day qualitative methods (such as grounded theory, IPA or discourse analysis) do better than the hermeneutic attempts of the past.

Qualitative research is more than a chat with participants

Qualitative research is also often misrepresented in texts that question its usefulness. Probably the most common misunderstanding is that qualitative methods involve nothing but a few interviews with people, after which the interviewer writes down his or her impressions. As we have indicated above, data collection in qualitative research methods is as rigorous as in quantitative research. The transcripts must be made available to everyone who wants to verify the outcome of the analysis. In addition, researchers are taught to be careful not to let their views bias the interview or the interpretation, and to incorporate controls to increase the validity of the findings. These include the following checks (cf. Silverman 2005):

1. *Representativeness*. Researchers must provide the criteria they used for their data analysis, so that the representativeness of the reported instances can be gauged.

2. *Confirmability*. Would someone else come to the same conclusions on the basis of an equivalent data analysis?

3. *Credibility*. Do the conclusions sound credible to the participants involved in the study?

4. *Comparison of situations that differ on one critical aspect*. Another way to check the validity of conclusions is to compare the data with those of similar cases that deviate in a critical aspect. Silverman (2005: 212–14), for instance, described a qualitative study that investigated what happened to Down's syndrome children in a heart hospital. In order to make sure that the study really addressed the concerns of those children, a comparison was made with consultations at the same clinic involving children without the syndrome.

5. *Alternative explanations*. Could the data be explained differently?

6. *Refutability*. Is there evidence that refutes the conclusions? This principle very much resembles the falsification test in quantitative psychology.

Personally, when preparing this chapter we were struck by the many similarities between what qualitative researchers do and what quantitative researchers do in a literature review. In both cases researchers:

- Try to leave their preconceptions behind and look with an open mind at the documents available.

- Start by reading through the various documents to get a feeling for the main themes and their connections.

- On the basis of several close re-readings, build up and refine a coding scheme that adequately summarises the various statements, always making reference to the original materials so that colleagues can check the conclusions.

- Look up extra sources in case of doubt, ambiguity or possible new leads.

- Make sure that no issues have been overlooked.

- Try to reach conclusions that go beyond the obvious but increase the understanding of the phenomenon and/or provide ideas for further exploration.

- Have the credibility of the synopsis checked by getting reviews from experienced people.
- Accept that the end product is to some extent influenced by the creator and limited in the degree to which the conclusions can be generalised.

The only difference is that in a literature review the raw materials are journal articles and book chapters, whereas in qualitative research one is dealing with transcripts of human interactions. So, if quantitative researchers question the value of qualitative methods, they also question the value of their own literature reviews that try to bring order to the many scattered findings and conjectures about a particular topic.

Weaknesses in quantitative research that can be addressed by the qualitative approach

If one accepts that there is no inherent incompatibility between quantitative and qualitative research (remember that not everybody does so!), it becomes worthwhile to search for ways in which one method can compensate for weaknesses in the other. As we have seen above, three weaknesses of quantitative psychology are (1) not enough interest in the participants, (2) research is too much driven by what can be measured and tested experimentally, and (3) too much focus on falsification at the expense of a pragmatic solution to the problem at hand. It is not so difficult to see how a qualitative approach can be fruitful here: (1) participants are the centre of focus in qualitative research, (2) qualitative research deals primarily with variables that are hard to quantify and that cannot be manipulated, and (3) given the correspondence between a qualitative analysis and the traditional literature review, one can see how the former can be used successfully for theory building and the solution of practical problems.

Weaknesses in qualitative research that can be addressed by the quantitative approach

Again, the three weaknesses we discussed with respect to qualitative research coincide with strengths of the quantitative approach. The quantitative approach is focused on falsification, which may form a welcome addition to the induction and verification of qualitative research, at least if the conclusion can be tested. Similarly, the quantitative approach is well suited to decide between theories (if they can be tested), and the quantitative approach has a wide arsenal of techniques to test whether the introspections of participants agree with their actions in relevant situations. Finally, statistical methods are much more powerful than the human mind to detect differences and correlations in large-scale datasets. This is interesting for qualitative researchers because quite often the data from a qualitative analysis exceed the human reasoning capacity. For instance, Lee *et al*. (1999) argued that qualitative research can be compared to an informal exploratory factor analysis. In their own words:

> Through a variety of qualitative techniques, for example, large amounts of qualitative data are subjectively evaluated (cf. intuitively correlated), simplified (cf. judgmentally combined into factors), and reconstituted (cf. subjectively rotated). If this is successful, the net result is greater understanding of the empirical evidence (cf. latent and causal traits are identified and defined).

(Lee *et al*. 1999: 164)

If this is true (and we see little reason to doubt their assessment), then whenever the data can be analysed statistically, there is overwhelming evidence that such an analysis will produce a more stable and detailed picture than human assessment. This is also the case when the data come from a qualitative study.

For the above reasons, an increasing number of psychologists have become convinced that progress in psychological research is better served by combining quantitative and qualitative methods rather than by trying to force research in one or the other direction. An interesting development in this respect will be what consequences this has for the underlying philosophies (the 'paradigms' of the opening citation).

What do you think?

Did the review of the different positions about the relationship of qualitative and quantitative research methods make you change your mind? In what ways? Or why not? What is your position now?

Interim summary

How do quantitative and qualitative research methods relate to each other?

- Some psychologists (both quantitative and qualitative) see them as incompatible and argue that psychology must make a choice:
  - the underlying philosophies (positivism vs. postmodernism) are mutually exclusive
  - attempts to combine both approaches are disguised attempts to improve the standing of the natural-science oriented research line or the hermeneutics oriented research line at the expense of the other.
- Other psychologists see both types of research methods as complementary; they focus more on the type of information provided by each method rather than on the philosophies that underlie them:
  - fervent supporters of each approach tend to depict an exaggerated view of the other approach
  - the weaknesses of one approach are the strengths of the other.

11.4 *Focus on*: Is too much respect for the philosophy of science bad for morale?

Psychology's rough treatment by philosophy of science

In Chapter 10 we saw how psychologists in the first half of the twentieth century turned to philosophers of science for inspiration on how to increase the scientific standing of their research. More than any other research discipline, they slavishly implemented the recommendations of the then prevailing positivists and logical positivists (observation, induction, verification), only to find themselves criticised 50 years later for a lack of theory. Repentantly, they listened to Popper and started to build cognitive theories that would enable them to test hypotheses, again to find themselves criticised 50 years later for not having an open mind. Both radical behaviourists (Chapter 5) and qualitative psychologists (this chapter) reproached cognitive psychologists for doing nothing but deductive theory testing, instead of looking properly at the raw data and using inductive reasoning to come to a better understanding. By the same time, mainstream psychology started to receive the 'gleeful' message from postmodernists that science after all was nothing special and that psychology had deluded itself thinking that adherence to the scientific method made any difference. This reignited the discussion between the natural-sciences oriented and the hermeneutics oriented movements in psychology (Chapter 10).

One would forgive those psychologists who begin to doubt whether listening to philosophers of science and following their advice has done any good for them! They might find themselves in agreement with the economist Paul Samuelson (1915–2009) who wrote:

> I rather shy away from discussions of Methodology with a capital M. To paraphrase Shaw, those who can, do science, those who can't, prattle about its methodology. Of course I cannot deny that I have a methodology. It is just that there seems little appeal in making it explicit to an outsider. Or, for that matter, in spelling it out to my own consciousness.
>
> (Samuelson 1992: 240)

Can we predict what governs scientific progress?

One of the reasons why it may be difficult to set up guidelines about how to achieve scientific progress is that doing good research is not a deterministic process that can be summarised in a few rules. As we saw above, a deterministic process is a process where the variability is so small that you can predict the outcome with high accuracy when you know the precursors. Its alternative is a stochastic process, a process where the variability in the possible determinants and the contribution of random noise is so big that it becomes impossible to exactly predict the next outcome. All you can do is estimate the probability with which various outcomes may occur.

Scientific creativity can hardly be considered a deterministic process, meaning that it is impossible to isolate a few factors that govern it. All you can do is point to a series of factors that (slightly) increase or decrease the probability of a new worthwhile finding. In addition, many of these factors are simply correlations, not causal influences. For instance, most scientists are hard-working people. However, this by itself does not mean that forcing people to work long hours will result in extra scientific progress. Only if the number of working hours is a causal factor of scientific progress will such a policy make a difference.

The evolutionary model of scientific progress

Interestingly, there is an account of scientific progress that fits within the view that there are very few ways in which progress can be stimulated. According to the evolutionary account, scientific progress follows Darwin's evolutionary principles of random variation (based on whatever method) followed by natural selection (Campbell 1960; Simonton 2011). In this view, scientific discoveries are nothing but blind (i.e. random) variations, similar to gene mutations. The subsequent selection determines whether a discovery will have an increasing number of descendants or whether it will be one of the many mutations that rapidly die out without leaving offspring.

According to the evolutionary account, the most important factor in scientific progress is the extent to which the environment favours reproduction. In an environment that stimulates reproduction, a lot of new variants will appear and start their struggle for life; an environment that stifles reproduction will only see a few variants come out, with low chances of success. A secondary variable that affects scientific progress is the fit between the offspring and the environment. A mutant that fits well in the environment will have a better chance of reproduction than a mutant that does not fit in the environment. Within this view, the only contribution philosophy of science can make is to help create an environment that favours the reproduction of ideas.

Worthwhile ideas in a pragmatic world

A factor that is likely to affect the fit of a new finding in the existing environment is the degree to which the finding is perceived as helpful to cope with the world. A randomly generated discovery that is seen to yield practical benefits is more likely to be reproduced than a discovery that does not seem to make a difference. As you may remember, this is the pragmatic criterion of knowledge growth discussed in Chapter 9. A worthwhile (true) finding is a finding that benefits human actions. Thus, there seems to be a remarkable match between the evolutionary theory of scientific progress and pragmatism. Only ideas that are seen as interesting by a sufficiently large group are supported and will survive.

A look at psychological research suggests that perceived usefulness indeed is an important criterion to decide which proposals are retained for further research (and textbooks) and which not. In both the quantitative and qualitative literature we regularly see reference being made to the practical impact of a finding as an index of its quality rather than a strict adherence to methodology. So, in the editorial of a mainstream, quantitative journal we read that:

> A former editor of the journal, Endel Tulving, recently recounted a rule he set for reviewing: Ask yourself, 'What did I learn from reading this paper? Was it worth learning?' If you get a positive response, accept; if not, reject. Tulving thought his admonition had little impact. I'm happy to contradict him. Most reviewers, most of the time, take the message to heart.
>
> (Bock 2008: 2)

Similarly, in a text describing the worth of qualitative research we read that:

> The decisive criterion by which any piece of research must be judged is, arguably, its impact and utility. It is not sufficient to develop a sensitive, thorough and plausible analysis, if the ideas propounded by the researcher have no influence on the beliefs or actions of anyone else.
>
> (Yardley 2000: 223)

The fact that the impact of a new insight depends more on the degree to which it is judged interesting by the readers than on the degree to which it followed the recommendations of philosophy of science can also be seen in the list of psychologists with the highest impact. In a review of the most eminent psychologists of the twentieth century (Haggbloom *et al.* 2002), the top positions were taken by respectively Skinner, Piaget, Freud, Bandura, Festinger and Rogers. Of these, at least three (Piaget, Freud and Rogers) would be classified as qualitative researchers in present-day terms. They did not come to their theories on the basis of rigid adherence to the hypothetico-deductive method, but on the basis of trying to understand their own functioning and that of a few others. Their ideas survived not because they were 'scientifically sound' or 'obviously true', but because a lot of people found them interesting and inspiring.

So, the ultimate criterion of scientific development may not be whether scientists did 'proper science' (according to philosophy of science) but whether their findings were perceived as relevant for the research community and society at large (i.e. fitted within the prevailing environment).

Needless to say, such a conclusion is nauseatingly ironic for psychologists. You may remember that this was exactly the advice given by Peirce and the first American psychologists, William James and John Dewey, when they founded American functionalism. In particular, James urged psychologists to aim for research that had practical relevance. The pragmatic criterion has been ignored by the philosophers of science (and the psychologists who listened to them) for most of the twentieth century, because it did not allow them to demarcate science from other ways of knowledge acquisition, but it may come to the foreground now as a result of the deadlock between realism and idealism (Chapter 9).

Interim summary

Is philosophy of science useful for psychology?

- Psychology has tried to follow the directives from philosophers of science on how to do 'proper' science, but has been confronted with changing and at times conflicting advice.

- The problem may be that philosophy of science in vain tries to distil a limited set of rules that would govern a process which is not deterministic.

- An alternative view that may be more in line with the stochastic nature of scientific discovery is the evolutionary account. According to this model, the rise and fall of scientific ideas follow Darwinian principles of random variation and natural selection.

- Because natural selection depends on the fit of an idea in the environment and because science depends on the wider culture to be financed, the ultimate criterion determining whether an idea will survive may be whether society at large finds the idea interesting and useful.

- This may entail a return to the pragmatic criterion put forward by James and Dewey at the beginning of psychology.

Recommended literature

Information about both quantitative and qualitative research methods can be found in Howitt, D. and Cramer, D. (2008) *Introduction to research methods in psychology* (2nd edn) (Harlow: Prentice Hall).

Further information about qualitative research methods can be found in Willig, C. (2008) *Introducing qualitative research in psychology* (2nd edn) (Maidenhead: McGraw-Hill/Open University Press), or in Smith, J.A. (ed.) (2008) *Qualitative psychology: A practical guide to research methods* (2nd edn) (London: Sage Publications).

References

Aegisdottir, S., White, M., Spengler, P.M., Mangherman, A.S. *et al.* (2006) 'The meta-analysis of clinical judgment project: Fifty-six years of accumulated research on clinical versus statistical prediction', *Counseling Psychologist,* **34**: 341–82.

Alvesson, M. (2000) 'Taking the linguistic turn in organizational research', *Journal of Applied Behavioral Science,* **36**: 136–58.

Anderson, C.A., Lindsay, J.J. & Bushman, B.J. (1999) 'Research in the psychological laboratory: Truth or triviality?' *Current Directions in Psychological Science,* **8**: 3–9.

Ashworth, P. (2003) 'The origins of qualitative psychology'. In J.A. Smith (ed.), *Qualitative psychology: A practical guide to research methods.* London: Sage, pp. 4–24.

Bock, K. (2008) Editorial. *Journal of Memory and Language,* **58**: 1–2.

Campbell, D.T. (1960) 'Blind variation and selective retention in creative thought as in other knowledge processes', *Psychological Review,* **67**: 380–400.

Danziger, K. (1990) *Constructing the subject: Historical origins of psychological research.* Cambridge: Cambridge University Press.

Dickson, A., Knussen, C. & Flowers, P. (2008) '"That was my old life; it's almost like a past-life now": Identity crisis, loss and adjustment amongst people living with Chronic Fatigue Syndrome', *Psychology & Health,* **23**: 459–76.

Doll, R., Peto, R., Boreham, J. & Sutherland, I. (2004) 'Mortality in relation to smoking: 50 years' observations on male British doctors', *British Medical Journal,* **328**: 1519–28.

Eysenck, M.W. & Keane, M.T. (2005) *Cognitive psychology: A student's handbook* (5th edn). Hove: Psychology Press.

Gergen, K.J. (2001) 'Psychological science in a postmodern context', *American Psychologist,* **56**: 803–13.

Glaser, B.G. & Strauss, A.L. (1967) *Discovery of grounded theory: Strategies for qualitative research.* New York: Aldine de Gruyter.

Greenhalgh, T. (1997) 'How to read a paper: Getting your bearings (deciding what the paper is about)', *British Medical Journal,* **315**: 243–46.

Grove, W.M., Zald, D.H., Lebow, B.S., Snitz, E. *et al.* (2000) 'Clinical versus mechanical prediction: A meta-analysis', *Psychological Assessment,* **12**: 19–30.

Haggbloom, S.J., Warnick, R., Warnick, J.E., Jones, V.K. *et al.* (2002) 'The 100 most eminent psychologists of the 20th century', *Review of General Psychology,* **6**: 139–52.

Hanson, R.K & Morton-Bourgon, K.E. (2009) 'The accuracy of recidivism risk assessments for sexual offenders: A meta-analysis of 118 prediction studies', *Psychological Assessment,* **21**: 1–21.

Hatch, J.A. (ed.) (1995) *Qualitative research in early childhood settings.* Westport, CT: Greenwood Publishing Group.

King, R.N. & Koehler, D.J. (2000) 'Illusory correlations in graphological inference', *Journal of Experimental Psychology: Applied,* **6**: 336–48.

Kuhn, T.S. (1962/1970) *The structure of scientific revolutions.* Chicago: University of Chicago Press.

Lee, T.W., Mitchell, T.R. & Sablynski, C.J. (1999) 'Qualitative research in organizational and vocational psychology 1979–1999', *Journal of Vocational Behavior,* **55**: 161–87.

Lemon, N. & Taylor, H. (1997) 'Caring in casualty: The phenomenology of nursing care.' In N. Hayes (ed.) *Doing qualitative analysis in psychology.* Hove: Psychology Press, pp. 227–43.

Maiers, W. (1991) 'Critical psychology: Historical background and task'. In C.W. Tolman and W. Maiers (eds) *Critical psychology: Contributions to an historical science of the subject.* Cambridge: Cambridge University Press.

Marecek, J. (2003) 'Dancing through minefields: Toward a qualitative stance in psychology.' In P.M. Camic, J.E. Rhodes & L. Yardley (eds), *Qualitative research in psychology: Expanding perspectives in methodology and design.* Washington DC: American Psychological Association, pp. 49–69.

Meehl, P.E. (1954) *Clinical vs. statistical prediction: A theoretical analysis and a review of the evidence.* Minneapolis: University of Minnesota Press.

Milgram, S. (1963) 'Behavioral study of obedience', *Journal of Abnormal and Social Psychology,* **67**: 371–8.

Modderaar, J. (1966) 'Over de validiteit van de selectie voor bedrijven [On the validity of selection for companies]', *Nederlands Tijdschrift voor de Psychologie,* **21**: 573–89.

Morgan, M. (1998) 'Qualitative research: Science or pseudo-science?' *The Psychologist,* **11**: 481–3 (and Postscript: 485).

Reid, K., Flowers, P. & Larkin, M. (2005) 'Exploring lived experience', *The Psychologist,* **18**: 20–23.

Rosenblueth, A. & Wiener, N. (1945) 'The role of models in science', *Philosophy of Science,* **12**: 316–21.

Rosenthal, R. & Rosnow, R.L. (2008) *Essentials of behavioral research: Methods and data analysis* (3rd edn). Boston, MA: McGraw-Hill.

Samuelson, P.A. (1992) 'My life philosophy: Policy credos and working days'. In M. Szenberg (ed.), *Eminent economists: Their life philosophies.* Cambridge: Cambridge University Press.

Schmidt, F.L. & Hunter, J.E. (1998) 'The validity and utility of selection methods in personnel psychology: Practical and theoretical implications of 85 years of research findings', *Psychological Bulletin,* **124**: 262–74.

Schraw, G., Wadkins, T. & Olafson, L. (2007) 'Doing the things we do: A grounded theory of academic procrastination', *Journal of Educational Psychology,* **99**: 12–25.

Sie, M. & Wouters, A. (2008) 'The real challenge to free will and responsibility', *Trends in Cognitive Sciences,* **12**: 3–4.

Silverman, D. (2005) *Doing qualitative research: A practical handbook* (2nd edn). London: Sage Publications.

Simonton, D.K. (2011) 'Creativity and discovery as blind variation: Campbell's (1960) BVSR model after the half-century mark', *Review of General Psychology,* **15**: 158–74.

Smith, J.A. (1996) 'Beyond the divide between cognition and discourse: Using interpretative phenomenological analysis in health psychology', *Psychology and Health,* **11**: 261–71.

Smith, J.A. (ed.) (2008) *Qualitative psychology: A practical guide to research methods* (2nd edn). London: Sage Publications.

Smith, M.B. (1994) 'Selfhood at risk: Postmodern perils and the perils of postmodernism', *American Psychologist,* **49**: 405–11.

Starks, H. & Trinidad, S.B. (2007) 'Choose your method: A comparison of phenomenology, discourse analysis, and grounded theory', *Qualitative Health Research,* **17**: 1372–80.

Stevenson, C. & Cooper, N. (1997) 'Qualitative and quantitative research', *The Psychologist,* **4**: 159–60.

Stratton, P. (1997) 'Attributional coding of interview data: Meeting the needs of long-haul passengers'. In N. Hayes (ed.), *Doing qualitative analysis in psychology.* Hove: Psychology Press, pp. 115–42.

Teigen, K.H. (2002) 'One hundred years of laws in psychology', *The American Journal of Psychology,* **115**: 103–18.

Todd, Z., Nerlich, B., McKeown, S. & Clarke, D.D. (2004) *Mixing methods in psychology: The integration of qualitative and quantitative methods in theory and practice.* Hove: Psychology Press.

Twenge, J.M., Campbell, W.K. & Foster, C.A. (2003) 'Parenthood and marital satisfaction: A meta-analytic review', *Journal of Marriage and the Family,* **65**: 574–83.

Vandenbroucke, J.P. (2008) 'Observational research, randomised trials, and two views of medical science', *PLoS Medicine,* **5**: e67, doi:10.1371/ journal.pmed.0050067.

Van Hezewijk, R. & Stam, H.J. (2008) 'Idols of the psychologist: Johannes Linschoten and the demise of phenomenological psychology in the Netherlands', *History of Psychology,* **11**: 185–207.

Van Strien, P.J. & Dane, J. (2001) *Driekwart eeuw psychotechniek in Nederland: De magie van het testen* [Three-quarters of a century of psychotechnics in the Netherlands: The magic of testing]. Assen: Koninklijke Van Gorcum.

Ward, N. (1998) 'Artificial intelligence and other approaches to speech understanding: Reflections on methodology', *Journal of Experimental and Theoretical Artificial Intelligence,* **10**: 487–93.

Willig, C. (2008) *Introducing qualitative research in psychology.* Maidenhead, UK: McGraw-Hill/Open University Press.

Wilson, T.D. & Dunn, E.W. (2004) 'Self-knowledge: Its limits, value, and potential for improvement', *Annual Review of Psychology,* **55**: 493–518.

Yardley, L. (2000) 'Dilemmas in qualitative health research', *Psychology and Health,* **15**: 215–28.

12 The precarious balance between biological, psychological and social influences

Questions to consider

?

Historical issue addressed in this chapter

- When did researchers start to include the impact of social relations in their theories?

Conceptual issues addressed in this chapter

- What does the biopsychosocial model of medicine imply? Does this have a psychological counterpart?
- Can human behaviour be explained on the basis of instincts?
- What evidence supports the view that mental life depends on biological factors?
- What has contributed to the current popularity of evolutionary psychology?
- What evidence supports the view that mental life depends on psychological factors?
- What evidence supports the view that mental life depends on socio-cultural factors?
- In what way does the diathesis–stress model relate to the biopsychosocial model?
- In what ways do people of various cultures differ?
- What causes aggression?

Introduction

> For far too long, behavioral genetics and socialization theory have been viewed as necessarily in opposition to one another. Researchers in both 'camps' have very rarely referred to studies from the other 'camp', other than to attack their concepts and findings. The result has been much fruitless dispute and serious misunderstandings of what each body of research has to contribute.
>
> (Rutter 2006: vi)

biopsychosocial model

model according to which the understanding of medical and psychological phenomena requires attention to biological and psychological as well as socio-cultural factors

In many introductory psychology books it is stressed that human functioning is affected by biological, psychological and socio-cultural factors. A person's actions, thoughts and feelings are influenced by his or her biological constitution, the way he or she perceives, interprets and remembers events, and the interactions he/she has with other people. In this discussion, reference is often made to Engel's (1977) biopsychosocial model of medicine. According to this model, medicine must take into account the psychological and social contributions to disease, as well as the biological involvement, in order to treat an illness properly. Similarly, according to the biopsychosocial model in psychology, mental functioning cannot be understood without taking into account the three types of influences (e.g. Peterson 1997).

However, a look at the literature beyond introductory books shows that although authors theoretically subscribe to the three sources of input, in practice they assign widely divergent weights to them. Most authors seem to pick out one influence (or at most two, as in the extract that opened this chapter), which they claim has not been given the full weight it deserves. So, throughout the history of psychology there have been psychologists stressing that the biological component of mental functioning is underestimated. Similarly, there have been psychologists emphasising that cognitive processes are the main forces behind human behaviour, both normal and abnormal, and that these processes overrule the biological and social constraints. Finally, there have been psychologists arguing that the social situation is a much stronger determinant of human behaviour than the opinions an individual has or the traits an individual inherits.

Because of the enduring quarrel between the three groups of researchers, the balance between biological, psychological and social forces is continuously shifting (hence the title of the chapter: 'the precarious balance'). At different times and within different branches of psychology, each group of variables has been given primacy. Sometimes the biological variables are on the winning side; then the psychological factors are in the spotlight; and finally there are epochs in which the social influences are centre stage. Some of the shifts follow cyclic movements with one group of variables getting most attention at one time, followed by a countermovement pointing to one of the other groups, again followed by a countermovement returning to the initial bias, and so on.

In this chapter we will review the arguments of the three groups, so that you have more background when you read books or articles by individual authors. We start with a historical example, before we have a look at the current situation. In that way, we hope to make clear that the discussion is not new, but has existed from the beginning of psychology.

What do you think?

On the basis of what we have already covered in this book (and lectures you have attended), you can probably indicate some of the biases that are present. Which line of approach has dominated, for instance, in functionalism, behaviourism, neuropsychology, feminist psychology, cognitive psychology or critical psychology?

12.1 What drives people? McDougall and his critics

McDougall's instincts and sentiments

You may remember William McDougall from Chapter 4. He was the British psychologist who was not allowed to start a laboratory in Oxford and eventually moved to the USA. One of his main contributions was that he brought research on motivation and emotion to the foreground. Before him, experimental psychologists examined intellectual processes such as sensation, perception, learning, memory and thinking, but eschewed issues like motivation and emotion, which according to McDougall were essential aspects of mental life. Why did people do the things they did? Why did they live in groups? Why did they follow leaders? The answers to such questions were left to anthropologists, sociologists, economists and historians.

McDougall is best known for his book *An introduction to social psychology*, first published in 1908. Despite its title, its main message was that humans were motivated by a limited set of innate motives from which all other motives were derived as a result of an individual's experience. (Like nearly all English psychologists of his time, McDougall was deeply influenced by Darwin's writings.) At first, McDougall called the primary motives instincts. He later regretted this, because most students interpreted them as automatic reflexes, whereas McDougall saw them as strivings to achieve particular goals. Therefore, he later called them *propensities*. In 1908, he listed 12 primary instincts (which in the subsequent revisions of the book he extended to 17). These were the instincts:

instinct

innate and fixed response that is automatically elicited by an appropriate stimulus; used around the turn of the twentieth century to explain motivation

1. to desire food periodically (hunger)
2. to reject certain substances (disgust)
3. to explore new places and things (curiosity)
4. to escape from danger (fear)
5. to fight when frustrated (anger)
6. to have sex (mating propensity)
7. to care for the young (mothering propensity)
8. to seek company (gregarious propensity)
9. to seek dominance (self-assertive propensity)
10. to accept inferiority (submissive propensity)
11. to make things (constructive propensity)
12. to collect things (acquisitive tendency).

McDougall further theorised that as a result of experience the primary instincts became modified. They could become activated upon thinking of a relevant object rather than seeing it, and they could be co-activated with other instincts as part of a blend, which McDougall called a *sentiment*. For instance, a husband's love for his wife was a sentiment including the mating propensity, the mothering propensity, and possibly others as well. Similarly, McDougall saw patriotism as a sentiment in which a man's native land had become the object of several instincts. McDougall argued that adult behaviours were primarily motivated by sentiments, rather than by instincts. Nevertheless, because the sentiments were derived from the instincts, they still possessed the emotional striving of the instincts. Social behaviour, for instance, was based on loyalties and interests resulting from the instincts combined into sentiments.

McDougall was not the first to use instincts – James had done so extensively in his *Principles* – but his system was the first in which instincts were seen as the basis of a coherent and structured set of motives that drove human actions. As McDougall himself wrote:

> Take away these instinctive dispositions with their powerful impulses, and the organism would become incapable of activity of any kind; it would lie inert and motionless like a wonderful clockwork whose mainspring had been removed.
>
> (McDougall 1948; as cited in Jahoda 2007: 159)

Reactions to McDougall

Woodworth (1948) describes the responses to McDougall's book. At first, they were largely positive. The book was a source of inspiration for the creation of social psychology as a separate branch of psychological research, rather than as part of sociology. The social sciences also took inspiration from the book, trying to show how a society emerged as a means to meet the instinctive demands of individuals, and how the instinctive cravings of individuals could be adapted to fit into an industrialised society.

Soon, however, McDougall's doctrine of instincts ran into what Woodworth called the 'professional bias of sociologists'. This is how he described the evolution:

> With their eyes fixed on the social group as the important object of study, [the sociologists] were less impressed with the natural demands of the individual than with another line of facts suggesting that the individual was molded by society. The individual derives his language, his manners and customs, and to a large extent his beliefs from the social environment . . . While to the psychologist it may be self-evident that society is composed of individuals and must meet their demands, to the sociologist the main fact is that society is there before any given individual and imposes on him its demands and standards. We behave alike and 'behave like human beings,' not in the main because of our instincts, but because of the culture we all receive.
>
> (Woodworth 1948: 223)

The sociological critique to McDougall reached its height in 1924 when Luther L. Bernard published a book entitled *Instinct, a study of social psychology,* in which he rejected instincts as the basis of human behaviour. He pointed out that no two psychologists agreed on the list of instincts and that instincts referred to complex activities that differed from culture to culture. Bernard argued, for instance, that a mother's care of her baby was not instinctive mothering behaviour but a complex activity taught by people in the environment. In his view, the highly artificial environment humankind had developed in the twentieth century was not primarily motivated by a desire to meet an individual's biological needs. Rather, the opposite was true: society expected individuals to adapt themselves to existing customs and institutions.

Not only sociologists took issue with McDougall's doctrine. Behaviourists attacked the theory as well, because they saw the instincts as too broad, unlikely to be a driving force throughout a person's life, and improbable as an explanation of the complex behaviour patterns shown by humans. How could complex behaviours be the result of inheritance? This, for instance, is what John Watson had to say about instincts:

> The behaviorist has found by his study that most of the things we see the adult doing are really learned. We used to think that a lot of them were instinctive, that is 'unlearned.' But we are now almost at the point of throwing away the word 'instinct.' Still there are a lot of things we do that we do not have to learn – to perspire, to breathe, to have our heart beat, to have digestion take place, to have our eyes turn toward a source of light, to have our pupils contract, to show a fear response when a loud sound is given. Let us keep as our second classification then 'learned responses,' and make it include all of the our complicated habits and all of our conditioned responses; and 'unlearned' responses, and mean by that all of the things that we do in earliest infancy before the processes of conditioning and habit formation get the upper hand.
>
> (Watson 1925: 15)

In Watson's eyes instincts were limited to the biological functions that were present at birth; all other behaviour was acquired through conditioning and habit formation.

The significance of McDougall's example: what are the weights of biological, psychological and social factors?

In Chapter 4 we discussed McDougall's views at some length, not because they are unavoidable in the history of psychology, but because they nicely illustrate the shifting balance of biological, psychological and socio-cultural contributions. McDougall started out with a predominantly biological view: motivations were based on innate instincts. This was questioned by the behaviourists, who emphasised that psychological processes (learning) should carry more weight. They also included socio-cultural influences (e.g. other people as the source of reinforcement and punishment), but these influences did not figure strongly in their thinking (as most of their theories were about the performance of individuals). Finally, the sociologists pointed to the importance of socio-cultural norms and expectations in human behaviour, at the expense of biological and psychological factors. As we will see in the following sections, the discussion about the relative weights of the different types of influence is still very much alive today.

Interim summary

- According to the biopsychosocial model, psychology has to take into account biological, psychological and socio-cultural factors if it wants to understand a topic fully.
- McDougall argued at the beginning of the twentieth century that humans are motivated by innate drives (instincts or propensities), which become modified and grouped into sentiments as a result of experience.
- At first, the reactions to McDougall's book were positive, but soon sociologists criticised it because it overlooked the social factors in human behaviour. At the same time, behaviourists criticised it because in their view behaviour was learned, not innate.
- McDougall's book and the reactions it provoked are typical of the constant discussion in psychology about the relative importance of biological, psychological and socio-cultural influences on human behaviour.

? What do you think?

Now that you have read about McDougall, how do you feel about the relative importance of biological, psychological and social factors? Are they equally important, or do you see a ranking of them? Discuss this with others. Do you all agree?

12.2 The biological perspective

According to the biological perspective, mental life is primarily determined by the biological processes in the brain. This perspective goes back at least as far as Hippocrates in Ancient Greece (Chapter 6). However, for most of recorded history its role was very limited, under the influence of the dualistic view defended by Plato and the Catholic Church. As you may remember from Chapter 7, dualism draws a sharp divide between the mind and the body. As a result, biological influences on mental functioning were seen as very minor. There was some surge in their perceived contribution in the nineteenth century and at the beginning of the twentieth century, when the relationship between aphasia and brain lesions was discovered (Chapter 6) and when Darwin's evolutionary theory started to have an impact (Chapter 3; see also McDougall above). However, within psychology the ascent of the biological perspective was blocked by the advent of behaviourism, which stressed the importance of learning.

Currently the biological perspective is gaining rapidly in power. Arguably its impact has never been as strong as now. Four main developments have led to this state of affairs: the discovery of psychoactive medication, the finding of a hereditary component in many psychological functions, the observation that certain types of human behaviour can be understood from an evolutionary point of view, and recent advances in neuroscience. Given that the last development has been dealt with extensively in Chapter 6, we discuss only the first three here.

The impact of psychoactive medication

Antipsychotics

An important argument for the influence of biological factors on mental life is the finding that chemical substances can affect psychological functions. Such influence was already known for many centuries in a negative way, particularly with respect to alcohol. However, in the middle of the twentieth century, as a result of the advances in medical science, medication became available that actively alleviated mental problems. One of the first drugs available was chlorpromazine for the treatment of hallucinations and delusions in schizophrenia (Chapter 8). Currently the contribution of antipsychotics in the treatment of schizophrenia is no longer questioned, despite their risk of side-effects such as drowsiness, involuntary movements and weight gain (e.g. Lehman & Steinwachs 1998).

Epilepsy

The biological approach had even more success in the treatment of some other mental disorders. A typical example is epilepsy. Epilepsy is a group of syndromes that have in common that part of the brain becomes active in an uncontrolled way. It affects up to 2% of the population at some point in their life (e.g. sometimes in old age). Symptoms during a seizure differ depending on the location of the source and the extent of the discharge. In the worst case patients faint and have convulsions (uncontrolled limb movements because of discharges in the motor cortex).

Because of the sudden onset of seizures, for a long time epilepsy was associated with demonic possession. As a result, the disorder carried a strong stigma (i.e. was socially discrediting for the patient). With the emergence of neurology in the nineteenth century, epilepsy increasingly became seen as a brain disorder and bromide was introduced in 1857 as the first effective anti-epileptic drug. Research received a further boost when scientists were able to measure the brain's electric activity with the use of EEG recordings (Chapter 6). This confirmed the presence of electrical discharges during a seizure and allowed researchers to better localise the site of the discharges. Bromide as the main drug for treatment was replaced by phenobarbitone (first used in 1912) and phenytoin (first used in 1938).

The increased understanding of the workings of the brain accelerated the development of still better drugs, which currently control seizures effectively in 70–80% of newly diagnosed patients. The remaining cases increasingly profit from high-precision surgery, helped by brain imaging, to remove or control the affected part of the brain. As a result of these evolutions, the treatment of epilepsy nowadays fully falls under the realm of biological treatments.

Ulcers

Another condition that for a long time was thought to have a strong psychological component but over time shifted to a biological treatment is that of stomach and intestinal ulcers. For a long time it was thought that lifestyle factors, in particular psychological stress, caused ulcers. As part of his research on the biological reactions to stress, the endocrinologist Hans Selye (1907–1982) noticed that rats he put under duress developed ulcers. For him, this seemed to agree with the correlation physicians observed between stress and stomach ulcers in humans. Consequently the proposed treatment of ulcers primarily included attempts to diminish the patient's stress.

In 1982, however, two Australian scientists, Robin Warren and Barry Marshall, discovered the presence of a new type of bacterium, *Helicobacter pylori,* as the cause of stomach and intestinal ulcers in the majority of patients. Warren and Marshall subsequently demonstrated that ulcers could be induced by injection of the bacteria into the stomach and could be cured with a treatment of antibiotics. In 2005 they were awarded the Nobel Prize for Medicine for their discoveries.

The importance of heredity in psychology

Heredity

Another finding that points to the impact of biological processes on mental functioning is the demonstration that differences between people are inherited to a large extent. There are two main ways to estimate the impact of heredity. The first is to compare identical twins with fraternal twins. Identical twins share the same genes, whereas fraternal twins do not share more genes with each other than brothers and sisters. So, if a trait is inherited, identical twins ought to resemble each other more than fraternal twins. The second method is to look at adopted children. If a trait is inherited, an adopted child should be more similar to the biological parents than to the adoptive parents. As you may remember from Chapters 8 and 11, similarity is expressed as a correlation coefficient. By comparing the correlations in different groups of individuals (e.g. identical twins vs. fraternal twins), it is possible to estimate how much of the variance is due to heredity and how much to the environment.

Needless to say, researchers have to make sure that there are no confounding variables biasing their figures. This has given rise to quite some discussion in the literature about how best to do this, although one cannot escape the impression that the controls nowadays tend to be much less strict than they were in the 1980–1990s, in line with the increased status of the biological perspective. Researchers seem to have accepted a strong genetic component in psychological variables and no longer question to what extent, for instance, the environment of identical twins can be compared to that of fraternal twins (e.g. it is likely that the environment is more similar for identical twins than for fraternal twins, given their similarity in appearance; in a good study, this should be controlled for).

Table 12.1 lists some of the heredity estimates that have been reported. In this figure, 0% variance explained means that all differences between individuals are due to differences in their environments (including biological factors such as the hormones to which the foetuses are exposed in the womb); 100% variance explained means that all individual differences are due to genetic variation.

Although there are interesting differences in estimated heritability between the characteristics (with a stronger genetic component in disorders such as ADHD (Attention Deficit Hyperactivity Disorder) and schizophrenia than in disorders such

Table 12.1 Heredity estimates reported (percentage of variance explained by the genetic constitution)

Although there are some differences between the characteristics (ADHD and schizophrenia have a stronger genetic component than alcohol dependence and life satisfaction), there is a clear contribution of heredity for all characteristics. This is in line with the biological perspective.

Characteristic	Percentage of variance	Source
ADHD	60–91%	Thapar *et al.* (2007)
Aggression	40–53%	Miles and Carey (1997)
Alcohol dependence	25–49%	Liu *et al.* (2004)
Depression (major)	31–42%	Sullivan *et al.* (2000)
Dyslexia	47–60%	Raskind (2001)
Feeling of loneliness	44–53%	Boomsma *et al.* (2005)
Intelligence	30–70%	Mackintosh (1998)
Life satisfaction	20–44%	Stubbe *et al.* (2005)
Obesity	64–84%	O'Rahilly & Farooqi (2006)
Personality disorders	50–60%	Torgersen *et al.* (2000)
Personality traits	41–51%	Bouchard (1994)
Schizophrenia	73–90%	Sullivan *et al.* (2003)
Sexual orientation	28–65%	Kendler *et al.* (2000)

as alcohol dependence and major depression), the most conspicuous finding is that for all characteristics genetic factors have a clear impact. There are even data on a strong genetic component in feeling lonely and being satisfied with one's life! Such findings are in line with the predictions of the biological perspective.

The importance of variation and selection: evolutionary psychology

Not only are the differences between individuals influenced by their biological make-up; human behaviours in general also seem to have a genetic component. There is a growing body of evidence indicating that many human behaviours are in line with what would be predicted on the basis of natural selection: behaviours that increase the chances of survival have a higher chance of being passed on to the next generation than behaviours that are less helpful. This message was first conveyed by the Harvard biologist Edward O. Wilson (1975) in a book called *Sociobiology: The new synthesis*. In this book, Wilson claimed that most social behaviours would eventually be understood on the basis of the reproductive advantage they give.

evolutionary psychology

approach in psychology that aims to understand human behaviour on the basis of natural selection and the evolutionary theory

The message was picked up by a group of psychologists and translated into a new research area, evolutionary psychology, which attempts to explain mental and psychological traits as a result of the 'struggle for life'. This was not a new perspective (see the functionalists in Chapter 4 and McDougall above), but the advances in evolutionary theory and the degree of knowledge available at the end of the twentieth century allowed the supporters to go well beyond what was achieved before. We summarise here some of the most important claims and findings.

Long-term partner selection

In order to pass on one's genes, it is important to choose a mate who not only produces viable offspring but is also willing to invest in the offspring until they can reproduce themselves. Humans in the past who were discerning in this respect have multiplied their genes, the others not. Buss (2004: 109) mentions the following features, which help to increase the chances of viable offspring:

- choose a mate who is able to invest,
- choose a mate who is willing to invest,
- choose a mate who is able to protect the children,
- choose a mate who will help raise the children,
- select a mate who is compatible with yourself,
- select a mate who is healthy.

Because humans for the most part of their history were hunter-gatherers with a clear division of labour between the sexes (men = hunting and achieving wealth and power in the group, women = bearing and raising children, gathering fruit and vegetables), the selection criteria for successful reproduction differed for men and women. For men the most important selection criteria were:

- identify a woman with high fertility and reproductive value (young, healthy, attractive),
- identify a woman who will stay loyal to you, so that you are not raising another man's children.

For women the following have been the most important criteria:

- make sure the man has the resources to raise the children or is likely to acquire them,
- make sure the man will commit himself to you and your children,
- make sure the man can protect you and your children (i.e. is healthy and has sufficient status in the group).

Buss (1989) noticed that these indeed were the main criteria men and women used to find a long-term partner in all 37 cultures he investigated. Men were particularly looking for youth, attractiveness (as an indicator of health) and signs of loyalty. Women were more interested in wealth, status, power and commitment. Buss further noted that any uncertainty a man has about the paternity of the children he is raising will lead to sexual jealousy in men, because husbands who in the past guarded their wives had more chances of passing on their genes than husbands who did not care. Other authors, however, have found less convincing evidence for these claims (Buller 2005; Richardson 2007).

In 1972, after comparing mate selection in different species, Robert Trivers noticed another regularity. He observed that in general the gender investing more in the upbringing of children is more discriminating about mating than the gender investing less. He called this the parental investment theory. For instance, among the Mormon crickets, where the males produce large, nutritious spermatophores at a considerable cost, the females compete with each other for access to the males, who then select which females they want.

In most other species, where the females bear the larger brunt of gestation and feeding, the roles are reversed: females are more selective and prudent with whom they will mate than males. According to Trivers, the parental investment theory also applies to humans. He further noticed that species in which the offspring requires a lot of care are likely to be monogamous (with the male and the female staying

parental investment theory

hypothesis in evolutionary psychology holding that the gender investing the most in the upbringing of offspring is more discriminating about mating together), whereas species in which the offspring requires little effort are usually characterised by polygyny (in which a relatively small number of males impregnate the females). Polygyny is present among nearly all mammal species. Monogamy is widespread among birds and humans.

Short-term partner selection

DNA research in bird colonies has shown that monogamy should be understood as 'male and female raise the offspring together', rather than as 'males and females are sexually loyal to each other'. In particular, partners of males with a low status tend to have intercourse with higher ranked males, presumably because this improves the quality (and hence the reproduction chances) of their offspring. Geary *et al.* (2004) suggested a similar pattern in humans. They pointed to studies showing 1% extramarital children in a rich quarter of a Swiss city against 30% in a disadvantaged British estate. Apparently, women who have ended up with a partner who does not rank high in the hierarchy are more likely to have an extramarital child than women with a highly desirable man. Along the same lines, McNulty *et al.* (2008) noticed that couples in which the husbands are rated as more attractive than the wives tend to be less stable.

What do you think?

For some years paternity tests have allowed fathers to be sure about their relationship to the children they are raising. Do you think this makes any difference to short-term partner strategies? Is having better offspring the only reason for short-term partnerships?

Inclusive fitness

inclusive fitness
hypothesis in evolutionary psychology that behaviour is motivated not only by the organism's own survival but also by the survival of organisms that are genetically related; the motivation depends on the degree of relatedness

William D. Hamilton (1964) launched a second idea that would be of importance to evolutionary psychology. He argued that individuals are not only motivated to promote their own genes, but also to help individuals with shared genes. The higher the genetic overlap, the more likely the support. Trivers called this inclusive fitness. It refers to the likelihood of passing on genes not only by direct reproduction but also by helping relatives to produce offspring. So, it is the sum of an individual's own reproductive success (the classical fitness in Darwin's theory) plus the effects of the individual's actions on the reproductive success of his or her next of kin (Buss 2004). Inclusive fitness enables evolutionary psychologists to understand altruistic behaviour. A parent who dies to save his/her child increases his/her inclusive fitness, especially if the parent is unlikely to have more children.

Inclusive fitness makes a number of interesting predictions, which have been borne out by the data (Buss 2004; but also see Buller 2005). One of them is that the probability of a human helping someone else depends on their genetic similarity. Another is that step-parents will be more likely to abuse and kill children than biological parents. The reason for this is the conflict that exists between the child, who is motivated to profit as much as possible from the parent, and the parent who is motivated to reproduce their own genes. In the case of biological children, inclusive fitness forms a counterweight which is absent in step-parents. Similarly, inclusive fitness predicts that parents will be more likely to kill their children when they themselves still have good chances of reproduction than when such chances are absent.

Inclusive fitness also explains why individuals will protect their next of kin (their own group) in case of danger. This is not only true in war and conflict. Van Vugt *et al.*

(2007) showed that it is also true in a virtual world. Male students were more likely to cooperate with their own group in an internet game, when there was perceived competition from a rival group at another university than when there was no such competition.

Cooperative alliances

Another question evolutionists have considered is what implications the struggle for life has for alliances between individuals who do not share many genes. At first sight, one would expect the struggle to result in selfishness. After all, individuals who constantly help others at the expense of their own reproduction fail to pass on their genes. In contrast, those who make sure they always get as much as possible out of the others are able to have many offspring and to multiply their genes. However, such a view overlooks the fact that most of the time individuals obtain more when they cooperate. Trivers (1971) called this *reciprocal altruism,* cooperation between two or more individuals for mutual benefit. As long as the individuals cooperate, the gains accrue. When one of them cheats and takes advantage of the others' cooperation, the gains for that person increase rapidly at the expense of the others. How to make sure, then, that the cheaters do not get the upper hand in a group?

tit-for-tat strategy

strategy proposed in evolutionary psychology to explain how evolutionarily motivated individuals cooperate in situations of mutual dependency and benefit

With the use of computer simulations Axelrod and Hamilton (1981) showed that a simple but very efficient strategy is the so-called tit-for-tat strategy. It consists of two simple rules:

1. start by cooperating,

2. thereafter, do the same as the other does (i.e. if they cooperate, continue cooperating; if they refuse to cooperate, refuse as well).

The strategy basically means that individuals will tend to cooperate when they encounter someone else for the first time, but will refuse to cooperate as soon as the other does not reciprocate. This refusal will continue until the other breaks the spell and offers collaboration. As long as individuals act according to the tit-for-tat strategy, they maximise their long-term profit (although there always will be the temptation of big short-term gains, offset by the prospect of possible ostracism). According to evolutionary psychologists, individuals who followed the tit-for-tat strategy had a higher overall reproduction rate and, therefore, became more and more frequent in subsequent generations. Hence, many social interactions in current society can be understood on the basis of this strategy.

KEY FIGURES in twentieth-century evolutionary theory

- **Edward O. Wilson:** American biologist who started sociobiology with the publication of his book *Sociobiology: The new synthesis* (1975), in which he claimed that many social behaviours can be understood on the basis of the reproduction advantage they have had for humans.

- **David Buss:** American psychologist who applied the evolutionary theory to mating strategies and was one of the founders of evolutionary psychology.

- **Robert Trivers:** American biologist who introduced the theories of parental investment and reciprocal altruism (which forms the basis of cooperative alliances).

- **William D. Hamilton:** British biologist who proposed the importance of inclusive fitness to understand altruism in the evolution theory. He also proposed the tit-for-tat strategy in collaboration with Robert Axelrod.

David Buss
Source: © David M. Buss, all rights reserved.

Innate knowledge

Evolutionary theory also provides an answer to a question that has vexed philosophy since the invention of empiricism, namely how the mind can absorb and structure empirical facts when it starts off as a blank slate. To translate this into a contemporary problem: why do human babies after a few years fluently understand human speech, whereas thus far it has proven impossible to implement such a feat on a computer? The computational power of computers easily outperforms that of the human brain. Still this is not enough to turn the blank slate of the computer into a talking machine. The cause probably is that the human brain processes speech information in a way we have not worked out yet. As a result, we don't yet know how to program a computer so that it learns like a human. However, this begs the question: how is the brain capable of doing so?

The German philosopher Immanuel Kant (1724–1804; see also Chapter 3) was the first to realise this. He argued that the only way in which the soul could absorb and structure empirical information was not by being a blank slate but by being an entity that from the onset imposed some organisation on the incoming information. Kant postulated 'innate categories' (e.g. of time, space and causality) as the foundation of such organisation. In his view, humans were able to perceive cause–effect relations because they had an innate category for them.

A frustrating aspect of Kant's theory was that he referred to divine or metaphysical input to explain the origin of the innate information. Evolutionary theory provides a scientifically more appealing answer. Just as the eye evolved to respond to certain electromagnetic rays emitted by the environment, so did the brain evolve to respond to certain stimuli emanating from the surroundings. Genes that caused a defence reaction upon seeing a snake or upon hearing a sudden loud noise increased the chances of survival and hence of reproduction. So, after they emerged, they were likely to stay and to pervade the species. Similarly, genes that increased the amount of information the brain could pick up from the environment resulted in a survival advantage and were likely to be passed on, once they had appeared on the basis of random variation. Eventually, this process of random variation and natural selection led to the brains we currently have, made in such a way that they are able to rapidly tune in to important signals in the surroundings and to learn from them. The learning component will be discussed in the next section.

Interim summary

The biological perspective

- According to the biological perspective, mental life is primarily determined by the biological processes in the brain.
- Four developments have increased the impact of the biological perspective in recent years:
  - the discovery of psychoactive medication
  - the finding of a hereditary component in many psychological functions
  - the observation that certain types of human behaviours can be understood from an evolutionary point of view (partner selection, inclusive fitness, cooperation, innate knowledge)
  - advances in neuroscience.

12.3 The psychological perspective

Adherents of the psychological perspective agree with the proponents of the biological perspective that some innate knowledge and behaviours may be the starting point of mental life. However, they disagree about the possibility of understanding human behaviour primarily on the basis of biological factors. In their view, to appreciate an individual's current functioning, it is much more important to know his or her ways of thinking. After all, a fundamental characteristic of people is that they gather knowledge all their life, which they use to carry on and improve their fate. Very few behaviours are purely instinctive, in the sense that they are elicited reflexively by the presence of a stimulus and need no learning. Organisms capable of learning have an enormous survival advantage, because they can take profit from their past experiences. They can avoid stimuli that previously caused negative sensations and approach stimuli that in the past led to positive experiences.

In addition, supporters of the psychological perspective point to the many aspects of human life that cannot be understood without assuming sophisticated psychological processes. This is true for the information processing emphasised by cognitive psychologists (Chapter 5), for emotions beyond reflexive fear and happiness (e.g. regret, shame, disappointment), and for the understanding of meaningful situations, as stressed in the hermeneutic approach.

Although we could have opted for examples in which psychological processing is pivotal, in the sections below we focus on functions close to biological and social functioning. In this way, we stay closer to the true message of the biopsychosocial model that biological, psychological and socio-cultural variables are involved in *each and every* aspect of human functioning.

Olfaction

Innate odours and survival

It is not difficult to find evidence for biological influences on olfaction. In line with evolutionary theory, researchers have found that some responses to odours are innate (e.g. Kobayakawa *et al.* 2007). From their first contact rodents are repulsed by the odours of spoiled food and by odorants associated with predators (e.g. the scent secreted by the anal gland of a fox). In contrast, they show instinctive attraction towards food smells and odours associated with their own species (e.g. the urine of females). Similarly, people show stable individual differences in their preferences for body odours, which have been linked to the immune system (Jacob *et al.* 2002).

At the same time, research on olfaction has provided some of the strongest evidence concerning the influences of learning and cognition on human behaviour. People respond differently to odours as a consequence of their learning histories and as a function of what they think the origin of the smell is.

Odours and associative learning

Odours that have been associated with negative events become conditioned stimuli that evoke an avoidance response; odours associated with positive events elicit an approach response. This is nicely illustrated by a study of Li *et al.* (2008). Participants smelled sets of three bottles (two containing the same odorant, one containing a barely distinguishable different odorant). At first, participants could not discriminate between the odours. However, after one of the odorants had repeatedly been paired with electrical shocks, participants' ability to discriminate the smells improved dramatically. Also their neural processing of the smells, as assessed with fMRI, changed.

Associations between odours and feelings or cognitions are capitalised upon by the fragrance industry, which aims to influence people's moods and buying behaviour with odours (cf. Chebat & Michon 2003). For instance, Spangenberg *et al.* (2006) observed that customers had a more favourable impression of a shop and bought more when the scent in the shop was congruent with the clothing sold (vanilla for women and rose maroc for men) than when it was not.

Odours and labelling

Interestingly, people's responses to odours do not require a lengthy learning process. Simply labelling an odour already has a strong impact. Djordjevic *et al.* (2008) asked participants to rate the pleasantness of an odour. Participants were presented with a total of 15 odours under three conditions: same odours were presented at different times with a positive, negative or neutral name. For example, in the positive name condition, participants were told for one of the odours that it came from parmesan cheese, in the negative name condition they were told that the same odour came from dry vomit, and in the neutral name position that it came from odour thirty-two. Figure 12.1 shows the dramatic differences in experience these labels induced. In another study, De Araujo *et al.* (2005) reported that a label (cheddar cheese vs. body odour) not only had an impact on the subjective ratings of the participants but also on their brain responses as measured with fMRI.

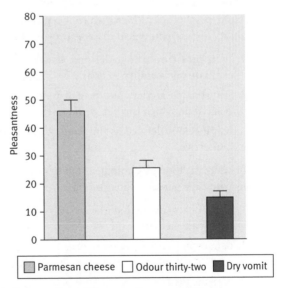

Figure 12.1 The influence of cognition on odour perception.

When participants are given an odour and asked to rate its pleasantness (0 = extremely unpleasant, 100 = extremely pleasant), they give much higher ratings when they are told the odour comes from parmesan cheese than when they are told it comes from odour thirty-two. Similarly, they give much lower ratings when they are told it comes from dry vomit. So, simply labelling the odours induces huge changes in perception.

Source: Adapted from Djordjevic *et al.* (2008), with permission.

The fact that simple sensory responses to odours so strongly depend on the way in which they are interpreted shows the impact of psychological factors on human functioning. In addition, responses to odours are not the only emotional responses subject to cognitive control. There is a considerable literature on how emotional responses to a wide variety of stimuli are influenced by cognitive processes (e.g. Ochsner & Gross 2005).

Cognitive modulation of pain

The gate control theory of pain

Another biological response that is modulated to a considerable extent by cognition is pain perception. Quite rapidly researchers noticed that there was very little correlation between the amount of tissue damage and the degree of pain experienced. Some people complain of unbearable, chronic pain with non-noticeable damage, whereas others continue to function at a high level despite obvious pain-inducing wounds. To account for these findings, Melzack and Wall (1965) proposed the gate control theory of pain. According to this theory, the nerve signals carrying the pain message have to pass through a gate before they reach the brain. At this gate they can be modulated. One source of inhibition consists of the endorphins released in the brain in emergency situations to help with the fight or flight response. The other attenuation occurs through cognitive modulation, in particular the attention paid to the pain signal and the interpretation of the pain signal. Sportspeople, for instance, endure a considerable amount of pain to improve their performance level.

gate control theory of pain

theory of pain perception which assumes that the nerve signals carrying the pain message have to pass through a gate before they reach the brain; at this gate the signals can be made stronger or weaker

Psychological factors in pain modulation

Three psychological factors have been reported to increase the level of physical disability and psychological distress provoked by pain (Keefe *et al.* 2004):

1. pain catastrophising, defined as the tendency to focus on pain and negatively evaluate one's ability to deal with pain,
2. pain-related anxiety and fear of pain, resulting in a high degree of fear avoidance behaviour, which further weakens the person,
3. helplessness, defined as the tendency to view all attempts to try to manage pain as ineffective.

In contrast, four psychological factors have been described that decrease the impact of pain on a person's functioning:

1. self-efficacy, defined as the person's confidence in his/her ability to find a way to deal with the pain,
2. pain coping strategies, defined as the variety of strategies used to deal with the pain,
3. readiness to change, defined as the willingness to take an active role in learning to manage the pain,
4. acceptance, defined as an active willingness to engage in meaningful activities in life regardless of the experience of pain; this is particularly needed in situations of persistent pain that cannot be controlled.

As a result of these findings, it is becoming clear that the treatment of chronic pain requires as much psychological help as biological interventions to decrease the impact of the pain signal. This is another argument in favour of the importance of psychological factors in human functioning. Even a biological process such as pain perception is more than a mere physiological registration of a biological change.

Cognitive processes in depression

Thoughts are an important factor in the origin and maintenance of mental health problems as well.

Irrational thoughts and maladaptive schemas

In particular with respect to depression there is good evidence for pathogenic thoughts as the core of the problem. Two independently working American cognitive therapists were central to this realization: Albert Ellis (1913–2007) and Aaron Beck (born in 1921). Ellis stressed that many patients with depression and generalised anxiety have irrational thoughts, such as 'everyone should love me and approve of me' and 'I should always be able, successful, and on top of things'. Beck pointed to the existence of maladaptive schemas in patients dealing with themselves, their future and the world. In Beck's view, the schemas (mostly the result of experiences in childhood and adolescence) become activated under the influence of situational stress and interfere with the person's coping strategies. Both Ellis and Beck showed that cognitive psychotherapies directed at correcting the irrational and maladaptive thoughts were highly effective in the treatment of the disorder.

Rumination

Another researcher stressing the importance of cognitive processes in depression is the American psychologist Susan Nolen-Hoeksema (2000). Her research focused on the relationship between mood regulation strategies and vulnerability to depression and other mental health problems. In particular she examined the effects of rumination, the tendency to respond to distress by focusing on the causes and consequences of the problems, without trying to actively solve the problems. Rumination exacerbates negative thinking and interferes with good problem-solving.

Treatment of depression

The relative contribution of biological and psychological factors in depression can be gauged by looking at the outcome of the therapies proposed by the two approaches. The biological perspective holds that depression is due to a biological imbalance in the brain and should be treated with medication. The psychological perspective maintains that medication is only indicated in the most severe cases (when the patients are too depressed to work on their problems) and that nothing much will change as long as patients do not alter their irrational and maladaptive thoughts. The latter is the explicit goal of the cognitive therapies of Ellis and Beck, but is also implicitly present in all other forms of psychotherapy.

An interesting study comparing the biological and the psychological approach was run at the outpatient psychiatric clinics of the University of Pennsylvania and Vanderbilt University (DeRubeis *et al.* 2005; Hollon *et al.* 2005). Patients were divided into three matched groups: the first group received medication; the second, cognitive psychotherapy. The third group was a placebo group that was treated in exactly the same way as the medication group, except for the fact that there was no active substance in the pills. For all patients, the severity of their depression was assessed bi-weekly by independent assessors (who were blind to the treatment condition). Figure 12.2a shows the improvement of the three groups over the first 8 weeks. As in the other studies published on this topic,

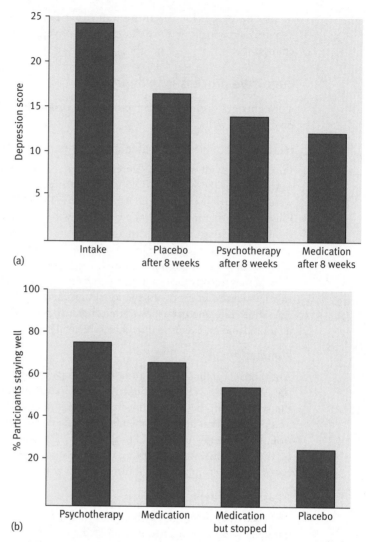

Figure 12.2 (a) Decrease of depression scores as a function of time in therapy and treatment group.

All three conditions show an improvement, including the placebo condition, but the improvement was bigger in the two treatment conditions. The differences started to become visible after four weeks.

(b) Percentage of patients who stay well in the year after the treatment.

Patients in the medication condition put on a placebo pill relapsed in 76% of cases (i.e. only 24% stayed well). Of the patients in the cognitive therapy condition 76% stayed well; of the patients who continued to receive medication less than 60% stayed well. Part of this figure was due to participants who stopped taking their medication.

the improvement was three-quarters due to a placebo effect and one-quarter due to the treatment used (see also Wampold *et al.* 2005; Kirsch *et al.* 2008). As for the treatment, no difference was observed between psychotherapy and medication.

The patients in the medication group and the psychotherapy group received treatment for 16 weeks and were subsequently followed for a year to see what happened to them. The patients in the medication condition were divided into two groups: one half was gradually placed on a placebo treatment, and the other half continued with the active substance. The patients in the cognitive therapy condition stopped their therapy and were allowed a maximum of three booster sessions when they felt a need for them. Each patient was seen once a month by an independent assessor who decided whether the treatment was still working or whether the patient had relapsed and needed more intensive therapy. Figure 12.2b shows the percentage of patients who stayed healthy for 12 months in the different conditions. Of the group that received medication followed by a placebo, 76% relapsed, against 24% of the patients who had been given psychotherapy. The group of patients who continued their medication fell between both groups, partly because a number of patients stopped taking their pills.

The above study is representative of the other studies on the treatment of depression: more than half of the improvement is due to a placebo effect and when patients on pills stop taking their medication, there is a high percentage of relapse. Both findings point to the importance of the psychological perspective in explaining and treating depression. The placebo effect is understandable in terms of cognitions (patients have renewed hope and force to tackle their problems) and the risk of relapse upon termination of medication is in line with the claim that persons remain vulnerable as long as they do not improve their irrational and maladaptive thoughts.

What do you think?

What is your way of coping when you feel down? Do you look for pills (biological perspective), do you try to change your thoughts (psychological perspective) or do you seek support from friends and family (socio-cultural perspective)? Why?

Social cognition

The importance of the implicit personality theory

The power of psychological processes is also exemplified by the way in which our perceptions of others influence our interactions with them. We have seen how the implicit personality theory governs our first impressions (Chapter 8). The implicit personality theory refers to the network of associations each person has about the correlations between various personal characteristics. They include characteristics related to the appearance of people (e.g. the presence of glasses, the clothes worn), information related to them (e.g. their name), the way they talk and behave, and the groups they belong to. All these factors determine the impression people will make on us and the way we will interact with them.

For instance, we are more likely to initiate contact with people who resemble us than with people who are different from us, a phenomenon called the *similarity-attraction hypothesis*. Nass and colleagues (1995) showed that this bias even works in interactions with computers. On the basis of a questionnaire they distinguished between a group of dominant college students and a group of submissive students. The students had to interact with a computer to solve problems. Half the students worked with a 'dominant' computer, called Max, who used strong language consisting of assertions and commands (e.g. 'You should definitely rate the flashlight higher. It is your only reliable night-signalling device.'). The other half interacted with a 'submissive' computer, Linus, who used weaker language consisting of questions and suggestions (e.g. 'Perhaps the flashlight should be rated higher? It may be your only reliable night-signalling device.'). After the task the participants were asked to indicate how much they appreciated the help from the computer. The computer received higher ratings when its personality matched that of the participant; it was also judged to be more competent.

Interim summary

The psychological perspective

- According to the psychological perspective, mental life (both normal and abnormal) is primarily determined by psychological processes. We have seen three examples of this:
  - the importance of learning and cognition in perception (olfaction)
  - the importance of cognitive modulation in pain perception
  - the role of irrational and maladaptive thoughts in depression.
- Psychological processes are also important in social interactions (social cognition).

12.4 The socio-cultural perspective

In the previous sections we saw evidence that human experiences and behaviour are influenced by biological factors and the way in which individuals perceive and process information. In addition to these two influences, people are also affected by the groups to which they belong and in which they move. Just think of it: how much of your time do you spend interacting with others? And how much of the time you spend alone is actually devoted to thoughts of others, or to trying to meet their expectations (e.g. with respect to your academic performance)? Social factors were first emphasised within sociology, but over the last century have become important in psychology as well (see the part on McDougall above). Below we discuss a few examples of social influences.

The first studies of social influences

The birth of sociology

Given that humans so often interact with others, it is surprising to see how long it took philosophers and scientists to pay attention to the influences people have on each other. Although there were a few isolated forerunners, the incorporation of social factors in thinking had to wait until the beginning of the nineteenth century when French scholars tried to understand what had happened during the French revolution. The best-known among them was Auguste Comte (1798–1857; Chapter 2), who coined the term 'sociology'. According to Comte, sociologists had to study existing (Western) society by means of the scientific method and try to steer it towards improvement. (Just as in psychology, Comte's scientific, positivist dogma would later be questioned by a hermeneutic line of thought.) The early French sociologists were joined by similarly minded scholars in Germany, Italy, Great Britain and – towards the end of the nineteenth century – the USA.

Although sociologists were interested in social structures, for most of them the people inhabiting society were of secondary importance. Society was their primary unit of analysis. It produced the individual through the process of socialisation and it provided individuals with roles, positions, relationships and structures within which they had to function.

Impact of the evolutionary theory on sociological thinking

At the turn of the twentieth century sociological thinking found itself confronted with Darwin's evolutionary theory. On the one hand, the theory offered interesting points of view for the organisation of society (cf. McDougall's ideas, discussed above). On the other hand, some conclusions went so diametrically against the sociological tenets that they were bound to elicit a negative response. Two lines of reasoning in particular provoked criticism.

social Darwinism

belief in Victorian England and the USA that progress in a society could be made by allowing the strong members to flourish and the weak members to die

The first development was social Darwinism, first propagated by Darwin's contemporary, Herbert Spencer (1820–1903).[1] Spencer defended the idea that a society evolved in the same way as living creatures did, on the basis of natural selection. However, in his view natural selection improved the rough material with which it set out (you may remember from Chapter 3 that the idea of cumulative progress is a common misunderstanding of the evolution theory). So, according to Spencer, societies were constantly improving under the influence of natural selection. They should not be tampered with. In particular, Spencer claimed that a society should not help individuals who were struggling, because these were the ones on the verge of being eliminated by the 'survival of the fittest' (a phrase coined by him). In the same vein, individuals who were doing well should not be hindered because they were the ones scoring high on the fitness scale. Although Spencer later softened some of his writings, the following quote illustrates what social Darwinism in its raw form implied:

> Fostering the good-for-nothing at the expense of the good, is an extreme cruelty. It is a deliberate stirring-up of miseries for future generations. There is no greater curse to posterity than that of bequeathing to them an increasing population of imbeciles and idlers and criminals . . . The whole effort of nature is to get rid of such, to clear the world of them, and make room for better.
>
> (Spencer, as cited in Ritzer & Goodman 2004: 43)

eugenics

social philosophy claiming that the fate of a nation can be improved by selective breeding of the inhabitants

Social Darwinism was swiftly joined by an even stronger version of how evolutionary theory could (or should) be applied to social issues: eugenics. According to this view, society should not be left free to do the natural selection, but it should be actively helped to produce more desirable individuals and get rid of the unwelcome elements. Originating in Britain with Francis Galton, eugenics would quickly capture the USA (Chapter 4) and be put into practice. It is estimated that several tens of thousands of people in the USA and Germany were sterilised against their will in the 1930s on the basis of the eugenic principle (Rutter 2006: 8).

Appalled by these excesses and influenced by the behaviourist manifesto that all behaviour is learned behaviour, psychologists would start to examine how human functioning was influenced by the presence of others. They became known as social psychologists. Below we list some of their main findings and tenets.

Social learning of cultural differences

Observational learning

observational learning

learning as a result of observing others performing actions and being rewarded or punished

A first important finding to help understand the influences people have on each other is the observation that automatic learning is not limited to classical conditioning and operant conditioning (see Chapter 5). For humans and animals it is often enough to observe others in order to learn. This form of learning is called observational learning or social learning and was introduced by the Canadian-American psychologist, Albert Bandura (born in 1925).

Observational learning means that individuals in a society learn the society's customs not by being rewarded for good behaviour and punished for bad behaviour, or by associating some activities with positive feelings and others with negative feelings, but simply by watching what others do and what consequences their behaviour has. As you may remember from Chapter 5, on the basis of his experiments Thorndike thought observational learning was impossible in cats. Since Thorndike's writings it has become clear, however, that this type of learning is quite prevalent and happens in all types of species.

A typical example of contemporary research on observational learning is Saggerson *et al.* (2005). In this study, naive pigeons observed other pigeons that had been trained to peck or step on a panel to obtain food. Two lights indicated when food would be delivered. If the red light went up, the 'expert' pigeon stepped on the panel to obtain food; if the green light went on, the 'expert' pigeon pecked on the panel to get food. The observers were in an adjacent cage and could see the demonstrator through walls of transparent plastic. They did not have a response panel in their cage (and they were hungry). The observers received repeated cycles of observational training and testing. For the latter, they were placed in the chamber of the 'expert' pigeon in the absence of the demonstrator and received presentations of the two lights. Saggerson *et al.* reasoned that if the naive pigeons had learned by observing the demonstrators, they should show the appropriate behaviour. This was indeed what happened.

Cultural differences

Observational learning explains many social phenomena, such as why people in different cultures prefer different types of food and why they eat more in some cultures than in others (Geier *et al.* 2006). It is also an important factor in perpetuating gender differences in accepted behaviour. Davis (2003), for instance, showed that the traditional division of roles between men and women is strongly promoted in television commercials targeted at children.

At a more general level, one of the most widely used schemes to understand cultural differences was proposed by the Dutch organisational psychologist Geert Hofstede (e.g. 2001). He distinguished four main dimensions along which cultures differ. They are:

1. *Power distance:* the extent to which the less powerful members (also in the family) accept and expect that power is distributed unequally; how much they are willing to honour the more powerful and show respect to them.

2. *Individualism vs. collectivism:* the degree to which individuals are integrated in groups. On the individualist side we have societies in which individuals primarily look after their own development. On the collectivist side, we have societies in which individuals primarily look at the interests of the group(s) to which they belong.

3. *Masculinity vs. femininity:* whether the values of the culture (in particular those for men) are biased towards assertive and competitive or towards modest and caring. On the masculine side of the dimension, there usually is a large gap between men's and women's values.

4. *Uncertainty avoidance:* the degree to which the society tolerates uncertainty. It indicates the extent to which individuals feel comfortable in unstructured, novel situations. Uncertainty avoiding cultures highly value traditions with strict laws and rules; they also prefer superiors from within their own cultures. Uncertainty accepting cultures are more tolerant of opinions different from those they are used to; they have fewer rules and more easily accept superiors from abroad.

Table 12.2 lists the values of the four dimensions for some countries. Go to **www.geert-hofstede.com** to find them for other countries. According to the social perspective, these values will have strong effects on how the individuals in different societies function.

Nature vs. nurture

nature–nurture debate
discussion about the respective contributions of genes and environment in the development of (human) qualities

The social perspective is adamant that many individual differences are not due to inherited, genetic traits, but to people's social experiences. The resulting discussion between the social and the biological perspective is known as the nature–nurture debate. At a general level (see below for provisos), the variance not accounted for by heredity in Table 12.1 can be ascribed to differences in the environment. In addition, proponents of the social perspective will question to what extent the heredity figures have been overestimated because of environmental confounds (e.g. because the environments of identical twins are more similar than those of fraternal twins).

Adoption and intelligence

One way to gauge the importance of the environment is to look at the consequences of adoption into a different environment. A particularly informative study in this respect was published by Capron and Duyme (1989). They looked at the intelligence of 14-year-old French children who had been adopted before the age of 6 months. On the basis of archives the authors were able to locate four groups of individuals. The

Table 12.2 **Degree to which different countries display differences in power, stress individualism, stress masculinity and uncertainty avoidance.**

Country	Power	Individualism	Masculinity	Uncertainty avoidance
Arab world	80	38	52	68
Australia	36	90	61	51
Brazil	69	38	49	76
Canada	39	80	52	48
China	80	20	66	30
France	68	71	43	86
Germany	35	67	66	65
India	77	48	56	40
Japan	54	46	95	92
Mexico	81	30	69	82
Netherlands	38	80	14	53
Poland	68	60	64	93
Russia	93	39	36	95
Sweden	31	71	5	29
United Kingdom	35	89	66	35
United States	40	91	62	46

Source: Adapted from Hofstede, G. (2005) *Cultures and organizations: Software of the mind,* 2nd edn, McGraw Hill USA; Cultures and organizations, Software of the mind 3rd edn, McGraw Hill, © Geert Hofstede B.V., quoted with permission.

Table 12.3 The combined effects of nature and nurture on the IQ scores of adopted children
This table shows that both heredity and environment have a substantial effect on the IQ scores of children who are adopted before the age of 6 months.

	Adoption family	
Biological parents	**Low intelligence**	**High intelligence**
Low intelligence	92	104
High intelligence	108	120

Source: Capron & Duyme (1989). Reprinted by permission from Macmillan Publishers Ltd: Assessment of effects of socioeconomic status on IQ in full cross-fostering design. *Nature*, **340**: 552–3.

first group had biological parents with low intelligence and went to adoption families with low intelligence. The second group of children had biological parents with low intelligence and were adopted by families with high intelligence. The third group of children had intelligent biological parents, and were adopted by less intelligent families. Finally, the fourth group had intelligent biological parents and were adopted by intelligent families. Table 12.3 shows the IQ scores of the four groups.

Table 12.3 clearly illustrates that both nature and nurture have a considerable impact on the intelligence of adoptive children. The children of biological parents with low intelligence scored on average 16 IQ points lower than the children of biological parents with high intelligence. At the same time, children who came into an adoptive family with high intelligence scored 12 IQ points higher than children who were adopted by a family with low intelligence.

A paradox in the nature–nurture debate

Within the nature–nurture debate, it is important to know that the relative importance of heredity and environment, as shown in Table 12.1, is not fixed, but depends on the way in which the society is organised. This can easily be illustrated with intelligence. Imagine a society where 10% of the population is extremely rich and can afford the best education for their children; the other 90% is extremely poor, is not nourished properly, and cannot afford schooling for their children. In such a society, the environment (i.e. the socioeconomic status of the parents) will have much more impact than the genes of the parents. That is, there will be a high correlation between the intelligence of the children and the socioeconomic status of their parents, and a low correlation between the intelligence of the children and environment-free intelligence measures of the parents. Now imagine a society in which each child has access to exactly the same type of good education, and where each child is supported to attain his or her full potential. In such a society, the intelligence differences between the children will have a low correlation with the socioeconomic status of their parents (the environment) but will have a high correlation with the genetic intelligence of the parents.

The above situation leads to a counterintuitive paradox in the nature–nurture debate. It is the following: *The more a society tries to give each child proper education, the higher the variance explained by heredity will be and the more it will look as if the environment has little impact on intelligence.* Harden and colleagues (2007) provided a powerful illustration of this paradox. They reported that high heredity estimates for intelligence (as reported in Table 12.1) are only observed in middle-class American families; they are not observed in families living near or below the poverty level. For these children, the environment explained most of the variance in intelligence scores. It may be good to keep this paradox in mind if in the future you read articles about the relative impact of genes and environment. A low correlation between intelligence and environment does not necessarily mean that the environment has no influence on intelligence; it may also mean that society has managed to wipe out the impact of the parents' socioeconomic status by providing first-class education to all the children. A similar paradox applies to all topics that form the subject of a nature–nurture debate.

Interactions in the nature–nurture debate

Although the contributions of nature and nurture are often presented in a simplified, either/or way, recent insights have depicted a much richer picture, full of interactions between genes and environment (Rutter 2006). For a start, very few genes have a deterministic outcome (i.e. invariably lead to a certain characteristic when they are present in one form, and to another characteristic when they are present in another form). Instead, most of the time genetic influences operate probabilistically. That is, they slightly increase or decrease the chances of having a certain condition or they slightly increase or decrease the severity of the condition (see the difference between stochastic and deterministic processes in Chapter 11 for an analogy).

Second, the influences of the environment are also probabilistic. They too slightly increase or decrease the likelihood and/or severity of a certain characteristic.

Third, the influences of nature and nurture do not simply add on, but can reinforce each other. For instance, in each cell only a small percentage of the genes are active. The genes involved in forming a nose, for example, are only active in one part of the body. Otherwise the whole body would consist of nose-like structures. So, every cell not only contains the DNA needed for the formation of all the different body parts, but also contains a complicated system of keys that determine which genes in a cell will become active and which not. In recent years, it is becoming clear that the activation of genes in cells may also depend on the environment in which a person grows up. Some gene-related personality features only become active in certain environments. In this way, genes and environment interact.

Finally, a person's genes to some extent determine the environment in which the person will dwell. People shape and select their environment partially as a function of their genetic constitution (e.g. people with high energy levels are more likely to find themselves in risky and demanding environments).

Notice that the interactions currently being investigated between nature and nurture are unlikely to be the only ones. If psychological processes are equally important for human functioning, as proposed by the biopsychosocial model, then we can expect interactions between all three types of influences.

Strong social situations

Another argument in favour of the social perspective is that in some social situations nearly all individuals act very much the same, despite differences in biological make-up and differences in learning history. Such situations are sometimes called **strong social situations**, because the situation overwhelms the differences in personal traits that people assume to be the controller of social behaviour. In Chapter 7 we saw an example of such a situation when we described Milgram's obedience research (1974).

strong social situation
a situation in which nearly all individuals act virtually the same, despite differences in biological make-up and differences in learning history

Another classic study is the Stanford Prison Experiment (Haney *et al.* 1973). In this study, students who had volunteered to take part in a psychological experiment, were 'arrested' without warning and 'jailed' in a basement of Stanford University, which looked like a real prison. They were guarded by peer students, who also had been selected randomly and been given this responsibility. The study was an attempt to examine what conformity pressures would do to groups of people functioning within the institutional setting of a prison, what power institutional environments had to influence those who passed through them.

This is how Haney and Zimbardo (1998) summarised the findings 25 years later:

> Twenty-five years ago, a group of psychologically healthy, normal college students (and several presumably mentally sound experimenters) were temporarily but dramatically transformed in the course of six days spent in a prison-like environment, in research that came to be known as the Stanford Prison Experiment . . . The outcome of our study was shocking and unexpected to us, our professional colleagues, and the general public. Otherwise emotionally strong college students who were randomly assigned to be mock-prisoners suffered acute psychological trauma and breakdowns. Some of the students begged to be released from the intense pains of less than a week of merely simulated imprisonment, whereas others adapted by becoming blindly obedient to the unjust authority of the guards. The guards, too—who also had been carefully chosen on the basis of their normal–average scores on a variety of personality measures—quickly internalized their randomly assigned role. Many of these seemingly gentle and caring young men, some of whom had described themselves as pacifists or Vietnam War 'doves,' soon began mistreating their peers and were indifferent to the obvious suffering that their actions produced. Several of them devised sadistically inventive ways to harass and degrade the prisoners, and none of the less actively cruel mock-guards ever intervened or complained about the abuses they witnessed. Most of the worst prisoner treatment came on the night shifts and other occasions when the guards thought they could avoid the surveillance and interference of the research team. Our planned two-week experiment had to be aborted after only six days because the experience dramatically and painfully transformed most of the participants in ways we did not anticipate, prepare for, or predict.
>
> (Haney & Zimbardo 1998: 709)

Haney and Zimbardo (1998) still subscribed to the conclusion they had drawn from the study 25 years earlier:

> The negative, anti-social reactions observed were not the product of an environment created by combining a collection of deviant personalities, but rather the result of an intrinsically pathological situation which could distort and rechannel the behaviour of essentially normal individuals. The abnormality here resided in the psychological nature of the situation and not in those who passed through it.
>
> (Haney & Zimbardo 1998: 710)

Indeed, Zimbardo (2004) referred to the same findings when he explained five years later why American soldiers had tortured Iraqi prisoners of war:

> The horrifying photos of young Iraqis abused by American soldiers have shocked the world with their depictions of human degradation, forcing us to acknowledge that some of our beloved soldiers have committed barbarous acts of cruelty and sadism. Now there is a rush to analyze human behavior, blaming flawed or pathological individuals for evil and ignoring other important factors. Unless we learn the dynamics of 'why,' we will never be able to counteract the powerful forces that can transform ordinary people into evil perpetrators.

Psychological research as a social enterprise?

Psychological research depends on the social context in which psychologists work

Social factors are particularly emphasised in critical psychology (Chapter 10), not only with respect to the participants in the studies but also with respect to the researchers themselves. Remember that according to postmodernists scientific knowledge is a social construction. Scientists do not study reality but construct reality (see also Chapter 13). This is how the American scholar Stephen Jay Gould formulated it:

> . . . science must be understood as a social phenomenon, a gutsy, human enterprise, not the work of robots programmed to collect pure information . . . Science, since people must do it, is a socially embedded activity.
>
> (Gould 1996: 53)

According to Gould, social embeddedness is particularly true for a discipline like psychology, because:

> . . . some topics are invested with enormous social importance but blessed with very little reliable information. When the ratio of data to social impact is so low, a history of scientific attitudes may be little more than an oblique record of social change.
>
> (Gould 1996: 54)

An argument in favour of this view is that psychological research knows a good deal of faddism: research issues come, are popular for some time, and go without leaving a trace. As noticed by Hunt (2005):

> mainstream experimental research in psychology can appear curiously faddish. Research central to one decade is all but gone from leading journals in the next, replaced by topics often entirely independent and noncumulative . . . Further, and in marked contrast to the usual energization of research in the physical sciences resulting from consensual resolution of major debates, in psychology research topics often seem to disappear precisely after research consensus has been reached.
>
> (Hunt 2005: 360)

According to critical psychologists, social factors will (co-)determine which view psychologists promote. There is some evidence for this. For instance, Gould (1996) noticed that biological factors in intelligence research tend to come to the fore each time there is a political turn to the right with promises of fewer taxes and fewer social services. Such a political shift is usually justified by a rhetoric stressing that people are born into their social classes because of their genetic endowment. Consequently, there is little point in helping those in the lower classes. In contrast, social factors in psychological theories are dominant when there is a massive economic expansion and upward social mobility (as in the USA at the beginning of the twentieth century, and Europe and the USA after World War II).

A critique of evolutionary psychology

According to critical psychologists, social factors are involved in the current popularity of evolutionary psychology as well. The argument is that evolutionary psychology has many followers, not because the evidence for it is stronger or scientifically more convincing, but because social factors make psychologists more inclined to adopt this view. The following social reasons have been mentioned (Gould and Lewontin, 1979; Fausto-Sterling *et al.* 1997; and Buller 2005; Jackson & Rees 2007):

- evolutionary psychology is popular because it focuses on the origin and history of humankind, which easily catches people's interest (e.g. it is the theme of most popular science books),
- the focus on sex and reproduction also has a strong appeal, certainly when the individual organism is seen as unconsciously engaged in strategies to maximise its opportunity to mate and to ensure survival of its offspring,
- the main principles of evolutionary psychology are simple 'just-so stories' that can be understood without much effort,

- evolutionary psychology has benefited from attracting a highly talented group of popular-science writers (e.g. Robert Wright and Steven Pinker),
- evolutionary psychology affirms existing gender inequalities and stereotypes (females are more sexually reserved than males, women are only interested in sex until they have children, women have less of men's innate ambition and willingness to take the risks needed for professional success),
- evolutionary psychology suggests an 'explanation' for why many people are unhappy (their body and mind are not adapted to modern society).

In Chapter 13 we will see more examples of how society and research interact.

What do you think?

How do you now feel about the relative importance of biological, psychological and socio-cultural factors? Has our discussion made you change your mind? In what way? Or why not?

Interim summary

The socio-cultural perspective

- First accentuated by sociologists (nineteenth century, Comte).
- Ambivalent relationship with evolutionary theory:
  - on the one hand, evolutionary theory provides interesting ideas
  - on the other hand, evolutionary theory gives rise to claims sociologists do not believe in (social Darwinism, eugenics).
- The influence of socio-cultural factors is due to the learning of cultural differences:
  - observational learning (form of associative learning)
  - according to Hofstede, cultures differ on four dimensions:
    - power distance
    - individualism vs. collectivism
    - masculinity vs. femininity
    - uncertainty avoidance.
- Nature–nurture debate: to what extent are individual differences in processing due to genes and to environment?
  - intelligence: adoption study showing impact of both
  - genes and environment are not each other's opposite; both influences are probabilistic (i.e. increase or decrease likelihoods) and interact with each other.
- The importance of social factors also clear in strong social situations, where the situation overwhelms the differences in biological constitution and learning history.
  - examples are Milgram's obedience studies and the Stanford Prison Experiment.
- Socio-cultural factors are emphasised in critical psychology, in particular with respect to the ways in which socio-cultural factors influence the hypotheses psychologists (and other scientists) are interested in.

12.5 *Focus on*: Why are people aggressive?

In the sections above we reviewed the ways psychologists have used to argue that mental life is the result of biological, psychological and social forces, and, therefore, requires a biopsychosocial model of explanation. We also mentioned that the balance between the three types of variables is a precarious one, constantly shifting as a function of the latest findings. For instance, in the past 10 years the biological perspective has gained considerably in strength, under the influence of brain imaging techniques, evolutionary psychology, and the biological treatment of mental disorders. A look at the past suggests that this surge in biological interest is likely to be followed by a rebound of the psychological and/or the social perspective at some point in the future.

So far we have illustrated the three perspectives with different topics. However, it is also possible (and instructive) to illustrate them with respect to the same topic. For instance, why are people aggressive? Why do they enforce harm on others who try to escape this? (For reviews, see Anderson & Bushman 2002; Geen 2001.)

Biological factors

The death drive in Freud's theory

One of the first explicit theories about aggression was presented by Freud. In some of his later writings he saw humans as driven by two innate drives: eros and a death drive (*Todestrieb*, later called *thanatos*). Eros was geared towards pleasure and the preservation of life; the death drive was directed towards destruction. The latter resulted in aggression and the refusal of pleasure. Both drives accumulated over time and needed to be discharged periodically, giving rise to a catharsis. As a result, both pleasure-seeking and aggression were inherent features of humans.

Lorenz's evolutionary theory

The idea of aggression as an innate feature, a drive, was also put forward by the Austrian animal researcher, Konrad Lorenz (1903–1989), and integrated within an evolutionary perspective. According to him, aggression was essential for the survival of the fittest because fighting for mates ensured that the offspring came from the strongest exemplars. Another advantage was that chased-off animals increased the dispersion of the species. Aggression built up over time and fired off whenever an appropriate stimulus was encountered. The resulting violence freed the energy, which was followed by a new accumulation.

Evidence for a biological component

Evidence for a biological contribution can be found in the fact that humans show individual differences in their degree of aggressiveness and that these differences are to a considerable extent inherited. As shown in Table 12.1, heredity is estimated to account for 40–53% of the variance in aggression encountered in humans. Other evidence for a biological contribution comes from the critical role of the limbic system in the regulation of aggression. This is an evolutionarily old part of the brain that is also involved in the regulation of emotions. An imbalance in the chemical substances that regulate the communication in this part of the brain results in an increased degree of aggression. A final biological factor is the availability of the male hormone testosterone. When female-to-male transsexuals were injected with testosterone as part of their gender-changing treatment, they reported a surge of aggressive feelings.

The opposite happened when male-to-female transsexuals received testosterone-lowering medication (Van Goozen *et al.* 1995).

Implications for treatment

Knowing about biological risk factors increases the possibility of medical treatment. At the same time, an exclusive reliance on the biological component drastically reduces the range of treatments, because the biological perspective does not offer much more than medicines to influence the communication in the limbic system and to lower the availability of testosterone in individuals with a high genetic risk. It also supplies tests to assess who has an enhanced risk, so that they can be watched. For the others, Freud and Lorenz recommended hard work and competitive sports to channel the aggressive energy towards more acceptable outlets.

Psychological factors

Learning aggressive behaviour

The psychological perspective stresses the importance of learning, perception and interpretation in aggression. Individuals who are reinforced for aggressive behaviour will increase it; individuals who are not reinforced (or punished) will decrease it. Patterson (1982), for instance, described circumstances in which children learn to behave aggressively, either because this leads to positive results or because it stops negative situations (which may happen, for instance, when a child notices that he is no longer bullied when he responds aggressively). According to the psychological perspective, much aggression (theft, fraud, extortion) is not elicited by aggression-provoking stimuli, as Freud and Lorenz claimed, but is due to the profit the perpetrator expects to extract from it.

Aggression is learned not only on the basis of one's own experiences, but also on the basis of what is observed in others. These can be real-life models, but also characters from movies and video games. There is a long tradition of research showing observational learning of aggression by watching violent films or taking part in brutal video games (Anderson *et al.* 2003). Observational learning is one of the main reasons why individuals who as children suffered from domestic violence are more likely to continue this behaviour in their new families (continuing a familial cycle of violence).

The importance of a person's perceptions

There is also good evidence that aggressive people have different perceptions than less aggressive individuals. They perceive more events as threatening, insulting or provocative. Dodge and Coie (1987) gave a review of the attributions that are likely to provoke aggression. An aggressive response is more likely,

- when a social situation is perceived as intentional rather than accidental,
- when a social situation is perceived as foreseeable rather than unforeseeable,
- when a social situation is perceived as freely chosen by the other rather than constrained.

A person who is biased to perceiving actions of others as intentional, foreseeable and of their own choice is more likely to respond aggressively than a person who is inclined to see actions as accidental, unforeseeable and due to circumstances.

The role of social skills

Finally, there is evidence that people with a high degree of aggression have more limited social skills. They have learned to solve their problems by resorting to violent behaviour and do not seem to have the normal range of responses. Nangle *et al.* (2002) reported that aggression is less likely in persons with skills:

● to negotiate conflict and influence peers,
● to participate and cooperate,
● to communicate (e.g. knowing that a listener ought to remain silent as long as a speaker is making a statement),
● to generate alternative solutions,
● to think of the consequences of actions,
● to pair solutions and consequences (both short term and long term),
● to appreciate that others have thoughts, feelings and motives in problem situations (i.e. perspective taking),
● to contain their anger and make use of self-instruction, relaxation and self-regulation.

Implications for treatment

The more individuals learn about possible causes of aggression and how to deal with them in a non-violent way, the more likely they are to resort to ways of settling their disagreements other than violence. Most children learn this from their natural environment (family, peers, school), but psychologists maintain that those skills can be learned throughout life and, therefore, should be part of rehabilitation programmes. Violent individuals often come from families where their parents were bad examples.

Social factors

Evidence for a social contribution

Because of the learning mentioned above, children who grow up in a social group with a high level of violence will be exposed to more aggression-related learning than children who grow up in more serene circumstances. An interesting study in this respect was published by Bohman (1996), who examined adopted children in Sweden. For each child, Bohman had information about the antisocial behaviour in the biological and the adoptive parents, and records about whether or not the children as adults got into trouble with the police. Table 12.4 lists the results.

When both the genes and the environment were aggression-free, only 3% of the adopted children got into trouble with the police by the time they were adults. Violence

Table 12.4 Aggression in adopted children as a function of antisocial behaviour in the biological and adoptive parents

These data show the combined effects of nature and nurture on aggression. When both influences were peaceful, only 3% of the children got in trouble with the police. The percentage rose both when either nature or nurture was a risk factor, and spiralled to 40% when both were negative.

Antisocial behaviour in adoptive parents	Antisocial behaviour in biological parents	
	Yes	No
Yes	40%	7%
No	12%	3%

Source: Bohman (1996).

in the biological parents increased the percentage to 12%; violence in the adoption family to 7%. However, the strongest effect was seen when both the biological and the adoption parents were prone to antisocial behaviour. Then, 40% of the children were known to the police for troublesome behaviour (which, incidentally, is an example of the interactions between genes and environment discussed above; they can reinforce each other).

The diathesis–stress model

diathesis–stress model

model claiming that the likelihood of a person having a disorder depends on the vulnerability of the person (diathesis) and the amount of stress experienced by the person

A model that has been proposed to explain the interaction between biological and social factors, as found by Bohman, is the diathesis–stress model (Zubin & Spring 1977). According to this model, the likelihood of a person having a disorder depends on the vulnerability of that person (the diathesis) and the amount of stress in the environment. The vulnerability is the outcome of genetic risk factors and previous experiences (e.g. child abuse). A highly vulnerable person will show the disorder even under low levels of stress. An individual with low vulnerability may still succumb to the disorder when his or her life circumstances are excessively stressful.

Other environmental factors that increase the probability of violence

Apart from the social environment, there are other factors that can increase the occurrence of violence. They are: frustration (being hindered in the achievement of a goal), provocation, threat, heat, noise, pain, the availability of weapons, alcohol and drugs. Social groups that are more exposed to these factors have a higher chance of acting violently. Finally, aggressive individuals will shape their environment so that it better fits their behaviour. A common phenomenon is that aggressive adolescents become isolated within their normal social groups (family, school, usual nightlife) and seek the company of gangs that highly value aggressive behaviour. Within these groups, the use of violence is further reinforced by the increase in status and power it brings.

Implications for treatment

Knowledge about the importance of social factors helps to organise communities in order to prevent violence, and is extremely useful in rehabilitation programmes to avoid relapse.

In summary, uncovering the various factors that contribute to aggression helps communities to deal with this problem. As the above review shows, progress is best made not by focusing on a single perspective at the exclusion of the others, but by taking into account all three types of factors: the biological, the psychological and the social.

Interim summary

Why are people aggressive?

- Biological contributions:
  - evolutionary advantage of aggressiveness
  - individual differences that to a large extent are inherited
  - chemical imbalances in the limbic system
  - impact of testosterone
  - points to a medical treatment (also preventive).

- Psychological contributions:
  - learning aggressive behaviour on the basis of observational learning and operant conditioning (positive results or the termination of a negative situation)
  - biases in the perception, so that more social situations are seen as provocative
  - limited social skills, so that there is no other response than a violent one
  - points to the importance of teaching new perceptions and responses in the treatment of aggression.
- Social contributions:
  - degree to which the environment exposes children to aggression-related learning
  - interacts with the person's vulnerability (diathesis–stress model)
  - series of other violence-provoking features in the environment
  - aggressive individuals seek the company of gang members who reinforce their behaviour
  - points to the need to change social influences in the treatment of aggression.

What do you think?

Given the many sources of evidence for the biopsychosocial model, it is surprising how little impact this model has in practice (both in research and in the treatment of diseases and disorders). Can you think of reasons for this? Why do more people seem to focus on the impact of a single factor than on the combined impacts of the different factors?

Recommended literature

A good book about evolutionary psychology is Buss, D.M. (2004) *Evolutionary psychology: The new science of the mind* (2nd edn) (Boston: Pearson Education). At the same time it may be interesting to read a more critical evaluation, such as Buller, D.J. (2005) *Adapting minds: Evolutionary psychology and the persistent quest for human nature* (Cambridge, MA: MIT Press).

A good book about learning and conditioning is Bouton, M.E. (2007) *Learning and behavior: A contemporary synthesis* (Sunderland, MA: Sinauer Associates Inc.).

An interesting book about the social and cultural influences on human behaviour is Matsumoto, D. and Juang, L. (2004), *Culture and psychology* (3rd edn) (London: Thomson Wadworth).

References

Anderson, C.A. & Bushman, B.J. (2002) 'Human aggression', *Annual Review of Psychology,* **53**: 27–51.

Anderson, C.A., Berkowitz, L., Donnerstein, E., Huesmann, L.R. *et al.* (2003) 'The influence of media violence on youth', *Psychological Science in the Public Interest,* **4**: 81–110.

Axelrod, R. & Hamilton, W.D. (1981) 'The evolution of cooperation', *Science,* **211**: 1390–6.

Bernard, L.L. (1924) *Instinct: A study of social psychology.* New York: Henry Holt & Co.

Bohman, M. (1996) 'Predisposition to criminality: Swedish adoption studies in retrospect.' In G.R. Bock & J.A. Goode (eds) *Genetics of criminal and antisocial behaviour.* Chichester: Wiley, pp. 99–114.

Boomsma, D.I., Willemsen, G., Dolan, C.V., Hawkley, L.C. *et al.* (2005) 'Genetic and environmental contributions to loneliness in adults: The Netherlands Twin Register study', *Behavior Genetics*, **35**: 745–52.

Bouchard, T.J. (1994) 'Genes, environment, and personality', *Science*, **264**: 1700–1.

Buller, D.J. (2005) *Adapting minds: Evolutionary psychology and the persistent quest for human nature*. Cambridge, MA: MIT Press.

Buss, D.M. (1989) 'Sex differences in human mate preference: Evolutionary hypotheses testing in 37 cultures', *Behavioral and Brain Sciences*, **12**: 1–49.

Buss, D.M. (2004) *Evolutionary psychology: The new science of the mind* (2nd edn). Boston, MA: Pearson Education.

Capron, C. & Duyme, M. (1989) 'Assessment of effects of socioeconomic status on IQ in a full cross-fostering design', *Nature*, **340**: 552–3.

Chebat, J.C. & Michon, R. (2003) 'Impact of ambient odors on mall shoppers' emotions, cognition, and spending: A test of competitive causal theories', *Journal of Business Research*, **56**: 529–39.

Davis, S.N. (2003) 'Sex stereotypes in commercials targeted toward children: A content analysis', *Sociological Spectrum*, **23**: 407–24.

De Araujo, I.E., Rolls, E.T., Velazco, M.I., Margot, C. *et al.* (2005) 'Cognitive modulation of olfactory processing', *Neuron*, **46**: 671–9.

DeRubeis, R.J., Hollon, S.D., Amsterdam, J.D., Shelton, R.C., *et al.* (2005) 'Cognitive therapy vs. medications in the treatment of moderate to severe depression', *Archives of General Psychiatry*, **62**: 409–16.

Djordjevic, J., Lundstrom, J.N., Clément, F., Boyle, J.A., *et al.* (2008) 'A rose by any other name: Would it smell as sweet?' *Journal of Neurophysiology*, **99**: 386–93.

Dodge, K.A. & Coie, J.D. (1987) 'Social-information-processing factors in reactive and proactive aggression in children's peer groups', *Journal of Personality and Social Psychology*, **53**: 1146–58.

Engel, G.L. (1977) 'The need for a new medical model: A challenge for biomedicine', *Science*, **196**: 129–36.

Fausto-Sterling, A., Gowaty, P.A. & Zuk, M. (1997) 'Evolutionary psychology and Darwinian feminism', *Feminist Studies*, **23**: 403–18.

Geary, D.C., Vigil, J. & Byrd-Craven, J. (2004) 'Evolution of human mate choice', *The Journal of Sex Research*, **41**: 27–42.

Geen, R.G. (2001) *Human aggression* (2nd edn). Buckingham, UK: Open University Press.

Geier, A.B., Rozin, P. & Doros, G. (2006) 'Unit bias: A new heuristic that helps explain the effect of portion size on food intake', *Psychological Science*, **17**: 521–5.

Gould, S.J. (1996) *The mismeasure of man* (2nd edn). New York: W.W. Norton & Co.

Gould, S.J. & Lewontin, R.C. (1979) 'The spandrels of San Marco and the panglossian paradigm: A critique of the adaptationist programme', *Proceedings of the Royal Society of London*, **B205**: 581–98.

Hamilton, W.D. (1964) 'The genetical evolution of social behavior I and II', *Journal of Theoretical Biology*, **7**: 1–52.

Haney, C. & Zimbardo, P. (1998) 'The past and future of US prison policy: Twenty-five years after the Stanford Prison Experiment', *American Psychologist*, **53**: 709–27.

Haney, C., Banks, W. & Zimbardo, P. (1973) 'Interpersonal dynamics in a simulated prison', *International Journal of Criminology and Penology*, **1**: 69–97.

Harden, K.P., Turkheimer, E. & Loehlin, J.C. (2007) 'Genotype by environment interaction in adolescents' cognitive aptitude', *Behavior Genetics*, **37**: 273–83.

Hofstede, G. (2001) *Culture's consequences: Comparing values, behaviors, institutions, and organizations across nations*. Thousand Oaks, CA: Sage Publications.

Hofstede, G. (2005) *Cultures and organizations: Software of the mind* (2nd edn). London: McGraw-Hill Professional.

Hollon, S.D., DeRubeis, R.J., Shelton, R.C., Amsterdam, J.D. *et al.* (2005) 'Prevention of relapse following cognitive therapy vs medications in moderate to severe depression', *Archives of General Psychiatry*, **62**: 417–22.

Hunt, H.T. (2005) 'Why psychology is/is not traditional science: The self-referential bases of psychological research and theory', *Review of General Psychology*, **9**: 358–74.

Jackson, S. & Rees, A. (2007) 'The appalling appeal of nature: The popular influence of evolutionary psychology as a problem for sociology', *Sociology*, **41**: 917–30.

Jacob, S., McClintock, M.K., Zelano, B. & Ober, C. (2002) 'Paternally inherited HLA alleles are associated with women's choice of male odor', *Nature Genetics*, **30**: 175–9.

Jahoda, G. (2007) *A history of social psychology*. Cambridge: Cambridge University Press.

Keefe, F.J., Rumble, M.E., Scipio, C.D., Giordano, L.A. *et al.* (2004) 'Psychological aspects of persistent pain: Current state of the science', *The Journal of Pain*, **5**: 195–211.

Kendler, K.S., Thornton, L.M., Gilman, S.E. & Kessler, R.C. (2000) 'Sexual orientation in a U.S. national sample of twin and nontwin sibling pairs', *American Journal of Psychiatry*, **157**: 1843–6.

Kirsch, I., Deacon, B.J., Huedo-Medina, T.B., Scoboria, A. *et al.* (2008) 'Initial severity and antidepressant benefits: A meta-analysis of data submitted to the Food and Drug Administration', *PLoS Med*, **5**(2): e45. doi:10.1371/journal.pmed.0050045.

Kobayakawa, K., Kobayakawa, R., Matsumoto, H., Oka, Y., *et al.* (2007) 'Innate versus learned odour processing in the mouse olfactory bulb', *Nature*, **450**: 503–8.

Lehman, A.F. & Steinwachs, D.M. (1998) 'At issue: Translating research into practice: The Schizophrenia Patient Outcomes Research Team (PORT) treatment recommendations', *Schizophrenia Bulletin*, **24**: 1–10.

Li, W., Howard, J.D., Parrish, T.B. & Gottfried, J.A. (2008) 'Aversive learning enhances perceptual and cortical discrimination of indiscriminable odor cues', *Science*, **319**: 1842–5.

Liu, I., Blacker, D.L., Xu, R., Fitzmaurice, G. *et al.* (2004) 'Genetic and environmental contributions to the development of alcohol dependence in male twins', *Archives of General Psychiatry*, **61**: 897–903.

Mackintosh, N.J. (1998) *IQ and human intelligence.* Oxford: Oxford University Press.

McNulty, J.K., Neff, L.A. & Karney, B.R. (2008) 'Beyond initial attraction: Physical attractiveness in newlywed marriage', *Journal of Family Psychology*, **22**: 135–43.

Melzack, R. & Wall, P.D. (1965) 'Pain mechanisms: A new theory', *Science*, **150**: 971–9.

Miles, D.R. & Carey, G. (1997) 'Genetic and environmental architecture of human aggression', *Journal of Personality and Social Psychology*, **72**: 207–17.

Milgram, S. (1974) *Obedience to authority: An experimental view.* New York: Harper & Row.

Nangle, D.W., Erdley, C.A., Carpenter, E.M. & Newman, J.E. (2002) 'Social skills training as a treatment for aggressive children and adolescents: A developmental–clinical integration', *Aggression and Violent Behavior*, **7**: 169–99.

Nass, C., Moon, Y., Fogg, B.J., Reeves, B. *et al.* (1995) 'Can computer personalities be human personalities?' *International Journal of Human–Computer Studies*, **43**: 223–39.

Nolen-Hoeksema, S. (2000) 'The role of rumination in depressive disorders and mixed anxiety/depressive symptoms', *Journal of Abnormal Psychology*, **109**: 504–11.

Ochsner, K.R. & Gross, J.J. (2005) 'The cognitive control of emotion', *Trends in Cognitive Sciences*, **9**: 242–9.

O'Rahilly, S. & Farooqi, I.S. (2006) 'Genetics of obesity', *Philosophical Transactions of the Royal Society B – Biological Sciences*, **361**: 1095–105.

Patterson, G.R. (1982) *Coercive family process.* Eugene, OR: Castalia.

Peterson, C. (1997) *Psychology: A biopsychosocial approach* (2nd edn). New York: Addison Wesley Longman.

Raskind, W.H. (2001) 'Current understanding of the genetic basis of reading and spelling disability', *Learning Disability Quarterly*, **24**: 141–57.

Richardson, R.C. (2007) *Evolutionary psychology as maladapted psychology.* Cambridge, MA: MIT Press.

Ritzer, G. & Goodman, D.J. (2004) *Modern sociological theory* (6th edn). Boston: McGraw-Hill.

Rutter, M. (2006) *Genes and behavior: Nature–nurture interplay explained.* Oxford: Blackwell Publishing.

Saggerson, A.L., George, D.N. & Honey, R.C. (2005) 'Imitative learning of stimulus–response and response–outcome associations in pigeons', *Journal of Experimental Psychology: Animal Behavior Processes*, **31**: 289–300.

Spangenberg, E.R., Sprott, D.E., Grohmann, B. & Tracy, D.L. (2006) 'Gender-congruent ambient scent influences on approach and avoidance behaviors in a retail store', *Journal of Business Research*, **59**: 1281–7.

Stubbe, J.H., Posthuma, D., Boomsma, D.I. & De Geus, E.J.C. (2005) 'Heritability of life satisfaction in adults: A twin-family study', *Psychological Medicine*, **35**: 1581–88.

Sullivan, P.F., Kendler, K.S. & Neale, M.C. (2003) 'Schizophrenia as a complex trait: Evidence from a meta-analyis of twin studies', *Archives of General Psychiatry*, **60**: 1187–92.

Sullivan, P.F., Neale, M.C. & Kendler, K.S. (2000) 'Genetic epidemiology and major depression: Review and meta-analysis', *American Journal of Psychiatry*, **157**: 1552–62.

Thapar, A., Langley, K., Owen, M.J. & O'Donavan, M.C. (2007) 'Advances in genetic findings on attention deficit hyperactivity disorder', *Psychological Medicine*, **37**: 1681–92.

Torgersen, S., Lygren, S., Dien, P.A., Skre, I. *et al.* (2000) 'A twin study of personality disorders', *Comprehensive Psychiatry*, **41**: 416–25.

Trivers, R.L. (1971) 'The evolution of reciprocal altruism', *Quarterly Review of Biology*, **46**: 35–57.

Trivers, R.L. (1972) 'Parental investment and sexual selection'. In B. Campbell (ed.), *Sexual selection and the descent of man: 1871–1971.* Chicago: Aldine, pp. 136–79.

Van Goozen, S.H.M., Cohen-Kettenis, P.T., Gooren, L.J.G., Frijda, N.H. *et al.* (1995) 'Gender differences in behaviour: Activating effects of cross-sex hormones', *Psychoneuroendocrinology*, **20**: 343–63.

Van Vugt, M., De Cremer, D. & Janssen, D.P. (2007) 'Gender differences in cooperation and competition: The male-warrior hypothesis', *Psychological Science*, **18**: 19–23.

Wampold, B.E., Minami, T., Tierney, S.C., Baskin, T.W. *et al.* (2005) 'The placebo is powerful: Estimating placebo effects in medicine and psychotherapy for randomized clinical trials', *Journal of Clinical Psychology*, **61**: 835–54.

Watson, J.B. (1925) *Behaviorism.* New York: People's Institute Publishing Company. (Reprinted in 1997 by Transaction Publishers.)

Wilson, E.O. (1975) *Sociobiology: The new synthesis.* Cambridge, MA: Harvard University Press.

Woodworth, R.S. (1948) *Contemporary schools of psychology* (revised edn). New York: The Ronald Press.

Zimbardo, P.G. (2004) 'Power turns good soldiers into "bad apples"'. Editorial in *The Boston Globe*, 9 May.

Zubin, J. & Spring, B. (1977) 'Vulnerability: A new view of schizophrenia', *Journal of Abnormal Psychology*, **86**: 103–26.

13 Psychology and society
The socio-political side

This chapter will cover . . .

Questions to consider

Historical issues addressed in this chapter

- Is the rise of psychology related to changes in religious convictions?
- Why does psychology today attach more interest to ethics in research and practice than in the first half of the twentieth century?

Conceptual issues addressed in this chapter

- Why are metaphors important in psychological research? Where do they come from?
- How has research on intelligence testing been influenced by social values in society?
- Are psychologists involved in power struggles between socio-political groups?
- In what way may postmodernism have contributed to the rise of pseudoscience?
- In what ways can psychological knowledge be misused?
- Does psychological research have an influence on the way in which people view themselves and interact with others?
- Do psychologists create needs rather than solve problems?
- Are psychologists politically neutral?
- Why does mental illness carry a stigma?

Introduction

> Many of the fundamental categories of twentieth-century psychology are, to all intents and purposes, twentieth-century inventions. Such concepts as 'intelligence', 'behaviour' and 'learning' were given such radically changed meanings by modern psychology that there simply are no earlier equivalents.
>
> (Danziger 1997: 36)

In the previous chapters we saw how psychology has developed and how it has been affected by a number of basic questions (conceptual issues). In this final chapter we look at the ways in which psychology and society have influenced each other. Psychology would not be around if society had not felt a need for this type of knowledge, and the Western world would look different without psychology. In the first part of the chapter we review a number of ways in which psychology has been influenced by socio-political tendencies in society. In the second part we see how psychology has changed society and has influenced the ways in which people perceive each other and interact with one another. This chapter focuses on the criticisms levied against psychology, which may not always be the nicest reading if you are an aspiring psychologist, but which is essential to fully understand psychology's perceived role in society. The 'focus on' section examines to what extent psychology has been able to remove the stigma of mental disorders.

13.1 Ways in which society has influenced psychology

Science overtakes religion in Western society

Initial strong links between psychological thinking and religion

As sketched in the first chapters, psychology as a separate branch of knowledge grew out of the rising role of scientific thinking in Western society. Without the scientific revolution and the increasing status of the natural sciences in the eighteenth and nineteenth centuries, there would never have been sufficient critical mass to start the scientific study of mental life. In all likelihood, psychology would have remained a subdiscipline of philosophy, secondary to religious writings. Education for a long time was controlled by the churches, which did not look favourably upon those who tried to examine the soul. This was the case in Europe, but also in the USA. As Fuchs (2000: 6) wrote:

> Seminaries provided the only graduate education available in the pre-Civil War period. Those who attended seminaries were prepared and chosen not only for the ministry but also for college professorships.

Unsurprisingly, many early psychologists had strong connections with religion. Carl Jung and Edward Thorndike, for instance, were sons of ministers. G. Stanley Hall and Carl Rogers came from very religious families and initially studied for the ministry. In 1904 Hall founded the *Journal of Religious Psychology*. Another early psychologist who stayed close to religion was William James, who in 1902 wrote the bestseller *The varieties of religious experience*.

Alliance formation with the expanding sciences

Rapidly, however, the experimental psychologists distanced themselves from religion, because it jeopardised their scientific credentials. They sought to align themselves with the rapidly growing natural sciences, by denouncing weaker fields that might contaminate them, such as religion, philosophy and sociology (Ward 2002: 53). The main exception was William James, who during his whole life felt as much attraction to mysticism as to scientific research, and in the end was felt by many of his colleagues to be an embarrassment rather than an asset to psychology (Hood 2000).

Within this perspective, psychology would never have sought to affiliate itself with the natural sciences if they had been perceived as weak by society (which they very much were until the seventeenth century; see Chapters 1 and 2).

Psychologists replace pastors

Another reason why the decline in religion contributed to the emergence of psychology is that fewer people felt comfortable discussing their mental health problems with religious authorities. Whereas for a long time the churches were the first port of call for mental health problems (and for many people still are), growing secularisation increased the need for non-religious counselling. At the same time, a growing number of clergy started to study psychology to improve the help they were able to provide.

Changes in society impinge on psychological practice

Impact on psychological research

The massive changes in the organisation of Western society in the nineteenth and twentieth centuries also generated ideas and research opportunities for psychologists. Kagan (2009a) lists six historical developments that affected psychological research:

1. The emergence of industrialization and increased numbers of European immigrants to the USA (which, for instance, led to the creation and use of intelligence tests; see below).

2. The historical commitment to a material basis for all natural phenomena (partly due to the biological discoveries about the physiological basis of the human mind; Chapter 6).

3. The Cold War and computers (leading to the rise of cognitive psychology – Chapter 5 – and the development of, for example, game theory, which tries to understand how an individual's success in making choices depends on the choices of others).

4. The entry of mothers into the workforce (which created a series of issues about the education of children).

5. The discovery of statistical techniques such as analysis of variance and regression (which determined the topics that could be investigated and the ways in which research was done).

6. The unique position of physics among the empirical sciences (which instilled in psychologists the desire to search for universal laws, free from individual variation and contextual constraints).

Kagan (2009b) further noticed that societal influences were not limited to the science-oriented track of psychology, but also shaped thought in the hermeneutic part (Chapter 10), for instance in psychoanalysis:

> If late nineteenth-century Europeans had held a more permissive attitude toward sexuality, Freud might not have written that repression of sexual urges was the primary cause of all neuroses. If the next generation of Europeans had not been rendered despondent by the shattering of illusions at the end of World War I and the reduction of mind to a set of mechanical parts, few would have questioned the possibility of attaining ideal states and Jung might not have argued that a spiritual outlook was needed to attain a form of Nirvana. If large numbers of American men raised in working-class families who served in World War II did not have the opportunity to attend college, Erik Erikson's suggestion that all persons must solve the difficult problem of 'finding their identity' would have been met with a puzzling, or lukewarm, reception. Had working mothers and divorce rates not increased dramatically in the twentieth century, John Bowlby's theory of attachment might not have gained popularity. Each of these original ideas required history to arrange a special constellation of conditions.
>
> (Kagan 2009b: 25)

Impact on clinical practice

Changes in society not only affect psychological research and theory, they also influence clinical practice. Mental disorders, like many other psychological phenomena, show cultural variation. This is not only true between cultures (with some conditions unique to a particular culture), but also across time within a culture. Reviewing the history of psychiatry in the West, Shorter (1992, 1997) noted historical peaks in certain diagnoses:

- nineteenth century: ovarian hysteria;
- nineteenth to twentieth century: conversion syndrome (hysteria with psycho-generated organic symptoms);
- 1940s–1950s: schizophrenia (particularly in America); and
- 1980s: multiple personality disorder.

According to Shorter (1992), each culture has a symptom pool, a collective memory of how to behave when ill. These include classical symptoms such as headache, tiredness, twitching limbs, but also new symptoms which doctors have just 'discovered'. At each time period patients with psychological problems gravitate towards the symptoms that at the time are thought to be legitimate indications of disease, as no patient wants to select illegitimate symptoms. So, if multiple personality disorder is seen as a common phenomenon by care takers (and described as such in the media), an increasing number of patients will show symptoms in line with the diagnosis (health workers will also be more likely to interpret symptoms as evidence for this condition). Consequently the symptoms observed by practitioners not only differ between cultures but also vary in time.

Society as a metaphor provider

metaphor
in science, stands for an analogy from another area that helps to map a new, complex problem by making reference to a better understood phenomenon

Another way in which the wider world has influenced psychology is by the provision of metaphors. Metaphors in science are analogies from other areas that help to map a new, complex problem by making reference to a better understood phenomenon. A typical example of a metaphor in science is that of electricity as a fluid streaming through cables and appliances and exerting a power against elements that resist the flow.

Examples of metaphors in psychology

Metaphors have had an influential role in psychological thinking as well. For instance, they have strongly shaped the ideas scholars had about memory (Draaisma 2000). Plato had already used the metaphor of a wax tablet to understand memory (a good memory consisted of a clear impression in the tablet and memories faded just like impressions on a tablet). From the Middle Ages onward, memory was often seen as a library, full of books. In the nineteenth century and the first half of the twentieth century, this metaphor was supplemented with those of new inventions that were made, such as the switchboard (from telephone exchanges), the mechanical piano (that 'remembered' a song and played it automatically), the phonograph and the photograph. In the mid-twentieth century, a completely new and exciting metaphor was found in the computer, giving rise, for example, to research on the difference between a short-term memory (a central processor) and a long-term memory (a hard disk on which information was stored and from which it was retrieved).

Metaphors have played a role in other areas of psychology as well (Leary 1995). For instance, when psychodynamic therapists attempt to relieve the pressure built up in a patient, they are following Freud's metaphor of the mind as a hydraulic device.

More generally, Gentner and Grudin (1985) argued that psychologists have used four types of metaphors:

1. the mind as an animal (e.g. ideas struggle or compete with each other),
2. the mind as a neural system (e.g. ideas are inhibited; disturbance of thought arises because of over-excitation in the brain),
3. the mind as a spatial container (e.g. memories that are in the background, fear that inundates the sympathetic nervous system),
4. the mind as a mechanical or computational system (e.g. serial, iterative operations going on in the brain).

What do you think?

Socrates compared memories with birds that you try to catch in a cage. To what extent does this metaphor differ from the library metaphor? And in what way does it differ from the computer metaphor?

The power of metaphors

It is important to realise that metaphors in science are not just comparisons. They allow researchers to formulate and test hypotheses on the basis of the analogy, which otherwise would have remained elusive. For instance, the library metaphor of memory made researchers alert to the way in which books are located in such a system. Each book has a particular location, which can be found by means of an index system (e.g. the author's name or a few keywords). Could it be that something similar was operating in the brain and that people needed memory cues in order to 'find' the memory traces? This type of question gave rise to a completely new area of memory research in the 1970s (e.g. Tulving & Thomson 1971).

Without doubt, the most influential metaphor in the history of psychology has been the computer. As we saw in Chapters 5 and 7, this metaphor was the catalyst both in the replacement of behaviourism by cognitive psychology, and in the ways psychologists and philosophers looked at the relationship between the mind and the brain.

Metaphors work because they transfer a complex knowledge system from a known theme to an unknown topic. At the same time, they include a danger, because often the phenomenon to be understood does not completely fit into the metaphor. The metaphor does not replace the reality; it only allows the researchers to get a grasp of some aspects of the phenomenon. The danger of overinterpreting metaphors can be illustrated with the library metaphor. In a library, as soon as the location of a book is known, all the information contained in the book becomes available. This is not the case with memory. Most of the time, only partial information can be retrieved from an address, and memory must continue its search. In addition, quite often it has to fill in missing gaps. The latter can be compared to the work of an archaeologist who tries to reconstruct a complete animal on the basis of a few recovered bones, another metaphor that has been used to grasp the workings of memory (Larsen 1987).

Throughout the history of psychology, scientific innovations have been a source of metaphors to understand the mechanisms of the mind. By applying them, psychologists got a better grip on the phenomena they tried to understand. At the same time, metaphors restrict understanding, because the phenomenon to be explained is rarely exactly the same as the analogy used.

Socio-political biases in psychological theories

In Chapters 10 and 12 we saw how scientific research does not happen in a void but is influenced by the culture in which the researchers live. In Chapter 10 we mentioned the type of advice psychologists gave on masturbation at the beginning of the twentieth century. In Chapter 12 we saw how the current popularity of evolutionary psychology might have other origins than the mere scientific supremacy of the theory.

The American scientist Stephen Jay Gould (1996) provided a series of other eye-opening examples related to the history of intelligence testing. He showed how socio-political biases twisted the conclusions that were drawn. Below we present a summary of his findings.

Intelligence testing in the French welfare state

As you may remember from Chapters 4 and 8, the first useful intelligence test was developed in France. This was no coincidence. On the one hand, there was the tradition of brain research initiated by scholars like Paul Broca (see Chapters 6 and 9). On the other hand, there was the political organisation of the French state, which not only aimed for a strong central authority but also felt responsible for the well-being of its citizens. The French state, together with other countries in Western Europe, was a strong proponent of the welfare system, in which inhabitants pay relatively high taxes as an insurance against adversity. Within this context, the Paris psychologists Alfred Binet and Théodore Simon started to design a test that would help to diagnose children who needed extra help in school. This became a particularly pressing issue at the beginning of the twentieth century, when compulsory primary education for all children began.

In line with their assignment and the socio-political system in which they lived, Binet and Simon saw their intelligence test as based on three principles:

1. The scores of the test were a practical device, showing how well a child grasped the skills needed within the education system. The scores did not define what intelligence was, because the tasks had simply been chosen because they worked better than anything else that was available.

2. The measure was meant as a rough guide for identifying mildly retarded and learning-disabled children who needed special help. It was not meant to rank children within the normal range.

3. The purpose of the scale was to provide extra help for children at risk. Mild retardation was not seen as a sign that children were incapable of studying.

Translation to the American context

Binet and Simon's intelligence test was brought to the USA, when Henry H. Goddard, the director of a School for Feeble-Minded Girls and Boys in New Jersey, heard about the test on a study visit to Belgium. He decided to translate and use the test, at first in his school, but soon in other contexts (e.g. with pupils attending regular schools and with immigrants). His popularisation efforts eventually led to the *Stanford–Binet test,* published by Lewis Terman in 1916, and to the *Army Tests* (Alpha and Beta), started under the direction of Robert M. Yerkes in 1917 (with the help of Goddard and Terman) and published in 1921.

The philosophy of the American tests, however, was not to identify children at risk so that they could receive extra help. The aim was to optimise the organisation of society by testing which children were intelligent enough for various types of schooling, and which adults were intelligent enough for various types of employment. For instance, in 1923, Terman (together with Yerkes and Thorndike) advertised a group of national intelligence tests on the basis of the Stanford–Binet and the Army Tests, to be used in schools for Grades 3–8. This is what the advert said:

> The direct result of the application of the army testing methods to school needs . . . the tests have been selected from a large group of tests after a try-out and a careful analysis by a statistical staff. The two scales prepared consist of five tests each (with practical exercises) and either may be administered in thirty minutes. They are simple in application, reliable, and immediately useful in classifying children in Grades 3 to 8 with respect to intellectual ability. Scoring is unusually simple.
>
> (Terman, as cited in Gould 1996: 208–9)

As for the test's use with employees, Terman wrote in 1916:

> Industrial concerns doubtless suffer enormous losses from the employment of persons whose mental ability is not equal to the tasks they are expected to perform . . . Any business employing as many as 500 or 1000 workers, as, for example, a large department store, could save in this way several times the salary of a well-trained psychologist.
>
> (Terman, as cited in Gould 1996: 211)

More generally, within the American socio-political context, Binet and Simon's principles became translated into the following tenets:

1. The various tasks identified by Binet and Simon and further extended by other researchers, all measure one single capacity, called 'general intelligence'.
2. The amount of intelligence in a person can be expressed by a single number (called IQ).
3. Individuals can be ranked linearly according to their IQ. This is true over the whole range of intelligences, not just in the subnormal range.
4. The IQ refers to an inborn quality, inherited from the previous generations.
5. A person's IQ is stable and permanent; that is, it will not change noticeably by a programme of social and educational intervention.
6. The IQ of a person correlates not only with the type of tasks the person can do, but also with his or her moral reasoning.

As for the latter claim, Goddard wrote in 1919:

> The intelligence controls the emotions and the emotions are controlled in proportion to the degree of intelligence . . . It follows that if there is little intelligence the emotions will be uncontrollable and whether they be strong or weak will result in actions that are unregulated, uncontrolled and, as experience proves, usually undesirable.
>
> (Goddard, as cited in Gould 1996: 190–1)

Given that black Americans on average scored substantially below white Americans, the IQ findings also had sweeping racial implications, as can be seen in the following excerpt from Terman (1916). It is part of a chapter in which Terman discussed the findings about people with IQ scores between 70 and 80 (i.e. the feeble-minded):

> Among laboring men and servant girls there are thousands like them . . . The tests have told the truth. These boys are ineducable beyond the merest rudiments of training. No amount of school instruction will ever make them intelligent voters or capable citizens . . . They represent the level of intelligence which is very, very common among Spanish-Indian and Mexican families of the Southwest and also among negroes. Their dullness seems to be racial, or at least inherent in the family stocks from which they came. The fact that one meets this type with such extraordinary frequency among Indians, Mexicans, and negroes suggests quite forcibly that the whole question of racial differences in mental traits will have to be taken up anew and by experimental methods . . . Children of this group should be segregated in special classes and be given instruction which is concrete and practical. They cannot master abstractions, but they can often be made efficient workers, able to look out for themselves. There is no possibility at present of convincing society that they should not be allowed to reproduce, although from a eugenic point of view they constitute a grave problem because of their unusually prolific breeding.
>
> (Terman, as cited in Gould 1996: 220–1)

When reading the above excerpts, it is important to keep in mind that the change in tone from the French to the American approach was not due to an increase in scientific knowledge in the first decades of the twentieth century. It was virtually all to do with differences in the socio-political climate between France and the USA. Many Americans were convinced that the white race was far superior to Native Americans and black people. They also had a much more competitive and individualistic approach to the organisation of the state.

What do you think?

Gould (1996) noted that the tenets of Goddard and Terman regain in popularity each time politics turns toward the right and the social services are slimmed down in order to reduce taxes. Can you find examples of this? Can you think of counter-examples?

Even measurements and data are not safe in the light of strong socio-political opinions: Gould vs. Morton

One objection scientists usually make to the criticism that their statements may be socio-politically biased is that their conclusions are based on sound empirical evidence (Chapters 9 and 10). Gould (1996) devoted a large part of his book to showing how easily 'objective' findings can be distorted by the researchers' expectations. Of the many examples he gave, we only mention the case of Samuel George Morton (1799–1851). Morton was an American physician and natural scientist, who was famous for his skull collection. In 1839, he published a volume on the brain sizes of Americans from different descent. As can be seen in Table 13.1, Morton's table clearly 'proved' that the mean skull size of white people (of Caucasian origin) was larger than that of Native Americans and black people.

Table 13.1 Morton's summary table of cranial capacity by race
This table clearly 'shows' that the brain size of American from Caucasian descent was larger than that of the other races.

Race	N	Internal capacity (in^3)		
		Mean	Largest	Smallest
Caucasian	52	87	109	75
Mongolian	10	83	93	69
Malay	18	81	89	64
American	144	82	100	60
Ethiopian	29	78	94	65

Source: Morton (1839) as cited in Gould (1996: 86).

From the lower cranial capacity of Native Americans (and the other races), Morton drew sweeping conclusions, such as: 'the benevolent mind may regret the inaptitude of the Indian for civilization' and '[Indians, i.e. Native Americans] are not only averse to the restraints of education, but for the most part are incapable of a continued process of reasoning on abstract subjects' (as cited in Gould 1996: 88–9). Throughout the nineteenth and the first part of the twentieth century, Morton's data were used as the decisive argument for race differences in intelligence.

Interestingly, Morton not only provided a summary table, but full information on each and every skull in his collection. Gould set out to re-analyse these data. His findings were:

1. The 144 skulls of the Native Americans belonged to many different groups, which differed in cranial capacity. Morton's sample was strongly biased towards the Inca Peruvians, who had smaller brains than the others but also smaller statures (just like with the other body parts, the size of the brain depends on the overall stature of a person). There were three skulls of Iroquois, who had brain sizes very close to those of the Caucasians.

2. Morton excluded the skulls of the Hindus from his Caucasian sample, because they were deemed 'too small to be acceptable'.

3. Morton measured the cranial capacity by pouring mustard seed in the skulls and measuring the amount that was required. This worked reasonably well, except for two problems. The first was that the seed was a bit sticky and sometimes did not fill cavities completely. The second was that mustard seed can be compressed. Because of these drawbacks, Morton later decided to redo his analyses with lead shot. However, he never published a clear summary table of these data. When Gould did so more than a century later, he found that the Caucasian cranial capacity stayed at 87 in^3, but that of the Native Americans increased to 86 in^3 and that of Africans to 83 in^3. According to Gould, Morton had more rigorously shaken and pressed the mustard seeds for his Caucasian skulls than for the other skulls.

When Gould corrected for the various biases, his estimates almost wiped out the racial differences in skull sizes as reported by Morton (the same was true for the other data reported by Morton in later publications on a total of 623 skulls). Gould thought it unlikely that manifest fraud was involved. Otherwise, Morton would never have published a full account of his raw materials. What probably happened was that Morton happily accepted the data that were in line with his expectations, whereas he double-checked and 'corrected' the data he did not understand. The end result was a set of 'scientific' measures that seemed to 'prove beyond doubt' the existence of racial differences in skull sizes (and, hence, intelligence) and that other researchers copied because it agreed with their beliefs.

There was a further interesting (and ironic) twist in the Gould vs. Morton dispute when Lewis *et al.* (2011) not only re-analysed the numbers used by Morton and Gould, but in addition redid the cranial measurements for 308 of Morton's skulls (something which Gould had not done). What they observed was that Morton's measurements were surprisingly accurate and that the few deviations between the initial measurements and the new measurements were not racially biased but randomly distributed. As it happened, Gould's 'corrections' to Morton's initial data were more systematic and theory-driven, making Lewis *et al.* (2011) conclude that Morton's description of the data was closer to the findings than Gould's. In their own words:

> Samuel George Morton, in the hands of Stephen Jay Gould, has served for 30 years as a textbook example of scientific misconduct . . . . The Morton case was used by Gould as the main support for his contention that 'unconscious or dimly perceived finagling is probably endemic in science, since scientists are human beings rooted in cultural contexts, not automatons directed toward external truth' . . . . This view has since achieved substantial popularity in 'science studies' . . . . But our results falsify Gould's hypothesis that Morton manipulated his data to conform with his *a priori* views. The data on cranial capacity gathered by Morton are generally reliable, and he reported them fully. Overall, we find that Morton's initial reputation as the objectivist of his era was well-deserved.
>
> (Lewis *et al.* 2011: 5–6)

Whichever will turn out to be the correct assessment of Morton's figures, the observation that the same data set can lead to different conclusions is a useful reminder of the fact that data collection and measurement involve selection and interpretation, which make scientific conclusions open to socio-political influences.

Money and Ehrhardt (1972): the trainability of gender identity

Socio-political biases in scientific conclusions are not limited to the biological perspective. The 1960s and 1970s were a time during which the social perspective dominated. The economy expanded rapidly, technological advances were breathtaking, and there was general optimism in American society. Suddenly it did not seem improbable that further gains could be made by improving the education system and providing better services to those in need. Maybe there was more merit in the social powers than initially acknowledged by Goddard and Terman in the heydays of eugenics? (Gould (1996) describes how these geneticists recanted some of their views towards the end of their careers.)

Within this period it was not surprising to see a book appear in which it was claimed that a person's gender identity was strongly influenced by education (Money & Ehrhardt 1972). A baby boy turned into a man, not only because of his Y-chromosome but also because of the way in which he was reared. The same was true for a baby girl. Again the conclusion was backed with 'sound' empirical evidence. A particularly revealing case in this respect was that of identical male twins, of whom one had his penis severed aged 8 months during a medical operation. The penis eventually was removed and replaced by a vulva, and the parents were advised to raise the boy as a girl. Money and Ehrhardt concluded that after these simple changes the boy happily grew up as a girl, proving that gender identity was not primarily due to genes, but to the ways in which education depended on the anatomical differences with which boys and girls were born.

Money and Ehrhardt's finding was seized upon by textbook authors who presented it as the decisive evidence for the power of social factors in mental and social life. However, with the growth of the biological perspective towards the end of the twentieth century, the case was revisited and found to have been misrepresented (Diamond & Sigmundson 1997). Brenda (previously Bruce) Reimer did not remember her childhood as a happy one. From the beginning she had difficulties with the fact that her parents treated her as a girl. She walked like a boy, fought with other boys, and had to change schools a few times because of bullying and behaviour problems. The crisis reached its peak when at puberty she had to take hormones and needed another operation to continue her female development. In the end, at the age of 14 she was told the truth about what had happened, and she experienced this as a huge relief. Later she had a sex change operation and became David, a name chosen for its analogy with the fight between David and Goliath. He married a single mother with three children and was happy with his renewed role. In the end, however, the story took a tragic turn. David's twin brother (who had mental health problems) committed suicide in 2002. Shortly afterwards David lost his job and savings, and was told by his wife that she wanted to end their marriage. In 2004, he committed suicide as well.

By that time, David's case had become famous again, because it had been seized upon by a journalist first to write a story in *Rolling Stone* magazine (in 1997), later to publish a book on it (in 2000), which was followed by an acclaimed BBC Horizon documentary (also in 2000). In line with the changed social climate, the case was now presented as evidence against the social perspective and in favour of a strict biological interpretation of the development of gender identity.

What do you think?

There is a lot of information available on Money and Ehrhardt's case study on the internet, under the titles 'David Reimer' and 'The boy who was turned into a girl'. Search for it, and see how it fits in with a changing socio-political context. Also notice the impact of the socio-political context on the media.

An example of current social influences: hidden racism

Socio-political influences are conspicuous for examples from the past, because the change in context makes the extent of the impact clearer. One cannot help but cringe and feel vicarious shame when reading some of Goddard's and Terman's texts. Surely such practices no longer exist in current-day psychological writings? Or do they, and are we simply not noticing them?

Teo (2005) acknowledges that blatant scientific racism, as found in the texts of Goddard and Terman, is no longer present in the current literature. However, in his view this does not preclude psychologists from still being influenced by the in-group bias, the belief that one's own group is superior in knowledge and skills to other groups. This bias shows itself in the fact that other groups are no longer explicitly denigrated, but they are ignored. Scientists from non-dominant groups find it harder to get their manuscripts accepted for publication and, if they do manage this, very few colleagues from the dominant group take notice of their articles. Teo calls this 'hidden colonial thinking' or **hidden racism**. As he writes:

> I suggest that most contemporary psychologists view scientific racism and blatant racial prejudices and actions as aberrations of the discipline's past. However, from a post-colonial perspective the major problem nowadays is not scientific racism . . . but hidden colonial thinking. Hidden colonial thinking in psychology, as hidden culture-centrism in general, expresses itself in terms of exclusion or disregard of non-Western psychologies.
>
> (Teo 2005: 166)

As a result, psychological research in all countries is dominated by what is thought to be interesting in the Anglo-Saxon world, as was observed by Gulerce (2006: 76) for Turkish psychology:

> The interpellation and normalization of American psychology is so strong in Turkish society . . . that Turkish psychologists do not get to study systematically and think about the long historical period prior to the common celebratory historical marker of the establishment of a Western chair of experimental psychology at a Turkish university. Furthermore, Turkish psychology is even more ahistorical, acultural, and asocial than American psychology, so that even the very idea of critical and cultural history of psychology in Turkey seems oxymoronic, as a good example of overidentification.

A similar criticism was raised by Rogers and Pilgrim (2005) and Watters (2010) about the treatment of mental health problems. They argue that currently a universal treatment based on Western research and values is being promoted throughout the world, irrespective of the cultural, social or economic context of the people involved (see also below).

hidden racism
advancing one's own race by non-conspicuous biases against other groups (usually by ignoring their contribution)

? What do you think?

According to Verhaeghe (2009), another example of current social influence is the tendency to blame people and the consequences this has for the relative importance of biological, psychological, and socio-cultural factors in the explanation of psychological phenomena (Chapter 12). Because it is easier to blame individuals for their biological and psychological faults than (powerful) social groups for their pathogenic values, the influence of social factors tends to be underplayed in the explanation of mental disorders. In addition, because it is less threatening for individuals in current society to blame their problems on a dysfunctional body than to a dysfunctional mind, biological explanations have an extra appeal. Consequently, biological factors nowadays dominate research on mental disorders. This not only relieves society and individuals of their responsibility to change their functioning; it also provides pharmaceutical companies with an opportunity to make money (see below). Do you agree with this assessment?

Socio-political influences on psychological practice

The socio-political context not only influences the theories built by psychologists, it also affects the conditions under which they work. Below we list two examples.

An increased interest in ethical issues

One of the developments of the last decades is an increased concern for ethical issues. Two big social changes lie at the heart of this shift. First, there was the acknowledgement that some experiments in the past (in particular medical experiments) were run despite knowing that they would harm the participants. An important catalyst in this respect was the large-scale medical research done in World War II, which came to light during the Nuremberg medical trials (1946–1947; Weindling 2004). The ethical issues raised at this trial (e.g. to what extent the forced sterilisations and experiments on inmates in Germany differed from those in the USA) resulted in the Nuremberg Code on the conduct of experiments with humans. A central principle in this code was informed consent. This principle stipulates that participants can only take part in an experiment after they have been informed about what will be involved (including the risks) and after they have explicitly and voluntarily given their consent to participate. Because of the vulnerable position in which individuals may find themselves when asked to give consent, it later became pivotal that an experiment not only involved informed consent from the participants, but also was approved by an independent body, an ethics committee.

The second social trend that made ethical issues central in research was the increased probability of legal action in case of a participant making a complaint. As a result, all official institutions introduced measures to ensure that no research could be carried out under their responsibility without proper ethical controls. Ethical codes of conduct were established and individual applications were checked to make sure they adhered to the code.

A typical example is the Code of Human Research Ethics established by The British Psychological Society, which can be downloaded from their website **www.bps. org.uk** (see also Kimmel 2007). It contains the following requirements for research with human participants:

informed consent

central principle in ethics, saying that people can only take part in a study after they have been informed of what will be involved and after they have explicitly and voluntarily agreed to participate

ethical code of conduct

protocol that includes all the ethics-related conditions to which a study must adhere

1. *Ethical approval for all research.* All research requires ethical approval by an independent body. This body makes sure that the research proposal adheres to the code.

2. *Protection of participants.* This not only involves protection from possible harm, but also preservation of the dignity and rights of the participants, and safeguards to ensure anonymity and confidentiality. Protection also requires competent supervision.

3. *Informed consent.* No research on a person may be carried out without the informed, free, express, specific and documented consent of the person. If the research cannot be done without concealing its true purpose, the ethics committee will make sure that the deception involved does not prevent the participants from giving informed consent.

4. *No coercion.* No participant should feel coerced to take part in a particular study.

5. *The right to withdraw.* Participants have the right to withdraw from any given research if they no longer feel comfortable. They can do so at any time without penalty and without providing a reason. Participants can also require that their data be withdrawn from the study.

6. *Anonymity and confidentiality*. Participants must be assured that all information they give will be treated with the utmost confidentiality and that their anonymity will be respected at all times unless otherwise determined by the law. Procedures for data storage must conform to the Data Protection Act.

7. *Appropriate exclusion criteria*. Researchers must make clear which participants cannot take part in the study (e.g. on the grounds of a pre-existing condition). These criteria must not involve arbitrary discrimination.

8. *Monitoring*. Researchers are obliged to monitor ongoing research for adverse effects on participants and to stop the research if there is cause for concern.

9. *Duty of care*. There is a duty of care on researchers to respect the knowledge of their participants and to ameliorate any adverse effects of their study. This involves the need for a debriefing at the end of the experiment. The debriefing consists of an explanation of the goals and the procedures of the study to the participants; it must also correct any form of deception that may have been included in the study.

10. *Additional safeguards for research with vulnerable populations*. Vulnerable populations include schoolchildren under the age of 18, people with learning or communication difficulties, patients, people in custody and probation, and people engaged in illegal activities. No research on these populations can be done without the additional written consent of the people responsible for them.

11. *Appropriate supervision*. Student investigators must be under the supervision of a member of academic staff and must be made aware of the relevant guidelines and of the need to observe them.

Codes of conduct are not only for those doing research. Similar codes have been established by professional societies to regulate the interactions between psychologists and clients. For instance, the British Psychological Society has a Code of Ethics and Conduct based on the following four domains of responsibility: respect, competence, responsibility and integrity. Each domain involves a number of values and is further defined by a set of standards (for further information, see the British Psychological Society 2006).

? What do you think?

An important aspect of everyday research in psychological departments is proper debriefing of the participants about the manipulations that were introduced and their possible effects/side-effects. After a review of existing practices Sharpe and Faye (2009) concluded, however, that debriefing is rarely detailed in research papers and often seems to have been minimal. Does this agree with your own experiences? Have a look at the recommendations given by Sharpe and Faye. Do you agree with them? Or are they unnecessarily prolonged for the majority of experiments you (have to) take part in? How much debriefing do you want or need after each experiment? Are there differences between experiments?

Litigation and the importance of documented evidence

One of the conclusions you may have drawn from this book thus far is that scientific knowledge is not to be trusted, because it is too tainted by the prevailing paradigm and the socio-political pressures that impinge on scientists. Such a conclusion can be defended and would put you in line with Feyerabend (who saw science as just another religion) and the postmodernists (who claimed that scientific knowledge is nothing but a social construction by the scientific community; see Chapter 9).

On the other hand, it is important to keep in mind that the very same biases apply to all kinds of knowledge and that the non-scientific approaches arguably have even fewer defences against them. Although scientists do make errors and from time to time and draw wrong conclusions on the basis of their findings, there are a number of mechanisms that allow others to evaluate the claims and to present counter-evidence. These are (see also Chapter 10):

- the requirement that the knowledge is coherent and cumulative (i.e. is related to the existing knowledge),
- the requirement that the knowledge is made available, so that it can be checked,
- the requirement to use well-defined and widely accepted methods of information gathering,
- the requirement of clarity of exposition (i.e. ambiguous statements are not accepted),
- the requirement that the knowledge is primarily based on prediction and falsification attempts,
- the requirement that the knowledge is not set in stone, but will be revised in the light of contradictory evidence.

Because of the above requirements, scientific knowledge is among the most trustworthy we have (though not fail-safe, as we have seen). Therefore, it is increasingly relied upon in Western society to make important decisions and to settle disagreements (e.g. in court). This brings us to a rather paradoxical situation: even though we are becoming increasingly aware of the relativity of scientific knowledge, we nevertheless rely more and more on it to make decisions, simply because the alternatives are more questionable. Although intelligence tests and achievement tests have their disadvantages, it is more acceptable to be excluded from a university on the basis of an achievement test taken by everyone, than on the basis of the whim of a single person deciding about the entry (e.g. Sacket *et al*. 2009). Students who have reason to believe the test was biased against them can search in the scientific literature for evidence to back their suspicion and can use this in their dispute. Similarly, groups that have good reason to question the usefulness of a test can campaign for another admission procedure (e.g. one no longer involving the initial selection of students) or for the use of another, better test.

On balance, the rising reliance on scientifically gathered evidence has been beneficial for psychologists, as their expertise has increasingly been called upon in situations that could give rise to appeals (Chapter 8). This led, for instance, to an explosion in the use of tests and psychological assessments in the judiciary system. An increasing number of verdicts are based on documented evidence by independent assessors rather than on subjective judgement alone.

Psychologists as pawns in power games

A main theme in sociology is the struggle for power between the various groups in society. Each group tries to increase its share of resources and its control over the others. Sometimes this results in an open conflict, but most of the time the tensions are sorted out by means of alliance formation. Psychologists as a group are entangled in this process. They try to improve their standing by manipulating others (see below), but at the same time they are constantly being used by other groups as part of their power struggle. An influential thinker about the use of power in societies was the French social historian and philosopher Michel Foucault (1926–1984).

Foucault and the power of discipline

In 1976 Foucault published a book, *Surveiller et punir* (Discipline and punish), in which he discussed how rulers discipline their inferiors. Until the eighteenth century, power was applied by brute force: by torturing, executing and burning those who defied the king's authority. This was often done in public to set an example. However, despite the use of brutality, the strategy was rather inefficient, because power was applied only sporadically, when a situation got out of hand.

A much better system was a constant surveillance system, in which minor deviances were immediately detected and corrected. An additional advantage of such a system was that it disciplined the subjects to such an extent that they automatically and unthinkingly followed the rules imposed upon them. Such an organisation became more and more dominant from the eighteenth century on, because in the industrial and the postindustrial world production started to depend on smooth interactions between large numbers of people who all performed specialised tasks.

One of the first examples of a surveillance system was the *Panopticon* proposed in 1785 by the British philosopher Jeremy Bentham. It consisted of a building with individual cells that could permanently be observed from a central tower. Bentham saw this as the ideal organisation for prisons, penitentiary houses, houses of industry, workhouses, poor-houses, factories, mad-houses, hospitals and schools. For efficiency purposes, he further proposed that the inmates must not be able to see into the observation tower, so that it was not necessary to permanently man the tower.

Another form of surveillance is to regularly check the workers. Medical (and later psychological) practitioners were brought in as part of this surveillance. The American sociologist F. Allan Hanson (1993) discussed two techniques that have been used in this respect. The first consisted of regular screenings with a lie detector. From time to time employees were required to take part in an interview about their functioning, while they were connected to a lie detector. Such a machine registers the physiological responses that accompany anxiety about lying (such as differences in blood pressure, sweating and changes in the voice). It was made clear to the employees that there was no point in trying to lie, because the machine would expose them. Lie detection tests became part of the working conditions in the USA in the 1980s. Hanson reported estimates of up to two million tests per year, until they were banned in 1988 for most purposes in the private sector (but not in the public sector), because they were experienced as too demeaning.

The second surveillance technique mentioned by Hanson (1993), and still in use, consisted of random drug tests, whereby the urine of employees is tested at random time intervals for the presence of illegal substances. Because of the unpredictable timing and the fact that they were able to trace drugs taken a few days before, these tests are extremely efficient within a surveillance system.

Within Foucault's world view, the primary role of psychologists is to help with the surveillance of mental health patients, students, employees and everyone else they are asked to assess and advise. The main task of psychologists is not to help clients, but to keep them in line with the prevailing social organisation. This also explains (part of) the popularity of their tests. As Hanson wrote:

What is unique about [medical and psychological] testing is that it has brought knowledge, control, and the social definition of the person to a new level of perfection and totality. Never before has any society deployed such a rich and ingenious panoply of dedicated techniques to scan, weigh, peruse, probe, and record the minutiae of its members' personal traits and life experiences. Never before has science, with all the power and prestige that have come to be associated with it, been brought so fully to bear on the problem of generating, storing, and retrieving precise knowledge about so many facets of the human individual. As a result of so much testing, it is certainly fair to say that more knowledge has been accumulated about individuals in contemporary society than at any previous time in history. This knowledge is used to control the behavior of individuals and also to characterize them in terms of their achievements and talents, their physical and mental characteristics, their normalities and abnormalities as measured along innumerable dimensions, many of which were not even recognized a century ago.

(Hanson 1993: 5)

Foucault's views on madness

Foucault's views about the treatment of mental disorders were even clearer in a previous book: *Folie et déraison* (Madness and civilization), published in 1961. In this book Foucault described how societies need outcasts, because their exclusion makes everyone else feel better. At first, the outcasts in the Western world were the people with contagious diseases, in particular leprosy. When they disappeared, society searched for a new group to exclude, which turned out to be the insane. Before, these people had been left alone, as they did not cause major problems. Under the new regime, however, they were locked up together with common criminals (Chapter 4).

With the rise of scientism and the fall of religion, mad people were no longer considered to be criminals, possessed by devils. However, this did not make them free again. Instead, the notion of mental illness was invented. The insane became subjects for diagnosis, discussion and regulation. They were locked up in asylums and put in the hands of hospital directors and psychiatrists. As happened in society at large, the way in which they were disciplined changed as well. They began to be managed through fear rather than through physical constraint. The wardens became the new social authority, both as judge and as representative of sanity. The insane were made aware of their madness by repeatedly being told of the irrationality of their fellow inmates.

Foucault (1961) further related the establishment of asylums to a change of values in Western society. Before the eighteenth century, the major sin was 'pride' (vanity); then it turned into 'idleness', the failure to work hard and utilise one's gifts and talents. Because of this change of values, idle people became perceived as rebels and, therefore, were confined to institutes where they were forced to work, even if the work did not result in utility or profit.

Again, in Foucault's world view, psychologists entered the system, not to change it but to continue it, to keep the insane obedient and tranquil at the outskirts of society.

What do you think?

What do you think of Foucault's assessment of psychologists as guardians and surveillants of the ruling powers?

KEY FIGURE Michel Foucault

- French philosopher and historian (1926–1984).
- Best known for his critical studies of social institutions, which he defined in terms of power seeking (e.g. the prison system, psychiatry and medicine).
- *Folie et déraison* (Madness and civilization): Book published in 1961, in which Foucault claimed that people suffering from mental disorders became treated as outcasts in the fifteenth–seventeenth centuries, because society needed such a stigmatised group after the gradual disappearance of the contagious illness leprosy.
- *Surveiller et punir* (Discipline and punish): Book published in 1976, in which Foucault argued that in current society power is no longer exerted by brute force but by constant surveillance and correction. Claimed that psychologists were part of the surveillance and correction machine.
- Also one of the first postmodernists to question the special status of science, and argue that scientific statements were social constructions, part of the constant power game in society.

Source: SIPA Press/ Rex Features.

The misuse of psychological knowledge by pseudoscientists

Another way in which psychologists have been used by society is that their knowledge has been hijacked by groups who did not subscribe to the scientific ethos. Arguably the most visible form of such misuse is the exploitation of psychological findings and tests by various types of alternative 'healers' and 'advisors' to strengthen their own claims, to give them credibility and to help them make money. Just as in many other sciences, psychological knowledge has been recycled by individuals who were not primarily interested in the truth of the findings (or at least in the fact that they were evidence-based), but in the extent to which they advanced their own case.

The knowledge spread by people who do not subscribe to the scientific ethos has variously been described as pop psychology, pseudopsychology and – more generally – pseudoscience, counterknowledge (Thompson 2008), mumbo-jumbo (Wheen 2004) or bullshit (Frankfurt 2005). The essential element of this type of knowledge is that evidence-based statements are freely combined with made-up statements, statements from dubious sources, and statements that are known to be wrong. As Frankfurt (2005) argued, such knowledge is worse than lying, because the user does not know what the truth is and does not care (unlike a liar). All that matters is whether a statement advances the case the person wants to make.

? What do you think?

Thompson (2008) holds that the internet has made the spreading of pseudoscience easier. As a result, he claims, this type of knowledge can rapidly gain power nowadays and turn into a 'counterknowledge industry', in which (big) money is made out of bogus science. Do you agree with this? Or do you think the internet helps people to become more critical, because they can more easily check the status of claims?

It can be argued that the status of pseudoscience has grown because of the post-modernist claim that science is nothing but a social construction by the community of scientists (see the 'science wars' in Chapter 9). Because postmodernists deny the objectiveness of scientific knowledge, they no longer make a distinction between evidence-based statements and made-up statements. The dangers of this attitude were illustrated by the American physicist Alan Sokal in 1996 when he submitted a manuscript for a special issue of the postmodernist journal *Social Text* devoted to the science wars. The manuscript, entitled 'Transgressing the boundaries: Toward a transformative hermeneutics of quantum gravity', defended an extreme form of cognitive relativism. It claimed that there was no external world, whose properties were 'independent of any individual human being and indeed of humanity as a whole'. As a result, it arrived at the conclusion that mathematical and physical notions such as Euclid's π (used for calculating the area and the circumference of a circle), formerly thought to be constant and universal, should be seen in their 'ineluctable historicity'.

The manuscript was accepted for publication without the need for any major revision, and published (Sokal 1996a). Sokal immediately wrote an accompanying article, in which he revealed the parody and showed how unfounded and nonsensical his claims were (Sokal 1996b). The original manuscript had been written with such leaps of logic 'that any competent physicist or mathematician (or undergraduate physics or math major) would realize that it is a spoof' (Sokal 1996b: 62). The fact that the paper was nevertheless published in a leading humanist journal showed how close the postmodernist view of science had come to pseudoscience (or any of the other words mentioned above), as can be seen in the following excerpts from Sokal:

> to test the prevailing intellectual standards, I decided to try a modest (though admittedly uncontrolled) experiment: Would a leading North American journal of cultural studies . . . publish an article liberally salted with nonsense if (a) it sounded good and (b) it flattered the editors' ideological preconceptions?
>
> The results of my little experiment demonstrate, at the very least, that some fashionable sectors of the American academic Left have been getting intellectually lazy. The editors of *Social Text* liked my article because they liked its conclusion: that 'the content and methodology of postmodern science provide powerful intellectual support for the progressive political project.' They apparently felt no need to analyse the quality of the evidence, the cogency of the arguments, or even the relevance of the arguments to the purported conclusion.
>
> (Sokal 1996b: 62)

In a later publication with the physicist, Jean Bricmont, Sokal stepped up his criticism. Sokal and Bricmont (1997) accused the postmodernists of abusing concepts and terminology coming from mathematics and physics by:

- referring to scientific theories about which they have, at best, an exceedingly hazy understanding; scientific terminology is used without bothering about what the words actually mean,

- importing concepts from the natural sciences without the slightest conceptual or empirical justification,

- displaying a superficial erudition by shamelessly throwing around technical terms in a context where they are completely irrelevant, with the sole goal to impress and intimidate the non-scientist reader.

Similar objections can be made against postmodernist revisions of psychology. 'Freeing psychology from its shackles of methods and theories' (Forshaw 2007) may be appealing (e.g. to students in exam times), but is unlikely to improve the quality of the services psychologists provide (APA Presidential Task Force on Evidence-based Practice 2006). There is no evidence that untrained managers are able to select personnel as well as qualified psychologists (quite on the contrary, as we have seen in Chapters 8 and 11) and the thought of having untutored people give therapy simply on the basis of their own intuitions and whims is not particularly reassuring either. There is a good deal of evidence that bona fide treatments (i.e. treatments based on therapies that have been validated and accepted in mainstream psychology) are better than non-bona fide treatments (Wampold *et al.* 2002; see also Messer 2004). Indeed, in most countries the main problem is not that existing psychologists are abusing their powers (although individual cases exist) but to protect clients from bogus therapists. Although scepticism of overdrawn scientific claims is healthy (Chapter 9), it may be good to keep in mind that a number of people are willing to assume scientific credentials (and the accompanying status in contemporary society) without the corresponding knowledge, training or ethics.

The misuse of psychological knowledge in times of war

An even more worrying concern is that psychological knowledge may become misused against people by psychologists themselves. An alleged example of such exploitation is the use of interrogation techniques based on learned helplessness in war prisoners (for a review, see Mayer 2008). Research in the 1960s showed that subjecting dogs to a series of electric shocks from which they could not escape destroyed them emotionally, so that they no longer tried to escape when, later, there was the possibility to do so. This research on learned helplessness was extremely important for the understanding of feelings of depression in individuals who no longer had control of their situation. Gradually it also became incorporated in the training of soldiers, to warn them in case they were captured.

At some point, however, according to Mayer the knowledge was reverse-engineered (by CIA psychologists) and used against so-called 'enemy combatants' in the American War on Terror. Although the charge provoked a sturdy response from the American Psychological Association, which issued a resolution reaffirming its position against torture or other cruel, inhuman or degrading treatment of enemy combatants (Resolution adopted by APA on 19 August 2007), concerns have been raised that the APA response was not fast enough and lacked the authority to prevent similar events in the future (e.g. Welch 2009). At least, the incident was a wake-up call that psychology is not immune to abuse of its knowledge and that psychologists may be actively involved in such mistreatment.

? What do you think?

Can you think of other examples in which psychologists may get involved in power struggles between social groups? Is there anything that can be done about this?

The meagre record of psychologists in power games so far

Although some authors are impressed by the impact psychologists have been able to make in society (e.g. Ward 2002 below), others are less overwhelmed. Cummings and O'Donohue (2008), for instance, point out that psychologists in America are among the worst-paid university graduates and that their financial situation is further deteriorating. They argue that psychologists have not played their cards well in the power games so far. They point to the following 'blunders' that have been made:

1. Psychologists have not been able to convince society that they have specific, worthwhile knowledge. In particular, they have failed to show that extra studies (e.g. a master's or PhD in clinical psychology) add further benefits.

2. Psychology has failed to form a proper alliance with medicine. There should be a psychologist in every primary care setting. The fact that this is not the case is due to the resistance of psychologists to the medical profession and to the fact that psychologists are single-minded about what treatment they are willing to offer (50-minute therapy sessions). The consequence is that functions psychologists should have (support, counselling, encouraging people to engage in health-improving activities, making sure patients adhere to their treatments, etc.) are taken up by nurses.

3. Psychology has failed to form a proper alliance with religion. As a result, its standing within church-related social and health services is compromised.

4. Academic and professional psychologists have failed to form a proper alliance, supporting and improving each other. As a result, education is less than optimal and practitioners have not been helped by academics to carve their niches.

5. Psychologists have a depreciating attitude to and deficient knowledge of money and economics. As a result they undersell themselves.

According to Cummings and O'Donohue psychologists must get their act together if they want to have a real standing in society. Currently they punch below their weight.

What do you think?

What do you think of Cummings and O'Donohue's assessment? Does it apply to your country as well, or do you find it exaggerated?

Interim summary

The ways in which society has influenced psychology

- A first factor in the growth of psychology was the decline of the impact of religion and the increase of scientific thinking in Western society.
- Society also provided topics and metaphors to the psychological researchers. Metaphors are analogies that help psychologists to better understand the phenomena they are investigating (e.g. the mind as a computer).
- Because science is a social enterprise, socio-political values have influenced the ideas psychologists put forward and the theories they examined. We illustrated this with the different views on intelligence testing and the changing roles of social and biological factors in gender identity.
- Society also influences the daily practice of psychologists. For instance, it has led to more interest in ethical issues and to an increased use of psychological tests in courts.

● According to sociologists, psychologists have been used in the power games that are going on in society. Foucault argued that psychologists were used for the surveillance of various groups. Psychology's findings have also been used by pseudo-scientists, who freely combined evidence-based statements with made-up claims. Furthermore, there is the concern that psychological knowledge may be misused against people (e.g. prisoners). Finally, some authors argue that psychologists have not played their cards well in the power games so far, so that their standing in society is lower than it could be.

13.2 Ways in which psychology has influenced society

In this section we will discuss ways in which psychology is thought to have influenced (Western) society. In particular we will focus on the critiques raised against psychology, as these tend to be covered less well in traditional psychology courses and help you to better understand the perceived role of psychologists in present-day life.

The psychologisation of society

Many psychologists do not realise it, but the impact psychology has on the way in which people interact is enormous. This is not due to the number of psychology students completing their studies each year (although psychology degrees are among the most popular at most universities), but to the number of other students who have psychology courses as part of their degrees, the number of articles devoted to psychology in newspapers and magazines, the number of radio and television programmes dedicated to psychological topics, and the frequency with which people talk to each other about psychological issues (see Chapter 8).

De Graaf and Kalmijn (2006) interviewed a large cohort of Dutch men and women who had been divorced, about their reasons for divorce. They found that the most frequently given reasons were psychology-related, such as 'we grew apart' (78% of respondents), 'we didn't pay enough attention to each other' (74%) and 'we were not able to talk' (73%). These reasons were given much more frequently than sexual problems (42%), physical violence (16%), alcohol or drugs problems (22%), infidelity of the spouse (37%) and division of household chores (22%). In addition, the impact of the psychology-related reasons showed a steady increase over the second half of the twentieth century: more people who had divorced towards the end of the century mentioned them than people who had divorced in the middle of the century.

The authors related these findings to what they called the psychologisation of society, the fact that economic ties in primary relationships have become less important over time, whereas emotional ties have grown in importance. The sociologist Steven Ward (2002), who critically reviewed the development of psychology, used the word in a slightly different way. In his view, psychologisation refers to the growing impact of psychology on society. This is how he started his final chapter, entitled 'The psychologization of the United States':

> Throughout this book I have tried to illustrate how over the course of the last century psychological categories and practices became 'naturalized.' As this happened, psychology, like other naturalized ideas and categories, 'disappeared into infrastructure, into habit, into the taken for granted' . . .

psychologisation

word used with two different meanings referring to: (1) the fact that emotional ties and personal well-being have become important in primary social relations, or (2) the growing impact of psychology on the way people see themselves and interact with others

Psychology's presence in schools, workplaces and homes is now an ordinary and seemingly indispensable feature of the cultural landscape. As a result of its presence we are now aware that there are children with varying IQ levels, that motivation can be enhanced through certain psychological techniques, that healthy marriages necessitate open communication, that people have certain psychological needs that require fulfillment, that aptitude can be gauged through psychological measurements and that self-esteem determines how we interact with others . . . As a result of this naturalization process, psychology is now 'part of the order of the universe'

(Ward 2002: 217)

A definition similar to Ward's was used by Gulerce (2006), who argued that psychologisation is not limited to the Western world, but is becoming a global phenomenon. It is also the definition we will use in this chapter. In the sections below we review some more examples of the ways in which psychology has influenced society.

Psychology has changed how people perceive each other

Labels introduced by psychology become real

One of the big social changes in the past centuries has been the growing individualisation (Chapter 8), the fact that people organise their lives more in terms of their own characteristics and ambitions rather than the groups they belong to. Psychology has been an important element in this transition, because many of the concepts through which people differentiate themselves come from psychological writings. For example, before Jung made a distinction between introverts and extroverts, nobody perceived people in these terms. Similarly, only after the concepts were introduced could people be seen as 'neurotic', 'depressed', 'intelligent', 'resilient', 'lacking in self-esteem', and so on.

Many psychological concepts became part of everyday life, once they had been coined. After psychiatrists and psychologists defined the concept 'depression' (actually major depression), people started to interpret their feelings with respect to this entity. The question was no longer whether people were sad or down, but whether they 'were depressed'. This was done first by psychiatrists and psychologists, later by popular psychology magazines, and in the end by everyone.

Another example is the concept of 'intelligence'. It can be argued that the present-day meaning of this word in terms of mental capacity did not exist before Galton and Binet started their research (Chapter 4). Indeed, in societies not yet influenced by Western thought there is no word for 'intelligent' with this particular meaning, in contrast to words referring to wise, handy and socially skilful. In Western society, however, the word has come to refer to what arguably is one of the most important qualities of an individual.

Labels introduced by psychology change the subject of psychology

It has been argued that the introduction of new concepts by psychologists not only changes the social reality for other people but also for (future) psychologists (Richards 2002; Tyson *et al.* 2011). Just like everyone else, new psychology students wrongly believe that the concepts currently used in psychology and the wider culture refer to 'natural personal qualities', which have always been there (because they are part of the person observed) and not to qualities that – to some extent – are the result of prior developments in psychological research.

As a result of previous research the subject matter observed by psychologists today is different from the subject matter observed in the past. Richards (2002) called this psychology's *reflexive relationship* with its subject matter (in sociology, reflexivity refers to a situation in which the act of examining changes the event that is examined). An example of this reflexive relationship can be seen in the research on performance differences between races. Before the concept 'racism' became used in the 1930s, researchers could comfortably examine such differences and interpret them as the outcome of innate differences (which some happily did, as we saw above). However, as soon as the concept of 'racism' became used as a person trait to explain the atrocities committed in the name of racial superiority, race-related research became charged and shifted from studying performance differences to studying prejudice (Teo 2008).

What do you think?

One of the purposes of this book is to show you the historical and socio-cultural relativity of (psychological) knowledge. Of the examples given, which one struck you as the most revealing? Can you think of others?

Psychological labels are to some extent arbitrary

The sociologist Hanson (1993) pointed out that new psychological concepts not only make new realities, but also define them in arbitrary ways, because the concepts have been introduced without a good understanding of what was involved. He argued that when Binet and Simon selected a few tasks to measure intelligence, they could not suspect that these tasks would become part of the definition of intelligence for the coming century. As Boring (1923) famously declared: 'intelligence is what an intelligence test measures'.

Hanson illustrated the arbitrariness of psychological concepts by giving the example of an alternative way in which intelligence could have been tested (Hanson 1993: 279–80). He called this test the New Intelligence Test (NIT). Instead of Binet and Simon's tasks (Chapter 4), the NIT contained the following scales:

1. *A name recall scale*: ability to remember the names of persons to whom one has just been introduced.

2. *A mathematics scale*: measures the subject's ability to do problems of arithmetic and algebra.

3. *The first impression scale*: measures the first impression the subject makes by having a panel of ordinary people evaluate him/her.

4. *An exposition of ideas scale*: the subject is given 5 minutes to read a page of text and 30 minutes to present a clear and accurate written account of it, including original examples and applications. A possible example of such a text is a page from the French philosopher Rousseau describing his distinction between self-love (*amour de soi*) and selfishness (*amour propre*).

5. *A small-talk scale*: evaluates the subject's ability to carry on an interesting conversation with someone he/she has never met.

6. *A bullshitting scale*: evaluates the subject's skill at participating in a discussion with two other people on a topic about which he/she knows nothing.

7. *A follow-the-directions scale*: the subject is told once, at the speed of ordinary conversation, to do a task that consists of six distinct steps and is evaluated on how well the task is accomplished.

8. *The adult sports scale*: measures the subject's ability to play golf or tennis.

9. *The SES scale*: is a rating of the subject according to the parental socioeconomic status.

Hanson argued that if this scale (which he purposely called the NITWIT scale) had attained the same status as Binet and Simon's, then this is how intelligence would have been defined by society. The resulting NITWIT score would have indicated whether a student was given entry to various schools and universities, whether s/he would be given particular jobs, and how much on average s/he would earn. As a result, people would see the NITWIT score as an indication of a unitary trait, representing the worth of a person. A further exciting development would be a distinction between culture-free NITWIT tests (measuring a person's potential and making it possible for psychologists to measure the heredity of the trait) and NITWIT achievement tests (making it possible to assess how well students master NITWIT).

Society adapts to the label

Hanson further argued that once a psychological label has become reality, society starts to adapt itself to the new measure, thereby further increasing the reality of the concept. With respect to the New Intelligence Test, Hanson mused how parents would agonise whether their children are NITWITty enough, how they could be helped to attain their maximum NITWIT potential, and how to make sure that children do not underestimate the importance of doing well on NITWIT tests. As Hanson wrote:

> They would review arithmetic and algebra, they would master techniques for remembering the names of strangers, they would practice bullshitting, they would take golf and tennis lessons, they would groom themselves to appear more likable on first sight. High school and college curricula would shift in the direction of more training in the areas covered by the NIT (if they did not, irate parents would demand to know why their children were not being taught something useful).

> (Hanson 1993: 280)

A complete industry of NITWIT study guides and training courses would become available, supervised by NITWIT specialists and also seized upon by pseudo-psychologists, who would try to make a good living out of it (possibly helped by their high scores on the scales of first impression, small-talk and bullshitting).

This, Hanson argued, is what has happened to the IQ test and the derived achievement tests. They have become all-invasive in Western society without anybody knowing what they were measuring and whether they really mattered. However, as a result of society's eagerness to adapt, year after year the test is becoming more inescapable, because it measures one of the most important aspects of Western society.

What do you think?

Sociologists have their own view of society. In sociological writings groups try to achieve power, despite the fact that they have nothing to offer. So, with respect to psychology, sociologists claim that society has been psychologised, not because this was good for society (or because society chose it), but because psychologists were instrumental in keeping the masses well behaved and within their social classes, because psychologists were good at befriending those in power, or because they were good at convincing people of the need for psychological advice. What answer would you give to the sociologists' assumption that psychology has nothing to offer? Is it true, for example, that IQ tests are completely arbitrary and in no way helpful to the individuals who take them?

Psychologists make friends

To make your way in society, according to sociologists it is imperative to have influential friends who can assist you. This is important not only for individuals and groups (e.g. the inhabitants of a village), but also for new branches of learning. As illustrated several times in this book, psychologists have vigorously tried to associate themselves with the natural sciences, despite the fact that most individuals did not perceive them that way (see Chapter 10). In turn, the natural sciences saw enough advantage in these advances to tolerate them (e.g. because a coalition with psychology increased the weight of the sciences in the culture, or because psychology brought many students to the science faculty, given that it was a popular study option). However, the position of psychology relative to the natural sciences was rarely one of equals. Therefore, according to Ward (2002), it was desirable for psychology to find other allies, preferably ones over which it had some say, ones who would agree that psychology had something they wanted and needed.

Educational psychology

The first group that welcomed input from psychology was the educationalists. In the late nineteenth century, the educational sector had a low status. The schooling of teachers was rudimentary and they were barely represented at university level. At the same time, the number of pupils was rising exponentially as a consequence of the compulsory education introduced in one country after the other. As Ward noted:

> With such a rapid expansion, educators yearned to obtain professional status, public respect and a means for managing the onslaught of new students. Psychologists were in the unique position of being able to offer assistance in all three of these objectives.
>
> (Ward 2002: 60)

Psychologists, eager to prove their usefulness, swiftly became involved in educational matters. Already in 1892, William James had given a series of public lectures to teachers. He was soon followed by Stanley Hall and, above all, by Edward Thorndike, who in 1906 published *The principles of teaching based on psychology* and in 1910 founded the *Journal of Educational Psychology*. Rapidly, psychologists and teachers agreed that psychology was a core component of a teacher's qualification.

In addition, psychology started to introduce its intelligence tests in schools and began to lobby for school counsellors. As Ward (2002) noted, schools were the first arena in which society was psychologised.

Advising parents

From its stronghold in schools, it was a small step to also raid the fledgling literature of parenting. Psychologists became involved in manuals about how to raise children. The pioneer here was Stanley Hall, who widely published about adolescents (Chapter 10). Another well-known psychologist venturing into the domain was the behaviourist John Watson, who urged parents to raise children according to behaviourist principles (Chapter 9). The end result was that new mothers felt less and less secure in relying on the advice of their own mothers, but took for granted that they needed 'expert' advice is order to properly educate their children.

Psychologists create needs

Institutions strive for monopolies by creating needs

A considerable part of the socio-political literature is devoted to the ways in which groups of people and institutions try to gain power. They do so by exaggerating the problems for which they claim to have a solution and by sending out alarming messages. When a government establishes a new institute to tackle a problem, one of the first things the institute will do is look for ways to increase the chances of its survival and prosperity (some sociologists would argue that most of the time this even comes before the real brief of solving the problem). So, the institute will initiate a number of actions stressing the gravity of the situation and the urgent need for action. It will organise workshops, publish flyers and reports, and lobby for extra funds. In a nutshell, it will do its best to convince others of the need for widespread action on the problems it comes to identify and for which it is providing solutions. (The same is true for charities and initiatives in the private sector.)

An interesting writer in this literature is the Austrian-born scholar Ivan Illich (1926–2002), who travelled between America (including Mexico and Latin America) and Europe. In a series of books, Illich (1971, 1973, 1976) argued that the greed for power is not limited to small-scale, starting initiatives, but is true for all sections of society. Once they are established, they try to increase their slice of the economy by creating new needs. They are not in the first place concerned with helping people, but with trying to make individuals dependent on their services. The following quote is typical of Illich's approach:

> Intensive education turns autodidacts into unemployables, intensive agriculture destroys the subsistence farmer, and the deployment of police undermines the community's self-control. The malignant spread of medicine has comparable results: it turns mutual care and self-medication into misdemeanors or felonies.
>
> (Illich 1976: 42)

Illich's account of medicine

Most interesting for us here is the 1976 book *Limits to medicine – Medical nemesis: The expropriation of health*. In this book Illich argues that the medical and pharmaceutical worlds enormously overstate their significance for the health of people (see Blech 2006 for a contemporary update). It is true that life expectancy has increased substantially in the last century, parallel to the development of medicine. However, the most important factors for this evolution, according to Illich, were the reduction of famine, the availability of clean water and fresh air, and improved sanitation (e.g. by the installation of sewers and by pointing doctors to the importance of washing their hands before attending to patients). Figure 13.1 shows one of the arguments Illich used for his claim. Though medicine is thought to have had a substantial impact on the incidence of tuberculosis, mortality rates due to tuberculosis decreased long before the origin and the cure for the disease were found. Neither of these events had a major influence on the rate of decrease.

On the basis of findings like these, Illich claimed that the best treatment of diseases would consist of (a) creating the conditions that prevent diseases (i.e. good hygiene, food and – as we now know – enough exercise), and (b) having a slimmed-down health service for emergencies in which it is known that short-term interventions can alleviate a lot of suffering. Illich reckons that a few dozens of medicines would suffice for this.

However, this is not how the medical world has developed. Instead of a modest profession, it has grown into a Moloch that makes doctors and pharmaceutical companies rich and that may take away up to one-fifth of the resources of a developed country. This was achieved in large part by doing needless tests and by inventing new illnesses for which cures were sold. Although Illich does not deny that medicine has known some successes, he claims that these are offset entirely by the following hidden costs:

1. medicine causes a lot of suffering in terminal patients,

2. medical gains are largely offset by doctor-inflicted injuries (e.g. side-effects of drugs, infections and accidents in hospitals, growth of new, more resistant organisms as a result of treatments),

3. medical practice promotes sickness by reinforcing a morbid society, which encourages people to become consumers of curative and preventive medicine,

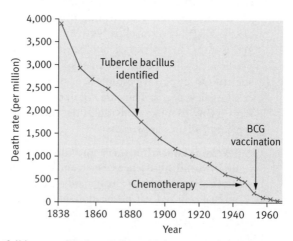

Figure 13.1 The fall in mortality from tuberculosis.

Notice how the decline started before the origin of the disease was discovered and before different types of treatment became available. According to Illich, this shows that the decline had little to do with the medical treatment of the disease, but rather with better hygiene and improved nutrition.

Source: McKeown (1979). Reproduced with permission.

4. health professionals have a health-denying effect insofar as they destroy the potential of people to deal with their human weakness, vulnerability and uniqueness in a personal and autonomous way.

Or as Illich summarised it:

> After a century of pursuit of medical utopia, and contrary to current conventional wisdom, medical services have not been important in producing the changes in life expectancy that have occurred. A vast amount of contemporary clinical care is incidental to the curing of disease, but the damage done by medicine to the health of individuals and populations is very significant. These facts are obvious, well documented, and well repressed.
>
> (Illich 1976: 14–15)

Marketing depression in Japan

The journalist Ethan Watters (2010: Chapter 4) documents how pharmaceutical companies, in line with Illich's analysis, promoted antidepressants in Japan in the early 2000s. The use of these drugs was much lower in Japan than in Western countries, despite comparable living standards. To understand this difference, a group of psychiatrists, psychologists and anthropologists specialising in health-related cultural differences was convened. At this conference it became clear that the American definition of depression was not universal. Many cultures did not share the American willingness to express distressful emotions and feelings to strangers and did not consider these as a health care issue. Rather they saw 'depression-related' symptoms as signs of social, spiritual or moral discord, which had to be sorted out through conversations with family members, community elders or spiritual leaders. As a result, they were unlikely to go to a physician asking for drugs to treat the condition.

Specifically with respect to Japanese people, it became clear that sad feelings for them were more related to others than the Western inward definition based on internal emotional states. The Japanese word for depression referred to a rare, severe condition thought to be inborn and incurable. As a result, Japanese psychiatrists felt little affinity with many Western writings about depression. The only equivalent they could think of was the term *melancholic personality type* introduced in the 1960s by a German professor. This term had caught on in Japan because its definition was close to a personality style well-known and respected in Japan: someone who was serious, diligent, thoughtful and concerned about the welfare of others, and who could become overwhelmed with sadness when upheaval threatened that welfare.

Adverts were launched alluding to the melancholic personality type (with its positive connotations of being sensitive to the welfare of others and to discord within the family or group). The adverts also compared depressive feelings to a 'cold of the soul', suggesting that it could happen to everyone and that it was perfectly treatable with drugs. Gradually, these messages were picked up by newspapers and magazines and, as hoped, the sales of antidepressants started to increase. At last, the Japanese population was convinced of the existence of 'depression' as defined in the Western world (in particular, by pharmaceutical companies).

The extension to psychology

Creating needs is not limited to the medical profession and pharmaceutical companies. According to sociologists, very much the same is true for psychologists. To them the extension is obvious: psychologists are not in the first place interested in helping people, but in creating needs so that they can expand their industry. This thinking can be found in several places, for instance in the following quote:

> In recent times, we have witnessed a marked rise in the discovery of numerous psychopathologies and syndromes. A wide variety of psychological difficulties and problems are now recognized as constituting identifiable symptoms or characteristics of syndromes previously unheard of. PreMenstrual Syndrome (PMS), battered woman syndrome, and attention-deficit disorder are just some of the disorders lately 'discovered' and offered up for public attention. Alongside this increase in the discovery and categorization of these types of problems is a parallel rise in the provision of counselling and therapy. Of course, if these syndromes are indeed unmitigated discoveries, the rise in therapy provision is an unambiguous blessing. However, it can be argued that the therapy industry, like any other, creates as well as serves a need.
>
> (Burr & Butt 2000: 186)

Another author very critical of the contribution of psychological therapy is the British sociologist Frank Furedi (e.g. Furedi 2004). In his view, normal everyday worries are given unnecessary psychological labels and put in line for psychological and medical treatment. A therapeutic ethos is pervading society, which can be summarised as follows. Currently people are exposed to much more stress than before. Only the strongest can withstand such stress without therapeutic help. Most individuals are biologically and psychologically vulnerable to developing some form of mental disorder. Help should primarily be geared towards the individual, to make him/her biologically and psychologically stronger by means of drugs and psychotherapy. People are told to avoid stressful situations and to expect severe emotional distress, otherwise:

> The expansion of therapeutic intervention into all areas of society has been remarkable. Even institutions which explicitly depend on the spirit of stoicism and sacrifice, such as the military, police and emergency services are now plagued with problems of emotion. It is often claimed that police and emergency personnel are particularly susceptible to stress-related illnesses, including post-traumatic stress disorder (PTSD). The very conduct of war is regularly portrayed through the language of mental illness.
>
> (Furedi 2004: 11)

The outcome of the therapeutic ethos is not, according to Furedi, that people feel better and stronger (as psychologists want them to believe) but weaker and anxious, dependent on psychology's services. The ethos is not making individuals more resilient, but installs in them maladaptive schemas and makes them prone to rumination (in line with suggestions made by Ellis, Beck and Nolen-Hoeksema; Chapter 12). People are taught to expect stress from all possible changes and to feel bad about it.

Ecclestone and Hayes (2009) argue that the same therapeutic ethos has pervaded (British) education. Education no longer is an enterprise in which young and energetic pupils are taught useful skills and knowledge by confident teachers. Instead, it has turned into a system of 'therapeutic education' in which cautious, hesitant adults try to guide vulnerable, at-risk children who are on the verge of losing their self-esteem. The bad feelings expected to result from school and life experiences are dealt with by forcing pupils into an endless series of therapeutic activities based on disclosing emotions to others (peers, teachers, tutors, counsellors and therapists). Challenges and transitions are no longer seen as opportunities but as sources of stress for which pupils need emotional support and guidance, even those who on the surface do not 'seem' to need help.

The end result, according to Eccleston and Hayes, is not that children feel happier and more resilient but turn into anxious and self-preoccupied individuals, afraid of taking initiative and devoid of proper subject knowledge, because 'teachers are also required to surrender their subject authority and to reveal their own uncertainties: indeed, too much commitment to subjects is now seen as "dysfunctional"' (2009: 80).

After having described the effects of therapeutic education in primary and secondary school, this is how Ecclestone and Hayes (2009: 87–89) depict students' entry into the 'therapeutic university':

> Students once went to school. They did not go there to receive therapy but went in the hope of receiving something called 'an education'. As we have shown in previous chapters, they will increasingly have experienced training in therapeutic activities. More and more young people are therefore increasingly likely to come to university with the expectations that reflect their therapeutic education. . . .
>
> Once, the experience of going to university was worthwhile precisely because of opportunities for new and challenging ideas, while the practical and personal challenges of moving away from home were insignificant in the excitement of facing intellectual challenge. Now, far from being a relief, these challenges make students anxious.
>
> Even if students do not come with parents holding their hands, paid professionals are there to act *in loco parentis*. Supporting students has now become a major focus of university work. There are transitional support groups and processes, explicit counselling to deal with personal problems, and courses to help students cope with examination stress. . . .
>
> Even if students leave their parents and their new professional parents behind and are ready for an intellectual challenge, they will learn that academic life is fraught with dangers that could affect their emotional health and well-being. Their first week will be spent on 'Induction' courses designed by administrators, student services and academics that will be about advice and support and little else. The assumption of such courses is that young people are increasingly unable to cope with the changes involved in leaving home and going to university.

The outcome of the therapeutic academic education for Eccleston and Hayes (2009: 104) has been more beneficial for psychologists than for students and lecturers. Universities no longer produce academics who are natural critics with confident, independent minds, but socially passive individuals with threatened selves. Lecturers are told no longer to consider courses as intellectual opportunities for students, but as possible stress generators that must be delivered carefully and cautiously. The only ones to profit from this situation are the psychologists and social workers who are called upon in ever increasing numbers to 'help' students cope with the stress, to 'support' staff and administrators trying to manage the torrent of emotional turmoil, and to evaluate the progress thus far.

? What do you think?

Does Ecclestone and Hayes's (2009) depiction of therapeutic education agree with your experiences? If yes, do you agree with their assessment that it has diminished your energy and resilience? If not, how have they misunderstood the situation?

Psychologists promote values

Psychologists spread Western views of wellness and healing around the world

Watters (2010) describes how psychologists, together with medical practitioners, contribute to spreading the therapeutic ethos across the world:

> Behind the promotion of Western ideas of mental health and healing lies a variety of cultural assumptions about human nature itself. Westerners share, for instance, beliefs about what type of life event is likely to make one psychologically traumatized, and we agree that venting emotions by talking is more healthy than stoic silence. We are certain that humans are innately fragile and should consider many emotional experiences as illnesses that require professional intervention. We're confident our biomedical approach to mental illness will reduce stigma for the sufferer and that our drugs are the best that science has to offer. We promise people in other cultures that mental health (and a modern style of self-awareness) can be found by throwing off traditional social roles and engaging in individualistic quests of introspection. These Western ideas of the mind are proving as seductive to the rest of the world as fast food and rap music, and we are spreading them with speed and vigor.
>
> (Watters 2010: 4)

Watters (Chapter 2) documents how the devastating tsunami of 2004 in Asia with its quarter-million dead not only brought material aid workers to the affected regions but also a stream of mental health workers. Psychologists and social workers were drawn to the region because they feared it would be faced with a gigantic post-traumatic stress disorder (PTSD) if no proper psychological help and prevention work was provided. Discussion groups and play groups (for the children) were organised amidst the rubble to relieve and neutralise the horrors gone through. Apart from questions about whether there is something like a genuine PTSD for natural disasters (the term was coined after the Vietnam War) and how effective psychotherapeutic help is for such a condition, Watters narrates how little these initiatives struck a chord with the locals:

> In the days after the disaster, reporters and clinicians arriving from the United States and elsewhere sometimes seemed confused, even concerned, when the local population didn't behave the way they'd expected. One trauma counselor being interviewed on BBC radio from a small coastal village expressed his worry that the local children appeared more interested in returning to school than discussing their experience of the tsunami. These children were 'clearly in denial,' the expert told the listening audience. The host of the program concurred, saying, 'Of course, everyone knows that children are the most vulnerable to trauma such as this.' The expert then confidently concluded that only later would the children 'experience the full emotional horror of what has happened to them.' Similarly, CNN reports expressed their amazement when tens of thousands of Sri Lankans attempted to abandon their refugee camps just days after the disaster, preferring to go back to their devastated villages or depend on friends or family.
>
> (Watters 2010: 77)

The mental health professionals disagreed with the locals on another aspect. Many victims of the disaster sought meaning and sense in religion and superstition. These too seemed examples of denial and problem avoidance (as if the Enlightenment never took place). The discrepancies between the health professionals and the locals made Watters (2010: 106) conclude that:

Although undertaken as humanitarian outreach, these efforts often look more like massive attempts at indoctrination. To accept the ideas of PTSD, other cultures first had to be 'educated' in the appropriate symptoms of PTSD and modern modes of healing.

According to Watters, the psychologists drawn to the devastated regions not only reached out to help; in the process they also imposed on the victims Western views of how to respond to disaster and to deal with its aftermath. They questioned the cultural narratives those people had to cope with tragedy. To drive the point home, Watters recounted the following analogy told to him:

> Imagine our reaction . . . if Mozambicans flew over after 9/11 and began telling survivors that they needed to engage in a certain set of rituals in order to sever their relationships with their deceased family members. How would that sit with us? Would that make sense?
>
> (2010: 107)

In particular, the Western psychologists were projecting their view that all responsibility for making sense of the world and dealing with adversity lay within the individual.

> By isolating trauma as a malfunction of the mind that can be connected to discrete symptoms and targeted with new and specialized treatments, we have removed the experience of trauma from other cultural narratives and beliefs that might otherwise give meaning to suffering. Being value-neutral to cultural beliefs is problematic given that these beliefs – be it God's plan for someone who's lost a child or patriotism for the soldier crippled in battle – are the very places where we once found solace and psychological strength.
>
> (Watters 2010: 121)

Psychologists are not politically neutral

A number of authors have argued that psychologists within the Western world are not politically neutral. For instance, the American lawyer and psychologist Richard Redding (2001) observed that although psychologists celebrate diversity, recognise the value and legitimacy of diverse beliefs and by their own admission strive to be inclusive, conservatives are a vastly underrepresented and marginalised minority in psychology (see Table 13.2 for ways in which conservative and liberal views differ). In an analysis of two social journals, Redding found that only 1 in 30 articles reflected conservative values; the others all advanced liberal themes and policies. Similarly, he noticed that in America psychology departments rank fifth in the percentage of staff who call themselves politically liberal.

Redding (2001) argued that as a consequence of their bias, psychology departments are a force in the promotion of left and liberal values in the society. He listed several ways in which this happens, the most important of which are:

● Research biases in policy research. Given that the way in which one defines a problem has an influence on the type of response one finds, Redding argues that if one asks liberal questions, one is likely to get liberal answers.

● Discrimination against students and scholars who do not share liberal attitudes and values. Redding lists examples of biases against students who mentioned their conservative convictions in the application forms to universities, and against researchers who apply for grants or submit manuscripts that are in line with conservative positions.

Table 13.2 Some differences between conservative (right-wing) and liberal
(left-wing) world views

	Conservative	Liberal
Individual differences	Mainly innate	Mainly the result of education
Remedies for social problems	Responsibility of the individual and his/her family	Responsibility of society
Responsibility for life circumstances	Individual	Society
Source of moral authority	Extrinsic (e.g. reliance on natural law or God)	Intrinsic (own morals)
Interpersonal relations	Ideal of tough-mindedness	Ideal of tender-mindedness
Ideal family model	Authoritarian – paternalistic	Egalitarian – nurturing

Source: Based on Redding (2001), 'Sociopolitical diversity in Psychology: The case for pluralism', *American Psychologist*, 56, 205–15.

- Biases in the educational contents. Students are not equally exposed to the different political perspectives on social issues and find it hard to defend conservative points of view in classroom debates. Given the strong influence lecturers have on students, this directs initially neutral students to the left.

- Biases in values promoted by psychotherapists. Partly because of their left-biased education, psychologists will promote liberal views in their own work. According to Redding (2001: 208): 'because a shifting process often occurs in therapy whereby the client's values gravitate toward those of the therapist . . . , there is the ethical concern that therapists may impose their liberal values on conservative clients.'

Redding (2001) further argued that the liberal bias of psychologists has consequences for psychology's standing in society. In particular, he argued:

- Psychologists have less influence on socio-political issues under conservative rule.

- Psychologists have less to offer to individuals with conservative socio-political values. For instance, given that the success of psychotherapy depends on the match between the client and the therapist, psychotherapists will be less good when it comes to treating conservative clients.

- Researchers are not critical enough when it comes to evaluating liberal policies. In contrast, they are hypercritical about the worth of rightward proposals.

A similar conclusion was reached by Cummings and O'Donohue (2008), who wrote:

> The consistently 'leftish' positions that APA [American Psychological Association] has taken on many political issues alienate the large majority of Americans who identify themselves as moderate or conservative. A recent AP-Ipsos poll found that only 6% of Americans described themselves as 'very liberal,' 15% as 'somewhat liberal,' 34% as 'moderate,' 27% as 'somewhat conservative,' and 14% as 'conservative.' The positions described by policy resolutions from the mental health field are slanted toward those describing themselves as 'very liberal.' Thus, these positions place the APA out of sync with the majority of the American public.

(Cummings & O'Donohue 2008: 181)

What do you think?

Do you agree with Redding and Cummings and O'Donohue that psychologists have a bias against right-wing ideas and opinions? Or is this view too strong? Why would such a bias exist? Try to think of a conservative proposal that might throw a different light on an issue discussed in one of your psychology courses and that could be an interesting starting point for thought or for an empirical study.

Psychology increases the weight of science in the competition with the humanities

Although in Chapter 10 we saw that a considerable segment of academic psychologists see themselves as humanists and that many psychology practitioners prefer to forget the scientific lessons once they have completed their studies, it cannot be denied that mainstream psychology has chosen the side of science in the two cultures' competition. Indeed, the *raison d'être* for psychology as a separate branch of knowledge was the *scientific* study of the human mind (Chapters 4 and 5).

As a result, psychology as a discipline has largely promoted the virtues of the scientific approach and downplayed the contribution of the humanities. Indeed, some psychologists have been among the most ardent promoters of the positivist movement, praising the progress of science as opposed to the standstill of humanist knowledge, as can be seen in the following citation:

> Greek physics and biology are now of historical interest only (no modern physicist or biologist would turn to Aristotle for help), but the dialogues of Plato are still assigned to students and cited as if they threw light on human behavior. Aristotle could not have understood a page of modern physics or biology, but Socrates and his friends would have little trouble in following most current discussions of human affairs. And as to technology, we have made immense strides in controlling the physical and biological worlds, but our practices in government, education, and much of economics, though adapted to very different conditions, have not greatly improved.
>
> (Skinner 1971: 11)

Similarly, many psychology researchers in their communication with the general public stress the superiority of their findings relative to common knowledge, because their findings are based on scientific evidence. In doing so, they use the positivistic discourse about scientific evidence (always correct and trustworthy) rather than the more correct Popperian or Kuhnian interpretation (Chapter 9). They most certainly are not referring to Feyerabend's (1975) recommendation that politicians must not be replaced by scientists, because the latter are too often carried away by their latest theories and hypotheses (which still have to be slaughtered by their peers or by a paradigm shift).

Psychologists are not neutral to religion

Authors who point to the liberal and scientific biases of psychologists also raise the issue of the consequences this has for psychologists' views about religion, which in general tend to be rather sceptical. This is how Cummings and O'Donohue (2008: 196) phrased it:

It never ceases to amaze me [sic] how many prominent, virulently antireligious psychologists I meet; it is also obvious that negative attitudes toward religion have become politically correct in psychology. . . . Unfortunately, this has damaged the APA's credibility as a scientific/professional body. It is increasingly viewed as just another political advocacy group that speaks from ideology rather than science.

As we saw above, Watters (2010), in a very different context, also noticed that few psychologists are able to see religion as a source giving meaning to life and adversity. Even if psychologists do not talk openly about their religious views, in subtle ways their attitudes impose values on the people they work with.

What do you think?

It could be argued that the biases discerned in psychologists (leftish, in favour of science, critical of religion) are not unique to this group but present in a large part of educated society. Does this mean that the biases cannot be attributed to psychology itself but to civilisation in general? Or would this be downplaying psychology's responsibility?

Interim summary

Critical views about the ways in which psychology has influenced society

- Psychology has contributed to the psychologisation of society. This word refers to two phenomena: first, to the fact that individuals have become seen as persons with their own thoughts and emotions, second, to the growing impact of psychology on the way people interact.
- Labels introduced by psychology have become social realities, because they influenced the way people saw themselves and others, and because society adapted itself to the new labels, despite the fact that they were to some extent arbitrary.
- Psychologists have tried to increase their power by making alliances with established groups, such as the natural sciences, and by extending their reach to new, upcoming groups (e.g. educationists).
- Psychologists also tried to increase their power by creating new needs for which they claimed to have solutions (Illich). They also export these values to the rest of the world.
- Psychologists are not politically neutral, but promote liberal values. This decreases the help they can give to people with conservative values.
- Psychologists also tend to promote science in the 'two cultures' competition and have difficulty endorsing religion as a meaning provider.

13.3   *Focus on*: To what extent have psychologists been able to change the negative image of mental disorders?

You may have noticed a contradiction in the first two parts of this chapter. On the one hand, psychologists are not portrayed as a powerful group with a high status. On the other hand, they are accused of having psychologised Western society and of now exporting their views to the rest of the world. How can we account for this contradiction?

Psychologisation is not steered by psychologists alone

One explanation may be that the psychologisation of society is not fully steered by psychologists, and that it is due as much to what the public thinks psychology is, as it is to what actually happens in psychological research. As we saw in Chapter 10, the public does not have a very accurate image of psychologists. Their opinions are a mish-mash of information from the media, stereotypes promoted in culture, and social biases. Still, these opinions are a powerful force in society, as pointed out by Ecclestone and Hayes (2009). At various places in their book they write that the rise of therapeutic education has not been directed in the first place by psychologists, but by political and social groups building on their understanding of psychological findings.

> The rise of therapeutic education reflects a political and social orthodoxy about how to deal with what is variously seen as 'emotional vulnerability', 'low self-esteem', and a 'fragile sense of self or identity'. This orthodoxy both creates and exaggerates popular concerns and, in turn, it legitimises and reinforces rapidly growing political and professional interest in the emotional well-being of whole communities and groups.
>
> (122)

> . . . by slowly coming to adopt a therapeutic ethos, state agencies can reinvent themselves in more relevant ways to the prevailing tone and concerns of the media, and cultural debates.
>
> (131)

> It is precisely because popular, caricatured therapy resonates so powerfully with cultural explanations about emotional problems that policy makers and the emotional well-being industry have seized on it. 'Robust' evidence and better validity and reliability of constructs are not simply irrelevant but their absence is integral to the rise of therapeutic education because popular 'evidence' is all that government needs to legitimise it.
>
> (157–8)

The stigma of mental disorders

The difference between popular psychology and evidence-based psychology becomes distressingly clear when we look at aggressiveness in people with mental disorders. Empirical evidence points to relatively low incidences of violence in persons with mental problems. It is true that some mental disorders are associated with a higher probability of aggression and violence, but these are mostly limited to antisocial personality disorders and dependence on various substances (in particular related to the need for money to buy the substance). Most other disorders (e.g. mood disorders, anxiety disorders) do not lead to a higher risk (e.g. Arboleda-Florez 1998), sometimes even the reverse (e.g. Bonta *et al*. 1998). Schizophrenia is associated with some increase in risk of violence, but this is largely confined to a subgroup with co-morbid substance misuse, medication non-compliance, active psychotic symptoms and a previous history of violence (e.g. Walsh *et al.* 2004). Walsh and Fahy (2002) reported that 2% of arrests in the USA involved schizophrenic patients (they make up about 1% of the population and are over-represented in lower socioeconomic groups). This can be compared with the fact that 16% of men aged 18–24 and from low economic classes in the USA are reported as being involved in violence.

How do these findings compare to popular opinion about aggressiveness in people with mental disorders? One way to investigate the perception of a social group is to work with vignettes. A vignette is a short story describing a particular person, such as:

> Becky is a second-year psychology student. She comes from Hampshire in the UK and her parents are both teachers. Most of the time she enjoys her studies, but some weeks are really hard due to the many deadlines that must be met. She has a part-time job in the college shop, to pay for her day-to-day expenses. Last year she broke up with her boyfriend, who had been her childhood sweetheart.

After reading the vignette, participants are given a number of questions and have to indicate on a Likert scale (e.g. 1 = very much, 4 = not at all) how interested they would be in interacting with this person. Typical questions could be:

- How willing would you be to move next door to Becky?
- How willing would you be to spend an evening socialising with Becky?
- How willing would you be to make friends with Becky?
- How willing would you be to work closely with Becky?
- How willing would you be to see Becky marry into the family?

Link and colleagues (1999) asked these questions to a large representative sample as part of a general social survey. However, they did not depict well-adjusted psychology students with middle-class backgrounds, but different types of mental disorders. This was their vignette for schizophrenia:

> Mary is a white woman with a college education. Up until a year ago, life was okay for Mary. But then, things started to change. She thought that people around her were making disapproving comments [about her] and talking behind her back. Mary was convinced that people were spying on her and that they could hear what she was thinking. Mary lost her drive to participate in her usual work and family activities and retreated to her home, eventually spending most of her day in her room. Mary was hearing voices even though no one else was around. These voices told her what to do and what to think. She has been living this way for six months.

When Link *et al.* (1999) asked their questions about willingness to interact with Mary, the answers they got shifted towards the alternative 'rather not' (mean score of 2.75), indicating that the participants preferred to keep their distance from Mary. Similar data were found for alcohol dependence (2.85), major depressive disorder (2.54) and cocaine dependence (3.20). On the basis of their findings, the authors concluded that the situation at the end of the twentieth century was still very much as Star had described it nearly half a century before:

> Mental illness is a very threatening, fearful thing and not an idea to be entertained lightly about anyone. Emotionally, it represents to people a loss of what they consider to be the distinctively human qualities of rationality and free will, and there is kind of

a horror in dehumanization. As both our data and other studies make clear, mental illness is something that people want to keep as far from themselves as possible.

(Star 1950 as cited in Link *et al.* 1999: 1331)

stigma
attribute that is deeply discrediting and that reduces the bearer to a tainted and discounted person

Many studies have since confirmed that mental health problems carry a stigma, defined by Goffman (1963) as an attribute that is deeply discrediting and that reduces the bearer from a whole and usual person to a tainted, discounted one (see also Link *et al.* 2004). To some extent this is surprising, given that the lifetime prevalence of mental disorders in the Western world is currently estimated at more than 40% (Kessler *et al.* 2005), meaning that nearly half the population at some point in their life may be diagnosed with a mental disorder, for which they are likely to seek help. The most prevalent disorders are major depressive disorder (17%), alcohol abuse (13%), specific phobias (12%) and social phobia (12%). It also shows that, whatever influence psychology has on society, at present it is not enough to counterbalance the deep negative attitude the public has towards individuals with mental problems.

Mechanisms behind the negative image

To understand why mental health problems continue to carry such a stigma in our society despite the meagre empirical evidence for it, we need to know what mechanisms underlie it. For instance, we could follow Foucault's argument that mad people have been singled out by society as outcasts, to make everyone else feel better and as a surveillance threat ('if you don't behave well, you will end up in the group of the mad'). In that case, the conclusion would have to be that no matter how much effort psychologists put into the case, it will be wasted energy. The group of the mad is needed for the other groups to feel better, and if the madness stigma were to disappear, a replacement group would have to be found.

Another view is that the stigma of mental illness is a social stereotype, due to the fact that the public has little veridical information about mental illnesses. There is considerable evidence for this. For instance, the public makes few distinctions between the different types of disorders and their impact on a person's life. When Angermeyer and Matschinger (2005) phoned a representative sample of 1,000 Germans to ask what a bipolar disorder was and gave four response alternatives, only 5% of the group knew the disorder referred to a mental health problem. The majority of the interviewees (61%) thought it had to do with global warming and the melting of the ice at the North and the South Poles.

A second finding is that few people indicate that they have direct experience with mental health patients (which incidentally suggests how much mental health problems are hidden). Most information seems to come from the media, in particular television and newspapers. They seem to be the major sources of the negative image, because they portray people with mental health problems as devoid of interesting attributes, severely affected and above all as dangerous (Nairn 2007). It starts as early as children's cartoons (Wilson *et al.* 2000), where characters with mental illnesses serve comic roles or act as evil villains, and where commonly occurring terms such as 'crazy', 'mad' and 'losing your mind' consistently denote loss of control.

Also in prime television series and films, people with mental health problems are predominantly portrayed as dangerous individuals. Of the 20 characters Wilson *et al.* (1999) randomly selected, 15 were portrayed as violent, unpredictable, unproductive, asocial, incompetent and unreliable. Corrigan *et al.* (2005) analysed American newspapers. Of the articles referring to mental health problems, 39% contained an association with violence. These usually figured on the front pages of tabloids (e.g. when a murder had been committed by someone who had been treated by the mental health services). The ones that gave a more representative picture were usually in the scientific sections of the more serious newspapers.

Nairn and Coverdale (2005) further observed that most articles relating to mental health problems were stories *about* people and not stories *of* people: there were few first-person stories based on the experiences and the perspectives of persons with mental health problems themselves. In a survey of more than 5,000 respondents, Angermeyer *et al.* (2005) observed that the stigma of mental illness was particularly strong among those who watched a lot of television and read tabloid newspapers.

This is how the mother of a son with schizophrenia experienced it:

> Just look how often and in what sort of magazines you can read something about cholesterol, for instance. Even in the tabloid press, and so often that you're getting sick and tired of it! And when you want to know something about a mental disorder, you only hear about it when a patient has committed a crime, and that's all. And this is a really big mistake!
>
> (Schulze & Angermeyer 2003: 306)

According to Link *et al.* (1999) the association in the media between mental health problems and danger is by far the strongest reason why the public wants to keep its distance from individuals with a mental illness. The fact that mental illnesses are so often associated with violence in the media means that even new patients themselves are scared of others on their first admissions. This is what a psychiatrist reported in her daily practice:

> Or what you see in crime series on TV. It seems there is a particular trend at the moment. Nearly every week, one of the perpetrators portrayed in these films ends up in a psychiatric hospital, because he's committed a horrific crime. And this shapes the public image, also among the patients. They're afraid they might find themselves attacking someone one day, and they'd rather not stay at the hospital because they're scared of the other patients.
>
> (Schulze & Angermeyer 2003: 305)

Finally, there are suggestions that the way people treat those with poor mental health has a significant influence on the outcomes of those individuals. This is how the American anthropologist Tanya Luhrmann (2007) described it:

> The primary conclusion of the ethnographic research on subjects with schizophrenia is that the daily experience of survival with serious psychotic illness is one of repeated social failure . . .
>
> You would expect individuals to experience social defeat when they have an encounter with another person who demeans them, humiliates them, subordinates them . . . Social defeat is not so much an idea that someone holds but a human encounter—an important distinction, because to alter individuals' ideas you can use psychotherapy, but to alter their encounters, you must change their social world.
>
> (Luhrmann 2007: 149, 151–2)

Luhrmann (2007) described how a considerable percentage of patients diagnosed with schizophrenia end up being homeless and dependent on charity. In her view, the reaction ex-patients receive from others is one of the reasons why the prospects of recovery are lower in Western countries than in Africa and India, where the extended family remains more involved in the treatment, where individuals do not have to be primary breadwinners or caretakers to be useful members of a household, and where fewer jobs are in fast-paced, high people-contact settings.

More importantly for our present discussion, however, is that all this research seems to have little impact on the responses people with mental illnesses get from the public. This brings us back to the original question of the section: how much of psychologisation is due to psychologists and how much to popular (mis)understanding of psychological findings?

> **? What do you think?**
>
> To what extent have your psychology studies formed a counterweight against the stigma of mental illness? Or do you see the same stereotypes among psychology students as in the general public?

Quo vadis, psychology?

The distressing discrepancy between the popular view of psychology and what evidence-based psychology actually stands for arguably confronts us with the biggest conceptual issue of the present book: do psychology studies matter? This issue can be translated into various sub-questions, such as: is the knowledge that psychological research generates helpful? Do psychological studies make a difference to those who research them (clients, relatives, schools, hospitals, companies, politicians)? Do they provide students with useful inform ation and skills? Does psychology require a dedicated degree? And maybe above all: can we imagine a twenty-first-century society without psychologists? Could the explosion of scientific knowledge in the past 300–400 years have taken place without the emergence of psychology as an independent discipline? And if so, how would our culture differ from the one we know now? These are the questions we leave you with at the end of this book.

Interim summary

To what extent is the psychologisation of society steered by psychologists?

- There is a discrepancy between the degree to which Western society has become psychologised and the impact of psychologists.
- This is because the psychologisation of society is driven to a larger extent by the popular image of psychology than by what happens in psychological research itself.
- Knowledge of psychology is largely driven by the media, which often brings a simplified and sensationalised story in line with popular beliefs and social biases. An example is the depiction of people with mental disorders and the consequences this has for the ways in which these persons are treated.
- The discrepancy between what psychology is and what the public thinks of it arguably confronts us with the biggest conceptual issue of this book: do psychology studies matter? Do they make a difference to those who research them?

Recommended literature

The influence of the socio-political context on psychology (in particular intelligence testing) is well described in Gould, S.J. (1996) *The mismeasure of man* (New York: W.W. Norton & Co.).

Good examples of the influences of psychology on society are Ward, S.C. (2002) *Modernizing the mind: Psychological knowledge and the remaking of society* (Westport, CT: Praeger), Hanson, F.A. (1993) *Testing testing: Social consequences of the examined life* (Berkeley: University of California Press), and Watters, E. (2010) *Crazy like us: The globalization of the American psyche* (New York: Free Press).

For the ways in which social groups try to increase their power, see in particular Illich, I. (1976) *Limits to medicine – Medical nemesis: The expropriation of health* (London: Marion Boyars Publishers).

Finally, for those who wonder whether at the end of the day psychology still has something to offer, an interesting article is Zimbardo, P.G. (2004) 'Does psychology make a significant difference in our lives?' (*American Psychologist*, 59: 339–51).

References

Angermeyer, M.C., Dietrich, S., Potl, D. & Matschinger, H. (2005) 'Media consumption and desire for social distance towards people with schizophrenia', *European Psychiatry*, 20: 246–50.

APA Presidential Task Force on Evidence-based Practice (2006) 'Evidence-based practice in psychology', *American Psychologist*, 61: 271–85.

Arboleda-Florez, J. (1998) 'Mental illness and violence: An epidemiological appraisal of the evidence', *Canadian Journal of Psychiatry – Revue Canadienne de Psychiatrie*, 43: 989–96.

Blech, J. (2006) *Inventing disease and pushing pills: Pharmaceutical companies and the medicalisation of normal life*. London: Routledge.

Bonta, J., Law, M. & Hanson, K. (1998) 'The prediction of criminal and violent recidivism among mentally disordered offenders: A meta-analysis', *Psychological Bulletin*, 123: 123–42.

Boring, E.G. (1923) 'Intelligence as the tests test it', *New Republic*, 6 June, 35–7.

Burr, V. & Butt, T. (2000) 'Psychological distress and post-modern thought.' In F. Dwight (ed.), *Pathology and the postmodern*. London: Sage Publications, pp. 186–206.

Colapinto, J. (1997) 'The true story of John/Joan', *Rolling Stone*, 775: 54–97.

Corrigan, P.W., Watson, A.C., Gracia, G., Slopen, N. *et al.* (2005) 'Newspaper stories as measures of structural stigma', *Psychiatric Services*, 56: 551–6.

Cummings, N.A. & O'Donohue, W.T. (2008) *Eleven blunders that cripple psychotherapy in America*. New York: Routledge.

Danziger, K. (1997) *Naming the mind: How psychology found its language*. London: Sage.

De Graaf, P.M. & Kalmijn, M. (2006) 'Divorce motives in a period of rising divorce: Evidence from a Dutch life-history survey', *Journal of Family Issues*, 27: 183–205.

Diamond, M. & Sigmundson, H.K. (1997) 'Sex reassignment at birth: Long-term review and clinical implications', *Archives of Pediatrics and Adolescent Medicine*, 151: 298–304.

Draaisma, D. (2000) *Metaphors of memory. A history of ideas about the mind*. Cambridge: Cambridge University Press.

Feyerabend, P.K. (1975/1993) *Against method: Outline of an anarchistic theory of knowledge*. London: New Left Books.

Forshaw, M.J. (2007) 'Free qualitative research from the shackles of method', *The Psychologist*, 20: 478–9.

Foucault, M. (1961) *Folie et déraison. Histoire de la folie à l'âge classique*. Paris: Librairie Plon. (English translation in 1965: *Madness and civilization: A history of insanity in the Age of Reason*; new translation in 2006: *History of madness*. London: Routledge.)

Foucault, M. (1976) *Surveiller et punir: Naissance de la prison*. Paris: Editions Gallimard. (English translation: Foucault, M. (1979) *Discipline and punish: The birth of the prison*. New York: Vintage.)

Frankfurt, H.G. (2005) *On bullshit*. Princeton, NJ: Princeton University Press.

Fuchs, A.H. (2000) 'Contributions of American mental philosophers to psychology in the United States', *History of Psychology*, 3: 3–19.

Furedi, F. (2004) *Therapy culture: Cultivating vulnerability in an uncertain age*. London: Routledge.

Gentner, D. & Grudin, J. (1985) 'The evolution of mental metaphors in psychology: A 90-year retrospective', *American Psychologist*, 40: 181–92.

Gould, S.J. (1996) *The mismeasure of man* (2nd edn). London: W.W. Norton & Co.

Gulerce, A. (2006) 'History of psychology in Turkey as a sign of diverse modernization and global psychologization.' In A.C. Brock (ed.), *Internationalizing the history of psychology*. New York: New York University Press, pp. 75–93.

Hanson, F.A. (1993) *Testing testing: Social consequences of the examined life*. Berkeley: University of California Press.

Hood, R.W. (2000) 'American psychology of religion and the *Journal for the Scientific Study of Religion*', *Journal for the Scientific Study of Religion*, 39: 531–43.

Illich, I. (1971) *Deschooling society*. London: Penguin Education.

Illich, I. (1973) *Tools for conviviality*. New York: Harper & Row (also available at http:// clevercycles.com/ tools_for_conviviality).

Illich, I. (1976) *Limits to medicine – Medical nemesis: The expropriation of health*. London: Marion Boyars (also available at www.soilandhealth.org).

Kagan, J. (2009a) 'Historical selection', *Review of General Psychology*, 13: 77–88.

Kagan, J. (2009b) *The three cultures: Natural sciences, social sciences, and the humanities in the 21st century*. Cambridge: Cambridge University Press.

Kimmel, A.J. (2007) *Ethical issues in behavioral research: Basic and applied perspectives* (2nd edn). Oxford: Blackwell Publishing.

Larsen, S.F. (1987) 'Remembering and the archaeology metaphor', *Metaphor and Symbol*, 2: 187–99.

Leary, D.E. (ed.) (1995) *Metaphors in the history of psychology*. Cambridge: Cambridge University Press.

Lewis, J.E., DeGusta, D., Meyer, M.R., Monge, J.M. *et al.* (2011) 'The mismeasure of science: Stephen Jay Gould versus Samuel George Morton on skulls and bias'; *PLoS Biol* 9(6): e1001071. doi:10.1371/journal.pbio.1001071.

Link, B.G., Phelan, J.C., Besnahan, M., Stueve, A. *et al.* (1999) 'Public conceptions of mental illness: Labels, causes, dangerousness, and social distance', *American Journal of Public Health*, 89: 1328–33.

Link, B.G., Yang, L.H., Phelan, J.C. & Collins, P.Y. (2004) 'Measuring mental illness stigma', *Schizophrenia Bulletin*, 30: 511–41.

Luhrmann, T.M. (2007) 'Social defeat and the culture of chronicity: Or, why schizophrenia does so well over there and so badly here', *Culture, Medicine and Psychiatry*, 31: 135–72.

Mayer, J. (2008) *The dark side: The inside story of how the war on terror turned into a war on American ideals*. Garden City, NY: Doubleday.

McKeown, T. (1979) *The role of medicine: Dream, mirage or nemesis?* (2nd edn). Oxford: Basil Blackwell.

Messer, S.B. (2004) 'Evidence-based practice: Beyond empirically supported treatments', *Professional Psychology: Research and Practice*, 35: 580–8.

Money, T. & Ehrhardt, A. (1972) *Man and woman, boy and girl, the differentiation and dimorphism of gender identity from conception to maturity*. Baltimore, MD: Johns Hopkins University Press.

Nairn, R.G. (2007) 'Media portrayals of mental illness, or is it madness? A review', *Australian Psychologist*, 42: 138–46.

Nairn, R.G. & Coverdale, J.H. (2005) 'People never see us living well: An appraisal of the personal stories about mental illness in a prospective print media sample', *Australian and New Zealand Journal of Psychiatry*, 39: 281–7.

Redding, R.E. (2001) 'Sociopolitical diversity in psychology: The case for pluralism', *American Psychologist*, 56: 205–15.

Richards, G. (2002) *Putting psychology in its place: A critical historical overview* (2nd edn). London: Routledge.

Rogers, A. & Pilgrim, D. (2005) *A sociology of mental health and illness* (3rd edn). Maidenhead, UK: Open University Press.

Sackett, P.R., Kuncel, N.R., Arneson, J.J., Cooper, S.R. *et al.* (2009) 'Does socioeconomic status explain the relationship between admissions tests and post-secondary academic performance?' *Psychological Bulletin*, 135: 1–22.

Schulze, B. & Angermeyer, M.C. (2003) 'Subjective experiences of stigma. A focus group study of schizophrenic patients, their relatives and mental health professionals', *Social Science & Medicine*, 56: 299–312.

Sharpe, D. & Faye, C. (2009) 'A second look at debriefing practices: Madness in our method?' *Ethics & Behavior*, 19(5): 432–47.

Shorter, E. (1992) *From paralysis to fatigue: A history of psychosomatic illness in the modern era*. New York: The Free Press.

Shorter, E. (1997) *A history of psychiatry*. New York: John Wiley & Sons.

Skinner, B.F. (1971) *Beyond freedom and dignity*. New York: Knopf.

Sokal, A. & Bricmont, J. (1997) *Impostures intellectuelles*. Paris: Editions Odile Jacob (English translation (1998, 2003) *Intellectual impostures*. London: Profile Books Ltd).

Sokal, A.D. (1996a) 'Transgressing the boundaries: Toward a transformative hermeneutics of quantum gravity', *Social Text*, **46/47**: 217–52 (also available at www.physics.nyu.edu/sokal/).

Sokal, A.D. (1996b) 'A physicist experiments with cultural studies', *Lingua Franca*, **May/June**: 62–64 (also available at www.physics.nyu.edu/sokal/).

Teo, T. (2005) *The critique of psychology: From Kant to postcolonial theory*. New York: Springer Science+Business Media, Inc.

Teo, T. (2008) 'Race and psychology'. In W.A. Darity (ed.) *International encyclopedia of the social sciences* (2nd edn). Detroit, MI: Macmillan, vol. 7, pp. 21–4.

The British Psychological Society (2004) *Guideline for minimum standards of ethical approval in psychological research*. Leicester, UK: The British Psychological Society.

The British Psychological Society (2006) *Code of ethics and conduct*. Leicester, UK: The British Psychological Society.

Thompson, D. (2008) *Counterknowledge: How we surrendered to conspiracy theories, quack medicine, bogus science and fake history*. London: Atlantic Books.

Tulving, E. & Thomson, D.M. (1971) 'Retrieval processes in recognition memory – Effects of associative context', *Journal of Experimental Psychology*, 87: 116–24.

Tyson, P.J., Jones, D. & Elcock, J. (2011) *Psychology in social context: Issues and debates*. Oxford: Blackwell Publishing.

Verhaeghe, P. (2009) *Het einde van de psychotherapie* (The end of psychotherapy). Amsterdam: De Bezige Bij.

Walsh, E. & Fahy, T. (2002) 'Violence in society: Contribution of mental illness is low', *British Medical Journal*, 325: 507–8.

Walsh, E., Gilvarry, C., Samele, C., Harvey, K. *et al.* (2004) 'Predicting violence in schizophrenia: A prospective study', *Schizophrenia Research*, 67: 247–52.

Wampold, B.E., Minami, T., Basking, T.W. & Tierney, S.C. (2002) 'A meta-(re)analysis of the effects of cognitive therapy versus "other therapies" for depression', *Journal of Affective Disorders*, 68: 159–65.

Ward, S.C. (2002) *Modernizing the mind: Psychological knowledge and the remaking of society*. Westport, CT: Praeger.

Watters, E. (2010) *Crazy like us: The globalization of the American psyche*. New York: Free Press.

Weindling, P.J. (2004) *Nazi medicine and the Nuremberg Trials: From medical war crimes to informed consent*. Basingstoke: Palgrave-Macmillan.

Welch, B. (2009) 'Torture, psychology, and Daniel Inouye: The true story behind psychology's role in torture', *Huffington Post*, 16 June (available at www.huffingtonpost.com/bryant-welch/torture-psychology-and-da_b_215612.html).

Wheen, F. (2004) *How mumbo-jumbo conquered the world: A short history of modern delusions*. London: Harper Perennial.

Wilson, C., Nairn, R., Coverdale, J. & Panapa, A. (1999) 'Mental illness depictions in prime-time drama: Identifying the discursive resources', *Australian and New Zealand Journal of Psychiatry*, 33: 232–9.

Wilson, C., Nairn, R., Coverdale, J. & Panapa, A. (2000) 'How mental illness is portrayed in children's television: A prospective study', *British Journal of Psychiatry*, 176: 440–3.

Epilogue

We have come to the end of our journey through the historical and conceptual issues in psychology. We hope you enjoyed it and found it intellectually stimulating. We have tried to strike a fair balance between two types of approaches that prevail in the literature. On the one hand, there are the celebratory reviews of psychology's achievements exalting the many precious gifts psychology has bestowed on society; on the other hand, there are the hypercritical reviews calling into question everything psychologists feel proud of and leaving students bewildered and depressed at the end of the reading.

For the record, we authors are both happy with our careers in psychology and never regretted our choice. However, this does not take away from the fact that from time to time it is good to stand back and take a critical look at what we are doing.

We are very well aware that similar reviews could be written about all the other academic disciplines. The fact that they do not seem to feel the same urge to put themselves into perspective may be seen as an illustration of a masochistic tendency in psychologists, although we ourselves tend to perceive it as an indication that psychologists are interested in all types of human functioning, including their own. We hope you will find the outcome of our enterprise helpful and inspiring for the continuation of your career!

Notes

Chapter 1

1. BCE stands for 'before the common era'; i.e. before the start of the Gregorian calendar used in the Western society (another notation in Christian cultures is BC [Before Christ]); CE means 'the common era' and begins with the start of the Gregorian calendar (indicated in Christian cultures as AD [Anno Domini]).

2. One of the debates relating to Aristotle is whether logic is best seen as part of theoretical or practical knowledge.

3. If this all sounds a bit obscure to you, comfort yourself with the following thought from Barnes (2000: 6): 'Let it be admitted that Aristotle can be not only tough but also vexing. Whatever does he mean here? How on earth is this conclusion supposed to follow from these premises? Why this sudden barrage of technical terms?' Recall, too, that for centuries higher education was largely devoted to trying to understand Aristotle.

Chapter 2

1. In England the change would only happen in 1752, when 11 days were dropped from the month of September. In the Eastern Orthodox Church the Julian calender is still in use and January 14 is a religious holiday in countries with this religion because it marks New Year in their Church.

2. Possibly because of the similarity between his first name and his surname, Galileo Galilei is usually called Galileo in Anglo-Saxon writings. We deliberately depart from this tradition, just like we do not use expressions such as 'Isaac's laws of physics' or 'Francis's *New Organon*'.

3. A saying that 200 years later would inspire the science writer Richard Dawkins to title one of his books *Unweaving the rainbow* (Dawkins 1998).

4. This was a European-wide coalition against the French King, Louis XIV.

Chapter 3

1. The Greek characters were used in the title, testament to the fact that the word was coined by combining the Greek words *psyche* (soul) and *logos* (word, study).

2. To illustrate the difficulties interpreting Aristotle, these two sentences are embedded in a text dealing with the question of how the soul can understand objects when it has no innate ideal forms to relate to. To answer this question, Aristotle made a distinction between potential knowledge and actual knowledge. The soul possessed potential knowledge but needed sensory input to translate this into actual knowledge. As Aristotle concluded in Part 8 of the same text: 'Knowledge and sensation are divided to correspond with the realities, potential knowledge and sensation answering to potentialities, actual knowledge and sensation to actualities. Within the soul the faculties of knowledge and sensation are potentially these objects, the one what is knowable, the other what is sensible . . . the soul is analogous to the hand; for as the hand is a tool of tools, so the mind is the form of forms and sense the form of sensible things.' The existence of potential knowledge is, arguably, why Aristotle thought humans could have certainty about the axioms forming the starting point of theoretical knowledge.

3. In 1734 Berkeley would be appointed Bishop of Cloyne in the Irish Anglican Church.

4. It should be noted, however, that Wolff's first writings on psychology date from 1719.

5. Incidentally, this is a study you can easily try out yourself. Put your thumb and index at a certain distance and briefly touch a friend's arm with them. Does your friend have the feeling of two points being touched or only one? Now increase or decrease the distance between your fingers.

6. In case you are not scared of a bit of maths: $\ln(30) \approx 3.40$, $\ln(36) \approx 3.58$, $\ln(43.5) \approx 3.77$, $\ln(52.2) \approx 3.95$. In other words, there is always a difference of about 0.18 between successive sensations, which you can expect given that $\ln(a \times x) = \ln(x) + \ln(a)$ and that $\ln(1.2) \approx 0.18$.

7. These data are to be found in Note IV of Donders' (1868/1969) article. They are given in the article as number of cycles produced by a tuning-fork vibrating at 261 Hz and recorded simultaneously with the stimulus and the response on a 'phonautograph'. For instance, for simple responses the time was 51.5 cycles, which equals to $1000 \times (51.5/261) = 197$ ms.

Chapter 4

1. The most likely reason for this title was that there already existed a journal called *Psychological Studies,* devoted to spiritualism and parapsychology (Fancher 1996).

2. Because the British Isles comprise lands that at various times fought against each other, different names are used to refer to them. Great Britain is used to refer to England, Scotland, and Wales. The United Kingdom denotes to the former three plus Northern Ireland. In Continental Europe the term 'England' is often used erroneously to refer to either Great Britain or the United Kingdom. This was the case, for instance, in Ribot's book, which was called *La psychologie anglaise contemporaine* (English contemporary psychology) rather than the intended *La psychologie Britannique contemporaine* (British contemporary psychology).

3. In the British system, there are three main categories of academic positions: lectureship, readership and professorship. The first is the lowest rank and the one in which young academics usually start. The second and the third position are conferred by the university on the basis of a strong research CV and recommendations by peers. Only the last category is allowed to use the title Professor. The former two must be referred to as Doctors.

Chapter 9

1. In 1659 Christiaan Huygens formulated a law of centripetal force, which formed the basis of Newton's second law of motion. In 1657 he also published what is considered the first mathematical textbook on probabilistic reasoning in games of chance.

2. Notice the references to Aristotle's *Organum* and Bacon's *Novum Organum.*

Chapter 12

1. For the sake of historical accuracy, it must be noted that the term 'social Darwinism' was rarely used in Spencer's time; it is a name that was given later to refer to this line of thought.

Glossary

access consciousness: access conscious information can be reported by the patient, used for reasoning and acted upon intentionally.

achievement test: standardised test which measures the knowledge of a particular topic or set of topics.

ad hoc modifications: modifications to a theory that according to Popper make the theory less falsifiable; decrease the scientific value of the theory.

Age of Enlightenment: name given to the Western philosophy and cultural life of the eighteenth century, in which autonomous thinking and observation became advocated as the primary sources of knowledge, rather than reliance on authority.

algorithm: list of instructions that converts a given input, via a fully defined series of intermediate steps, into the desired output.

animal spirits: spirits that were thought by Galen to travel over the nerves between the ventricles in the brain and the body.

animism: explanation of the workings of the world and the universe by means of spirits with humanlike characteristics.

anthropomorphic interpretation: interpreting behaviour of non-human living creatures by attributing human motives and human-like intelligence to them.

antipsychiatry movement: a pressure group starting in the 1960s that called into question the usefulness of the prevailing psychiatric treatments.

applied psychology: the application of psychological knowledge and research methods to solve practical problems.

associative learning: learning of simple associations (correlations) between all types of events; thought to be the basis of automatic, type I thinking.

asylum: name given to the institutions for the insane established from the sixteenth century on; first modelled after prisons, later after hospitals for chronic patients.

authenticity test: test to determine whether a person is who he/she pretends to be and to ascertain guilt or innocence.

behaviourism: movement in psychology arguing that observable behaviours are the most important aspect of human functioning to be understood; denies to various extents the relevance of information processing going on in the mind; particularly strong in the USA in the first half of the twentieth century.

biopsychosocial model: model according to which the understanding of medical and psychological phenomena requires attention to biological, psychological as well as socio-cultural factors.

boxes-and-arrows diagram: flowchart outlining the different information stores (boxes) and information transformations (arrows) involved in the execution of a particular task with observable input and output; used by cognitive psychologists to detail the information processing involved in the task.

bracketing: requirement in qualitative research to look at a phenomenon with an open mind and to free oneself from preconceptions.

brain equipotentiality theory: theory saying that all parts of the brain have equal significance and are involved in each task; first thought to apply to the complete brain; since the nineteenth century limited to the cerebral hemispheres.

case study: within medicine and clinical psychology, the intensive study of an individual patient within the context of his/her own world and relations, to understand and help the individual patient.

Chinese room: thought experiment proposed by Searle to illustrate the difference between information processing in humans and information processing in computers.

classical conditioning: form of learning discovered by Pavlov in which an association is made between two events in the environment; usually studied with a stimulus that elicits a reflex-like response (e.g. food in mouth → salivation) to which a second, initially neutral stimulus is coupled.

clinical psychology: branch of psychology applying psychological knowledge to the assessment and treatment of mental disorders.

cognitive neuropsychiatry: subfield that tries to understand consequences of mental disorders in terms of breakdowns in the cognitive models of normal psychological functioning.

cognitive neuropsychology: part of neuropsychology aimed at understanding and treating the behavioural consequences of brain damage within the information processing models proposed by cognitive psychologists.

cognitive neuroscience: the scientific study of the biological mechanisms underlying cognition; largely based on brain imaging techniques, TMS and the measurement of electrical activity.

cognitive psychology: movement in psychology arguing that observable behaviours are the result of information processing in the mind; started in the 1950s and currently the dominant form of mainstream psychology.

comparative psychology: study of behaviour of animals, usually with the intention to shed light on human functioning within the framework of the evolutionary theory.

computational model: computer program simulating the human information processing assumed to be involved in the execution of a particular task; requires researchers to be much more precise about of what going on than in a boxes-and-arrows model.

confirmation bias: tendency people have to search for evidence that confirms their opinion; goes against falsificationism.

confounding variable: variable that was not taken into account in the study and that may be the origin of the effect observed.

consciousness: word referring to the private, first-person experiences an individual lives through; contains all the mental states a person is aware of; part of the mind that can be examined with introspection.

correspondence theory of truth: a statement is true when it corresponds with reality. Assumes that there is a physical reality which has priority and which the human mind tries to understand. First formulated by Aristotle.

critical psychology: movement in psychology that criticises mainstream psychology for failing to understand that knowledge does not refer to an outside reality (idealism), that scientific knowledge is not cumulative but consists of social constructions, and that psychological theories and claims have an impact on the world in which people live.

Dark Ages: name given in the Renaissance to the Middle Ages, to refer to the lack of independent and scientific thinking in that age.

deductive reasoning: form of reasoning in which one starts from a number of indisputable premises (known statements), from which new, true conclusions can be drawn if the rules of logic are followed.

degenerative research programme: notion introduced by Lakatos to indicate a paradigm that does not allow researchers to make new predictions and that requires an increasing number of ad hoc modifications to account for the empirical findings.

demarcation: setting and marking the boundaries of a concept; used, for instance, in the philosophy of science to denote attempts to define the specificity of science.

diagnostic tests: tests to determine which condition a person has.

diathesis–stress model: model claiming that the likelihood of a person having a disorder depends on the vulnerability of the person (diathesis) and the amount of stress experienced by the person.

discourse analysis: qualitative research method that aims to discover how social relations between people are determined by the language they use.

dualism: view of the mind–body relation according to which the mind is immaterial and completely independent of the body; central within religions and also in Descartes' philosophy.

Edwin Smith papyrus: papyrus from Ancient Egypt that contains short descriptions of the symptoms and treatment of different forms of brain injury; named after the person who bought the papyrus in Egypt and had it analysed.

EEG: electroencephalogram: outcome of measurement of electrical brain activity by means of sensors placed on the scalp; routinely used in hospitals for the detection of epilepsy.

efficacy of therapies: measure to indicate how much improvement a therapy brings to patients.

embodied cognition: the conviction that the interactions between the human body and the environment form the grounding (meaning) of human cognition.

empiricism: view according to which knowledge is obtained by means of perceptual experiences; usually involves idea of associations between ideas to combine the individual perceptions; also emphasis on inductive reasoning.

epistemology: branch of philosophy concerned with the nature of knowledge.

ethical code of conduct: protocol that includes all the ethics-related conditions to which a study must adhere.

eugenics: social philosophy claiming that the fate of a nation can be improved by selective breeding of the inhabitants.

Event Related Potential (ERP): signal obtained by averaging the EEG signals to stimuli that are repeated a number of times; allows researchers to look for differences in the signal as a function of characteristics of the stimulus.

evolutionary psychology: approach in psychology that aims to understand human behaviour on the basis of natural selection and the evolutionary theory.

experimental history: method introduced by Bacon in which the natural philosopher extracts the truth from Nature by active manipulation and examining the consequences of the intervention.

face validity: estimating the validity of a test by estimating to what extent the items of the test agree with one's own beliefs; is not evidence-based.

falsificationism: view within the philosophy of science that statements are scientific only if they can be falsified empirically.

feminist psychology: movement in psychology aimed at understanding women; is particularly concerned with the way in which women are treated in mainstream psychology

Fertile Crescent: region in the Middle East with a high level of civilisation around 3,000 BCE; included the Ancient Mesopotamian and the Ancient Egyptian civilisations.

fMRI: brain imaging technique based on the measurement of blood with oxygen vs. blood without oxygen; currently the most popular imaging technique because of its high spatial resolution (allows good localisation); has rather low temporal resolution (cannot trace what is happening at a speed of hundreds of registrations per second)

focus group: technique in which a group of participants freely discuss a limited set of questions.

folk psychology: collection of beliefs lay people have about psychological functioning; no efforts made to verify them empirically or to check them for their internal coherence.

free will: situation in which individuals can choose their course of action from a number of alternatives; choice is the outcome of an informed deliberation.

functionalism: name given to an approach in early American psychology research, that examined the practical functions of the human mind inspired by the evolutionary theory.

functionalism: in philosophy, view about the relationship between the mind and brain that considers the mind as a separate layer of information implemented on a Turing machine; predicts that the mind can be copied onto another Turing machine.

gate control theory of pain: theory of pain perception which assumes that the nerve signals carrying the pain message have to pass through a gate before they reach the brain; at this gate the signals can be made stronger or weaker.

geocentric model: model of the universe in which the Earth is at the centre; was dominant until the seventeenth century.

Gestalt psychology: group of psychologists who argued that the human mind could not be understood by breaking down the experiences into their constituting elements; perception is more than the sensation of stimuli, it involves organisation.

global workspace model: model that explains the role of consciousness by analogy to a theatre: consciousness is meant to make some information available to the whole brain (i.e. the play), so that the various background processes can align their functioning to what is going on centrally.

grounded theory: qualitative research method that tries to understand what is going on in a particular situation and which, on the basis of a qualitative analysis and induction, tries to come to a theoretical insight grounded in the data.

hard problem: name given by Chalmers to refer to the difficulty of explaining in what respects consciousness is more than accounted for on the basis of functionalism.

heliocentric model: model of the universe in which the Sun is at the centre.

hermeneutics: approach in psychology according to which the task of the psychologist is to interpret and understand persons on the basis of their personal and socio-cultural history.

heuristic-based thinkers: those who think based on heuristics, rules of thumb that do not require as much effort as the scientific method and that most of the time result in good decisions, but that are subject to a number of biases.

hidden racism: advancing one's own race by non-conspicuous biases against other groups (usually by ignoring their contribution).

historical method: one of the three research methods introduced by Wundt; consists of studying the human mind by investigating the products of human cultures; according to Wundt particularly well suited to investigate the 'higher' functions of the mind.

homunculus: word (meaning 'little man') used to refer to the difficulty of explaining goal-oriented behaviour without making use of an ultimate intelligent (human-like) control centre.

humanistic psychology: psychological movement promoted by Rogers and Maslow as a reaction against psychoanalysis and behaviourism; stressed that people are human, inherently positive, endowed with free will and living within a socio-cultural context.

humanities: academic disciplines that continued the traditional study of the ancient classics, increasingly supplemented with teachings of contemporary literature and art.

human relations movement: second main theory of how work should be organised; stressed the humanity of the employees and the importance of social relations.

human resource movement: third main theory of how work should be organised; stressed the desire for self-actualisation in employees; employees will perform best if given autonomy and authority.

hypothetico-deductive method: model introduced by Popper to understand the scientific method; on the basis of observation, induction and educated guesswork, a theory of a phenomenon is formulated; the correctness of the theory is evaluated by the formulation of a testable prediction (hypothesis) on the basis of deductive reasoning; the prediction is subsequently put to a falsification test, which provides new observational data for further theorising.

idealism: view within philosophy that human knowledge is a construction of the mind and does not necessarily correspond to an outside world; the truth of knowledge depends on the coherence with rest of the knowledge in the social group.

ideographic approach: the conclusions of a study stay limited to the phenomenon under study.

identity problem: the difficulty the materialistic theory of the mind–brain relationship has to explain how two events can be experienced as the same despite the fact that their realisation in the brain differs.

illusory correlation: perception of a correlation between events for which no independent evidence can be found.

implicit personality theory: mixture of stereotypes and individuating information about the associations of person characteristics that people use to make predictions about how others will behave in social relations.

inclusive fitness: hypothesis in evolutionary psychology that behaviour is motivated not only by the organism's own survival but also by the survival of organisms that are genetically related; the motivation depends on the degree of relatedness.

individualisation: trend in a society towards looser social relations and a greater focus by individuals on themselves than on the groups they belong to.

inductive reasoning: form of reasoning in which one starts from observations and tries to reach general conclusions on the basis of convergences in the observations; is needed in science to turn observed phenomena into scientific laws; no guarantee that the conclusions are true.

industrial psychology: first theory about how work should be organised; strongly influenced by Taylor's scientific management: employees were the hands of the company that would accept any work if remunerated enough; tasks had to be made simple so that everyone could do them without much practice.

industrial revolution: name to refer to the socioeconomic and cultural changes in the nineteenth century caused by the invention of machines; involved, among other things, the replacement of the labour of peasants and craftsmen by mass production in factories and the resulting massive relocation from the countryside to the towns.

information feedback: mechanism in which the current performance level is compared to the desired end-state and the discrepancy is used to bring the performance closer to the end-state aimed for; important for psychology because it explained a great deal of goal-directed behaviour that previously seemed to require a homunculus explanation.

information processing: encoding mental representations, transforming them by means of algorithms, and integrating them with existing knowledge; forms the core of cognitive psychology.

informed consent: central principle in ethics, saying that people can only take part in a study after they have been informed of what will be involved and after they have explicitly and voluntarily agreed to participate.

instinct: innate and fixed response that is automatically elicited by an appropriate stimulus; used around the turn of the twentieth century to explain motivation.

instrumental conditioning: name introduced by Thorndike to refer to learning on the basis of the law of effect; called operant conditioning by Skinner.

interpretative phenomenological analysis: qualitative research method in psychology that tries to understand how a phenomenon is experienced by the people involved.

introspection: research method in psychology consisting of a person looking inward and reporting what he/she is experiencing; usually done under controlled circumstances.

IQ-test: test which is supposed to measure the intelligence of a person; focuses on learning potential; results correlate with school performance and suitability for intellectually demanding occupations.

law of effect: behavioural law introduced by Thorndike to refer to the fact that behaviours followed by positive consequences are strengthened and more likely to be repeated.

localisation theory: theory saying that brain processes are localised, meaning that only part of the brain underlies a particular mental function.

logical positivism: philosophical movement in the first half of the twentieth century, claiming that philosophy should stop thinking about metaphysics, and instead try to understand the essence of the scientific approach; central tenet was the verification principle.

logograph: a sign representing a spoken word, which no longer has a physical resemblance to the word's meaning.

magnetoencephalography (MEG): measurement of the electrical brain activity by means of measurement of the magnetic field around the head; is one of the most promising brain imaging techniques, because it has the potential of both a high temporal and spatial resolution.

masked priming: experimental technique to investigate unconscious information processing, consisting of briefly presenting a prime between a forward meaningless mask and a subsequent target, and examining the effect of the prime on the processing of the target.

materialism: view about the relationship between the mind and brain that considers the mind as the brain in operation.

Matthew effect: the tendency to give more credit to well-known scientists than they deserve; increases the perceived impact of these scientists.

mechanistic view: world view according to which everything in the material universe can be understood as a complicated machine; discards the notion that things have goals and intentions as assumed by the animistic view; identified with Descartes.

meme: information unit proposed by Dawkins that reproduces itself according to the principles of the evolutionary theory (variation, selection and replication).

mental chronometry: using reaction times to measure the time needed for various mental tasks; on the basis of a comparison of different tasks, models of the mental processes involved in the tasks are postulated.

mental representation: information pattern in the mind representing knowledge obtained through observation or the application of an algorithm; forms a realm separate from the brain and could in principle be copied to another brain (or in a more extreme version, to a Turing machine).

metaphor: in science, stands for an analogy from another area that helps to map a new, complex problem by making reference to a better understood phenomenon.

methodolatry or **methodologism:** tendency to see methodological rigour as the only requirement for scientific research, at the expense of theory formation.

mind: aggregate of faculties humans (and animals) have to perceive, feel, think, remember and want.

mind-brain problem: issue of how the mind is related to the brain; three main views: dualism, materialism and functionalism.

natural selection: process in Darwin's evolutionary theory by which the environment results in the continuation and multiplication of organisms with certain genetic features and hinders the reproduction of organisms with other genetic features; the first type of features are called favourable (within the prevailing environment), the second type unfavourable.

nature–nurture debate: discussion about the respective contributions of genes and environment in the development of (human) qualities.

neurologist: name used at the end of the nineteenth century by physicians who were interested in the treatment of milder forms of mental problems outside the asylum; the term was later used to refer to specialists of the nervous system, when the original neurologists merged with the psychiatrists and took up the latter's name.

neuron: brain cell; basic unit of the nervous system; contains a cell body, dendrites and an axon.

neuropsychology: branch of psychological research and practice that looks at the relationship between brain and behaviour; research traditionally focused on understanding the consequences of brain damage and localising the affected tissue; practice aimed at assessing the behavioural and mental consequences of the injury and administering the rehabilitation programme.

neurotransmitter: chemical substance used to communicate between neurons; is released from the synapse when a signal arrives through the axon; can be affected by drugs.

nomothetic approach: a study is run in search for universal principles that exceed the confines of the study.

non-invasive techniques: methods in neuroscience that allow the study of the workings of the brain without surgery or the use of irreversible interventions.

observational learning: learning as a result of observing others performing actions and being rewarded or punished.

operational definition: definition of a variable in terms of how the variable has been measured; allows description of the variable in quantitative form.

paradigm: notion introduced by Kuhn to refer to the fact that scientists share a set of common views of what the discipline is about and how problems must be investigated.

parental investment theory: hypothesis in evolutionary psychology holding that the gender investing the most in the upbringing of offspring is more discriminating about mating.

personality test: test to measure relatively stable and distinctive patterns of behaviour that characterise individuals and their reactions to the environment.

personality trait: basic dimension used to describe differences in personality between people; is often bipolar with opposites at the extremes (e.g. introvert vs. extrovert).

phenomenological consciousness: refers to the fact that human experiences possess subjective qualities that seem to defy description; experiences have a meaning that goes beyond formal report (semantics instead of syntax).

philosophy: critical reflection on the universe and human functioning; started in Ancient Greece.

philosophy of science: branch of philosophy that studies the foundations of scientific research, to better understand the position of scientific research relative to other forms of information acquisition and generation.

phlogiston: substance that was believed to make materials flammable before the chemical processes of combustion were understood.

phonogram: a sign that represents a sound or a syllable of spoken language; forms the basis of writing systems.

phrenology: view that mental functions are localised in the brain and that the capacity of a function corresponds to the size of the brain part devoted to it; gave rise to personality assessment by means of analysing bumps on the skull; initiated by Gall and Spurzheim at the beginning of the nineteenth century.

physiognomy: belief that the personality of an individual can be deduced from their appearance, in particular from the shape of the head and the face.

pictogram: an information-conveying sign that consists of a picture resembling the person, animal or object it represents.

place coding system: system in which the meaning of a sign not only depends on its form but also on its position in a string; is used for instance in Arabic numerals.

positivism: view that authentic knowledge can only be obtained by means of the scientific method; saw religion and philosophy as inferior forms of explanation.

positron emission tomography (PET): brain imaging technique based on measurement of radioactive tracer injected into the bloodstream.

postcolonial psychology: movement in psychology addressing the issues of racism and the ways in which dominant groups treat other groups.

postmodernist: in the philosophy of science, someone who questions the special status of science and sees scientific explanations as stories told by a particular group of scientists.

pragmatism: view within philosophy that human knowledge is information about how to cope with the world; the truth of knowledge depends on the success one has in engaging with the world, on what works.

preliterate civilisation: civilisation before writing was invented.

Principia mathematica: book in which Newton presented his laws of physics (1687); considered to be the primary reason for the increased status of science.

progressive research programme: notion introduced by Lakatos to indicate a paradigm that allows researchers to make new, hitherto unexpected predictions that can be tested empirically.

Protestant Reformation: movement against the Roman Catholic Church, which was important for the development of science, because it emphasised the need for education, critical thinking, hard work and worldly success.

pseudohistory of science: text that looks like a history of science, but that contains systematic errors because of a desire to present the research as more impressive and important than it was and to depict the scientist as a genius who has to battle against the lack of understanding and appreciation by the peers.

pseudoscience: branch of knowledge that pretends to be scientific but violates the scientific method on essential aspects, such as lack of openness to testing by others and reliance on confirmation rather than falsification.

psychoactive drugs: medicines prescribed for mental disorders.

psychoanalysis: name given to Freud's theory and therapy.

psychological treatment: treatment of mental health problems consisting of conversations between the patient and the therapist; initiated by Freud as an alternative to the prevailing medical and educational treatments.

psychologisation: word used with two different meanings referring to: (1) the fact that emotional ties and personal well-being become important in primary social relations, or (2) the growing impact of psychology on the way people see themselves and interact with others.

psychophysics: part of psychological research dealing with the relationship between physical stimuli and the corresponding sensation.

purposive behaviourism: version of behaviourism, defended by Tolman, which saw behaviour as goal-related (means to an end); agreed with other behaviourists that psychology should be based on observable behaviour.

qualia: qualities of conscious thoughts that give the thoughts a rich and vivid meaning, grounded in the interactions with the world.

qualifying test: test to find the best person for a task.

qualitative research methods: research methods based on understanding phenomena in their historical and socio-cultural context; are associated with the hermeneutic approach based on understanding the meaning of a situation.

quantitative imperative: a bias only to find measurable topics interesting because quantitative research methods require numerical data.

quantitative research methods: research methods based on quantifiable data; are associated with the natural-science approach based on the hypothetico-deductive model.

radical behaviourism: strong version of behaviourism, defended by Skinner, which denies the relevance of information processing in the mind and holds that all human behaviour can be understood on the basis of S-R associations.

rationalism: view according to which knowledge is obtained by means of reasoning; usually through deductive reasoning on the basis of innate knowledge.

realism: view within philosophy that human knowledge tries to reveal real properties of the outside world; the truth of knowledge is determined by the correspondence of the knowledge with the real world.

reflex arc: notion introduced in the nineteenth century to describe the processes underlying a reflex: a signal is picked up by sensory receptors, transmitted to the spinal cord through an afferent nerve, transferred to interneurons, which activate motor neurons that send a motor command over an efferent nerve to initiate the withdrawal movement.

reliability: in test research, the degree to which the outcome of a test is the same if the test is repeated under unchanged circumstances or if an equivalent test is used.

Renaissance: cultural movement from the fourteenth to the seventeenth century based on a rediscovery and imitation of the classical Greek and Roman civilisations.

Romantic movement: movement in the late 1700s to early 1800s that reacted against the mechanistic world view and the emphasis on reason preached by Enlightenment; it saw the universe as a changing organism and stressed everything that deviated from rationalism: the individual, the irrational, the imaginative, the emotional, the natural and the transcendental.

scepticism: philosophical view that does not deny the existence of a physical reality, but denies that humans can have reliable knowledge of it; first formulated by Pyrrho of Ellis.

scholastic method: study method in which students unquestioningly memorise and recite texts that are thought to convey unchanging truths.

science wars: notion used by the postmodernists to refer to their attacks against the special status of science and their unmasking of scientific knowledge as a social construction.

scientific revolution: name given to a series of discoveries in the seventeenth century, involving Galilei, Descartes and Newton, that enhanced the status of science in society.

self: the feeling of being an individual with private experiences, feelings and beliefs, who interacts in a coherent and purposeful way with the environment.

semi-structured interview: interview in which each interviewee gets a small set of core questions, but for the rest is encouraged to speak freely; achieved by making use of open-ended, non-directive questions.

shell-shock: anxiety response on battlefield that prevents soldiers from functioning properly; was one of the first topics addressed by applied psychology.

social construction: notion used by postmodernists to indicate that scientific knowledge is not objective knowledge discovering the workings of an external reality, but a story told by a particular scientific community on the basis of their language and culture.

social Darwinism: belief in Victorian England and the USA that progress in a society could be made by allowing the strong members to flourish and the weak members to die.

social desirability: bias people have to present themselves in a manner they think will be viewed favourably by others.

social management: management and control of deviant individuals and individuals in need by official social services.

spiritualism: belief that the spirits of the dead can he contacted by mediums; flourished in English-speaking countries at the end of the nineteenth and the beginning of the twentieth century.

standardised psychological test: test that psychologists have examined for reliability and validity, for which they have information about the expected performance, and which is administered in a uniform way.

stigma: attribute that is deeply discrediting and that reduces the bearer to a tainted and discounted person.

strong social situation: a situation in which nearly all individuals act virtually the same, despite differences in biological make-up and differences in learning history.

structuralism: name given by Titchener to his approach to psychology, consisting of trying to discover the structure of the human mind by means of introspection.

structured interview: interview in which all interviewees receive the same set of questions.

survival of the fittest: term introduced by Herbert Spencer to describe the outcome of natural selection: only organisms that fit within the environment and can produce viable offspring survive.

syllogism: argument consisting of three propositions: the major premise, the minor premise, and the conclusion. The goal of logic is to determine which syllogisms lead to valid conclusions and which not.

symbol grounding problem: the finding that representations (symbols) used in computations require a reference to some external reality in order to get meaning.

The origin of species: book by Charles Darwin (1859) in which he presented the evolutionary theory.

thought experiment: hypothetical scenario that helps with the understanding of a philosophical argument.

tit-for-tat strategy: strategy proposed in evolutionary psychology to explain how evolutionarily motivated individuals cooperate in situations of mutual dependency and benefit.

top-down process: process by which information from a higher processing stage is fed back to previous processing stages and influences the processing at these stages; found to be a helpful (and even essential) element in many computational models.

transcranial magnetic stimulation (TMS): stimulation of a brain region by means of a coil placed on the head; allows temporary interference with the processing of a small part of the brain.

Turing machine: basic (hypothetical) machine operating on the basis of Boolean logic and able to simulate the processing of more complex machines operating according to these principles.

Turing test: test described by Alan Turing, which involves a human interacting with a machine and another human without being able to discriminate the machine from the human; machines that pass the Turing test are seen as the goal of artificial intelligence.

unconscious plagiarism: term used by Bornstein to indicate how the scientific and the hermeneutic approach in psychology have influenced each other without the proponents being aware of it.

validity: in test research, the degree to which a test measures what it claims to measure; determined by correlating the test results with an external criterion.

ventricles: apertures in the middle of the brain, which for a long time were thought to contain perceptions, memories and thoughts; seat of the animal spirits.

verification: principle that up to the 1950s formed the core of the scientific method: a proposition was meaningful (scientific) if its truth could he empirically verified.

verificationism: adherence to the principle that a proposition is meaningful only if it can be verified as true or false; with respect to science states that a proposition is scientific only if it can be verified through objective, value-free observation.

vital force: animistic substance thought to be present in living matter before the chemical and biological differences between living and non-living matter were understood.

welfare state: socio-political system in which individuals insure themselves against setbacks via taxes, which are used by the state to provide welfare services.

Würzburg school: group of psychologists at the University of Würzburg who used introspection as the research method, but came to different conclusions from those of Wundt and Titchener; in particular they claimed that many thought processes were not available to introspection (imageless thoughts).

zeitgeist: word used in the history of science to indicate that the time was right for a certain discovery; the discovery did not originate from a single genius, but from a much wider development leading to the discovery.

zombie thought experiment: thought experiment proposed by Chalmers to illustrate that consciousness is more than the working of the brain or the implementation of information on a Turing machine because it involves a subjective component with qualia.

Bibliography

Abma, R. (2004) 'Madness and mental health.' In J. Jansz and P. van Drunen (eds) *A social history of psychology*. Oxford: Blackwell, pp. 93–128.

Achterhuis, H. (1979) *De markt van welzijn en geluk* [The market of well-being and happiness]. The Netherlands: Uitgeverij Ambo.

Adair, J.G. (1984) 'The Hawthorne effect: A reconsideration of the methodological artifact', *Journal of Applied Psychology*, 69: 334–45.

Aegisdottir, S. *et al.* (2006) 'The meta-analysis of clinical judgment project: Fifty-six years of accumulated research on clinical versus statistical prediction', *Counseling Psychologist*, 34: 341–382.

Allchin, D. (2002) 'To err and win a Nobel Prize: Paul Boyer, ATP synthase and the emergence of bioenergetics', *Journal of the History of Biology*, 35: 149–72.

Allchin, D. (2003) 'Scientific myth-conceptions', *Science Education*, 87: 329–51.

Allchin, D. (2004) 'Pseudohistory and pseudoscience', *Science & Education*, 13: 179–95.

Allport, G.W. (1947) 'Scientific models and human morals', *Psychological Review*, 54: 182–92.

Allport, G.W. & Odbert, H.S. (1936) 'Trait-names, a psycho-lexical study', *Psychological Monographs*, 47(1).

Alvesson, M. (2000) 'Taking the linguistic turn in organizational research', *Journal of Applied Behavioral Science*, 36: 136–58.

Anderson, C.A. & Bushman, B.J. (2002) 'Human aggression', *Annual Review of Psychology*, 53: 27–51.

Anderson, C.A. *et al.* (2003) 'The influence of media violence on youth', *Psychological Science in the Public Interest*, 4: 81–110.

Anderson, C.A., Lindsay, J.J. & Bushman, B.J. (1999) 'Research in the psychological laboratory: Truth or triviality?' *Current Directions in Psychological Science*, 8: 3–9.

Anderson, M.L. (2003) 'Embodied cognition: A field guide', *Artificial Intelligence*, 149: 91–130.

Andrewes, D.G. (2002) *Neuropsychology: From theory to practice*. Hove: Psychology Press.

Andrews, R. (1987) *The Routledge dictionary of quotations*. London: Routledge.

Angermeyer, M.C., Dietrich, S., Potl, D. & Matschinger, H. (2005) 'Media consumption and desire for social distance towards people with schizophrenia', *European Psychiatry*, 20: 246–50.

Angermeyer, M.C. & Matschinger, H. (2005) 'What is a bipolar disorder? Results of a representative survey of the German population', *Psychiatrische Praxis,* 32: 289–91.

Annas, J. (2003) *Plato: A very short introduction*. Oxford, UK; Oxford University Press.

APA Presidential Task Force on Evidence-based Practice (2006) 'Evidence-based practice in psychology', *American Psychologist*, 61: 271–85.

Appelbaum, P.S., Robbins, P.C. & Roth, L.H. (1999) 'Dimensional approach to delusions: Comparisons across types and diagnoses', *American Journal of Psychiatry*, 156: 1938–1943.

Arboleda-Florez, J. (1998) 'Mental illness and violence: An epidemiological appraisal of the evidence', *Canadian Journal of Psychiatry – Revue Canadienne de Psychiatrie*, 43: 989–96.

Ashworth, P. (2003) 'The origins of qualitative psychology'. In J.A. Smith (ed.) *Qualitative psychology: A practical guide to research methods*. London: Sage, pp. 4–24.

Axelrod, R. & Hamilton, W.D. (1981) 'The evolution of cooperation', *Science*, 211: 1390–6.

Baars, B.J. (1986) *The cognitive revolution in psychology*. New York: Guilford Press.

Baars, B.J. (1997) *In the theater of consciousness: The workspace of the mind*. New York: Oxford University Press.

Bacon, F. (1620) *Novum organum scientiarum*.

Baker, T.B., McFall, R.M. & Shoham, V. (2009) 'Current status and future prospects of clinical psychology: Toward a scientifically principled approach to mental and behavioral health care', *Psychological Science in the Public Interest*, 9: 67–103.

Bargh, J.A. & Chartrand, T. (1999) 'The unbearable automaticity of being', *American Psychologist*, 54: 462–79.

Bargh, J.A., Gollwitzer, P.M., Lee-Chai, A., Barndollar, K. & Trötschel, R. (2001) 'The automated will: Nonconscious activation and pursuit of behavioral goals', *Journal of Personality and Social Psychology*, 81: 1014–27.

Barnes, J. (2000) *Aristotle: A very short introduction.* Oxford: Oxford University Press.

Barrick, M.R., Shaffer, J.A. & DeGrassi, S.W. (2009) 'What you see may not be what you get: Relationships among self-presentation tactics and ratings of interview and job performance', *Journal of Applied Psychology*, 94: 1394–1411.

Barrow, R. (2000) 'Determining stereotypical images of psychologists: the Draw A Psychologist Checklist', *College Student Journal*, 34: 123–33.

Bauer, R.M. (1984) 'Autonomic recognition of names and faces in prosopagnosia: A neuropsychological application of the guilty knowledge test', *Neuropsychologia*, 22: 457–69.

Baumeister, R.F., Masicampo, E.J. & Vohs, K.D. (2011) 'Do conscious thoughts cause behavior?', *Annual Review of Psychology*, 62: 331–61.

Beck, D.M. (2010) 'The appeal of the brain in the popular press', *Perspectives on Psychological Science*, 5: 762–66.

Bem, S. & Looren de Jong, H. (2006) *Theoretical issues in psychology: An introduction.* London: Sage Publications.

Benjafield, J.G. (2005) *A history of psychology.* Oxford: Oxford University Press.

Benjamin, L.T., Jr. (2000) 'The psychology laboratory at the turn of the 20th century', *American Psychologist*, 55: 318–21.

Berger, H. (1969) 'Hans Berger on the electroencephalogram of man: The fourteen original reports on the human electroencephalogram', *EEG & Clinical Neurophysiology*, Supp. 28.

Berlin, I. (1999) *The roots of Romanticism* (ed. Henry Hardy). London: Pimlico.

Bernard, L.L. (1924) *Instinct: A study of social psychology.* New York: Henry Holt & Co.

Binet, A. (1904) 'A propos de la mesure de l'intelligence', *L'Année Psychologique*, 11: 69–82 (available on http://www.persee.fr/web/revues/ home/prescript/revue/psy).

Binet, A. & Simon, T. (1904a) 'Sur la nécessité d'établir un diagnostic scientifique des états inférieurs de l'intelligence', *L'Année Psychologique*, 11: 163–190 (available on http://www.persee.fr/web/revues/ home/ prescript/revue/psy).

Binet, A. & Simon, T. (1904b) 'Méthodes nouvelles pour le diagnostic du niveau intellectuel des anormaux', *L'Année Psychologique*, 11: 191–244 (available on http:// www.persee.fr/web/revues/ home/prescript/revue/psy).

Binet, A. & Simon, T. (1904c) 'Application des méthodes nouvelles au diagnostic du niveau intellectuel chez des enfants normaux en anormaux d'hospice et d'école primaire', *L'Année Psychologique*, 11: 245–336 (available on http://www.persee.fr/web/revues/ home/prescript/ revue/psy).

Binet, A. & Simon, T. (1907) 'Le dévelopement de l'intelligence chez les enfants', *L'Année Psychologique*, 14: 1–94 (available on http://www.persee.fr/web/revues/ home/prescript/revue/psy).

Bird-David, N. (1999) '"Animism" revisited: Personhood, environment, and relational epistemology', *Current Anthropology*, 40: S67–S91.

Birnbaum, L.C. (1955) 'Behaviorism in the 1920's', *American Quarterly*, 7: 15–30.

Blackwood's Edinburgh Magazine (1858), October, pp. 506–7. At http://books.google.be/books?id=sggHAQA AIAAJ&pg=PA506&dq=hamilton+%22phenomena+ of+memory%22+intitle:Edinburgh+intitle:Magazine& hl=nl&sa=X&ei=lJyET7DUI9CeOtSp3M0I&ved=0C DcQ6AEwAA#v=onepage&q&f=false.

Blech, J. (2006) *Inventing disease and pushing pills: Pharmaceutical companies and the medicalisation of normal life.* London: Routledge.

Block, N. (1995) 'On a confusion about a function of consciousness', *Behavioral and Brain Sciences*, 18: 227–87.

Block, N. (2004) *Qualia.* In R. Gregory (ed.) *Oxford companion to the mind* (2nd edn). Oxford: Oxford University Press.

Blodgett, H.C. (1929) 'The effect of the introduction of reward upon the maze performance of rats'. *Univ Calif Publ Psychol*, 4: 113–34.

Bock, K. (2008) Editorial. *Journal of Memory and Language*, 58: 1–2.

Bohman, M. (1996) 'Predisposition to criminality: Swedish adoption studies in retrospect.' In G.R. Bock and J.A. Goode (eds) *Genetics of criminal and antisocial behaviour.* Chichester: Wiley, pp. 99–114.

Bonta, J., Law, M. & Hanson, K. (1998) 'The prediction of criminal and violent recidivism among mentally disordered offenders: A meta-analysis', *Psychological Bulletin*, 123: 123–42.

Boomsma, D.I., Willemsen, G., Dolan, C.V., Hawkley, L.C. & Cacioppo, J.T. (2005) 'Genetic and environmental contributions to loneliness in adults: The Netherlands Twin Register study', *Behavior Genetics*, 35: 745–52.

Boring, E.G. (1923) 'Intelligence as the tests test it', *New Republic*, 6 June 1923, 35–7.

Boring, E.G. (1933) *The physical dimensions of consciousness.* New York: Appleton-Century.

Boring, E.G. (1950) *A history of experimental psychology* (2nd edn). New York: Appleton-Century-Crofts.

Bornstein, R.F. (2005) 'Reconnecting psychoanalysis to mainstream psychology: Challenges and opportunities', *Psychoanalytic Psychology*, **22**: 323–40.

Bouchard, T.J. (1994) 'Genes, environment, and personality', *Science*, **264**: 1700–1.

Bouton, M.E. (2007) *Learning and behavior: A contemporary synthesis*. Sunderland, MA: Sinauer Associates.

Boyack, K.W., Klavans, R. & Börner, K. (2005) 'Mapping the backbone of science', *Scientometrics*, **64**: 351–74.

Breasted, J.H. (1930) *The Edwin Smith surgical papyrus*. Chicago: University of Chicago Press (2 vols).

Breeuwsma, G. (2008) 'Het vergeten weten: De teloorgang van klassiekers in de psychologie'. [Forgotten knowledge: The decline of classics in psychology]. *De Psycholoog*, **43**: 202–209.

Bridgman, P.W. (1927) *The logic of modern physics*. Chicago: University of Chicago Press.

Broadbent, D.E. (1958) *Perception and communication*. Elmsford, NY: Pergamon Press.

Broca, P. (1863) 'Sur les caractères des cranes basques', *Extrait des Bulletins de la Société d'anthropologie de Paris*. Retrieved on 10 January 2008, from books.google.com.

Brysbaert, M. (2006) *Psychologie*. Gent, Belgium: Academia Press.

Bryson, B. (2003) *A short history of nearly everything*. London: Doubleday.

Buckingham, H.W. (2006) 'The Marc Dax (1770–1837)/ Paul Broca (1824–1880) controversy over priority in science: Left hemisphere specificity for seat of articulate language and for lesions that cause aphemia', *Clinical Linguistics & Phonetics*, **20**: 613–19.

Buller, D.J. (2005) *Adapting minds: Evolutionary psychology and the persistent quest for human nature*. Cambridge, MA: MIT Press.

Burr, V. & Butt, T. (2000) 'Psychological distress and postmodern thought.' In F. Dwight (ed.) *Pathology and the postmodern*. London: Sage Publications, pp. 186–206.

Buss, D.M. (1989) 'Sex differences in human mate preference: Evolutionary hypotheses testing in 37 cultures', *Behavioral and Brain Sciences*, **12**: 1–49.

Buss, D.M. (2004) *Evolutionary psychology: The new science of the mind* (2nd edn). Boston, MA: Pearson Education.

Buss, D.M. (2008) *Evolutionary psychology: The new science of the mind*. Harlow, UK: Pearson Education.

Butterworth, B. (1999) *The mathematical brain*. London: Macmillan.

Cahan, E.D. & White, S.H. (1992) 'Proposals for a second psychology', *American Psychologist*, **47**: 224–35.

Cajori, F. (ed.) (1934) *Sir Isaac Newton's Mathematical Principles of natural philosophy and his system of the world*. Berkeley: University of California Press.

Campbell, D.T. (1960) 'Blind variation and selective retention in creative thought as in other knowledge processes', *Psychological Review*, **67**: 380–400.

Capgras, J. & Reboul-Lachaux, J. (1923) 'L'Illusion des "sosies" dans un délire systématisé chronique', *Bulletin de la Société de Médecine Mentale*, **11**: 6–16. (Translated into English in Ellis, H.D., Whitley, J. and Luauté, J.-P. (1994) 'Delusional misidentification. The three original papers on the Capgras, Frégoli and intermetamorphosis delusions', *History of Psychiatry*, **5**: 117–46. If you read Dutch, also available in Draaisma, D. (2006) *Ontregelde geesten*. Groningen: Historische Uitgeverij.)

Capron, C. & Duyme, M. (1989) 'Assessment of effects of socioeconomic status on IQ in a full cross-fostering design', *Nature*, **340**: 552–3.

Carless, S.A., Rasiah, J. & Irmer B.E. (2009) Discrepancy between human resource research and practice: Comparison of industrial/organisational psychologists and human resource practitioners' beliefs. *Australian Psychologist*, **44**: 105–111.

Carnap, R. (1966) *Philosophical foundations of physics: An introduction to the philosophy of science*. New York: Basic Books.

Catholicon, or the Christian Philosopher (1815) *Roman Catholic Magazine*, 4 (at books.google.co.uk/books?ei=8zRjT_ipHOWa0QWH0uWKCA&id=yC4EAAAAQAAJ).

Cattell, J.M. (1888) 'The psychological laboratory at Leipsic', *Mind*, **13**: 37–51 (at psychclassics.yorku.ca).

Cattell, R.B. (1956) 'Validation and intensification of the Sixteen Personality Factor Questionnaire', *Journal of Clinical Psychology*, **12**: 205–14.

Cerullo, J.J. (1988) 'E.G. Boring: Reflections on a discipline builder', *The American Journal of Psychology*, **101**: 561–75.

Chadwick, O. (1990) *The secularization of the European mind in the nineteenth century*. Cambridge: Cambridge University Press.

Chalmers, A.F. (1999) *What is this thing called science?* (3rd edn). Maidenhead, UK: Open University Press.

Chalmers, D.J. (1966) *The conscious mind: In search of a fundamental theory*. New York: Oxford University Press.

Changeux, J.P. (1997) *Neuronal man: The biology of mind*, translated by Laurence Garey. Princeton, NJ: Princeton University Press.

Charles, E.P. (2008) 'Eight things wrong with introductory psychology courses in America: A warning to my European colleagues', *Journal für Psychologie*, **16**(1).

Chebat, J.C. & Michon, R. (2003) 'Impact of ambient odors on mall shoppers' emotions, cognition, and spending: A test of competitive causal theories', *Journal of Business Research*, **56**: 529–39.

Chiesa, M. (1994) *Radical behaviorism: The philosophy and the science*. Sarasota, FL: Authors Cooperative, Publishers.

Churchland, P. (1981) 'Eliminative materialism and the propositional attitudes', *Journal of Philosophy*, **78**: 67–90.

Clarke, E. & Jacyna, L.S. (1987) *Nineteenth-century origins of neuroscientific concepts*. Berkeley: University of California Press.

Cohen, H.F. (1994) *The scientific revolution: A historiographical inquiry*. Chicago: University of Chicago Press.

Cohen, H.F. (2010) *How modern science came into the world: Four civilizations, one 17th-century breakthrough*. Amsterdam: Amsterdam University Press.

Colapinto, J. (1997) 'The true story of John/Joan', *Rolling Stone*, **775**: 54–97.

Coles, P. (2001) 'Einstein, Eddington and the 1919 eclipse', *Historical Development of Modern Cosmology*, ASP Conference Series, 252.

Collini, S. (1998) *Introduction to C.P. Snow's The two cultures*. Cambridge: Cambridge University Press.

Collins, A. (1703) Letter to John Locke. As cited in Woolhouse, R.S. (2007) *Locke: A Biography*, p. 441. Cambridge: Cambridge University Press.

Coltheart, M. (2004) 'Are there lexicons?', *Quarterly Journal of Experimental Psychology*, **57A**: 1153–71.

Coltheart, M. (2004) 'Brain imaging, connectionism and cognitive neuropsychology', *Cognitive Neuropsychology*, **21**: 21–5.

Coltheart, M. (2006) 'What has functional neuroimaging told us about the mind (so far)?', *Cortex*, **42**: 323–31.

Coltheart, M. (2007) 'The 33rd Sir Frederick Bartlett Lecture: Cognitive neuropsychiatry and delusional belief', *Quarterly Journal of Experimental Psychology*, **60**: 1041–62.

Coltheart, M., Patterson, K. & Marshall, J.C. (eds) (1980) *Deep dyslexia*. London: Routledge & Kegan Paul.

Comte, A. (1830) *Cours de philosophie positive*. Paris: Bachelier.

Coon, D.J. (1992) 'Testing the limits of sense and science: American experimental psychologists combat spiritualism 1880–1920', *American Psychologist*, **47**: 143–51.

Corkin, S. (2002) 'What's new with the amnesic patient H.M.?', *Nature Reviews Neuroscience*, **3**: 153–160.

Corrigan, P.W. *et al.* (2005) 'Newspaper stories as measures of structural stigma', *Psychiatric Services*, **56**: 551–6.

Costall, A. (2001) 'Pear and his peers', In G.C. Bunn, A.D. Lovie & G.D. Richards (eds) *Psychology in Britain* (pp. 188–204). Leicester: BPS Books.

Costall, A. (2006) '"Introspectionism" and the mythical origins of scientific psychology', *Consciousness and Cognition*, **15**: 634–54.

Coyne, J.C. & Palmer, S.C. (2007) 'Does anyone read the classic studies they cite? Reflections on claims that psychotherapy promotes the survival of cancer patients', *The European Health Psychology*, **9**: 46–9.

Crick, F. (1995) *The astonishing hypothesis: The scientific search for the soul*. London: Touchstone Books.

Cubberley, E.P. (1920) *The history of education*. London: Constable & Co.

Cubelli, R. & De Bastiani, P. (2011) '150 Years after Leborgne: Why is Paul Broca so important in the history of neuropsychology?', *Cortex*, **47**: 146–147.

Cubelli, R. & Montagna, C.G. (1994) 'A reappraisal of the controversy of Dax and Broca', *Journal of the History of the Neurosciences*, **3**: 215–26.

Cummings, N.A. & O'Donohue, W.T. (2008) *Eleven blunders that crippled psychotherapy in America*. New York: Routledge.

Danziger, K. (1990) *Constructing the subject: Historical origins of psychological research*. Cambridge: Cambridge University Press.

Danziger, K. (1997) *Naming the mind: How psychology found its language*. London: Sage.

Darley, J.M. & Latané, B. (1968) 'Bystander intervention in emergencies: Diffusion of responsibility', *Journal of Personality and Social Psychology*, **8**: 377–83.

Davis, S.N. (2003) 'Sex stereotypes in commercials targeted toward children: A content analysis', *Sociological Spectrum*, **23**: 407–24.

Dawes, R.B. (1994) *House of cards: Psychology and psychotherapy built on myth*. New York: The Free Press.

Dawkins, R. (1976/2006) *The selfish gene: 30th anniversary edition – with a new Introduction by the author*. Oxford: Oxford University Press.

Dawkins, R. (1998) *Unweaving the rainbow: Science, delusion, and the appetite for wonder*. Boston: Houghton Mifflin.

Deary, I.J. (1994) 'Sensory discrimination and intelligence: Postmortem or resurrection?', *The American Journal of Psychology*, 107: 95–115.

De Araujo, I.E. Rolls, E.T., Velazco, M.I., Margot, C. & Cayeux, I. (2005) 'Cognitive modulation of olfactory processing', *Neuron*, 46: 671–9.

De Gelder, B., Vroomen, J., Pourtois, G. & Weiskrantz, L. (1999) 'Non-conscious recognition of affect in the absence of striate cortex', *Neuroreport*, 10: 3759–63.

De Graaf, P.M. & Kalmijn, M. (2006) 'Divorce motives in a period of rising divorce: Evidence from a Dutch life-history survey', *Journal of Family Issues*, 27: 183–205.

De Houwer, J. (2011) 'Why the cognitive approach in psychology would profit from a functional approach and vice versa', *Perspectives on Psychological Science*, 6: 202–9.

Dehaene, S., Naccache, L., Cohen, L., Le Bihan, D., Mangin, J.F., Poline, J.B. & Riviere, D. (2001) 'Cerebral mechanisms of word masking and unconscious repetition priming', *Nature Neuroscience*, 4: 752–8.

Dehaene, S., Sergent, C. & Changeux, J.P. (2003) 'A neuronal network model linking subjective reports and objective physiologi cal data during conscious perception', *Proceedings of the National Academy of Sciences of the United States of America*, 100: 8520–5.

Delboeuf, J.R.L. (1873) *Etude psychophysique: recherches théoriques et expérimentales sur la mesure des sensations et spécialement des sensations de lumière et de fatigue*. Bruxelles: l'Académie Royale de sciences, des lettres et des beaux-arts de Belgique.

Dennett, D.C. (2003) *Freedom evolves*. New York: Penguin.

Dennis, P.M. (2011) 'Press coverage of the new psychology by the New York Times during the progressive era', *History of Psychology*, 14: 113–36.

DeRubeis, R.J. *et al.* (2005) 'Cognitive therapy vs. medications in the treatment of moderate to severe depression', *Archives of General Psychiatry*, 62: 409–16.

Dewey, J. (1887) *Psychology*. New York: Harper & Brothers.

Dewey, J. (1896) 'The reflex are concept in psychology', *Psychological Review*, 3: 357–70. Retrieved on 12 November 2007 from http:// psychclassics.yorku.ca.

Diamond, M. & Sigmundson, H.K. (1997) 'Sex reassignment at birth: Long-term review and clinical implications', *Archives of Pediatrics and Adolescent Medicine*, 151: 298–304.

Dickson, A., Knussen, C. & Flowers, P. (2008) '"That was my old life; it's almost like a past-life now": Identity crisis, loss and adjustment amongst people living with Chronic Fatigue Syndrome', *Psychology & Health*, 23: 459–76.

Dienes, Z. (2008) *Understanding psychology as a science: An introduction to scientific and statistical inference*. Basingstoke: Palgrave Macmillan.

Dijksterhuis, A. & Nordgren, L.F. (2006) 'A theory of unconscious thought', *Perspectives on Psychological Science*, 1: 95–109.

Dijksterhuis, A., Bos, M.W., Nordgren, L.F. & van Baaren, R.B. (2006) 'On making the right choice: The deliberation-without-attention effect', *Science*, 311: 1005–7.

Dijksterhuis, A., Smith, P.K., van Baaren, R.B. & Wigboldus, D.H.J. (2005) 'The unconscious consumer: Effects of environment on consumer behavior', *Journal of Consumer Psychology*, 15: 193–202.

Djordjevic, J. *et al.* (2008) 'A rose by any other name: Would it smell as sweet?' *Journal of Neurophysiology*, 99: 386–93.

Dodge, K.A. & Coie, J.D. (1987) 'Social-information-processing factors in reactive and proactive aggression in children's peer groups', *Journal of Personality and Social Psychology*, 53: 1146–58.

Doll, R., Peto, R., Boreham, J. & Sutherland, I. (2004) 'Mortality in relation to smoking: 50 years' observations on male British doctors', *British Medical Journal*, 328: 1519–28.

Donders, F.C. (1868) 'Over de snelheid van psychische processen'. Translated by Koster, W.G. (1968). 'On the speed of mental processes', *Acta Psychologica*, 30: 412–31.

Donders, F. C. (1969[1868]) 'On the speed of mental processes', *Acta Psychologica*, 30: 413–21.

Dougherty, T.W., Turban, D.B. & Callender, J.C. (1994) 'Confirming first impression in the employment interview: A field-study of interviewer behavior', *Journal of Applied Psychology*, 79: 659–65.

Douglas, K.S., Guy, L.S. & Hart, S.D. (2009) Psychosis as a risk factor for violence to others: A meta-analysis. *Psychological Bulletin*, 135: 679–706.

Draaisma, D. (2000) *Metaphors of memory. A history of ideas about the mind*. Cambridge: Cambridge University Press.

Draaisma, D. (2009) *Disturbances of the mind*. Cambridge: Cambridge University Press.

Draper, J.W. (1847) *A textbook on natural philosophy for the use of schools and colleges*. New York: Harper & Brothers.

Driver-Linn, E. (2003) 'Where is psychology going? Structural fault lines revealed by psychologists' use of Kuhn', *American Psychologist*, 58: 269–78.

Dupuy, J.P. (2009) *On the origins of cognitive science: The mechanization of the mind.* Cambridge, MA: MIT Press.

Eagly, A.H., Ashmore, R.D., Makhijani, M.G. & Longo, L.C. (1991) 'What is beautiful is good, but . . . : A meta-analytic review of research on the physical attractiveness stereotype', *Psychological Bulletin*, **110**: 109–28.

Ebbinghaus, H. (1908/1973) *Psychology: An elementary textbook.* New York: Arno Press.

Ecclestone, K. & Hayes, D. (2009) *The dangerous rise of therapeutic education.* London: Routledge.

Edgell, B. (1947) 'The British Psychological Society', *British Journal of Psychology*, **37**: 113–32. (Reprinted in **2001**: *British Journal of Psychology*, **92**: 3–22.)

Eling, P. (2005) 'Baginsky on aphasia', *Journal of Neurolinguistics*, **18**: 301–15.

Eling, P. (2006a) 'Meynert on Wernicke's aphasia', *Cortex*, **42**: 811–6.

Eling, P. (2006b) 'The psycholinguistic approach to aphasia of Chajim Steinthal', *Aphasiology*, **20**: 1072–84.

Ellingson, T. (2001) *The myth of the Noble Savage.* Berkeley: University of California Press.

Ellis, H.D. & Florence, M. (1990) 'Bodamer's (1947) paper on prosopagnosia', *Cognitive Neuropsychology*, **7**: 81–105.

Ellis, H.D. & Lewis, M.B. (2001) 'Capgras delusion: A window on face recognition', *Trends in Cognitive Sciences*, **5**: 149–56.

Ellis, H.D. & Young, A.W. (1990) 'Accounting for delusional misidentifications', *British Journal of Psychology*, **157**: 239–48.

Ellis, H.D., Young, A.W., Quayle, A.H. & de Pauw, K.W. (1997) 'Reduced autonomic responses to faces in Capgras delusion', *Proceedings of the Royal Society London: Biological Sciences*, **264**: 1085–92.

Encyclopedia Britannica (1773) London: Dilly.

Endersby, J. (2007) *A guinea pig's history of biology: The plants and animals who taught us the facts of life.* London: William Heinemann.

Engel, G.L. (1977) 'The need for a new medical model: A challenge for biomedicine', *Science*, **196**: 129–36.

Evans, J.S.B.T. (2002) 'Logic and human reasoning: An assessment of the deduction paradigm', *Psychological Bulletin*, **128**: 978–96.

Eysenck, H.J. (1952/1992) 'The effects of psychotherapy: An evaluation', *Journal of Consulting Psychology*, **16**: 319–24. Reprinted in *Journal of Consulting and Clinical Psychology*, **60**: 659–63.

Eysenck, H.J. (1976) 'Learning theory model of neurosis: New approach', *Behaviour Research and Therapy*, **14**: 251–67.

Eysenck, H.J. & Eysenck, M.W. (1975) *Manual of the Eysenck Personality Questionnaire.* San Diego: Educational and Industrial Testing Service.

Eysenck, H.J., Eysenck, S.B.G. & Barrett, P. (1985) 'A revised version of the psychoticism scale', *Personality and Individual Differences*, **6**: 21–9.

Eysenck, M.W. & Keane, M.T. (2005) *Cognitive psychology: A student's handbook* (5th edn). Hove: Psychology Press.

Fancher, R.E. (1996) *Pioneers of psychology* (3rd edn). New York: Norton.

Fancher, R.E. (2009) 'Scientific cousins: The relationship between Charles Darwin and Francis Galton', *American Psychologist*, **64**: 84–92.

Fausto-Sterling, A., Gowaty, P.A. & Zuk, M. (1997) 'Evolutionary psychology and Darwinian feminism', *Feminist Studies*, **23**: 403–18.

Fechner, G.T. (1860) *Elemente der Psychophysik.* Leipzig: Breitkopf & Härtel.

Ferngren, G.B. (2002) *Science & religion: A historical introduction.* Baltimore, MD: The Johns Hopkins University Press.

Feyerabend, P.K. (1975/1993) *Against method: Outline of an anarchistic theory of knowledge.* London: New Left Books.

Fine, G.A. (1987) 'Joseph Jacobs: A sociological folklorist', *Folklore*, **98**: 183–93.

Finston, K.D., Beaver, J.B. & Cramond, B.L. (1995) 'Development and field test of a checklist for the Draw-a-scientist test', *School Science and Mathematics*, **95**: 195–205.

Fisher, G.H. (1968) 'Ambiguity of form – old and new', *Perception & Psychophysics*, **4**(3): 189–92.

Fodor, J.A. (1981) 'The mind–body problem', *Scientific American*, **244**(1): 124–32.

Forshaw, M.J. (2007) 'Free qualitative research from the shackles of method', *The Psychologist*, **20**: 478–79.

Foucault, M. (1961) *Folie et déraison. Histoire de la folie à l'âge classique.* Paris: Librairie Plon. [English translation in 1965: *Madness and civilization: A history of insanity in the Age of Reason*; new translation in 2006: *History of madness*, Routledge.]

Foucault, M. (1961/2006) *The history of madness.* Oxford: Routledge (original title: *Folie et déraison. Histoire de la folie à l'âge classique.* Paris: Libraire Plon).

Foucault, M. (1976) *Surveiller et punir: Naissance de la prison.* Paris: Editions Gallimard (English translation: Foucault, M. (1979) *Discipline and punish: The birth of the prison.* New York: Vintage).

Fox, D., Prilleltensky, I. & Austin, S. (eds) (2009) *Critical psychology: An introduction* (2nd edn). Los Angeles: Sage Publications.

Fox, M.C., Ericsson, K.A. & Best, R. (2011) Do procedures for verbal reporting of thinking have to be reactive? A meta-analysis and recommendations for best reporting methods. *Psychological Bulletin*, 137: 316–44.

Frankfurt, H.G. (2005) *On bullshit*. Princeton, NJ: Princeton University Press.

Freud, S. (1900/1913) *The interpretation of dreams* (English translation by A.A. Brill). New York: Macmillan (at psychclassics.yorku.ca).

Friedman, M. (2004) *Kant: Metaphysical Foundations of Natural Science (Cambridge Texts in the History of Philosophy*. Cambridge: Cambridge University Press.

Frith, C. (1992) *The cognitive neuropsychology of schizophrenia*. Hove: Erlbaum.

Fuchs, A.H. (2000) 'Contributions of American mental philosophers to psychology in the United States', *History of Psychology*, 3: 3–19.

Fuchs, A.H. (2000) 'Teaching the introductory course in Psychology circa 1900', *American Psychologist*, 55: 492–5.

Furedi, F. (2004) *Therapy culture: Cultivating vulnerability in an uncertain age*. London: Routledge.

Furumoto, L. (1989) 'The new history of psychology.' In I. Cohen (ed.) The G. Stanley Hall Lecture Series (Vol. 9). Washington, DC: APA.

Gabbard, G.O. & Gabbard, K. (1999) *Psychiatry and the cinema* (2nd edn). Washington, DC: American Psychiatric Press.

Galef, B.G. (1998) 'Edward Thorndike: Revolutionary psychologist, ambiguous biologist', *American Psychologist*, 53: 1128–34.

Gardner, H. (1987) *The mind's new science: A history of the cognitive revolution*. New York: Basic Books.

Garroutte, E.M. (2003) 'The positivist attach on Baconian science and religious knowledge in the 1870s'. In C. Smith (ed.) *The secular revolution: Power, interests, and conflict in the secularization of American public life* (pp. 197–215). Berkeley: University of California Press.

Gauch, H.G. (2003) *Scientific method in practice*. Cambridge: Cambridge University Press.

Gazzaniga, M.S., Ivry, R. & Mangun, G.R. (1998) *Fundamentals of cognitive neuroscience*. New York: W.W. Norton.

Geary, D.C., Vigil, J. & Byrd-Craven, J. (2004) 'Evolution of human mate choice', *The Journal of Sex Research*, 41: 27–42.

Geen, R.G. (2001) *Human aggression* (2nd edn). Buckingham, UK: Open University Press.

Geertz, C. (2000) *Available light: Anthropological reflections on philosophical topics*. Princeton, NJ: Princeton University Press.

Geier, A.B., Rozin, P. & Doros, G. (2006) 'Unit bias: A new heuristic that helps explain the effect of portion size on food intake', *Psychological Science*, 17: 521–5.

Gentner, D. & Grudin, J. (1985) 'The evolution of mental metaphors in psychology: A 90-year retrospective', *American Psychologist*, 40: 181–92.

Gergen, K.J. (1973) 'Social psychology as history', *Journal of Personality and Social Psychology*, 26: 309–20.

Gergen, K.J. (2001) 'Psychological science in a postmodern context', *American Psychologist*, 56: 803–13.

Gerteis, L.S. (1991) 'Book review of *Abolitionist, actuary, atheist: Elizur Wright and the reform impulse*, by Lawrence B. Goodheart', *The Journal of American History*, 77: 1360–1.

Geschwind, N. (1972) 'Language and the brain', *Scientific American*, 226: 76–83.

Gilles, D. (1996) *Artificial intelligence and scientific method*. Oxford: Oxford University Press.

Giorgi, A. (1970) *Psychology as a human science*. New York: Harper & Row.

Glaser, B.G. & Strauss, A.L. (1967) *Discovery of grounded theory: Strategies for qualitative research*. New York: Aldine de Gruyter.

Glenberg, A.M. & Robertson, D.A. (2000) Symbol grounding and meaning: A comparison of high-dimensional and embodied theories of meaning. *Journal of Memory and Language*, 43: 379–401.

Goffman, E. (1963) *Stigma: Notes on the management of spoiled identity*. Englewood Cliffs, NJ: Prentice Hall.

Goldberg, L.R. (1990) 'An alternative "description of personality": The big-five factor structure', *Journal of Personality and Social Psychology*, 59: 1216–29.

Goodglass, H. (1983) 'Linguistic aspects of aphasia', *Trends in Neuroscience*, **June**: 241–3.

Goodglass, H. & Kaplan, E. (1983) *The assessment of aphasia and related disorders*. Philadelphia: Lea & Febiger.

Goodwin, C.J. (1991) 'Misportraying Pavlov's apparatus', *The American Journal of Psychology*, 104: 135–41.

Gould, S.J. (1996) *The mismeasure of man* (2nd edn). London: W.W. Norton & Co.

Gould, S.J. & R.C. Lewontin (1979) 'The spandrels of San Marco and the panglossian paradigm: A critique of the adaptationist programme', *Proceedings of the Royal Society of London*, B205: 581–98.

Gower, B. (1997) *Scientific method: An historical and philosophical introduction*. London: Routledge.

Graham, J., Haidt, J. & Nosek, B.A. (2009) Liberals and conservatives rely on different sets of moral foundations. *Journal of Personality and Social Psychology*, **96**: 1029–46.

Gratzer, W. (2002) *Eurekas and euphorias: The Oxford book of scientific anecdotes*. Oxford: Oxford University Press.

Green, C.D. (2009) 'Darwinian theory, functionalism, and the first American psychological revolution', *American Psychologist*, **64**: 75–83.

Greenhalgh, T. (1997) 'How to read a paper: Getting your bearings (deciding what the paper is about)', *British Medical Journal*, **315**: 243–46.

Greenwald, A.G. (1992) 'New look 3: Unconscious cognition reclaimed', *American Psychologist*, **47**: 766–79.

Greenwald, A.G., Draine, S.C. & Abrams, R.L. (1996) 'Three cognitive markers of unconscious semantic activation', *Science*, **273**: 1699–702.

Greenwald, A.G., Spangenberg, E.R., Pratkanis, A.R. & Eskenazi, J. (1991) 'Double-blind tests of subliminal self-help audiotapes', *Psychological Science*, **2**: 119–22.

Griffith, C.R. (1921) 'Some neglected aspects of a history of psychology', *Psychological Monographs*, **30**: 17–29 (available on http:// psychclassics.yorku.ca).

Gross, C.G. (1998) *Brain, vision, memory: Tales in the history of neuroscience*. Cambridge, MA: The MIT Press.

Gross, R. (2003) *Themes, issues and debates in psychology* (2nd edn). Abingdon, UK: Hodder Arnold.

Grove, W.M., Zald, D.H., Lebow, B.S., Snitz, E. & Nelson, C. (2000) 'Clinical versus mechanical prediction: A meta-analysis', *Psychological Assessment*, **12**: 19–30.

Grüsser, O.J. (1989) Quantitative visual psychophysics during the period of European enlightenment. The studies of astronomer and mathematician Tobias Mayer (1723–1762) on visual acuity and colour perception. *Documenta Ophthalmologica*, **71**: 93–111.

Guillin, V. (2004) 'Théodule Ribot's ambiguous positivism: Philosophical and epistemological strategies in the founding of French scientific psychology', *Journal of the History of the Behavioral Sciences*, **40**: 165–81.

Gulerce, A. (2006) 'History of psychology in Turkey as a sign of diverse modernization and global psychologization.' In A.C. Brock (ed.) *Internationalizing the history of psychology*. New York: New York University Press, pp. 75–93.

Gupta, K. (1932) A few hints on the teaching of mathematics. *Indian Journal of Psychology*, **7**: 75–86.

Haggard, P. (2005) 'Conscious intention and motor cognition', *Trends in Cognitive Sciences*, **6**: 290–5.

Haggbloom, S.J. *et al.* (2002) 'The 100 most eminent psychologists of the 20th century', *Review of General Psychology*, **6**: 139–52.

Halligan, P.W. & Marshall, J.C. (1996) *Method in madness: Case studies in cognitive neuropsychiatry*. Hove: Psychology Press.

Hamilton, W.D. (1964) 'The genetical evolution of social behavior I and II', *Journal of Theoretical Biology*, **7**: 1–52.

Haney, C. & Zimbardo, P. (1998) 'The past and future of US prison policy: Twenty-five years after the Stanford Prison Experiment', *American Psychologist*, **53**: 709–27.

Haney, C., Banks, W. & Zimbardo, P. (1973) 'Interpersonal dynamics in a simulated prison', *International Journal of Criminology and Penology*, **1**: 69–97.

Hanley, J.R., Masterson, J., Spencer, L.H. & Evans, D. (2004) 'How long do the advantages of learning to read a transparent orthography last? An investigation of the reading skills and reading impairment of Welsh children at 10 years of age', *Quarterly Journal of Experimental Psychology*, **57**A: 1393–410.

Hannam, J. (2009) *God's philosophers: How the medieval world lay the foundations of modern science*. London: Icon Books.

Hanson, F.A. (1993) *Testing testing: Social consequences of the examined life*. Berkeley: University of California Press.

Hanson, R.K & Morton-Bourgon, K.E. (2009) 'The accuracy of recidivism risk assessments for sexual offenders: A meta-analysis of 118 prediction studies', *Psychological Assessment*, **21**: 1–21.

Hanssen, M., Bak, M., Bijl, R., Vollebergh, W. & van Os, J. (2005) 'The incidence and outcome of subclinical psychotic experiences in the general population', *British Journal of Clinical Psychology*, **44**: 181–91.

Harden, K.P., Turkheimer, E. & Loehlin, J.C. (2007) 'Genotype by environment interaction in adolescents' cognitive aptitude', *Behavior Genetics*, **37**: 273–83.

Harley, T.A. (2004) 'Does cognitive neuropsychology have a future?', *Cognitive Neuropsychology*, **21**: 2–16.

Harnad, S. (1990) 'The symbol grounding problem', *Physica D*, **42**: 335–346.

Harris, B. (1979) 'Whatever happened to Little Albert?', *American Psychologist*, **34**: 151–60.

Hartwig, S.G. (2002) 'Surveying psychologists' public image with drawings of a "typical" psychologist', *South Pacific Journal of Psychology*, **14**: 69–75.

Hatch, J.A. (ed.) (1995) *Qualitative research in early childhood settings*. Westport, CT: Greenwood Publishing Group.

Hatfield, G. (1998) 'Kant and empirical psychology in the 18th century', *Psychological Science*, **9**: 423–8.

Hatfield, G. (2000) 'The brain's "new" science: Psychology, neurophysiology, and constraint', *Philosophy of Science*, **67**: S388–S403.

Haynes, R. (2003) 'From alchemy to artificial intelligence: Stereotypes of the scientist in Western literature', *Public Understanding of Science*, **12**: 243–53.

Hearnshaw, L. (1964) *A short history of British psychology, 1840–1948*. London: Methuen.

Hell, B., Trapmann, S., Weigand, S. & Schuler, H. (2007) 'The validity of admission interviews – a meta-analysis', *Psychologische Rundschau*, **58**: 93–102.

Helm-Estabrooks, N., Fitzpatrick, P.M. & Barresi, B. (1981) 'Response of an agrammatic patient to a syntax stimulation program for aphasia', *Journal of Hearing and Speech Disorders*, **46**: 422–7.

Henson, R. (2005) 'What can functional neuroimaging tell the experimental psychologist?' *The Quarterly Journal of Experimental Psychology*, **58A**: 193–233.

Herschel, J.F.W. (1831) *A preliminary discourse on the study of natural philosophy*. London.

Hicks, G.D. (1928) 'A century of philosophy at University College, London', *Journal of Philosophical Studies*, **3**: 468–82.

Hoffman, J.L. (1949) 'Clinical observations concerning schizophrenic patients treated by prefrontal leukotomy', *New England Journal of Medicine*, **241**: 233–6.

Hofstede, G. (2001) *Culture's consequences: Comparing values, behaviors, institutions, and organizations across nations*. Thousand Oaks, CA: Sage Publications.

Hofstede, G. (2005) *Cultures and organizations: Software of the mind* (2nd edn). London: McGraw-Hill Professional.

Holender, D. (1986) 'Semantic activation without conscious identification in dichotic listening, parafoveal vision, and visual masking: A survey and appraisal', *Behavioral and Brain Sciences*, **9**: 1–23.

Holland, T. (2008) *Millennium*. London: Little, Brown.

Hollingworth, H.L. (1922) *Judging human character*. New York: Appleton & Company.

Hollon, S.D. *et al.* (2005) 'Prevention of relapse following cognitive therapy vs medications in moderate to severe depression', *Archives of General Psychiatry*, **62**: 417–22.

Holmes, G.M. (1918) 'Disturbance of vision by cerebral lesions', *British Journal of Ophthalmology*, **2**: 353–84.

Holmes, R. (2008) *The age of wonder: How the Romantic generation discovered the beauty and terror of science*. London: Harper Press.

Hood, R.W. (2000) 'American psychology of religion and the *Journal for the Scientific Study of Religion*, *Journal for the Scientific Study of Religion*, **39**: 531–43.

Hosoda, M., Stone-Romero, E.F. & Coats, G. (2003) 'The effects of physical attractiveness on job-related outcomes: A meta-analysis of experimental studies', *Personnel Psychology*, **56**: 431–62.

Hulett, J.E. (1955) 'Book review of *Psychotherapy and personality change: Coordinated research studies in the client-centered approach*, by Carl R. Rogers and Rosalind F. Dymond', *American Sociological Review*, **20**: 369–70.

Hume, D. (1779) *Dialogues concerning natural religion* (2nd edn). London.

Hunt, H.T. (2005) 'Why psychology is/is not traditional science: The self-referential bases of psychological research and theory', *Review of General Psychology*, **9**: 358–74.

Hunter, Z.R., Brysbaert, M. & Knecht, S. (2007) 'Foveal word reading requires interhemispheric communication', *Journal of Cognitive Neuroscience*, **19**: 1373–87.

Huylebrouck, D. (2006) 'Mathematics in (central) Africa before colonization', *Anthropologica et Praehistorica*, **117**: 135–62.

Ifrah, G. (1998) *The universal history of numbers: From prehistory to the invention of the computer*. London: The Harvill Press. (Translation of the French original (1994): *Histoire Universelle des chiffres*. Paris: Editions Robert Laffont.)

Illich, I. (1971) *Deschooling society*. London: Penguin Education.

Illich, I. (1973) *Tools for conviviality*. New York: Harper & Row (also available on http://clevercycles.com/tools_for_conviviality).

Illich, I. (1976) *Limits to medicine – Medical nemesis: The expropriation of health*. London: Marion Boyars (also available on www. soilandhealth.org).

Ioannidis, J.P.A. (2005) 'Contradicted and initially stronger effects in highly cited clinical research', *Journal of the American Medical Association*, **294**: 218–28.

Jack, A.I. & Roepstorff, A. (2002) 'Introspection and cognitive brain mapping: From stimulus-response to script-report', *Trends in Cognitive Sciences*, **6**: 333–9.

Jackson, F. (1982) 'Epiphenomenal qualia', *Philosophical Quarterly*, **32**: 127–36.

Jackson, S. & Rees, A. (2007) 'The appalling appeal of nature: The popular influence of evolutionary psychology as a problem for sociology', *Sociology*, **41**: 917–30.

Jacob, S. *et al.* (2002) 'Paternally inherited HLA alleles are associated with women's choice of male odor', *Nature Genetics*, **30**: 175–9.

Jacobs, J. (1887) 'Experiments on "Prehension"', *Mind*, **12**: 75–9.

Jahoda, G. (2007) *A history of social psychology*. Cambridge: Cambridge University Press.

James, W. (1890) *The principles of psychology* (2 vols) New York: Henry Holt (at psychclassics.yorku.ca).

James, W. (1892) 'A plea for psychology as a "natural science"', *The Philosophical Review*, **1**: 146–53.

Janda, L.H., England, K., Lovejoy, D. & Drury, K. (1998) 'Attitudes toward psychology relative to other disciplines', *Professional Psychology: Research and Practice*, **29**: 140–3.

Jansz, J. & Van Drunen, P. (eds) (2004) *A social history of psychology*. Oxford: Blackwell Publishing.

Jensen, R. (2006) Behaviorism, latent learning, and cognitive maps: Needed revisions in introductory psychology textbooks. *Behavior Analyst*, **29**: 187–209.

Johnson, B. (2007) 'Twenty-eight people ask Hugh MacLeod to be their friend each day. What's so special about him? Answer: he may be Britain's most successful Facebooker'. *The Guardian*, 15 December, p. 3.

Johnston, L. (2002) 'Behavioral mimicry and stigmatization', *Social Cognition*, **20**: 18–35.

Jolley, N. (2005) *Leibniz*. London: Routledge.

Jones, S. (1999) *Almost like a whale: The origin of species updated*. London: Doubleday.

Jost, J.T., Glaser, J., Kruglanski, A.W. & Sulloway, F.J. (2003) 'Political conservatism as motivated social cognition', *Psychological Bulletin*, **129**: 339–75.

Kagan, J. (2009) *The three cultures: Natural Sciences, Social Sciences, and the Humanities in the 21st century*. Cambridge, MA: Cambridge University Press.

Kagan, J. (2009a) 'Historical selection', *Review of General Psychology*, **13**: 77–88.

Kagan, J. (2009b) *The three cultures: Natural Sciences, Social Sciences, and the Humanities in the 21st century*. Cambridge: Cambridge University Press.

Kagitcibasi, C. (2002) 'A model of family change in cultural context'. In *Online Readings in Psychology and Culture*. Retrieved on December 10, 2007 from http://www.ac.wwu.edu/~culture/ contents_complete.htm.

Kahneman, D. & Tversky, A. (1974) 'Judgment under uncertainty: Heuristics and biases', *Science*, **185**: 1124–31.

Kahneman, D. & Tversky, A. (1979) 'Prospect theory: Analysis of decision under risk', *Econometrica*, **47**: 263–91.

Kane, R. (2005) *A contemporary introduction to free will*. Oxford University Press.

Kant (1994) *Metaphysical foundations of natural science* (trans. M. Freeman). Cambridge: Cambridge University Press.

Kaplan, R.M. & Saccuzzo, D.P. (2005) *Psychological testing: Principles, applications, and issues* (6th edn). Belmont, CA: Thomson Wadsworth.

Keefe, F.J., Rumble, M.E., Scipio, C.D., Giordano, L.A. & Perri, L.M. (2004) 'Psychological aspects of persistent pain: Current state of the science', *The Journal of Pain*, **5**: 195–211.

Keil, F.C. (2003) 'Folkscience: Coarse interpretations of a complex reality', *Trends in Cognitive Sciences*, **7**: 368–73.

Keil, F.C., Lockhart, K.L. & Schlegel, E. (2010) 'A bump on a bump? Emerging intuitions concerning the relative difficulties of the sciences', *Journal of Experimental Psychology: General*, **139**: 1–15.

Kendler, K.S., Thornton, L.M., Gilman, S.E. & Kessler, R.C. (2000) 'Sexual orientation in a U.S. national sample of twin and nontwin sibling pairs', *American Journal of Psychiatry*, **157**: 1843–6.

Kessels, U., Rau, M. & Hannover, B. (2006) 'What goes well with physics? Measuring and altering the image of science', *British Journal of Educational Psychology*, **76**: 761–80.

Kessler, R.C., Berglund, P., Demler, O., Jin, R. *et al.* (2005) 'Lifetime prevalence and age-of-onset distributions of DSM-IV disorders in the national comorbidity survey replication', *Archives of General Psychiatry*, **62**: 593–602.

Kihlstrom, J.F. (2007) *Social neuroscience: The footprints of Phineas Gage*. Retrieved on 11 November, 2007 from http://socrates.berkeley .edu/~kihlstrm/ SocialNeuroscience07.htm.

Kihlstrom, J.F. (2010) 'Social neuroscience: The footprints of Phineas Gage', *Social Cognition*, **28**: 757–83.

Kimmel, A.J. (2007) *Ethical issues in behavioral research: Basic and applied perspectives* (2nd edn). Oxford: Blackwell Publishing.

King, R.N. & Koehler, D.J. (2000) 'Illusory correlations in graphological inference', *Journal of Experimental Psychology: Applied*, **6**: 336–48.

Kirsch, I., Deacon, B.J., Huedo-Medina, T.B., Scoboria, A., Moore, T.J. & Johnson, B.T. (2008) 'Initial severity and antidepressant benefits: A metaanalysis of data submitted to the Food and Drug Administration', *PLoS Med* **5**(2): e45. doi:10.1371/journal.pmed.0050045.

Kobayakawa, K. *et al.* (2007) 'Innate versus learned odour processing in the mouse olfactory bulb', *Nature*, **450**: 503–8.

Koch, S. (1961) 'Psychological science versus the science-humanism antinomy: Intimations of a significant science of man', *American Psychologist*, **16**: 629–39.

Kompier, M.A.J. (2006) 'The "Hawthorne effect" is a myth, but what keeps the story going?', *Scandinavian Journal of Work, Environment & Health*, **32**: 402–12.

Kotowicz, Z. (2007) 'The strange case of Phineas Gage', *History of the Human Sciences*, **20**: 115–31.

Kreiner, D.S., Altis, N.A. & Voss, C.W. (2003) 'A test of the effect of reverse speech on priming', *Journal of Psychology*, **137**: 224–32.

Krstić, K. (1964) 'Marko Marulic: The author of the term "psychology"', *Acta Instituti Psychologici Universitatis Zagrabiensis*, **36**: 7–13 (at psychclassics.yorku.ca).

Kuhn, T.S. (1962/1970) *The structure of scientific revolutions*. Chicago: University of Chicago Press.

Kunda, Z. & Thagard, P. (1996) 'Forming impressions from stereotypes, traits, and behaviors: A parallel-constraint-satisfaction theory', *Psychological Review*, 103: 284–308.

Kunst-Wilson, W.R. & Zajonc, R.B. (1980) 'Affective discrimination of stimuli that cannot be recognized', *Science*, 207: 557–8.

Laing, R.D. (1960) *The divided self: An existential study in sanity and madness*. Harmondsworth: Penguin.

Lakatos, I. (1970) 'Falsification and the methodology of scientific research programs.' In I. Lakatos and A. Musgrave (eds) *Criticism and the growth of knowledge*. New York: Cambridge University Press.

Lakoff, G. & Johnson, M. (1980) *Metaphors we live by*. Chicago, IL: University of Chicago.

Lakoff, G. & Johnson, M. (1999) *Philosophy in the flesh: The embodied mind and its challenge to Western thought*. New York: Basic Books.

Lamme, V.A.F. (2006) 'Towards a true neural stance on consciousness', *Trends in Cognitive Sciences*, 10: 494–501.

Lamme, V.A.F. (2010) 'How neuroscience will change our view on consciousness (plus subsequent commentaries)', *Cognitive Neuroscience*, 1: 204–240.

Langner, T.S. (1962) 'A twenty-two item screening score of psychiatric symptoms indicating impairment', *Journal of Health and Human Behavior*, 3: 269–76.

Larsen, S.F. (1987) 'Remembering and the archaeology metaphor', *Metaphor and Symbol*, 2: 187–99.

Lawrence, W. (1817) *Lectures on physiology, zoology, and the natural history of man*. London: James Smith.

Leahey, T.H. (1992) 'The mythical revolutions of American psychology', *American Psychologist*, 47: 308–18.

Leahey, T.H. (2004) *A history of psychology* (6th edn). Upper Saddle River, NJ: Pearson Prentice Hall.

Leakey, R. & Lewin, R. (1992) *Origins reconsidered: In search of what makes us human*. London: Doubleday.

Leary, D.E. (ed.) (1995) *Metaphors in the history of psychology*. Cambridge: Cambridge University Press.

Lee, T.W., Mitchell, T.R. & Sablynski, C.J. (1999) 'Qualitative research in organizational and vocational psychology 1979–1999', *Journal of Vocational Behavior*, 55: 161–87.

Lehman, A.F. & Steinwachs, D.M. (1998) 'At issue: Translating research into practice: The Schizophrenia Patient Outcomes Research Team (PORT) treatment recommendations', *Schizophrenia Bulletin*, 24: 1–10.

Leibniz, G.W. (1765) *Nouveaux essais sur l'entendement human* (New essays on human understanding). First appeared in Raspe, R.E. (ed.) (1765) *Oeuvre philosophiques, latines et françaises, de feu Mr. de Leibniz, tirées de ses manuscrits, qui se conservent dans la bibliothèque royale à Hanovre*. Amsterdam and Leipzig.

Lemon, N. & Taylor, H. (1997) 'Caring in casualty: The phenomenology of nursing care.' In N. Hayes (ed.) *Doing qualitative analysis in psychology*. Hove: Psychology Press, pp. 227–43.

Lewin, K., Lippitt, R. & White, R. (1939) 'Patterns of aggressive behaviour in experimentally created "social climates"', *Journal of Social Psychology*, 10: 271–99.

Lewis, J.E., DeGusta, D., Meyer, M.R., Monge, J.M., Mann, A.E. *et al.* (2011) 'The mismeasure of science: Stephen Jay Gould versus Samuel George Morton on skulls and bias', *PLoS Biol* 9(6): e1001071. doi:10.1371/journal.pbio.1001071.

Li, W., Howard, J.D., Parrish, T.B. & Gottfried, J.A. (2008) 'Aversive learning enhances perceptual and cortical discrimination of indiscriminable odor cues', *Science*, 319: 1842–5.

Libet, B. (1985) 'Unconscious cerebral initiative and the role of conscious will in voluntary action', *Behavioral and Brain Sciences*, 8: 529–39.

Libet, B. (1999) 'Do we have free will?' *Journal of Consciousness Studies*, 6: 47–55.

Lieberman, M.D. (2000) 'Intuition: A social cognitive neuroscience approach', *Psychological Bulletin*, 126: 109–37.

Lieberman, M.D. (2007) 'Social cognitive neuroscience: A review of the core processes', *Annual Review of Psychology*, 58: 259–89.

Liebig, J. von (1863) *Ueber Francis Bacon von Verulam und die Methode der Naturforschung*. Munich.

Lilienfeld, S.O., Lynn, S.J., Ruscio, J. & Beyerstein, B.L. (2010) *50 great myths of popular psychology: Shattering widespread misconceptions about human behaviour*. Chichester: Wiley-Blackwell.

Lindberg, D.C. (1992) *The beginnings of Western science: The European scientific tradition in philosophical, religious, and institutional context, 600 BC to AD 1450*. Chicago: The University of Chicago Press.

Link, B.G., Phelan, J.C., Besnahan, M., Stueve, A. & Pescosolido, B.A. (1999) 'Public conceptions of mental illness: Labels, causes, dangerousness, and social distance', *American Journal of Public Health*, 89: 1328–33.

Link, B.G., Yang, L.H., Phelan, J.C. & Collins, P.Y. (2004) 'Measuring mental illness stigma', *Schizophrenia Bulletin*, 30: 511–41.

Liu, I., Blacker, D.L., Xu, R., Fitzmaurice, G., Lyons, M.J. & Tsuang, M.T. (2004) 'Genetic and environmental contributions to the development of alcohol dependence in male twins', *Archives of General Psychiatry*, 61: 897–903.

Locke, E.A. (2009) 'It's time we brought introspection out of the closet', *Perspectives on Psychological Science*, **4**: 24–25.

Locke, J. (1690) *Essay concerning human understanding*. London.

Loftus, E.F. & Klinger, M.R. (1992) 'Is the unconscious smart or dumb?' *American Psychologist*, **47**: 761–5.

Lott, B. (1985) 'The potential enrichment of social personality psychology through feminist research and vice versa', *American Psychologist*, **40**: 155–64.

Louden, R.B. (ed.) (2006) *Immanuel Kant: Anthropology from a pragmatic point of view*. Cambridge: Cambridge University Press.

Lovie, S. (2001) 'Three steps to heaven: How the British Psychological Society attained its place in the sun'. In G.C. Bunn, A.D. Lovie & G.D. Richards (eds) *Psychology in Britain* (pp. 95–114). Leicester: BPS Books.

Lowery, B.S., Eisenberger, N.I., Hardin, C.D. & Sinclair, S. (2007) 'Long-term effects of subliminal priming on academic performance', *Basic and Applied Social Psychology*, **29**: 151–7.

Luhrmann, T.M. (2007) 'Social defeat and the culture of chronicity: Or, why schizophrenia does so well over there and so badly here', *Culture, Medicine and Psychiatry*, **31**: 135–72.

Luyten, P., Blatt, S.J. & Corveleyn, J. (2006) 'Minding the gap between positivism and hermeneutics in psychoanalytic research', *Journal of the American Psychoanalytic Association*, **54**: 571–610.

Lyons, W. (2001) *Matters of the mind*. New York: Routledge.

Mackenzie, D.B. (1977) *Behaviorism and the limits of scientific method*. London: Routledge & Kegan Paul.

Mackintosh, N.J. (1998) *IQ and human intelligence*. Oxford: Oxford University Press.

Mahajan, S.K., Machhan, P.C., Sood, B.R., Kuman, S., Sharma, D.D., Mokta, J. & Pal, L.S. (2004) 'Neurocysticercosis presenting with psychosis', *Journal of the Association of Physicians in India*, **52**: 663–66.

Maiers, W. (1991) 'Critical psychology: Historical background and task'. In C.W. Tolman and W. Maiers (eds) *Critical psychology: Contributions to an historical science of the subject*. Cambridge: Cambridge University Press.

Malone, J.C. & Cruchon, N.M. (2001) 'Radical behaviorism and the rest of psychology: A review/précis of Skinner's *About Behaviorism*', *Behavior and Philosophy*, **29**: 31–57.

Mandler, G. (2007) *A history of modern experimental psychology*. *Cambridge*, MA: The MIT Press.

Manguel, A. (1996) *A history of reading*. London: HarperCollins.

Mann, N. (1996) 'The origins of humanism'. In J. Kraye (ed.) *The Cambridge companion to Renaissance humanism* (pp. 1–19). Cambridge: Cambridge University Press.

Manning, R., Levine, M. & Collins, A. (2007) 'The Kitty Genovese Murder and the social psychology of helping: The parable of the 38 witnesses', *American Psychologist*, **62**: 555–62.

Marcel, A.J. (1983) 'Conscious and unconscious perception: Experiments on visual masking and word recognition', *Cognitive Psychology*, **15**: 197–237.

Marecek, J. (2003) 'Dancing through minefields: Toward a qualitative stance in psychology'. In P.M. Camic, J.E. Rhodes & L. Yardley (eds) *Qualitative research in psychology: Expanding perspectives in methodology and design*. Washington DC: American Psychological Association, pp. 49–69.

Marr, D. (1982) *Vision*. San Francisco: Freeman.

Marti, S., Sackur, J., Sigman, M. & Dehaene, S. (2010) 'Mapping introspection's blind spot: Reconstruction of dual-task phenomenology using quantified introspection', *Cognition*, **115**: 303–13.

Martin, L. (1986) '"Eskimo words for snow": A case study in the genesis and decay of an anthropological example', *American Anthropologist*, **88**: 418–23.

Martineau, H. (1858) *The positive philosophy of Auguste Compte*. New York: Calvin Blanchard.

Maslow, A.H. (1966) *Psychology of science*. New York: Harper and Row.

Mayer, B. & Merckelbach, H. (1999) 'Unconscious processes, subliminal stimulation, and anxiety', *Clinical Psychology Review*, **19**: 571–90.

Mayer, J. (2008) *The dark side: The inside story of how the war on terror turned into a war on American ideals*. Garden City, NY: Doubleday.

Mayo, E. (1945) *The social problems of an industrial civilization*. Cambridge, MA: Harvard University Press.

McCabe, D.P. & Castel, A.D. (2008) 'Seeing is believing: The effect of brain images on judgments of scientific reasoning', *Cognition*, **107**: 343–52.

McComas, W.F. (ed.) (1998) *The nature of science in science education*. Dordrecht: Kluwer Academic Publishers.

McCulloch, W.S. & Pitts, W.H. (1943) 'A logical calculus of the ideas immanent in nervous activity', *Bulletin of Mathematical Biophysics*, **5**: 115–33.

McDaniel, M.A., Whetzel, D.L., Schmidt, F.L. & Maurer, S.D. (1994) 'The validity of employment interviews: A comprehensive review and meta-analysis', *Journal of Applied Psychology*, **79**: 599–616.

McDougall, W. (1930) *William McDougall*. In Murchison C. (ed.) *A history of psychology in autobiography*, I, Clark University Press, 191–223.

McDuffie, T.E. (2001) 'Scientists – geeks & nerds? Dispelling teachers' stereotypes of scientists', *Science and Children*, 38: 16–19.

McKeown, T. (1979) *The role of medicine: Dream, mirage or nemesis?* (2nd edn). Oxford: Basil Blackwell.

McNulty, J.K., Neff, L.A. & Karney, B.R. (2008) 'Beyond initial attraction: Physical attractiveness in newlywed marriage', *Journal of Family Psychology*, 22: 135–43.

McReynolds, P. (1987) 'Lightner Witmer: Little-known founder of clinical psychology', *American Psychologist*, **42**: 849–58.

Medawar, P.B. (1969) *Induction and intuition in scientific thought*. London: Methuen. As cited in R. Rosenthal & R.L. Rosnow (2008) *Essentials of behavioral research: Methods and data analysis* (3rd edn). Boston: McGraw Hill.

Meehl, P.E. (1954) *Clinical vs. statistical prediction: A theoretical analysis and a review of the evidence*. Minneapolis: University of Minnesota Press.

Meerman, E.E., Verkuil, B. & Brosschot, J.F. (2011) 'Decreasing pain tolerance outside of awareness', *Journal of Psychosomatic Research*, 70: 250–7.

Melzack, R. & Wall, P.D. (1965) 'Pain mechanisms: A new theory', *Science*, 150: 971–9.

Merikle, P.M., Smilek, D. & Eastwood, J.D. (2001) 'Perception without awareness: Perspectives from cognitive psychology', *Cognition*, 79: 115–134.

Messer, S.B. (2004) 'Evidence-based practice: Beyond empirically supported treatments', *Professional Psychology: Research and Practice*, 35: 580–8.

Miles, D.R. & Carey, G. (1997) 'Genetic and environmental architecture of human aggression', *Journal of Personality and Social Psychology*, 72: 207–17.

Miles, L.K., Nind, L.K. & Macrae, C.N. (2010) 'Moving through time', *Psychological Science*, 21: 222–3.

Milgram, S. (1963) 'Behavioral study of obedience', *Journal of Abnormal and Social Psychology*, 67: 371–8.

Milgram, S. (1974) *Obedience to authority: An experimental view*. New York: Harper & Row.

Miller, G.A. (1956) 'The magical number seven, plus or minus two', *Psychological Review*, 63: 81–97.

Miller, G.A. (2003) 'The cognitive revolution: A historical perspective', *Trends in Cognitive Sciences*, 7: 141–4.

Miller, G.A. (2010) 'Mistreating psychology in the decades of the brain', *Perspectives on Psychological Science*, 5: 716–43.

Milner, B. (1962) 'Les troubles de la mémoire accompagnant les lesions hippocampiques bilatérales'. In *Physiologie de l'hippocampe*. Paris: Centre National de la Recherche Scientifique.

Minto, W. (1893) *Logic: Inductive and deductive*. London: John Murray.

Modderaar, J. (1966) 'Over de validiteit van de selectie voor bedrijven [On the validity of selection for companies]', *Nederlands Tijdschrift voor de Psychologie*, 21: 573–89.

Monahan, J. (1981) *The clinical prediction of violent behavior*. Washington, DC: Government Printing Office.

Money, T. & Ehrhardt, A. (1972) *Man and woman, boy and girl, the differentiation and dimorphism of gender identity from conception to maturity*. Baltimore, MD: Johns Hopkins University Press.

Morgan, M. (1998) 'Qualitative research: Science or pseudo-science?' *The Psychologist*, **11**: 481–3 (and Postscript on p. 485).

Morgeson, F.P., Campion, M.A., Dipboye, R.L., Hollenbeck, J.R., Murphy, K. & Schmitt, N. (2007) 'Reconsidering the use of personality tests in personnel selection contexts', *Personnel Psychology*, **60**: 683–729.

Morton, J. & Patterson, K. (1980) 'A new attempt at an interpretation, or, an attempt at a new interpretation'. In M. Coltheart *et al.* (eds) *Deep dyslexia*. London: Routledge & Kegan Paul.

Müller, J.P. (1838) *Elements of physiology* (translated by W. Baly). London.

Münsterberg, H. (1915) *Psychology: General and applied*. New York: D. Appleton & Co.

Myers-Scotton, C. (2006) *Multiple voices: An introduction to bilingualism*. Malden, MA: Blackwell Publishing.

Nagel, T. (1974) 'What is it like to be a bat?' *Philosophical Review*, 4: 435–50.

Nairn, R.G. (2007) 'Media portrayals of mental illness, or is it madness? A review', *Australian Psychologist*, **42**: 138–46.

Nairn, R.G. & Coverdale, J.H. (2005) 'People never see us living well: An appraisal of the personal stories about mental illness in a prospective print media sample', *Australian and New Zealand Journal of Psychiatry*, **39**: 281–7.

Nangle, D.W., Erdley, C.A., Carpenter, E.M. & Newman, J.E. (2002) 'Social skills training as a treatment for aggressive children and adolescents: A developmental-clinical integration', *Aggression and Violent Behavior*, 7: 169–99.

Nass, C., Moon, Y., Fogg, B.J., Reeves, B. & Dryer, D.C. (1995) 'Can computer personalities be human personalities?' *International Journal of Human–Computer Studies*, 43: 223–39.

Neisser, U. (1967) *Cognitive psychology*. New York: Appleton-Century-Crofts.

Nicholls, A. & Liebscher, M. (2010) *Thinking the unconscious: Nineteenth-century German thought.* Cambridge: Cambridge University Press.

Nicolas, S. (2004) *L'hypnose: L'école de la Salpêtrière face à l'école de Nancy.* Paris: L'Harmattan.

Nicolas, S. & Ferrand, L. (1999) 'Wundt's laboratory at Leipzig in 1891', *History of Psychology*, 2: 194–203.

Nicolas, S. & Ferrand, L. (2011) 'La psychologie cognitive d'Alfred Binet', L'Année Psychologique, 111: 87–116.

Nisbett, R. & Ross, L. (1980) *Human inference: Strategies and shortcomings of social judgment.* Englewood Cliffs, NJ: Prentice-Hall.

Nisbett, R. & Wilson, T. (1977) 'Telling more than we can know: Verbal reports on mental processes', *Psychological Review*, 84: 231–59.

Nolen-Hoeksema, S. (2000) 'The role of rumination in depressive disorders and mixed anxiety/depressive symptoms', *Journal of Abnormal Psychology*, 109: 504–11.

Nordgren, L.F., Bos, M.W. & Dijksterhuis, A. (2011) 'The best of both worlds: Integrating conscious and unconscious thought best solves complex decisions', *Journal of Experimental Social Psychology*, 47: 509–11.

Numbers, R.L. (2009) *Galileo goes to jail and other myths about science and religion.* Boston, MA: Harvard University Press.

Ochsner, K.R. & Gross, J.J. (2005) 'The cognitive control of emotion', *Trends in Cognitive Sciences*, 9: 242–9.

OECD (2007) 'Multiple comparisons of mean performance on the science scale', *PISA 2006: Science competencies for tomorrow's world*, 1.

Ones, D.S., Viswesvaran, C. & Reiss, A.D. (1996) 'Role of social desirability in personality testing for personnel selection: The red herring', *Journal of Applied Psychology*, 81: 660–79.

O'Rahilly, S. & Farooqi, I.S. (2006) 'Genetics of obesity', *Philosophical Transaction of the Royal Society B – Biological Sciences*, 361: 1095–105.

Orchowski, L.M., Spickard, B.A. & McNamara, J.R. (2006) 'Cinema and the valuing of psychotherapy: Implications for clinical practice', *Professional Psychology: Research and Practice*, 37: 506–14.

Park, S.W. & Auchincloss, E.L. (2006) 'Psychoanalysis in textbooks of introductory psychology: A review', *Journal of the American Psychoanalytic Association*, 54: 1361–80.

Patterson, G.R. (1982) *Coercive family process.* Eugene, OR: Castalia.

Peirce, C.S. (1877) 'The fixation of belief', *Popular Science Monthly*, 12: (November) 1–15.

Pereboom, D. (2001) *Living without free will.* Cambridge University Press.

Peretz, I. & Zatorre, R.J. (2005) 'Brain organization for music processing', *Annual Review of Psychology*, 56: 89–114.

Peterson, C. (1997) *Psychology: A biopsychosocial approach* (2nd edn). New York: Addison Wesley Longman.

Pickren, W.E. & Rutherford, A. (2010) *A history of modern psychology in context.* Hoboken, NJ: John Wiley & Sons.

Poldrack, R.A. (2010) Mapping mental function to brain structure: How can cognitive neuroimaging succeed? *Perspectives on Psychological Science*, 5: 753–61.

Pomerantz, J.R. & Kubovy, M. (1986) 'Theoretical approaches in organization', in Boff, J.P., Kaufman, L. and Thomas, J.P. (eds) *Handbook of perception and human performance*. New York, NY Wiley.

Popper, K.R. (1970) 'Normal science and its dangers.' In I. Lakatos & A. Musgrave (eds) *Criticism and growth of knowledge*. New York: Cambridge University Press.

Porter, R. (2006) 'Medical science'. In R. Porter (ed.) *The Cambridge history of medicine*. Cambridge: Cambridge University Press.

Porter, R. (ed.) (2006) *The Cambridge history of medicine*. Cambridge: Cambridge University Press.

Powell, A.G. & Frankenstein, M. (1997) *Ethnomathematics: Challenging Eurocentrism in mathematics education.* New York: SUNY Press.

Prins, R. & Bastiaanse, R. (2006) 'The early history of aphasiology: From the Egyptian surgeons (c. 1700 BC) to Broca (1861)', *Aphasiology*, 20: 762–91.

Proceedings of the First Annual Convention of the American Normal School Association (1859). At http://books.google.co.uk/books?id=-PxBAAAAIAAJ&printsec=frontcover#v=onepage&q&f=false.

Puhl, R. & Brownell, K.D. (2001) 'Bias, discrimination, and obesity', *Obesity Research*, 9: 788–805.

Pulvermüller, F. (2005) 'Brain mechanisms linking language and action', *Nature Reviews Neuroscience*, 6: 576–82.

Raskind, W.H. (2001) 'Current understanding of the genetic basis of reading and spelling disability', *Learning Disability Quarterly*, 24: 141–57.

Redding, R.E. (2001) 'Sociopolitical diversity in psychology: The case for pluralism', *American Psychologist*, 56: 205–15.

Rehman, S.U., Nietert, P.J., Cope, D.W. & Kilpatrick, A.O. (2005) 'What to wear today? Effects of doctor's attire on the trust and confidence of patients', *The American Journal of Medicine*, **118**: 1279–86.

Reid, K., Flowers, P. & Larkin, M. (2005) 'Exploring lived experience', *The Psychologist*, **18**: 20–23.

Ribot, T.A. (1870) *La psychologie anglaise contemporaine*. Librairie philosophique de Ladrange.

Richards, G. (1996) *Putting psychology in its place: An introduction from a critical historical perspective*. London: Routledge.

Richards, G. (2001) 'Edward Cox, the Psychological Society of Great Britain (1875-1879) and the meaning of institutional failure'. In G.C. Bunn, A.D. Lovie & G.D. Richards (eds) *Psychology in Britain* (pp. 33–53). Leicester: BPS Books.

Richards, G. (2002) *Putting psychology in its place: A critical historical overview* (2nd edn). London: Routledge.

Richards, G. (2009) *Psychology: The key concepts*. London: Routledge.

Richards, R.J. (1980) 'Christian Wolff's prolegomena to empirical and rational psychology: Translation and commentary', *Proceedings of the American Philosophical Society*, **124**: 227–39.

Richards, R.J. (1981) 'Natural selection and other models in the historiography of science'. In M.B. Brewer & B.E. Collins (eds) *Scientific inquiry and the social sciences* (pp. 37–76). San Francisco: Jossey-Bass Publishers.

Richards, R.J. (2002) *The Romantic conception of life: Science and philosophy in the age of Goethe*. Chicago: University of Chicago Press.

Richardson, R.C. (2007) *Evolutionary psychology as maladapted psychology*. Cambridge, MA: MIT Press.

Rissmiller, D.J. & Rissmiller, J.H. (2006) 'Evolution of the antipsychiatry movement into mental health consumerism', *Psychiatric Services*, **57**: 863–6.

Ritzer, G. & Goodman, D.J. (2004) *Modern sociological theory* (6th edn). Boston: McGraw Hill.

Robinson, D.K. (2001) Reaction-time experiments in Wundt's Institute and beyond. In R.W. Rieber & D.K. Robinson (eds) *Wilhelm Wundt in history: The making of a scientific psychology* (pp. 161–204). New York: Kluwer/Plenum.

Rochberg-Halton, E. (1987) 'Why pragmatism now?' *Sociological Theory*, **5**: 194–200.

Rogers, A. & Pilgrim, D. (2005) *A sociology of mental health and illness* (3rd edn). Maidenhead, UK: Open University Press.

Rogers, C.R. (1942) *Counseling and psychotherapy*. Boston, MA: Houghton Mifflin.

Rogers, C.R. & Dymond, R.F. (eds) (1954) *Psychotherapy and personality change: Coordinated research studies in the client-centered approach*. Chicago: The University of Chicago Press.

Rosenblueth, A. & Wiener, N. (1945) 'The role of models in science', *Philosophy of Science*, **12**: 316–21.

Rosenhan, D.L. (1973) 'On being sane in insane places', *Science*, **179**: 250–8.

Rosenthal, R. & Rosnow, R.L. (2008) *Essentials of behavioral research: Methods and data analysis* (3rd edn). Boston: McGraw-Hill.

Rosenthal, R. (1963) 'On the social psychology of the psychological experiment: The experimenter's hypothesis as unintended determinant of experimental results', *American Scientist*, **51**: 268–83.

Rosenthal, R. (1966) *Experimenter effects in behavioral research*. New York: AppletonCentury-Crofts.

Ross, E.H. & Murray, D.J. (1996) *E.H. Weber on the tactile senses* (2nd edn). Hove (UK): Taylor & Francis.

Rowe, F.B. (1983) 'Whatever became of poor Kinnebrook?', *American Psychologist,* **38**: 851–52.

Rowe, W. (1993) *Philosophy of religion*. Belmont, CA: Wadsworth Publishing.

Rust, J. (2008) First psychometric laboratory: Cambridge 1886–1889. At www.psychometrics.ppsis.cam.ac.uk/page/217/first-psychometric-laboratory.htm.

Rutter, M. (2006) *Genes and behavior: Nature–nurture interplay explained*. Oxford: Blackwell Publishing.

Rynes, S.L., Colbert, A.E. & Brown, K.G. (2002) 'HR professionals' beliefs about effective human resource practices: Correspondence between research and practice', *Human Resource Management*, **41**: 149–74.

Sackett, P.R., Kuncel, N.R., Arneson, J.J., Cooper, S.R. & Waters, S.D. (2009) 'Does socioeconomic status explain the relationship between admissions tests and post-secondary academic performance?', *Psychological Bulletin*, **135**: 1–22.

Saenger, P. (1997) *Space between words: The origins of silent reading*. Stanford, CA: Stanford University Press.

Saggerson, A.L., George, D.N. & Honey, R.C. (2005) 'Imitative learning of stimulus–response and response–outcome associations in pigeons', *Journal of Experimental Psychology: Animal Behavior Processes*, **31**: 289–300.

Salsburg, D. (2001) *The lady tasting tea: How statistics revolutionized science in the twentieth century*. New York: Freeman.

Samuelson, P.A. (1992) 'My life philosophy: Policy credos and working days', In M. Szenberg (ed.) *Eminent economists: Their life philosophies*. Cambridge: Cambridge University Press.

Sanders, K., van Riemsdijk, M. & Groen, B. (2008) 'The gap between research and practice: A replication study on the HR professionals' beliefs about effective human resource practices', *International Journal of Human Research Management*, **19**: 1976–88.

Sandoval, W.A. (2005) 'Understanding students' practical epistemologies and their influence on learning through inquiry', *Science Education*, **89**: 634–56.

Sarton, G. (1937) *The history of science and the new humanism*. Cambridge, MA: Harvard University Press. (1988 reprint from Brunswick: Transaction Books)

Schacter, D.L. (1987) 'Implicit memory: History and current status', *Journal of Experimental Psychology: Learning, Memory, and Cognition*, **13**: 501–18.

Schiller, F. (1979) *Paul Broca: Founder of French anthropology, explorer of the brain*. Berkeley, CA: University of California Press.

Schimit, D. (2005) 'Re-visioning antebellum American psychology: The dissemination of mesmerism, 1836–1854', *History of Psychology*, **8**: 403–34.

Schlimm, D. & Neth, H. (2008) 'Modeling ancient and modern arithmetic practices: Addition and multiplication with Arabic and Roman numerals', In V. Sloutsky, B. Love & K. McRae (eds) *Proceedings of the 30th Annual Meeting of the Cognitive Science Society* (pp. 2007–2012). Austin, TX: Cognitive Science Society.

Schmidt, F.L. & Hunter, J.E. (1998) 'The validity and utility of selection methods in personnel psychology: Practical and theoretical implications of 85 years of research findings', *Psychological Bulletin*, **124**: 262–74.

Schneider, D.J. (1973) 'Implicit personality theory: Review', *Psychological Bulletin*, **79**: 294–309.

Schraw, G., Wadkins, T. & Olafson, L. (2007) 'Doing the things we do: A grounded theory of academic procrastination', *Journal of Educational Psychology*, **99**: 12–25.

Schulze, B. & Angermeyer, M.C. (2003) 'Subjective experiences of stigma. A focus group study of schizophrenic patients, their relatives and mental health professionals', *Social Science & Medicine*, **56**: 299–312.

Schütz, A. (1964) 'The well-informed citizen', In: *Collected papers. Vol. II. Studies in social theory* (ed. A. Broderson). The Hague: Martinus Nijhoff.

Scruton, R. (2001) *Kant: A very short introduction*. Oxford: Oxford University Press.

Searle, J. (1980) 'Minds, brains, and programs', *Behavioral and Brain Sciences*, **3**: 417–57.

Seife, C. (2000) *Zero: The biography of a dangerous idea*. London: Souvenir Press.

Shallice, T. (1988) *From neuropsychology to mental structure*. Cambridge: Cambridge University Press.

Shapin, S. (1996) *The scientific revolution*. Chicago: University of Chicago Press.

Sharpe, D. & Faye, C. (2009) 'A second look at debriefing practices: Madness in our method?', *Ethics & Behavior*, **19**(5): 432–47.

Shepherd, G.M. (1991) *Foundations of the neuron doctrine*. New York: Oxford University Press.

Shorter, E. (1992) *From paralysis to fatigue: A history of psychosomatic illness in the modern era*. New York: The Free Press.

Shorter, E. (1997) *A history of psychiatry: from the era of the asylum to the age of Prozac*. New York: John Wiley & Sons.

Shorter, E. (2006) 'Primary care'. In R. Porter (ed.) *The Cambridge history of medicine* (pp. 103–135). Cambridge: Cambridge University Press.

Sie, M. & Wouters, A. (2008) 'The real challenge to free will and responsibility', *Trends in Cognitive Sciences*, **12**: 3–4.

Silverman, D. (2005) *Doing qualitative research: A practical handbook* (2nd edn). London: Sage Publications.

Sim, S. (ed.) (1998) *The Routledge companion to postmodernism* (2nd edn). London: Routledge.

Simonton, D.K. (2011) 'Creativity and discovery as blind variation: Campbell's (1960) BVSR model after the half-century mark', *Review of General Psychology*, **15**: 158–74.

Skinner, B.F. (1971) *Beyond freedom and dignity*. New York: Knopf.

Skinner, B.F. (1974) *About behaviorism*. New York: Knopf.

Skolnick-Weisberg, D., Keil, F.C., Goodstein, J., Rawson, E. & Gray, J.R. (2008) 'The seductive allure of neuroscience explanations', *Journal of Cognitive Neuroscience*, **20**: 470–7.

Smith, J.A. (1996) 'Beyond the divide between cognition and discourse: Using interpretative phenomenological analysis in health psychology', *Psychology and Health*, **11**: 261–71.

Smith, J.A. (ed.) (2008) *Qualitative psychology: A practical guide to research methods* (2nd edn). London: Sage Publications.

Smith, M.B. (1994) 'Selfhood at risk: Postmodern perils and the perils of postmodernism', *American Psychologist*, **49**: 405–11.

Smith, M.K. (1901) (translator) *A text-book in psychology: An attempt to found the science of psychology on experience, metaphysics, and mathematics by Johann Friedrich Herbart*. New York: Appleton and Company.

Smith, R. (2005) 'The history of psychological categories', *Studies in History and Philosophy of Biological and Biomedical Sciences,* **36**: 55–94.

Snow, C.P. (1959/1998) *The two cultures* (with introduction by Stefan Collini). Cambridge: Cambridge University Press.

Sokal, A. & Bricmont, J. (1997) *Impostures intellectuelles*. Paris: Editions Odile Jacob. Translated into English (1998, 2003) as *Intellectual impostures*. London: Profile Books Ltd.

Sokal, A.D. (1996a) 'Transgressing the boundaries: Toward a transformative hermeneutics of quantum gravity', *Social Text*, **46/47**: 217–52 (also available on http://www.physics.nyu.edu/sokal/).

Sokal, A.D. (1996b) 'A physicist experiments with cultural studies', *Lingua Franca*, **May/June**, 62–64 (also available on http://www.physics. nyu.edu/sokal/).

Sokal, M.M. (1972) 'Psychology at Victorian Cambridge – The unofficial laboratory of 1887–1888', *Proceedings of the American Philosophical Society*, **116**: 145–7.

Sokal, M.M. (1981) *An education in psychology: James McKeen Cattell's Journal and Letters from Germany and England, 1880–1888*. Cambridge, MA: MIT Press.

Sokal, M.M. (2006) 'The origins of the new psychology in the United States', *Physis: Rivista internazionale di storia della scienza*, **43**: 273–300.

Soon, S.C., Brass, M., Heinze, H.J. & Haynes, J.D. (2008) 'Unconscious determinants of free decisions in the human brain', *Nature Neuroscience*, **11**: 543–5.

Spangenberg, E.R., Sprott, D.E., Grohmann, B. & Tracy, D.L. (2006) 'Gender-congruent ambient scent influences on approach and avoidance behaviors in a retail store', *Journal of Business Research*, **59**: 1281–7.

Sperling, G. (1960) 'The information available in brief visual presentations', *Psychological Monographs*, **74**: 1–29.

Spurzheim, J.G. (1834) *Phrenology of the doctrine of the mental phenomenon* (3rd edn). Boston: Marsh, Caper and Lyon.

Stangor, C. (2006) *Research methods for the behavioral sciences*. Boston, MA: Houghton Mifflin.

Stanovich, K.E. (2004) *The robot's rebellion: Finding meaning in the age of Darwin*. Chicago: The University of Chicago Press.

Stanovich, K.E. (2010) *How to think straight about psychology?* (9th International Edition). Harlow, UK: Pearson.

Starks, H. & Trinidad, S.B. (2007) 'Choose your method: A comparison of phenomenology, discourse analysis, and grounded theory', *Qualitative Health Research*, **17**: 1372–80.

Sternberg, R.J. (1999) 'Twenty tips for teaching introductory psychology.' In B. Perlman, L.I. McCann & S.H. McFadden (eds) *Lessons learned: Practical advice for the teaching of psychology* (vol. 1). Washington, D.C.: American Psychological Society, pp. 99–104.

Stevens, S.S. (1935) 'The operational definition of psychological concepts', *Psychological Review*, **42**: 517–27.

Stevenson, C. & Cooper, N. (1997) 'Qualitative and quantitative research', *The Psychologist*, **4**: 159–60.

Stratton, P. (1997) 'Attributional coding of interview data: Meeting the needs of long-haul passengers.' In N. Hayes (ed.) *Doing qualitative analysis in psychology*. Hove: Psychology Press, pp. 115–42.

Stroop, J.R. (1935) 'Studies of interference in serial verbal reactions', *Journal of Experimental Psychology*, **18**: 643–62 (reprinted 1992 in *Journal of Experimental Psychology: General*, **121**: 15–23).

Stubbe, J.H., Posthuma, D., Boomsma, D.I. & De Geus, E.J.C. (2005) 'Heritability of life satisfaction in adults: A twin-family study', *Psychological Medicine*, **35**: 1581–88.

Sturm, T. (2006) 'Is there a problem with mathematical psychology in the eighteenth century? A fresh look at Kant's old argument', *Journal of the History of the Behavioral Sciences*, **42**: 353–77.

Sullivan, P.F., Kendler, K.S. & Neale, M.C. (2003) 'Schizophrenia as a complex trait: Evidence from a meta-analyis of twin studies', *Archives of General Psychiatry*, **60**: 1187–92.

Sullivan, P.F., Neale, M.C. & Kendler, K.S. (2000) 'Genetic epidemiology and major depression: Review and meta-analysis', *American Journal of Psychiatry*, **157**: 1552–62.

Swinkels, A. (2003) 'An effective exercise for teaching cognitive heuristics', *Teaching of Psychology*, **30**: 120–2.

Szasz, T.S. (1960) 'The myth of mental illness', *American Psychologist*, **15**: 113–18.

Tait, W. (1854) *Tait's Edinburgh magazine*. Edinburgh: Sutherland & Knox (at www.archive.org/details/taitsedinburghm04taitgoog).

Taleb, N.N. (2007) *The black swan: The impact of the highly improbable*. New York: Random House.

Talisse, R.B. & Aikin, S.F. (eds) (2011) *The pragmatism reader: From Peirce to the present*. Princeton, NJ: Princeton University Press.

Taylor, F.W. (1911) *Scientific management*. New York: Harper & Brothers.

Teigen, K.H. (2002) 'One hundred years of laws in psychology', *The American Journal of Psychology*, **115**: 103–18.

Teo, T. (2005) *The critique of psychology: From Kant to postcolonial theory*. New York: Springer Science+Business Media, Inc.

Teo, T. (2007) 'Local institutionalization, discontinuity, and German textbooks of psychology, 1816–1854', *Journal of the History of the Behavioral Sciences*, **43**: 135–57.

Teo, T. (2008) 'Race and psychology'. In W.A. Darity (ed.) *International encyclopedia of the social sciences* (2nd edn). Detroit, MI: Macmillan, Vol. 7, pp. 21–4.

Thapar, A., Langley, K., Owen, M.J. & O'Donavan, M.C. (2007) 'Advances in genetic findings on attention deficit hyperactivity disorder', *Psychological Medicine*, 37: 1681–92.

The British Psychological Society (2004) *Guideline for minimum standards of ethical approval in psychological research*. Leicester, UK: The British Psychological Society.

The British Psychological Society (2006) *Code of ethics and conduct*. Leicester, UK: The British Psychological Society.

Thomas, R.K. (2007) 'Recurring errors among recent history of psychology textbooks', *American Journal of Psychology*, 120: 477–95.

Thompson, D. (2008) *Counterknowledge: How we surrendered to conspiracy theories, quack medicine, bogus science and fake history*. London: Atlantic Books.

Thomson, J.A. (1922) *The outline of science: A plain story simply told*. New York: G.P. Putnam's Sons.

Thorndike, E.L. (1911) *Animal intelligence*. New York: Macmillan.

Tizard, B. (1959) 'Theories of brain localization from Flourens to Lashley', *Medical History*, 3: 132–45.

Todd, Z., Nerlich, B., McKeown, S. & Clarke, D.D. (2004) *Mixing methods in psychology: The integration of qualitative and quantitative methods in theory and practice*. Hove: Psychology Press.

Tolman, E.C. (1948) 'Cognitive maps in rats and men', *Psychological Review*, 55: 189–209 (available at psych-classics.yorku.ca).

Torgersen, S. *et al.* (2000) 'A twin study of personality disorders', *Comprehensive Psychiatry*, 41: 416–25.

Trivers, R.L. (1971) 'The evolution of reciprocal altruism,' *Quarterly Review of Biology*, 46: 35–57.

Trivers, R.L. (1972) 'Parental investment and sexual selection'. In B. Campbell (ed.) *Sexual selection and the descent of man: 1871–1971*. Chicago: Aldine, pp. 136–79.

Tulving, E. & Thomson, D.M. (1971) 'Retrieval processes in recognition memory – Effects of associative context', *Journal of Experimental Psychology*, 87: 116–24.

Turing, A. (1950) 'Computing machinery and intelligence', *Mind*, 59: 434–60.

Twenge, J.M., Campbell, W.K. & Foster, C.A. (2003) 'Parenthood and marital satisfaction: A meta-analytic review', *Journal of Marriage and the Family*, 65: 574–83.

Tyson, P.J., Jones, D. & Elcock, J. (2011) *Psychology in social context: Issues and debates*. Oxford: Blackwell Publishing.

Uglow, J. (2002) *The lunar men: The friends who made the future*. London: Faber and Faber.

UK ECT Review Group (2003) 'Efficacy and safety of electroconvulsive therapy in depressive disorders: A systematic review and meta-analysis', *The Lancet*, 361: 799–808.

Uttal, W.R. (2001) *The new phrenology: The limits of localizing cognitive processes*. Cambridge, MA: MIT Press.

Valentine, E.R. (1999) 'The founding of the psychological laboratory, University College London: "Dear Galton... Yours truly, J Sully"', *History of Psychology*, 2: 204–18.

Valentine, E.R. (2000) 'Metaphysics', In A.E. Kazdin (ed.) *Encyclopedia of psychology*, Vol. 5, (pp. 204–9). Oxford: Oxford University Press.

Van Drunen, P., Van Strien, P.J. & Haas, E. (2004) 'Work and organization'. In J. Jansz and P. Van Drunen (eds) (2004) *A social history of psychology*. Oxford: Blackwell Publishing.

Van Goozen, S.H.M., Cohen-Kettenis, P.T., Gooren, L.J.G., Frijda, N.H. & Van de Poll, N.E. (1995) 'Gender differences in behaviour: Activating effects of cross-sex hormones', *Psychoneuroendocrinology*, 20: 343–63.

Van Hezewijk, R. & Stam, H.J. (2008) 'Idols of the psychologist: Johannes Linschoten and the demise of phenomenological psychology in the Netherlands', *History of Psychology*, 11: 185–207.

Van Strien, P.J. & Dane, J. (2001) *Driekwart eeuw psychotechniek in Nederland: De magie van het testen* [Three-quarters of a century of psychotechnics in the Netherlands: The magic of testing]. Assen: Koninklijke Van Gorcum.

Van Vugt, M., De Cremer, D. & Janssen, D.P. (2007) 'Gender differences in cooperation and competition: The male-warrior hypothesis', *Psychological Science*, 18: 19–23.

Vandenbroucke, J.P. (2008) 'Observational research, randomised trials, and two views of medical science', *PLoS Medicine*, 5: e67, doi:10.1371/journal.pmed.0050067.

Verhaeghe, P. (2009) *Het einde van de psychotherapie* [The end of psychotherapy]. Amsterdam: De Bezige Bij.

Vilchez-Gonzalez, J.M. & Parales Palacios, F.J. (2006) 'Image of science in cartoons and its relationship with the image in comics', *Physics Education*, 41: 240–9.

Von Sydow, K. (2007) 'The public image of psychologists, psychotherapists, and psychiatrists', *Psychotherapeut*, 52: 322–33.

Vul, E., Harris, C., Winkielman, P. & Pashler, H. (2009) 'Puzzlingly high correlations in fMRI studies of emotion, personality, and social cognition', *Perspectives on Psychological Science*, **4**: 274–290.

Wade, N.J. (2007) 'Image, eye, and retina (invited review)', *Journal of the Optical Society of America*, **24**: 1229–49).

Walsh, E. & Fahy, T. (2002) 'Violence in society: Contribution of mental illness is low', *British Medical Journal*, **325**: 507–8.

Walsh, E. *et al.* (2004) 'Predicting violence in schizophrenia: A prospective study', *Schizophrenia Research*, **67**: 247–52.

Walter, H. (2001) *Neurophilosophy of free will.* Cambridge, MA: MIT Press.

Wampold, B.E. *et al.* (1997) 'A meta-analysis of outcome studies comparing bona fide psychotherapies: Empirically, "all must have prizes"', *Psychological Bulletin*, **122**: 203–15.

Wampold, B.E., Minami, T., Baskin, T.W. & Tierney, S.C. (2002) 'A meta-(re)analysis of the effects of cognitive therapy versus "other therapies" for depression', *Journal of Affective Disorders*, **68**: 159–65.

Wampold, B.E., Minami, T., Tierney, S.C., Baskin, T.W. & Bhati, K.S. (2005) 'The placebo is powerful: Estimating placebo effects in medicine and psychotherapy for randomized clinical trials', *Journal of Clinical Psychology*, **61**: 835–54.

Ward, N. (1998) 'Artificial intelligence and other approaches to speech understanding: Reflections on methodology', *Journal of Experimental and Theoretical Artificial Intelligence*, **10**: 487–93.

Ward, S.C. (2002) *Modernizing the mind: Psychological knowledge and the remaking of society.* Westport, CT: Praeger.

Warrington, E.K. & Weiskrantz, L. (1978) Further analysis of the prior learning effect in amnesic patients. *Neuropsychologia*, **16**: 169–176.

Wason, P.C. (1960) 'On the failure to eliminate hypotheses in a conceptual task', *Quarterly Journal of Experimental Psychology*, **12**: 129–40.

Watson, J.B. (1907) 'Studying the mind of animals', *The World Today,* **12**: 421–6 (available at psychclassics. yorku.ca).

Watson, J.B. (1913) 'Psychology as the behaviorist views it', *Psychological Review*, **20**: 158–77.

Watson, J.B. (1925) *Behaviorism.* New York: People's Institute Publishing Company. (Reprinted in 1997 by Transaction Publishers.)

Watson, J.B. & Rayner, R. (1920) 'Conditioned emotional reactions', *Journal of Experimental Psychology,* **3**: 1–14 (available at psychclassics.yorku.ca).

Watters, E. (2010) *Crazy like us: The globalization of the American psyche.* New York: Free Press.

Weber, M. (1904/1905) 'Die protestantische Ethik und der Geist des Kapitalismus' (translated in 1905 as '*The Protestant ethic and the spirit of capitalism*'). *Archiv für Sozialwissenschraft und Sozialpolitik*, **20**: 1–54; **21**: 1–110.

Wegner, D.M. (2004) 'Précis of "The illusion of conscious will"', *Behavioral and Brain Sciences*, **27**: 649–59.

Weindling, P.J. (2004) *Nazi medicine and the Nuremberg Trials: From medical war crimes to informed consent.* Basingstoke: Palgrave-Macmillan.

Weisbord, M.R. (1985) 'Participative work design: A personal odyssey', *Organizational Dynamics*, **13**: 4–20. (Table adapted from Trist, E. (1981) *The evolution of socio-technical systems – A conceptual framework and an action research program.* Toronto: Ontario Ministry of Labour.)

Weiten, W. (2010) Interview. *APS Observers,* **23**(4).

Welch, B. (2009) 'Torture, psychology, and Daniel Inouye: The true story behind psychology's role in torture. *Huffington Post*, June 16, 2009 (available on http://www. huffingtonpost.com/bryant-welch/torture-psychology-and-da_b_215612.html; retrieved on July 28, 2011).

Wheen, F. (2004) *How mumbo-jumbo conquered the world: A short history of modern delusions.* London: Harper Perennial.

Whewell, W. (1837) *History of inductive sciences.* London: Parker & Strand.

Whitaker, H.A. & Etlinger, S.C. (1993) 'Theodor Meynert's contribution to classical 19th century aphasia studies', *Brain and Language*, **45**: 560–71.

Whittle, P. (2000) 'W.H.R. Rivers and the early history of psychology at Cambridge'. In A. Saito (ed.) *Bartlett, culture and cognition.* Hove, UK: Psychology Press, pp. 21–35.

Willig, C. (2008) *Introducing qualitative research in psychology.* Maidenhead: McGraw-Hill/ Open University Press.

Willis, R. (1847) *The works of William Harvey, M.D. translated from the Latin with a life of the author.* London: Sydenham Society.

Wilson, C., Nairn, R., Coverdale, J. & Panapa, A. (1999) 'Mental illness depictions in prime-time drama: Identifying the discursive resources', *Australian and New Zealand Journal of Psychiatry*, **33**: 232–9.

Wilson, C., Nairn, R., Coverdale, J. & Panapa, A. (2000) 'How mental illness is portrayed in children's television: A prospective study', *British Journal of Psychiatry*, **176**: 440–3.

Wilson, E.O. (1975) *Sociobiology: The new synthesis.* Cambridge, MA: Harvard University Press.

Wilson, T.D. & Dunn, E.W. (2004) 'Self- knowledge: Its limits, value, and potential for improvement', *Annual Review of Psychology*, 55: 493–518.

Wissler, C. (1901) 'The correlation of mental and physical tests', *Psychological Review Monograph Supplements*, 3(6).

Wittgenstein, L. (1953) *Philosophical investigations*. (trans. G.E.M. Anscombe). Oxford: Basil Blackwell.

Wolf, T.H. (1964) 'Alfred Binet: A time of crisis', *American Psychologist,* 19: 762–71.

Wolff, G. (1732) *Psychologia empirica*. Frankfurt-Leipzig.

Woodworth, R.S. (1948) *Contemporary schools of psychology* (Revised edn). New York: The Ronald Press.

Wooldridge, A. (1994) *Measuring the mind: Education and psychology in England, c. 1860–c. 1990*. Cambridge: Cambridge University Press.

Workman, L. & Reader, W. (2008) *Evolutionary psychology: An introduction* (2nd edn). Cambridge: Cambridge University Press.

Wright, T.R. (2008) *The religion of humanity: The impact of Comtean positivism on Victorian Britain*. Cambridge: Cambridge University Press.

Wundt, W.M. (1896/1897) *Outlines of psychology* (English translation by C.H. Judd). Leipzig: Wilhelm Engelmann (at psychclassics.yorku.ca).

Yardley, L. (2000) 'Dilemmas in qualitative health research', *Psychology and Health*, 15: 215–28.

Yasar, S., Baker, D., Robinson-Kurpius, S., Krause, S. & Roberts, C. (2006) 'Development of a survey to assess K-12 teachers' perceptions of engineers and familiarity with teaching design, engineering, and technology', *Journal of Education*, 95: 205–16.

Young, M. (1994) *The rise of the meritocracy* (with a new introduction by the author). London: Transaction Publishers.

Zehr, D. (2000) 'Portrayals of Wundt and Titchener in introductory psychology texts: a content analysis', *Teaching of Psychology*, 27: 122–5.

Zeldow, P.B. (2009) 'In defense of clinical judgment, credentialed clinicians, and reflective practice', *Psychotherapy Theory, Research, Practice, Training*, 46: 1–10.

Ziegler, J.C., Bertrand, D., Toth, D., Csepe, V., Reis, A., Faisca, L., Saine, N., Lyytinen, H., Vaessen, A. & Blomert, L. (2010) 'Orthographic depth and its impact on universal predictors of reading: A cross-language investigation', *Psychological Science*, 21: 551–9.

Zimbardo, P.G. (2004) 'Power turns good soldiers into "bad apples".' Editorial in *The Boston Globe*, May 9.

Zubin, J. & Spring, B. (1977) 'Vulnerability: A new view of schizophrenia', *Journal of Abnormal Psychology*, 86: 103–26.

Index

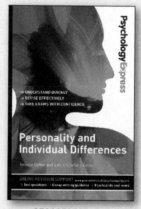

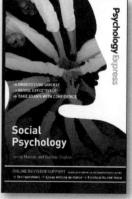